CONECTADOS

Communication Manual

Patti J. Marinelli

University of South Carolina

Karin Fajardo

CENGAGE
Learning

Australia • Brazil • Mexico • Singapore • United Kingdom • United States

CENGAGE
Learning®

Conectados

Patti Marinelli & Karin Fajardo

Product Director: Beth Kramer

Senior Product Manager: Heather Bradley Cole

Product Development Manager: Katie Wade

Associate Content Developer: Daniel Cruse

Product Assistant: Julie Allen

Managing Content Developer: Patrick Brand

Marketing Manager: Jennifer Castillo

Senior Content Project Manager: Aileen Mason

Senior Art Director: Linda Jurras

Manufacturing Planner: Betsy Donaghey

IP Analyst: Jessica Elias

IP Project Manager: Farah Fard

Production Service: Lumina Datamatics, Inc.

Compositor: Lumina Datamatics, Inc.

Cover and Text Designer: Polo Barrera

Cover Image: © Shutterstock

For product information and technology assistance, contact us at **Cengage Learning Customer & Sales Support, 1-800-354-9706**

For permission to use material from this text or product, submit all requests online at **cengage.com/permissions.** Further permissions questions can be emailed to **permissionrequest@cengage.com**

Library of Congress Control Number: 2014947912

ISBN-978-1-111-35084-0

Cengage Learning
20 Channel Center Street
Boston, MA 02210
USA

Cengage Learning is a leading provider of customized learning solutions with office locations around the globe, including Singapore, the United Kingdom, Australia, Mexico, Brazil, and Japan. Locate your local office at: **www.cengage.com/global.**

Cengage Learning products are represented in Canada by Nelson Education, Ltd.

To learn more about Cengage Learning Solutions, visit **www.cengage.com**.

Purchase any of our products at your local college store or at our preferred online store **www.cengagebrain.com.**

Printed in the United States of America

Print Number: 02   Print Year: 2016

Acknowledgments

μεράκι (may-rah-kee) Greek loan word from the Turkish merak; to do something from the heart, with one's whole being

Conectados is a labor of love, the result of more than seven years of creative effort. We extend our sincere thanks to everyone who has contributed to this project, from inception to conclusion.

We are especially grateful to Beth Kramer, Product Director, for the vision and support that moved *Conectados* from idea to reality. Our deep appreciation also goes to Heather Bradley Cole, Senior Product Manager, for guiding our team with great acumen through many years of development. We thank you both for sticking with us through thick and thin!

We want to acknowledge the entire *Conectados* team for their invaluable contributions to this project. We thank you all for your keen insights, perceptive suggestions, and consummate professionalism. It is impossible to mention here all the ways in which you have guided and supported us. We hope that you realize how much we admire and appreciate the talent, creativity and energy you've brought to bear in *Conectados*. We're especially indebted to Katie Wade, Product Development Manager; Gabriela Ferland, Freelance Content Developer; Daniel Cruse, Associate Content Developer; Patrick Brand, Managing Content Developer; Andrew Tabor, Senior Product Development Specialist; and Michelle Williams, Marketing Director.

We would also like to express our appreciation to our fine contributing writers. Our thanks go to Catherine Wiskes for her creative activities in the **Vocabulario** and **Gramática** sections online; to Martín Gaspar for his work in the **Conectados con...** authentic reading activities online; to Max Ehrsam and Paula Orrego for their hard work on the chapter exams; Marissa Vargas for her precision on the **Paso** quizzes; Gabriela Ferland for her excellent work on the self-tests; and Anne Prucha from the University of Central Florida for her thoughtful design of the Preview PowerPoints.

Of course the creation of the content for *Conectados* was only part of the picture. We are indebted to the *Conectados* design and production team for meticulously transforming over 5000 pages of manuscript into a beautiful Classroom Manual and a state-of-the-art Online Program. Our special thanks go to Aileen Mason, Senior Content Project Manager, for her expert supervision over each detail of that process; and to Jenna Vittorioso, Project Manager at Lumina Datamatics, Inc., for the day-to-day coordination of the many production elements. Thanks also go to each of the following for their unique and valued contributions: Poyee Oster, for image research and permissions; Melissa Flamson, for text research permissions; Jessica Elias, rights acquisition specialist; Linda Jurras, art director; Polo Barrera, designer; and Lumina Datamatics, Inc., compositor. We also thank the native reader, copyeditor, proofreaders, and illustrator for their detailed work.

We are indebted to the incredibly talented professionals at IXL for the creation of the *Conectados* technological platform. In particular, we would like to thank Christine Pasetes, Lead Book Developer, for her leadership and collaboration. We are also appreciative of the precise work of the following IXL professionals: Gayane Lachinyan, Senior Book Developer, Yen Nguyen, Senior Book Development Specialist, Megan Horner, Senior Book Developer, Julia Clark, Associate Book Developer, and Michael Houser, Editor. Thank you for your meticulous attention to detail and for the superbly reliable and user-friendly interface. We are also grateful to Soundscape Productions for producing the audio files and to A/T Media Services for creating the videos for **Perspectivas** and the *Conectados* Integrated Performance Assessments.

We want to acknowledge all our colleagues from around the country who participated in reviews and focus groups for **Conectados**. Because your observations and suggestions helped shape **Conectados**, we consider you integral members of our team. Thank you for your candid remarks, helpful criticism, and enthusiastic support.

Reviewer List

James Abraham, *Glendale Community College*

Claudia Acosta, *College of the Canyons*

Amy Adrian, *Ivy Tech Community College*

Ana Afzali, *Citrus College*

Susana Alaiz Losada, *Queensborough Community College*

Pilar Alcalde, *The University of Memphis*

Juan Alcarria, *Georgia College*

Frances Alpren, *Vanderbilt University*

Tim Altanero, *Austin Community College*

Daniel Althoff, *Southeastern Oklahoma State University*

Carlos C. Amaya, *Eastern Illinois University*

Rafael Arias, *Los Angeles Valley College*

Teresa Arrington, *Blue Mountain College*

Clara Arroyo, *Case Western Reserve University*

Yuly Asención, *Northern Arizona University*

Carlos Báez, *North Hennepin Community College*

Graciela Báez, *New York University*

Ann Baker, *University of Evansville*

Clare Bennett, *University of Alaska Southeast - Ketchikan*

Antonio Barbagallo, *Stonehill College*

Erika Barragan, *Tarrant County College - Northeast*

Sonia Barrios Tinoco, *Seattle University*

Roschelle Bautista, *Dalten State College*

Anne Becher, *University of Colorado-Boulder*

Maritza Bell-Corales, *Middle Georgia State College*

David Beltrán, *Harold Washington College*

Ana Benito, *Indiana University-Purdue University - Fort Wayne*

Hsiao-Ping Biehl, *La Salle University*

Graciela Susana Boruszko, *Pepperdine University*

Catherine Briggs, *North Lake College*

Suzanne Buck, *Central New Mexico Community College*

Steven Budge, *Mesa Community College*

Oscar Cabrera, *Community College of Philadelphia*

Elizabeth Calvera, *Virginia Tech*

Kellie Campbell, *Saint Michael's College*

Douglas Canfield, *University of Tennessee*

Antonio Cardenas, *Mesa Community College*

Aurora Castillo, *Georgia College & State University*

Francisca Castillo, *Lee College*

Esther Castro, *San Diego State University*

Isabel Castro, *Towson University*

An Chung Cheng, *University of Toledo*

Ralph Cherry, *Wayland Baptist University*

Selfa Chew, *University of Texas at El Paso and UTEP - Spain*

Silvia Choi, *Georgia Gwinnett College*

Kellye Church, *University of North Texas*

Robert Colvin, *Brigham Young University-Idaho*

Elizabeth Combier, *University of North Georgia*

Norma Corrales-Martin, *Temple University*

William Cowan, *University of Texas - Arlington*

Angela Cresswell, *Holy Family University*

Adam Crofts, *College of Southern Idaho*

José Cruz, *Fayetteville Technical Community College*

Marius Cucurny, *Golden West College*

Cathleen Cuppett, *Coker College*

Elena Davidiak, *Stony Brook University*

Kelly Davidson, *Clemson University*

Dulce De Castro, *Collin College*

Luis Delgado, *Olive-Harvey College*

David Detwiler, *MiraCosta College*

John Deveny, *Oklahoma State University*

Michael Dillon, *Morehouse College*

Vilma Dones de Herrera, *Grand Canyon University*

Bill Dooley, *Baylor University*

Indira Dortolina, *Lone Star College - Cy Fair*

Judith Downing, *Rutgers University - Camden*

Kimberly Eherenman, *University of San Diego*

John Ellis, *Scottsdale Community College*

Maria Enciso, *Saddleback College*

Hector Enriquez, *University of Texas at El Paso*

Margaret Eomurian, *Houston Community College - Central*

Angela Erickson-Grussing, *College of St. Benedict & Saint John's University*

Luz Marina Escobar, *Tarrant County College - Southeast Campus*

Deborah Esparza, *Milwaukee Area Technical College*

Angela Felix, *Rio Salado College*

Francisco J. Fernández-Rubiera, *University of Central Florida*

Daniel Figueroa, *University of Dayton*

Leah Fonder-Solano, *University of Southern Mississippi*

Alberto Fonseca, *North Central College*

Vasant Gadre, *Richland College*

Carmen Garcia, *Texas Southern University*

Gerardo García-Muñoz, *Prairie View A&M University*

Danielle Geary, *Georgia Institute of Technology*

Amy George-Hirons, *Tulane University*

Carolina Ghanem-Cameron, *Georgia Perimeter College*

Alicia Gignoux, *University of Montana*

Jennifer Góngora, *Sam Houston State University*

Charlene Grant, *Skidmore College*

Susan Griffin, *Boston University*

Sergio Guzmán, *College of Southern Nevada*

Judy Haisten, *College of Central Florida*

Devon Hanahan, *College of Charleston*

Michelle Harkins, *Burlington County College*

Luis Hermosilla, *Kent State University*

Dianne Hobbs, *Texas Christian University*

Michael Hubert, *Washington State university*

Michael Hughes, *California State University, San Marcos*

Alfonso Illingworth-Rico, *Eastern Michigan University*

Franklin Inojosa, *Harold Washington College*

Casilde Isabelli, *University of Nevada, Reno*

Becky Jaimes, *Austin Community College - Hays*

Carmen Jany, *California State University, San Bernardino*

Bruce Johnson, *Chandler-Gilbert Community College*

Armand Jones, *Spelman College*

João Junqueira, *National University*

Esther Kahn, *Northern Virginia Community College*

Jorge Koochoi, *Central Piedmont Community College*

Jason Krieger, *North Lake College*

Barbara Kruger, *Finger Lakes Community College*

Ryan LaBrozzi, *Bridgewater State University*

Ute Lahaie, *Gardner-Webb University*

Todd Lakin, *City Colleges of Chicago*

Luis Latoja, *Columbus State Community College*

Suzanne LaVenture, *Davidson County Community College*

Lance Lee, *Durham Technical Community College*

Raul Llorente, *Georgia State University*

Ceydy Ludovina, *American River College*

Monica Malamud, *Cañada College*

Pedro Maligo, *Columbus State University*

Marilyn Manley, *Rowan University*

Lily Martinez, *Bakersfield College*

Rob Martinsen, *Brigham Young University*

María Matz, *University of Massachusetts Lowell*

Andrew Maughan, *Kent State University*

Marco Mena, *Massachusetts Bay Community College*

Lilia Mendoza, *Waubonsee Community College*

Dulce Menes, *University of New Orleans*

Joseph Menig, *Valencia College*

Deanna Mihaly, *Eastern Michigan University*

Mónica Millán, *Eastern Michigan University*

Dennis Miller, *Clayton State University*

Gabriela Miranda-Recinos, *Steven F. Austin State University*

Charles H. Molano, *Lehigh Carbon Community College*

Monica Montalvo, *University of Central Florida*

Luis Mora, *Georgia Gwinnett College*

Nallely Morales, *Paradise Valley Community College*

Rosa-Maria Moreno, *Cincinnati State Technical and Community College*

Bridget Morgan, *Indiana University South Bend*

Danie Moss-Velasco, *Delaware County Community College*

Markus Muller, *California State University, Long Beach*

Yanci Murphy, *Chandler-Gilbert Community College*

Ruth Navarro, *Grossmont College*

German Negron, *University of Nevada*

Oksana Nemirovski, *Tarrant County College*

Antonio Noguera, *University of Wisconsin - Madison*

Janet Nuñez, *University of Georgia - Athens*

Sandy Oakley, *Palm Beach State College*

María de los Santos Onofre-Madrid, *Angelo State University*

Ana Oskoz, *University of Maryland, Baltimore County*

Luisa Ossa, *La Salle University*

Larbi Oukada, *Georgia College*

Mirta Pagnucci, *College of Dupage*

Alberto Pastor, *Southern Methodist University*

Peggy Patterson, *Rice University*

Sue Pechter, *Northwestern University*

José Carlos Pedroza, *Palomar College*

Teresa Pérez-Gamboa, *University of Georgia - Athens*

Michelle Petersen, *Arizona State University*

Andrea Petri, *MiraCosta College*

Christine Poteau, *Alvernia University*

Stacey Powell, *Auburn University / Troy University*

Belgica Quiros-Winemiller, *Glendale Community College*

Lea Ramsdell, *Towson University*

Kay Raymond, *Sam Houston State University*

José Neftalí Recinos, *Steven F. Austin State University*

José Recinos, *San Bernardino Valley College*

Maria Redmon, *University of Central Florida*

Devon Reed, *Kent State University*

Hernán Restrepo, *Virginia Commonwealth University / J. Sergeant Reynolds Community College*

Miguel Reyes-Mariano, *Genesee Community College*

Danielle Richardson, *Davidson County Community College*

Anthony Robb, *Rowan University*

Maria Rocha, *Houston Community College*

David Rock, *Brigham Young University - Idaho*

Judy Rodríguez, *California State University, Sacramento*

Dawn Rogodzinski-Lisa, *Northern Illinois University*

Mirna Rosende, *County College of Morris*

Marta Rosso, *Tufts University*

Laura Ruiz-Scott, *Scottsdale Community College*

Jeff Ruth, *East Stroudsburg University*

Carmen Rygg, *University of North Dakota*

Linda Saborío, *Northern Illinois University*

David Sanchez, *Fullerton College / Chapman University*

Laura Sánchez, *Longwood University*

Ruth Sánchez-Imizcoz, *Sewanee: The University of the South*

Nandini Sarma, *Carleton University*

Sarah Schaaf, *College of St. Benedict & Saint John's University*

Jean Scheppers, *College of Central Florida*

Paul Schroeder, *Northeastern Illinois University*

Linda Schumacher, *Harper College*

Paul Sebastian, *College of Idaho*

Janet Sedlar, *University of Chicago*

Gabriela Segal, *Arcadia University*

Íñigo Serna, *Washington State University*

Albert Shank, *Maricopa Community Colleges*

Steve Sheppard, *University of North Texas*

Sara Smith, *Colorado Mountain College*

Stuart Smith, *Austin Community College*

Alfredo J. Sosa-Velasco, *Southern Connecticut State University*

Karen Stone, *Gateway Community College*

Nancy Stucker, *Cabrillo College*

Haiqing Sun, *Texas Southern University*

Mingyu Sun, *University of Wisconsin - Milwaukee*

Linda Tracy, *Santa Rosa Junior College*

Toni Trives, *Santa Monica College*

Walteria Tucker, *South Florida State College*

Contenido / Contents

	Comunicación	Vocabulario

- Say what classes you have
- Follow your professor's instructions

Gramática

Cultura y conexiones

Estrategias y destrezas

- **Nuestro mundo**: The Spanish-speaking world
- **Conectados con... la geografía: Cinco maravillas geográficas del mundo hispano**
- **Conectados con... la neurociencia: ¡Jugar es bueno para ti!** (infographic)
- ▶ **Reportaje**: Bolivia's Madidi National Park
- ▶ **Perspectivas**: Where are you from?
- 🌐 **Exploración**: Famous people

- **Composición**: A message to a former roommate
- **Pronunciación**: Vowels
- **Estrategias:**
  Reading: Recognizing cognates
  Listening-Viewing: Viewing a segment several times
  Writing: Using tildes, accent marks, and punctuation

- **Nuestro mundo**: Spain
- **Conectados con... la cinematografía: El cine español**
- **Conectados con... la sociología: Adictos a las redes sociales** (infographic)
- ▶ **Reportaje**: Barcelona's street life
- ▶ **Perspectivas**: Social life at the university
- 🌐 **Exploración**: University curricula

- **Composición**: A message to an exchange student
- **Pronunciación**: The letters **ll, ñ, r,** and **rr**
- **Estrategias:**
  Reading: Scanning for specific information
  Listening-Viewing: Listening for cognates and keywords
  Writing: Creating statements and questions

- **Nuestro mundo**: Cuba, Dominican Republic, and Puerto Rico
- **Conectados con... la biología: Cuatro especies en peligro de extinción**
- **Conectados con... las ciencias: ¿Qué es la ciencia?** (infographic)
- ▶ **Reportaje**: Cuba through the eyes of photographer David Alan Harvey
- ▶ **Perspectivas**: Birthday celebrations
- 🌐 **Exploración**: Pets

- **Composición**: A letter to a host family
- **Pronunciación**: The letters **j, h,** and **ch**
- **Estrategias:**
  Reading: Using prior knowledge
  Listening-Viewing: Watching without sound
  Writing: Connecting sentences

Contenido / Contents

	Comunicación	Vocabulario

Gramática

Cultura y conexiones

Estrategias y destrezas

- **Nuestro mundo**: Mexico
- **Conectados con... la música: La música del mundo hispano**
- **Conectados con... la religión: Homenaje a los muertos** (infographic)
- ▶ **Reportaje**: Mexico's culture and natural wonders
- ▶ **Perspectivas**: Tourist destinations
- 🌐 **Exploración**: A trip to Los Cabos

- **Composición**: An article on a popular vacation destination
- **Pronunciación**: Intonation of statements and questions
- **Estrategias:**
  Reading: Identifying key information
  Listening-Viewing: Using visuals to aid comprehension
  Writing: Composing paragraphs

- **Nuestro mundo**: Guatemala and Honduras
- **Conectados con... la arquitectura: La arquitectura colonial, neoclásica y modernista**
- **Conectados con... la arqueología: Descubren espectacular friso maya de 1400 años en Petén** (article)
- ▶ **Reportaje**: Guatemala's Mayan ruins
- ▶ **Perspectivas**: Household chores
- 🌐 **Exploración**: Vacation home in Guatemala

- **Composición**: A message about your summer job
- **Pronunciación**: The letter **g**
- **Estrategias:**
  Reading: Focusing on the time frame
  Listening-Viewing: Listening for the main idea
  Writing: Writing longer sentences

- **Nuestro mundo**: El Salvador and Nicaragua
- **Conectados con... la agricultura: El arte del cultivo**
- **Conectados con... las artes culinarias: Breve historia del chocolate** (article)
- ▶ **Reportaje**: Nicaragua's history, nature, and architecture
- ▶ **Perspectivas**: Typical dishes
- 🌐 **Exploración**: Restaurants in Nicaragua

- **Composición**: A blog entry about healthy dining advice
- **Pronunciación**: The letters **z** and **c**
- **Estrategias:**
  Reading: Review of reading strategies
  Listening-Viewing: Using background knowledge to anticipate content
  Writing: Review of writing strategies

Contenido / Contents

	Comunicación	Vocabulario **V**

Gramática	Cultura y conexiones	Estrategias y destrezas

Contenido / Contents

	Comunicación	Vocabulario

Gramática	Cultura y conexiones	Estrategias y destrezas

Appendix

Icons

 Colaborar — Collaborative work with a partner

 Oral communication with a partner

 Oral communication with two or more classmates

 Clase — Oral class activity

 Video segment accessed online

 Share It! activity

 Web-based activity

 Activity that recycles material from previous chapters

Note to Student

Dear Student,

We wrote *Conectados* with you in mind. We wanted you to easily comprehend the language concepts; that's why we broke each topic into small, digestible bits. We wanted to make the practice activities as enjoyable as possible; that's why you won't find repetitive drills but instead, thought-provoking activities, real-life tasks, and—occasionally—games. And we wanted you to feel part of the global Spanish-speaking community; that's why we included interviews with your Spanish-speaking peers as well as explorations using Spanish-language websites. We also wanted to help build a classroom community, so we created an online forum for you to share posts with your classmates. Above all, we wanted to share with you our love for the Spanish language and cultures. We hope to inspire you to become a lifelong learner of Spanish and an admirer of its incredible cultures!

Sincerely,

P.J.M. and K.F.

P.S. *Conectados* means *connected*. In *Conectados* not only will you be connected to the internet, but you will also be connected with the Spanish-speaking world, with other academic disciplines, and with your classmates and instructor. Language, after all, connects us all, regardless of our differences.

¡Hola!

© urbancow/Getty Images

Objetivos Motivation is a key factor in learning a language. Think about why you are studying Spanish and then ask yourself exactly what you want to accomplish. Set specific and realistic goals for yourself, and feel proud of each achievement!

Online Take note of the learning outcomes for each section of the lesson. At the end of each **Paso**, use the self-assessment activity to reflect on and evaluate what you have learned and what you need to work on.

LP-1 **Mi meta.** Why are you studying Spanish? What is your goal for this class? Think about these questions and then complete the statements.

1. I want to study Spanish because . . . (Check all that apply.)

☐ Spanish is spoken by 50 million people in the United States and by over 400 million people worldwide. It's everywhere!

☐ I want to connect with my cultural heritage.

☐ I want to travel / work in a Spanish-speaking country.

☐ I will be able to use Spanish in my career.

☐ I want to make new friends and meet new people.

☐ I have to take Spanish as a graduation requirement.

2. By the end of this course, I want to be able to _____.

Para presentarte
To introduce yourself

¡Hola! ¿Cómo te llamas?

Me llamo Nico. ¿Y tú?

© Sam Edwards/Getty Images

Me llamo Lucía.

© Sam Edwards/Getty Images

V **Vocabulario** We need vocabulary—words and phrases that make up a language—to communicate with others. When you encounter new vocabulary, try to guess what the words and phrases mean by using visual cues and words you do know. In the dialogue above; what do you think **Me llamo Lucía** means? If you guessed *My name is Lucía*, you're right!

Learning vocabulary is perhaps the most important task in learning a new language. The more words you know, the more you understand, and the more you can say. The best way to learn new words and phrases is to see and hear them in sentences, to say them, write them, and use them in various situations. Consistent, regular practice is important to your success.

Online Take the time to click and hear the vocabulary multiple times, until the words and phrases sound familiar. Then, work thoughtfully through the assigned activities. This study plan will help you move from recognizing the words to using them to express your own thoughts.

 LP-2 **¿Cómo te llamas?** It's time to meet your classmates! Walk around the classroom and ask five fellow students their names.

Modelo **Estudiante A:** Hola. ¿Cómo te llamas?
Estudiante B: Me llamo *(name)*. ¿Y tú?
Estudiante A: Me llamo *(name)*.

Para deletrear

To spell

¿Cómo se escribe tu nombre?

Se escribe ene-i-ce-o.

© Sam Edwards/Getty Images

© Sam Edwards/Getty Images

El alfabeto

a	a	h	hache	ñ	eñe	u	u
b	be	i	i	o	o	v	uve
c	ce	j	jota	p	pe	w	uve doble
d	de	k	ka	q	cu	x	equis
e	e	l	ele	r	erre	y	ye
f	efe	m	eme	s	ese	z	zeta
g	ge	n	ene	t	te		

Pronunciación y Composición Part of learning a language is learning its sounds and symbols—how to pronounce it and how to write it. What have you noticed so far? In the written language, which Spanish letter doesn't exist in the English alphabet? What punctuation marks are unique to the Spanish language? And what about spoken Spanish? How does it sound to you compared to English?

Online You will have many opportunities to train your ear by listening to audio recordings of native speakers and watching short authentic videos. Be sure to practice your pronunciation by repeating the words and phrases you hear. Next, write sentences with those new words and phrases. And always keep this in mind: It is normal to make mistakes as you learn a new language, and practice does make perfect!

 LP-3 **¿Cómo se escribe?** Find out the names of four classmates you haven't met yet. Ask how their names are spelled and write them in the chart.

Modelo
Estudiante A: Hola. ¿Cómo te llamas?
Estudiante B: Me llamo Jayden.
Estudiante A: ¿Cómo se escribe Jayden?
Estudiante B: Se escribe jota-a-ye-de-e-ene. ¿Y tú? ¿Cómo te llamas?

	Nombre
1.	
2.	
3.	
4.	

Para saludar
To greet someone

¡Hola! ¿Cómo estás?

Bien, gracias. ¿Y tú?

¿Cómo está usted, doctora Pérez?

Bien, gracias. ¿Y usted?

Títulos	Titles				
Señor (Sr.)	*Mr.*	Profesor	*Professor (male)*	Doctor (Dr.)	*Doctor (male)*
Señora (Sra.)	*Mrs.; Ms.*	Profesora	*Professor (female)*	Doctora (Dra.)	*Doctor (female)*
Señorita (Srta.)	*Miss; Ms.*				

 Cultura Learning a new language is closely tied to learning about the people who speak that language and their way of life—in other words, their culture. Culture is a broad term; it encompasses everything from customs and habits of daily life to religious and political institutions to artistic and literary creations.

One important cultural concept is the notion of *formal* and *informal* speech. In Spanish, the two words for *you*—**tú** and **usted**—signal this difference. In the dialogues above, which is used in the more formal situation?

Online You will use Google Earth to visit the regions where Spanish is spoken. You will also explore daily life as well as the great achievements of Spanish-speaking people from around the world through videos and readings.

Colaborar

LP-4 **¿Cómo estás?** How would you ask each of the following people in Spanish how he or she is doing? Working with a classmate, decide whether you should use a formal or an informal greeting. Use the name of the person in the picture and say the greeting aloud.

Modelo ¿Cómo está usted, señor Calvo?

Señor Calvo

1. Sofía

2. Doctora Moreno

3. Profesor García

4. Juan

4 Lección preliminar

Las asignaturas
Academic subjects

Las ciencias naturales	*Science*		la informática	*computer science*
la biología	*biology*		la ingeniería	*engineering*
la física	*physics*		**Las humanidades y**	***Humanities and***
la química	*chemistry*		**bellas artes**	***fine arts***
Las ciencias sociales	***Social sciences***		el arte	*art*
las ciencias políticas	*political science*		la cinematografía	*film-making*
la historia	*history*		las lenguas	*languages*
la psicología	*psychology*		la literatura	*literature*
Los estudios profesionales	***Professional studies***		la música	*music*
la administración de	*business*		el teatro	*theater*
empresas	*administration*		**Las matemáticas**	***Math***
la comunicación	*communication*		el álgebra	*algebra*
el derecho	*law*		el cálculo	*calculus*
la educación	*education*		la geometría	*geometry*

 Conexiones By learning another language, you also open the door to a world of new information. Imagine being able to use your Spanish to learn about other subjects of interest to you! To help you do this, keep in mind that many words are similar in Spanish and English. These cognates, or **cognados** as they are known in Spanish, have the same meanings but slight differences in spelling and pronunciation.

Online You will learn new information drawn from other academic disciplines by watching brief documentary-style videos and by reading short articles from newspapers, magazines, and internet sites.

Colaborar

LP-5 **Las asignaturas.** What academic subject do you associate with each of the following terms? Working with a classmate, read each list of terms, select the corresponding academic subject, and say it aloud in Spanish. How many cognates do you recognize?

1. los experimentos, los elementos, las reacciones
2. las repúblicas, la democracia, la constitución
3. las computadoras, los programas, los sistemas binarios
4. el español, el inglés, el italiano, el chino, el árabe
5. las ecuaciones, los factores, $a + b = c$

Colaborar

LP-6 **¿Qué clase es?** What do you think these people are studying? Working with a partner, say the name of each class aloud in Spanish. Then say aloud the name of the corresponding course category (such as **las ciencias naturales** or **las humanidades**).

 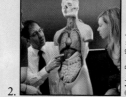  

1.   2.   3.   4.

Para hablar de las clases

To talk about classes

¿Qué clases tienes?

Tengo historia, inglés, biología y español.

G **Gramática** To communicate effectively, you need to know how to put words together to create sentences. In both English and Spanish, verbs—words like *have*, *is*, *read*, and *watch*—are a key part of every sentence. In Spanish, verbs have different forms. For example, in the dialogue above, two verb forms are used: **tengo** and **tienes**. Which one means *I have*? Which one means *do you have*?

Online You will learn more about the structures and word order of Spanish in the **Gramática** sections. Take time to observe how language is used in the model conversations, where new grammar is presented. Work through each point of the explanation and test your comprehension by completing the **Try it!** questions before you begin the assigned practice activities.

 LP-7 Las clases. Ask four classmates what classes they are taking. Fill in the chart in Spanish with at least two courses (aside from Spanish!) for each person.

Modelo   **Estudiante A:** Hola. ¿Cómo te llamas?

              Estudiante B: Hola. Me llamo Kelly.

              Estudiante A: ¿Qué clases tienes, Kelly?

              Estudiante B: Tengo español, química, inglés y música.

Nombre	Clases
1.	
2.	
3.	
4.	

Para entender en clase

To understand in class

¿Entienden? ¿Sí? ¡Excelente!

© Rubberball/Getty Images

Las instrucciones del profesor	Professor's instructions
Su atención, por favor.	*Your attention, please.*
Abran los libros en la página (cinco).	*Open your books to page (five).*
Cierren los libros.	*Close your books.*
Escuchen.	*Listen.*
Repitan.	*Repeat.*
Miren acá.	*Look over here.*
Escriban la respuesta.	*Write the answer.*
Contesten las preguntas.	*Answer the questions.*
¿Entienden?	*Do you understand?*
Trabajen con un(a) compañero(a) de clase.	*Work with a classmate.*

Comunidad In class, you will join with your classmates and instructor to form a new community where you use your Spanish to learn together and share ideas.

Online To build your class community, you may be asked to post your own videos and photos or to work with a partner to make a recording. To connect to the global community, take advantage of Skype, Facebook Chat, or Google to connect with other Spanish speakers and learners.

Colaborar

LP-8 **Las instrucciones del profesor.** What might your Spanish instructor say in each situation? With a partner, match the appropriate expression to the situation.

_____ 1. To introduce new words to the class

_____ 2. If several class members appear confused

_____ 3. Before passing out a quiz

_____ 4. To organize the class members for an activity

_____ 5. To make sure everyone is listening

_____ 6. While pointing to a drawing

a. Cierren los libros, por favor.

b. Escuchen y repitan.

c. Trabajen con un compañero de clase.

d. ¿Entienden?

e. Su atención, por favor.

f. Miren acá.

Vocabulario

Congratulations! You now know how to do the following:

- Say hello and ask someone's name
- State your name and spell it
- Greet people in informal and formal situations
- Say what classes you have
- Follow your professor's instructions

Para aprender mejor

Study vocabulary according to your learning style preference. For example, visual learners like to see the words written; auditory learners benefit from hearing and repeating words aloud; kinesthetic learners prefer to act out the words. In addition, some learners prefer to study by themselves while others study better in groups. As you begin your study of Spanish, try different styles and see what works best for you.

Preguntas / Questions

Preguntas	Questions
¿Cómo está usted?	*How are you? (formal)*
¿Cómo estás?	*How are you? (informal)*
¿Cómo se escribe tu nombre?	*How do you spell your name?*
¿Cómo te llamas?	*What's your name?*
¿Qué clases tienes?	*What classes do you have?*
¿Y tú?	*And you? (informal)*
¿Y usted?	*And you? (formal)*

Palabras útiles / Useful words

Palabras útiles	Useful words
Bien.	*Fine; Good.*
Gracias.	*Thank you; Thanks.*
Hola.	*Hi; Hello.*
Me llamo...	*My name is . . .*
No. / Sí.	*No. / Yes.*
Se escribe...	*It's spelled . . .*
Tengo...	*I have . . .*
y	*and*

Títulos / Titles

Títulos	Titles
Doctor (Dr.)	*Doctor (male)*
Doctora (Dra.)	*Doctor (female)*
Profesor	*Professor (male)*
Profesora	*Professor (female)*
Señor (Sr.)	*Mr.*
Señora (Sra.)	*Mrs.; Ms.*
Señorita (Srta.)	*Miss; Ms.*

Las asignaturas / Academic subjects

Las asignaturas	Academic subjects
Las ciencias naturales	*Science*
la biología	*biology*
la física	*physics*
la química	*chemistry*
Las ciencias sociales	*Social sciences*
las ciencias políticas	*political science*
la historia	*history*
la psicología	*psychology*
Los estudios profesionales	*Professional studies*
la administración de empresas	*business administration*
la comunicación	*communication*
el derecho	*law*
la educación	*education*
la informática	*computer science*
la ingeniería	*engineering*
Las humanidades y bellas artes	*Humanities and fine arts*
el arte	*art*
la cinematografía	*film-making*
las lenguas	*languages*
la literatura	*literature*
la música	*music*
el teatro	*theater*
Las matemáticas	*Math*
el álgebra	*algebra*
el cálculo	*calculus*
la geometría	*geometry*

El alfabeto: p. 3

¡Vamos a conocernos!

CAPÍTULO 1

 Conexiones a la comunidad
Become friends with a native Spanish speaker on your campus or in your community.

In this chapter you will . . .

- explore the Spanish-speaking world
- introduce yourself and others
- greet others and ask how they're feeling
- count and exchange basic personal information

- describe your classroom and campus
- say where you're going around campus
- learn about five geographical wonders
- get to know your classmates through the social site *Share It!*

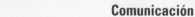

 NUESTRO MUNDO

Cultura
Spanish-speaking world, p. 10

Comunicación

 VOCABULARIO   **GRAMÁTICA**

Paso 1
Greetings, introductions, and personal information, p. 12
Numbers 0–100, p. 16
Subject pronouns and the verb **estar**, p. 19

 VOCABULARIO   **GRAMÁTICA**

Paso 2
Classroom objects and expressions, p. 22
Nouns and articles, p. 26
The verb **ser**, p. 29

 VOCABULARIO   **GRAMÁTICA**

Paso 3
Places around campus, p. 32
The verb **tener**, p. 36
The verb **ir**, p. 39

 COMPOSICIÓN   **PRONUNCIACIÓN**

Composición: A message, p. 43
  Estrategia: Using tildes, accent marks, and punctuation
Pronunciación: Vowels, p. 47

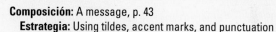

SÍNTESIS

Interpersonal, presentational, and interpretive communication, p. 45

 CONECTADOS CON...

Conexiones y Comparaciones
Conectados con... la geografía, p. 42
  Estrategia: Recognizing cognates
<u>Conectados con... la neurociencia</u>
▶ <u>Reportaje: Bolivia</u>
  Estrategia: <u>Viewing a segment several times</u>

 NUESTRA COMUNIDAD

Comunidad
Nosotros / *Share It!*: Our online community, p. 44
▶ **Perspectivas:** Where are you from?, p. 44
Exploración: Famous people, p. 44

NUESTRO **MUNDO**

El mundo hispanohablante

© Cengage Learning 2016

Spanish is the national language of twenty countries around the globe. It places second in the world, after Mandarin, for the number of native speakers.

Number of native speakers of Spanish: about 400 million

Spanish is the primary language: Argentina, Bolivia, Chile, Colombia, Costa Rica, Cuba, Ecuador, El Salvador, España, Guatemala, Guinea Ecuatorial, Honduras, México, Nicaragua, Panamá, Paraguay, Perú, Puerto Rico, República Dominicana, Uruguay, Venezuela

Significant Spanish-speaking communities: Estados Unidos, Canadá, Andorra, Belice, Filipinas, Marruecos

© Blend Images/Shutterstock

El mundo hispanohablante es muy diverso.

Although they share a common language, native speakers of Spanish are among the most diverse in the world. Depending on the country, they trace their roots to a variety of European, Amerindian, Asian, and African cultures. In Latin America, many Spanish speakers are **mestizos**, of mixed European and Amerindian heritage.

Historia

El español tiene su origen en la Península Ibérica, en España.

The Spanish language originated in the Iberian Peninsula, where it evolved from Latin, the language of the Roman Empire. Through colonization, Spain carried the language to the New World and beyond, to Africa (Equatorial Guinea) and Asia (the Philippines). Today, although pronunciation, grammar, and vocabulary vary somewhat among the Spanish-speaking countries, these differences rarely cause problems in communication.

Religión

In most Spanish-speaking regions, the majority of the inhabitants consider themselves Christians—most often, Roman Catholics. Other world religions—including Judaism, Buddhism, and Islam—are practiced as well. In countries such as Mexico, Guatemala, Ecuador, Bolivia, and Peru, many cherish their Amerindian beliefs and rituals.

El catolicismo es la religión principal del mundo hispanohablante.

El fútbol es el deporte más popular del mundo hispanohablante.

Deporte

Without a doubt, the most popular sport in the Spanish-speaking world is soccer. People of all ages and social classes play the game, and millions more watch it. Baseball is the national pastime in many Spanish-speaking countries of the Caribbean, while basketball continues to draw more and more fans, especially in Argentina and Spain.

1-1 **¿Qué sabes?** What do you know about the Spanish-speaking world? Read the information on these two pages and match the information in the two columns.

_____ 1. Number of countries where Spanish is the predominant language

_____ 2. Ethnic and cultural heritage of native speakers of Spanish

_____ 3. Language from which Spanish evolved

_____ 4. How Spanish came to be spoken in the Americas

_____ 5. Main religion of the Spanish-speaking world

_____ 6. Most popular sport in Spain and Latin America

a. colonization

b. Latin

c. soccer

d. twenty

e. Catholicism

f. European, Amerindian, African, Asian

El primer día de clase

In this *Paso*, you will . . .
- greet others and say good-bye
- introduce yourself and others
- exchange phone numbers, emails, and addresses
- describe how you and others feel

Entre profesores y estudiantes

Saludos	*Greetings*
Buenos días.	*Good morning.*
Buenas tardes.	*Good afternoon.*
Buenas noches.	*Good evening.*
¿Qué tal?	*How's it going? (informal)*
Muy bien.	*Very well; Great.*
No muy bien.	*Not so well.*
Regular.	*So-so.*
¿Qué hay de nuevo?	*What's new?*
Nada.	*Nothing.*
Todo bien.	*Everything's fine; Everything's okay.*

Reacciones	*Reactions*
Lo siento (mucho).	*I'm (very) sorry.*
Me alegro (mucho).	*I'm (really) glad.*

Entre profesores y estudiantes (cont.)

Presentaciones	*Introductions*
¿Cómo se llama usted?	*What's your name? (formal)*
¿Cómo te llamas?	*What's your name? (informal)*
Le presento a...	*I'd like you to meet . . . (formal)*
Te presento a...	*I'd like you to meet . . . (informal)*
Mucho gusto.	*Nice to meet you.*
Igualmente.	*Same here; Likewise.*

Despedidas	*Leave-Takings*
Adiós.	*Good-bye.*
Buenas noches.	*Good night.*
Chao.	*Bye; Ciao. (informal)*
Hasta luego.	*See you later.*
Hasta mañana.	*See you tomorrow.*
¡Nos vemos (en clase)!	*See you (in class)!*
¡Te llamo más tarde!	*I'll call you later!*

PASO 1 VOCABULARIO V

¡Aplícalo!

↻ Basic greetings and titles of address, **Lección preliminar**

 Colaborar

1-2 **Categorías.** How many of the following basic phrases do you understand? Working with a classmate, take turns reading each list aloud; then circle the words and phrases that fit each category. The number of correct answers per category will vary.

Modelo Alfabeto: (jota) / (equis) / nada / sí / (ye)

1. **Saludos:** ¡Hola! / Hasta mañana. / Buenas noches. / Chao. / Buenos días.

2. **Despedidas:** ¡Nos vemos! / Hasta luego. / Buenas noches. / ¿Qué tal? / Igualmente.

3. **Títulos:** Profesora / Regular / Srta. / Señora / Doctor

4. **Presentaciones:** Me llamo Ana. / Lo siento mucho. / Te presento a José. / Mucho gusto. / Regular.

5. **Variantes de "¿Cómo estás?":** ¿Qué tal? / ¿Cómo se llama usted? / ¿Qué hay de nuevo? / ¿Y usted? / ¿Cómo se escribe?

6. **Respuestas a (Responses to) "¿Cómo estás?":** Bien, gracias. / Igualmente. / No muy bien. / Mucho gusto. / Adiós.

Colaborar

1-3 **Lo lógico.** How would you respond to the following questions and statements? Write the letter of the most logical response in each blank. Then read each conversational exchange aloud with a classmate and decide whether each one is formal, informal, or possibly both!

_____ 1. Buenas tardes. ¿Cómo está usted?

_____ 2. Te presento a Tamisha.

_____ 3. ¿Cómo te llamas?

_____ 4. ¿Qué hay de nuevo?

_____ 5. Todo bien, gracias.

_____ 6. Mucho gusto, señor.

_____ 7. Hasta luego.

a. Me alegro mucho.

b. Bien. ¿Y usted?

c. Te llamo más tarde.

d. Hola, mucho gusto.

e. Igualmente.

f. Nada.

g. Me llamo Hugo.

 Colaborar

1-4 **Una conversación.** Working with a classmate, read the following conversation between two students. As you read your part, choose the more logical words in parentheses.

ROSA (1. Adiós / Hola), Paco. ¿Qué (2. estás / hay de nuevo)?

PACO Todo bien, (3. igualmente / gracias). ¿Y tú? ¿Cómo (4. estás / está)?

ROSA No (5. regular / muy bien).

PACO Ah... ¡(6. Me alegro / Lo siento)!

ROSA Bueno, (7. nos vemos / mucho gusto) en clase.

PACO (8. Buenos días / Chao).

© Kadettmann/Dreamstime.com

14 Capítulo 1

¡Exprésate!

The alphabet, **Lección preliminar**

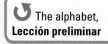 **1-5** **El primer día de clase.** With two classmates, complete the following dialogue among three university students with words and phrases from the **Vocabulario** section on pages 12–13. When you finish, practice reading it aloud.

ALEX ¡Hola, Sam! ¿Qué hay de nuevo?

SAM (1) _____. ¿Y tú?

ALEX (2) _____.

SAM Me alegro mucho. Mira, te presento a Jordan.

ALEX (3) _____.

JORDAN Igualmente.

SAM Bueno, nos vemos en clase.

ALEX (4) _____.

JORDAN (5)¡_____!

 **1-6** **En una fiesta.** In groups of three, write a dialogue for each of the following situations. Be prepared to act these out in front of the class.

1.  2.  3.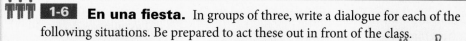

Illustrations © Cengage Learning 2016

 1-7 **Presentaciones.** Working in groups of three, take turns introducing the person to your left.

Modelo

Te presento a Nicole.

Mucho gusto, Nicole.

Igualmente.

Nota cultural

In Spain and Latin America, relatives usually greet each other with a kiss on the cheek. Male friends generally greet each other with several pats on the back, while female friends kiss each other on the cheek. Friends and peers of opposite sexes will also kiss—an "air" kiss with touching cheeks. In more formal situations, men and women shake hands.

1-8 **Los países.** How many Spanish-speaking countries do you recall? Try this guessing game:

Clase

- Everyone stands up.
- Your instructor starts to spell aloud the name of a Spanish-speaking country.
- As soon as you recognize the country, sit down.
- The instructor will ask one person for the correct answer.

Los números del 0 al 100

LUIS	¡Hola, Carmen!
MABEL	¿Carmen? Soy Mabel.
LUIS	¿Es el cuatro, sesenta y cinco, cero, tres, veinte?
MABEL	No, es el cuatro, sesenta y cinco, cero, tres, veintiuno.

■ ■ ■

Descúbrelo

- What telephone number is Luis trying to call?

- Did he call the correct number? Which digit did he get wrong?

- What number in the conversation is written as three separate words?

1. In Spanish, the numbers (**los números**) 0–30 and 40, 50, 60 . . . 100 are each generally written as one word. The numbers 31–39, 41–49, 51–59, etc. are each written as three separate words.

Los números del 0 al 100							
0	cero						
1	uno	11	once	21	veintiuno	31	treinta y uno
2	dos	12	doce	22	veintidós	32	treinta y dos
3	tres	13	trece	23	veintitrés	33	treinta y tres
4	cuatro	14	catorce	24	veinticuatro	40	cuarenta
5	cinco	15	quince	25	veinticinco	50	cincuenta
6	seis	16	dieciséis	26	veintiséis	60	sesenta
7	siete	17	diecisiete	27	veintisiete	70	setenta
8	ocho	18	dieciocho	28	veintiocho	80	ochenta
9	nueve	19	diecinueve	29	veintinueve	90	noventa
10	diez	20	veinte	30	treinta	100	cien

2. There are common patterns for how numbers are used in phone numbers, home addresses, and email addresses.

- Telephone numbers are often stated in groups of two. If there is an uneven number of digits, the first digit is stated, then the pairs. For example, 516-8596 is said: "five, sixteen, eighty-five, ninety-six."

MARTA	**¿Cuál es tu número de teléfono?**	*What's your phone number?*
LUIS	**Es el dos, veintidós, treinta y tres, cincuenta.**	*It's 222-3350.*

- When saying a street address, the building number is given after the name of the street.

JUAN	**¿Cuál es tu dirección?**	*What's your address?*
PACO	**Es calle Colón, número ochenta y seis.**	*It's 86 Colón Street.*

- The words **arroba** (@) and **punto com** are used in email addresses.

ELENA	**¿Cuál es tu correo electrónico?**	*What's your email?*
CLARA	**Es vargas99@yahoo.com (vargas, noventa y nueve, arroba, yahoo punto com)**	*It's . . .*

3. The number **uno** and numbers that end in **uno** have different forms depending on the gender of the noun that follows.

- **Uno** becomes **un** before a masculine noun. Notice the accent mark over **veintiún**.

un libro	veintiún libros	cincuenta y un libros

- **Uno** becomes **una** before a feminine noun.

una página	veintiuna páginas	cincuenta y una páginas

The alphabet, **Lección preliminar**

Colaborar

1-9 **Las secuencias.** With a partner, read the following sequences of numbers aloud in Spanish and fill in the gaps.

1. 2, 4, 6, 8... 20
2. 100, 90, 80... 20
3. 21, 24, 27... 45
4. 50, 55, 60... 90
5. 19, 18, 17... 11
6. 63, 62, 61... 55
7. (Create your own sequence and have your partner finish it with 5 more numbers.)

Colaborar

1-10 **En el café.** How many people came to the coffee shop this week? Write out each number in words. Afterwards, check your answers by using the Spanish alphabet to spell each number aloud to a classmate.

1. 21 estudiantes   2. 1 doctora   3. 31 profesores

4. 1 doctor   5. 21 profesoras

Illustrations © Cengage Learning 2016

Colaborar

1-11 **Información básica.** Working with a partner, complete the following dialogue between the department secretary and a student. Use logical words and phrases from the **Gramática** section on pages 16–17. Afterwards, read it aloud again and substitute your own personal information for Felicia's.

SECRETARIA ¿Cómo se llama usted?

FELICIA Felicia Torres.

SECRETARIA ¿Cuál es su (1) _____ de teléfono?

FELICIA (2) _____ el 762-0897.

SECRETARIA ¿(3) _____ es su dirección?

FELICIA Es (4) _____ Jacinto, número 41.

SECRETARIA ¿Cuál es su (5) _____ electrónico?

FELICIA Es felicia dos (6) _____ gmail punto com.

SECRETARIA Gracias.

¡Exprésate!

1-12 **Caracoles.** With four to six classmates, sit in a circle and play the number game "**Caracoles**."

- One student starts counting: **uno**.
- The person to his/her right says the next number: **dos**. Continue counting in a circle.
- When the number is 7, has a 7 in it, or is a multiple of 7, the person says **caracoles** instead of the number. For example: ... **10, 11, 12, 13, caracoles, 15, 16, caracoles, 18**...
- When someone makes a mistake, start over with **uno**. The first group to reach **cien** wins the game.

1-13 **Tarjetas de presentación.** You've just returned from a meeting of the Chamber of Commerce. With a partner, look at the business cards you collected. Take turns reading a phone number, address, or email at random. Your partner needs to say whose it is.

Modelo **Estudiante A:** El número de teléfono es el cuarenta y nueve, cuarenta y uno, setenta y ocho, once.
Estudiante B: Gregorio López Blanco.

GREGORIO LÓPEZ BLANCO
Gerente Director

Tel. 4941-7811
GLB@importadoraperusa.com

María Echeverry Cabrera
Agente de turismo

www.viaturs.com
Calle Princesa, 310
Celulares: 2483-4524
　　　　　5941-0399

LORENZO CASTAÑO RUIZ
MERCADÓLOGO

Sintex S.A.
Calle San Francisco, 13
lcastaño@sintex.com
Teléfono: 3367-2115

Mónica Alejandra Casona
Fotógrafa

Calle 23, #55
Cel. 2176-5042
acasona123@gmail.com

Illustrations © Cengage Learning 2016

1-14 **El directorio.** Fill out the directory by doing the following:

- Introduce yourself to four classmates you don't know very well.
- Ask for and write each person's name, local address, phone number, and email.
- For extra practice, follow the Hispanic custom of using two last names.
- To ask for the spelling, say **¿Cómo se escribe... ?**

Nombre	Dirección	Teléfono	Correo electrónico

Los pronombres de sujeto y el verbo *estar*

NURIA ¡Hola, Pablo! ¿Cómo estás?

PABLO Bien, pero *(but)*... ¿dónde está Diego?

NURIA Él está en Nueva York.

PABLO ¿Y Ana?

NURIA Ella está en Miami.

PABLO ¡Suertudos! *(Lucky ones!)*

1. The subject of a sentence is the person who performs the action or is the topic of the sentence. It can be a name (such as **Diego**), a noun (such as **amigo**), or a subject pronoun, such as *I* or *we* in English. Here are the subject pronouns in Spanish. Notice that there is no Spanish equivalent for the subject pronoun *it*.

Descúbrelo

- Where are Diego and Ana?
- What word is used to ask and tell where Diego is?
- To whom does the subject pronoun **ella** refer?

Los pronombres de sujeto	
Singular	**Plural**
yo *I*	**nosotros** *we (males / mixed group)* **nosotras** *we (females)*
tú *you (informal)* **usted (Ud.)** *you (formal)*	**vosotros** *you (males / mixed group; informal; used in Spain)* **vosotras** *you (females; informal; used in Spain)* **ustedes (Uds.)** *you (formal; also informal in Latin America)*
él *he* **ella** *she*	**ellos** *they (males / mixed group)* **ellas** *they (females)*

2. Spanish has several ways of expressing the subject pronoun *you*.

- Use the informal **tú** to address someone you're on a first-name basis with, such as a friend, a family member, a classmate, or a peer.

- Use the more formal **usted**, oftentimes written as **Ud.**, to address an older person, an acquaintance, or an authority figure.

- In Latin America, use **ustedes (Uds.)** to address a group of two or more people, in all circumstances. In Spain, use **vosotros** and **vosotras** to address two or more friends, family members, classmates, or peers; use **ustedes** to address two or more authority figures or people much older than yourself.

3. Because there are different verb forms for most subject pronouns, subject pronouns are not used when the meaning is clear. Instead, subject pronouns are added primarily to clarify or emphasize their meaning. In the following sentence, for example, the understood subject is **yo: Estoy bien.**

4. Here are the forms for the verb **estar** *(to be)* in the present tense. **Estar** *(to be)* is the basic form, called the infinitive. The different verb forms, called conjugations, correspond to different subjects: *I am, you are, he is*, etc. When the subject is *it*, the form **está** is used.

El presente del verbo *estar* *to be*			
yo	**estoy**	nosotros/nosotras	**estamos**
tú	**estás**	vosotros/vosotras	**estáis**
usted	**está**	ustedes	**están**
él/ella	**está**	ellos/ellas	**están**

5. The verb **estar** is used to express where someone or something is located. To ask about a location, begin your question with **¿Dónde... ?** For example: **¿Dónde está Guinea Ecuatorial?**

6. The verb **estar** is also used to express how someone feels. Here are some key words for physical and emotional conditions. Notice that nearly all these adjectives have two forms: Use the word ending in **-o** to refer to a male, and the one ending in **-a** to refer to a female. Adjectives that end in **-e**, such as **triste**, can refer to a male or a female.

cansado / cansada sad
contento / contenta happy
emocionado / emocionada excited
enfermo / enferma sick
enojado / enojada Angry/grumpy

estresado / estresada stressed
ocupado / ocupada occupied/busy
preocupado / preocupada concerned/worried
triste sad

¡Aplícalo!

 1-15 **De vacaciones.** Where are you and your family vacationing? Working with a classmate, create six short conversations with the verb **estar** like the one in the model. Can you identify the country that corresponds to each capital city?

Modelo Quito
Estudiante A: Mi familia y yo estamos en Quito.
Estudiante B: ¡Ah! Están en Ecuador.

1. Madrid
2. San José
3. Buenos Aires
4. Lima
5. Santiago
6. Bogotá

1-16 **Situaciones.** How do you feel in the following situations? Compare your answers with those of a classmate. (Don't forget: Use the appropriate **-o** or **-a** ending!)

Modelo The police stop you on the highway.
Estudiante A *(male):* ¡Estoy estresado!
Estudiante B *(female):* ¡Estoy preocupada!

1. Your dog died.
2. You have 5 classes and 3 meetings.
3. Your roommate lost your iPod.
4. You ate some bad food.
5. Your parents are buying you a car.
6. Your favorite aunt is in the hospital.

1-17 ¡**Agarra** *(Catch)*! In groups of four or five, play the following conjugation game.

- The instructor will give each group a small ball (or a crumpled piece of paper).
- The person holding the ball calls out a subject (look at the list below or invent your own) and gently tosses the ball to another player.
- That player needs to say the corresponding form of **estar**, then call out another subject, toss the ball to someone else, and so on.

Sujetos			
Ana y yo	nosotros	Sergio	usted
el doctor Tobías	la profesora	la Srta. Ruiz	ustedes
Marta y Ana	los señores	tú	yo

1-18 **Ta-Te-Ti con emociones.** With a partner, play two games of tic-tac-toe. Taking turns, pretend you are each one of the people in the drawings and say how you feel. If you give the correct expression, mark the corresponding box with **X** or **O**. Think before choosing a drawing so that your partner doesn't get three in a row!

Modelo If you are male, you say: **Estoy contento**.
If you are female, you say: **Estoy contenta**.

© Cengage Learning 2016

1-19 **Dramatización.** With a partner, role-play the following situation, **en español**, of course! Be prepared to present it to the class.

Professor Ramírez	Alicia, an employee in the dean's office
1. You walk into your dean's office and greet his assistant.	2. You greet the professor who just walked in and whom you don't know.
3. Say who you are and ask where the dean, **el doctor Blanco**, is.	4. The dean, **el doctor Blanco**, is in the hospital (**en el hospital**); he's ill.
5. React to the news.	6. Say that you are worried.
7. Ask where the hospital is located.	8. The hospital is on Alamos Street.
9. Say thank you and good-bye.	10. Reply appropriately.

En el salón de clase

In this *Paso*, you will . . .
- identify classroom objects
- use common classroom expressions
- ask and tell where someone is from
- express possession

El salón

un calendario

un mapa del mundo

Septiembre

un televisor

un reloj

una pizarra digital

una pizarra

¿Entienden?

No. ¿Puede repetirlo?

un libro

una profesora

una mesa

una silla

DICCIONARIO

un diccionario

una computadora (portátil)

© Cengage Learning 2016

¿Qué hay en el salón de clase?	What's in the classroom?
Hay...	*There is / There are . . .*
También hay...	*Also, there is / there are . . .*
Expresiones de cortesía	*Courtesy expressions*
Por favor.	*Please.*
Gracias.	*Thank you.*
De nada.	*You're welcome; No problem.*
Perdón.	*Excuse me; Sorry.*

El salón (cont.)

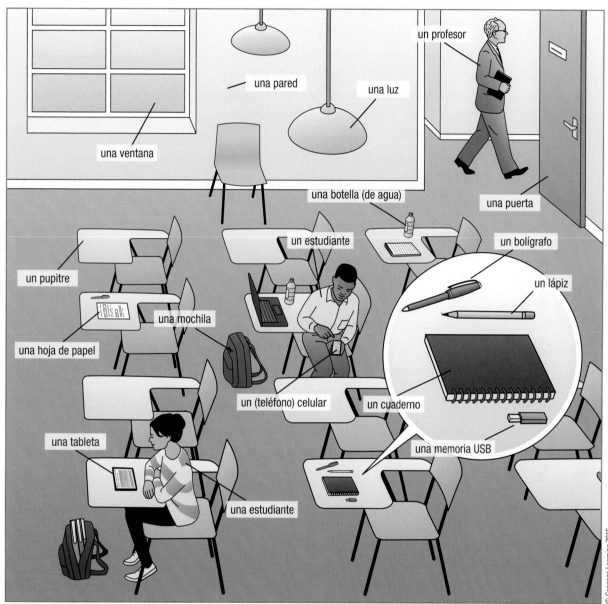

una pared
una luz
un profesor
una ventana
una botella (de agua)
una puerta
un estudiante
un bolígrafo
un pupitre
un lápiz
una mochila
una hoja de papel
un (teléfono) celular
un cuaderno
una tableta
una memoria USB
una estudiante

Expresiones útiles en una clase

¿Cómo se dice... ?	*How do you say . . . ?*
¿Qué significa... ?	*What does . . . mean?*
¿Qué es esto?	*What is this?*
Tengo una pregunta.	*I have a question.*
No entiendo.	*I don't understand.*
No sé.	*I don't know.*
¿Puede repetirlo?	*Can you repeat that? (formal)*
¿Puedes repetirlo?	*Can you repeat that? (informal)*
¿En qué página estamos?	*What page are we on?*

Useful classroom expressions

© Cengage Learning 2016

¡Aplícalo!

Colaborar

1-20 Categorías. With a partner, take turns reading all the words in each category aloud. Then, identify one word that isn't related to the category.

1. **Para tomar apuntes** *(To take notes)*: un bolígrafo / una botella de agua / una computadora portátil / un cuaderno

2. **Para indicar la fecha / la hora** *(To tell the date / time)*: un calendario / un teléfono celular / un reloj / una mesa

3. **Dentro de una mochila** *(Inside a backpack)*: una ventana / un lápiz / una botella de agua / una memoria USB

4. **Muebles** *(Furniture)*: una silla / un estudiante / una mesa / un pupitre

5. **Para estudiar** *(To study)*: un mapa / un diccionario / un libro / una puerta

6. **Aparatos electrónicos** *(Electronic devices)*: una pizarra digital / una tableta / una pared / una computadora

Colaborar

1-21 Expresiones útiles. What are these students saying to their instructor during Spanish class? With a partner, read the three conversations aloud and complete each one in a logical way. Refer to the **Vocabulario** section on pages 22–23.

1.
SARA Profesora Ramos, tengo una _____.

PROFESORA RAMOS ¿Sí? Dime. *(Tell me.)*

SARA ¿_____ significa "pared"?

PROFESORA RAMOS Significa *wall.*

2.
KEISHA Profesora, ¿en qué página _____?

PROFESORA RAMOS En la página diez.

KEISHA Perdón, ¿_____ repetirlo?

PROFESORA RAMOS Sí, claro. Estamos en la página diez.

3.
CARL Profesora, ¿_____ se dice *tomorrow* en español?

PROFESORA RAMOS Se dice "mañana".

CARL Ah, sí. Muchas _____.

PROFESORA RAMOS De nada.

Colaborar

1-22 En el salón de clase. What objects are in your Spanish classroom? With a partner, take turns stating whether each object in the list is in the classroom. Follow the model.

Modelo una computadora
Hay una computadora. / No hay una computadora.

1. un mapa del mundo
2. una pizarra digital
3. un televisor
4. un calendario

5. un reloj en la pared
6. un diccionario
7. una puerta
8. un escritorio

¡Exprésate!

Clase

1-23 **¿Dónde está?** Your Spanish instructor has hidden some objects around the room. Can you and your classmates find them?

- Divide the class into two or three teams.
- Listen to your instructor's question and raise your hand as soon as you see the object.
- Your instructor will call on someone on the first team to have three or more people with their hands up.

Modelo **Profesor(a):** ¿Dónde está mi libro?
Estudiante: Aquí está *(Here it is)*, profesor(a). *(pointing to the book)*
Profesor(a): Muchas gracias.
Estudiante: De nada.

> **Algunos objetos en el salón de clase:**
>
> el bolígrafo
> la botella de agua
> el cuaderno
> el lápiz
> el libro
> el mapa
> la memoria USB
> el teléfono celular

1-24 **El ahorcado.** Using the expressions in **Frases útiles**, invite a classmate to work with you. Then, play a game of Hangman using the names of classroom objects.

- Think of a word and draw a line for every letter in that word.
- Your partner will guess one letter at a time.
- If the letter is correct, write it on the appropriate line. If it's wrong, write the letter on the page and draw a body part on the gallows.

Are you ready for a bigger challenge? Try using short phrases in addition to classroom objects.

> **Frases útiles**
>
> ¿Quieres trabajar conmigo? *Do you want to work together?*
> Claro que sí. *Sure.*
> Te toca a ti. *It's your turn.*
> Está bien. *Okay.*

© Cengage Learning 2016

Colaborar

1-25 **Hablando con el profesor.** During class, your instructor says the following. Working with a partner, say how you would respond.

1. ¿Cómo se dice *notebook* en español?
2. ¿Qué hay en la mesa?
3. ¿Qué significa "mochila"?
4. ¿Qué es esto? *(pointing to a chair)*

5. Abran el libro.
6. Gracias.
7. ¿Entienden?

1-26 **¿Cómo se dice... ?** With a partner, take turns asking the Spanish names for six objects in the classroom. Ask **¿Cómo se dice** (+ word in English)? Your partner replies **Se dice** (+ word in Spanish).

Los sustantivos y los artículos

RAMONA	Tengo todo *(everything)* para las clases: la computadora portátil, unos cuadernos, un bolígrafo...
PACO	¿Y los libros?
RAMONA	¡Ay, no! ¿Dónde están los libros?
PACO	¡Mira! *(Look!)* Están en la mesa.

■ ■ ■
Descúbrelo

- What materials does Ramona have ready for class? What seems to be missing?
- What do you think **la** and **los** mean?
- Which words mean *a* or *some*?
- Which of these is a plural noun: **computadora**, **cuadernos**, or **bolígrafo**?

1. Nouns (**los sustantivos**) are words that identify people, places, things, and abstract concepts. In Spanish, all nouns have gender (**género**) and are referred to as masculine or feminine. Here's a general rule.

Masculino	Femenino
• Words that end in **-o** are usually masculine: **un libro**	• Words that end in **-a** are usually feminine: **una computadora**
• Words that refer to males are masculine, regardless of ending: **un profesor, un estudiante, un artista**	• Words that refer to females are feminine, regardless of ending: **una profesora, una estudiante, una artista**

2. Some nouns don't follow the general rule.

- Nouns that end in **-e** or a consonant may be masculine or feminine. You must memorize the genders of these nouns individually.

  Masculine: **un pupitre, un reloj**   Feminine: **una serie, una luz**

- A few nouns must be memorized as exceptions. For example, **el día** *(day)* and **el mapa** end in **-a** but are masculine.

3. Nouns are either singular or plural. To make a noun plural:

- Add **-s** if the noun ends in a vowel: **cuaderno → cuadernos**
- Add **-es** if the noun ends in a consonant: **profesor → profesores**
- If the final consonant is **z**, change **z** to **c** and add **-es**: **luz → luces**

To refer to a mixed group of males and females, use the masculine plural: **profesores** *(male and female professors)*

4. Nouns are often used with definite articles (**los artículos definidos**), which express *the*. You must choose the article that matches the noun in gender and number.

Los libros están en **la** mesa.   *The books are on the table.*

Los artículos definidos		
	Masculino	**Femenino**
Singular	**el** libro	**la** mesa
Plural	**los** libros	**las** mesas

- Definite articles are used before titles such as **señor**, **profesora**, etc. when you talk about a person, but not when you talk directly to a person.

  La señora Perales está enferma. *but* ¿Cómo está usted, señora Perales?

- English 's (apostrophe s) is never used in Spanish to express possession. Use this formula instead:

DEFINITE ARTICLE	+	THING POSSESSED	+ ***DE*** +	POSSESSOR	
el	+	libro	+ **de** +	Juan	*Juan's book*

5. Indefinite articles (**los artículos indefinidos**) are used with nouns and express *a/an* and *some*. You must choose the article that matches the noun in gender and number.

   Hay **unos** bolígrafos y **una** botella en la mesa.   *There are **some** pens and **a** bottle on the table.*

Los artículos indefinidos		
	Masculino	**Femenino**
Singular	**un** bolígrafo	**una** botella
Plural	**unos** bolígrafos	**unas** botellas

Colaborar
1-27 **En la mochila.** What's in this backpack? Challenge a classmate to see which of you unscrambles all the words faster. Afterwards, take turns saying each word aloud with its indefinite article: **un**, **una**, **unos**, or **unas**.

¡Aplícalo!

1. llastebo
2. dcarlnioea
3. fogarlíbos
4. spálice

5. onfoelté cruella
6. emmoair BSU
7. slobir
8. draunoce

Kim Reinick/Shutterstock

1-28 **¿Qué número?** Working with a partner, play a guessing game. The first person randomly selects a drawing and identifies the object. The second person listens and says the corresponding number of that object. Don't forget to include the appropriate definite article: **el**, **la**, **los**, or **las**.

Modelo **Estudiante A:** el pupitre
          Estudiante B: número 8
          Estudiante A: ¡Correcto!

1.   2.   3.   4.   5.

6.   7.   8.   9.   10.

© Cengage Learning 2016

1-29 ¿Qué es esto? Find out how many words your classmate remembers. Taking turns, do the following.

- Point to different items in your classroom and ask **¿Qué es esto?** You can also point to items in drawings in your book. (But be sure to cover up the labels!)
- Your classmate should first identify the object together with the corresponding indefinite article (**un, una, unos, unas**), and then give the plural.

Modelo Estudiante A: ¿Qué es esto? *(pointing to a backpack)*
Estudiante B: una mochila
Estudiante A: ¿Y en plural?
Estudiante B: unas mochilas

Nota lingüística

Use the preposition **en** to mean *in* or *on*. For example: **en la mochila** *in the backpack*, **en la pared** *on the wall*.

1-30 ¿Dónde está? Form a group with three or four classmates. Look at the drawing of the office of **Profesor Caos**. Taking turns, ask **¿Dónde está / Dónde están** *(name of object(s) in drawing)*? The person to your right replies and the others say whether the answer is correct.

Modelo Estudiante A: ¿Dónde están los mapas?
Estudiante B: Los mapas están en la mochila.
Estudiante C: No. Los mapas están en la pared.

© Cengage Learning 2016

1-31 Nuestro salón de clase. What does your Spanish classroom look like? What is in it? Play this true-false game with a classmate or with two teams of two.

- First, each of you (or each team) should write ten statements about what is in your classroom; these statements may be true or false. For example:

    Hay veinte estudiantes en nuestro salón de clase.

    No hay un mapa.

- Next, take turns reading the statements aloud. Your partner (or opposing team) must say whether the statement is true (**cierto**) or false (**falso**). Each correct answer scores one point.
- Want to make the game more challenging? Make it a rule that the players cannot look around the room and must say from memory whether each statement is true or false.

El verbo *ser*

CARLA   ¿Profesor Jones? Yo soy Carla Aguado y ella es mi amiga Alicia Ríos. Estamos en su clase de inglés.

PROF. JONES   ¡Mucho gusto! Eh... ¿De dónde son ustedes?

ALICIA   Somos de Colombia. Yo soy de Cartagena y Carla es de Bogotá.

1. The verb **ser** means *to be.* Here are its forms in the present tense.

El presente del verbo *ser* to be			
yo	**soy**	nosotros/nosotras	**somos**
tú	**eres**	vosotros/vosotras	**sois**
usted	**es**	ustedes	**son**
él/ella	**es**	ellos/ellas	**son**

2. The verb **ser** is known as a linking verb because it connects two parts of the sentence together. It is often used before nouns to identify people, places, or things. Notice the question words that are used to request identification: **¿qué?** *(what?)* and **¿quién?** *(who?)*

DAVID	¿Qué **es** esto?	*What **is** this?*
PROFESOR	**Es** una tableta.	*It's a tablet computer.*
ANA	¿Quién **es** ese señor?	*Who **is** that man?*
LUISA	**Es** el Profesor Sánchez.	*He's Professor Sánchez.*

3. **Ser** is used with the preposition **de** to tell where somebody or something is from. Notice the question words **¿De dónde... ?** *(Where . . . from?)*

PACO	**¿De** dónde **eres?**	*Where **are you from?***
JUAN	**Soy de** México.	*I'm from Mexico.*

4. **Ser** is also used with the preposition **de** to express to whom something belongs. Notice the question words **¿De quién... ?** *(Whose . . . ?/ To whom . . . ?)*

RITA	**¿De** quién **son** los cuadernos?	***Whose** notebooks **are** these? / To whom do the notebooks belong?*
ANITA	**Son de** Rafael.	***They are** Rafael's. / They belong to Rafael.*

5. While the verb **ser** is used in many cases to express *is* and *are*, Spanish uses the word **hay** to say *There is . . .* and *There are . . . .* **Hay** is a present tense form of the verb **haber.**

Hay veinticinco estudiantes en la clase de español.
There are twenty-five students in Spanish class.

■ ■ ■
Descúbrelo

■ With whom are Carla and Alicia speaking?

■ What question is used to ask Carla and Alicia where they are from?

■ What three verb forms does Alicia use to explain where the two women are from?

¡Aplícalo!

👤👤👤 **1-32** **El primer día de clase.** What are these students talking about on the first day of class? Working in groups of three, each person should read aloud the lines for one of the students in the dialogue. Complete each sentence with the appropriate form of the verb **ser**.

ANA   Marcos, te presento a Rafael. Rafael (1) _____ un nuevo *(new)* estudiante.

MARCOS   Hola, Rafael. ¿De dónde (2) _____ *(tú)*?

RAFAEL   Yo (3) _____ de Chile.

MARCOS   ¿Sí? Ana y yo (4) _____ de Chile, también. ¡Qué casualidad! *(What a coincidence!)*

RAFAEL   Oye *(Listen)*, ¿quién (5) _____ la señora rubia *(blond)*?

ANA   (6) _____ la Sra. Smith, nuestra *(our)* profesora de inglés.

RAFAEL   ¿De dónde (7) _____ ella?

ANA   De Estados Unidos. Ella y su esposo *(her husband)* (8) _____ de Nueva York.

👤👤👤 **1-33** **Concentración.** Test your memory! Form groups of three or four and do the following.

- One person begins by completing this sentence: **Yo soy de** *(any city that begins with A).*

- The next person repeats the sentence (**Yo soy de...**) and says: **Tú eres de** *(any city that begins with B).*

- The third person repeats both sentences and then says: **Usted es de** *(any city that begins with C).*

- The game continues until all subject pronouns are used.

Modelo   Yo soy de Acapulco. Tú eres de Bogotá. ...

Colaborar **1-34** **¿Qué es esto?** Working with a classmate, read the descriptions of the mystery people, places, and things. Many of the unfamiliar words look like English words, so try to guess their meanings as you read. Then, identify what or who is being described. Use the proper form of **ser** in your response.

Modelo   **Estudiante A:** Es un papel. Indica continentes y océanos. ¿Qué es?
              Estudiante B: Es un mapa.

1. Es el primer *(first)* presidente de Estados Unidos. ¿Quién es?
2. Son libros con *(with)* definiciones. ¿Qué son?
3. Está en la Polinesia. La capital es Honolulú. ¿Qué es?
4. Es estudiante en el Colegio de Hogwarts. Los padres *(parents)* son Lily y James. ¿Quién es?
5. Son similares a los lápices. ¿Qué son?
6. Está en el salón de clase. Habla *(He/She speaks)* español bien. ¿Quién es?

¡Exprésate!

Clase

1-35 **Mis compañeros y yo.** Walk around the class and talk to four different classmates to complete the chart below. To request spelling, say **¿Cómo se escribe... ?**

Modelo **Estudiante A:** Hola. ¿Cómo te llamas?
Estudiante B: Me llamo Kelly.
Estudiante A: ¿De dónde eres, Kelly?
Estudiante B: Soy de Augusta, Georgia. ¿Y tú? ¿Cómo te llamas?

	Nombre	**Ciudad** (*City*) **y estado** (*state*)
Estudiante 1		
Estudiante 2		
Estudiante 3		
Estudiante 4		

Colaborar

1-36 **Superestrellas.** Do you recognize these stars? With a partner, follow the model to exchange information about each one.

Profesiones: actriz (*actress*), autora, cantante (*singer*), director, futbolista, jugador de béisbol, tenista

Modelo **Estudiante A:** ¿Quién es? (*pointing to the photograph*)
Estudiante B: Es Alfonso Cuarón.
Estudiante A: ¿Cuál es su profesión?
Estudiante B: Es director.
Estudiante A: ¿De dónde es?
Estudiante B: Es de México.

Alfonso Cuarón, México

1. Daddy Yankee, Puerto Rico

2. Albert Pujols, República Dominicana

3. Sofía Vergara, Colombia

4. Rafael Nadal, España

5. Isabel Allende, Chile

6. Lionel Messi, Argentina

Clase

1-37 **¿De quién es?** Your instructor is going to borrow some things from several of you and then place them on the desk. Do you recall what belongs to whom?

Modelo **Profesor(a):** ¿De quién es (*name of object in Spanish*)?
Estudiante: Es de (*name of student*).

PASO 2 **31**

PASO 3 VOCABULARIO

Por el campus

In this _Paso_, you will . . .
- identify places around campus
- say where buildings are located
- say where someone is going
- say what you have

Nuestro campus

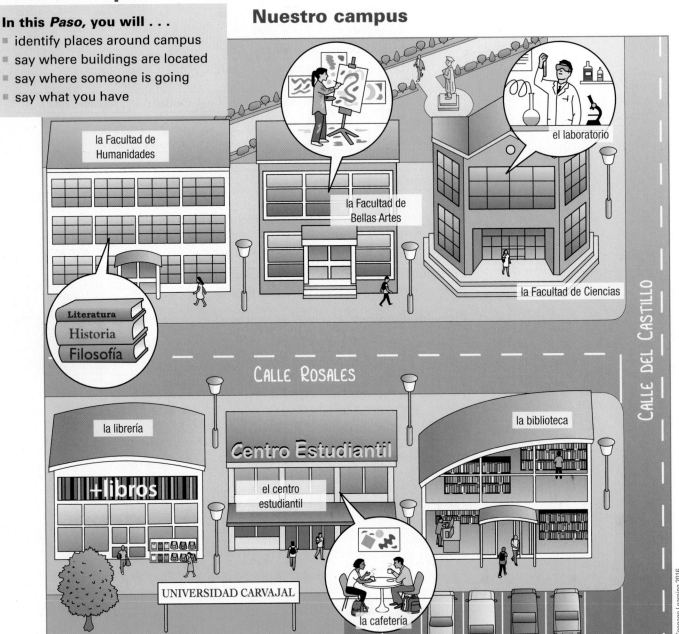

la Facultad de Humanidades

la Facultad de Bellas Artes

el laboratorio

la Facultad de Ciencias

Literatura
Historia
Filosofía

CALLE ROSALES

CALLE DEL CASTILLO

la librería

+libros

Centro Estudiantil

el centro estudiantil

la biblioteca

UNIVERSIDAD CARVAJAL

la cafetería

© Cengage Learning 2016

Para expresar ubicación	To express location
¿Dónde está... ?	Where is . . . ?
Está...	It's . . .
aquí / allí	here / there
en la calle / la avenida...	on . . . street / avenue
cerca de...	close to . . .
lejos de...	far from . . .
al lado de...	next to . . .; beside . . .
enfrente de...	across from . . .; facing . . .

Nuestro campus (cont.)

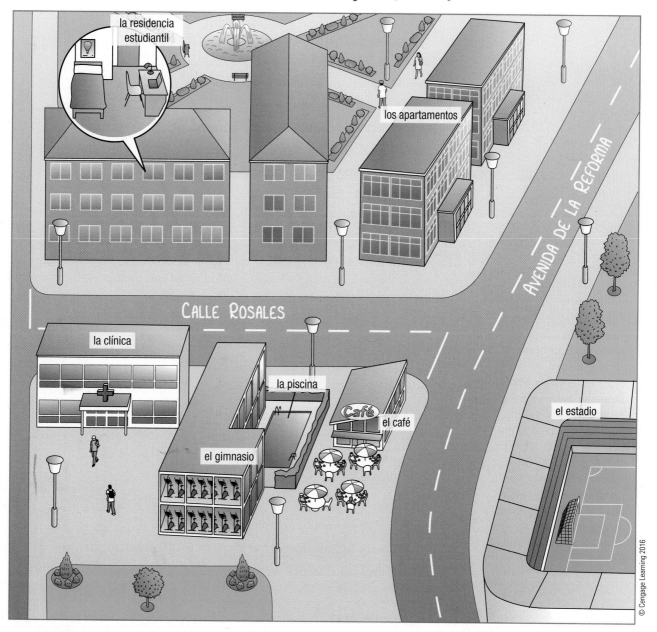

Para hablar de tu domicilio

¿Dónde vives?
    Vivo con mi familia.
    Vivo en una residencia / un apartamento.
¿Cómo es tu cuarto?
    Es (muy) grande. / Es (muy) pequeño.
¿Tienes compañero(a) de cuarto?
    Sí, se llama...
    No, no tengo compañero(a) de cuarto.

To talk about where you live

Where do you live?
    I live with my family.
    I live in a dorm / an apartment.
What's your room like?
    It's (very) big. / It's (very) small.
Do you have a roommate?
    Yes, his/her name is . . .
    No, I don't have a roommate.

¡Aplícalo!

Colaborar

1-38 ¿Dónde? Working with a partner, complete the sentences with places around campus.

1. Sirven (*They serve*) pizza en la _____.

2. Venden (*They sell*) libros en la _____.

3. Muchos estudiantes viven (*live*) en la _____ estudiantil.

4. La competición de natación (*swimming*) es en la _____.

5. Los doctores y los pacientes están en la _____.

6. Hay actividades para estudiantes en el _____ estudiantil.

7. La clase de biología es en el _____.

8. La profesora de español está en la Facultad de _____.

9. La clase de Pilates es en el _____.

10. El partido de fútbol (*soccer match*) es en el _____.

Colaborar

1-39 Este semestre. Victoria and Eugenio are talking about where they live. Working with a partner, read their conversation aloud and complete it by choosing the most logical words in parentheses.

EUGENIO ¿(1. Dónde / Cómo) vives este semestre (*this semester*), Victoria?

VICTORIA (2. Pequeño / Vivo) en una residencia.

EUGENIO Ah, ¿sí? ¿Cómo es tu (3. cuarto / familia)?

VICTORIA Es un poco (4. al lado / pequeño).

EUGENIO ¿Tienes (5. familia / compañera) de cuarto?

VICTORIA Sí. (6. Me llamo / Se llama) Sabrina y es de México. ¿Y tú, Eugenio? ¿Dónde vives?

EUGENIO Vivo en un (7. facultad / apartamento).

VICTORIA ¡Qué bien! (*That's great!*) ¿Está (8. cerca / la calle) del campus?

EUGENIO Sí. Está (9. avenida / enfrente) del estadio.

VICTORIA Bueno, Eugenio, tengo clase ahora (*now*). ¡Te llamo más tarde!

EUGENIO ¡Chao! (10. Buenos días. / ¡Hasta luego!)

> **Nota cultural**
> Students in Spanish-speaking countries choose from a variety of housing options. Many students live with their families and commute to classes; others share apartments with friends. While university-run dormitories are not as common as they are in the U.S., privately-owned residence halls are available in many cities.

Colaborar

1-40 ¿Dónde está? Imagine that you are studying at the **Universidad Carvajal**, pictured on pages 32–33. Taking turns with a classmate, describe the campus by completing the statements with street names (**en la calle...**) or logical phrases of location (**cerca de, al lado de, enfrente de**).

Modelo Los apartamentos están... **cerca del estadio.**

1. El gimnasio está...

2. La librería está...

3. Las residencias están...

4. El estadio está...

5. La Facultad de Ciencias está...

6. La Facultad de Humanidades está...

7. La clínica está...

8. El centro estudiantil está...

¡Exprésate! 👤👤👤 **1-41** **Charadas.** In groups of three or four, play a game of charades with places on campus. (Names of common places are found on pages 32–33.) One person uses pantomime and the others try to guess where on campus she or he is. The person who guesses correctly goes next.

Modelo **Estudiante A:** *(moving arms in a swimming motion)*
Estudiante B: Estás en la piscina.
Estudiante A: ¡Sí!

👤👤 **1-42** **¿Dónde está?** A Spanish-speaking student would like to know where these places are located on your campus. With a classmate, follow the model and create short dialogues.

Modelo el gimnasio
Estudiante A: Perdón, ¿dónde está el gimnasio?
Estudiante B: Está en la calle Franklin, enfrente de la Residencia Jefferson.
Estudiante A: Gracias.
Estudiante B: ¡De nada!

1. el centro estudiantil
2. la clínica
3. el estadio
4. la librería
5. la Facultad de Humanidades
6. la residencia *(Add the name of a dorm on your campus.)*

👤👤👤 **1-43** **Una encuesta.** What is the most popular kind of living arrangement in your class? Interview four classmates with these questions and take notes on their answers.

¿Dónde vives?

¿Cómo es tu cuarto?

¿Tienes compañero(a) de cuarto?

👤👤 **1-44** **Por nuestro campus.** Role-play the following situation with a classmate. One of you (**Estudiante A**) is a new student from Colombia who doesn't know his/her way around campus. The other (**Estudiante B**) is a local student walking around campus.

Estudiante A	Estudiante B
1. You (a student from Colombia) stop a student (**Estudiante B**) and find out whether he/she speaks Spanish: **¿Hablas español?**	2. Respond appropriately.
3. Ask where the library is.	4. Respond and then introduce yourself.
5. Reply to the introduction and introduce yourself. Say where you're from and ask where he/she's from.	6. Say where you're from and where you're living; then, ask where he/she's living.
7. Reply and close the conversation by thanking the student.	8. Respond appropriately and say good-bye.

PASO 3 GRAMÁTICA A

El verbo *tener*

IVÁN ¿Tienes clase ahora *(now)*?

JUAN MANUEL No. Estoy en la cafetería. ¡Tengo hambre!

IVÁN Yo tengo hambre también. ¡Muuuucha hambre!

© Cengage Learning 2016

Descúbrelo

- Does Juan Manuel have class now?
- Where is Juan Manuel?
- What verb form is used to ask a friend whether he/she *has* something?
- What expression is used to say *I'm hungry*?

1. The verb **tener** means *to have*. Here are its forms in the present tense.

El presente del verbo *tener* to have			
yo	**tengo**	nosotros/nosotras	**tenemos**
tú	**tienes**	vosotros/vosotras	**tenéis**
usted	**tiene**	ustedes	**tienen**
él/ella	**tiene**	ellos/ellas	**tienen**

2. The verb **tener** is used to express what somebody has.

¿**Tienes** clase ahora?   ***Do you have*** class now?

3. **Tener** is also used to express age. Notice that in English *to be* is used for this purpose.

¿Cuántos años **tiene** Elisa?   *How old **is** Elisa?*
Tiene veinte años.   *She's twenty (years old).*

4. Here are other common expressions that use **tener**.

LOLA ¿**Tienes** hambre?   *Are you hungry?*
ELVIRA No, pero **tengo** mucha sed.   *No, but I'm really thirsty.*

tener (mucho) calor	*to be (very) hot*
tener (mucho) frío	*to be (very) cold*
tener (mucha) hambre	*to be (very) hungry*
tener (mucha) sed	*to be (very) thirsty*
tener (mucho) cuidado	*to be (very) careful*
tener (mucho) miedo	*to be (very) afraid*
tener (mucha) prisa	*to be in a (big) hurry*
tener razón	*to be right / correct*
tener (mucho) sueño	*to be (very) sleepy*
tener que (+ *infinitive*)	*to have to (do something)*

 **¡Aplícalo!**

 1-45 **Ta-Te-Ti con _tener_.** With a partner, play two games of tic-tac-toe using the verb **tener**. Before you place your **X** or **O** on the first board, you have to conjugate and write the verb correctly with the subject in that square. For example: **ella → ella tiene.**

Carlos y yo	ella	los profesores
tú	yo	usted
ustedes	los compañeros de cuarto	Marcos

yo	Ana y yo	él
usted	tú	ustedes
Juan y David	Claudia	Miguel y yo

Colaborar

1-46 **Motivo de ruptura _(Deal-breaker)_.** Beatriz and Carla are talking with a woman who has a room to rent in her large house. With a partner, choose the correct words in parentheses as you read the dialogue aloud.

BEATRIZ Me llamo Beatriz Calvo y ella es Carla Molino. Somos estudiantes.
Yo (1. tengo / tienes) veinte (2. cuidado / años) y Carla tiene diecinueve.

SEÑORA Muy bien... Aquí está el cuarto. (3. Es / Eres) grande y tiene mucha luz.

CARLA Sí, tiene (4. prisa / razón), señora. Es muy grande.

BEATRIZ Tengo (5. una pregunta / mucha hambre): ¿Hay teléfono en el cuarto?

SEÑORA No, pero _(but)_ ¿ustedes no (6. tienes / tienen) celular?

BEATRIZ Sí, nosotras (7. tienen / tenemos) celular...

CARLA ¡Uy! ¡La temperatura está a 100 grados Fahrenheit! Tengo (8. calor / frío).

BEATRIZ Yo también. ¿El cuarto no (9. tengo / tiene) aire acondicionado?

SEÑORA No, pero _(but)_...

CARLA Lo siento, señora...

Colaborar

1-47 **La vida del estudiante.** Student life can present many challenges. Use the verb **tener** and take turns reacting to each situation.

Modelo It's midnight and you're walking alone through a dark part of campus.
Estudiante A: ¡Tengo miedo!
Estudiante B: Tengo miedo y ¡tengo cuidado!

1. It's 2:30 a.m. and you've been studying for hours for a big chemistry test.

2. As you wake up the next day, you're shocked to see that it's already 9:55. Your chemistry test is at 10:00!

3. You made it to chemistry class and the next two classes after that. But there was no time to have breakfast or to stop for coffee.

4. You finally get to have lunch. But as you leave the restaurant, you notice that the temperature has dropped to 45°. What's with the weather?

5. Back in your super-heated dorm, you settle in for another night of studying. You wonder whether they'll ever fix the thermostat.

1-48 **Personas de renombre.** With a partner, take turns talking about these well-known individuals and guessing who they are.

Modelo   **Estudiante A:** Tiene *(number)* años y es de *(country)*. ¿Quién es?
             Estudiante B: ¿Es *(name of person)*?

Lorena Ochoa, exgolfista / México / 1981

Rodolfo Neri Vela, científico y astronauta / México / 1952

Shakira, cantante y compositora / Colombia / 1977

Juanes, cantante y compositor / Colombia / 1972

Óscar Hijuelos, escritor / Estados Unidos / 1951

Sonia Sotomayor, juez asociada / Estados Unidos / 1954

1-49 **En la mochila.** What is in the typical student's backpack? Interview three classmates by asking **¿Tienes... ?** Record your answers in the chart.

	Yo	Estudiante 1	Estudiante 2	Estudiante 3
una botella de agua				
una tableta				
muchos libros				
un teléfono celular				
(another item)				

Colaborar

1-50 **¿Cómo se sienten?** It's Friday, and who can possibly concentrate under these conditions? Working with a partner, take turns describing how these students feel by creating sentences with the verb **tener** and words such as **hambre**, **miedo**, **sueño**, etc.

El verbo *ir*

ALONSO ¡Hola, Jimena! ¿Adónde vas?

JIMENA Voy al gimnasio. ¿Y tú?

ALONSO Yo voy a mi cuarto. Estoy muy cansado.

JIMENA Bueno, ¡hasta luego!

1. The verb **ir** means *to go*. Here are its forms in the present tense.

El presente del verbo *ir* *to go*			
yo	**voy**	nosotros/nosotras	**vamos**
tú	**vas**	vosotros/vosotras	**vais**
usted	**va**	ustedes	**van**
él/ella	**va**	ellos/ellas	**van**

2. To say where somebody is going, use **ir** + **a** + destination. To ask where someone is going, use the question word **¿adónde?**

SERGIO **¿Adónde** vas, Cristal?   **Where** are you going, Cristal?

CRISTAL **Voy a** clase.   *I am going to* class.

3. If the destination is preceded by the definite article **el**, combine **a** + **el** → **al**.

Van **al** café.   *They're going **to the** coffee shop.*

4. To say *Let's go!*, use the expression **¡Vamos!**

CLARA ¿Vamos a la piscina?   *Shall we go to the pool?*

JOSÉ Sí, **¡vamos!**   *Yes, **let's go!***

Colaborar **1-51** **Una conversación en el campus.** With a partner, read the following conversation aloud. As you read, choose the correct forms of the verb **ir**.

PEDRO ¡Hola, Leila! ¡Hola, Zaida! ¿Adónde (1. voy / van) ustedes?

ZAIDA Nosotras (2. van / vamos) a la Facultad de Bellas Artes.

PEDRO ¡Está lejos! Yo (3. vas / voy) a la biblioteca.

LEILA ¿No (4. vas / voy) al laboratorio, Pedro? ¿Y la clase de química?

PEDRO ¡Tienes razón! ¡Tengo que (5. va / ir) al laboratorio! ¡Chao!

LEILA ¡Hasta luego, Pedro! *(a Zaida)* ¡Oh, no! El laboratorio está en la calle Alameda ¡y Pedro (6. va / van) a la calle Cádiz!

¡Aplícalo!

1-52 **¿Adónde vas?** Take turns with a classmate asking each other where you are going. The person then says one of the places pictured below and the other one identifies the number of the drawing.

Modelo **Estudiante A:** ¿Adónde vas?

Estudiante B: Voy al laboratorio.

Estudiante A: Número 2

Estudiante B: ¡Correcto! ¿Adónde vas tú?

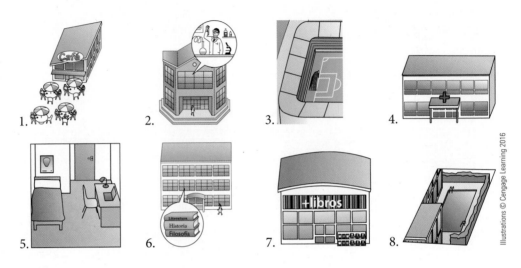

1. 2. 3. 4.

5. 6. 7. 8.

Illustrations © Cengage Learning 2016

1-53 **Cuatro en línea.** Challenge a classmate to a game of four-in-a-row. The object of this game is to get four marks (**X** or **O**) in a row, either horizontally, vertically, or diagonally. In order to put your mark in a square, you must first say a sentence with the correct form of the verb **ir**.

- To start each sentence, choose a subject from the left-hand column and add the corresponding form of the verb **ir**.

- To complete the sentence, choose the destination from the top row and add **a** before it.

Modelo **Estudiante A:** Doña Rosa va a Panamá.

Estudiante B: ¡Correcto!

	Panamá	el salón de clase	la clínica	la piscina	el café	España	el gimnasio
doña Rosa							
yo							
tú							
los profesores							
mi compañero y yo							
Julio Paz							
ustedes							

¡Exprésate!

1-54 **¿Adónde van los estudiantes?** With a partner, take turns asking and telling where the following students are going to study abroad. Each city is given on the map; be sure to add the names of the corresponding countries.

Modelo **Estudiante A:** ¿Adónde va Susana?
Estudiante B: Susana va a Quito, Ecuador.

1-55 **¿Adónde van ustedes?** You and a clasmate bump into each other on campus. Ask each other where you're going. Do this three times, in each instance pretending it's the time of day shown on the clock. Answer according to where you would normally go on campus at that time of day.

Modelo **Estudiante A:** ¡Hola! ¿Adónde vas?
Estudiante B: Voy a la Facultad de Ciencias. ¿Y tú?

Son las dos.

1. Son las diez y diez.

2. Son las doce y dos.

3. Son las cuatro y media.

1-56 **¡Vamos!** With a partner, use each of the statements below as a starting point to create a short conversation. Be sure to choose a logical place to go.

Modelo **Estudiante A:** Tengo hambre.
Estudiante B: Yo también. ¿Vamos a la cafetería?
Estudiante A: ¡Sí! ¡Vamos!

1. Tengo sed.

2. Tengo sueño.

3. Estoy enfermo(a).

4. Tengo que estudiar *(study)*.

5. ¡Ay, no! ¡Mi tableta está en mi cuarto!

6. Necesito *(I need)* unos bolígrafos para las clases.

7. Tengo que hablar *(speak)* con mi profesor de historia.

CONECTADOS CON...
LA GEOGRAFÍA

Cinco maravillas geográficas del mundo hispano

La geografía del mundo hispano es muy variada: hay selvas, desiertos, montañas y costas. Entre sus muchos atractivos naturales, están estas cinco maravillas, únicas en el mundo.

Salar de Uyuni, Bolivia

© Chris Howey/Shutterstock

1. **Salar de Uyuni, Bolivia.** Este lago prehistórico es el mayor *(largest)* desierto de sal *(salt)* del mundo. Contiene 10 mil millones *(billions)* de toneladas de minerales.

2. **Salto Ángel, Venezuela.** Es la catarata *(waterfall)* más alta *(tallest)* del mundo. Cae *(It falls)* de un "tepuy", o montaña mesa, al río Churún, 980 metros abajo.

3. **Barrancas del Cobre, México.** Este grupo de cañones es más extenso y más profundo que *(deeper than)* el Gran Cañón *(Grand Canyon)* de Estados Unidos. Están en el estado de Chihuahua, México.

Estrategia: Recognizing cognates

To instantly expand your vocabulary in Spanish, always look for cognates when you read. Cognates **(los cognados)** are words in two different languages that resemble one another and have the same meaning. The Spanish word **geografía** and the English word *geography*, for instance, are cognates. As you read the article, find and circle eight more cognates.

Palabras de geografía

el desierto	*desert*
el lago	*lake*
la montaña	*mountain*
el mundo	*world*
el río	*river*
la selva	*rainforest; jungle*

1-57 Comprensión. For each statement, change one word to make it true.

1. El Salto Ángel es la montaña más alta del mundo.

2. Barrancas del Cobre es un grupo de glaciares en Chihuahua, México.

3. Uyuni, el mayor desierto de sal del planeta, está en Argentina.

4. El río Amazonas nace en las montañas de Bolivia.

5. El Glaciar Perito Moreno es una reserva de petróleo muy importante.

6. Un "tepuy" es una montaña tropical.

Clase

1-58 ¿Y tú? Discuss the following questions with your classmates.

1. ¿Cuál es el dato más sorprendente de la lectura *(the most surprising fact in the reading)*?

2. ¿Cuál de las cinco maravillas geográficas quieres conocer *(do you want to visit)*? ¿En qué país *(country)* está?

3. ¿Cuál es una maravilla geográfica de tu estado *(home state)*?

4. **Glaciar Perito Moreno, Argentina.** Este famoso y colosal glaciar forma parte de una reserva de agua potable *(drinking water)* muy importante. La ruptura de los grandes bloques de hielo *(ice)* produce un espectáculo increíble y único *(unique)* en el mundo.

5. **Río Amazonas, América del Sur.** Es el río más grande del planeta en volumen *(volume)*. Nace *(It has its source)* en los Andes de Perú y desemboca en *(flows into)* el océano Atlántico.

Salto Ángel, Venezuela

Río Amazonas

Composición: Un mensaje

Write a message to your former roommate, who is now studying in Argentina. Include a salutation (**Hola, *name:***), a greeting, a description of your living arrangements (including roommates), a question about where he/she is living this semester, final remarks, and a closing (**Saludos, *your name***).

Revisión en pareja. Exchange papers with a classmate and edit each other's work.

- Does the message include all the information mentioned above? Write one positive comment and one suggestion for improvement.

- Are the spelling and punctuation correct? Circle any possible errors. Check carefully for accent marks, any words with the letter **ñ**, and question marks (**¿ ?**).

Estrategia
Using tildes, accent marks, and punctuation

- The letter **ñ** is written with a wavy mark, known as a tilde: **mañana**

- Accent marks are sometimes required over vowels; memorize the accent mark as part of the spelling: **estás, cómo**

- An inverted question mark is used at the beginning of a question: **¿Dónde vives?**

- An inverted exclamation point is used at the beginning of an exclamatory statement: **¡Hasta mañana!**

1-59 Nosotros / *Share It!* Who are the members of our online community? What did you learn about your classmates? Working with two or three classmates, discuss the posts on *Share It!* and answer the following questions.

1. ¿Cuántas personas hay en nuestra comunidad?
2. ¿Quién es de un estado *(a state)* lejos de aquí? ¿Quién es de este estado *(this state)*?
3. ¿Quién tiene una imagen interesante en *Share It!*?

1-60 Perspectivas: ¿De dónde eres? Online, you watched a video of nine Spanish-speaking students as they answered the question **¿De dónde eres?** How did the interviewees respond? With two or three classmates, compare the responses you selected when you watched that video. Then, interview the members of your group with the questions that follow and jot down the information.

- ¿Cómo te llamas?
- ¿De dónde eres?
- ¿Dónde vives?

1-61 Exploración: Personas famosas. Online, you visited a website and read about a famous person. Share your findings with two or three classmates in a brief presentation. Say the name of your celebrity and answer the following questions about him/her.

- ¿Cómo se llama? (Se llama...)
- ¿Cuál es su profesión?
- ¿De dónde es?
- ¿Cuántos años tiene?

1-62 Conectados con... la neurociencia. Online, you read an article about the neurological and other effects of videogames. With two or three classmates, share the results of your research on popular videogames or on the effects of playing these games.

Modelo

En México los videojuegos más populares son... / Según *(According to)* mi investigación, los videojuegos...

1-63 **En el café.** You (**Estudiante A**) and your partner (**Estudiante B**) have two similar but not identical drawings. Your task is to describe them and find the differences between them without looking at each other's drawings.

- There are eight differences between the two drawings.

- The differences might include the number, kind, and location of objects, the appearance of the room, the answers to questions, or how the people feel.

- You (**Estudiante A**) will begin by saying: **En mi dibujo** *(drawing)*, **los estudiantes están en un café.**

This is a pair activity for **Estudiante A** and **Estudiante B**.

If you are **Estudiante A**, use the information on this page.

If you are **Estudiante B**, turn to p. S-1 at the back of the book.

Estudiante A

Las ocho diferencias:

1. _____
2. _____
3. _____
4. _____
5. _____
6. _____
7. _____
8. _____

SÍNTESIS

Colaborar · 👥 **1-64** **Los murales de O'Gorman.** Have you seen these murals before? With a partner, read the information about them and answer the questions.

1. ¿Cómo se llama el artista?

2. ¿De dónde es el artista?

3. ¿Dónde están los murales?

4. ¿Cómo son los murales: grandes o pequeños?

5. ¿Cuántos años tienen los murales?

6. ¿Hay murales en tu *(your)* campus? (¿Dónde?)

Los murales de la Biblioteca Central de la Universidad Nacional Autónoma de México (UNAM)

La Universidad Nacional Autónoma de México es la universidad más grande de México. Su biblioteca es famosa por los murales sobre la historia y la cultura mexicanas.

Dirección: Coyoacán, D.F.
Inauguración: 1956
Artista: Juan O'Gorman (Ciudad de México, 1905–1982)
Tamaño: 4000 m^2
Número de mosaicos: más de tres millones

👥👥 **1-65** **Una conversación en el campus.** In groups of four, assign the roles of Daniela, Mario, Santiago, and Claudia. Then complete the following conversation, in which Daniela introduces her friends Santiago and Claudia to Mario and they all talk. Read through the whole conversation to be sure that your additions are logical. Be prepared to read this aloud to the class.

DANIELA ¡Hola, Mario! ¿(1) _____?

MARIO Hola, Daniela. Muy bien, gracias. ¿Y tú? ¿(2) _____?

DANIELA Todo bien. Mario, (3) _____ a Santiago y a Claudia. Ellos son estudiantes aquí.

Photos: (l) csp/Shutterstock; (r) AFP/Getty Images

© Cengage Learning 2016;

MARIO	Mucho gusto. ¿(4) _____?
SANTIAGO	Nosotros somos de Venezuela. ¿(5) _____?
MARIO	Yo soy de México, del D.F.
CLAUDIA	*(picking up a flash drive from the floor)* ¿(6) _____?
DANIELA	Es una memoria USB.
SANTIAGO	¿(7) _____?
DANIELA	Es de Mario.
MARIO	*(as Claudia hands him the flash drive)* ¡(8) _____!
CLAUDIA	De nada.
DANIELA	Bueno, Mario, ¿dónde vives este semestre *(this semester)*?
MARIO	(9) _____.
SANTIAGO	¡Qué casualidad! *(What a coincidence!)* Yo vivo allí también.
CLAUDIA	Perdón, chicos, pero *(but)* yo tengo sed. ¿(10) _____?
DANIELA	¡Buena idea! ¡Vamos!

 1-66 **Situación: Una recepción.** This semester you've decided to live in **La Casa Hispana**, a special residence hall where all the students have pledged to speak only Spanish. You are attending a beginning-of-the-year reception where all the residents get to know one another. With your classmates, do the following:

- Introduce yourself to one of the residents and find out where he or she is from.

- Next, introduce this person to someone else in the group.

- Finish the conversation and then approach someone else in the class.

- Keep meeting and greeting people until your instructor calls time.

- To start the conversation, say: **Hola. Me llamo...**

- To end the conversation, say: **Bueno, mucho gusto,** *(friends' names).* **¡Nos vemos en clase!**

Pronunciación: Las vocales

Colaborar Working with a classmate, take turns reading aloud the verses of this children's song to practice the pronunciation of **a, e, i, o,** and **u.**

> **La mar estaba serena, serena estaba la mar.**
> **¡Con A!**
> **La mar astaba sarana, sarana astaba la mar.**
> **¡Con E!**
> **Le mer estebe serene, serene estebe le mer.**
> **¡Con I!**
> **Li mir istibi sirini, sirini istibi li mir.**
> **¡Con O!**
> **Lo mor ostobo sorono, sorono ostobo lo mor.**
> **¡Con U!**
> **Lu mur ustubu surunu, surunu ustubu lu mur.**

VOCABULARIO

Para aprender mejor

Before studying long lists of words, classify them into meaningful categories. The words in this section are organized by parts of speech (nouns, verbs, adjectives), but you could also classify them as *things in my backpack*, *cognates*, etc.

Sustantivos

el apartamento *apartment*

la arroba *@*

la avenida *avenue*

la biblioteca *library*

el bolígrafo *pen*

la botella (de agua) *(water) bottle*

el café *coffee shop*

la cafetería *cafeteria*

el calendario *calendar*

la calle *street*

el campus *campus*

el (teléfono) celular *cell phone*

el centro estudiantil *student center*

la clínica *health center*

la compañera (de clase, de cuarto) *partner, classmate, roommate (female)*

el compañero (de clase, de cuarto) *partner, classmate, roommate (male)*

la computadora (portátil) *(laptop) computer*

el correo electrónico *email*

el cuaderno *spiral notebook*

el cuarto *room*

el diccionario *dictionary*

la dirección *address*

el estadio *stadium*

el estudiante *student (male)*

la estudiante *student (female)*

la facultad *college*

la familia *family*

el gimnasio *gym, fitness center*

la hoja de papel *sheet of paper*

el laboratorio *lab*

el lápiz *pencil*

la librería *bookstore*

el libro *book*

la luz *light*

el mapa (del mundo) *(world) map*

la memoria USB *flash drive*

la mesa *table*

la mochila *backpack*

el número (de teléfono) *(telephone) number*

la pared *wall*

la piscina *swimming pool*

la pizarra (digital) *(interactive) board*

el profesor *professor (male)*

la profesora *professor (female)*

la puerta *door*

el punto *dot*

el pupitre *desk*

el reloj *clock*

la residencia estudiantil *dorm*

el salón de clase *classroom*

la silla *chair*

la tableta *tablet (computer)*

el televisor *television, TV*

la universidad *university*

la ventana *window*

Verbos

estar *to be*

hay *there is/there are*

ir *to go*

ser *to be*

tener *to have*

Vivo... *I live...*

Adjetivos

cansado(a) *tired*

contento(a) *happy*

emocionado(a) *excited*

enfermo(a) *ill, sick*

enojado(a) *angry, mad*

estresado(a) *stressed*

grande *big, large*

mucho(a) *a lot of, many*

ocupado(a) *busy, occupied*

pequeño(a) *small*

preocupado(a) *worried, concerned*

triste *sad*

Adverbios

allí *there*

aquí *here*

muy *very*

también *also, too*

un poco *a little*

Preposiciones

al lado de *next to, beside*

cerca de *close to*

con *with*

en *on, in*

enfrente de *across from, facing*

lejos de *far from*

Preguntas

¿Adónde...? *Where...?*

¿Cómo...? *How...?*

¿Cuál...? *What...?*

¿De dónde...? *Where...from?*

¿De quién...? *Who...belong to?*

¿Dónde...? *Where...?*

¿Quién...? *Who...?*

Greetings and reactions, p. 12

Introductions, p. 13

Leave-takings, p. 13

Numbers 0–100, p. 16

Subject pronouns, p. 19

Courtesy expressions, p. 22

Classroom expressions, p. 23

Definite and indefinite articles, pp. 26–27

Expressions with *tener*, p. 36

La vida estudiantil

> **Conexiones a la comunidad**
> Attend the next meeting of your school's Spanish Club. Find out what activities are planned for the semester.

In this chapter you will . . .
- explore Spain
- describe your classes and professors
- tell time
- talk about weekday and weekend activities

- extend, accept, and decline invitations
- make statements and ask questions
- learn about filmmaking in Spain
- share experiences about student life

NUESTRO **MUNDO**

España

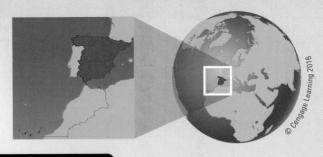

España es un país europeo muy diverso. Está compuesto de diecisiete comunidades autónomas y dos ciudades autónomas.

Población: 47 300 000
Capital: Madrid
Gobierno: monarquía parlamentaria

Moneda: el euro
Industrias: textiles, comidas *(foods)*, metales, turismo

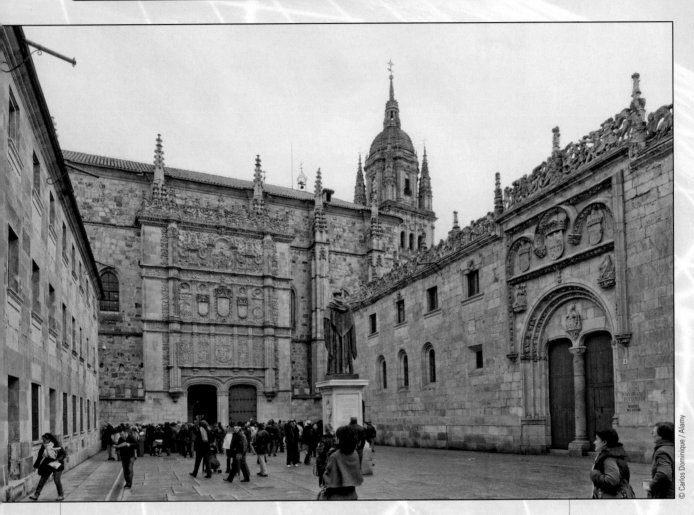

La Universidad de Salamanca, fundada *(founded)* en 1218, es la universidad más antigua *(oldest)* de España en funcionamiento *(still open)*. Dos de sus estudiantes famosos son el conquistador Hernán Cortés y el autor Miguel de Unamuno. Hoy *(Today)*, aproximadamente 30 mil *(thousand)* estudiantes de España y de numerosos países estudian en la Universidad de Salamanca.

Lenguas

España tiene varias lenguas cooficiales: el castellano o español, el catalán, el gallego y el euskera. La música *(musician)* de la foto es de Galicia y habla *(she speaks)* gallego.

Historia

Entre los años 711 y 1492, los árabes controlan parte de España. La Alhambra, en Granada, es un palacio de esa época *(that time period)*. Las columnas, los arcos y el patio son un importante legado *(legacy)* árabe en la arquitectura española.

Celebraciones

La Feria de Abril es un famoso festival de Sevilla, España. Hay paseos de caballos *(parades of horses)*, corridas de toros *(bullfights)* y música flamenca. ¡Olé!

2-1 **¿Qué sabes?** What have you learned about Spain? Choose the correct completion for each sentence.

_____ 1. El gobierno de España es...

_____ 2. España tiene diecisiete...

_____ 3. Las lenguas cooficiales de España son el castellano, el catalán,...

_____ 4. La universidad más antigua de España está en...

_____ 5. La Alhambra fue construida por *(was built by)*...

_____ 6. La Feria de Abril se celebra *(is celebrated)* en...

a. los árabes.

b. el gallego y el euskera.

c. Sevilla.

d. comunidades autónomas.

e. una monarquía parlamentaria.

f. Salamanca.

▶ **2-2** **Videomundo.** After watching the video, compare Madrid to your nearest city. Mention the architecture, signage, police officers, and parks.

Háblame de tus clases

In this *Paso*, you will . . .
- describe your classes and professors
- talk about the days of the week
- create affirmative and negative sentences

Las carreras

¿Qué carrera estudias?

Estudio historia.

¿Es difícil?

No, pero hay mucha tarea.

Para describir las clases	*Describing classes*
¿Cómo es la clase de... ?	*What's . . . class like?*
Es...	*It's . . .*
interesante / aburrida	*interesting / boring*
fácil / difícil	*easy / difficult*
divertida	*fun*
No está mal.	*It's okay.*
... pero (no) hay...	*. . . but . . . there is(n't) / there are(n't) . . .*
muchos / pocos exámenes	*a lot of / few tests*
mucha / poca tarea	*a lot of / little homework*
muchos / pocos informes	*a lot of / few papers, reports*

Para hablar de las clases	*Talking about classes*
¿Cuál es tu clase preferida?	*What's your favorite class?*
Mi clase preferida es... porque...	*My favorite class is . . . because . . .*
Me gusta la clase de (música).	*I like (music) class.*

© Cengage Learning 2016

Las clases

lunes	martes	miércoles	jueves	viernes	sábado	domingo
inglés	historia	inglés	historia	inglés		
arte	cálculo	arte	cálculo	arte		
biología		biología		biología		

¿Qué clases tienes este semestre?

Los lunes, miércoles y viernes tengo inglés, arte y biología. Los martes y jueves tengo historia y cálculo.

Para describir a los profesores

¿Qué tal el profesor (la profesora)?
Él/Ella es...
    simpático(a) / antipático(a)
    bueno(a) / malo(a)
    organizado(a) / despistado(a)
    amable
    exigente

Describing professors

What do you think of the professor?
He/She is . . .
    nice / mean, unpleasant
    good / bad
    organized / scatterbrained, absentminded
    kind and helpful
    demanding, strict

Para hablar de los días de la semana

¿Qué día es?
Hoy / Mañana es (lunes).
¿Cuándo tienes la clase de (inglés)?
    Tengo inglés los (martes) y (jueves).
¿Cuándo es el examen de biología?
    Es el (miércoles).

Talking about days of the week

What day is it?
Today / Tomorrow is (Monday).
When do you have (English) class?
    I have English on (Tuesdays) and (Thursdays).
When is the biology exam?
    It's this (Wednesday).

¡Aplícalo! Colaborar **2-3** **¿Cómo es?** Work with a partner to choose the best words to describe the classes and professors depicted below.

1. La profesora Rojas es (organizada / despistada / fácil).
2. La clase de lenguas clásicas es (fácil / buena / difícil).
3. La clase de historia del arte es (interesante / divertida / aburrida).
4. El profesor Yepes es (divertido / exigente / despistado).

¿Dónde está mi bolígrafo? Ah, sí, aquí está. ¿Y el libro de texto? ¿Dónde está mi libro?

Estoy estresada porque ¡no entiendo!

Profesora Rojas

Clase de lenguas clásicas

El profesor es amable, pero la clase es bla, bla, bla. Tengo sueño.

Su atención, por favor. Mañana hay examen. Y la tarea es un informe de diez páginas.

Clase de historia del arte

Profesor Yepes

 Colaborar **2-4** **¿Qué carrera estudias?** With a partner, choose the correct words in parentheses and then read the dialogue aloud.

CAMILO ¿Qué (1. día / carrera) estudias, Malena?

MALENA Estudio (2. administración / comunicación) de empresas.

CAMILO ¡Yo también! ¿Qué (3. clases / informes) tienes?

MALENA Los lunes y miércoles tengo (4. historia / semana), lenguas y sociología. Los (5. días / martes) y jueves tengo cálculo y economía.

CAMILO ¿Qué (6. cómo / tal) la clase de economía? ¿Es difícil?

MALENA No, es (7. fácil / amable). No hay (8. muy / mucha) tarea y la profesora es muy buena. Es mi clase (9. antipática / preferida).

2-5 **Los días de la semana.** Work in groups of four to six to practice the days of the week. How fast can your group name the days?

- One of you begins by saying **Hoy es martes** and points to a classmate.
- That student replies **Mañana es miércoles.** He/She then chooses a different day, says **Hoy es (+ día),** and points to someone else.
- If you can't reply, say **¡Paso!** and point to another person.

Nota cultural

Students in Spain and Latin America have to declare majors before entering universities. That is why there is no exact equivalent to *undeclared major* or *undecided major* in Spanish. If a Spanish speaker asks you **¿Qué carrera estudias?** and you're an undeclared major, simply reply **Todavía no sé.** *(I don't know yet.)*

¡Exprésate!

↻ Academic subjects, **Lección preliminar**

 2-6 **¿Qué clase tienes?** How many of your classmates have course schedules like yours? Create a chart on paper like the one here and fill it out with your classes. Then, circulate among your classmates and, for each of your classes, try to find somebody who has a similar class on the same day. Have that person sign his/her name next to the class.

Modelo **Estudiante A:** ¿Tienes inglés los lunes?

Estudiante B: Sí. Tengo inglés los lunes, miércoles y viernes. / No, lo siento.

Estudiante A: Firma aquí *(Sign here)*. / Gracias.

lunes	martes	miércoles	jueves	viernes

2-7 **Opiniones.** What do you think of your classes this semester? Complete each of the following statements with the name of a class or professor. Then share your opinions with two other classmates. How many responses were the same?

1. En la clase de _____ hay mucha tarea pero no es muy difícil.

2. El (La) profesor(a) _____ es inteligente y muy amable.

3. Los exámenes son muy difíciles en la clase de _____.

4. La clase de _____ es interesante pero hay muchos informes.

5. Me gusta la clase de _____ porque hay mucha interacción con los compañeros.

6. Mi clase preferida este semestre es _____.

↻ Exchanging basic information, **Capítulo 1 Paso 1**

2-8 **En la oficina de admisión.** Imagine you work in the Admissions Office and that your partner is a transfer student. Interview him/her to fill out the following information sheet. Then switch roles.

▪ Begin the interview by asking **¿Cómo te llamas?**

▪ To ask for spelling, say **¿Cómo se escribe?**

▪ To request repetition, say **¿Puedes repetirlo?**

ADMISIÓN A LA FACULTAD DE HUMANIDADES

Nombre: _____

Teléfono: _____

Correo electrónico: _____

Carrera: _____

Cursos este semestre: _____

_____

_____

© Cengage Learning 2016; Photo: Seamartini Graphics/ Shutterstock

PASO 1 GRAMÁTICA A

Los adjetivos

MANOLO   La doctora Zolé es una profesora muy simpática.

VICTORIA   Sí, pero sus exámenes son muy difíciles.

MANOLO   Yo te ayudo. *(I'll help you.)*

VICTORIA   Eres un buen amigo, Manolo. ¡Gracias!

■ ■ ■
Descúbrelo

- What does Victoria think of her class with Doctor Zolé?

- What kind of friend is Manolo?

- What adjective does Manolo use to describe his professor? What letter does that adjective end in? Is that adjective placed before or after the word for *professor*?

1. Adjetives (**los adjetivos**) are words that describe people, places, or things.

- Use masculine adjective endings with masculine nouns and feminine endings with feminine nouns.

El Sr. Calvo es **organizado**.	*Mr. Calvo is **organized**.*
La Sra. García es **simpática**.	*Mrs. García is **nice**.*

- Additionally, use the plural endings when the noun is plural.

Tengo dos clases **difíciles**.	*I have two **hard** classes.*

2. Follow this chart to choose the correct adjective endings.

Adjective ends in:	Masculine		Feminine	
	Singular	**Plural**	**Singular**	**Plural**
-o	buen**o**	buen**os**	buen**a**	buen**as**
-e	amab**le**	amab**les**	amab**le**	amab**les**
a consonant	inform**al**	inform**ales**	inform**al**	inform**ales**
-dor	trabaja**dor**	trabaja**dores**	trabaja**dora**	trabaja**doras**
-ista	optim**ista**	optim**istas**	optim**ista**	optim**istas**

3. Descriptive adjectives are normally placed *after* the nouns they describe. They can also be placed after the linking verbs **ser** and **estar**.

Tengo unas clases **interesantes**.	*I have some **interesting** classes.*
El profesor de inglés es **amable**.	*The English professor is **kind**.*

4. Adjectives that express *how many* (**muchos / muchas, pocos / pocas**) or *how much* (**mucho / mucha, poco / poca**) are placed *before* nouns.

Hay **pocos** exámenes en arte.	*There are **few** exams in art.*
Hay **mucha** tarea en historia.	*There's **a lot of** homework in history.*

© Cengage Learning 2016

5. The adjectives **bueno** and **malo** can be placed before or after nouns. When placed before a masculine singular noun, these adjectives drop the final **-o**.

un **buen** amigo	*a **good** friend (male)*	una **buena** amiga	*a **good** friend (female)*
un **mal** ejemplo	*a **bad** example*	unos **malos** ejemplos	*some **bad** examples*

6. The meaning of the adjective **grande** changes slightly depending on its placement. **Grande** is shortened to **gran** before a singular noun of either gender.

Before the noun:	una **gran** universidad	*a **great** university*
After the noun:	una universidad **grande**	*a **large** university*

Colaborar

2-9 **Las clases de Blanca y Lucas.** Blanca and Lucas are talking about their classes this semester. Working with a partner, choose the correct form of the adjective in each case and then read the conversation aloud.

¡Aplícalo!

LUCAS ¿Qué tal tus clases este semestre, Blanca? ¿Son (1. buenos / buenas)?

BLANCA No están mal, pero ¡estoy (2. estresado / estresada) porque son muy (3. difícil / difíciles)!

LUCAS Sí, entiendo. Yo también tengo profesores muy (4. exigente / exigentes). Estoy (5. preocupado / preocupada) por mis notas *(grades)*.

BLANCA ¿Cuál es tu clase (6. preferido / preferida)?

LUCAS La informática. Hay (7. mucha / muchas) tarea, pero la profesora es (8. organizado / organizada).

BLANCA Mi profesor de informática es muy (9. despistado / despistada). Peor aún *(Even worse)*, hay un examen el lunes y no entiendo el material.

LUCAS Yo te ayudo *(I'll help you)*.

BLANCA Eres un (10. buen / bueno) amigo, Lucas.

2-10 **Ta-Te-Ti con adjetivos.** Challenge a classmate to a game of adjective tic-tac-toe. To mark your square with X or O, you must first say the phrase with the adjective in its correct form. For example: **unas clases (informal)** → **unas clases informales**.

unas clases (informal)	un cuarto (pequeño)	unos libros (interesante)		unos profesores (exigente)	un gimnasio (grande)	unas universidades (central)
un examen (fácil)	una profesora (simpático)	una tarea (aburrido)		una clase (organizado)	una compañera (antipático)	un amigo (despistado)
una universidad (importante)	unos compañeros (divertido)	un diccionario (grande)		una residencia (divertido)	unos informes (difícil)	unas amigas (simpático)

¡Exprésate!

Frases útiles

Para mí *For me, In my view*

En mi opinión *In my opinion*

¿Qué piensan ustedes? *What do you think?*

(No) Estoy de acuerdo. *I (dis)agree.*

2-11 Encuesta. Which courses and professors fit the descriptions below? Compare opinions with several classmates.

Modelo una clase aburrida pero fácil

Estudiante A: En mi opinión, la clase de historia es aburrida pero fácil. ¿Qué piensan ustedes?

Estudiante B: Estoy de acuerdo.

Estudiante C: Para mí, la clase de historia es muy interesante.

1. una clase aburrida pero fácil
2. una cafetería buena
3. dos clases muy divertidas
4. dos compañeros de clase muy simpáticos
5. una residencia estudiantil grande pero aburrida
6. una clase difícil pero interesante

2-12 ¿Cierto o falso? With a partner, take turns making either true or false statements about the drawing. Say **cierto** (if it's true) or **falso** (if it's false).

Some useful words: **amable, antipático, bueno, despistado, difícil, divertido, exigente, grande, malo, organizado, pequeño, simpático.**

Modelo **Estudiante A:** El profesor es **aburrido**.

Estudiante B: Falso. El profesor es divertido.

2-13 Situación. With a partner, role-play the following situation between two students who meet at Spanish Club. Take turns and follow the numbering.

Estudiante A	Estudiante B
1. You are a new student from Barcelona, Spain. Introduce yourself to the student in front of you.	2. Greet the new student and ask where he/she is from.
3. Respond and then find out what classes he/she is taking.	4. Answer the question. Then say what your favorite class is.
5. Say you are also taking that class, but it's boring and the tests are hard.	6. Your class is the opposite. Describe it and then ask who the professor is.
7. Answer the question and describe the professor with two unflattering adjectives.	8. Describe your professor, **el profesor Soto**, with two positive adjectives.
9. To close, say you have to take (**Tengo que tomar...**) the class with Professor Soto.	10. Say yes, he's very good, and then say good-bye.

PASO 1 GRAMÁTICA B

La oración y la negación

ALICIA	Mi clase preferida es cálculo.
ENRIQUE	Mi clase preferida no es cálculo. Es literatura.
ALICIA	Cada loco con su tema *(To each his own).*

1. A complete sentence (**una oración**) consists of a subject (**el sujeto**) and a verb (**el verbo**); other elements may be added to complete the thought.

SUBJECT	+	CONJUGATED VERB	+	OTHER ELEMENTS
Mi clase preferida		es		literatura.
My favorite class		*is*		*literature.*

2. The verb in a complete sentence is always conjugated. That is, the verb is changed from its infinitive form (**estar, ir, ser, tener**) to a new form that corresponds to the subject of the sentence. For example, in the sentence below, **está** is the form of **estar** that corresponds to the subject **Marta (ella)**.

> Marta **está** en la biblioteca.   *Marta **is** in the library.*

3. The conjugated form of a verb also indicates *when* the action takes place. In the sentence below, for instance, the verb is conjugated in the present tense (**el presente de indicativo**); this verb tense tells us that the action is taking place now or that it takes place regularly.

> Alicia y Enrique **van** al gimnasio los martes y jueves.
> *Alicia and Enrique **go** to the gym on Tuesdays and Thursdays.*

4. Subjects may be nouns (**María, los estudiantes**) or subject pronouns (**yo, tú, él, ella, nosotros, nosotras, ellos, ellas**). In Spanish, the subject pronoun is not stated if the verb ending and the context of the conversation make the subject clear. This is known as an understood subject.

> Alicia está en la cafetería. **Tiene** hambre. *(understood subject = **ella**)*
> *Alicia is in the cafeteria. **She is** hungry.*

5. A negative sentence (**una oración negativa**) conveys the idea that somebody *doesn't* do something. To make a sentence negative, add **no** before the verb. In negative sentences in Spanish, the words *do* and *does* are not expressed.

> Enrique **no** tiene clase hoy.   *Enrique **doesn't** have class today.*

■ ■ ■
Descúbrelo

- Does Alicia like mathematics?
- Who likes literature?
- What is the verb in the first sentence? Does it come before or after the subject of the sentence?
- To say that something *isn't*, what word is placed before the verb **es**?

¡Aplícalo!

Colaborar

2-14 **En España.** Ingrid is studying Spanish in Spain this semester. To find out why she's enjoying this experience, work with a classmate to unscramble each group of words and use them to write a complete sentence.

Modelo buena / la / es / universidad
La universidad es buena.

1. son / los / amables / profesores
2. los / viernes / clase / no / tenemos
3. cerca / campus / residencia / la / del / está
4. fiestas *(parties)* / vamos / a / sábados / los
5. es / no / tarea / la / difícil

Colaborar

2-15 **Magaly y yo.** What is Penélope saying about campus life? Working with a partner, take turns reading the sentences aloud. For the second sentence in each set, you must decide what the understood subject is and conjugate the verb in parentheses in the present tense.

1. Mi compañera de cuarto se llama Magaly. (Ser) _____ de Sevilla, España.
2. Magaly está muy ocupada este semestre. (Tener) _____ seis clases.
3. Yo no estoy muy ocupada este semestre. (Tener) _____ solo *(only)* cuatro clases.
4. Magaly y yo tenemos muchos amigos en la universidad. (Ir) _____ al gimnasio con ellos *(with them)* los lunes y jueves.
5. Me gusta la universidad. Los profesores son muy buenos. También (ser) _____ muy amables.

Colaborar

2-16 **España.** Working with a partner, make the statements about Spain negative and then provide the correct information from the list, as in the model.

Modelo España es una república.
España **no** es una república. Es una monarquía parlamentaria.

1. España está en América del Sur.
2. La capital es Salamanca.
3. Tiene siete comunidades autónomas.
4. La moneda *(currency)* es el dólar.
5. La bandera *(flag)* tiene cuatro colores principales.

Información sobre España

Es Madrid.
Es el euro.
Tiene diecisiete comunidades autónomas.
Es una monarquía parlamentaria.
Está en Europa.
Tiene dos colores principales.

¡Exprésate! **Colaborar**

2-17 **¡No!** You disagree with almost everything your friend Marcos says. With a partner, take turns reading aloud and responding to his remarks. First, create a negative sentence that contradicts Marcos; then, create an affirmative one with your opinion.

Modelo **Estudiante A (Marcos):** La clase de biología es difícil.

Estudiante B: ¡No es verdad! *(That's not true!)* La clase de biología **no** es difícil. Es fácil y hay poca tarea.

1. El profesor de inglés es aburrido.
2. Las residencias son pequeñas.
3. La cafetería es mala.
4. Tenemos un examen de informática hoy.
5. La biblioteca está lejos de las residencias.
6. Hay mucha tarea en la clase de psicología.

2-18 **Muy lógico.** With a partner, create as many logical sentences as you can in three minutes. Select one word or phrase from each group and be sure to conjugate the verbs. Follow the model.

Modelo **Estudiante A:** *(Chooses a subject)* La clase de química...

Estudiante B: *(Repeats the subject and chooses a logical verb)* La clase de química es...

Estudiante A: *(Repeats the subject and the verb, and adds an element to complete the thought.)* La clase de química es aburrida.

Sujeto	Verbo	Otros elementos	
Yo	ser	a la biblioteca	divertido(a)(s)
Mi compañero(a) de cuarto	ir	aburrido(a)(s)	fácil(es)
Los profesores		al café	grande(s)
La clase de (...)		al estadio	interesante(s)
Las residencias		bueno(a)(s)	simpático(a)(s)
Mis compañeros de clase y yo		difícil(es)	

 The verb **tener,** Capítulo 1 Paso 3

2-19 **¿Qué tienen?** Take turns with a partner. One person uses the verb **tener** to create a statement about one of the photos, but without saying the name indicated in the drawing. Then the other person identifies which photo was described.

Modelo **Estudiante A:** Tiene hambre.

Estudiante B: ¿Juan?

Estudiante A: ¡Correcto!

Julia

Marina

Armando

Juan

Lola

Mariluz

Un día típico entre semana

La hora

¿Qué hora es?

¡Ay, no! ¡Tengo clase en cinco minutos!

Son las tres.

Iván

Puri

© Cengage Learning 2016

Es la una.

Son las tres.

Son las seis y cuarto.

Son las siete y media.

Son las nueve menos diez. / Son las ocho y cincuenta.

Para decir la hora	Telling time
¿Qué hora es?	*What time is it?*
Es mediodía. / Es medianoche.	*It's noon. / It's midnight.*
de la mañana	*a.m. (6 a.m. to noon)*
de la tarde	*p.m. (noon to sundown)*
de la noche	*p.m. (sundown to midnight)*
de la madrugada	*a.m. (late night, early morning hours)*
Son las tres y cincuenta de la madrugada.	*It's 3:50 a.m.*
Son las cuatro menos diez de la madrugada.	*It's ten 'til four in the morning.*

Para hablar de los horarios	Talking about schedules
¿A qué hora es tu primera / última clase?	*What time is your first / last class?*
Mi primera / última clase es a (las nueve).	*My first / last class is at (9:00).*
No tengo clases por la mañana / tarde / noche.	*I don't have classes in the morning / afternoon / evening.*

Un día típico

Hola, soy Nuria. **Normalmente, llego** a la universidad a las nueve.

Paso la mañana en clases. **¡Tomo** muchos **apuntes**!

Por la tarde, **practico deportes**.

También **trabajo de** tres **a** seis.

Por la noche, **estudio** por dos horas.

También **miro la tele**.

Illustrations © Cengage Learning 2016

Actividades cotidianas	*Everyday activities*
descansar	*to relax*
escuchar música	*to listen to music*
hablar por teléfono	*to talk on the phone*
participar en un grupo estudiantil	*to participate in a student organization*
pasar el rato con amigos	*to spend time / to hang out with friends*
pasar horas en Internet	*to spend hours online*
regresar a casa	*to go back home*
terminar la tarea	*to finish up homework*
tocar (la guitarra, el piano)	*to play (the guitar, the piano)*

cuarto = 15 min.

PASO 2 VOCABULARIO

¡Aplícalo!

Nota lingüística

To give times up to 30 minutes past the hour, use **y**.

Son las tres y veinte. (3:20)

To give times more than 30 minutes past the hour, use **menos** and subtract from the next hour.

Son las cuatro menos veinte. (3:40). You can also say **Son las tres y cuarenta.**

 Places around campus, **Capítulo 1 Paso 3**

2-20 **¿Qué hora es?** Working with a partner, take turns asking and answering what time it is. When one partner says the time, the other indicates which image corresponds to that time. Add the appropriate phrase for a.m. or p.m. (**de la mañana, de la tarde, de la noche, de la madrugada**).

Modelo Estudiante A: ¿Qué hora es?
Estudiante B: Son las nueve y diez de la mañana.
Estudiante A: *(Pointing to the image with the time mentioned)* Es este. *(It's this one.)*

Illustrations © Cengage Learning 2016

2-21 **¿Dónde están?** Where are these students when they do these things? With a partner, take turns reading aloud the descriptions of their activities and saying where they most likely are.

Modelo Estudiante A: Bárbara estudia y termina la tarea.
Estudiante B: Está en la biblioteca.

la biblioteca	el estadio	la librería
el café	el gimnasio	la piscina
la clase de historia	el laboratorio	la residencia

1. Dulce María escucha al profesor y toma apuntes.
2. José Luis practica el hockey con amigos.
3. Mariana pasa horas en los experimentos de biología.
4. Paulina mira sus programas favoritos en la tele.
5. Eduardo mira los partidos de fútbol *(soccer matches)* con los amigos.
6. Ana pasa el rato con amigos.

2-22 **Un día típico.** What is a typical Monday like for Lili? With a partner, put the statements in the most logical order by numbering them from 1 to 8.

_____ a. A las doce y media tengo hambre y voy a la cafetería.

_____ b. También tengo biología por la mañana, de once a doce.

_____ c. Regreso a casa a las seis.

_____ d. Llego a la universidad a las nueve menos cuarto.

_____ e. Mi primera clase es historia. Es a las nueve.

_____ f. Por la noche, descanso en casa.

_____ g. Por la tarde estudio en la biblioteca por dos o tres horas.

_____ h. También practico deportes con amigos de cinco a seis.

¡Exprésate!

Colaborar

2-23 **El horario de clases.** Pablo Castillo is getting a degree in social work (**trabajo social**). With a partner, look at his class schedule and complete the sentences by adding a number, a time, or the name of a class.

Facultad de Ciencias Sociales			HORARIO 1° TRABAJO SOCIAL		
HORARIOS	LUNES	MARTES	MIÉRCOLES	JUEVES	VIERNES
14.30–16.00			Prácticas de Trabajo Social		Prácticas de Trabajo Social
16.00–17.30	Psicología General	Introducción a la Antropología		Introducción al Trabajo Social	
17.30–19.00	Introducción al Trabajo Social	Derecho	Introducción a la Antropología	Sociología	Sociología
19.00–20.30		Introducción a los Servicios Sociales	Introducción a los Servicios Sociales	Psicología General	Derecho

1. Pablo tiene _____ clases en total.
2. Los lunes, la primera clase es a las _____ de la tarde y la última es de _____ a _____ de la noche.
3. Las prácticas son los _____ y _____ a las _____ de la tarde.
4. La clase de antropología es los _____ a las _____ de la tarde y los _____ a las _____ de la tarde.
5. Los jueves, antes de *(before)* ir a la clase de psicología, Pablo tiene _____.
6. Los viernes, la última clase de Pablo es _____, de _____ a _____ de la noche.

2-24 **Nuestras actividades.** What do you and your partner do on a typical day? Take turns completing the sentences aloud and comparing your activities.

1. Yo escucho música (hip hop / clásica / rock). ¿Y tú?
2. Yo hablo mucho de (política / clases / problemas) con mis amigos. ¿Y tú?
3. Yo descanso en casa los domingos por la (mañana / tarde / noche). ¿Y tú?
4. Yo practico (el tenis / el voleibol / el básquetbol). ¿Y tú?
5. Yo paso horas (en Internet / en la biblioteca / en el café). ¿Y tú?
6. Yo miro videos de (YouTube / Netflix / mis amigos). ¿Y tú?

2-25 **¿Dónde están?** In small groups, talk about where you are at certain hours. Taking turns, first say a day and a time; then ask the others where they are.

Modelo **Estudiante A:** Es martes y son las ocho de la noche. ¿Dónde están ustedes?
Estudiante B: Normalmente estoy en la residencia estudiantil.
Estudiante C: Por lo general *(Generally)*, yo estoy en el gimnasio.

El presente de los verbos regulares *-ar*

HORACIO	¿Trabajas este semestre?
BEATRIZ	Sí. Normalmente trabajo de seis a nueve de la noche. ¿Y tú?
HORACIO	No trabajo, pero estudio mucho. ¡Soy un comelibros *(bookworm)*!

■ ■ ■

Descúbrelo

- Which of the two students has a job?
- Does this person work three hours routinely or rarely?
- What ending does the verb have when Horacio asks Beatriz whether she works?
- What ending does the verb have when Beatriz answers Horacio's question?

1. The present tense (**el presente de indicativo**) expresses these notions:

- an action that occurs regularly or routinely

  Trabajo los lunes y los martes.   *I work on Mondays and Tuesdays.*

- an ongoing action or condition

  Tomo cuatro clases este semestre.   *I'm taking four classes this semester.*

- an action that will take place in the near future

  Hablo con el profesor mañana.   *I'm talking with the professor tomorrow.*

2. Here are the endings for the *-ar* verbs in the present tense. These endings are used with all the new verbs in this **Paso: contestar, descansar, escuchar, estudiar, hablar, llegar, mirar, participar, pasar, practicar, regresar, terminar, tocar, tomar,** and **trabajar**.

El presente indicativo de los verbos regulares *-ar*			
tomar *to take*			
yo	tom**o**	nosotros/nosotras	tom**amos**
tú	tom**as**	vosotros/vosotras	tom**áis**
usted	tom**a**	ustedes	tom**an**
él/ella	tom**a**	ellos/ellas	tom**an**

3. To create a complete sentence with any of these verbs, first say the subject (who is doing the action), then add the conjugated verb (the action itself), and finally finish with the rest of the thought.

SUBJECT	+	VERB	+	OTHER ELEMENTS
Muchos estudiantes		trabaj**an**		por la noche.
Many students		*work*		*in the evenings.*

Subject pronouns are often omitted because the verb ending indicates who the subject is.

Estudio por la tarde.   *I study in the afternoons.*

2-26 **¡A jugar!** Play this conjugation game with your classmates.

Clase

- The class is divided into two (or more) teams.
- Your instructor will say a subject and a verb. Taking turns, one person from each team runs to the board and writes the answer.
- The first person to write a correct answer earns two points for the team. All teams with a correct answer win one point.

2-27 **El blog de Diana.** With a partner, complete Diana's blog about a typical day at the **Universidad de Salamanca**. Choose the more logical verb in each case and write it in the present tense.

Colaborar

www.uni.es/blogs/diana						
Vida en el Campus	Blogs	Visitas	Coste	Matricular	Aceptado	Consejeros

Inicio ▾ Blogs ▾ Diana 　　　　　　　　　　　　　　　 Buscar

En un día típico yo (1. regresar / llegar) _____ a la universidad a las nueve. Mis compañeros y yo (2. pasar / trabajar) _____ la mañana en clase. En clase, nosotros (3. tocar / estudiar) _____ la gramática. Yo (4. tomar / escuchar) _____ muchos apuntes en esa[1] clase porque el profesor Cruz (5. ser / ir) _____ muy exigente. A las once, yo (6. ir / trabajar) _____ a la clase de cultura española con la profesora Sánchez. Ella (7. participar / hablar) _____ mucho de la historia de España. ¡(8. Tener / Ser) _____ muy interesante! Por la tarde, normalmente yo (9. pasar / mirar) _____ el rato con amigos.

© Cengage Learning 2016

[1]*that*

2-28 **Nuria Carrillo.** Imagine you are studying abroad in Spain. What is life like there for you and your friend Nuria? With a partner, complete the sentences with logical verbs in the present tense. Add other words where you see this cue: (¿ ... ?)

Colaborar

1. Nuria Carrillo _____ la carrera de psicología. Yo _____ la carrera de (¿ ... ?) _____.

2. Nuria llega a la universidad (¿ ... ?) _____, pero yo _____ por la tarde.

3. Nuria y yo _____ deportes los domingos o (*or*) los (¿ ... ?) _____.

4. Los martes y jueves, Nuria _____ en una cafetería, pero yo no _____.

5. Nuria no _____ mucho la tele porque está ocupada. Yo _____ la tele (¿ ... ?) _____.

6. Nuria y yo estudiamos horas en (¿ ... ?) _____.

Illustrations © Cengage Learning 2016

2-29 Un lunes típico. What time do you and your partner do these things on a typical Monday? Interview a classmate by creating questions with the phrases in the chart. Listen to each response and then check the appropriate column.

Note: If you do not engage in the activity you're asked about, reply with **no**; for example: **No voy a la cafetería.**

Modelo **llegar** a la universidad
Estudiante A: ¿A qué hora llegas a la universidad?
Estudiante B: Llego a la universidad a las ocho. ¿Y tú? *(Estudiante A checks **Por la mañana**.)*
Estudiante A: Yo llego a la universidad a la una. *(Estudiante B checks **Por la tarde**.)*

Actividad	Por la mañana	Por la tarde	Por la noche
1. **tener** la primera clase			
2. **regresar** a casa			
3. **ir** a la cafetería			
4. **trabajar**			
5. **pasar** el rato con amigos			
6. **mirar** la televisión			
7. **terminar** la tarea normalmente			
8. **descansar** en casa			

2-30 El estudiante modelo. What does a model student usually do? Take turns creating sentences and responding by saying **cierto** *(true)* or **falso** *(false)*.

Modelo mirar la tele todas las noches *(every night)*
Estudiante A: El estudiante modelo mira la tele todas las noches.
Estudiante B: Falso.

tomar buenos apuntes en clase	estar en Twitter en clase
ir a fiestas todas las noches	ser organizado
llegar a clase tarde *(late)*	pasar horas y horas en la biblioteca
no escuchar a los profesores en clase	hablar por teléfono en clase
estudiar mucho para los exámenes	no terminar la tarea normalmente

2-31 Estamos súper ocupados. Form teams of two to three people and compete with another team to see which one is the busiest—and remembers the most! The winner is the last student (and team) that is able to remember everything and add another statement.

- **Estudiante A** from Team 1 begins by making up a sentence saying what his/her team does on Tuesdays. (**Los martes tenemos tres clases.**)
- Next, **Estudiante A** from Team 2 repeats that statement and adds another activity. (**Los martes nosotros tenemos tres clases y trabajamos por la tarde.**)
- **Estudiante B** from Team 1 repeats and adds on even more. (**Los martes nosotros tenemos tres clases, trabajamos por la tarde y participamos en un grupo estudiantil.**)
- Continue alternating team members and teams until one person can no longer remember all the statements.

Las preguntas de sí/no

© Cengage Learning 2016

CARLOS	¿Toca Miguel la guitarra?
MARÍA	No, no toca la guitarra. Toca el piano.
CARLOS	¡Ah! ¿Y tú, María? ¿Tocas el piano también?
MARÍA	Un poco. ¡No soy Alicia Keys!

1. There are three main patterns for yes/no questions (**preguntas**).

> ¿CONJUGATED VERB + SUBJECT + OTHER ELEMENTS?
> ¿Toca   Miguel   el piano?
>
> *Does Miguel play the piano?*

> ¿CONJUGATED VERB + OTHER ELEMENTS + SUBJECT?
> ¿Toca   la guitarra   Miguel?
>
> *Does Miguel play the guitar?*

> ¿SUBJECT + CONJUGATED VERB + OTHER ELEMENTS?
> ¿Miguel   toca   el violín?
>
> *Miguel plays the violin?*

2. The subject of a yes/no question may also be understood rather than stated.

> ¿Tocas el violín?   *Do you play the violin?*

3. Yes/No questions may also be negative. In this case, the word **no** is added just before the conjugated verb. The words *doesn't* and *don't* are not expressed in Spanish.

> ¿**No** toca Miguel el piano?   ***Doesn't*** *Miguel play the piano?*

4. To answer a yes/no question in the affirmative, say **sí** *(yes)* and then add a statement with more information.

CARLOS	¿Estudias mucho?	*Do you study a lot?*
MARÍA	**Sí**, normalmente estudio por tres horas.	*Yes, I usually study for three hours.*

5. To answer a yes/no question in the negative, say **no** and add a negative statement, or say **no** and add the correct information.

CARLOS	¿Estudias química?	*Do you study chemistry?*
MARÍA	**No, no** estudio química.	*No, I **don't** study chemistry.*

■ ■ ■
Descúbrelo

- What instrument does Miguel play?
- Who else plays the piano?
- When Carlos asks whether Miguel plays the guitar, which word comes first—the subject or the verb?
- To say that somebody *doesn't* do something, what word is placed before the verb?

PASO 2 GRAMÁTICA B

¡Aplícalo! Colaborar **2-32** **Universidad de Sevilla.** Would you like to study abroad one day in Seville, Spain? Taking turns with a classmate, one person reads aloud a question about the **Universidad de Sevilla** and the other gives the most logical response.

Preguntas	Respuestas
_____ 1. ¿Es pequeña la universidad?	a. Sí, practican rugby, hockey, fútbol y más.
_____ 2. ¿Está cerca de Madrid?	b. No, no tengo, pero hay uno en Internet.
_____ 3. ¿Tiene muchas bibliotecas?	c. Sí, y también apartamentos.
_____ 4. ¿Practican los estudiantes deportes?	d. No, es grande. Tiene 70 000 (setenta mil) estudiantes.
_____ 5. ¿Hay residencias estudiantiles?	e. No, está lejos.
_____ 6. ¿Tienes un mapa del campus?	f. Sí, tiene veinte.

Colaborar **2-33** **Cuatro personas, dos conversaciones.** What are the people in the photos talking about? With a partner, first decide which lines go with which pictures. Then, put the lines in order to form one short conversation for each photo. Write the two short exchanges on a piece of paper and read them aloud with a classmate.

¿Escuchas música flamenca?	No, no mucho. ¿Y tú?	Sí, es muy buena.
No, es el lunes.	Sí. ¿Es el examen el viernes?	¿Tienes una pregunta?

© Diego Cervo/Shutterstock

© Yellow Dog Productions/Getty Images

2-34 **Por teléfono.** Work with a classmate to complete the following telephone conversation. First, read it through to get the gist. Then create logical yes/no questions for the missing lines. Finally, read the dialogue aloud with your partner.

ALE   ¡Hola, Cris! Habla Ale. ¿(1) _____?

CRIS   Sí, muy ocupado. Tengo tarea de español. ¿(2) _____?

ALE   No, no tengo tarea hoy. ¿(3) _____?

CRIS   No, estoy en el centro estudiantil.

ALE   ¡Yo también estoy en el centro estudiantil!

CRIS   ¿(4) _____?

ALE   Sí, estoy enfrente del televisor. ¿Y tú? ¿(5) _____?

CRIS   Sí, estoy en el café, cerca de la puerta. ¿(6) _____?

ALE   Sí, miro deportes. Cris, ¡tienes que hacer la tarea aquí!

¡Exprésate!

Colaborar

2-35 **Combinaciones.** Work with a classmate to create as many different yes/ no questions as you can using the words in the boxes. Use this pattern: **¿Conjugated verb + subject + other elements?**

Modelo **Estudiante A:** *(Chooses a subject.)* la profesora de español

Estudiante B: *(Chooses and conjugates a logical verb.)* ¿Es la profesora de español... ?

Estudiante A: *(Finishes the question.)* ¿Es la profesora de español divertida?

Verbos	Sujetos	Otros elementos
ser	tú	divertido(a)(s)
estudiar	tus amigos	muchos deportes
practicar	*(name of a classmate)*	difícil(es)
mirar	el (la) profesor(a) de español	muchas horas en Internet
trabajar	el (la) profesor(a) de *(class)*	en la residencia
descansar	la clase de español	ciencias naturales
pasar	la clase de *(class)*	de España

Clase

2-36 **¿Qué haces?** Circulate around the class and ask your fellow students yes/no questions formed from the phrases in the chart. When somebody answers **sí** to a question, ask that person to sign his/her name. The first person to get all the items signed is the winner.

¡Ojo! A maximum of two signatures per person is allowed.

Modelo **tener** inglés los lunes

Estudiante A: Hola, *(name)*. ¿Tienes inglés los lunes?

Estudiante B: ¡Sí!, tengo inglés los lunes. / No, lo siento. No tengo inglés los lunes.

Estudiante A: Firma *(Sign)* aquí, por favor. / Gracias.

Actividad	Firma *(Signature)*
escuchar música clásica	
tomar buenos apuntes en historia	
tocar bien el piano	
participar en un grupo estudiantil	
mirar deportes en la televisión	
estudiar los sábados	

2-37 **¡Sí!** Ask a partner ten yes/no questions that you think he/she will answer with **sí**. The person who gets the most **sí** answers wins the game.

Modelo **Estudiante A:** ¿Escuchas música reggaetón?

Estudiante B: Sí. ¿Estudias en la biblioteca?

Estudiante A: ¡No! ¿Participas... ?

El fin de semana

In this *Paso*, you will . . .
- extend, accept, and decline invitations
- talk about weekend activities
- say how often you do things
- ask information questions

Una invitación

Invitaciones	*Invitations*
¿Por qué no... ?	*Why don't we . . . ?*
¿Qué tal si... ?	*What if we . . . ?*
¿Tienes ganas de... ?	*Do you feel like . . . ?*
¡Buena idea!	*Good idea!*
¡Claro que sí!	*Of course!*
De acuerdo.	*Okay.*
Lo siento, pero tengo que...	*I'm sorry, but I have to . . .*
Tal vez otro día.	*Perhaps another day.*

Actividades de ocio	*Leisure activities*
asistir a los partidos de (fútbol)	*to go to (soccer) games*
fútbol americano / béisbol / baloncesto	*football / baseball / basketball*
bailar en un club	*to dance at a club*
correr en el parque	*to run in the park*

Un fin de semana típico

Los viernes casi siempre **como en un restaurante chino** con mis amigos.

Los sábados normalmente **asisto a los partidos de baloncesto**.

A veces **lavo la ropa**.

Nunca **limpio el cuarto**.

Illustrations © Cengage Learning 2016

Actividades de ocio	*Leisure activities*
escribir un blog	*to write a blog*
ir a un concierto / a una fiesta / al cine	*to go to a concert / to a party / to the movies*
ir de compras	*to go shopping*
leer una novela	*to read a novel*
mandar mensajes de texto a mis amigos	*to text my friends*
tuitear	*to tweet*
visitar a mi familia	*to visit my family*

Expresiones de frecuencia	*Expressions of frequency*
normalmente	*normally, usually*
por lo general	*generally, in general*
(casi) todos los días	*(almost) every day*
(casi) siempre	*(almost) always*
a menudo	*often*
a veces	*sometimes*
nunca / no... nunca	*never*

¡Aplícalo!

Colaborar

2-38 **Una invitación.** Working with a partner, choose the more logical word or phrase in each set of parentheses; then read the conversation aloud.

CELSO Margarita, ¿(1. por qué / cómo) no vamos a un concierto el viernes? La orquesta sinfónica toca una obra *(work)* de Manuel de Falla.

MARGARITA (2. ¡Buena idea! / Lo siento), Celso. Tengo que trabajar el viernes por la noche.

CELSO Entonces *(Then)*, ¿(3. me gusta / tienes ganas de) ir al partido de fútbol el sábado?

MARGARITA (4. ¡Claro que sí! / Te llamo más tarde.) ¿A qué hora es?

CELSO A las cuatro (5. de la tarde / de la madrugada).

MARGARITA Muy bien. Y por la noche, ¿(6. qué tal / cómo) si comemos en un restaurante chino?

CELSO (7. Adiós / De acuerdo).

2-39 **Unas excusas.** You keep inviting a friend to do things together and he/she keeps turning you down! Working with a classmate, follow the model and create four short conversations.

- To invite, say: **¿Tienes ganas de** *(verb in infinitive form + other elements)*?
- To make an excuse, say: **Tengo que** *(verb in infinitive form + other elements)*.

Modelo Estudiante A: ¿Tienes ganas de comer en Taco Bell el sábado?
Estudiante B: Lo siento. Tengo que estudiar para un examen.
Estudiante A: Tal vez otro día.

> **Nota lingüística**
> - Most expressions of frequency can appear before or after a verb, at the beginning or at the end of a sentence:
>   **Mis amigos siempre van a fiestas.**
>   **Mis amigos van a fiestas siempre.**
> - When **nunca** goes after a verb, the word **no** must be used before the verb:
>   **Nunca trabajo los fines de semana.**
>   **No trabajo nunca los fines de semana.**

2-40 **¿Con qué frecuencia?** How often do you do these things on weekends? Describe your habits by completing each sentence with one of the expressions in the list; ask your partner **¿Y tú?** to find out his/her response.

Modelo Asisto a los partidos de fútbol americano.
Estudiante A: Asisto a los partidos de fútbol americano **a menudo**. **¿Y tú?**
Estudiante B: **Nunca** asisto a los partidos de fútbol americano.

(casi) todos los días	a menudo
a veces	nunca (+ *verb*)
(casi) todas las semanas	no (+ *verb*) nunca

1. Asisto a los partidos de fútbol.
2. Voy a fiestas.
3. Lavo la ropa.
4. Voy al cine.
5. Tuiteo.
6. Visito a mi familia.
7. Limpio mi cuarto.
8. Como en un restaurante chino.

¡Exprésate!

Numbers 0–100, Capítulo 1, Paso 3

ᵗᵗ 2-41 Actividades de ocio entre la juventud española. This bar graph depicts how young Spaniards (from ages 15 to 29) spend their free time. How do they compare to young people in the United States?

■ With a partner, summarize the information in the chart by creating ten sentences in the **ellos** form of the present tense. For example: **El 92% (noventa y dos por ciento) de los jóvenes escuchan música.**

■ After completing your summary, answer these questions.

1. ¿Cuáles son las tres actividades más populares entre *(most popular among)* los españoles?

2. ¿Cuáles son las tres actividades más populares entre tus amigos *(among your friends)*?

3. ¿Cuáles de las actividades son tus preferidas?

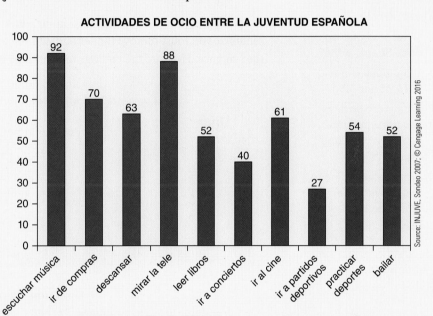

ACTIVIDADES DE OCIO ENTRE LA JUVENTUD ESPAÑOLA

Source: INJUVE, Sondeo 2007; © Cengage Learning 2016

ᵗᵗ 2-42 Las invitaciones. Working with a partner, first read about the likes and dislikes of Sofía, Jorge, Alejandra, and Luis. Then, assume the identity of one of these characters and invite one of the others—role-played by your partner—to do something together. The dialogue you create together should reflect the preferences of the characters. Repeat this activity with several different pairings of characters.

Sofía: Es muy sociable. Sus actividades preferidas son bailar, hablar con amigos y escuchar música. Sofía nunca pasa los fines de semana en casa.

Jorge: Para él, una noche perfecta consiste en *(consists of)* ir a comer con amigos o a bailar en un club. También va al cine a menudo.

Alejandra: Es muy atlética. Practica el fútbol y el tenis a menudo. También tiene talento para la música; toca la guitarra y el violín.

Luis: Pasa muchas horas en Internet. Lee blogs y visita los sitios de redes sociales *(networking sites)*. A veces asiste a partidos de fútbol o de béisbol.

El presente de los verbos regulares -*er* / -*ir*

HORACIO ¿Lees blogs a menudo?

BEATRIZ Sí, y también escribo un blog, "Crítica de política".

HORACIO ¡Leo tu blog todos los días! Es muy interesante.

■ ■ ■ Descúbrelo

- What kind of blog does Beatriz write?
- What does Horacio think of her blog?
- What verb ending is used when the subject of **leer** and **escribir** is **yo**?
- What verb ending is used with **leer** when the subject is **tú**?

1. In Spanish, verb infinitives may end in -**ar**, -**er**, or -**ir**. To use a regular -**er** verb in a sentence, you must remove the -**er** and add the ending that matches the subject of the sentence. Here are the endings for -**er** verbs in the present tense.

El presente indicativo de los verbos regulares -*er*			
comer *to eat*			
yo	com**o**	nosotros/nosotras	com**emos**
tú	com**es**	vosotros/vosotras	com**éis**
usted	com**e**	ustedes	com**en**
él/ella	com**e**	ellos/ellas	com**en**

Common -*er* verbs					
aprender	*to learn*	**comer**	*to eat*	**comprender**	*to understand*
correr	*to run*	**leer**	*to read*		

2. To use a regular -**ir** verb in a sentence, you must remove the -**ir** and add the ending that matches the subject of the sentence. Here are the endings for -**ir** verbs in the present tense.

El presente indicativo de los verbos regulares -*ir*			
vivir *to live*			
yo	viv**o**	nosotros/nosotras	viv**imos**
tú	viv**es**	vosotros/vosotras	viv**ís**
usted	viv**e**	ustedes	viv**en**
él/ella	viv**e**	ellos/ellas	viv**en**

Common -*ir* verbs			
asistir (a)	*to attend*	**escribir**	*to write*
recibir	*to receive, to get*	**vivir**	*to live*

© Cengage Learning 2016

3. Verbs that end in **-er** and **-ir** use the same word order in sentences as **-ar** verbs do. When the context is clear, the subject pronoun is usually omitted.

SUBJECT	+ (NO)	+ CONJUGATED VERB	+ OTHER ELEMENTS
Mis amigos y yo	(no)	**comemos**	en la cafetería.
My friends and I	*(don't)*	***eat***	*in the cafeteria.*

👥 2-43 El estudiante típico. What is the typical student like at your school? Are you a typical student? Working with a partner, complete these two activities.

¡Aplícalo!

Primera parte: First, take turns conjugating the verbs in the present tense and reading the descriptions. Then check the appropriate column to indicate whether or not each statement describes the typical student at your school.

El estudiante típico...	Sí	No
1. (asistir) _____ a clase de lunes a viernes.		
2. (leer) _____ dos o tres horas todos los días.		
3. (vivir) _____ en una residencia estudiantil en el campus.		
4. (comer) _____ en la cafetería casi todos los días.		
5. (recibir) _____ mensajes de texto en clase.		
6. (comprender) _____ bien a los profesores.		
7. (aprender) _____ una lengua extranjera *(foreign)*.		

Segunda parte: Using the phrases in the chart, ask your partner whether the activities mentioned apply to him/her. To ask the question, use the **tú** form of the verb; to answer, use the **yo** form. Are either of you "typical students"?

Modelo Estudiante A: ¿Asistes a clase de lunes a viernes?
Estudiante B: No, asisto a clase de lunes a jueves. ¿Y tú?

👥 2-44 Unas opiniones. What do you think of your classes this semester? What's the workload like? Working with a partner, share your opinions by taking turns reading each statement aloud. First, identify the subject; then, conjugate each verb to match the subject; finally, finish the sentence by naming a class.

🔄 Academic subjects, **Lección preliminar**

Modelo Estudiante A: Mis compañeros y yo (escribir) **escribimos** mucho en la clase de **inglés**.
Estudiante B: Mis compañeros y yo (escribir) **escribimos** mucho en la clase de **historia**.

1. Mis compañeros de clase y yo (leer) _____ mucho en la clase de _____.
2. (Nosotros: escribir) _____ muchos informes en la clase de _____.
3. (Nosotros: aprender) _____ información interesante en la clase de _____.
4. A veces (yo: estar) _____ estresado(a) en la clase de _____.
5. No (yo: comprender) _____ muy bien al profesor (a la profesora) en la clase de _____.
6. (Yo: recibir) _____ mucho correo electrónico de mi profesor(a) de _____.

¡**Exprésate!** **2-45** **Los fines de semana del profe.** What do you think your
Colaborar instructor does on weekends?

- With a partner, read the list of weekend activities in the chart. Indicate how often the two of you think that your instructor engages in each of the activities by marking the appropriate column with a **P** (for **predicción**).
- After everyone has marked his or her predictions, take turns asking your instructor questions about these activities. For example: **¿Con qué frecuencia come usted en restaurantes mexicanos?**
- As you listen to your instructor's responses, record his or her answers with a check mark. How many of your predictions were correct?

	Todos los fines de semana	A menudo	A veces	Nunca
comer en restaurantes mexicanos				
ir al cine				
asistir a partidos (de fútbol, etcétera)				
escribir un blog				
practicar deportes con otros profesores				
correr en el parque				
escuchar música en vivo (live)				
leer novelas en español				

2-46 **Dos verdades y una mentira** *(Two truths and a lie).* Write three sentences describing what you do on the weekends: Two must be true and one must be a lie. Then, working in small groups, take turns reading your sentences aloud. Your classmates have to guess which one is a lie. How well do you know one another?

Modelo **Estudiante A:** Toco la guitarra en una banda. Tuiteo todos los días. A veces asisto a conciertos de jazz.

Estudiantes B y C: No tocas la guitarra en una banda.

Estudiante A: Sí toco la guitarra en una banda, pero nunca tuiteo.

2-47 **¿Cierto o falso?** With a partner, take turns making either true or false statements about what the people are doing in the drawing. Say **cierto** (if it's true) or **falso** (if it's false).

Some useful verbs: **comer, correr, escribir, leer, practicar, tocar.**

Modelo **Estudiante A:** La familia Ruiz practica deportes.

Estudiante B: Falso. La familia Ruiz come pizza.

78 Capítulo 2

Las preguntas de información y de confirmación

LORENA	¿Dónde comemos?
SAMANTHA	Normalmente comemos comida china los viernes, ¿verdad?
LORENA	Sí.
SAMANTHA	Entonces, ¿por qué no vamos al nuevo *(new)* restaurante Pekín?
LORENA	¡Buena idea!

© Cengage Learning 2016

1. Tag questions (**las preguntas de confirmación**) are a variation of yes/no questions. They are formed by adding a short confirming word at the end of a statement.

> AFFIRMATIVE STATEMENT, + **¿VERDAD?** OR **¿NO?**
> La comida italiana es buena, **¿verdad?**   *Italian food is good, **isn't it?***

> NEGATIVE STATEMENT, + **¿VERDAD?**
> **No** tenemos clase mañana, **¿verdad?**   *We don't have class tomorrow, **right?***

2. Information questions (**las preguntas de información**) require answers with specific information rather than a simple *yes* or *no*. They start with interrogative words (**interrogativos**), such as the following. Notice that all these question words use accent marks. Also, unlike English, Spanish uses **quiénes**—a plural version of *who*—to refer to more than one person.

Los interrogativos

¿A qué hora? *At what time?*	**¿Cuántos? / ¿Cuántas?** *How many?*
¿Adónde? *To where?*	**¿De dónde?** *From where?*
¿Cómo? *How?*	**¿Dónde?** *Where?*
¿Con qué frecuencia? *How often?*	**¿Para qué?** *What for?*
¿Cuál? / ¿Cuáles? *Which one(s)?*	**¿Por qué?** *Why? How come?*
¿Cuándo? *When?*	**¿Qué?** *What?*
¿Cuánto? / ¿Cuánta? *How much?*	**¿Quién? / ¿Quiénes?** *Who?*

3. To form information questions, use the following pattern. Recall that subjects may be understood rather than stated.

> ¿INTERROGATIVE + CONJUGATED VERB + SUBJECT + OTHER ELEMENTS?
>   **¿Dónde**   viven   Marcela y José   este semestre?
> **Where** *are Marcela and José living this semester?*

4. In informal English it is acceptable to place a preposition at the end of a question; however, in Spanish, prepositions (**a**, **de**, **con**, etc.) always appear before interrogative words, at the beginning of questions.

> **¿Con quién** vas a la fiesta?   *Who are you going to the party **with?** /*
>   ***With whom** are you going to the party?*

5. Use the appropriate endings for gender and number with **cuánto(a)**, **cuántos(as)**, **cuál(es)**, and **quién(es)**.

¿Cuán**tos** partid**os** hay esta semana?   *How many games are there this week?*

6. In Spanish there are two ways to express *What is / What are . . . ?*

- To ask for definitions and explanations or to identify an object, use **¿Qué es... ?**

¿**Qué es** un blog?   *What's a blog?*

- To inquire about specific details or information (but not a definition), use **¿Cuál es... ? / ¿Cuáles son... ?**

¿**Cuáles son** tus clases preferidas?   *What / Which are your favorite classes?*

¡Aplícalo! **2-48** **Una invitación.** With a partner, play the roles of Andrea and Rubén, two friends from Barcelona, Spain. As you read your roles, choose the correct question words from the list below. Some of the question words will be used more than once and some not at all.

cómo	cuál	cuándo	cuántas	de dónde
no	por qué	qué	quiénes	verdad

RUBÉN   Oye, Andrea, tú no trabajas hoy, ¿(1) _____?

ANDREA   No. ¿(2) _____ preguntas?

RUBÉN   Pues, ¿(3) _____ no vamos de compras a El Corte Inglés?

ANDREA   Buena idea. ¿A (4) _____ vamos? Porque hay muchos.

RUBÉN   Vamos a El Corte Inglés de la Plaza de Cataluña. Está muy cerca.

ANDREA   De acuerdo. ¿(5) _____ van con nosotros? ¿Martina? ¿Jesús? ¿Arnau?

RUBÉN   Tú, Arnau y yo: ¡los tres mosqueteros (*musketeers*)!

 2-49 **El club de español.** The Spanish Club skyped a student in Spain to learn about her experiences at the **Universidad de Murcia**. Below are her responses during the Q&A session. With a partner, create a logical question for each response. Hint: Choose a question word that corresponds to the underlined information.

Modelo   Estudio en Murcia.
            ¿Dónde estudias?

1. El programa se llama Erasmus.
2. Hay dos campus: el campus de Espinardo y el campus de la Merced.
3. La Facultad de Matemáticas está en el campus de Espinardo.
4. Vivo con Carola y Flavia, dos estudiantes de Italia.
5. Las fiestas son los jueves, viernes y sábados.
6. No hay muchos clubs de deportes o música porque muchos estudiantes regresan a sus casas los fines de semana.

¡Exprésate!

 2-50 **¡Adivina *(Guess)* la actividad!** With a partner, take turns choosing one of the listed activities. Your partner needs to guess which activity you selected by using any three interrogative words (not complete questions) to get more information.

Modelo Estudiante A: *(Chooses "estudiar para la clase de español" but does not reveal it.)*
Estudiante B: ¿Dónde?
Estudiante A: en la biblioteca o en el cuarto
Estudiante B: ¿Cuándo?
Estudiante A: por la noche
Estudiante B: ¿Qué?
Estudiante A: el vocabulario
Estudiante B: ¿Estudiar para la clase de español?
Estudiante A: ¡Sí!

bailar salsa	**lavar la ropa**
comer en un restaurante con amigos	**leer una novela**
correr un maratón	**mandar mensajes de texto a mis amigos**
estudiar para la clase de español	**practicar el baloncesto**
ir de compras	**visitar a mi familia**

 2-51 **¿Verdad?** Find a classmate with whom you haven't partnered yet. Taking turns, make five statements about your partner and attach a tag question at the end. Your partner will then affirm or deny your statements. How many correct assumptions did you make?

Modelo Estudiante A: Asistes a los partidos de béisbol a menudo, ¿no?
Estudiante B: No, nunca asisto a los partidos de béisbol. / Sí, asisto a casi todos los partidos.

Clase

2-52 **¡Jeopardy® en español!** Your instructor will divide the class into three to five teams to play a game.

- Taking turns, one team chooses a category and dollar amount (for example: **Un día típico por cincuenta dólares**), and the instructor reads an answer aloud.
- The first team to raise hands and give the correct question wins the dollar amount and chooses next.
- The team with the highest dollar amount at the end of the game wins.

Nuestra clase de español	Un día típico	Las actividades de ocio	España
$25	$25	$25	$25
$50	$50	$50	$50
$75	$75	$75	$75
$100	$100	$100	$100

CONECTADOS CON...
LA CINEMATOGRAFÍA

El cine español

El cine español es reconocido *(recognized)* internacionalmente por el talento artístico, la calidad *(quality)* y la originalidad. Su historia empieza *(begins)* en 1896 con películas mudas *(silent)*. En 1928 aparece el cine experimental con la película surrealista de Luis Buñuel y Salvador Dalí, *Un perro andaluz*.

Dos grandes directores

- Luis Buñuel (1900–1983) es considerado uno de los directores más *(most)* originales de la historia. En 1972, Buñuel es el primer *(first)* director español en recibir un Óscar por *El discreto encanto de la burguesía*.

- Pedro Almodóvar (1949–) es un director de cine español de gran prestigio internacional. Su filmografía es muy extensa e incluye películas ganadoras *(winning)* de premios internacionales, como por ejemplo, *Volver* (2006). Sus millones de fans adoran su humor irreverente y sus personajes no convencionales.

Estrategia Scanning for specific information

In order to find specific information in a reading, use the strategy of scanning **(la búsqueda rápida)**. Move your eyes quickly over the words until you find the word, phrase, or number you're looking for.

Palabras de cinematografía

el actor	*actor*
la actriz	*actress*
la estrella	*star*
la película	*movie*
el personaje	*character*
el premio	*award*
protagonizar	*to play the lead in*

2-53 **Comprensión.** Identify the following things and people from the reading.

1. Es una película surrealista de 1928.
2. Es el primer *(first)* director español en recibir un Óscar.
3. Es un director español famoso por su humor irreverente.
4. Son tres actores españoles que *(that)* trabajan en Hollywood.
5. Es un premio de la cinematografía de España similar al premio Óscar.

Clase

2-54 **¿Y tú?** Discuss the following questions with your classmates.

1. ¿Miras muchas películas? ¿Con qué frecuencia vas al cine?
2. ¿Estás familiarizado(a) con el cine español? ¿Qué películas españolas has visto *(have you seen)*?
3. ¿Quiénes son tus actores preferidos? ¿Y tu director(a) preferido(a)?

España en Hollywood

Antonio Banderas, Penélope Cruz y Javier Bardem son tres actores españoles que *(that)* protagonizan películas de Almodóvar y se convierten en *(become)* estrellas de Hollywood. En 2008, Penélope Cruz es la primera *(first)* actriz española en ganar un premio Óscar.

Penélope Cruz recibe el premio Goya, un prestigioso premio de la Academia de las Artes y las Ciencias Cinematográficas de España.

© AFP/Getty Images

Composición: Un mensaje

Paloma, an exchange student from Spain, is eager to meet U.S. students. She sounds interesting, so you decide to respond to her post on the website of your university's Association for International Students. Include a saluation (**Hola, Paloma:**), a greeting, information about yourself (name, major, and free time activites), an invitation to go out for coffee, and a closing (**Saludos,** *your name*).

Revisión en pareja. Exchange papers with a classmate and edit each other's work.

- Does the message include all the information mentioned above? Write one positive comment and one suggestion for improvement.

- Does every sentence have a subject and a corresponding conjugated verb? Are the words in the proper order? Write short comments to point out possible mistakes.

Estrategia:
Creating statements and questions

Statements and questions are the building blocks of compositions.

- **Statement:** Subject + (no) conjugated verb + other elements.
- **Yes/No question:** ¿(No) Conjugated verb + subject + other elements?
- **Information question:** ¿Question word + conjugated verb + subject + other elements?

NUESTRA COMUNIDAD

2-55 **Nosotros / *Share It!*** Online, you posted a photo and a description (or a video) of your favorite place on or near campus. What did you learn as you viewed your classmates' posts? With two or three classmates, discuss the posts on *Share It!* and answer these questions.

1. ¿Cuáles son los lugares *(places)* más populares en el campus? ¿Cuáles son los lugares más populares cerca del campus? ¿Dónde están? ¿Por qué son populares?

2. ¿Quiénes de ustedes tienen una opinión contraria *(opposing)* sobre los lugares mencionados?

3. ¿Qué foto (o video) es muy divertida o interesante? ¿Por qué?

2-56 **Perspectivas: ¿Cómo es la vida social?** Online, you watched a video of three Spanish-speaking students as they answered the questions **¿Cómo es la vida social en la universidad? ¿En qué grupos estudiantiles participas?** How did the interviewees respond? With two or three classmates, compare the notes you took when you watched that video. Then, interview the others in your group with the questions that follow and jot down the information.

- ¿Cómo te llamas?
- En tu opinión, ¿cómo es la vida social en la universidad?
- ¿En qué grupos estudiantiles participas?

2-57 **Exploración: Planes de estudio.** Online, you visited the website of a university in Spain and explored the classes offered in your current major (or another major of your choice). Using your notes from your online investigations, share your findings with your classmates in a brief presentation. After your presentations, discuss these questions: How many courses do students take in Spain? And in your university? How many of these classes are electives?

Modelo

La universidad se llama... Mi carrera *(major)* es... y está en la Facultad de... En el primer ciclo, hay... asignaturas. Tres clases o materias troncales *(core classes)* son... En mi opinión, la clase de... parece *(seems)* muy interesante.

2-58 **Conectados con... la sociología.** Online, you read about addiction to social media. With two or three classsmates, share the results of your research on the use of social media or on the prevalance of other kinds of addiction.

Modelo

(Type of social media) es muy popular en... / En Estados Unidos, la adicción...

2-59 **La invitación.** You (**Estudiante A**) and your partner (**Estudiante B**) want to go out and do something fun this week. Using the information in the entertainment guide and the appointment calendar, find an activity you both enjoy and can attend.

- **Estudiante A** will use the entertainment guide to choose an activity and invite **Estudiante B**.

- **Estudiante B** will use the appointment calendar to check his or her availability and will accept or decline the invitation.

- **Estudiante A** should start the conversation with **¿Qué tal si... ?** and propose an activity. (**¿Qué tal si vamos a un concierto?**)

- **Estudiante B** should ask about the activity (**¿Qué día es? ¿A qué hora es?**) and describe any other obligations or plans that he or she has (**El miércoles a las siete tengo que... / voy a...**).

> This is a pair activity for **Estudiante A** and **Estudiante B**.
>
> If you are **Estudiante A**, use the information on this page.
>
> If you are **Estudiante B**, turn to p. S-2 at the back of the book.

GUÍA DEL OCIO
Esta semana

Música
Concierto de Rodrigo y Gabriela
Sala Bikini, miércoles 26 a las 20.30 h

Arte
Exposición de Picasso
Fundación Botín, de martes a jueves, de 10 a 20 h

Restaurantes
Bodega La Andaluza
Tiene como protagonistas a las tapas. Abre todos los días de 14 h a 0.30 h madrugada.

Cine
Festival de Cine de Terror
Cine Universitario, viernes 28 a las 18 h

Deportes
Partido de fútbol LA Galaxy–FC Barcelona
Estadio Camp Nou, domingo 30 a las 17 h

Noche
Club Camelot
Discoteca con un espíritu alternativo. Abre todos los sábados hasta la madrugada.

Colaborar **2-60 La educación en la historia.** The aims and approaches to education in Spain have changed over the years. Look at the poster **(el cartel)** from the time of the Spanish Civil War and read the information beside it. Then answer the questions below with a partner.

1. ¿Cuál es el tema *(theme; topic)* de este cartel?

2. ¿Qué hacen los niños *(What are the children doing)* en el cartel?

3. ¿De qué región española es el cartel? ¿Dónde está esta región? ¿Qué lengua hablan?

4. ¿Qué tipos de reformas recomienda el CENU?

5. ¿Cómo son las escuelas en tu comunidad *(your community)*? ¿Privadas o públicas? ¿Religiosas o laicas? ¿Mixtas o separadas *(Co-ed or single gender)*?

Durante la Guerra Civil Española (1936–1939), se proponen muchas reformas,[1] incluso la transformación de la educación pública. En Cataluña, el Consejo[2] de la Escuela Nueva Unificada (CENU) recomienda varias innovaciones como[3] la educación laica (no religiosa) y la coeducación (mixta, o con los dos sexos). Este cartel de Cataluña presenta estas ideas de forma concisa en la lengua de la región: el catalán.

[1]*many reforms are proposed*   [2]*Council*   [3]*such as*

Pronunciación: Las letras *ll, ñ, r, rr*

How quickly and correctly can you and your classmates say these tongue twisters and silly sentences in Spanish? Pay close attention to the sounds corresponding to **ll, ñ, r,** and **rr**.

1. **El perro de Rosa y Roque no tiene rabo, porque Ramón Ramírez se lo ha cortado.**

   Rosa and Roque's dog doesn't have a tail because Ramón Ramírez cut it off.

2. **Yo lloro si lloras, si lloras yo lloro. Si tú ya no lloras, tampoco yo lloro.**

   I cry if you cry, if you cry I cry. If you are no longer crying, I won't cry either.

3. **Ñoño Yáñez come ñame en las mañanas con el niño.**

   Ñoño Yáñez eats yams in the mornings with the boy.

ϯϯϯ **2-61** **¿Quién es?** Play this guessing game with two or three classmates. First, each group member silently chooses one of the people pictured below and creates a five-sentence description of that person's typical day. Then, each person takes a turn presenting that description. The rest of the group listens and tries to guess whose routine is being described.

Modelo Llega a la universidad a las ocho de la mañana. Pasa la mañana en...

El rector (*dean*) de la universidad

Una profesora

Una estudiante seria

Un estudiante juerguista (*fun-loving*)

Un atleta

Una bibliotecaria (*librarian*)

Clase

2-62 **Situación: El centro de consejería.** With your classmates, turn your classroom into a peer-counseling center for new students. About a third of your class should take the roles of peer counselors and be seated at desks. The rest of the class should be the new students; they walk around the classroom, talk with the "counselors," and make small talk with other students.

Consejeros	Nuevos (*New*) estudiantes
• Greet the new students as they approach your desk.	• Approach a peer-counselor and greet him/her.
• Introduce yourself.	• Introduce yourself.
• Make small talk: Ask the new students where they are from, what they are majoring in, and what classes they are taking.	• Ask several questions about classes, professors, class times, locations of buildings on campus, etc.
• Answer questions they have about your campus, classes, professors, and free-time activities on campus.	• If all the peer-counselors are busy, introduce yourself to other new students and make small talk: Find out where they are from, what classes they are taking, what they think of their classes, etc.
• As they leave, say good-bye and wish them good luck (**¡Buena suerte!**).	

VOCABULARIO

RECURSOS

Para aprender mejor

Learn words in pairs. They can be pairs of opposite meanings (**aburrido / interesante**), pairs of related words (**música / concierto**), or verbs that commonly occur with certain nouns (**practicar deportes**).

Sustantivos

los apuntes *notes*
el baloncesto *basketball*
el béisbol *baseball*
el blog *blog*
la carrera *major, degree*
el cine *movies, movie theater*
el club *club*
el concierto *concert*
el examen *test*
la familia *family*
la fiesta *party*
el fútbol *soccer*
el fútbol americano *football*
el grupo estudiantil *student organization*
la guitarra *guitar*
la hora *time; hour*
el horario *schedule*
el informe *paper, report*
el mensaje de texto *text message*
la música *music*
la novela *novel*
el parque *park*
el partido *game*
el piano *piano*
el restaurante *restaurant*
el semestre *semester*
la tarea *homework*

Verbos

aprender (a) *to learn (how)*
asistir a *to go to, to attend*
bailar *to dance*
comer *to eat*
comprender *to understand*
contestar *to answer, to reply*
correr *to run*
descansar *to relax*
escribir *to write*

escuchar música *to listen to music*
estudiar *to study*
hablar (por teléfono) *to talk (on the phone)*
ir de compras *to go shopping*
lavar (la ropa) *to wash (clothes)*
leer *to read*
limpiar *to clean*
llegar *to arrive*
mandar mensajes de texto *to text, to send a text message*
mirar (la tele) *to watch TV*
participar *to participate*
pasar (horas, el rato) *to spend (hours, time)*
practicar (un deporte) *to play (a sport)*
recibir *to receive, to get*
regresar *to go back*
terminar *to finish*
tocar *to play (a musical instrument)*
tomar *to take*
trabajar *to work*
tuitear *to tweet*
visitar *to visit*
vivir *to live*

Adjetivos

aburrido(a) *boring*
amable *kind and helpful*
antipático(a) *mean, unpleasant*
bueno(a) *good*
chino(a) *Chinese*
despistado(a) *absentminded, scatterbrained*
difícil *difficult*
divertido(a) *fun*
exigente *strict, demanding*
fácil *easy*
interesante *interesting*

malo(a) *bad*
organizado(a) *organized*
perfecto(a) *perfect*
poco(a) *little, not much*
pocos(as) *few, not many*
preferido(a) *favorite*
simpático(a) *nice*
típico(a) *typical*

Los días de la semana

el lunes *Monday*
el martes *Tuesday*
el miércoles *Wednesday*
el jueves *Thursday*
el viernes *Friday*
el sábado *Saturday*
el domingo *Sunday*
entre semana *during the week, on weekdays*
el fin de semana *weekend*

Expresiones útiles

a menudo *often*
a veces *sometimes*
hoy *today*
mañana *tomorrow*
me gusta *I like*
No está mal. *It's okay.*
normalmente *usually*
nunca *never*
por la mañana *in the morning*
por la noche *in the evening*
por la tarde *in the afternoon*
por lo general *usually*
porque *because*
(casi) siempre *(almost) always*
todos los días *every day*

Telling time, p. 62
Invitations, p. 72
Question words, p. 79

Entre familia y amigos

Conexiones a la comunidad
Watch a Spanish movie. Movies about family and friendships include *Todo lo que tú quieras, Cinco días sin Nora,* and *Viva Cuba.*

In this chapter you will . . .

- explore Cuba, the Dominican Republic, and Puerto Rico
- talk about family, friends, and pets
- express possession
- describe people and make comparisons
- describe some gatherings and celebrations
- express likes and dislikes
- learn about endangered species in the Caribbean
- share family memories

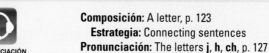

NUESTRO**MUNDO**

Cuba, República Dominicana y Puerto Rico

Estas tres islas *(islands)* hispanohablantes
están en el mar Caribe, cerca de Estados
Unidos. Su cultura tiene influencias españolas,
indígenas y africanas.

© Cengage Learning 2016

República de Cuba
Población: 11 100 000
Capital: La Habana
Gobierno: estado
  comunista

Moneda: el peso cubano
Exportaciones: azúcar
  (sugar), níquel, tabaco

República Dominicana
Población: 10 200 000
Capital: Santo Domingo
Gobierno: república
  democrática
Moneda: el peso
  dominicano

Exportaciones:
  ferroníquel *(nickel and
  iron alloy)*, azúcar,
  oro *(gold)*

Estado Libre Asociado de Puerto Rico
Población: 3 700 000
Capital: San Juan
Gobierno: estado libre
  asociado
  (commonwealth)

Moneda: el dólar
  americano
Exportaciones:
  químicos, electrónicos,
  ropa *(clothing)*

© Danita Delimont/Getty Images

En el Caribe, una actividad preferida entre *(among)* familia y amigos es ir al
malecón. Un malecón es un paseo marítimo *(seafront promenade)*: un lugar ideal
para pasear *(stroll)*, contemplar el océano y pasar el rato. El malecón de la foto está
en La Habana, Cuba, y es ocho kilómetros de largo *(long)*.

Astronomía

El Observatorio de Arecibo, Puerto Rico, es un centro de investigación importante en la astronomía. Este gigantesco telescopio mide *(measures)* 305 metros de diámetro y es el radiotelescopio más *(most)* sensitivo del mundo. Con este enorme instrumento, los científicos estudian los planetas y las galaxias.

Agricultura

En 1493 Cristóbal Colón lleva una planta asiática —la caña de azúcar *(sugar cane)*— a la isla La Española (hoy, Haití y República Dominicana). Así empieza *(begins)* el cultivo de esta planta en el Caribe y la trata de esclavos *(slave trade)* en el Nuevo Mundo *(New World)*.

Música

El Caribe hispánico ha producido *(has produced)* muchos estilos de música popular: el mambo, la salsa, el merengue, la bachata y muchos más. Esta música es el producto de la fusión de ritmos españoles, africanos e indígenas. La influencia africana, por ejemplo *(for example)*, es evidente en los ritmos sincopados y el uso de instrumentos de percusión.

3-1 **¿Qué sabes?** Compare and contrast **Cuba**, **República Dominicana**, and **Puerto Rico** by creating a Venn diagram for the three countries and filling it with the following phrases.

la caña de azúcar
el dólar americano
la influencia africana en la música
el radiotelescopio más sensitivo
  del mundo

el mar Caribe
un estado comunista
cerca de Estados Unidos
pasear por el malecón
una república democrática

3-2 **Videomundo.** After watching the videos on Cuba, the Dominican Republic, and Puerto Rico, brainstorm a list of at least ten sights and sounds (**escenas y sonidos**) associated with these three Caribbean regions.

La familia, los amigos y las mascotas

Mi familia

In this *Paso*, you will . . .
- talk about family, friends, and pets
- describe family relationships
- express possession

mi abuela, Celia	mi abuelo, Justo

mi mamá, Irene	mi papá, Ernesto

mi tía, Teresa	mi tío, Roberto

mi hermana, Maya	mi hermano, Antonio	**Yo soy Eva.**

mi prima, Adriana	mi primo, Daniel

Otros parientes — Other relatives

el esposo / la esposa — *husband / wife; spouse*
el hijo / la hija — *son / daugther*
el hijo único / la hija única — *only child*
el nieto / la nieta — *grandson / granddaughter*
el padre / la madre — *father / mother*
los padres — *parents*
el sobrino / la sobrina — *nephew / niece*

Los amigos — Friends

el mejor amigo / la mejor amiga — *best friend*
el novio / la novia — *boyfriend; groom / girlfriend; bride*

Las mascotas — Pets

el perro / el gato / el pájaro — *dog / cat / bird*
el pez, los peces — *fish*

Mis fotos

Este es **mi novio** David. Tiene dos **perros** muy **cariñosos**.

Esta es **mi mejor amiga**, Gabi. Su familia es de Venezuela pero **llevan muchos años aquí** en República Dominicana.

Aquí estamos **todos** en **la boda** de mi prima Inés. **¡Qué día más emocionante!**

Esta soy yo **de bebé**, en mi fiesta de **cumpleaños**. **Qué linda**, ¿verdad?

Para hablar sobre las fotos

¿Quién es este señor / esta señora?

¿Quiénes son estos chicos / estas chicas?

¡Qué foto más bonita / tierna / divertida!

¡Qué día más emocionante / inolvidable!

el hombre / la mujer

el niño / la niña

Más información sobre la familia

¿Cómo es tu familia?

    Es bastante loca, pero nos queremos.

    Es muy unida; nos llevamos bien.

Quiero (mucho) a... / No soporto (a)...

Falleció hace unos años.

estar soltero(a) / casado(a) / divorciado(a)

llevar años aquí / allí

Talking about photos

Who's this man / woman?

Who are these guys (boys) / young women (girls)?

What a pretty / sweet / fun picture!

What an exciting / memorable day!

man / woman

little boy / little girl

More family information

What's your family like?

    It's pretty crazy, but we love one another.

    We're very close; we get along well.

I love . . . (a lot). / I can't stand . . .

He/She passed away a few years ago.

to be single / married / divorced

to have been living here / there for years

¡Aplícalo!

🔄 Affirmative and negative sentences, **Capítulo 2 Paso 1**

Colaborar

3-3 **¡Qué foto más linda!** Leticia is asking you about the photos that your friend Eva has posted. Working with a partner, take turns answering her questions. Refer to the photos on page 93 and follow the model.

Modelo Leticia: "David es el hermano de Eva, ¿verdad?"
Estudiante A: No, David es el novio de Eva.

1. "Gabi es la prima de Eva, ¿verdad?"

2. "La familia de Gabi es de Cuba, ¿no?"

3. "¿Lleva muchos años en República Dominicana la familia de Gabi?"

4. "¿Quién es la novia en esta foto de la boda? Es Inés, ¿verdad?"

5. "Inés es la hermana de Eva, ¿no?"

6. "¡Qué foto más tierna! ¿Quién es el bebé? ¿Es Inés?"

7. "En esta foto, Eva tiene uno o dos años, ¿verdad?"

8. "Mi foto preferida es la de David y los perros. ¿Cuál es tu foto preferida?"

Colaborar

3-4 **Una celebración.** Angélica is describing one of her favorite pictures. With a partner, select the more logical words and read the description aloud.

Mi familia es muy (1. unida / soltera) y siempre tenemos reuniones familiares para celebrar (2. los cumpleaños / las mascotas). Aquí estamos en la (3. boda / fiesta) de mi sobrina, Lisette. Ella está con su papá, mi (4. hermano / primo). Los señores son mis (5. hijos / abuelos). Son muy (6. emocionantes / cariñosos), ¿verdad? (7. Quiero / No soporto) mucho a mis abuelos, especialmente a mi abuela. Mi mamá (8. falleció / lleva) hace unos años y mi abuela es como una segunda *(second)* mamá. Los otros chicos en la foto son los (9. tíos / primos) de Lisette. Qué foto más (10. tierna / divorciada), ¿verdad?

© Tim Dolan Photography/Getty Images

Nota cultural

Spanish, like English, has specific words for members of blended families: **padrastro** *step-father;* **madrastra** *stepmother;* **hermanastro(a)** *stepbrother (sister);* **medio(a) hermano(a)** *half brother (sister);* etc. However, these terms are rarely used in everyday conversation. Instead, most people call these members of their families **padre**, **madre**, or **hermano(a)**.

3-5 **El árbol genealógico.** Working with a partner, take turns describing your family trees; include each person's name and age.

- First, **Estudiante A** describes his/her family—beginning with the grandparents—while **Estudiante B** listens and draws a family tree based upon that description.

- Next, switch roles. When you are both done, swap papers and check the results.

¡Exprésate!

🔄 Yes/No questions,
Capítulo 2 Paso 2

3-6 **Adivina la palabra.** With three or four classmates, form a circle and play a guessing game with words from the **Vocabulario** on pages 92–93. The goal is to guess the hidden word you're holding by asking ten or fewer yes/no questions.

- First, each person writes the word for a family member or pet on a piece of paper.
- Next, each member of the group passes his/her card to the left, face down.
- The first player holds the card facing out so that he/she cannot see the word, but the rest of the group can.
- This player asks the group yes/no questions until he/she guesses the word correctly.

Modelo   **Estudiante A:** ¿Es una mascota?
Estudiante B: No, es un pariente.
Estudiante A: ¿Es un hombre?
Estudiante C: No, es una mujer. ...

3-7 **Las fotos.** Imagine these are pictures of your friends and family. With a partner, take turns asking questions and making comments about them. For example, talk about the relationship, age, event, etc. Afterwards, do the same with some real pictures you have with you.

Modelo   **Estudiante A:** *(pointing to the little girl)* ¿Quién es esta niña?
Estudiante B: Es mi sobrina Mariana. Tiene tres años. Es una foto de su fiesta de cumpleaños.
Estudiante A: ¡Qué foto más divertida!

Nota lingüística

To say *this* or *these* in Spanish use these forms:

este chico *this boy*
esta chica *this girl*
estos chicos *these boys*
estas chicas *these girls*

The same forms are used when the person or thing is understood: **Este** es mi tío. *This (man) is my uncle.*

1.   2.   3.

3-8 **¿Cómo es tu familia?** Working with a classmate, ask each other these questions to find out more about your respective families.

1. ¿Cómo es tu familia? ¿Es muy unida? ¿Un poco loca?
2. ¿Dónde vive tu familia? ¿Llevan muchos años allí?
3. ¿Tienes hermanos o eres hijo(a) único(a)? *(If your partner has siblings, ask:)* ¿Cuántos?
4. ¿Visitas con frecuencia a tus abuelos? ¿Cuántos años tienen?
5. ¿Tienes muchos tíos y primos? ¿Pasas mucho tiempo con ellos?
6. ¿Cuál de tus amigos es como parte de tu familia *(is like part of your family)*? ¿Asiste a muchas fiestas de tu familia?
7. ¿Qué mascotas tienes? ¿Cómo se llaman?

Los adjetivos y los pronombres posesivos

SALMA   Tu familia tiene muchas mascotas, ¿verdad?

DEX   Sí, mira esta foto. Aquí está mi hermanito con sus perros.

SALMA   ¡Qué foto más divertida! ¿De quién son el gato y el pájaro?

DEX   El gato es mío y el pájaro es de nuestra abuela.

■ ■ ■
Descúbrelo

- What are Salma and Dex talking about?

- Which pets belong to Dex? To his brother? To his grandmother?

- What are the Spanish words for *your*, *his*, and *our*?

- What are the Spanish words for *my* and *mine*?

1. Possessive adjectives (**los adjetivos posesivos**) are words such as *my*, *his*, and *our* that indicate possession, ownership, and relationships.

   Aquí está **mi** hermanito con **sus** perros. *Here's **my** little brother with **his** dogs.*

Los adjetivos posesivos

mi(s)	*my*	**nuestro(s) / nuestra(s)**	*our*
tu(s)	*your (informal)*	**vuestro(s) / vuestra(s)**	*your (informal, Spain)*
su(s)	*your (formal)*	**su(s)**	*your (informal / formal)*
su(s)	*his/her/its*	**su(s)**	*their*

2. Possessive adjectives are placed in front of nouns and match these nouns in number. For example: **mis perros** *(my dogs)*.

   Two of the possessive adjectives, **nuestro** and **vuestro**, match nouns in both number and gender. For example: **nuestra tía** *(our aunt)*.

3. Spanish has several equivalents for *your*.

   - To refer to a friend or family member (informal): **tu(s)**

   - To refer to a stranger, an older person, or someone in authority (formal): **su(s)**

   - When *your* refers to more than one person: **su(s)** *(informal or formal in Latin America; formal in Spain)*; **vuestro(s) / vuestra(s)** *(informal in Spain)*

4. **Su(s)** has several meanings: *your, his, her, its,* and *their*. When the context is not clear, replace **su** with the phrase: **de + él / ella / ellos / ellas / usted / ustedes**.

Enrique y Alicia viven en Georgia.	*Enrique and Alicia live in Georgia.*
La casa **de él** está en Atlanta.	***His** house is in Atlánta.*
La casa **de ella** está en Augusta.	***Her** house is in Augusta.*

5. Possessive pronouns (**los pronombres posesivos**) are used when a noun is understood, rather than stated. Like possessive adjectives, possessive pronouns agree in gender and number with the nouns they refer to. For example: **Mis perros son muy cariñosos. ¿Cómo son los tuyos?**

Los pronombres posesivos				
	Masculino singular	Masculino plural	Femenino singular	Femenino plural
mine	el mío	los míos	la mía	las mías
yours (inf.)	el tuyo	los tuyos	la tuya	las tuyas
yours (form.)/his/hers/its	el suyo	los suyos	la suya	las suyas
ours	el nuestro	los nuestros	la nuestra	las nuestras
yours (inf., Spain)	el vuestro	los vuestros	la vuestra	las vuestras
yours (inf. / form., Lat. Am.; form., Spain)/theirs	el suyo	los suyos	la suya	las suyas

Colaborar

3-9 **Una familia grande.** Eduardo is asking his friend Adela about her family. Working with a partner, play the roles of the two friends and complete their conversation in a logical way.

¡Aplícalo!

EDUARDO ¿Dónde vive (1. tu / su) familia, Adela?

ADELA Es un poco complicado porque (2. mi / mis) padres están divorciados. Yo vivo aquí con mi mamá y (3. nuestros / mis) dos hermanos.

EDUARDO ¿Y (4. tu / tus) papá? ¿Vive aquí?

ADELA No, él está en Nueva York, con (5. su / sus) nueva *(new)* esposa, Rosa.

EDUARDO ¿Están casados (6. nuestros / tus) hermanos?

ADELA Mi hermano Rubén sí está casado. Él, (7. tu / su) esposa Linda y (8. su / sus) tres hijos tienen una casa muy cerca de la nuestra.

EDUARDO ¡(9. Tu / Tus) familia es muy interesante, Adela!

ADELA Bueno, (10. nuestro / nuestra) familia es un poco loca, pero nos queremos mucho.

3-10 **Comparaciones.** How do your family and friends compare to César's? With a partner, take turns reading César's statements aloud; then each of you should make a similar statement using a possessive pronoun.

Modelo "Mi mejor amigo se llama Osvaldo".

Estudiante A: El mío se llama Austin.

Estudiante B: El mío se llama Patrick.

1. "Mi familia vive en Florida".

2. "Nuestra familia es grande y unida".

3. "Nuestros abuelos viven muy cerca".

4. "Mi mejor amigo tiene 21 años".

5. "Mis tíos tienen un gato y tres pájaros".

6. "Mi prima preferida se llama Lidia y está casada".

¡Exprésate!

 Colaborar

3-11 **¿Quién es?** Taking turns, one of you reads a clue and the other says what family relationship that person has.

> **Modelo** **Estudiante A:** Es la hermana de tu padre. ¿Quién es?
>
> **Estudiante B:** Es mi tía.

1. Es la hija de tus tíos. ¿Quién es?

2. Son las esposas de tus tíos. ¿Quiénes son?

3. Es la madre de mi madre. ¿Quién es?

4. Son las primas de mi hija. ¿Quiénes son?

5. Son las hijas de nuestros padres. ¿Quiénes son?

6. Es el hermano de nuestra madre. ¿Quién es?

Colaborar

3-12 **Esmeralda Santiago.** Read the following article on a well-known Puerto Rican writer and answer the questions. Compare answers with a partner.

1. ¿Por qué es Esmeralda Santiago bicultural? ¿Te consideras tú *(Do you consider yourself)* bicultural también? ¿Por qué sí o por qué no?

2. ¿Cómo se llama su primer libro? ¿Cómo se llamaría *(would be called)* tu primer libro?

3. ¿Cómo es su familia: grande o pequeña? ¿Cómo es la tuya?

4. ¿Qué apodo *(nickname)* usa su familia para hablar con Esmeralda? ¿Qué apodo usa tu familia para hablar contigo?

5. ¿Con quiénes vive Esmeralda ahora *(now)*? ¿Con quién(es) vives tú ahora?

Conozca a Esmeralda Santiago: una escritora entre dos culturas

Esmeralda Santiago nació[1] en Puerto Rico en 1948 pero lleva muchos años en Estados Unidos. Sus experiencias como inmigrante latina y su identidad bicultural son temas[2] de muchas de sus novelas autobiográficas. En su primer libro, *Cuando era puertorriqueña*, Esmeralda narra[3] sobre su niñez[4]. "Negi", como su familia la llama, es la mayor[5] de once hijos. Cuando tiene trece años, emigra a Nueva York con su madre y siete hermanos. La vida de inmigrante no es fácil pero Esmeralda logra[6] "el sueño americano": estudia en la Universidad de Harvard y es una prominente escritora. Hoy, vive en Nueva York con su esposo Frank, su hijo Lucas y su hija Ila.

© Cengage Learning 2016. Photo: © ZUMA Press, Inc. / Alamy

[1]*was born* [2]*subjects* [3]*narrates* [4]*childhood* [5]*oldest* [6]*achieves*

3-13 **Los preferidos.** Get together with a classmate and share information about your favorites. Follow the model. Be prepared to tell the class the results.

> **Modelo** parientes
>
> **Estudiante A:** Mis parientes preferidos son mis abuelos. ¿Cuáles son los tuyos?
>
> **Estudiante B:** Los míos son mis primos de Miami.

1. deporte
2. música
3. clase
4. mascotas
5. programas de televisión
6. restaurantes en el campus
7. lugar donde estudiar
8. película *(movie)*

Los verbos *ser* y *estar*

NIÑA   ¿Por qué estás enojado, abuelito?

ABUELO   ¡Porque los programas de televisión son muy aburridos!

NIÑA   No es un televisor, abuelito, ¡es un microondas *(microwave)*!

ABUELO   ¡Ay bendito *(Good grief)*! ¿Dónde están mis anteojos *(glasses)*?

1. **Ser** and **estar** both mean *to be* but have different uses. You should use **estar** to say or ask about the following:

   - Where someone is or where something is located

     Mi tío **está** <u>en el hospital</u>.   *My uncle **is** <u>in the hospital</u>.*

   - How people (or animals) are feeling or how they are doing

     Mi tía **está** <u>preocupada</u>.   *My aunt **is** <u>worried</u>.*

   - Someone's marital status

     Mis padres **están** <u>divorciados</u>.   *My parents **are** <u>divorced</u>.*

2. You should use **ser** in these cases:

   - In front of a noun phrase, to identify people and things

     Luis **es** <u>mi hermano</u>.   *Luis **is** <u>my brother</u>.*

   - Before an adjective, to describe what someone or something is like

     Mis hermanos **son** <u>inteligentes</u>.   *My brothers **are** <u>smart</u>.*

   - Before **de**, to tell where someone / something is from or to whom something belongs

     Mis abuelos **son** <u>de Bonao</u>.   *My grandparents **are** <u>from Bonao</u>.*

   - To say where an event is taking place

     La boda **es** <u>en la catedral</u>.   *The wedding **is** <u>at the cathedral</u>.*

   - To give the day, date, time, and information such as addresses and phone numbers

     Mi teléfono **es** <u>el 555-0671</u>.   *My phone number **is** <u>555-0671</u>.*

3. Here are three important questions that use **ser** and **estar**:

ser	¿De quién **es**... (este perro)?	*Whose (dog) is this?*
ser	¿Cómo **es**... (tu sobrino)?	*What is (your nephew) like?*
estar	¿Cómo **está**... (tu sobrino)?	*How is (your nephew) doing / feeling?*

■ ■ ■
Descúbrelo

- Why is the grandfather angry? What was he really doing?

- Does the grandfather use a form of **ser** or **estar** to describe the TV shows? And to refer to the location of the glasses?

- What verb does the girl use to ask her grandfather why he's angry: **ser** or **estar**? And to identify the microwave?

© Cengage Learning 2016

PASO 1 GRAMÁTICA B G

¡Aplícalo! | Colaborar | **3-14** **Una conversación por teléfono.** Work with a partner to complete this telephone conversation.

- First, complete Armando's questions with the correct forms of **ser** and **estar**.
- Then match each question to Casandra's answers.
- Finally, read the exchanges aloud.

Las preguntas de Armando

1. Hola. ¿Cómo _____ (tú)?

2. ¿Dónde _____ (tú)?

3. Ah, ¿sí? ¿_____ muy ocupada?

4. ¿A qué hora _____ la fiesta y dónde _____?

5. ¿Quién _____ Rita?

6. ¿Dónde _____ la casa de Rita?

Las respuestas de Casandra

a. En la casa de Rita a las ocho de la noche.

b. Bien, pero un poco cansada.

c. Es mi amiga de Santo Domingo.

d. En la biblioteca. Tengo mucha tarea.

e. Sí. Pero, después de *(after)* terminar la tarea, voy a una fiesta.

f. En la calle Central, cerca del campus.

Clase | **3-15** **Firma, por favor.** Time to collect signatures! Circulate around the class and ask your classmates yes/no questions formed from the phrases in the chart. When somebody answers **sí**, ask that person to sign. **¡Ojo!** You can only collect two signatures per person.

Modelo **estar** enfermo(a)
    Estudiante A: Hola, Ada. ¿Estás enferma?
    Estudiante B: Sí, estoy enferma. / No, no estoy enferma.
    Estudiante A: Firma aquí *(Sign here)*, por favor. / Gracias.

Condiciones y descripciones	Firma *(Signature)*
1. **estar** enfermo(a)	
2. **ser** hijo(a) único(a)	
3. **ser** de otro estado *(another state)*	
4. **estar** un poco estresado(a) hoy	
5. **ser** muy organizado(a)	
6. **estar** contento(a)	
7. **estar** cerca de la puerta	
8. **ser** un poco despistado(a)	
9. **ser** de esta ciudad *(city)*	
10. **estar** enfrente de la ventana	

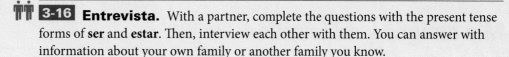

¡Exprésate!

3-16 Entrevista. With a partner, complete the questions with the present tense forms of **ser** and **estar**. Then, interview each other with them. You can answer with information about your own family or another family you know.

1. ¿En qué ciudad *(town)* _____ la casa de tus padres?

2. ¿Cuál _____ la dirección de la casa?

3. ¿Cómo _____ tu familia? ¿Grande o pequeña?

4. ¿De dónde _____ tus padres?

5. ¿Cómo _____ tus padres? ¿Estrictos o flexibles?

6. ¿_____ (tú) emocionado(a) cuando tus padres visitan la universidad?

7. ¿_____ (tú) buen hijo (buena hija)?

3-17 ¡Qué día más inolvidable! Get together in groups of four or six people and divide your group into two teams to play this game.

- Alternating turns, each team member says one sentence describing the scene in the drawing. For example: **La familia está en un parque.**

- Each sentence with a correct use of **ser** or **estar** earns two points for the team. A logical sentence without **ser** or **estar** earns one point.

© Cengage Learning 2016

3-18 ¡Qué absurdo! Working in small groups, create absurd mini-stories by following these steps:

- First, each person writes his/her answer to question #1 at the top of a sheet of paper.

- Each person folds the paper to cover what was written and passes it to the person on the right.

- Next, each person writes his or her answer to question #2, folds the paper, and passes it again. Continue in this way until all six questions are answered.

- Finally, each person takes a turn unfolding the paper he or she ends up with and reads the mini-story. Which one is the most absurd?

Preguntas

1. ¿Quién es el chico?   4. ¿Qué hora es?

2. ¿Con quién está?   5. ¿Qué hacen *(are they doing)*?

3. ¿Dónde están?   6. ¿Cómo están o cómo se sienten? *(How do they feel?)*

PASO 2 VOCABULARIO

Mis amigos y mi familia

In this *Paso*, you will . . .
- describe physical characteristics and personality traits
- make comparisons
- refer to an extreme quality

Unas fotos

¡Hola! Soy Juan. Mira las fotos de mis amigos y mi familia.

Estos son mis amigos.

El **rubio** se llama Luis. Es **callado** pero muy **buena gente**.

El **moreno** se llama Ángel y es muy **bromista**.

El **de barba** se llama Juan, **como yo**. Es el **más intelectual de todos**.

Los rasgos físicos	Physical characteristics
¿Cómo es físicamente?	What does he (she) look like?
Es...	He (She) is . . .
joven / viejo(a), mayor	young / old
alto(a) / bajo(a)	tall / short
gordo(a) / delgado(a)	fat / thin
rubio(a) / moreno(a) / pelirrojo(a)	blond / dark-haired / red-headed
calvo(a) / canoso(a)	bald / white-haired
guapo(a) / feo(a)	good-looking / ugly
Usa gafas / anteojos.	He (She) wears glasses.
Tiene bigote / barba.	He has a moustache / a beard.
¿Es alto(a) como tú?	Is he (she) tall like you are?
Sí, es alto(a) como yo.	Yes, he's (she's) tall like me.
¿Tiene el pelo... ?	Does he (she) have . . . hair?
largo / corto	long / short
rubio / castaño / negro	blond / brown / black
¿Tiene los ojos... ?	Does he (she) have . . . eyes?
castaños / azules / verdes	brown / blue / green

Unas fotos (cont.)

Estos son mis abuelos. Mi abuelita es **un amor**. Es muy **comprensiva** y **generosa**.

Mi abuelo —para ser **sincero**— **tiene mal genio**. Bueno, aquí está contento.

Esta es mi novia Valeria. Es **guapísima**, ¿verdad?

Aquí está con sus gatas, Princesa y Reina. ¡Son muy **mimadas**!

La edad
Age

¿Son ustedes de la misma edad? — *Are you the same age? / Is he (she) as old as you are?*
  Sí, somos (casi) de la misma edad. — *Yes, we're (almost) the same age.*
  No, yo soy mayor / menor. — *No, I'm older / younger.*

El carácter y la personalidad
Character and personality traits

¿Cómo es? — *What is he (she) like?*
Tiene mal genio. — *He (She) is bad-tempered.*
Es... — *He (She) is . . .*
  atlético(a) — *athletic*
  buena gente — *a good person, "good people"*
  callado(a) — *quiet*
  extrovertido(a) / tímido(a) — *outgoing / shy*
  inteligente / tonto(a) — *smart / dumb, silly*
  optimista / pesimista — *optimistic / pessimistic*
  serio(a) / bromista — *serious / a jokester*
  trabajador(a) / perezoso(a) — *hardworking / lazy*
¿Es como tú? — *Is he (she) like you?*
  No, no somos (nada) parecidos(as). — *No, we're not much alike (at all).*

 Adjectives,
Capítulo 2 Paso 1

3-19 **¿Cierto o falso?** With a partner, take turns reading aloud the following statements based on the photographs on pages 102–103. As you read each statement, use the form of the adjective that agrees with the noun. Then say whether it's **cierto** (*true*) or **falso** (*false*) and correct the false statements.

Modelo   La abuela tiene los ojos _____. (azul)
    Estudiante A: La abuela tiene los ojos azules.
    Estudiante B: Falso. La abuela tiene los ojos castaños.

1. Luis es _____. (moreno)
2. Luis y Juan no son muy _____. (alto)
3. Ángel es _____. (rubio)
4. Valeria es muy _____. (guapo)
5. Valeria tiene los ojos _____. (castaño)
6. Las gatas son _____. (bonito)
7. La abuela es muy _____. (joven)
8. El abuelo tiene el pelo _____. (largo)

3-20 **Los nuevos *(new)* compañeros.** José Luis is studying abroad in Santo Domingo and has met a number of new classmates. What are they like? Work with a classmate to complete his description with the most appropriate words from the list.

atlético(a)	~~comprensivo(a)~~	perezoso(a)
~~buen~~	~~extrovertido(a)~~	pesimista
~~callado(a)~~	~~mal~~	

Me gusta el grupo de compañeros de la universidad. Mi mejor amigo se llama Rafael. Él practica muchos deportes: ¡es muy (1) _____! Su novia, Odalys, es guapa pero no habla mucho; es bastante (2) _____. Ramona es muy diferente. ¡Habla todo el día! Es muy expresiva y (3) _____. Juan Carlos es un (4) _____ amigo. Siempre escucha con paciencia y tolerancia; es muy (5) _____. Hay dos compañeros de clase que *(that)* no son muy simpáticos. Roberto tiene una actitud muy negativa; es muy (6) _____. Y Caridad siempre está enojada; tiene (7) _____ genio. Ella nunca estudia; es (8) _____. Pero por lo general, los estudiantes son muy amables y divertidos.

3-21 **Mi mejor amigo(a).** What is your best friend like?

■ Complete the sentences below and share the information with a classmate.

■ Your classmate should ask you two follow-up questions about your friend.

> Mi mejor amigo(a) se llama...
> Es de...
> Tiene... años.
> Físicamente, es... y...
> Tiene el pelo... y los ojos...
> Tiene una personalidad interesante. Es... y... También es muy...

¡Exprésate!

3-22 Memoria fotográfica. Let's put your memory to the test!

- In pairs, look at the following photograph closely for twenty seconds. When your instructor says time is up, close your books.
- Then, with your partner, write sentences with as much as you remember about the people in the photograph. After a few minutes your instructor will call time again.
- You should then get together with another pair and compare notes. Which pair has a better photographic memory?

© Lisa F. Young/Shutterstock

3-23 Nuestros ideales. With a classmate, compare your notions of the following ideal people.

Modelo   el compañero de cuarto ideal

> **Estudiante A:** El compañero de cuarto ideal es sociable y extrovertido.
>
> **Estudiante B:** Estoy de acuerdo (*I agree*). También es organizado y sincero. / No estoy de acuerdo (*I don't agree*). El compañero de cuarto ideal es callado y serio.

1. el profesor ideal
2. los amigos ideales
3. los padres ideales
4. el hermano / la hermana ideal
5. el novio / la novia ideal
6. la compañera de trabajo ideal

3-24 El ladrón (*The thief*). A "robbery" has been committed in your classroom and you need to figure out who did it!

- First, everyone puts their heads down, eyes closed, and your instructor—the victim and witness of the crime—will tap someone on the shoulder. That person is **el ladrón** or **la ladrona**.
- Then, everyone opens their eyes and become detectives. Each detective (including the "thief"!) asks the witness (your instructor) one yes/no question about the thief's appearance. For example: **¿Tiene pelo corto?**
- At the end of the interrogation, write down the name of the thief. Who's a good detective?

Los comparativos

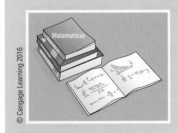

AMAYA	Yo tengo **más** tarea **que** tú.
ERNESTO	No, yo tengo **tanta** tarea **como** tú.
AMAYA	Pero tu tarea es **menos** difícil **que** la mía.
ERNESTO	¡¿**Menos** difícil?! ¡Mi tarea es **más** complicada **que** calzoncillo de pulpo *(octopus's underwear)*!

■ ■ ■

Descúbrelo

- What are Amaya and Ernesto arguing about?

- Who thinks he or she has more homework than the other person? What Spanish phrase means *more homework than you*?

- What words does Ernesto use to say *as much . . . as*?

- What words does Amaya use to say *less . . . than*?

1. Comparisons of inequality are used when two people / animals / things have different amounts of something. To express the notion of *more . . . than*, use this phrase:

> **MÁS** + (ADJECTIVE / ADVERB / NOUN) + **QUE**
>
> adjective: Mi perro es **más** <u>cariñoso</u> **que** mi gato.
> *My dog is **more** <u>affectionate</u> **than** my cat.*
>
> adverb: Mi perro come **más** <u>rápidamente</u> **que** mi gato.
> *My dog eats **more** <u>quickly</u> **than** my cat (does).*
>
> noun: Mi perro tiene **más** <u>energía</u> **que** mi gato.
> *My dog has **more** <u>energy</u> **than** my cat (does).*

2. To express the idea of *less . . . than*, use this phrase:

> **MENOS** + (ADJECTIVE / ADVERB / NOUN) + **QUE**
>
> adjective: Mi gato es **menos** <u>inteligente</u> **que** mi perro.
> *My cat is **less** <u>intelligent</u> **than** my dog.*
>
> adverb: Mi perro duerme **menos** <u>tranquilamente</u> **que** mi gato.
> *My dog sleeps **less** <u>peacefully</u> **than** my cat.*
>
> noun: Mi perro tiene **menos** <u>juguetes</u> **que** mi gato.
> *My dog has **fewer** <u>toys</u> **than** my cat does.*

3. Some comparative expressions have irregular forms: **Mi prima es <u>menor que</u> yo.**
My cousin is <u>younger than</u> I am.

> | | |
> |---|---|
> | **joven → menor que** | *younger than* |
> | **viejo → mayor que** | *older than* |
> | **bueno → mejor que** | *better than* |
> | **malo → peor que** | *worse than* |

4. Comparisons of equality are used when two people / animals / things have the same amount of something.

To compare equal quantities of nouns and express the notion *as much / many . . . as*, choose the form of **tanto** that agrees with the noun:

> **TANTO / TANTA / TANTOS / TANTAS** + (NOUN) + **COMO**
> Carlos tiene **tantos** <u>hermanos</u> **como** yo. *Carlos has **as many** <u>siblings</u> **as** I do.*

5. To compare adjectives and adverbs and express the idea *as . . . as*, use this phrase:

> TAN + (ADJECTIVE / ADVERB) + COMO
>
> **adjective:**   Mi perro es **tan** <u>viejo</u> **como** mi gato.
> *My dog is **as** <u>old</u> **as** my cat.*
>
> **adverb:**   Elisa juega al tenis casi **tan** <u>bien</u> **como** su hermano.
> *Elisa plays tennis almost **as** <u>well</u> **as** her brother.*

6. To express *as much as* with verbs, use **tanto como**.

> Yo <u>estudio</u> **tanto como** tú.   *I <u>study</u> **as much as** you do.*

Colaborar

3-25 **Dos amigas.** What are Alicia and Casandra like? With a partner, complete the comparisons with the most logical words and phrases from the list.

mayor que	mejor que	menos	tan	tantos

1. Alicia es un año _____ Casandra.

2. Casandra tiene _____ hermanos como Alicia.

3. Alicia toca la guitarra _____ Casandra.

4. Casandra es _____ atlética que Alicia.

5. Alicia no es _____ extrovertida como Casandra.

3-26 **Comparaciones.** How do you compare to your classmate? First, ask each other the questions in the first column. Then, compare yourself to your classmate by completing the sentence in the second column. Are the two of you somewhat alike or very different?

Pregunta	Comparación
1. ¿Cuántos años tienes?	Yo soy (**mayor que / menor que**) mi compañero(a). O: Somos de la misma edad.
2. ¿Cuántas horas estudias o trabajas en un día típico?	Yo soy (**más / tan / menos**) trabajador(a) (**que / como**) mi compañero(a).
3. ¿Cuántas mascotas tienes?	Yo tengo (**más / tantas / menos**) mascotas (**que / como**) mi compañero(a).
4. ¿Cuántos hermanos tienes?	Yo tengo (**más / tantos / menos**) hermanos (**que / como**) mi compañero(a).
5. ¿Cuántas horas practicas deportes en una semana típica?	Yo soy (**más / tan / menos**) atlético(a) (**que / como**) mi compañero(a).
6. ¿Eres alto(a) o bajo(a)? ¿Cuánto mides *(How tall are you)*?	Yo soy (**más / tan / menos**) alto(a) (**que / como**) mi compañero(a).

¡Aplícalo!

¡Exprésate!

3-27 La familia Quintana.

How are these family members alike or different? With a partner, take turns creating true (**cierto**) / false (**falso**) statements that compare their physical and personal qualities.

Modelo   **Estudiante A:** Natalia es tan guapa como su hermano Héctor.
               Estudiante B: Cierto. Jorge es...

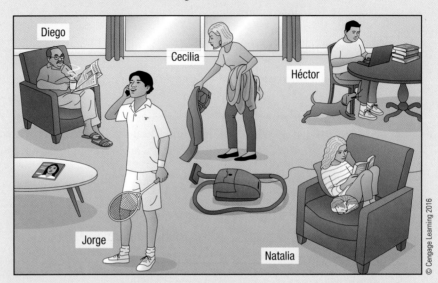

3-28 Las quejas (Complaints).

Life is hard! With a classmate, take turns complaining and exaggerating. The first person complains about some real or imaginary problem, and the second creates a comparison that shows how his/her problem is even worse!

Modelo   **Estudiante A:** Tengo un problema. Mi perro es gordo.
               Estudiante B: ¡Mi perro es más gordo que el tuyo! Tengo otro problema. Solo tengo $20.
               Estudiante A: ¡Yo tengo $10! ¡Tengo menos dinero que tú! Tengo otro problema...

3-29 La escuela secundaria y la universidad.

How does life at college compare to life in high school? With a partner, make comparisons and share your opinions, as in the model.

Modelo   la vida social
               Estudiante A: Para mí, la vida social en la universidad es más divertida que la vida social en la escuela secundaria. Hay más fiestas, partidos, grupos estudiantiles y otras actividades. ¿Qué piensas tú?
               Estudiante B: No estoy de acuerdo. En mi opinión, la vida social en la escuela secundaria es tan divertida como la vida social en la universidad.

Frases útiles

Para mí *For me, In my view*
En mi opinión *In my opinion*
¿Qué piensas tú? *What do you think?*
(No) Estoy de acuerdo. *I (dis)agree.*

1. la vida social
2. los profesores
3. la tarea
4. el programa deportivo
5. los grupos estudiantiles
6. la cafetería
7. las oportunidades para conocer gente nueva (*meet new people*)

PASO 2 GRAMÁTICA B

Los superlativos

© Cengage Learning 2016

LEOPOLDO ¿Cómo son tus tres gatos, Ramona?

RAMONA Cada uno *(Each one)* es diferente. Garfield es el más perezoso y el más gordo de los tres. Condesa es la más bonita. ¡Tiene los ojos grandísimos! Silvestre es el menos inteligente pero es el más cariñoso.

LEOPOLDO ¡Son parecidos a mis tres hermanos!

1. Superlatives are similar to comparatives, but are used to refer to the extremes within a group, such as the *tallest* person, the *least playful* animal, the *best* dormitories, or the *worst* classes.

> Garfield es **el más gordo de** mis gatos.   *Garfield is **the fattest** of my cats.*

2. To say that someone / something has the most of a quality, use this phrasing:

> **EL / LA / LOS / LAS** (NOUN) + **MÁS** (ADJECTIVE) + **DE** (GROUP / PLACE)
> Felicia es **la (chica) más cariñosa de** su familia.
> *Felicia **is the most affectionate (girl)** in her family.*

3. To indicate that someone / something has the least of a quality, use this phrasing:

> **EL / LA / LOS / LAS** (NOUN) + **MENOS** (ADJECTIVE) + **DE** (GROUP / PLACE)
> Carlos y Elisa son **los menos serios de** todos.
> *Carlos and Elisa are **the least serious ones** of all.*

4. These irregular forms are also used with definite articles to form the superlative.

el (la) mejor	los (las) mejores	*the best*
el (la) peor	los (las) peores	*the worst*
el (la) mayor	los (las) mayores	*the oldest* (with people)
el (la) menor	los (las) menores	*the youngest* (with people)

5. Another kind of superlative—the absolute superlative—expresses the idea of *very, very,* or *extremely.* This is formed by adding to an adjective the new ending that matches the gender and number of the noun: **-ísimo / -ísima / -ísimos / -ísimas.** If the adjective ends in a vowel, drop the last vowel before adding the ending.

> Mi gata Condesa tiene los ojos **grandísimos**. (grande + ísimos = grandísimos)
> *My cat, Condesa, has **extremely large** eyes.*

■ ■ ■
Descúbrelo

- Which of Ramona's cats is the laziest? The prettiest? The least intelligent?

- What do the cats remind Leopoldo of?

- What phrase indicates that someone / something has the most of a particular quality? The least of a quality?

- What ending is added to **grande** to mean *extremely*?

If we use ísimo/a it is very general!

PASO 2 GRAMÁTICA B

¡Aplícalo!

👥 3-30 ***People* en español.** *People* magazine is taking a survey on the best and the worst. How would you respond to the poll? Working with a partner, take turns expressing your opinions on each topic by completing the sentences aloud.

1. El actor más guapo de Hollywood es...
2. La actriz *(actress)* más guapa de Hollywood es...
3. El programa más divertido de la televisión es...
4. La película *(movie)* más tonta del año es...
5. El atleta profesional menos simpático es...
6. La celebridad *(celebrity)* con el peor pelo es...
7. La celebridad más loca es...
8. El mejor programa de telerealidad *(reality show)* es...
9. Los mejores futbolistas *(soccer players)* del momento son...
10. El evento más triste del año es...

👥 3-31 La fiesta de Roberto. An interesting mix of people is attending Roberto's birthday party.

- Write down as many sentences as you can describing the extremes in the drawing.
- When your instructor calls time, take turns reading your sentences aloud to a classmate.
- You earn one point for each extreme that your classmate does *not* have. The person with more points wins the game.

Modelo El abuelo es el mayor de la familia.

la mamá

el abuelo

el padre

Roberto

la abuela

el hermano, Timoteo

la hermana, Arlenis

el amigo, Manny

© Cengage Learning 2016

110 Capítulo 3

3-32 **Lo mejor y lo peor.** What are the best and worst aspects of your campus? Follow the model and compare answers with two or three classmates.

Modelo la mejor residencia

Estudiante A: La mejor residencia del campus es Hampton Hall.

Estudiante B: Estoy de acuerdo. Es muy moderna y bonita.

Estudiante C: No estoy de acuerdo. Para mí...

1. la clase más aburrida
2. la residencia menos moderna
3. el peor lugar (*place*) para estudiar
4. el evento más popular
5. los mejores apartamentos
6. las actividades menos populares

3-33 **Los extremos.** With a classmate, share information about your family and friends. Talk about who among them are the most and the least athletic, hardworking, etc., and add details to explain your choices.

Modelo atlético(a)

Estudiante A: Mi hermana Amanda es la más atlética de nuestra familia. Practica el tenis a menudo y el fútbol todos los fines de semana. Mi mamá es la menos atlética. Su actividad preferida es leer.

Estudiante B: Mi amigo Sam es el más atlético de mis amigos...

1. atlético(a)
2. trabajador(a)
3. extrovertido(a)
4. intelectual
5. mimado(a)
6. organizado(a)

3-34 **El concurso de mascotas.** You and two classmates are the judges for the local pet show. Compare the physical and personal attributes of the contestants and award prizes for the top animal in each category. Follow the model.

- the largest
- the smallest
- the cutest
- the ugliest
- the fattest
- the skinniest
- the most affectionate
- the overall best

Modelo **Estudiante A:** Tarzán es el perro más grande.

Estudiante B: Sí, ¡Tarzán es grandísimo!

© Ermolaew Alexander/Shutterstock

Las fiestas

In this *Paso*, you will . . .

- discuss party preparations
- describe family gatherings and celebrations
- make a toast and offer good wishes
- express likes and dislikes

Los preparativos para una fiesta sorpresa

mandar las invitaciones

envolver los regalos

decorar la casa con globos

preparar el pastel de cumpleaños

poner la mesa

comprar flores

Las celebraciones	Celebrations
el aniversario (de bodas)	*(wedding) anniversary*
la boda	*wedding*
el cumpleaños	*birthday*
la graduación	*graduation*
el picnic / la barbacoa	*picnic / barbecue*
la reunión familiar	*family reunion; family gathering*

Actividades en una reunión	Activities at a get-together
almorzar	*to have lunch*
charlar con los invitados	*to chat with guests*
contar chistes / cuentos	*to tell jokes / stories*
disfrutar (de la música / de la fiesta)	*to enjoy (the music / the party)*
jugar al voleibol / a las cartas / a los videojuegos	*to play volleyball / cards / videogames*
recordar los viejos tiempos	*to remember old times*
servir la merienda / la cena	*to serve snacks / supper*

La fiesta sorpresa

La familia García **festeja el cumpleaños** de María. Todos **cantan "cumpleaños feliz"**. María **pide un deseo** y **apaga las velas**.

Cumpleaños feliz,
te deseamos a ti,
cumpleaños María,
cumpleaños feliz.

abrir los regalos

probar la comida y la bebida

sacar fotos

La invitación

¿Quieres venir a mi fiesta el próximo (sábado)?
  Me encantaría. ¿A qué hora empieza?

Expresiones de felicitación

¡Feliz cumpleaños / aniversario!
¡Muchas felicidades!
¡Sorpresa!

Hacer un brindis

Brindo por...
  la feliz pareja.
  la salud de (José).
¡Salud! / ¡Chin chin!

Al anfitrión / A la anfitriona

Gracias por todo.
Lo pasé / Lo pasamos muy bien.

Invitation

Do you want to come to my party next (Saturday)?
  I'd love to. At what time does it start?

Expressions of congratulations

Happy birthday / anniversary!
Congratulations!
Surprise!

Making a toast

Here's to . . .
  the happy couple.
  the health of (José).
Cheers!

To the host / hostess

Thanks for everything.
I had / We had a great time.

¡Aplícalo!

Colaborar

3-35 ¿Cuándo? Time to brush up on your "party phrases"! With a partner, take turns reading the expressions aloud and indicating in which of the three situations they would be said.

- **en una invitación**   - **en la fiesta**   - **al final de la fiesta**

1. "¡Sorpresa!"
2. "Gracias por todo".
3. "Lo pasé muy bien".
4. "¡Chin chin!"

5. "Brindo por la salud de Juan".
6. "Muchas felicidades".
7. "¿Quieres venir a mi fiesta?"
8. "¿A qué hora empieza?"

Expressions
of frequency,
Capítulo 2 Paso 3

Colaborar

3-36 Las celebraciones. What celebrations do you associate with the following activities? With a partner, create sentences with **nosotros** as the subject; include the kind of celebration and an expression of frequency (**normalmente, por lo general, a menudo, a veces, nunca**).

Modelo   comprar flores
Normalmente compramos flores para una boda o para una fiesta de aniversario de bodas. A veces compramos flores para una fiesta de cumpleaños.

una boda	una reunión familiar
una fiesta de cumpleaños	una fiesta típica entre estudiantes
una barbacoa / un picnic	una fiesta de aniversario de bodas

1. comer sándwiches
2. jugar a los videojuegos
3. contar chistes
4. hacer un brindis

5. recordar los viejos tiempos
6. decorar un pastel
7. servir una cena elegante
8. recibir regalos

Colaborar

3-37 Mini conversaciones. Role-play the following four exchanges with a classmate. As you read your lines aloud, choose the best word in parentheses.

1. MARÍA   ¡Hola, Tomás! ¿(Quieres / Pasas) venir a mi fiesta de cumpleaños el (aniversario / próximo) sábado? Empieza a las ocho.

   TOMÁS   Sí, ¡me (felicidades / encantaría)! Gracias por la (merienda / invitación).

2. MAMÁ   Hijo, tenemos que decorar la casa con muchos (globos / invitados).

   HIJO   Sí, y también tenemos que envolver los (regalos / cuentos).

3. JULIA   El (anfitrión / pastel) de cumpleaños es muy bonito y tiene muchísimas (velas / bodas).

   ULISES   Sí, ¿por qué no le sacas (fotos / chistes)?

4. TÍO   Brindo por la feliz (mesa / pareja).

   LORENA   Gracias, tío, por el brindis y por (todo / salud).

3-38 Los preparativos. You and your classmates are planning a surprise party for your Spanish instructor. What do you have to do to get ready?

■ Form a circle with three or four classmates.

■ Using the phrase **Tenemos que...**, the first person mentions something that has to be done: **Tenemos que mandar las invitaciones.**

■ Each student repeats the previous list and adds to it until everyone has had two turns. **Tenemos que mandar las invitaciones. También tenemos que... etcétera.**

3-39 Una noche inolvidable. What do you think each of the characters in each drawing is saying? Incorporate phrases from the bottom of page 113 as you act out the scenes with a partner.

aniversario de mis abuelos

1.

2.

3.

Illustrations © Cengage Learning 2016

3-40 Una invitación. You're throwing a surprise birthday party for your roommate! With a classmate, role-play an invitation to this party. **Estudiante A** should begin.

Estudiante A	Estudiante B
1. Greet your friend; ask how he/she is doing.	2. Return the greeting.
3. Invite your friend to a surprise party on Sunday.	4. Accept and ask what time the party will start.
5. Tell him/her the starting time of the party.	6. Ask who the party is for (**¿Para quién... ?**)
7. Tell him/her that it is for your roommate.	8. Thank your friend for the invitation.
9. Say good-bye.	10. Tell your friend that you'll see him/her at the party.

Nota cultural

A country's geography can greatly influence the culture of its people. In Puerto Rico and the Dominican Republic, for example, the traditional **bizcocho de boda** or **bizcocho de cumpleaños** is a yellow sponge cake with a filling made of pineapple, one of their major crops. Sometimes, wedding cakes are decorated with seashells, sea stars, and other marine objects familiar to island-dwellers.

PASO 3 GRAMÁTICA A **G**

Los verbos con cambio de raíz en el tiempo presente

NINA ¿Quieres venir a mi fiesta esta noche?

LUIS Sí quiero pero no puedo. Lo siento, Nina, tengo que estudiar.

NINA ¡Bah! Querer es poder. *(Where there's a will, there's a way.)**

*Literally: To want is to be able to.

■ ■ ■
Descúbrelo

- Why can't Luis go to Nina's party?
- What familiar saying does Nina use to respond to Luis's excuse?
- What two infinitives are used in this saying?
- When Luis uses the conjugated forms of these two verbs, what happens to the **e** and the **o**?

1. As you have learned, conjugated verbs use endings that correspond to the subject of the sentence. Some verbs undergo an additional change in the front part of the verb, known as the *stem* or *root*. These verbs are known as *stem-changing verbs* (**los verbos con cambio de raíz**).

INFINITIVE	=	STEM	+	ENDING →	CONJUGATED VERB	
querer		**quer**	+	er	Qui**e**ro...	*I want to . . .*
poder		**pod**	+	er	... pero no p**ue**do.	*. . . but I can't.*

2. There are three kinds of stem-changing verbs in the present tense. The three kinds of stem-changes occur in every form of the present tense except **nosotros** and **vosotros**.

Cambio de e → ie			
qu_e_rer (ie) *to want, to love*			
yo	qui**e**ro	nosotros/nosotras	qu**e**remos
tú	qui**e**res	vosotros/vosotras	qu**e**réis
usted	qui**e**re	ustedes	qui**e**ren
él/ella	qui**e**re	ellos/ellas	qui**e**ren

Otros verbos e → ie:

emp**e**zar	*to start, to begin*
entender	*to understand*
pensar	*to think*
preferir	*to prefer*
sentir	*to be sorry, to regret; to feel*

Cambio de o → ue			
alm_o_rzar (ue) *to have lunch*			
yo	alm**ue**rzo	nosotros/nosotras	alm**o**rzamos
tú	alm**ue**rzas	vosotros/vosotras	alm**o**rzáis
usted	alm**ue**rza	ustedes	alm**ue**rzan
él/ella	alm**ue**rza	ellos/ellas	alm**ue**rzan

Otros verbos o → ue:

contar	*to tell; to count*
dormir	*to sleep*
envolver	*to wrap*
poder	*to be able to, can*
probar	*to taste, to try*
recordar	*to remember, to recall*
volver	*to return, to go back*

Cambio de e → i			
p_e_dir (i) *to ask for, to request*			
yo	p**i**do	nosotros/nosotras	p**e**dimos
tú	p**i**des	vosotros/vosotras	p**e**dís
usted	p**i**de	ustedes	p**i**den
él/ella	p**i**de	ellos/ellas	p**i**den

Otros verbos e → i:

repetir	*to repeat*
seguir (sigo)	*to follow, to continue*
servir	*to serve*

3. There is a unique stem-changing verb, **jugar**, that changes **u → ue**: <u>jue</u>go, <u>jue</u>gas, <u>jue</u>ga, jugamos, jugáis, <u>jue</u>gan.

3-41 **Ta-Te-Ti con verbos.** Challenge a classmate to two games of tic-tac-toe. To mark your square with X or O, you must conjugate the verb in the present tense with the subject indicated. For example: **dormir (ue): tú → duermes.**

¡Aplícalo!

dormir (ue): tú	recordar (ue): ustedes	pedir (i): nosotros	jugar (ue): tú	empezar (ie): la fiesta	probar (ue): Ana y yo
contar (ue): nosotros	pensar (ie): yo	preferir (ie): los chicos	querer (ie): usted	volver (ue): yo	repetir (i): tú
sentir (ie): ellos	servir (i): tú	jugar (ue): ella	seguir (i): David	poder (ue): tú	entender (ie): ellos

Colaborar **3-42** **Un domingo típico.** Juliana, who spent a vacation in Puerto Rico, is talking to Rogelio, a native from the "Island of Enchantment". She wants to know how he usually spends Sundays. To complete their conversation, choose appropriate verbs from the list and conjugate them in the present tense. Then, read the conversation aloud with a partner.

~~almorzar~~	dormir	jugar	querer
~~contar~~	~~entender~~	pedir	recordar

JULIANA   ¿Cómo es un domingo típico?

ROGELIO   Mi familia y yo siempre vamos a Playa Luquillo. Tú (1) _____ Playa Luquillo, ¿verdad?

JULIANA   ¡Claro que sí! Es una playa muy bonita. ¿Hacen *(Do you have)* un picnic en la playa o (2) _____ ustedes en un restaurante?

ROGELIO   Nosotros siempre hacemos un picnic. La comida de mi tía es buenísima y yo siempre (3) _____ más.

JULIANA   ¿Y después de *(after)* comer?

ROGELIO   Los adultos (4) _____ la siesta y los niños (5) _____ al fútbol o al voleibol. Luego *(Later)* escuchamos música y charlamos.

JULIANA   Tú (6) _____ mucho a tu familia, ¿no?

ROGELIO   Sí, por supuesto. Mi tío Mario es muy divertido: siempre (7) _____ chistes. Y mis primos son mis mejores amigos.

JULIANA   Sí, yo (8) _____ perfectamente. Mi familia es muy unida también.

© L.A. Nature Graphics/Shutterstock

¡Exprésate!

3-43 **Firma aquí *(Sign here)*.** Walk around the classroom and ask your classmates yes/no questions formed from the phrases in the chart. If someone answers **sí**, ask him/her to sign your chart. Only two signatures from the same person are allowed.

Modelo   **jugar** al voleibol a menudo
  Estudiante A: ¿Juegas al voleibol a menudo?
  Estudiante B: Sí. Juego al voleibol a menudo. / No, no juego al voleibol a menudo.
  Estudiante A: Firma *(Sign)* aquí, por favor. / Gracias.

Actividad	Firma *(Signature)*
1. **jugar** al voleibol a menudo	
2. normalmente **dormir** ocho horas	
3. **servir** comida mexicana en las fiestas a veces	
4. siempre **pedir** un deseo cuando apagas las velas	
5. siempre **probar** el pastel en las fiestas	
6. para tu cumpleaños, **preferir** las fiestas sorpresa	

3-44 **¿Lógico o ilógico?** Take turns constructing sentences by choosing one element from each column and conjugating the verb in the present tense. Your partner must say whether the sentence is logical or not.

Modelo   **Estudiante A:** Yo pido el pastel de chocolate.
  Estudiante B: ¡Lógico! / (¡No es lógico!)

mis amigos y yo	**jugar**	a las nueve de la noche
yo	**almorzar**	una cena formal
mis abuelos	**querer**	a mi novio / novia
mis compañeros de clase	**dormir**	una siesta todos los días
mi mejor amigo(a)	**pedir**	a las cartas
la fiesta	**servir**	en un restaurante cubano
tú	**empezar**	el pastel de chocolate

3-45 **¿Conoces al profesor?** Are you getting to know your instructor well? With one or two classmates, read the questions and predict how your instructor will answer each one. Then, take turns with your classmates asking him/her the questions. Which group had the most correct predictions?

1. ¿A qué hora empieza Ud. su día en la universidad?

2. ¿Dónde almuerza Ud. normalmente?

3. ¿A qué hora vuelve Ud. a casa?

4. ¿Cómo prefiere Ud. festejar su cumpleaños?

5. ¿Qué deportes juega a menudo?

6. ¿Qué sirve Ud. en las reuniones familiares?

El verbo *gustar*

© Cengage Learning 2016

GLORIA	¿Te gustan las fiestas, Martín?
MARTÍN	Sí, me gustan, pero no me gusta bailar. ¿Y a ti?
GLORIA	A mí me gusta mucho bailar. ¡Bailo como un trompo *(like a top)*!

■ ■ ■
Descúbrelo
- Does Martín like parties?
- Who likes to dance?
- What two verb forms does Martín use to talk about what he likes?
- What little word expresses the notion that <u>I</u> like something?

1. The verb **gustar** is used to express what somebody does or doesn't like. The literal meaning of this verb is *to be pleasing*.

> ¿Te **gusta** la bachata?   *Do you **like** bachata (music)? (Literally: Is bachata music pleasing to you?)*

2. With the verb **gustar**, the thing that you like is the subject of the sentence. The subject is generally placed after the verb.

> VERB SUBJECT
> ¡Me gusta **la música**!   *I like **music**!*

3. Two verb forms are commonly used: **gusta** and **gustan**.

- Use **gusta** when the subject is a singular noun, an infinitive, or a series of infinitives.

> | | | |
> |---|---|---|
> | Subject = a singular noun: | Me **gusta** la fiesta. | *I **like** the party.* |
> | Subject = infinitive(s): | Me **gusta** bailar. | *I **like** to dance.* |

- Use the verb form **gustan** when the subject is a plural noun or a series of singular nouns.

> | | | |
> |---|---|---|
> | Subject = a plural noun: | Me **gustan** mis regalos. | *I **like** my gifts.* |
> | Subject = two or more nouns: | Me **gustan** el rap y la salsa. | *I **like** rap and salsa.* |

4. To say *who* likes something, place the pronoun **me**, **te**, **le**, **nos**, **os**, or **les** in front of **gusta / gustan**. To make the sentence negative, add **no** in front of the pronoun.

> | | | |
> |---|---|---|
> | Affirmative sentence: | **Nos** gusta esta barbacoa. | *We **like** this barbecue.* |
> | Negative sentence: | <u>**No nos**</u> gusta el pastel. | *We <u>**don't**</u> like the cake.* |

gustar to like			
me gusta (gustan)	*I like*	**nos** gusta (gustan)	*we like*
te gusta (gustan)	*you (inf.) like*	**os** gusta (gustan)	*you (pl., inf., Sp.) like*
le gusta (gustan)	*you (form.) like*	**les** gusta (gustan)	*you (pl.) like*
le gusta (gustan)	*he/she likes*	**les** gusta (gustan)	*they like*

5. To name specific people, follow these patterns:

- For one person: **a** + *(name / singular noun)* + **le** + **gusta / gustan**

  A Martín le gustan las fiestas sorpresa.   *Martín likes surprise parties.*

- For more than one person: **a** + *(names / plural noun)* + **les** + **gusta / gustan**

  A Rosa y a Lorenzo les gusta bailar.   *Rosa and Lorenzo like to dance.*

6. To clarify or emphasize *who* likes something, prepositional phrases are used.

A mí me gusta(n)...	**A nosotros** nos gusta(n)...
A ti te gusta(n)...	**A vosotros(as)** os gusta(n)...
A usted le gusta(n)...	**A ustedes** les gusta(n)...
A él le gusta(n)...	**A ellos** les gusta(n)...
A ella le gusta(n)...	**A ellas** les gusta(n)...

¡Aplícalo!

Colaborar

3-46 **El cumpleaños de Juan.** Penélope and Simón are discussing Juan's upcoming birthday. Complete their conversation with the correct pronouns (**me, te, le, nos, les**) and then read it aloud with a partner.

PENÉLOPE   El cumpleaños de Juan es el jueves. ¡Tenemos que organizar una fiesta sorpresa!

SIMÓN   ¡Mala idea! A Juan no (1) _____ gustan las fiestas sorpresa.

PENÉLOPE   ¡Bah! A todos mis amigos (2) _les___ gustan mucho las fiestas sorpresa. ¿Qué tal si la fiesta es en tu apartamento?

SIMÓN   A mi compañero de cuarto y a mí no (3) _____ gusta tener fiestas en nuestro apartamento porque es muy pequeño. Lo siento.

PENÉLOPE   ¡Eres un aguafiestas *(party pooper)*, Simón! ¿Por qué no (4) _____ gustan las fiestas?

SIMÓN   A mí sí (5) _____ gustan, pero a Juan no. Él prefiere salir al cine o a un restaurante.

PENÉLOPE   ¡Perfecto! La fiesta sorpresa de Juan será *(will be)* en el restaurante Mi Familia.

Colaborar

3-47 **¡Me gusta!** Which of the following aspects of parties do you like? Which do you not like? Follow the model and share your preferences with a classmate.

Modelo   bailar
Me gusta bailar. / No me gusta bailar.

1. escuchar música
2. los regalos tontos
3. el pastel

4. sacar fotos espontáneas
5. cantar con karaoke
6. las comidas exóticas

¡Exprésate!

 3-48 **Las preferencias.** You are planning a party for your classmate's birthday. Use these questions to find out his/her preferences. Then, your classmate will ask you about your preferences.

1. ¿Te gusta festejar tu cumpleaños con tu familia o con tus amigos?

2. ¿Te gustan los picnics o las fiestas en casa?

3. ¿Te gustan los globos o las flores?

4. ¿Te gustan los pasteles de chocolate o de vainilla?

5. ¿Te gusta bailar o charlar?

6. ¿Te gusta recibir regalos o dinero?

7. ¿Te gusta apagar las velas o no?

8. ¿Te gustan las fiestas sorpresa o no?

 3-49 **Nuestras impresiones.** What aspects of student life do you like or dislike? Working with a classmate, take turns combining the phrases in the three columns to create complete sentences about the university. How many different sentences can you create together?

Modelo   A mí no me gusta el cuarto en la residencia.
A mi compañera de cuarto le gusta ir al gimnasio.

A mí (no) me	gusta	las clases interactivas
A ti (no) te	gustan	los profesores exigentes
A mi compañero(a) de		el cuarto en la residencia
cuarto (no) le		los restaurantes en el campus
A mis amigos y a mí (no) nos		la tarea en línea
A mis amigos (no) les		la vida *(life)* social
A mis profesores (no) les		ir al gimnasio
		tener fiestas los sábados
		ir al café con amigos
		tener exámenes los lunes

3-50 **El regalo ideal.** Which of these is the best gift for your classmate? Working with a partner, first ask each other several questions about what you like to do; for example: **¿Te gusta leer? ¿Te gustan las plantas?** Then, based on your partner's responses, say which is the ideal gift: **El regalo ideal para ti *(for you)* es un libro.**

una pecera

un libro

un balón de fútbol

una planta en maceta

unos zapatos para correr

una caja de chocolates

CONECTADOS CON...
LA BIOLOGÍA

Cuatro especies en peligro de extinción

La biodiversidad del Caribe es grande. Existen más de 600 especies de aves, 500 especies de reptiles y 90 especies de mamíferos. Desafortunadamente, muchas de estas especies están en peligro de extinción.

El manatí de las Antillas

El manatí es un mamífero marino herbívoro. Es un animal tímido y no agresivo. Su cuerpo *(body)* es grande y cilíndrico: el adulto pesa *(it weighs)* aproximadamente 1400 libras *(pounds)*. Los manatíes viven en las costas y los estuarios. Están en peligro de extinción por la destrucción de su hábitat y también por colisiones con vehículos acuáticos.

La cotorra de La Española

La cotorra es un ave nativa de la isla La Española. Es muy querida por los dominicanos porque es colorida y "habla". Su amenaza principal es la captura para el comercio ilegal como mascota. Su hábitat natural es el bosque *(forest)* donde come semillas *(seeds)* y frutas *(fruits)*.

Estrategia: Using prior knowledge

Your prior knowledge, or **conocimientos previos**, is your personal experience and knowledge about the world. Look at the photos on these two pages and ask yourself what you already know about these animals. Use your prior knowledge to anticipate the content of the reading.

Palabras de biología

la amenaza	*threat*
el anfibio	*amphibian*
el ave	*bird*
el cambio climático	*climate change*
la especie	*species*
el mamífero	*mammal*
el peligro de extinción	*danger of extinction*
el reptil	*reptile*

3-51 **Comprensión.** Fill in the chart with facts in Spanish from the reading.

Especie	Clase de vertebrado	Características	Amenaza principal
manatí			
cotorra			
tortuga carey			
coquí			

3-52 **¿Y tú?** Working with a classmate, share your responses to these questions.

1. ¿Es grande la biodiversidad en tu estado o región?

2. ¿Qué especies están en peligro de extinción en tu área?

La tortuga carey

La tortuga carey es un reptil muy bonito. Su caparazón *(shell)*, de color ámbar, se usa para objetos de decoración aunque *(even though)* es ilegal. Muchas de estas tortugas marinas viven en los arrecifes *(reefs)* de coral tropicales cerca de Cuba. Su comida preferida es la esponja de mar *(sea sponge)*.

© Rich Carey/Shutterstock

El coquí duende

El coquí es el símbolo de Puerto Rico. Estas pequeñas ranas *(frogs)* no ponen huevos *(lay eggs)* en el agua y no pasan por la etapa de renacuajo *(tadpole)*. Hay muchas especies de coquíes, algunas *(some)* en peligro de extinción. El coquí duende, por ejemplo, no canta y no se reproduce cuando tiene calor. El cambio climático es la principal amenaza de este diminuto animal.

© Joseph/Shutterstock

Composición: Una carta

You're planning to spend the semester studying Spanish in the Dominican Republic. Write a message to your host family and tell them about yourself. Begin with a salutation (**Querida familia:**) and a self-introduction (who you are, what you are like, what you study, what you do in your free time). In this section, use three different connectors. To conclude, write two questions and a closing (**Saludos,** *your name*).

 Revisión en pareja. Exchange papers with a classmate and edit each other's work.

- Does the message include all the requested information? Write one positive comment and one suggestion for improvement.
- Are three different connectors used? Point out any place where another connector could be added.
- Are **ser** and **estar** used correctly? Do the adjectives agree with the nouns they describe? Circle any possible errors of this kind.

Estrategia:

Connecting sentences

To create longer sentences, join short, related sentences with connectors like these:

- **así que** *so*
- **aunque** *although*
- **o** *or*
- **pero** *but*
- **porque** *because*
- **y** *and*

NUESTRA COMUNIDAD

 3-53 **Nosotros /** *Share It!* Online, you posted a picture of a party or celebration. As you viewed your classmates' posts, what did you find especially interesting? Discuss the posts that you viewed and answer these questions:

1. ¿Qué celebraciones / reuniones hay en las fotos?
2. ¿Hay más fotos de celebraciones con amigos o con familiares *(family members)*?
3. ¿Quién tiene una foto muy divertida? ¿Quién tiene una foto sentimental? ¿Y una tierna? Describe las fotos.
4. ¿Cuál es tu foto preferida? ¿Por qué te gusta?

 3-54 **Perspectivas: ¿Cómo festejas los cumpleaños?** Online, you watched a video of three Spanish-speaking students as they answer the question **¿Cómo festejas los cumpleaños?** How do the interviewees respond? Working with two or three classmates, compare the notes you took when you watched that video. Then, interview the others in your group with the same question—**¿Cómo festejas los cumpleaños?**—and jot down the information.

 3-55 **Exploración: Mascotas.** Online, you read about pets available for adoption and selected one that you would like to have or that you'd like to give to a friend or family member. Share your findings with your classmates. Make a brief presentation in which you include the following information about your new pet.

- ¿Qué tipo de mascota es?
- ¿Cómo se llama?
- ¿Cómo es?
- ¿Por qué te gusta?

 3-56 **Conectados con... las ciencias.** Online, you read an article about the scientific method and important scientists. With two or three classmates, share the results of your research on an important Hispanic scientist or describe the role science plays in your life.

Modelo

(Name) es un(a) científico(a) importante de... / Estudio...

3-57 El árbol. How are your powers of deduction? You (**Estudiante A**) and your partner (**Estudiante B**) have two different sets of clues. Your task is to exchange information and decipher the clues so that you completely fill out this tree for the Rodríguez family from the Dominican Republic. Write your responses in Spanish.

> This is a pair activity for **Estudiante A** and **Estudiante B**.
>
> If you are **Estudiante A**, use the information on this page.
>
> If you are **Estudiante B**, turn to p. S-3 at the back of the book.

Estudiante A

Las pistas (clues):

- El abuelo se llama José.
- Emilia tiene cuatro nietos y le gusta recordar los viejos tiempos.
- Vanesa es la hermana de Jesús y Julián.
- Laura tiene la misma edad que su primo Julián.
- La sobrina de Antonia tiene 10 años.
- A la hija de Manuel le gusta tocar la guitarra.
- Antonia tiene 40 años y su esposo tiene cinco más.
- Gloria vive en Santo Domingo con su esposo y sus hijos.
- A la esposa de Felipe le gusta jugar a las cartas.
- Los padres de Laura viven en Puerto Plata.

- Nombre: _____
- Edad: _____
- Residencia: San Cristóbal
- Actividades: _____

- Nombre: Emilia
- Edad: _____
- Residencia: _____
- Actividades: _____

- Nombre: _____
- Edad: 40 años
- Residencia: _____
- Actividades: _____

- Nombre: _____
- Edad: _____
- Residencia: Puerto Plata
- Actividades: _____

- Nombre: _____
- Edad: _____
- Residencia: _____
- Actividades: _____

- Nombre: Gloria
- Edad: _____
- Residencia: _____
- Actividades: _____

- Nombre: _____
- Edad: 14 años
- Actividades: _____

- Nombre: Julián
- Edad: _____
- Actividades: jugar al fútbol

- Nombre: _____
- Edad: _____
- Actividades: _____

- Nombre: Vanesa
- Edad: _____
- Actividades: _____

3-58 **La madre.** Imagine you and your partner are volunteers at an art museum. Look at the following painting **(el cuadro)** by Dominican artist Cándido Bidó. Together, prepare a brief presentation about this work of art for a group of local Spanish-speaking school children that will come for a tour. In your presentation, identify the painting and describe the subject: Who she is, what country she is in, what she looks like, how she probably feels, and who's with her. Be prepared to present this to your classmates.

La dama del sombrero rojo (2009), Cándido Bidó

Clase

3-59 **Situación: ¡De fiesta!** With your classmates, have a "birthday party" in your classroom. Your instructor will select one person to be the guest of honor and the rest of the class will be guests. During the party, do the following.

The guest of honor:

- Greet the guests and thank them for their good wishes.
- Ask the guests whether they are hungry or thirsty **(¿Tienes hambre? ¿Tienes sed?)** and offer them some sandwiches **(sándwiches)** or soft drinks **(refrescos)**.
- Introduce people to one another, as needed.
- At the end of the party, say good-bye and thank everyone for the presents.

The guests:

- Greet the guest of honor and wish him/her a happy birthday.
- Introduce yourselves to other guests and make small talk **(¿De dónde eres? ¿Qué estudias? ¿Te gustan tus clases? ¿Qué música te gusta escuchar?** etc.)
- Ask for the names of people you don't know. **(¿Cómo se llama la chica alta y morena? ¿Quién es el chico rubio?)**
- At the end of the party, thank the host for everything and say that you had a good time.

3-60 Las personalidades. With two or three classmates, read the following magazine article about how children's personalities may vary according to their birth order within a family. How much of this information holds true for you? Taking turns, explain which of your personality traits the article correctly predicted and which it got wrong.

Modelo   Yo soy hija única. Soy una persona muy creativa porque me gusta dibujar *(draw)* y escribir cuentos. Pero no soy mimada y ¡no soy egoísta! Soy la más generosa de mis amigos...

La personalidad de los hijos

¿**C**ómo es tu personalidad? Muchos expertos piensan que eso depende de si eres hijo único, el mayor, el del medio[1] o el menor. Cada uno tiene rasgos específicos.

Los hijos únicos son hijos mimados que desarrollan[2] personalidades egoístas pero que también son organizados, responsables y creativos. Tienen gran imaginación y un vocabulario más sofisticado que los hijos de familias grandes.

Los mayores tienen muchas expectativas.[3] Estas personas son muy responsables pero también son muy exigentes. No les gustan los cambios[4] y por lo general, mantienen las tradiciones de la familia.

Los del medio son los más independientes y sociables de los hermanos. Normalmente son personas innovadoras y un poco rebeldes.

Quieren ser el centro de atención y por eso son competitivos y celosos.[5]

Los menores son personas muy cariñosas pero de carácter fuerte.[6] De todos los hermanos, son los más perezosos. Dependen de sus hermanos mayores y de sus padres para todo. Generalmente son muy buenos en los estudios y tienen éxito[7] en el trabajo, siempre y cuando puedan mandar.[8]

[1]*middle child* [2]*develop* [3]*expectations* [4]*changes* [5]*jealous* [6]*strong personality* [7]*success*
[8]*tell others what to do*

Pronunciación: Las letras *j, h, ch*

Challenge your classmates to a pronunciation contest. Working in groups of three or four, how quickly and correctly can you say the following tongue twisters? Focus especially on the proper pronunciation of **j**, **h**, and **ch**.

1. El hipopótamo Hipo está con hipo. *The hippopotamus Hipo has the hiccups.*

2. Pancha plancha con cuatro planchas. ¿Con cuántas planchas plancha Pancha? *Pancha irons with four irons. With how many irons does Pancha iron?*

3. Juan junta juncos junto a la zanja. *Juan gathers reeds next to the ditch.*

VOCABULARIO

RECURSOS

Para aprender mejor
As you watch people walk by, practice Spanish vocabulary by describing each person in your mind in Spanish.

Sustantivos

el (la) abuelo(a) *grandfather / grandmother*

el (la) (mejor) amigo(a) *(best) friend*

el amor *love*

la bebida *drink*

las cartas *playing cards*

la casa *house*

la celebración *celebration*

la cena *supper*

el chiste *joke*

la comida *food*

el cuento *story*

el deseo *wish*

la familia *family*

la flor *flower*

el globo *balloon*

el (la) hermano(a) *brother / sister, sibling*

el (la) invitado(a) *guest*

la mamá *mom*

la merienda *snack*

el (la) novio(a) *boyfriend; groom / girlfriend; bride*

el ojo *eye*

el papá *dad*

el pariente *relative*

el pastel *cake*

el pelo *hair*

el (la) primo(a) *cousin*

el regalo *gift*

el (la) tío(a) *uncle / aunt*

la vela *candle*

el videojuego *videogame*

el voleibol *volleyball*

Verbos

abrir *to open*

almorzar (ue) *to have lunch*

apagar *to blow out, to turn off*

cantar *to sing*

charlar *to chat*

comprar *to buy*

contar (ue) *to tell; to count*

decorar *to decorate*

disfrutar de *to enjoy*

dormir (ue) *to sleep*

empezar (ie) *to start, to begin*

entender (ie) *to understand*

envolver (ue) *to wrap*

festejar *to celebrate*

gustar *to like, to be pleasing to*

jugar (ue) *to play*

llevar años aquí *to have been living here for years*

mandar *to send*

pedir (i) *to ask for, to request*

pensar (ie) *to think*

poder (ue) *to be able to, can*

poner la mesa *to set the table*

preferir (ie) *to prefer*

preparar *to prepare, to make*

probar (ue) *to taste, to try*

querer (ie) *to want; to love (people, pets)*

recordar (ue) *to remember, to recall*

repetir (i) *to repeat*

sacar fotos *to take pictures*

seguir (i) *to follow, to continue*

sentir (ie) *to be sorry, to regret; to feel*

servir (i) *to serve*

tener mal genio *to be ill-tempered*

volver (ue) *to return, to go back, to come back*

Adjetivos

alto(a) *tall*

azul *blue*

bajo(a) *short*

bromista *jokester*

calvo(a) *bald*

canoso(a) *white-haired*

cariñoso(a) *loving, affectionate*

casado(a) *married*

castaño(a) *brown*

comprensivo(a) *understanding*

corto(a) *short*

delgado(a) *thin*

divorciado(a) *divorced*

feo(a) *ugly*

generoso(a) *generous*

gordo(a) *fat*

guapo(a) *good-looking*

intelectual *intellectual*

joven *young*

largo(a) *long*

lindo(a) *cute*

mimado(a) *spoiled*

moreno(a) *dark-haired*

negro(a) *black*

parecido(a) *alike*

pelirrojo(a) *red-headed*

perezoso(a) *lazy*

rubio(a) *blond(e)*

sincero(a) *sincere, honest*

soltero(a) *single*

verde *green*

viejo(a) *old*

¡Buen viaje!

Conexiones a la comunidad
Search the internet for travel packages or alternative spring break opportunities in Mexico (or Puerto Rico, if you don't have a passport).

CAPÍTULO

4

In this chapter you will . . .

- explore Mexico
- discuss vacation plans and activities
- talk about dates, weather, and seasons
- express what is going on

- plan travel, lodging, and sightseeing
- express plans, preferences, and obligations
- learn about popular music
- share your vacation experiences

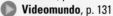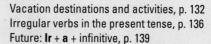

NUESTRO **MUNDO**

México

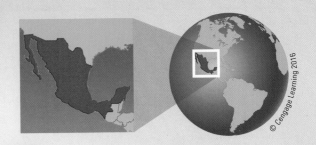

México, país vecino *(neighboring)* de Estados Unidos, tiene la población más grande de hispanohablantes del mundo.

Población: 121 000 000
Capital: México, D.F.
Gobierno: república federal
Moneda: el peso mexicano

Exportaciones: productos manufacturados, petróleo, plata *(silver)*, frutas

© Cosmo Condina/Getty Images

Muchos turistas visitan Chichén Itzá, una antigua ciudad maya en Yucatán, México. La principal construcción de esta zona arqueológica es el Templo de Kukulkán. Esta pirámide demuestra *(shows)* la precisión astronómica y matemática de los mayas. En los equinoccios *(equinoxes)*, la luz forma la imagen de una serpiente bajando las escaleras *(descending the stairs)*: ¡es espectacular!

130 Capítulo 4

David Alfaro Siqueiros, "La March de la humanidad" (Detail). © Schalkwijk/Art Resource, NY. © 2014 Artists Rights Society (ARS), New York/SOMAAP, Mexico City.

Arte

El muralismo mexicano es un movimiento artístico que se origina después de *(after)* la Revolución de 1910. Tres grandes muralistas son Diego Rivera, David Alfaro Siqueiros y José Clemente Orozco. Sus murales en edificios públicos cuentan del gran pasado indígena, de eventos históricos y de la lucha *(struggle)* social.

Geología

En el estado de Chihuahua, las montañas de la Sierra Madre Occidental crean una topografía espectacular. El sistema de cañones se llama Barrancas del Cobre y son más grandes que el Gran Cañón de Arizona. Tienen su origen en una erupción volcánica hace más de 20 millones de años.

© arturo salcido/iStockphoto

© Nathalie Speliers Ufermann/Shutterstock

Gastronomía

La comida mexicana —una combinación de tradiciones culinarias indígenas y europeas— es muy variada. Los ingredientes más comunes son el maíz *(corn)*, el frijol *(bean)* y el chile. El plato típico de la foto, el chile en nogada, se prepara el 16 de septiembre para celebrar la independencia porque tiene los colores de la bandera *(flag)*.

4-1 **¿Qué sabes?** Indica si la oración es **cierta** *(true)* o **falsa** *(false)*. Corrige *(Correct)* las oraciones falsas.

1. México es el país con el número mayor de hispanohablantes del mundo.

2. La moneda oficial de México es el dólar.

3. La zona arqueológica de Chichén Itzá está en México, D.F.

4. Chichén Itzá es una antigua ciudad azteca.

5. Los muralistas pintan murales en edificios públicos.

6. Diego Rivera y Frida Kahlo son grandes muralistas.

7. Las Barrancas del Cobre están en Arizona.

8. Muchos mexicanos comen chiles en nogada para celebrar la independencia.

4-2 **Videomundo.** Mira el video de México. Usa cuatro adjetivos para describir la capital de México. Luego *(Then)*, usa cuatro adjetivos para describir la capital de tu estado. ¿Son similares o diferentes?

Las vacaciones

De vacaciones en la playa

In this *Paso*, you will . . .
- discuss vacation destinations and activities
- talk about vacation plans

esquiar en el agua

dar un paseo en velero

pescar

ir en lancha

montar a caballo

nadar en el mar

bucear

dar un paseo

tomar el sol

© Cengage Learning 2016

Para hablar de las vacaciones	Talking about vacations
¿Qué te gusta hacer en las vacaciones?	*What do you like to do on vacation?*
Me gusta ir a la playa / a las montañas.	*I like to go to the beach / to the mountains.*
Me gusta conocer nuevos lugares.	*I like to see new places.*
Me encanta viajar.	*I love to travel.*
¿Adónde vas en tus próximas vacaciones?	*Where are you going on your next vacation?*
Voy a (México).	*I'm going to (Mexico).*
Me muero por...	*I'm dying to . . .*
hacer un crucero	*go on a cruise*
hacer turismo de aventura	*do adventure tourism*
No veo la hora de irme de vacaciones.	*I can't wait to go on vacation.*
¡Quiero ir contigo!	*I want to go with you!*
¡Buen viaje!	*Have a good trip!*

De vacaciones en la ciudad

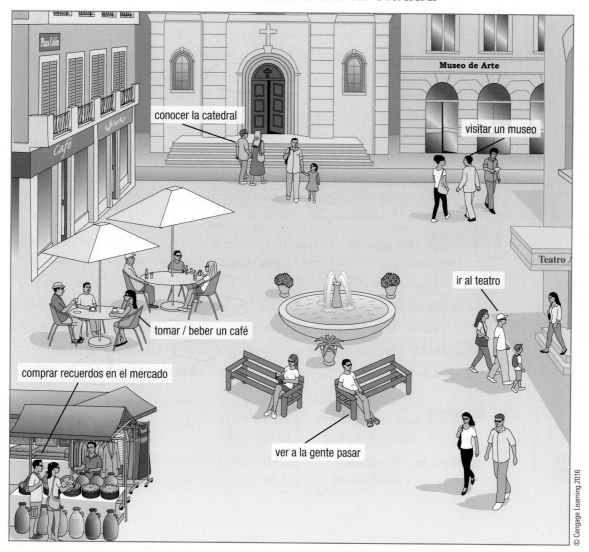

conocer la catedral

visitar un museo

tomar / beber un café

ir al teatro

comprar recuerdos en el mercado

ver a la gente pasar

Museo de Arte

Plaza Colón

Café

Teatro

© Cengage Learning 2016

Otras actividades	*Other activities*
acampar	*to camp*
caminar por la plaza	*to walk in the main square*
esquiar en la nieve	*to ski in the snow*
explorar las zonas arqueológicas	*to explore archaeological sites*
hacer senderismo	*to hike*
hacer surf	*to surf*
ir a un parque de diversiones	*to go to an amusement park*
montar en bicicleta	*to ride a bike*
recorrer la ciudad	*to go all around the city*
tomar / beber un refresco	*have / drink a soda*
ver un espectáculo	*to see a show*

¡Aplícalo!

Colaborar

4-3 Categorías. Con un(a) compañero(a) de clase, tomen turnos *(take turns)* para leer en voz alta *(read aloud)* los grupos de palabras. ¿Qué expresión **no** corresponde a la categoría?

Modelo   En una ciudad: ver a la gente pasar / ir al teatro /(hacer surf)/ dar un paseo

1. **En el mar:** (nadar) / pescar / recorrer la ciudad / ir en lancha
2. **En las montañas:** acampar /(hacer un crucero)/ esquiar en la nieve / hacer senderismo
3. **En una ciudad:** dar un paseo en velero / caminar por la plaza / comprar recuerdos / visitar un museo
4. **En la playa:** tomar el sol / montar a caballo /(esquiar en la nieve)/ bucear
5. **En un parque de diversiones:** tomar un refresco / conocer la catedral / ver un espectáculo / comer comida basura *(junk food)*

Colaborar

4-4 Los planes. Con un(a) compañero(a), completen la conversación con las palabras más apropiadas. Luego *(Then)* lean la conversación en voz alta *(read aloud)*.

LINA   ¡Estoy cansadísima! No veo (1.(la hora)/ el día) de irme de vacaciones.

ALBERTO   Sí, entiendo. ¿(2. De dónde /(Adónde)) vas en tus próximas vacaciones?

LINA   No sé. Me encanta viajar y (3. pescar /(conocer)) nuevos lugares.

ALBERTO   ¿Por qué no haces un (4. parque /(crucero))? Así visitas Puerto Rico.

LINA   ¡Buena idea! Las aguas del Caribe son perfectas para (5.(bucear)/ recorrer).

4-5 Las vacaciones. ¿Con qué frecuencia participan tú y tu compañero(a) en estas actividades? Sigan *(Follow)* el modelo.

Modelo   Estudiante A: ¿Con qué frecuencia vas a un parque de diversiones?
Estudiante B: Voy a un parque de diversiones **a menudo**. Me gusta ir a Six Flags. ¿Y tú?

Expressions of frequency, **Capítulo 2 Paso 3**

¿Con qué frecuencia... ?	todos los años	a menudo	a veces	No... nunca.
1. **ir** a un parque de diversiones		\		
2. **explorar** zonas arqueológicas		\		
3. **pescar** en el mar				\
4. **acampar** en las montañas	\			
5. **visitar** museos		\		
6. **esquiar** en la nieve			\	
7. **recorrer** una ciudad grande		\		
8. **bucear**		\		

Nota lingüística

Notice that the verb **esquiar** needs accent marks:

esquío
esquías
esquía
esquiamos
esquiáis
esquían

¡Exprésate!

4-6 Charadas locas. ¡Vamos a jugar a las charadas!

- Primero (*First*), todos Uds. escriben en papel dos actividades de las páginas 132 y 133. Por ejemplo: **pescar y tomar un café**.

- Su profesor(a) va a recoger (*collect*) y redistribuir (*redistribute*) los papeles a personas diferentes.

- En groups de cuatro o cinco, cada persona toma un turno y dramatiza las actividades en su papel. El resto del grupo tiene que adivinar (*guess*) las actividades. ¿Cuál es la combinación de actividades más loca?

Nota cultural

Although official Spanish words do exist, many adventuresome activities are expressed in everyday Spanish with the verbs **hacer** or **practicar** and the English words.

hacer canopy
hacer jet ski
hacer parasailing
hacer snorkel
hacer windsurf
practicar wakeboard

4-7 El turismo de aventura. ¿Te gusta el turismo de aventura? En México hay muchas oportunidades fabulosas. Trabaja con un(a) compañero(a) para crear pequeñas conversaciones.

Modelo **Estudiante A:** Me muero por bucear.
Estudiante B: ¿Por qué no vas a Cozumel?

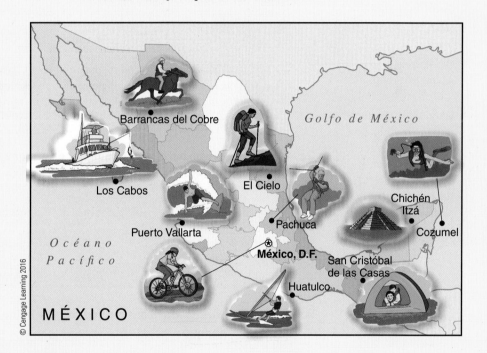

4-8 Nuestras vacaciones. Entrevístense (*Interview each other*) con las preguntas. ¿Qué actividades les gusta hacer a los dos en las vacaciones?

1. Normalmente, ¿pasas las vacaciones con tu familia o con amigos?
2. ¿Prefieres las vacaciones activas o tranquilas?
3. Para ti, ¿es interesante visitar lugares históricos?
4. ¿Prefieres la playa o las montañas?
5. ¿Qué haces cuando estás en la playa?
6. ¿Te gusta hacer turismo de aventura?
7. ¿Qué ciudades grandes te gustan?
8. ¿Qué haces cuando estás en una ciudad grande?

LUIS ÁNGEL	Voy a Ixtapa este fin de semana. ¡No veo la hora!
EDUARDO	No conozco Ixtapa. ¿Qué te gusta hacer allí?
LUIS ÁNGEL	Todos los deportes acuáticos. Doy paseos en velero, buceo, hago windsurf...
EDUARDO	¡Qué padre! *(Cool!)*

■■■

Descúbrelo

■ How does Luis Ángel feel about his upcoming trip?

■ Has Eduardo ever been to Ixtapa?

■ What does Luis Ángel like to do there?

■ What verb forms in the conversation correspond to these infinitives—**ver**, **conocer**, **dar**, and **hacer**? What is the subject for each of these verb forms?

1. Spanish has several kinds of irregular verbs (**los verbos irregulares**). One kind, the -**go** verbs, has irregular **yo** forms in the present tense. The forms for the other persons (**tú**, **él**, **nosotros**, etc.) are regular.

Infinitive	*yo* "-go" form	Other forms are regular
hacer *to do, to make*	**hago**	haces, hace, hacemos, hacéis, hacen
poner *to put, to place*	**pongo**	pones, pone, ponemos, ponéis, ponen
salir *to leave, to go out*	**salgo**	sales, sale, salimos, salís, salen
traer *to bring*	**traigo**	traes, trae, traemos, traéis, traen

2. Some -**go** verbs also have a stem change of **e → ie** or **e → i** in the forms for **tú**, **Ud./él/ella**, and **Uds./ellos/ellas**.

Infinitive	*yo* "-go" form	Some forms have stem-changes
tener (ie) *to have*	**tengo**	tienes, tiene, tenemos, tenéis, tienen
venir (ie) *to come*	**vengo**	vienes, viene, venimos, venís, vienen
decir (i) *to say, to tell*	**digo**	dices, dice, decimos, decís, dicen

3. One -**go** verb, **oír** *(to hear)*, has spelling changes in the other persons: **oigo, oyes, oye, oímos, oís, oyen**.

4. The following verbs also have irregular forms for **yo** in the present tense. The forms for the other persons (**tú**, **él**, **nosotros**, etc.) are regular.

Infinitive	*yo* form	Other forms are regular
dar *to give*	**doy**	das, da, damos, dais, dan
saber *to know*	**sé**	sabes, sabe, sabemos, sabéis, saben
ver *to see, to watch*	**veo**	ves, ve, vemos, veis, ven
conocer *to know*	**conozco**	conoces, conoce, conocemos, conocéis, conocen
conducir *to drive*	**conduzco**	conduces, conduce, conducimos, conducís, conducen

5. Saber and **conocer** both mean *to know*, but they are not interchangeable.

saber *to know, to know how (to do something)*	**conocer** *to know, to meet (be introduced to), to be familiar with*
• information: **Sé la respuesta.**	• people: **Conozco bien a Julia.**
• **saber** + infinitive: **No sé esquiar.**	• places: **¿Conoces Cancún?**
	• artistic works: **No conozco esa novela.**

Nota lingüística
Always use the word **a** after the verb **conocer** to refer to someone you know. You'll learn more about this in **Capítulo 5.**

6. Some of the irregular verbs are used in idioms (**los modismos**).

Change firsword "irregular" to its Right form

dar un paseo	*to stroll, to go for a walk*
dar un paseo en velero	*to go sailing*
hacer un crucero	*to go on a cruise*
hacer la maleta	*to pack one's suitcase*
hacer un viaje / una excursión	*to take a trip / an excursion*
no ver la hora de + infinitivo	*to be eager to, can't wait to*
poner la mesa	*to set the table*
poner la tele / la radio	*to turn on the TV / the radio*

Colaborar

4-9 **De vacaciones.** ¿Qué haces normalmente cuando estás de vacaciones? Conjuga los verbos en la forma **yo.** Luego pon *(Then put)* las oraciones en el orden más lógico. Toma turnos con tu compañero(a) para leer las oraciones.

¡Aplícalo!

_____ a. Primero *(First)*, (conducir) _Conduzco_ al hotel.

_____ b. Por la noche (salir) _____ a un club y (oír) _____ música.

_____ c. Cuando llego al hotel, (ir) _Voy_ directamente al cuarto.

_____ d. Por la tarde, (dar) _doy_ un paseo por la ciudad.

_____ e. A las seis, voy a un café y (ver) _voy_ a la gente pasar.

_____ f. En el club (conocer) _conozco_ a unos nuevos amigos y bailamos mucho.

_____ g. (Poner) _pongo_ mis cosas en el clóset y luego *(then)* (almorzar) _Almuerzo_ a la una.

_____ h. A la una de la madrugada, (volver) _volvo_ al hotel.

Colaborar

4-10 **El sabelotodo.** Ronaldo es un sabelotodo *(know-it-all)*. Con un(a) compañero(a), completen la conversación con **saber** o **conocer.**

RONALDO ¿(1. _Conozco_) qué, Modesto? Yo (2. _conozco_) a Luis Miguel.

MODESTO ¡¿El famoso cantante *(singer)*?! ¡También (3. _conoces_) su casa?

RONALDO No, pero yo (4. _Se_) dónde vive. También (5. _Sé_) su correo electrónico.

MODESTO ¿Tus hermanos también (6. _conocen_) a Luis Miguel?

RONALDO No, no. Yo soy el único de mi familia. Yo (7. _conozco_) a muchas personas famosas.

MODESTO Pues, yo (8. _Sé_) la música de Luis Miguel pero no a él.

Clase

4-11 **Las predicciones.** ¿Conocen Uds. bien a su profesor(a)?

- Primero, con un(a) compañero(a), escriban seis preguntas con verbos de la lista. Usen la forma de **Ud.** (Por ejemplo: **¿Hace Ud. senderismo?**)
- ¿Cómo va a contestar las preguntas su profesor(a)? Escriban sus predicciones.
- Entrevisten (*Interview*) a su profesor(a) con las preguntas. ¿Quiénes tienen el mayor número de predicciones correctas?

(hacer) senderismo	(conocer) muchos países de Centroamérica
(venir) al campus en bicicleta	(ver) espectáculos musicales a menudo
(saber) bucear en el mar	(salir) de casa a las ocho de la mañana

Clase

4-12 **Firma aquí, por favor.** Circula por el salón para entrevistar (*interview*) a tus compañeros. Si contestan "Sí", tienen que firmar (*sign*) en la tabla. ¡Ojo! Hay un límite de dos preguntas para cada (*each*) estudiante.

Modelo **Estudiante A:** ¿Conoces Acapulco?
Estudiante B: No, no conozco Acapulco. / Sí, conozco Acapulco.
Estudiante A: Está bien. / Firma aquí (*Sign here*), por favor.

Actividad	Firma
1. **conocer** Cancún, México	No conozco cancun Mexico
2. **traer** una computadora a clase	Trieno
3. **saber** esquiar en la nieve	No, No se
4. **venir** al campus en motocicleta	no, no vengo
5. **poner** la tele cuando estudias	pongo
6. **ver** a tu familia los fines de semana	
7. **conducir** un auto híbrido	No conduzco
8. **hacer** cruceros a veces	hago
9. **salir** de casa a las nueve de la mañana	sale
10. **decir** "Hola" a tus compañeros de clase	digo

4-13 **La mentira.** En grupos de tres o cuatro estudiantes, cada estudiante dice tres oraciones con los verbos **conocer** y **saber** en la forma **yo**: dos oraciones son verdades (*the truth*) y una es mentira (*a lie*). Los compañeros tienen que indicar cuál de las oraciones es mentira. ¿Quién puede engañar (*trick*) al grupo?

Modelo **Estudiante A:** Conozco Roma, Italia. Sé bucear. Conozco al presidente de nuestra universidad.
Estudiante B: No conoces Roma.
Estudiante A: ¡Ajá! Sí conozco Roma, pero no sé bucear.

El futuro: ir + a + infinitivo

MOISÉS ¡No veo la hora de llegar a Cancún!

AMANDA Sí, va a ser muy divertido. Esta noche vamos a ver un espectáculo. Mañana vamos a pescar. Pasado mañana vamos a montar a caballo…

MOISÉS ¿Pero por qué dices "vamos"? ¡Yo voy a descansar!

1. To express what somebody is going to do in the near future, use the present tense of **ir** followed by the word **a** and an infinitive. This construction corresponds to the English *to be going to + infinitive.*

> EL PRESENTE DE **ir** + **a** + INFINITIVO + OTROS ELEMENTOS
> **Vamos   a   ver   un espectáculo.**
> *We're going to see a show.*

2. Recall that the verb **ir** is irregular in the present tense. Its forms are **voy, vas, va, vamos, vais, van**.

LUIS	¿Qué **vas a hacer** esta noche?	*What **are you going to do** tonight?*
ANA	**Voy a tomar** un café con unos amigos.	***I'm going to have** coffee with some friends.*

3. Certain expressions of time are often used with **ir** + **a** + **infinitivo** to talk about the future.

MOISÉS	¿Vas a trabajar **mañana**?	*Are you going to work **tomorrow**?*
AMANDA	Sí, pero **la semana que viene** voy a hacer un crucero.	*Yes, but **next week** I'm going to go on a cruise.*

Expresiones de tiempo futuro

esta tarde	*this afternoon*
esta noche	*tonight*
mañana	*tomorrow*
pasado mañana	*the day after tomorrow*
la próxima semana / la semana que viene	*next week*
el próximo mes / el mes que viene	*next month*
el próximo año / el año que viene	*next year*

■ ■ ■
Descúbrelo

- According to Amanda, what are she and Moisés going to do in Cancun?

- What does Moisés say that he is going to do?

- What two words does Amanda use to express *we're going to*?

- What verb form follows this construction?

¡Aplícalo! 👥 **4-14** **La familia Trotamundos.** ¿Qué va a hacer la familia Trotamundos en
Colaborar las próximas vacaciones? Trabaja con un(a) compañero(a) para completar el blog con
ir + a + infinitivos de la lista.

dar	explorar	leer	recorrer
escribir	hacer	montar	sacar

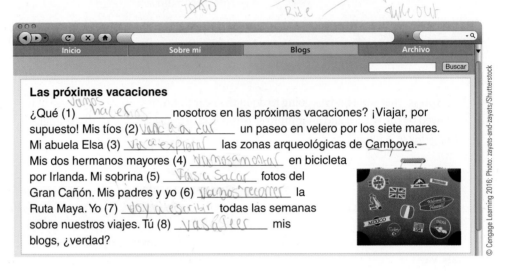

Las próximas vacaciones

¿Qué (1) _____ nosotros en las próximas vacaciones? ¡Viajar, por
supuesto! Mis tíos (2) _____ un paseo en velero por los siete mares.
Mi abuela Elsa (3) _____ las zonas arqueológicas de Camboya.
Mis dos hermanos mayores (4) _____ en bicicleta
por Irlanda. Mi sobrina (5) _____ fotos del
Gran Cañón. Mis padres y yo (6) _____ la
Ruta Maya. Yo (7) _____ todas las semanas
sobre nuestros viajes. Tú (8) _____ mis
blogs, ¿verdad?

👥 **4-15** **¿Qué van a hacer?** Tomando turnos *(Taking turns),* tú dices qué vas a
hacer y tu compañero(a) dice adónde vas.

Modelo **Estudiante A:** Voy a estudiar.

Estudiante B: Vas a la biblioteca, ¿verdad?

Estudiante A: Sí, voy a la biblioteca.

Actividades	
comer con mi novio(a)	nadar
comprar un diccionario	practicar yoga
estudiar	ver un partido de fútbol
ir de compras	tomar un refresco

Lugares	
la biblioteca	la librería
el café	el mercado
el estadio	la piscina
el gimnasio	el restaurante

 Days of the
week, **Capítulo 2
Paso 1**

👥 **4-16** **Una semana ocupada.** ¡Tú y tu compañero(a) tienen una semana
muy ocupada! Tomen turnos *(Take turns)* para preguntar cuándo van a hacer las
actividades de la lista.

Modelo **Estudiante A:** ¿Cuándo vas a visitar a tu familia?

Estudiante B: Voy a visitar a mi familia el jueves.

1. visitar a tu familia

2. lavar la ropa

3. practicar un deporte

4. mirar un partido

5. asistir a una fiesta

6. estudiar para un examen

7. comer en un restaurante

8. ir de compras

¡Exprésate! **4-17** **En mis próximas vacaciones.** ¡Vamos a jugar!

Clase

- ¿Adónde vas en tus próximas vacaciones? ¿Qué vas a hacer? Escribe la respuesta en papel. Por ejemplo: **Voy a Nueva York. Voy a visitar los museos.**
- Después *(Then)*, entrega *(hand in)* el papel a tu profesor(a). Él/Ella va a redistribuir los papeles.
- Circula por la clase y haz preguntas a tus compañeros hasta encontrar *(until you find)* quién tiene tu papel. Por ejemplo: **¿Adóndes vas? ¿Qué vas a hacer?**

4-18 **Lo siento, pero...** Tú invitas a tu compañero(a) a hacer algo, pero tu compañero(a) da muchas excusas para no aceptar tu invitación. Después *(Then)*, cambien de papel *(change roles)*.

Modelo   Estudiante A: ¿Quieres ir al teatro esta noche?
Estudiante B: Lo siento, pero esta noche voy a una fiesta.
Estudiante A: Entonces ¿qué tal si vamos a bailar mañana? Nuestra banda favorita va a tocar en el club Iguana.
Estudiante B: Lo siento, pero mañana voy a visitar a mi abuela en el hospital...

4-19 **¡Vamos a la Ciudad de México!** Tú y tu compañero(a) van a estar en México, D.F. por tres días: del viernes por la mañana al domingo por la tarde. ¿Qué van a visitar?

- Miren el folleto *(brochure)*.
- Preparen un itinerario *(itinerary)* con el día, la hora y el lugar.
- Estén preparados *(Be prepared)* para presentar su itinerario a la clase.

Modelo   El viernes vamos a visitar el Palacio Nacional a las diez de la mañana. Por la tarde, vamos a...

Ciudad de México | Atracciones turísticas

Templo Mayor
Plaza de la Constitución
Tel: (55) 5542 0606 o 4784
Horario: martes–domingo (09:00–17:00)

Palacio Nacional
Plaza de la Constitución
Tel: (55) 3688 1255
Horario: lunes–sábado (10:00–17:00)

Parque Zoológico de Chapultepec
Tel: (55) 5553 6229 o 6263
Horario: martes–domingo (09:00–16:00)

Museo Nacional de Antropología
Paseo de la Reforma y Calzada Gandhi
Tel: (55) 5553 6381
Horario: martes–sábado (09:00–19:00),
domingos (09:00–18:00)

Museo Casa de Frida Kahlo
Londres 247, Coyoacán
Tel: (55) 5554 5999
Horario: martes–domingo (10:00–18:00)

Museo Rufino Tamayo
Paseo de la Reforma 51
Horario: martes–domingo (10:00–18:00)

© Cengage Learning 2016; Photo: Irafael/Shutterstock

El tiempo, las estaciones y las fechas

In this *Paso*, you will . . .

- talk about the weather and seasons
- ask and tell what date it is
- use numbers over 100
- express what is going on right now

¿Qué tiempo hace?

Hoy en la zona arqueológica de Teotihuacán, México, **hace buen tiempo. Hace sol y hace un poco de calor.**

Hoy en las montañas de Bariloche, Argentina, **es un día perfecto** para esquiar. **Está nevando pero no hace mucho frío.**

Hoy en el Parque Nacional de Ordesa, España, **hace mal tiempo. Está lloviendo y hace mucho viento.**

Illustrations © Cengage Learning 2016

Otras expresiones de tiempo

Nieva...
Llueve...
Hace fresco.
Está nublado.

Comentarios sobre el tiempo

¡Qué calor / frío!
¡Qué día más bonito!
Si no llueve, vamos a...

Los meses del año

enero	mayo	septiembre
febrero	junio	octubre
marzo	julio	noviembre
abril	agosto	diciembre

Other weather expressions

It snows . . .
It rains . . .
It's cool.
It's cloudy.

Commenting on the weather

It's so hot / cold!
What a beautiful day!
If it doesn't rain, we're going to . . .

Months of the year

January	*May*	*September*
February	*June*	*October*
March	*July*	*November*
April	*August*	*December*

¿Cuál es el pronóstico del tiempo?

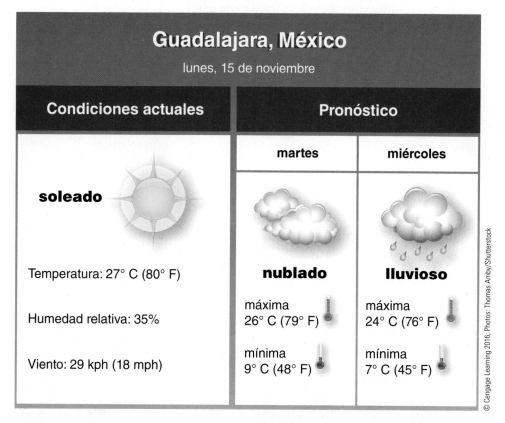

Guadalajara, México
lunes, 15 de noviembre

Condiciones actuales	Pronóstico	
	martes	miércoles

soleado

Temperatura: 27° C (80° F)

Humedad relativa: 35%

Viento: 29 kph (18 mph)

nublado

máxima 26° C (79° F)

mínima 9° C (48° F)

lluvioso

máxima 24° C (76° F)

mínima 7° C (45° F)

© Cengage Learning 2016; Photos: Thomas Amby/Shutterstock

Hoy es lunes, quince de noviembre. **Hace sol y la temperatura está a 27 grados.**

Mañana va a **estar nublado. Según el pronóstico, va a llover** pasado mañana.

Las estaciones	*Seasons*
la primavera	*spring*
el verano	*summer*
el otoño	*fall*
el invierno	*winter*
la estación de lluvia	*rainy season*
la estación seca	*dry season*

Las fechas	*Dates*
¿Qué fecha es hoy?	*What's today's date?*
Hoy es jueves, 11 de octubre.	*Today is Thursday, October 11.*
Mañana es el 12 de octubre.	*Tomorrow is October 12.*
¿En qué fecha empiezan las vacaciones de primavera?	*When does spring break begin?*
Empiezan el 25 de marzo.	*It begins on March 25.*

¡Aplícalo!

Nota cultural

In Spanish-speaking countries, dates are expressed by mentioning the day first, then the month. Consequently, dates are written in a different order than in English. For example, **3/10 = el tres de octubre** (not March 10, as in English).

4-20 Día de la Independencia. ¿Qué fecha es el Día de la Independencia de cada uno de los siguientes países? Trabaja con un(a) compañero(a). Tomando turnos *(Taking turns)*, uno dice una fecha y el otro nombra el país.

Modelo **Estudiante A:** El dieciséis de septiembre.

Estudiante B: Es el Día de la Independencia de México.

País	Día de la Independencia
Cuba	20/5
México	16/9
Panamá	28/11
Colombia	20/7
Ecuador	10/8
Paraguay	15/5
Uruguay	25/8
Argentina	9/7
Chile	18/9
República Dominicana	27/2

4-21 Las descripciones. Observa las fotos. ¿Qué estación es? ¿Qué tiempo hace? Trabajando con un(a) compañero(a), una persona describe una de las fotos y la otra persona identifica la foto.

a.

b.

c.

d.

4-22 ¿Cuál es tu estación preferida? Usa las preguntas para entrevistar *(interview)* a tu compañero(a) de clase. ¿Tienen Uds. las mismas *(same)* opiniones?

1. ¿Cuál es tu estación preferida? ¿Por qué?
2. ¿Cuál es tu estación menos preferida? ¿Por qué no te gusta mucho?
3. ¿En qué mes es tu cumpleaños? ¿Qué tiempo hace normalmente?
4. ¿Qué actividades te gusta hacer en el verano? ¿Y en el invierno?
5. ¿Vas a viajar en las vacaciones de primavera? ¿Adónde? ¿Qué tiempo hace allí?
6. ¿Qué vas a hacer el sábado si llueve? ¿Y si hace buen tiempo?
7. ¿Prefieres el calor o el frío? ¿Dónde hace muchísimo calor? ¿Y muchísimo frío?

¡Exprésate!

4-23 Reportes del tiempo. Formen grupos de dos o tres personas. Tomando turnos *(Taking turns)*, una persona describe el tiempo de una de las ocho ciudades pero no dice *(doesn't say)* qué ciudad es. Los compañeros escuchan e identifican la ciudad.

Modelo **Estudiante A:** Hoy hace sol. ¡Hace mucho calor! La temperatura está a treinta y cinco grados.

Estudiante B: Madrid, España

Nota cultural

Temperatures in Spanish-speaking countries are generally expressed in Celsius. Temperatures at 0° C and below are freezing; temperatures around 10° C are cool; and temperatures above 30° C are hot.

EL TIEMPO

México, D.F.	Quito	Miami	Nueva York
Máx: 23° C	Máx: 11° C	Máx: 34° C	Máx: 26° C
Mín: 15° C	Mín: 6° C	Mín: 26° C	Mín: 15° C

Madrid	Lima	Bariloche	Buenos Aires
Máx: 35° C	Máx: 19° C	Máx: 6° C	Máx: 11° C
Mín: 19° C	Mín: 16° C	Mín: 0° C	Mín: 6° C

© Cengage Learning 2016; Photos: TyBy/Shutterstock

4-24 Los cumpleaños por orden. ¿Cuándo son los cumpleaños de los estudiantes en esta clase? ¿En qué mes hay más cumpleaños?

Clase

- Formen grupos de ocho a diez estudiantes.
- Pregúntense *(Ask one another)*, **¿Cuándo es tu cumpleaños?**
- Formen una fila *(Line up)* por orden de las fechas de sus cumpleaños: de enero a diciembre.

4-25 Una visita especial. Tú y tu amigo(a) mexicano(a) están hablando por teléfono sobre sus planes. Dramatiza esta situación con un(a) compañero(a).

Amigo(a) mexicano(a)	Estudiante de tu universidad
1. Greet your friend and ask how he/she is doing.	2. Respond and ask what's new.
3. Say you have good news (**Tengo buenas noticias.**) Tell him/her that you're going to visit in February.	4. React to the good news. Then, say what season it'll be and describe what the weather will be like here.
5. React to the weather description.	6. Ask what he/she feels like doing. Mention two or three activities. (For example: **¿Tienes ganas de bailar en un club?**)
7. Say which of the activities you feel like doing. (**Tengo ganas de...**)	8. Say you can't wait! (**¡No veo la hora!**) Then say you have to study for a test and end the conversation.

Los números mayores de 100

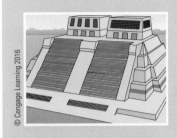

ARELI "Tenochtitlán, capital del imperio Azteca. Fundada en el año mil trescientos veinticinco".

ELÍAS "Población: entre cien mil y trescientos mil habitantes". ¡Qué grande!

ARELI Sí. Era *(It was)* la ciudad más grande de Mesoamérica.

■ ■ ■
Descúbrelo

- What are Areli and Elías reading and talking about?
- What happened in 1325?
- What number do you think **mil** represents?
- What words in the dialogue express 300,000?

1. Here are the numbers from one hundred to one million.

Los números mayores de cien			
100	cien	1001	mil uno
101	ciento uno	2000	dos mil
150	ciento cincuenta	3000	tres mil
200	doscientos	10 000	diez mil
300	trescientos	15 000	quince mil
400	cuatrocientos	50 000	cincuenta mil
500	quinientos	75 500	setenta y cinco mil quinientos
600	seiscientos	99 999	noventa y nueve mil novecientos noventa y nueve
700	setecientos	100 000	cien mil
800	ochocientos	200 000	doscientos mil
900	novecientos	300 600	trescientos mil seiscientos
1000	mil	1 000 000	un millón

2. Here are some rules to remember.

- Use **ciento** for counting from 101 to 199: **ciento uno**.
- Use **cien** for numbers that are *not* between 101 and 199: **cien mil**.
- For percentages *(percent)*, use **por ciento**: **cincuenta por ciento**.
- Before a noun, the words for hundreds agree in gender: **doscient<u>as</u> personas**.
- Years are *not* grouped by twos, as in English: **mil cuatrocientos noventa y dos** (1492).
- The word **y** *(and)* is used only between tens and ones: **doscientos setenta y cinco**.
- When a noun follows **millón** or **millones,** the word **de** is added: **un millón de pesos**.
- Numbers may be punctuated with spaces or periods: **50 000** or **50.000**.

© Cengage Learning 2016

ŤŤ `4-26` **Excursiones en México.** Hay muchas excursiones desde la Ciudad de México al mar. Con un(a) compañero(a), tomen turnos para preguntar el precio *(price)* y las fechas de salida *(departure)* y de regreso *(return)*. Sigan el modelo.

¡Aplícalo!

Modelo   **Estudiante A:** ¿Cuánto cuesta la excursión a Guayabitos?

Estudiante B: Cuesta seiscientos cincuenta pesos.

Estudiante A: ¿Qué día sale?

Estudiante B: Sale el veinte de mayo.

Estudiante A: ¿Qué día regresa?

Estudiante B: Regresa el veintidós de mayo.

Excursiones desde la Ciudad de México

RIVIERA MAYA
Fecha: del 10/4 al 24/4
Costo: $5800 pesos

PASEO A QUIROGA, PÁTZCUARO, JANITZIO
Salida el 24/7. Regreso el 28/7.
Costo: $750 pesos por persona

VERACRUZ
Fecha: del 29/7 al 6/8
Costo: $3350 pesos

GUAYABITOS
2 días, 1 noche
del viernes 20/5 al
domingo 22/5
$650 pesos,
incluye transporte

ACAPULCO
7 noches, 8 días
$12 650 pesos por persona
Sale el 1/8 o el 15/8

Pide el itinerario y más información a Excursiones Al-Mar. Tels: 1591 7404 y 1591 7245

© Cengage Learning 2016; Photo: Humberto Ortega/Shutterstock

`4-27` **Cifras interesantes.** ¿Qué sabes de México?

Primera parte: Tu profesor(a) va a decir seis números grandes; escribe los números en los espacios en blanco *(blanks)*.

a. _____   d. _____

b. _____   e. _____

c. _____   f. _____

ŤˣŤ
Colaborar
Segunda parte: Trabaja con un(a) compañero(a) para relacionar *(match)* los números con la información sobre México.

1. México recibe más de _____ de turistas todos los años.

2. La primera universidad en América del Norte se fundó *(was founded)* en el año _____ en la capital de México.

3. El zacahuil —el tamal más grande del mundo— pesa *(weighs)* aproximadamente _____ libras *(lbs.)*.

4. La capital de México está a una altitud de _____ pies *(ft.)* sobre el nivel del mar.

5. Hay aproximadamente _____ especies de plantas y animales en México.

6. La superficie de México es de _____ kilómetros cuadrados *(square kilometers)*.

PASO 2   **147**

¡Exprésate!

 4-28 La historia de México. ¿Eres bueno(a) en historia? Con un(a) compañero(a), digan en qué año ocurren los siguientes eventos.

Modelo **Estudiante A:** Yo creo que *(I think that)* Hernán Cortés conquista la capital de los aztecas en 1521.

Estudiante B: Estoy de acuerdo. / No estoy de acuerdo.

> **Los años: 1325   1492   1521   1810   1910   1992**

1. Hernán Cortés conquista la capital de los aztecas en _____.
2. Los líderes de México, Estados Unidos y Canadá firman *(sign)* el Tratado de Libre Comercio *(NAFTA)* en _____.
3. Cristóbal Colón llega a América y así se inicia el contacto entre dos continentes en _____.
4. Los aztecas fundan Tenochtitlán, la capital de su imperio, en _____.
5. Varios grupos se rebelan contra la dictadura *(dictatorship)* de Porfirio Díaz y la Revolución Mexicana empieza en _____.
6. El padre Miguel Hidalgo y Costilla empieza la lucha por la independencia de México en _____.

Colaborar **4-29 El turismo en México.** Trabaja con tu compañero(a) para leer el artículo en voz alta *(aloud)*. Después *(Then)*, contesten las preguntas.

1. ¿Qué porcentaje de los turistas en México es de Estados Unidos? ¿Qué tienen estos dos países en común?
2. ¿Cuáles son dos destinos populares de México?
3. ¿Cuántos años tiene Cancún? ¿Cuántos hoteles hay allí?
4. ¿Qué es Xcaret? ¿Cuántos turistas pueden visitar este lugar en un día normal?
5. México, D.F. es una ciudad muy grande. Da cuatro ejemplos que demuestran esto *(show how big it is)*.

México: grande en turismo

México tiene más de 3000 kilómetros de frontera común[1] con Estados Unidos. No es gran sorpresa que las personas de Estados Unidos representan aproximadamente el 65% de los turistas que visitan México. Uno de los destinos más populares es Cancún, fundada en 1970. Cancún tiene más de 140 hoteles y su parque ecológico Xcaret (ish-ka-ret) recibe más de 2300 visitantes al día. Otro destino importante es la capital, centro económico y cultural del país. Según un estudio reciente, el D.F. tiene 10 671 cuartos de hotel de cinco estrellas[2], 438 salas de cine, 110 museos y más de 100 000 taxis.

[1]*shared border* [2]*stars*

© Cengage Learning 2016; Photo: © BrettCharlton/iStockphoto

El presente progresivo

ROBERTO Hola, Juan. ¿Qué estás haciendo?

JUAN Nada especial. Estoy mirando la tele.

ROBERTO ¿Quieres venir a mi casa? Marta y Rosa están aquí y estamos comiendo pizza.

JUAN ¡Gracias! ¡Ya voy! (*I'm on my way!*)

© Cengage Learning 2016

1. The present progressive tense (**el presente progresivo**) is used to describe what is going on at the present moment in time.

| ROBERTO | ¿Qué **estás haciendo**? | *What **are you doing**?* |
| JUAN | **Estoy mirando** la tele. | *I'm watching TV.* |

2. The present progressive tense is made up of two parts: the present tense of the verb **estar** and a present participle (**gerundio**). You already know the present tense of **estar** (**estoy, estás, está, estamos, estáis, están**). To form the present participle for most regular verbs, follow this process.

- For **-ar** verbs, drop the **-ar** and add **-ando**: mira**r** + **ando** → **mirando**
- For **-er** verbs, drop the **-er** and add **-iendo**: come**r** + **iendo** → **comiendo**
- For **-ir** verbs, drop the **-ir** and add **-iendo**: escribi**r** + **iendo** → **escribiendo**

■ ■ ■
Descúbrelo

- What is Juan doing?
- What are his friends doing?
- Which verb is used to express that somebody *is doing* something—**ser** or **estar**?
- What two endings in Spanish correspond to *-ing*, as in *watching* or *eating*?

El presente progresivo			
yo	**estoy mirando (comiendo, etc.)**	nosotros(as)	**estamos mirando (comiendo, etc.)**
tú	**estás mirando (comiendo, etc.)**	vosotros(as)	**estáis mirando (comiendo, etc.)**
Ud./él/ella	**está mirando (comiendo, etc.)**	Uds./ellos/ellas	**están mirando (comiendo, etc.)**

3. Stem-changing **-ir** verbs also undergo a stem change in the present progressive. The **e** changes to **i**, and the **o** to **u** in the present participle.

Los gerundios con cambio de raíz	
e → i	**o → u**
decir → d**i**ciendo *saying* pedir → p**i**diendo *asking for* repetir → rep**i**tiendo *repeating* seguir → s**i**guiendo *following* sentir → s**i**ntiendo *feeling* servir → s**i**rviendo *serving*	dormir → d**u**rmiendo *sleeping* morir → m**u**riendo *dying*

Email Question

4. If the infinitive has a vowel before the **-er** or **-ir** ending, the ending for the present participle is spelled -**yendo**.

Algunos gerundios que terminan en -*yendo*		
leer	le**yendo**	*reading*
oír	o**yendo**	*hearing*
traer	tra**yendo**	*bringing*

¡Aplícalo!
Colaborar

4-30 **La Feria del Tamal.** Estás mirando un informe especial en la televisión sobre un festival en México. ¿Qué está diciendo la presentadora? Con un(a) compañero(a), lean el informe en voz alta, completándolo con el presente progresivo de los verbos.

© keellla

Buenas tardes, amigos. Estamos aquí en Coyoacán en la Feria del Tamal. Como Uds. ven, (1. hacer) _____ mucho sol y yo (2. disfrutar) _____ de este gran festival, junto con *(along with)* miles de visitantes. En el escenario *(stage)* principal, en este momento un conjunto de mariachis (3. tocar) _____ música norteña y varios niños (4. bailar) _____. ¡Qué lindos!

En otra sección del festival hay un mercado y muchas personas (5. comprar) _____ recuerdos típicos. Pero, claro, la estrella *(star)* del festival es el tamal. Más de 30 expositores (6. participar) _____ en el evento y cada uno *(each one)* (7. preparar) _____ tamales con diferentes ingredientes. Y como es de esperar *(as is to be expected)*, ¡todos nosotros (8. comer) _____ tamales! Mmm...

4-31 **Charadas.** ¡Tú y tu compañero(a) van a ser actores! La primera persona dramatiza una acción de la lista (por ejemplo, **tomar un refresco**). La otra persona usa el presente progresivo para describir la acción (por ejemplo, **Estás tomando un refresco.**).

↻ Party preparations and activities, **Capítulo 3 Paso 3**

decorar la casa con globos	jugar a los videojuegos
descansar en casa	lavar los platos
envolver un regalo	limpiar el cuarto
escribir una invitación	pedir un deseo y apagar las velas
hacer un brindis	poner la mesa
hacer un pastel	tomar un refresco

4-32 Haciendo turismo. ¿Dónde están los turistas? ¿Qué están haciendo? Toma turnos con un(a) compañero(a) para describir los dibujos *(the drawings)*.

Modelo La mujer está en un velero. Está pescando.

 1.
 2.
 3.
4.

 5.
6.
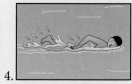 7.
8.

Illustrations © Cengage Learning 2016

4-33 ¿Cuál es la estación? En grupos de tres o cuatro personas, van a jugar a "¿Cuál es la estación?".

- Tomando turnos, una persona menciona dos actividades en el presente progresivo.
- Los otros tienen que adivinar *(guess)* cuál es la estación más lógica.

Modelo **Estudiante A:** Estoy jugando al béisbol. También estoy estudiando para los exámenes finales.
Estudiante B: ¿Es la primavera?
Estudiante A: ¡Sí!

4-34 Entrevista con una celebridad. Con un(a) compañero(a), escriban y dramaticen una escena del programa "Estilo de vida de los ricos y famosos". El episodio de esta semana es "Vacaciones glamorosas". Tienen que incluir un mínimo de tres oraciones en el presente progresivo.

Estudiante A: Tú eres reportero(a) para el programa de televisión "Estilo de vida de los ricos y famosos".	**Estudiante B:** Tú eres una persona rica y famosa. Estás de vacaciones en un lugar exótico. Un(a) reportero(a) va a entrevistarte *(interview you)*.
■ Explica dónde estás y quién es la celebridad. ■ Menciona qué está haciendo la celebridad en este momento. ■ Entrevista a la celebridad sobre sus extravagantes vacaciones y cómo está pasando el rato.	■ Describe el lugar exótico. ■ Explica con detalles qué estás haciendo en este fabuloso lugar. ■ Contesta todas las preguntas del reportero / de la reportera.

De viaje

In this *Paso*, you will . . .

- make travel and hotel arrangements
- ask for travel-related information, such as prices and schedules
- express plans, preferences, and obligations

En el hotel

> Buenas noches. ¿Tiene alguna habitación libre para esta noche?

> Sí, señor. ¿Quiere una habitación sencilla o doble?

Recepción

© Cengage Learning 2016

En la oficina de turismo

> ¿Cuánto cuesta la entrada?

> Cuesta 30 pesos pero hay descuento para estudiantes.

México VIVA México VIVA México Museo de Arte México México

© Cengage Learning 2016

Expresiones en el hotel

¿Tiene baño privado / aire acondicionado?
¿Cuánto cuesta la noche?
¿Puedo pagar... ?
   con tarjeta de crédito / débito
   en efectivo

Expresiones en la oficina de turismo

Estoy buscando...
   un restaurante típico
   un hotel económico
   un cajero automático
¿Qué se puede hacer por aquí?
¿Qué excursión nos recomienda?
¿A qué hora abre / cierra (el museo)?

Expressions in a hotel

Does it have a private bathroom / A/C?
How much does one night cost?
Can I pay . . . ?
   with a credit / debit card
   in cash

Expressions in a tourist office

I'm looking for . . .
   a typical restaurant
   an inexpensive hotel
   an ATM
What is there to do around here?
What tour do you recommend (to us)?
What time does (the museum) open / close?

En la estación de tren

Por favor, quiero comprar un boleto de ida y vuelta a Veracruz.

Aquí tiene. El tren sale a las diez y cuarto.

En la ciudad

Disculpe, señor, ¿hay una farmacia por aquí?

Sí, hay una en la esquina.

El transporte	*Transportation*
el avión / el aeropuerto	*airplane / airport*
el tren / la estación de tren	*train / train station*
el autobús / la parada de autobús	*bus / bus stop*
el metro / la estación de metro	*subway / subway station*

Indicaciones	*Directions*
¿Dónde puedo cambiar dinero?	*Where can I exchange money?*
Disculpe. ¿Hay... por aquí?	*Excuse me. Is there . . . around here?*
una farmacia	* a pharmacy, a drugstore*
un banco	* a bank*
Hay uno(a)...	*There's one . . .*
en la esquina	* on the corner*
a dos cuadras	* two blocks away*
¿Puedo ir a pie o debo tomar un taxi?	*Can I walk there or should I take a taxi?*

¡Aplícalo!

Colaborar

4-35 **Gran Hotel Ciudad de México.** Con un(a) compañero(a), lean el anuncio y contesten las preguntas.

1. ¿Qué se puede hacer en la zona del Gran Hotel?
2. ¿Qué amenidades *(amenities)* tiene el hotel? ¿Qué tienen las habitaciones?
3. ¿Cuánto cuesta la noche? ¿Cómo se puede pagar? ¿Hay descuentos?
4. En tu opinión, ¿es un hotel económico? ¿Quieres pasar la noche en este hotel?

★★★★★

Gran Hotel Ciudad de México
Avenida 16 de septiembre, 82, Ciudad de México, C.P. 06000

Nuestro hotel cuenta con gimnasio, salas de conferencias y mucho más. Las habitaciones tienen aire acondicionado, televisor, Internet, baño privado. Estamos en el Centro Histórico cerca de museos y restaurantes.

Habitación doble *Super Saver* (con una cama[1]): **$1263 pesos***

Habitación de lujo doble (con dos camas): **$1415 pesos***

*Aceptamos todas las tarjetas de crédito.

[1] *bed*

Colaborar

4-36 **En la oficina de turismo.** Tú y tu compañero(a) están en la Oficina de Turismo. Completen la conversación de una manera lógica.

ESTUDIANTE A Esta es nuestra primera visita a Guanajuato. ¿(1. _____)?

EMPLEADO Les recomiendo el Museo Casa Diego Rivera.

ESTUDIANTE B ¡Buena idea! ¿(2. _____)?

EMPLEADO Abre a las 10 de la mañana, de martes a domingo.

ESTUDIANTE A Muy bien. ¿Está lejos? ¿(3. _____)?

EMPLEADO No necesitan tomar un taxi. Está a tres cuadras de aquí.

ESTUDIANTE B También (4. _____).

EMPLEADO El restaurante La Fonda tiene comida típica.

ESTUDIANTE A Vamos a estar aquí por tres días. ¿(5. _____)?

EMPLEADO Tienen que hacer una excursión a San Miguel de Allende.

↻ Asking and telling time, **Capítulo 2 Paso 2**

4-37 **De viaje en autobús.** Con un(a) compañero(a), preparen tres pequeños diálogos. Sigan el modelo.

Destino	Tarifa	Hora de salida
Durango	$675	16:30 h
Matamoros	$390	5:40 h
Puerto Vallarta	$910	21:30 h
Reynosa	$285	3:45 h

Modelo **Turista:** Quiero comprar un boleto de ida y vuelta a **Durango**.
Empleado: Muy bien. Cuesta **$675**.
Turista: ¿A qué hora sale?
Empleado: Sale a **las cuatro y media de la tarde**.
Turista: Gracias, muy amable.

Clase

4-38 **¿Cuál es la pregunta?** ¡Vamos a jugar a Jeopardy™ en español!

- Su profesor(a) va a dividir la clase en tres o cuatro equipos.
- El primer equipo tiene que elegir *(pick)* una categoría y una cantidad de dinero. Por ejemplo: **Queremos *En el aeropuerto* por cincuenta dólares.**
- Después *(Then)*, su profesor(a) va a leer la respuesta. Todos los equipos tienen 45 segundos para escribir la pregunta en papel. Si la pregunta es correcta y lógica, el equipo gana el dinero.

En el hotel	En el aeropuerto	En la oficina de turismo	Por la calle	Las vacaciones
$50	$50	$50	$50	$50
$100	$100	$100	$100	$100
$250	$250	$250	$250	$250
$500	$500	$500	$500	$500

4-39 **De viaje.** Varios turistas están de viaje. ¿Qué están diciendo? Con un(a) compañero(a), dramaticen breves conversaciones para cada escena.

1. En el hotel

2. En la estación de tren

3. En la oficina de turismo

Illustrations © Cengage Learning 2016

Las frases verbales

GUADALUPE ¿Qué quieres hacer mañana?

EMILIANO Me gustaría ir al parque de diversiones.

GUADALUPE A mí también, pero según el pronóstico, va a llover.

EMILIANO Ah, entonces podemos ir al museo de arqueología.

GUADALUPE ¡Buena idea!

■ ■ ■
Descúbrelo

- What does Emiliano want to do tomorrow?
- Why is his first suggestion not a good idea?
- What form of the verb is used after **quieres**, **va a**, and **podemos**?
- Do you think **me gustaría** means *I like to* or *I'd like to*?

1. As you know, every sentence must have a conjugated verb. Sometimes a verb phrase (**frase verbal**) is used instead of a single verb. Verb phrases consist of the combination of a conjugated verb and an infinitive.

> CONJUGATED VERB + INFINITIVE
>
> Mañana **pensamos visitar** el museo.   *Tomorrow **we plan to visit** the museum.*
> También **esperamos conocer** la catedral.   *We also **hope to see** the cathedral.*

2. Here are common verb phrases.

- **esperar + infinitivo**   *to hope to do something*
- **pensar (ie) + infinitivo**   *to plan to do something*
- **deber + infinitivo**   *must / should / ought to do something*
- **necesitar + infinitivo**   *to need to do something*
- **tener + que + infinitivo**   *to have to do something*
- **poder (ue) + infinitivo**   *to be able to do something; can do something*
- **preferir (ie) + infinitivo**   *to prefer to do something*
- **querer (ie) + infinitivo**   *to want to do something*

3. To say what somebody *would like to*, use the verb form **gustaría** + infinitive. To indicate *who* would like to do this, place the appropriate pronoun before the verb (**me, te, le, nos, os, les**).

> **Nos gustaría comprar** recuerdos.   ***We'd like to buy** souvenirs.*

Para expresar *would like*	
me gustaría + infinitivo	*I'd like to*
te gustaría + infinitivo	*you'd (inf.) like to*
le gustaría + infinitivo	*you'd (form.) like to*
le gustaría + infinitivo	*he/she would like to*
nos gustaría + infinitivo	*we'd like to*
os gustaría + infinitivo	*you'd (pl., inf.) like to*
les gustaría + infinitivo	*you'd (pl., form.) like to*
les gustaría + infinitivo	*they'd like to*

¡Aplícalo!

4-40 Las próximas vacaciones. ¿Qué planes tienes para las próximas vacaciones? Completa las siguientes oraciones; luego *(then)* compara tus planes con los de un(a) compañero(a) de clase.

1. Las próximas vacaciones, pienso ir a (destino). *Florida*
2. Voy a viajar en (medio de transporte). *Bus*
3. Quiero salir el (día) de (mes) y regresar el (día) de (mes). *vente siempre Quince cinco*
4. El primer día de mis vacaciones, espero (actividad). *nadar*
5. Otro día, quiero (actividad).
6. Antes de *(Before)* viajar, necesito (obligación). *Cambiar dinero*
7. También debo (obligación) antes de *(before)* salir. *buy tickets*
8. En este viaje no puedo, pero algún día, me gustaría conocer (destino). *España*

4-41 Los planes académicos. Trabaja con tres compañeros de clase para crear seis oraciones lógicas sobre los planes académicos. Sigan las instrucciones y tomen turnos siendo *(being)* estudiantes A, B, C y D.

- Primero, Estudiante A selecciona un sujeto de la columna 1. (**Los estudiantes...**)
- Después *(Then)*, Estudiante B selecciona un verbo de la columna 2 y lo conjuga. (**Los estudiantes deben...**)
- Estudiante C selecciona un infinitivo de la columna 3. (**Los estudiantes deben hacer...**)
- Finalmente Estudiante D selecciona una terminación lógica de la columna 4. (**Los estudiantes deben hacer la tarea de español.**)

1	2	3	4
yo	deber *To have To*	estudiar *study*	horas en la biblioteca
tú	esperar *To hope*	hacer *To do*	en un grupo estudiantil
los estudiantes	pensar *To think*	participar *To Participate*	la tarea de español
mi amigo(a)	poder *To be able to*	pasar *To Pass (Time)*	en el laboratorio
mis amigos y yo	preferir *To prefer*	tomar *To take*	una presentación oral
Uds.	querer *To want*	trabajar *To work*	una clase de historia

4-42 El fin de semana. ¿Qué vas a hacer el próximo fin de semana? Trabajando con un(a) compañero(a), háganse *(ask each other)* estas preguntas. ¿Quién de Uds. tiene los planes más divertidos?

1. ¿Qué piensas hacer el viernes por la noche?
2. ¿Qué quieres hacer el sábado por la mañana? ¿Y por la tarde? *Yo Quiero Trabajar*
3. ¿Qué esperan hacer tú y tus amigos el sábado por la noche?
4. ¿Qué te gustaría hacer el domingo? *me gustaría estudiar la clases lunes*
5. ¿Qué necesitas hacer el domingo para prepararte *(to get ready)* para tus clases del lunes?

4-43 **¿Qué les recomiendan?** Varios turistas piensan visitar tu región. ¿Adónde deben ir? ¿Qué pueden hacer allí? Con un(a) compañero(a), usen los verbos **deber** y **poder** en sus recomendaciones.

Modelo   Paco es un joven de 16 años. Le gustan muchísimo los deportes de aventura.
 Estudiante A: Paco **debe** ir al lago Dillon. Allí **puede** ir en kayak.
 Estudiante B: Boulder es el destino perfecto. **Puede** acampar y escalar rocas.

1. A Carolina y a su esposo Juan les gusta mucho el teatro y la música clásica.
2. Silvia y Antonio prefieren un lugar con muchas actividades para sus dos hijos.
3. A Rafael y a sus amigos les gustan los deportes acuáticos.
4. Noemí y su esposo disfrutan de la naturaleza *(nature)*.
5. Samanta y Viviana son estudiantes de historia.

Colaborar **4-44** **Ideas muy diferentes.** ¿Qué quieren hacer en Hawái los miembros de la familia Godoy? Trabajando con un(a) compañero(a), usen los verbos **pensar**, **preferir**, **esperar**, **querer** y **gustaría** para expresar los planes de cada persona. Después *(Then)*, imaginen que tú y tu compañero(a) van a Hawái. ¿Qué quieren hacer Uds.?

Modelo   El padre **piensa** hacer una excursión a un parque nacional.

pensar   preferir   esperar   querer   gustaría

© Cengage Learning 2016

 4-45 **Los preparativos.** ¿Qué necesitan Uds. hacer en estas situaciones? En grupos de tres o cuatro, tomen turnos para mencionar una actividad diferente para cada situación. Usen los verbos **tener que**, **necesitar**, **deber** y **pensar**.

Modelo   **Situación:** Mañana voy a visitar a mi tía en el hospital.
 Estudiante A: **Pienso** llevar un DVD cómico porque probablemente está aburrida.
 Estudiante B: Antes de *(Before)* llegar al hospital, **necesito** comprar flores.
 Estudiante C: También **quiero**...

Situación 1: La próxima semana vamos a Europa de vacaciones.

Situación 2: El próximo fin de semana voy a la playa.

Situación 3: Pasado mañana voy a la fiesta de cumpleaños de mi mejor amigo(a).

PASO 3 GRAMÁTICA B

Las expresiones indefinidas y negativas

Hotel Cabañas El Bosque

© Cengage Learning 2016

AURA ¡Qué hotel más aburrido! No hay nadie.

RUBÉN Yo soy alguien.

AURA El hotel no tiene ningún restaurante, ningún gimnasio, ninguna piscina, ¡nada!

RUBÉN Sí, es muy romántico.

1. Negative expressions (**las expresiones negativas**) are words and phrases like *nobody* and *nothing*; indefinite expressions (**las expresiones indefinidas**) are their opposites, like *somebody* and *something*.

Expresiones negativas		Expresiones indefinidas	
nada	*nothing, not anything*	**algo**	*something, anything*
nadie	*nobody / no one; not anybody / not anyone*	**alguien**	*somebody / someone; anybody / anyone*
nunca	*never, not . . . ever*	**siempre**	*always*
casi nunca	*hardly ever*	**casi siempre**	*almost always*
ninguno	*none, not any*	**alguno**	*some, any*
tampoco	*neither, not . . . either*	**también**	*also, too*
(ni...) ni	*(neither . . .) nor*	**(o...) o**	*(either . . .) or*

■ ■ ■
Descúbrelo

- What doesn't Aura like about the hotel?
- What does Rubén think about the hotel?
- What is the opposite word for **nadie**? What do you think it means?
- What happens to the word **ningún** when it is in front of a feminine noun?

2. Negative expressions can be placed *before* or *after* the verb. When negative expressions are placed *after* the verb, the word **no** must be added before the verb.

Mis abuelos **nunca** viajan.   Mis abuelos **no** viajan **nunca**.

3. When used as an adjective directly before a noun, **alguno** has four forms: **algún**, **alguna**, **algunos**, **algunas**. When used as a pronoun, the forms are: **alguno**, **alguna**, **algunos**, **algunas**.

¿Hay **algún** hotel por aquí?   **Algunos** de mis amigos van a acampar en El Cielo.

4. When used as an adjective directly before a noun, **ninguno** has two forms: **ningún** and **ninguna**. When used as a pronoun, the two forms are **ninguno** (with the **-o**) and **ninguna**.

No hay **ningún** hotel aquí.   **Ninguno** de mis amigos quiere acampar.

PASO 3 GRAMÁTICA B

¡Aplícalo! Colaborar **4-46 En la oficina de turismo.** Con un(a) compañero(a) de clase, completen los diálogos con las palabras más lógicas de la lista.

> algo   alguien   alguna   nada   nadie   ninguna   también   tampoco

TURISTA 1 ¿Hay _Alguna_ farmacia por aquí?

EMPLEADO Lo siento, no hay _Ninguna_ cerca de aquí.

****

TURISTA 2 Necesito un mapa y _También_ necesito cambiar dinero.

EMPLEADO Lo siento. No tenemos mapas; _Tampoco_ cambiamos dinero.

****

TURISTA 3 Disculpe. ¿Están los baños libres o hay _Alguien_ en ellos?

EMPLEADO No hay _nadie_ porque no hay baños. Son clósets.

****

TURISTA 4 Me gustaría hacer _Algo_ interesante esta noche. ¿Qué me recomienda?

EMPLEADO Para ser sincero, no hay _nada_ interesante en este pueblo. Todo *(Everything)* cierra a las siete.

 Colaborar **4-47 Una fiesta sorpresa.** ¿Cómo es la fiesta sorpresa de Xavier? Mira las imágenes y contesta las preguntas. Trabaja con un(a) compañero(a).

1. Cuando llega Xavier, ¿hay alguien en casa? ¿Qué piensa él?

2. ¿Cómo es el comedor *(dining room)* de la casa? ¿Tiene alguna ventana?

3. ¿Dicen los amigos de Xavier algo? ¿Qué dice Xavier?

4. ¿Hay alguna decoración? ¿Hay globos o flores? ¿Hay un pastel? ¿Hay regalos?

Illustrations © Cengage Learning 2016

4-48 El turista. Con un(a) compañero(a), indiquen si cada oración describe a un turista optimista o a un turista pesimista. Luego expliquen si Uds. son optimistas o pesimistas en cada caso. Sigan el modelo.

Modelo El turista (optimista / pesimista) no hace reservaciones en ningún hotel.
    Estudiante A: En este caso, soy optimista. **Nunca** hago reservaciones en ningún hotel.
    Estudiante B: Yo soy pesimista. **Siempre** hago reservaciones.

1. El turista (optimista / pesimista) siempre llega al aeropuerto tres horas antes.
2. El turista (optimista / pesimista) siempre está muy nervioso cuando viaja por avión.
3. El turista (optimista / pesimista) no tiene ninguna fotocopia de su pasaporte.
4. El turista (optimista / pesimista) tiene muchas medicinas en la mochila.
5. El turista (optimista / pesimista) nunca está preocupado por nada.
6. El turista (optimista / pesimista) lleva mucho dinero en efectivo en la mochila.

4-49 Comportamiento del viajero. Entrevista *(Interview)* a dos compañeros para completar la tabla sobre el comportamiento *(behavior)*.

Modelo **Tú:** Cuando viajas, ¿con qué frecuencia sacas fotos de monumentos?
    Estudiante A: Yo saco fotos de monumentos a veces.
    Estudiante B: Yo nunca saco fotos de monumentos.

Cuando viajas, ¿con qué frecuencia... ?	siempre	a veces	nunca
1. **sacar** fotos de monumentos		\	
2. **almorzar** en restaurantes típicos		\	
3. **hacer** excursiones en autobús			\
4. **dormir** en hoteles económicos		\	
5. **dar** una propina *(tip)* al taxista	\		
6. **pedir** direcciones		\	

Almuerzas
es
duermes
do
Pides

4-50 ¡Qué pésimo hotel! Con un(a) compañero(a), preparen una lista de cinco quejas *(complaints)* para el gerente *(manager)* de este hotel. En la lista, describan los problemas usando palabras como **algo**, **nada**, **nadie**, **nunca**, **ninguno(a)** y **siempre**.

Colaborar

Modelo Ninguna ventana abre.

1.

2.

3.

4.

5.

Illustrations © Cengage Learning 2016

CONECTADOS CON...
LA MÚSICA

La música del mundo hispano

La música del mundo hispano se caracteriza por su infinita variedad de géneros, instrumentos y estilos. Algunas de las canciones contemporáneas más populares tienen sus bases en tradiciones muy antiguas *(old)*. Las siguientes tres canciones representan lo nuevo *(new)* y lo eterno de la música hispana.

Como quien pierde una estrella: música ranchera de México

Las rancheras son un género icónico de la música mexicana, un símbolo del país. Tienen sus raíces *(roots)* en el siglo XIX, pero ganan *(gain)* en popularidad después de *(after)* la Revolución Mexicana de 1910. La instrumentación incluye la guitarra, el violín, el acordeón y la trompeta. Alejandro Fernández es un ejemplo de un artista contemporáneo de este género. Su interpretación de la canción *Como quien pierde una estrella* es moderna y apasionada.

Alejandro Fernández realiza conciertos por todo el mundo.

Estrategia **Identifying key information**

When you approach a reading, identify first the key points of information **(los puntos clave)**. Ask yourself: Who? What? When? Where? Why? Once you know the answers to these essential questions, you can reread to discover more detail.

Palabras de música

el (la) artista	*performer*
la canción, las canciones	*song, songs*
el (la) cantante	*singer*
el conjunto	*musical group, band*
el género	*genre*
el instrumento	*musical instrument*

4-51 **Comprensión.** Lee el artículo y contesta las preguntas con oraciones completas.

1. ¿Quién canta la canción ranchera *Como quien pierde una estrella*?
2. ¿Cuándo ganó *(won)* popularidad la música ranchera en México?
3. ¿Qué representa el flamenco?
4. ¿De dónde es la música flamenca?
5. ¿Por qué es *Guantanamera* considerada el himno nacional "no oficial" de Cuba?

4-52 **¿Y tú?** En grupos de tres o cuatro, comparen sus respuestas a las preguntas.

1. ¿Quién es uno(a) de tus artistas favoritos(as)?
2. ¿Cuál es uno de tus conjuntos preferidos?
3. ¿Qué canción te gusta mucho?

Volver: una fusión del flamenco con el tango

El flamenco, un género de música popular de España, tiene sus orígenes en Andalucía. El flamenco representa una fusión de influencias gitanas *(gypsy),* africanas, árabes y peninsulares. Hoy en día *(In present times),* el flamenco continúa su evolución. Por ejemplo, en su interpretación de la canción *Volver,* la famosa cantante española Estrella Morente combina el flamenco de España con el tango de Argentina y Uruguay.

Guantanamera: una canción folclórica ¡con salsa!

La música folclórica se considera la música de la gente. Un ejemplo de fama internacional es la canción cubana *Guantanamera.* Una de sus numerosas versiones incorpora los versos del poeta cubano José Martí, y por eso es considerada el himno *(anthem)* nacional "no oficial" de Cuba. En una interpretación, la cantante cubana Celia Cruz transforma esta canción tradicional con los ritmos de la música salsa. La salsa, popular por toda Latinoamérica, combina elementos caribeños y africanos.

Las castañuelas son un instrumento de percusión. Se usan en la música flamenca.

Composición: Un artículo

Your university is preparing a special travel edition of its newspaper. Select a popular vacation destination and write a one-paragraph article about it.

 Revisión en pareja. Exchange papers with a classmate and edit each other's work.

- Does the paragraph have a topic sentence? Is the paragraph well-developed? Write one positive comment and one suggestion for improvement.
- Are the verbs conjugated correctly? Circle any verbs that might be incorrect.
- Do the adjectives and articles match the nouns in number and gender? Underline any that might be incorrect.

Estrategia
Composing paragraphs
- State the main idea in a topic sentence (**oración temática**).
- Develop the main idea with related information and examples.

NUESTRA COMUNIDAD

 4-53 **Nosotros / *Share It!*** En línea, subiste *(you posted)* una foto de tus vacaciones. También viste *(You also saw)* las publicaciones *(posts)* de varios compañeros de clase. Ahora *(Now)*, con dos o tres compañeros, comenten sobre estas publicaciones y contesten las preguntas.

1. ¿Cuáles son algunos de los lugares en las fotos?
2. ¿Hay más fotos de playa, montaña o ciudad?
3. ¿Qué están haciendo las personas en las fotos?
4. ¿Qué atracciones turísticas hay en las fotos?
5. ¿Quién tiene una foto muy divertida? Describe la foto.

 4-54 **Perspectivas: Lugares turísticos populares.** En línea, miraste *(you watched)* un video en el que *(in which)* tres estudiantes describen los lugares turísticos más populares de sus respectivos países. ¿Qué dicen los estudiantes? Con dos compañeros, comparen sus respuestas sobre el video. Después *(Then)*, entrevístense *(interview one another)* con estas preguntas:

- ¿Cuáles son algunos lugares turísticos populares en tu estado o región?
- ¿Cuál es la mejor temporada *(time of year)* para visitar esos lugares?

 4-55 **Exploración: Un viaje a Los Cabos.** En Internet, planeaste un viaje a Los Cabos. Ahora *(Now)*, formen grupos de tres o cuatro estudiantes. Tomen turnos haciendo breves presentaciones sobre sus planes. Las otras personas escuchan y hacen preguntas.

Modelo

Voy a salir para Los Cabos el ___ de ___ a las ___. Voy a volver el ___ de ___ a las ___. Mi vuelo *(flight)* es el número ___. El boleto de ida y vuelta cuesta ___. Mi hotel se llama ___. Me gusta este hotel porque tiene ___. La habitación cuesta ___ por noche. El primer día, quiero ___. El segundo día, pienso ___. El tercer día, espero ___. El viaje, en total, va a costar ___.

 4-56 **Conectados con... la religión.** En línea, leíste un artículo sobre el Día de los Muertos. Con dos o tres compañeros(as), compartan *(share)* información de sus investigaciones sobre este tema.

Modelo

En Albuquerque, la comunidad mexicana festeja... / En Perú, las personas celebran...

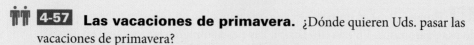

SÍNTESIS

††† **4-57** **Las vacaciones de primavera.** ¿Dónde quieren Uds. pasar las vacaciones de primavera?

- Tú **(Estudiante A)** y tu compañero(a) **(Estudiante B)** tienen información sobre dos paquetes *(vacation packages)* para México.

- Primero tienen que intercambiar y apuntar *(jot down)* los detalles de los viajes.

- Después *(Then)*, necesitan comparar los dos paquetes y decidir cuál prefieren.

> This is a pair activity for **Estudiante A** and **Estudiante B**.
>
> If you are **Estudiante A**, use the information on this page.
>
> If you are **Estudiante B**, turn to p. S-4 at the back of the book.

Estudiante A

Destinos en México
Paquete Especial Vacaciones de Primavera – Cozumel para Estudiantes

Gran Solaris Cozumel

5 días, 4 noches
(habitación cuádruple)

Todas las comidas incluidas:
- desayuno
- almuerzo
- cena

Traslados en autobús
(aeropuerto–hotel–aeropuerto)

1 Noche de fiesta con espectáculo

Solo
$4500*
pesos por persona

*Tarifas incluyen todos los impuestos. Precio NO incluye boleto de avión.

¡Disfruta de unas vacaciones inolvidables en el Caribe mexicano! Con sus aguas cristalinas, Cozumel es un paraíso para los aficionados de los deportes acuáticos. Las actividades más populares de esta isla caribeña son nadar, bucear, pescar, hacer windsurf y dar paseos en velero. Para las personas que prefieren las actividades en tierra, hay tenis, paseos a caballo y senderismo.

© Cengage Learning 2016; Photo: Vilainecrevette/Shutterstock

Información sobre el paquete del Estudiante B
Destino:
Actividades en el área:
Hotel:
Duración del viaje:
Precio *(Price)*:
El precio incluye:
Aspectos interesantes:

SÍNTESIS

Colaborar **4-58** **Pepe.** Pepe, el protagonista de este cómic, es un señor mexicano que no habla, solo usa pantomima. En esta tira *(strip)*, Pepe es náufrago *(shipwrecked)* en una isla desierta. Con un(a) compañero(a), contesten las preguntas y describan el cómic.

1. ¿De dónde es Pepe? ¿Cómo es?
2. ¿Dónde está ahora *(now)*?
3. ¿Qué está haciendo?

4. ¿Tiene hambre o sed? ¿Por qué?
5. ¿Qué tiene que usar para pescar?

4-59 **Cuento loco.** ¡Vamos a inventar un cuento loco! Formen grupos de tres o cuatro personas y sigan las instrucciones.

- Uno(a) de Uds. es el (la) secretario(a) y la única *(only)* persona que puede ver el cuento.
- El (La) secretario(a) pide una palabra para cada espacio en blanco *(blank)*. **(Por ejemplo: Una fecha, por favor.)** Tomen turnos para contestar.
- Al final, lean el cuento completo. ¿Es absurdo?

Nuestras vacaciones

Nuestras próximas vacaciones empiezan el _____. En ese mes la
_____(una fecha)_____
temperatura es de _____ grados y _____. Nuestro grupo va
_____(número)_____ _____(expresión de tiempo)_____
a ir a _____, porque es muy _____. Primero, pensamos
_____(nombre de ciudad)_____ _____(adjetivo, singular)_____
_____ y después *(afterward)* queremos _____ en
_____(verbo, infinitivo)_____ _____(verbo, infinitivo)_____
_____. Por la noche, vamos a tomar un _____ para ir al teatro
_____(un lugar)_____ _____(medio de transporte)_____
y ver un espectáculo _____. Antes de *(Before)* regresar, debemos
_____(adjetivo, masculino singular)_____
comprar _____ para nuestro profesor de _____.
_____(sustantivo, plural)_____ _____(clase)_____

4-60 **Situación: En un tren.** Hoy, el salón de clase es un tren y tú tienes una misión.

© Graur Razvan/Shutterstock

1. Antes de empezar *(Before beginning)*:

   ▪ Formen grupos de cuatro y coloquen *(position)* dos sillas enfrente de dos sillas: este es su compartimiento del tren.

   ▪ Su profesor(a) va a dar a cada estudiante una oración secreta. Uds. van a tener que usar esta oración durante la conversación. Memorícenla *(Memorize it)*.

2. El viaje en tren:

   ▪ Tengan una conversación normal entre desconocidos *(strangers)* en un compartimiento del tren: hablen sobre el tiempo, de dónde son, adónde van, a quién van a visitar, etcétera.

   ▪ Digan *(Say)* sus oraciones secretas de manera natural *(naturally)*. Nadie debe saber cuál es la oración secreta.

3. La llegada:

   ▪ Su profesor(a) va a decir cuándo llega el tren a la estación. Paren *(Stop)* la conversación.

   ▪ Adivinen *(Guess)* cuáles son las oraciones secretas de sus compañeros. ¿Quién cumplió *(accomplished)* la misión?

Pronunciación: La entonación

Colaborar

Con un(a) compañero(a), lean en voz alta *(aloud)* el chiste para practicar la entonación.

PACIENTE	Doctor, ¿cree usted que puedo vivir 40 años más?
DOCTOR	Depende. ¿Usted va de parranda *(go out partying)* todas las noches?
PACIENTE	No, doctor.
DOCTOR	¿Bebe?
PACIENTE	No, doctor.
DOCTOR	¿Tiene novia?
PACIENTE	No, doctor.
DOCTOR	¿Come comida basura *(junk food)*?
PACIENTE	No, doctor.
DOCTOR	¿Y para qué quiere usted vivir 40 años más?

VOCABULARIO

RECURSOS

Para aprender mejor
You don't need to travel abroad to practice Spanish. Befriend a native Spanish speaker in your own community. Tell the person, **Estoy aprendiendo español y me gustaría practicarlo con alguien** and see what happens!

Sustantivos

el aeropuerto *airport*
el aire acondicionado *A/C*
el autobús *bus*
el avión *airplane*
el banco *bank*
el baño *bathroom*
el boleto (de ida y vuelta) *(round-trip) ticket*
el café *coffee*
el cajero automático *ATM*
la catedral *cathedral*
la ciudad *city*
el crucero *cruise; cruise ship*
el descuento *discount*
el dinero *money*
la entrada *admission, entrance, ticket*
el espectáculo *show*
la estación *season; station*
la estación de lluvia *rainy season*
la estación seca *dry season*
la excursión *excursion, tour*
la farmacia *pharmacy*
la gente *people*
la habitación *room*
el hotel *hotel*
el invierno *winter*
la lancha *motorboat*
el lugar *place*
el mar *sea*
el mercado *market*
el metro *subway*
la montaña *mountain*
el museo *museum*
la nieve *snow*
la oficina de turismo *tourist office*
el otoño *fall*
la parada (de autobús) *(bus) stop*
el parque de diversiones *amusement park*
la playa *beach*

la plaza *main square*
la primavera *spring*
el recuerdo *souvenir*
el refresco *soft drink*
la tarjeta de crédito / débito *credit / debit card*
el taxi *taxi, cab*
el teatro *theater*
el tren *train*
el turismo (de aventura) *(adventure) tourism*
las vacaciones *vacation*
el velero *sailboat*
el verano *summer*
el viaje *trip*
la zona arqueológica *archaeological site*

Verbos

abrir *to open*
acampar *to camp*
beber *to drink*
bucear *to scuba dive*
cambiar *to exchange*
caminar *to walk*
cerrar (ie) *to close*
conducir *to drive*
conocer *to know; to meet*
costar (ue) *to cost*
dar *to give*
dar un paseo *to go for a walk*
dar un paseo en velero *to go sailing*
decir (i) *to say, to tell*
deber *must, should, ought to*
esperar *to hope*
esquiar *to ski*
explorar *to explore*
hacer *to do, to make*
hacer la maleta *to pack a suitcase*
hacer senderismo *to go hiking*
hacer surf *to surf*
ir a pie *to walk, to go on foot*

montar a caballo *to ride a horse*
montar en bicicleta *to ride a bike*
morir (ue) *to die*
nadar *to swim*
necesitar *to need*
oír *to hear*
pagar (en efectivo) *to pay (in cash)*
pensar (ie) *to plan*
pescar *to fish*
poder *to be able, can*
poner *to put, to place*
poner la tele / la radio *to turn on the TV / the radio*
recomendar (ie) *to recommend*
recorrer *to go all over*
saber *to know*
salir *to leave, to go out*
tomar *to drink*
tomar el sol *to sunbathe*
traer *to bring*
venir (ie) *to come*
ver *to see, to watch*
viajar *to travel*

Expresiones útiles

¡Buen viaje! *Have a good trip!*
Me encanta... *I love to . . .*
Me muero por... *I'm dying to . . .*
No veo la hora de... *I can't wait to . . .*
próximo(a) *next*
Quiero ir contigo. *I want to go with you.*
Si... *If . . .*

Time expressions, p. 139
Weather expressions, p. 142
Months and dates, p. 143
Numbers over 100, p. 146
Adjectives, p. 152
Directions, p. 153
Indefinite and negative expressions, p. 159

Todo en un día

Conexiones a la comunidad
Visit the ethnic aisle of your local supermarket or a Latin American market. Read the Spanish labels of products you use on a daily basis.

In this chapter you will . . .

- explore Guatemala and Honduras
- describe your daily routine
- talk about your room and chores
- describe a house and its furnishings

- say where things are located
- talk about past actions
- learn about three architectural styles in Latin America
- share information about where you live

NUESTRO MUNDO
Guatemala y Honduras

Guatemala y Honduras son dos países de Centroamérica. Tienen ciudades coloniales, ruinas arqueológicas mayas y una geografía espectacular.

República de Guatemala
Población: 14 100 000
Capital: Ciudad de Guatemala
Moneda: el quetzal
Exportaciones: café, azúcar *(sugar)*, petróleo

República de Honduras
Población: 8 300 000
Capital: Tegucigalpa
Moneda: el lempira
Exportaciones: ropa, café, camarones *(shrimp)*

Tradicionalmente, las mujeres mayas pasan tres o cuatro horas al día tejiendo *(weaving)*. Esta joven maya teje un bonito huipil *(indigenous blouse)* en un telar de cintura *(backstrap loom)*. Con este tipo de telar, las mujeres pueden realizar otros quehaceres *(chores)* mientras tejen.

Geografía

El majestuoso volcán Atitlán, con un cono casi perfecto, está al lado del lago de Atitlán, en Guatemala. Atitlán es uno de 32 volcanes de Guatemala. El más alto es Tajumulco (4200 metros) y los dos más activos son Pacaya y de Fuego. Honduras, en cambio *(on the other hand)*, no tiene ningún volcán activo.

Celebraciones

En Semana Santa *(Holy Week)*, las calles de Antigua, Guatemala, están adornadas con magníficas alfombras *(carpets)* de aserrín teñido *(dyed sawdust)*. Grupos de voluntarios elaboran estas alfombras para las procesiones religiosas. La tarea, que lleva de diez a quince horas, es una forma de demostrar su devoción católica. Naturalmente, cuando la procesión pasa por las alfombras, todo el trabajo se destruye *(is destroyed)*.

Arqueología

El parque arqueológico de Copán está en Honduras occidental, muy cerca de Guatemala. Muchos lo llaman el París del mundo maya por su importancia artística y cultural. Unos ejemplares de la perfección artística de los antiguos mayas son las estelas, figuras de piedra *(stone)* que narran eventos históricos.

5-1 **¿Qué sabes?** Completa las oraciones sobre Guatemala y Honduras.

1. Guatemala y Honduras están en...

2. Un producto que ambos *(both)* países exportan es...

3. Una actividad artística de las mujeres mayas es...

4. Una diferencia geográfica entre Guatemala y Honduras es que...

5. Una tradición de Semana Santa en Antigua, Guatemala, es elaborar...

6. Copán es el París del mundo maya porque fue *(it was)*...

5-2 **Videomundo.** Mira los videos de Guatemala y Honduras. Describe la geografía, la arquitectura, la artesanía *(arts and crafts)* y la influencia maya de estos dos países.

La rutina

In this *Paso*, you will . . .
- talk about your daily routine
- express sequence and frequency
- express changes in emotional states

Mi rutina entre semana

Por lo general, **me levanto** a las siete.

Desayuno rápido y salgo a correr.

Me ducho antes de ir a clase.

Estoy en clase **hasta** las cuatro.

Luego, por la noche, tengo que estudiar.

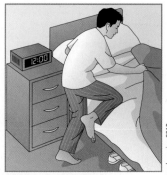

Me acuesto a la medianoche.

© Cengage Learning 2016

La rutina diaria	Daily routine
¿Cómo es tu rutina diaria?	*What's your daily routine?*
Me despierto...	*I wake up . . .*
Me lavo los dientes.	*I brush my teeth.*
Me lavo la cara / las manos / el pelo.	*I wash my face / my hands / my hair.*
Me baño...	*I take a bath . . .*
Me afeito...	*I shave . . .*
Me visto...	*I get dressed . . .*
Me pongo...	*I put on . . .*
Me peino...	*I comb my hair . . .*
Me maquillo...	*I put on make-up . . .*

Otras actividades	Other activities
desayunar	*to have breakfast*
almorzar (ue)	*to have lunch*
cenar	*to have supper*

Los fines de semana

Me quedo en cama hasta el mediodía.

Almuerzo con mis amigos.

Por la tarde, **me relajo**.

Siempre **me arreglo** para salir a bailar.

¡**Me divierto** mucho en el club!

Nunca **me duermo** antes de las dos.

© Cengage Learning 2016

Palabras de secuencia	*Sequence words*
primero ✓	*first*
luego	*then, next*
antes de (+ infinitivo)	*before (. . . -ing)*
después de (+ infinitivo)	*after (. . . -ing)*
mientras	*while*
por último	*finally, last*

Palabras de frecuencia y de tiempo	*Expressions of frequency and time*
temprano ✓	*early*
tarde ✓	*late*
todos los días ✓	*every day*
una vez al día / a la semana / al mes	*once a day / a week / a month*
dos veces / tres veces al día	*twice / three times a day*

¡Aplícalo! Colaborar **5-3** **Un cambio de rutina.** ¿Cómo es la rutina de Alicia? Con un(a) compañero(a), completen la descripción de su rutina.

_____ 1. Entre semana me despierto...

_____ 2. Luego me levanto, me lavo...

_____ 3. Después de arreglarme,...

_____ 4. Los fines de semana me quedo...

_____ 5. Por la noche voy a un club...

_____ 6. Regreso a casa muy tarde y...

a. me acuesto.

b. los dientes y me ducho.

c. en cama hasta las once.

d. temprano, a las seis y media.

e. salgo para la universidad.

f. para bailar y me divierto con mis amigos.

 Colaborar **5-4** **Todo en orden.** ¿Cómo es tu rutina entre semana? ¿En qué orden haces estas cosas? Con un(a) compañero(a), sigan el modelo y comparen sus rutinas. Incluyan estas tres expresiones: **primero, luego, por último**.

First   Next   finally/last

Modelo Por la mañana: me levanto / desayuno / me ducho

Estudiante A: Por la mañana, **primero** me levanto, **luego** me ducho y **por último** desayuno.

Estudiante B: Yo también. / Yo no: **primero** me levanto, **luego** desayuno y **por último** me ducho.

1. Por la mañana: me despierto / pienso en mis planes para el día / me levanto

2. Por la mañana: desayuno / me visto / me ducho

3. Por la mañana: me peino / me lavo la cara / me lavo los dientes

4. Por la tarde: me relajo / estudio / ceno

5. Por la noche: me pongo el pijama / miro la tele / me acuesto

 Colaborar **5-5** **Mi rutina.** ¿Cómo es tu rutina los sábados? Con un(a) compañero(a), tomen turnos y completen las oraciones con su información personal. Hay que incluir un verbo lógico para cada imagen.

1. Los sábados, normalmente yo _____ hasta _la seis horas_
me Quedo

2. Por lo general, después de levantarme, _una vez al día_

3. A menudo yo _____ con _Montses_ a las _Deborah_
como

4. Por la tarde, a menudo yo _Miro_ la tele

5. A veces _Yo Leo_

6. Casi nunca _____ antes de _dos noche_
voy a dormir

¡Exprésate!

 5-6 **¿Con qué frecuencia?** ¿Con qué frecuencia hacen estas actividades tú y tu compañero(a) de clase? Completen las oraciones con una expresión de frecuencia y comparen sus respuestas. ¿Tienen Uds. rutinas muy similares?

Modelo Me despierto muy temprano por la mañana...

Estudiante A: **No** me despierto muy temprano por la mañana **nunca.** ¿Y tú?

Estudiante B: Me despierto muy temprano **una o dos veces a la semana.**

todos los días / todas las noches	una o dos veces a la semana
una vez al día	tres o cuatro veces a la semana
dos o tres veces al día	una o dos veces al mes
más de tres veces al día	no... (casi) nunca

1. Me levanto muy temprano...
2. Me quedo en cama hasta el mediodía...
3. Me lavo los dientes...
4. Desayuno...
5. Me duermo con música...
6. Me ducho con agua fría...
7. Me acuesto muy tarde...

 **5-7** **¡Qué locura!** ¿Qué haces con estos productos? Tomando turnos, una persona crea una oración con uno de los productos; la otra persona indica si la oración es lógica o ilógica.

Modelo **Estudiante A:** Me lavo el pelo con crema de afeitar.

Estudiante B: ¡Qué locura! *(That's crazy!)* ¡Es ilógico!

1. 2. 3.

4. 5. 6.

↺ Telling time, **Capítulo 2 Paso 2**

 5-8 **El día más ajetreado.** ¿Cuál es tu día más ajetreado *(hectic)*? Con un(a) compañero(a), entrevístense *(interview each other)* con estas preguntas.

1. ¿Cuál es tu día más ajetreado?
2. ¿A qué hora te levantas ese día *(on that day)*?
3. ¿Qué haces antes de salir de tu casa?
4. ¿A qué hora y dónde almuerzas?
5. ¿Qué haces por la tarde?
6. ¿A qué hora cenas? ¿Con quién(es)?
7. ¿Qué haces para relajarte?
8. ¿A qué hora te acuestas?

Illustrations: © Cengage Learning 2016

Los verbos reflexivos en el tiempo presente

ANDREA ¿Cómo va todo con tu bebé, María? ¿Duerme por la noche?

MARÍA Sí, como un ángel. Yo acuesto a Sarita a las nueve, luego yo me acuesto a las diez. Mi esposo se acuesta a las once y los tres dormimos ¡hasta las seis de la mañana!

ANDREA ¡Increíble!

■ ■ ■

Descúbrelo

- What time does María put her baby to bed?
- What time does María go to bed? And her husband?
- When does María use **me** before the verb—when talking about going to bed or about putting her baby to bed?

1. Many verbs can be used both reflexively and non-reflexively. The reflexive use refers to an action that we do to or for ourselves; the infinitive ends in **-se**. The non-reflexive use refers to an action that we do to or for someone else.

Reflexive use: **despertarse**	**Me despierto** temprano. *I wake up early.* *(Literally: I wake myself up early.)*

Non-reflexive use: **despertar**	**Despierto** a mi hija a las nueve. *I wake up my daughter at nine o'clock.*

2. Some reflexive verbs refer to feelings or to changes in emotional and mental states.

ponerse:	**Me pongo** triste cuando llueve mucho. *I get sad when it rains a lot.*
enojarse:	**Me enojo** cuando mi compañero usa mis cosas. *I get mad when my roommate uses my stuff.*
preocuparse:	**Me preocupo** cuando él regresa a casa tarde. *I get worried when he comes home late.*
sentirse:	**Me siento** nervioso cuando tengo un examen. *I feel nervous when I have a test.*

3. A reflexive verb always uses a reflexive pronoun that matches the subject of the sentence. This pronoun is placed before the conjugated verb in a sentence.

El presente del verbo *levantarse* to get up			
yo	**me levanto**	nosotros(as)	**nos levantamos**
tú	**te levantas**	vosotros(as)	**os levantáis**
Ud./él/ella	**se levanta**	Uds./ellos/ellas	**se levantan**

4. When reflexive verbs refer to parts of the body, Spanish uses the definite article (**el, la, los, las**) instead of a possessive (**mi, tu, su, nuestro**).

Nos lavamos **el** pelo todos los días.	*We wash our hair every day.*

5. The following reflexive verbs are regular and use the usual present-tense endings for **-ar**, **-er**, and **-ir** verbs. One verb—**ponerse**—has an irregular **yo** form: **me pongo**.

Common Reflexive Verbs

afeitarse _to shave_	**lavarse los dientes** _to brush one's teeth_
arreglarse _to get oneself ready_	**levantarse** _to get up_
bañarse _to take a bath, to bathe_	**maquillarse** _to put on make-up_
ducharse _to take a shower_	**peinarse** _to comb one's hair_
enojarse _to get angry, to get mad_	**ponerse** _to put on (clothing, perfume,_
lavarse la cara / las manos / el pelo	_etc.)_
to wash one's face / hands / hair	**preocuparse (por)** _to get worried, to_
	worry (about)

6. Many reflexive verbs are stem-changing. The stressed vowel in the stem undergoes a change in all persons except **nosotros** and **vosotros**, just like non-reflexive verbs.

e → ie	**o → ue**	**e → i**
despertarse _to wake up_	**acostarse** _to go to bed_	**vestirse** _to get dressed_
divertirse _to have a good time_	**dormirse** _to fall asleep_	
sentirse _to feel_		

5-9 **Un joven padre.** Con un(a) compañero(a), completen la descripción de una mañana típica para Enrique y su pequeño hijo. En cada caso, ¿es necesario usar un verbo reflexivo o no?

Colaborar

Todos los días mi esposa y yo (1. nos levantamos / levantamos) muy temprano, a las seis. Yo (2. me ducho / ducho) y (3. me visto / visto) rápido mientras mi esposa (4. se levanta / levanta) a nuestro hijo Luisito. Luego, mi esposa (5. se ducha / ducha) y yo (6. me visto / visto) a Luisito. Después Luisito y yo desayunamos, yo (7. me lavo / lavo) los dientes y salimos para la guardería (_day care center_).

5-10 **¿Cómo se siente Noelia?** Con un(a) compañero(a), completen la conversación por teléfono entre Noelia y su madre con las formas apropiadas de los verbos entre paréntesis.

Colaborar

NOELIA   Ay, (1. sentirse: yo) _____ muy estresada.

MADRE   Tienes un examen, ¿verdad? Tú siempre (2. ponerse) _____ nerviosa antes de tomar un examen, y después sacas (_you get_) una A.

NOELIA   ¡No entiendes! ¡Los exámenes de cálculo son súper difíciles!

MADRE   Bueno, pero ¿por qué (3. enojarse: tú) _____ conmigo (_with me_)?

NOELIA   Lo siento, mamá. Siempre (4. ponerse: yo) _____ de mal humor cuando no duermo.

MADRE   Sabes, tu padre y yo (5. preocuparse) _____ cuando estudias toda la noche.

NOELIA   Uds. (6. preocuparse) _____ mucho. Estoy bien. Gracias por llamar, mamá. ¡Chao!

¡Aplícalo!

¡Exprésate!

5-11 Mi rutina. ¡Vamos a jugar a las charadas! Tomando turnos, Estudiante A actúa *(acts out)* una acción reflexiva de la lista y Estudiante B describe la acción en el tiempo presente. Por ejemplo: **Te duermes en una clase aburrida**.

acostarse en una cama muy pequeña	**ducharse con agua fría**
afeitarse en la oscuridad *(dark)*	**lavarse los dientes en un tren**
despertarse a las cinco de la madrugada	**sentarse en una silla rota**
divertirse en una piscina	**sentirse enfermo(a) en un avión**
dormirse en una clase aburrida	**vestirse para una cita** *(date)*

5-12 ¿Cómo te sientes? Tu compañero(a) va a leer una situación y tú tienes que decir cómo te sientes en esa situación. Luego, tú lees una situación y tu compañero(a) dice cómo se siente, y así sucesivamente. ¡Ojo! Usen **enojarse**, **preocuparse**, **sentirse** o **ponerse**.

Modelo   **Estudiante A:** Tomas un examen muy difícil y cuando terminas, piensas "¡Qué desastre *(disaster)*!" Pero en la próxima clase, ves que tienes una nota *(grade)* muy buena.

   Estudiante B: Me pongo muy contento(a) y salgo a celebrar con mis amigos.

1. Son las tres de la madrugada. Estás caminando a tu residencia, solo(a) *(alone)*. Oyes un ruido *(noise)*.
2. Preparas un pastel para la fiesta de cumpleaños de tu mejor amigo(a). Tu compañero(a) de cuarto prueba el pastel ¡antes de la fiesta!
3. Te despiertas muy temprano y te arreglas para ir a clase. Antes de salir, miras el calendario y ves que es sábado.
4. Es domingo y decides lavar la ropa. Mientras lavas, ves algo en un bolsillo *(pocket)*: ¡cien dólares!
5. Es martes y son las diez de la noche. El miércoles por la mañana tienes un examen de literatura y no tienes idea de qué trata la novela *(what the novel is about)*.

Colaborar

5-13 En la peluquería canina. La familia Ramírez tiene una peluquería canina *(dog salon)*. Con un(a) compañero(a) de clase, describan qué hace cada persona o animal. Usen verbos reflexivos o no reflexivos, dependiendo de la situación.

Modelo   El papá baña al dálmata...

Palabras útiles

el bóxer
el caniche *(poodle)*
el collie
el dálmata *(Dalmatian)*
afeitar(se)
bañar(se)
despertar(se)
maquillar(se)
peinar(se)

© Cengage Learning 2016

Los verbos reflexivos en el infinitivo y el presente progresivo

VICTORIA ¿Te estás arreglando? La fiesta empieza en media hora.

JACOBO Sí, amor, me estoy afeitando y luego tengo que peinarme.

VICTORIA ¿Qué es ese ruido *(noise)*? ¿Estás arreglándote o estás jugando?

JACOBO ¿Puedes repetir la pregunta? La conexión está mala...

1. The present progressive tense (**estar** + *present participle*) expresses an action that is taking place at the moment you are speaking. When reflexive verbs are conjugated in this tense, the reflexive pronoun may be placed before the conjugated verb **estar** or be attached to the end of the present participle. When the pronoun is attached, an accent mark is added: **-ándo-** / **-iéndo-**.

Carla **se** está bañando.	*Carla is taking a bath.*
Carla está bañándo**se**.	*Carla is taking a bath.*

2. Reflexive verbs are also used in verb phrases *(conjugated verb + infinitive)*. In those instances, the reflexive pronoun may be placed in either of two positions: before the conjugated verb or attached to the infinitive at the end of the phrase.

Me voy a vestir.	*I'm going to get dressed.*
Voy a vestir**me**.	*I'm going to get dressed.*

3. Prepositions such as **antes de** *(before)* and **después de** *(after)* are often followed by infinitives. With reflexive infinitives, the pronoun is always attached to the end. Notice that both parts of the sentence refer to the same person.

Después de levantar**me**, desayuno.	*After I get up, I eat breakfast.*

▪▪▪
Descúbrelo

- What verb tense does Jacobo use to tell his girlfriend what he's doing to get ready for the party?

- Is Jacobo telling the truth? What is he really doing?

- Where is the reflexive pronoun when Victoria asks whether he's getting ready? Where is it the second time she asks the question?

- What other verb form has the reflexive pronoun attached to the end of it?

5-14 **Mi rutina.** ¿Cómo es tu rutina normalmente? Completa las siguientes
Colaborar oraciones con infinitivos. Incluye el pronombre **me** cuando el infinitivo es reflexivo. Después, compara tus oraciones con las de un(a) compañero(a).

¡Aplícalo!

Modelo Normalmente me lavo la cara antes de **acostarme**.

1. Normalmente me ducho antes de...

2. Por lo general me lavo los dientes después de...

3. Normalmente desayuno después de...

4. Me gusta escuchar música para...

5. Por lo general me arreglo para...

6. A menudo me baño después de...

5-15 Por la mañana. ¿Qué están haciendo las personas en los dibujos *(drawings)*? Tomando turnos, una persona describe una acción en el presente progresivo sin *(without)* mencionar el sujeto. Por ejemplo: **Me estoy levantando. / Estoy levantándome.** La otra persona indica *(points out)* el dibujo correspondiente.

yo   él   Uds.   Mario   Maritza

tú   Ud.   mis amigos   nosotros

Illustrations: © Cengage Learning 2016

5-16 ¡Qué torta! *(What a mess!)* Después de estos pequeños accidentes, ¿qué planes tienen las personas en las ilustraciones? Con un(a) compañero(a), formen oraciones completas con los sujetos y las frases verbales indicados.

Colaborar

Modelo   Voy a lavarme las manos. / Me voy a lavar las manos.

yo / ir a

1. tú / deber

2. Ricardo / necesitar

3. Ana / querer

4. mis amigos / ir a

5. el Sr. Alba / pensar

6. yo / tener que

Illustrations: © Cengage Learning 2016

¡Exprésate!

5-17 **Al revés.** ¿Qué hacen tú y tus compañeros en un día típico, al revés *(backwards, from finish to start)*? Hagan lo siguiente *(Do the following)*:

- Formen un círculo con cuatro o cinco estudiantes.
- Estudiante A empieza así: **Me acuesto a la medianoche.**
- Estudiante B dice qué hace antes de eso *(what he/she does before that)*. Por ejemplo: **Antes de acostarme, me lavo los dientes.**
- Estudiante C dice qué hace antes de eso (**Antes de lavarme los dientes...**) y así sucesivamente hasta llegar a la mañana, cuando se levantan.

5-18 **Una excursión a Tikal.** Tú y tu compañero(a) están en Antigua, Guatemala, y mañana van a hacer una excursión a Tikal. Lean el itinerario y luego tomen turnos para hacer las preguntas y contestarlas.

1. El autobús sale a las cuatro de la madrugada. ¿A qué hora piensas levantarte?
2. Para desayuno podemos pedir servicio a la habitación. ¿Quieres desayunar antes o después de arreglarte?
3. ¿A qué hora llegamos a Tikal? ¿Vamos a tener tiempo para ver todas las ruinas?
4. ¿A qué hora vamos a almorzar? ¿Y a qué hora vamos a cenar?
5. La excursión va a ser muy divertida, pero va a ser un día muy largo. ¿Cuándo podemos relajarnos?

Nota cultural

Tikal, located in the jungles of northern Guatemala, is a major Classic Mayan site with magnificient temples. From 250 to 900 AD, Tikal was the largest city in the Americas. Today, the National Park covers an area of over 200 square miles, with thousands of structures, many of them still being excavated.

EXCURSIÓN A TIKAL: Itinerario	
4:00 a.m.	Transporte en autobús del hotel al aeropuerto en Ciudad de Guatemala
6:30 a.m.	Viaje en avión a Flores
7:30 a.m.	Transporte en autobús del aeropuerto en Flores a Tikal
9:00 a.m.	Visita del parque arqueológico Tikal
1:00 p.m.	Almuerzo
2:30 p.m.	Transporte al aeropuerto en Flores
5:00 p.m.	Viaje en avión a Ciudad de Guatemala
6:00 p.m.	Regreso al hotel en Antigua

© Cengage Learning 2016; Photo: Tomasz Pado/Shutterstock

5-19 **Tuiteando.** Vamos a hacer un juego relacionado con Twitter.

- un tenista profesional, antes de jugar al tenis
- una novia, antes de la boda
- un(a) estudiante, antes de ir a la universidad
- un actor de teatro, antes de un espectáculo *(show)*

- Imagina que eres una persona de la lista. Escribe un mensaje de 140 carácteres o menos. Describe cómo te estás arreglando para el evento; usa el presente progresivo. Por ejemplo: **Me estoy maquillando. Estoy sintiéndome muy nerviosa.**
- Después, formen grupos pequeños. Tomando turnos, lean sus mensajes. Los compañeros tienen que adivinar *(guess)* a quién corresponde cada *(each)* mensaje.

Cuartos y quehaceres

Mi cuarto

In this *Paso*, you will . . .

- describe your room
- discuss and complain about chores
- talk about past actions

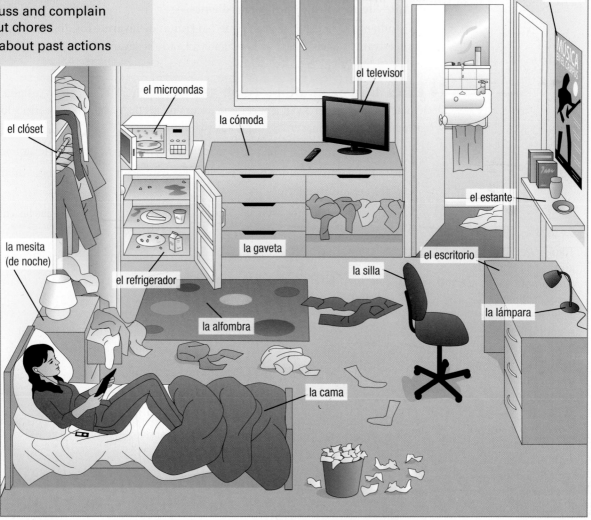

el cartel

el televisor

el microondas

el clóset

la cómoda

el estante

el escritorio

la silla

el refrigerador

la gaveta

la lámpara

la mesita (de noche)

la alfombra

la cama

© Cengage Learning 2016

Para describir el cuarto

¿Cómo es tu cuarto?
  Es grande y tiene mucha luz.
  Es pequeño pero muy acogedor.
El cuarto está...
  limpio / sucio
  ordenado / desordenado

Quejas

El cuarto es un desastre.
Hay una montaña de ropa sucia.
Odio (el desorden).
¡Qué fastidio!
Estoy harto(a) de (tus quejas).

Describing a room

What's your room like?
  It's big and full of light.
  It's small but very cozy.
The room is . . .
  clean / dirty
  tidy / messy

Complaining

The room's a mess.
There's a pile of dirty clothes.
I hate (untidiness).
What a bother!
I'm fed up with (your complaining).

Los quehaceres

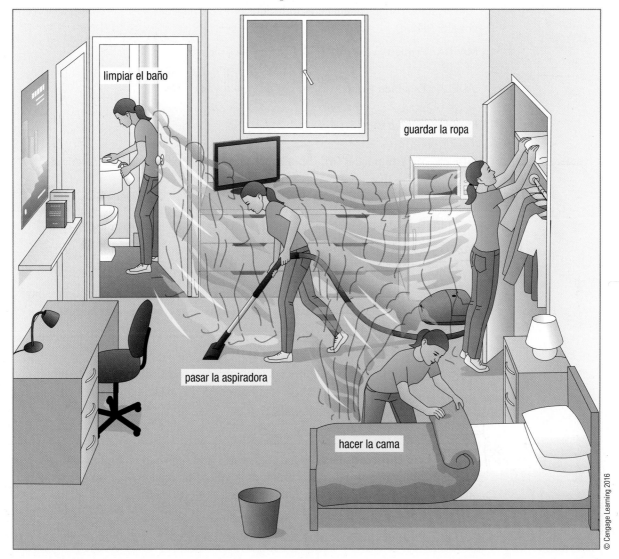

limpiar el baño

guardar la ropa

pasar la aspiradora

hacer la cama

© Cengage Learning 2016

Para hablar de los quehaceres

¿Me puedes ayudar con los quehaceres?
¿Prefieres limpiar el baño o pasar
   la aspiradora?
No me importa.
Acabo de...
   lavar los platos
   ordenar el cuarto
   planchar la ropa
Todavía tengo que...
   barrer el piso
   regar (ie) las plantas
   sacar la basura

Talking about chores

Can you help with chores?
Would you rather clean the bathroom or
   vacuum?
I don't care.
I have just . . .
   done the dishes
   tidied up the room
   ironed the clothes
I still have to . . .
   sweep the floor
   water the plants
   take out the trash

PASO 2 VOCABULARIO

¡Aplícalo!

Colaborar **5-20** **¡Tenemos que limpiar!** Mayra y Adela están hablando sobre cómo dividir el trabajo de limpiar el apartamento. Con un(a) compañero(a), completen la conversación con los quehaceres indicados por las imágenes. Lean la conversación en voz alta (aloud).

MAYRA   Primero, voy a (1) [🛏️]. Después pienso (2) [🧹] .

ADELA   Está bien y mientras, yo voy a (3) [🗑️] y (4) [🚰] .

MAYRA   ¿Quién va a (5) [🧹] ?

ADELA   Yo. Y tú puedes (6) [🪞] porque, bueno, porque a mí no me gusta.

Photos: ekler /Shutterstock; majson/Shutterstock

Colaborar **5-21** **¡Qué fastidio!** Pascual y Axel son compañeros de cuarto con conceptos muy diferentes del orden. Con un(a) compañero(a), completen su conversación.

PASCUAL   Axel, tenemos que ordenar el cuarto. ¿Me puedes (1. ayudar / regar)?

AXEL   Pero, ¿por qué? El cuarto no está (2. desordenado / piso).

PASCUAL   ¿Qué dices? ¡El cuarto es un (3. limpio / desastre)! Mira la alfombra: hay una (4. queja / montaña) de ropa sucia. Tenemos que lavar la ropa.

AXEL   ¡Qué (5. estante / fastidio)! (6. Odio / Todavía) lavar. Prefiero comprar ropa nueva.

PASCUAL   ¡Qué bromista eres! Bueno, si no quieres lavar tu ropa, va a la basura porque estoy (7. quehaceres / harto) del desorden.

AXEL   No me (8. importa / cómoda).

5-22 **Los quehaceres.** ¿Qué quehaceres necesitas hacer? Tomando turnos con un(a) compañero(a) de clase, una persona dice una oración que empieza con **Acabo de (+ infinitivo).** La otra persona dice si es cierto o falso.

Modelo   **Estudiante A:** Acabo de regar las plantas.
          Estudiante B: Falso. Necesitas regar las plantas.

Palabras útiles

guardar la ropa
hacer la cama
lavar las ventanas
limpiar el baño
pasar la aspiradora
planchar la ropa
regar las plantas
sacar la basura

© Cengage Learning 2016

¡Exprésate!

5-23 Un lugar para vivir. Tú y tu compañero(a) buscan un lugar para vivir el próximo semestre. Reciben estos mensajes de texto de algunos amigos. Lean los mensajes y decidan cuál de los dos lugares prefieren. Expliquen por qué.

Modelo **Estudiante A:** Prefiero el apartamento (la residencia) porque...
Estudiante B: (No) Estoy de acuerdo...

> El apartamento es pequeño y un poco viejo pero está a tres cuadras del campus y se permiten mascotas. Hay una piscina para los residentes y un lugar especial para guardar bicicletas. Los cuartos son básicos: tienen una cama, una cómoda, un escritorio y una silla. También hay un televisor ¡y tenemos cable con más de 100 canales!

> La residencia es súper moderna, con Wi-Fi y diseño industrial. Está un poco lejos del campus, pero el autobús pasa con frecuencia. Los cuartos son grandes y tienen muchas ventanas. También tienen un clóset enorme. No hay microondas pero sí hay un pequeño refrigerador. En esta residencia, no tienen que preocuparse por alergias: no hay alfombras y tampoco mascotas.

5-24 Encuesta sobre los quehaceres. Con dos o tres compañeros, miren los resultados de una encuesta *(survey)* y contesten las preguntas.

¿Cuál es el quehacer doméstico que odias?

Quehacer	Porcentaje
Barrer	13%
Lavar los platos	17%
Limpiar el baño	19%
Sacar la basura	14%
Hacer la cama	4%
Lavar la ropa	8%
Planchar	10%
Poner la mesa	7%
Otros	8%

© Cengage Learning 2016

1. ¿Cuál es el quehacer doméstico que más participantes odian? ¿Cuál es el tuyo?

2. ¿Cuál es el quehacer doméstico que menos participantes odian? ¿Cuál es el tuyo?

3. ¿Los participantes odian menos barrer o planchar? ¿Y tú? ¿Cuál prefieres hacer?

4. ¿Los participantes odian más limpiar el baño o sacar la basura? ¿Y tú? ¿Por qué?

5. ¿Los quehaceres causan conflictos entre tú y tu compañero(a) de cuarto? Explica.

5-25 Teatro improvisado. Con un(a) compañero(a) de clase, dramaticen una escena *(scene)* entre dos amigos(as) que viven en un apartamento. Estudiante A empieza la conversación así: **Tenemos que hablar. Como sabes, mis padres...**

Estudiante A	Estudiante B
Situación: Tus padres vienen esta tarde y el apartamento es un desastre.	**Situación:** Es sábado por la mañana y quieres descansar.
Personalidad: Te gusta el orden y quieres impresionar a tus padres.	**Personalidad:** Eres despreocupado(a) *(carefree)*. El desorden... ¿qué desorden?
Meta *(Goal)*: Quieres la ayuda de Estudiante B. Esperas dividir los quehaceres entre los dos.	**Meta *(Goal)*:** Quieres hacer lo menos posible *(as little as possible)*.

Pronouns for direct object (handwritten)

Los pronombres de complemento directo

BRUNO   Pienso comprar esta planta para mi apartamento.

DIANA   **La** tienes que regar.

BRUNO   Sí, sí, **la** voy a regar una vez al mes.

DIANA   Hmm. El cactus es más bonito. ¿Por qué no **lo** compras?

■■■
Descúbrelo

- What does Bruno want to buy? Why does Diana suggest a cactus instead?

- What does the word **la** refer to? What does the word **lo** refer to?

- Where are **la** and **lo** positioned in the sentences—before or after the conjugated verbs?

1. A direct object (**complemento directo**) is an optional sentence element that answers the question *whom?* or *what?* with respect to the verb. In the sentence below, the direct object is *what* the person plans to buy—**un cactus**.

   (Yo) Pienso comprar **un cactus**.   *I want to buy **a cactus**.*

   An object / thing (handwritten)

2. Direct objects can be things or people. In Spanish, when the direct object is a specific person, the word **a** is placed in front of it. This is known as the *personal a*.

   Bruno conoce a Diana.   *Bruno knows Diana.*

   A person (handwritten)

3. Direct objects can be replaced by pronouns. When a pronoun replaces a direct object, it agrees in number and gender with the noun it replaces.

   Limpio **mi casa** los sábados.   *I clean **my house** on Saturdays.*
   Nunca **la** limpio entre semana.   *I never clean **it** during the week.*

Los pronombres de complemento directo			
me	*me*	**nos**	*us*
te	*you (sing., inf.)*	**os**	*you (pl., inf. in Spain)*
lo, la	*you (sing., form.)*	**los, las**	*you (pl.; form. in Spain)*
lo	*him, it*	**los**	*them*
la	*her, it*	**las**	*them*

4. The location of direct object pronouns within a sentence varies.

   - With a single conjugated verb: before the verb.

     ¿El baño? **Lo** limpio todos los días.   *The bathroom? I clean **it** every day.*

   - With a verb phrase: before the conjugated verb or attached to the infinitive.

     ¿Mi cuarto? **Lo** voy a limpiar mañana. / Voy a limpiar**lo** mañana.
     *My room? I'm going to clean **it** tomorrow.*

© Cengage Learning 2016

- With the present progressive tense: before the conjugated verb or attached to the present participle with an accent mark: **-ándo-** / **-iéndo-**.

> ¿La mesa? **La** estoy poniendo ahora mismo. / Estoy poniéndo**la** ahora mismo.
> *The table? I'm setting **it** right now.*

5-26 La venta de garaje. Tú y tu compañero(a) van a una venta de garaje *(garage sale)* para comprar cosas para su apartamento. Uds. tienen $100. ¿Qué van a comprar? Creen *(Create)* conversaciones como las del modelo.

Modelo **Estudiante A:** La lámpara cuesta $3 (tres dólares).
Estudiante B: Está bien. **La** compro. El escritorio cuesta $25.
Estudiante A: No, no **lo** quiero.

© Cengage Learning 2016

5-27 ¡Ay, mamá! Tu mamá (o tu papá) insiste en recordarte todo *(remind you of everything)*. Con un(a) compañero(a), preparen diálogos con la frase **Acabo de...**

Colaborar

Modelo **Estudiante A (mamá / papá):** ¿Cuándo vas a hacer la tarea para tus clases?
Estudiante B (tú): ¡No te preocupes! Acabo de hacer**la**.

1. ¿No vas a llamar a tu abuela?
2. ¿Cuándo vas a envolver los regalos para el cumpleaños de tu hermana?
3. ¿Por qué no ordenas tu cuarto un poco?
4. ¿Puedes ayudar a tu hermanito? Su tarea de matemáticas es muy difícil.
5. El picnic es pasado mañana. ¿No piensas invitar a tus primas?

5-28 ¡Cuánto trabajo! Tú y tu compañero(a) están trabajando en una pequeña pensión *(bed and breakfast / inn)*. ¿Qué tienen que hacer hoy? Miren las dos listas. Sigan el modelo; incluyan pronombres de complemento directo.

Modelo **Estudiante A:** ¿Quién tiene que limpiar los baños?
Estudiante B: Tú tienes que limpiar**los**. ¿Quién tiene que...?

Estudiante A

limpiar los baños   ordenar el comedor
limpiar la piscina   comprar las flores
ayudar al jardinero

Estudiante B

servir el desayuno   hacer las camas
regar las plantas   sacar la basura
ayudar a la recepcionista

¡Exprésate!

Palabras útiles

todos los días
una vez al día
una o dos veces a la semana
dos o tres veces al mes
no... nunca

5-29 Súper limpio. ¿Quién hace estos quehaceres con más frecuencia: tú o tu compañero(a) de clase? Entrevístense *(Interview each other)* sobre las actividades y anoten *(jot down)* las respuestas. Usen pronombres de complemento directo.

Modelo **barrer** el piso
Estudiante A: ¿Con qué frecuencia barres el piso?
Estudiante B: **Lo** barro una vez a la semana. ¿Y tú?

Quehaceres	Yo	Mi compañero(a)
barrer el piso		
lavar la ropa		
limpiar el baño		
hacer la cama		
sacar la basura		
ordenar el cuarto		
limpiar las alfombras		

5-30 La vida diaria. Con un(a) compañero(a), entrevístense *(interview each other)* con estas preguntas sobre la vida diaria *(daily life)*. En sus respuestas, hay que usar pronombres de complemento directo.

1. Por lo general, ¿dónde comes el almuerzo? ¿A qué hora lo comes?

2. ¿Haces la tarea por la mañana, por la tarde o por la noche? ¿Dónde la haces?

3. ¿Miras televisión solo(a) *(alone)* o con amigos? ¿Cuántas horas la miras en un día normal?

4. ¿Lees las noticias *(news)* todos los días? Por lo general, ¿las lees en Internet o en algún periódico *(newspaper)*?

5. Normalmente, ¿a qué hora tomas café? ¿Lo tomas cuando estás estudiando tarde por la noche?

Party preparations, **Capítulo 3 Paso 3**

5-31 Los preparativos. Tú y tus compañeros de clase quieren hacer una fiesta para su profesor(a) porque él/ella se muda *(is moving away)*. ¿Cómo van a dividir los preparativos para la fiesta? Formen grupos pequeños y sigan el modelo.

Modelo mandar las invitaciones
Estudiante A: ¿Quién va a mandar las invitaciones?
Estudiante B: Yo las voy a mandar. / Yo voy a mandarlas. ¿Quién va a... ?
Estudiante C: Yo voy a...

ayudarme a limpiar	**invitar a todos los estudiantes**
comprar las bebidas	**limpiar la casa**
comprar las flores	**traer el pastel**
decorar la casa	**preparar los sándwiches**
envolver el regalo	**sacar unas fotos**

El pretérito de verbos regulares

MAMÁ Estoy muy preocupada. Esta *(This)* mañana Miguel se levantó a las cinco y salió a correr.

PAPÁ ¿Qué dices? ¿Nuestro hijo se levantó a las cinco?

MAMÁ Sí, y cuando regresó a casa, ¡limpió su cuarto!

PAPÁ ¡Dios mío! ¡O está enfermo o está enamorado *(in love)*!

■ ■ ■
Descúbrelo

■ What did Miguel do this morning that surprised his parents?

■ What does Miguel's father think is behind this change in routine?

■ Do these verbs refer to the present, the past, or the future? **se levantó, salió, limpió**

1. The preterite (**el pretérito**) is used to express what happened or what someone did at some particular point of time in the past, such as *yesterday* or *ten years ago*.

> Normalmente cenan a las seis pero anoche **cenaron** a las ocho.
> *They usually have supper at 6:00 but last night **they had supper** at 8:00.*

2. The preterite has two sets of endings: one for **-ar** verbs, and another for **-er** and **-ir** verbs.

El pretérito de los verbos regulares

	lavar *to wash*	**comer** *to eat*	**salir** *to leave, go out*
yo	lav**é**	com**í**	sal**í**
tú	lav**aste**	com**iste**	sal**iste**
Ud./él/ella	lav**ó**	com**ió**	sal**ió**
nosotros(as)	lav**amos**	com**imos**	sal**imos**
vosotros(as)	lav**asteis**	com**isteis**	sal**isteis**
Uds./ellos/ellas	lav**aron**	com**ieron**	sal**ieron**

3. With a reflexive verb, include the appropriate reflexive pronoun before the conjugated verb: **me, te, se, nos, os, se.** For example: **Me levanté.**

4. The verb **gustar** normally uses just two forms in the preterite—**gustó** and **gustaron.** For example: **Me gustó la película.** *I liked the movie.*

5. Some **-ar** verbs have spelling changes only in the **yo** form of the preterite.

Only in the "I" form

■ Infinitives ending in **-car** change **c** to **qu:**

> bus**car** *to look for:* yo bus**qué** (buscaste, buscó, buscamos, buscasteis, buscaron)

■ Infinitives ending in **-gar** change **g** to **gu:**

> lle**gar** *to arrive:* yo lle**gué** (llegaste, llegó, llegamos, llegasteis, llegaron)

■ Infinitives ending in **-zar** change **z** to **c:**

> empe**zar** *to begin:* yo empe**cé** (empezaste, empezó, empezamos, empezasteis, empezaron)

6. Some **-er** / **-ir** verbs have spelling changes only with the following subjects: **Ud./él/ ella** and **Uds./ellos/ellas**.

- Infinitives ending in *vowel* + **-er** / **-ir** change **i** to **y**:

> constr**uir** *(to build)*: construí, construiste, constru**y**ó, construimos, construisteis, constru**y**eron

¡Aplícalo!

5-32 **¡A conjugar!** Para practicar las conjugaciones del pretérito, formen círculos de cuatro o cinco personas.

- La primera persona dice un verbo y un sujeto de la lista; por ejemplo, **tomar: tú**. Luego, indica a otra persona *(points to another person)*.
- Esta persona conjuga el verbo en el pretérito (**tomaste**); después, dice otro verbo y sujeto (**correr: nosotros**) e indica a otra persona; y así sucesivamente.

> **Verbos:** tomar / comer / escribir / levantarse / correr / vivir / limpiar / barrer / bañarse / trabajar
> **Sujetos:** yo / tú / él / ella / nosotros / ellos / Ud. / Uds. / los estudiantes / el profesor

5-33 **Ayer.** ¿Qué hiciste ayer? *(What did you do yesterday?)* Con un(a) compañero(a), completen las oraciones y háganse *(ask each other)* las preguntas. (Nota: *If yesterday was not a class day, talk about the most recent day you had classes.*)

1. Ayer me levanté a las ___Diez y nueve alanoveijante de la mañana___. ¿A qué hora te levantaste tú?
2. Me arreglé y salí de casa a las ___siete a la hora de la mañana___. ¿A qué hora saliste de casa tú? *dress up go out*
3. Pasé la mañana en _____. ¿Dónde pasaste tú la mañana?
4. Almorcé a las _____ en _____. ¿A qué hora y dónde almorzaste tú?
5. Por la tarde, (estudié / asistí a clase / trabajé / descansé / ¿ ... ?). ¿Y tú?
6. Luego, cené con _____. ¿Con quién cenaste tú?
7. Por la noche (estudié / miré la tele / jugué deportes / trabajé / ¿ ... ?). ¿Y tú?
8. Por último, me acosté a la(s) _____. ¿A qué hora te acostaste tú?

Colaborar

5-34 **Un viaje.** Imagina que tú y tu compañero(a) están en un centro turístico. ¿Qué hicieron *(What did you do)* el primer día de sus vacaciones allí?

- Primero, conjuguen los verbos en el pretérito en la forma **nosotros**.
- Después, pongan *(put)* las expresiones en un orden lógico.
- Escriban un pequeño párrafo e incluyan dos o tres de estas expresiones: **primero, luego, después de, antes de, por la tarde, por último**.

buscar un restaurante	**llegar** al hotel
escoger un plato típico	**pagar**
jugar al golf	**pescar**
leer el menú	**sacar** la tarjeta de crédito

¡Exprésate!

Clase

5-35 **Firma aquí, por favor.** ¿Cuáles de tus compañeros hicieron *(did)* estas actividades ayer *(yesterday)*? Circula por el salón para entrevistar a varios compañeros. Si contestan "Sí", tienen que firmar *(sign)* en la tabla.

Modelo **Estudiante A:** ¿Estudiaste por más de dos horas ayer?

Estudiante B: Lo siento. No estudié ayer. / ¡Sí! Estudié mucho.

Estudiante A: Está bien. / Firma aquí *(Sign here)*, por favor.

Actividad	Firma
1. **estudiar** por más de dos horas	
2. **comer** algo horrible en la cafetería	
3. **ordenar** el cuarto	
4. **salir** a bailar con amigos	
5. **correr** más de una milla	
6. **conocer** a una persona interesante	

Colaborar

5-36 **El sábado pasado.** Con un(a) compañero(a), describan las actividades de Néstor y sus amigos el sábado pasado *(last Saturday)*. Usen el pretérito. Por ejemplo: **César se despertó a las once.**

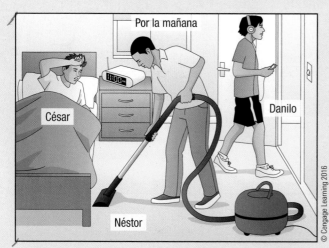

5-37 **Tipos y estereotipos.** ¿Qué hicieron anoche *(last night)* las personas indicadas en la lista? Menciona tres actividades en el pretérito y tu compañero(a) tiene que adivinar quién lo hizo *(guess who did it)*. Sigan el modelo.

Modelo **Estudiante A:** Anoche se quedó en casa, leyó tres libros y estudió hasta la medianoche.

Estudiante B: ¿Marcos, un estudiante súper dedicado?

Estudiante A: ¡Sí! / No. Vuelve a adivinar. *(Guess again.)*

un(a) turista en nuestra ciudad	nuestro(a) profesor(a) de español
Marcos, un estudiante súper dedicado	Antonio, un estudiante perezoso
Platón, un gato muy mimado	Tatiana, una niña de ocho años
Alexa, una atleta	Lili, una estudiante muy sociable

PASO 3 VOCABULARIO

Casas

Una casa colonial

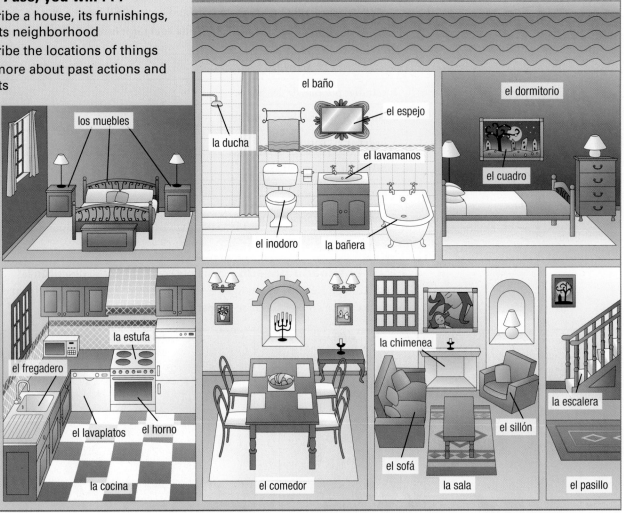

los muebles

el baño

el espejo

la ducha

el lavamanos

el dormitorio

el cuadro

el inodoro   la bañera

el fregadero

la estufa

el lavaplatos   el horno

la cocina

el comedor

la chimenea

el sillón

el sofá   la sala

la escalera

el pasillo

© Cengage Learning 2016

Para describir donde vives	*Describing where you live*
¿Cómo es tu casa?	*What's your house like?*
Es...	*It's . . .*
de estilo colonial / de estilo moderno	*a colonial / modern (house)*
de un piso / de dos pisos	*a one-story / two-story (house)*
nueva / antigua	*new / very old*
Tiene un jardín grande.	*It has a big yard.*
¿Te gusta donde vives?	*Do you like where you live?*
Sí, vivo en un barrio...	*Yes, I live in a . . . neighborhood*
tranquilo / seguro	*quiet / safe*
La verdad es que no. Quiero mudarme.	*Actually, I don't. I want to move away.*
Los vecinos hacen mucho ruido.	*The neighbors make a lot of noise.*

En el patio, hay un periquito...

en la fuente

en medio del patio

en el rincón

delante de la fuente

encima de la silla

sobre la mesita

detrás de la silla

debajo de la mesita

entre las plantas

© Cengage Learning 2016

Para indicar relaciones espaciales

No encuentro mis llaves.
¿Sabes dónde están?
Sí, están...
    encima de (la cómoda)
    a la derecha de...
    a la izquierda de...
    al lado de...
    cerca de / lejos de...

Para dar la bienvenida

¡Bienvenido(a)!
Pasa adelante.
Estás en tu casa.

Describing spatial relationships

I can't find my keys.
Do you know where they are?
Yes, they're . . .
    on top of (the dresser)
    to the right of . . .
    to the left of . . .
    next to . . .
    near / far from . . .

Welcoming a friend

Welcome!
Come in. (informal)
Make yourself at home. (informal)

¡Aplícalo!

Colaborar

5-38 **Comparando casas.** En las páginas 192 y 193 puedes ver la casa de la familia Monterroso. ¿Es muy similar o muy diferente a tu casa? Con un(a) compañero(a), tomen turnos para comparar esa casa con las casas de Uds.

1. La casa de los Monterroso es de estilo (colonial / moderno / tradicional).	Mi casa es de estilo _____.
2. La casa de los Monterroso es de (un / dos) piso(s).	Mi casa es de _____ piso(s).
3. Los Monterroso tienen (dos / tres / cuatro) dormitorios y (un / dos / tres) baño(s).	Nosotros tenemos _____ dormitorios y _____ baño(s).
4. La cocina de su casa es (pequeña / grande) y bastante (moderna / vieja).	La cocina de mi casa es _____ y _____.
5. La sala de los Monterroso es (bonita / fea) y normalmente está muy (ordenada / desordenada).	La sala de mi casa es _____ y normalmente está muy _____.
6. En el jardín de la casa hay una (fuente / piscina) y (unas plantas / una casa para los perros).	En el jardín de mi casa hay _____ y _____. / No tengo un jardín.

Colaborar

5-39 **¡Bienvenido!** Estás en la puerta de la casa de tu familia anfitriona *(host family)* en Honduras. Con un(a) compañero(a), lean la conversación y escojan las palabras más lógicas.

TÚ   Hola, soy *(tu nombre)*. ¿Es Ud. la señora Palacios?

SRA. PALACIOS   Sí, soy yo. ¡(1. Bienvenido / Bienvenida) a nuestra casa! Pasa (2. adelante / entre).

TÚ   Muchas gracias, señora. ¡Qué casa más (3. bonita / sucia)!

SRA. PALACIOS   La casa es bastante (4. limpia / antigua) pero me gusta. Este barrio es muy (5. seguro / ordenado) también y los vecinos no hacen mucho (6. ruido / llave).

TÚ   Yo sé que voy a estar muy (7. contento / contenta) aquí con Uds.

SRA. PALACIOS   Y nosotros también. Ahora *(Now)* vamos por el pasillo y... ¡aquí tienes tu dormitorio! Puedes poner tus cosas (8. encima de la cama / debajo del horno) por el momento.

TÚ   Gracias, señora. ¡Ah! Hay un escritorio (9. en el rincón / debajo de la cama). ¡Un lugar perfecto para estudiar!

SRA. PALACIOS   Hay otro lugar donde puedes estudiar —en el patio. Vamos por aquí. ¿Ves la silla (10. delante de la fuente / sobre la mesita)? Es un lugar perfecto para leer.

TÚ   Sí, tiene razón. Y la pequeña estatua *(statue)* (11. al lado de la bañera / entre las plantas) es preciosa.

SRA. PALACIOS   Recuerda, estás en tu (12. casa / condominio).

¡Exprésate!

5-40 **La casa ideal.** ¿Cómo es tu casa ideal? Trabajando en grupos de tres o cuatro, entrevístense *(interview one another)* con estas preguntas.

1. ¿Dónde está tu casa ideal? ¿En la ciudad, en la playa o en la montaña?

2. ¿De qué estilo es? ¿Cuántos pisos tiene? ¿Prefieres una casa nueva o una casa antigua o histórica?

3. Para ti, ¿es importante tener una casa "verde"?

4. ¿Cuántos baños tiene la casa? ¿Cuántos dormitorios? ¿Cómo es la cocina?

5. ¿Tiene un jardín grande o pequeño? ¿Hay piscina en el jardín?

6. ¿Cómo es el barrio? ¿Cómo son los vecinos?

5-41 **La mudanza.** Tú y tu compañero(a) tienen un nuevo apartamento. ¿Dónde van a poner sus cosas *(all your stuff)*? Sigan el modelo y completen el plano con todos los artículos de la lista.

Modelo   **Estudiante A:** ¿Dónde ponemos el refrigerador?
                  Estudiante B: Podemos ponerlo en la cocina al lado de la ventana.
                            (Estudiante A draws a refrigerator next to the window.)

Muebles y artículos

alfombra	cuadro
sofá	refrigerador
sillón	mesita de noche
cama	lámpara
espejo	escritorio
cómoda	microondas
mesa	televisor
sillas	estante para libros

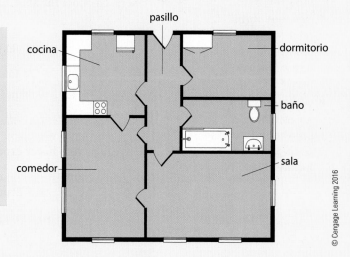

5-42 **Dos casas.** Con un(a) compañero(a) de clase, inventen y dramaticen una conversación para cada imagen.

1. Para hablar de dónde vives

2. Para dar la bienvenida

PASO 3 GRAMÁTICA A

El pretérito de *ir, ser, hacer* y *tener*

ERNESTO ¿Qué hiciste anoche *(last night)*?

MILTON Nada especial. Tuve que trabajar. ¿Y tú?

ERNESTO Fui a la ópera para mi clase de música. ¡Qué noche más aburrida!

MILTON ¡Y siempre dicen que la vida estudiantil es divertida!

■ ■ ■
Descúbrelo

- What did Milton have to do last night?
- Where did Ernesto go?
- Do these verbs refer to the present, the past, or the future? **hiciste / tuve / fui**
- What infinitives do you think correspond to these conjugated verbs? **hiciste / tuve / fui**

1. Many common verbs, such as **ir** and **ser**, are irregular in the preterite. Since the preterite verb forms for these two verbs are identical, their meaning is clarified through the context.

ir: Ernesto **fue** a la ópera.	*Ernesto **went** to the opera.*
ser: La ópera **fue** aburrida.	*The opera **was** boring.*

El pretérito de *ir to go* y *ser to be*			
yo	fui	nosotros(as)	fuimos
tú	fuiste	vosotros(as)	fuisteis
Ud./él/ella	fue	Uds./ellos/ellas	fueron

2. The irregular verb **hacer** expresses what somebody did or made.

El pretérito de *hacer to do, to make*			
yo	hice	nosotros(as)	hicimos
tú	hiciste	vosotros(as)	hicisteis
Ud./él/ella	hizo	Uds./ellos/ellas	hicieron

3. The irregular verb **tener**, when followed by **que** (*+ infinitive*) expresses that somebody had to do something and did it. When used alone, **tener** means *had* in the sense of *got* or *received*.

Milton **tuvo que trabajar** anoche.	*Milton **had to work** last night.*
Tuve más de 200 mensajes de texto ayer.	*I **had / got** more than 200 texts yesterday.*

El pretérito de *tener to have*			
yo	tuve	nosotros(as)	tuvimos
tú	tuviste	vosotros(as)	tuvisteis
Ud./él/ella	tuvo	Uds./ellos/ellas	tuvieron

5-43 **Los preparativos.** En la Residencia Hispana —donde tú vives— todos los residentes hablan español todo el tiempo. Recientemente, Uds. celebraron una jornada a puertas abiertas *(open house)*. ¿Qué tuvieron que hacer Uds. para prepararse para este evento? Trabajando con un(a) compañero(a), observen las fotos y formen oraciones completas en el pretérito con **tener** + **que** + **(infinitivo)**.

Colaborar

 **¡Aplícalo!**

Modelo Lucía tuvo que pasar la aspiradora.

Lucía

1. yo

2. Eduardo

3. Rosita y Manuela

4. Jazmín y yo

5. tú

6. Jamal

 5-44 **El miércoles por la noche.** Con un(a) compañero(a), sigan el modelo y preparen cinco diálogos en el pretérito. (¡Ojo! **a** + **el** → **al**)

Modelo **Estudiante A:** *(Escoge una persona de la columna A.)* ¿Adónde fueron Natalia y Annalise?

Estudiante B: *(Escoge un lugar de la columna B.)* Fueron al gimnasio.

Estudiante A: ¿Qué hicieron allí?

Estudiante B: *(Escoge actividades lógicas de la columna C.)* Jugaron al baloncesto y corrieron.

A: Personas	B: Lugares	C: Actividades
tú	el gimnasio	leer unos artículos y pasar horas en línea
Natalia y Annalise	la biblioteca	tomar un café y charlar con unos amigos
Luis Manuel	el café	jugar al baloncesto y correr
tú y tus amigos	el centro estudiantil	mirar una película y comer pizza
tu compañero(a) de cuarto	la librería	hacer unos experimentos y escribir un informe
Roberto y Sonia	el laboratorio	buscar una calculadora y comprar unos libros

Colaborar

5-45 **Causa y efecto.** La relación causa y efecto define muchas de nuestras acciones. Con un(a) compañero(a), miren la lista de causas. Para cada una *(each one)*, piensen en un efecto lógico. Usen **tener que** en el pretérito.

Modelo Mi compañero de cuarto se mudó. → Tuve que buscar un nuevo compañero de cuarto.

1. Anoche, te sentiste enfermo. →

2. Esta mañana, no había *(there wasn't)* agua caliente *(hot)*. →

3. No lavé ropa en muchas semanas. →

4. Alberto no encontró las llaves de su auto. →

5. La cafetería cerró hoy. →

6. Dejaste tu tarjeta de crédito en casa. →

7. Llovió a cántaros *(It rained cats and dogs)* en el picnic. →

8. Mis vecinos hicieron mucho ruido toda la noche. →

5-46 **¿A qué cuarto fuiste y qué hiciste?** Con dos o tres compañeros, formen un círculo para hacer la siguiente actividad:

- Estudiante A dice a qué cuarto de la casa fue y qué hizo allí. Por ejemplo: **Fui al baño y me lavé los dientes.**

- Estudiante B repite la oración y añade *(adds)* otra: **Fui al baño y me lavé los dientes. Luego fui a la cocina y desayuné.**

- Estudiante C repite las oraciones y añade otra y así sucesivamente.

- El juego continúa hasta que todos los estudiantes tengan dos turnos *(until everyone goes twice)*.

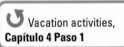
Vacation activities,
Capítulo 4 Paso 1

5-47 **Unas vacaciones fantásticas.** Tú y tu compañero(a) acaban de llegar de unas vacaciones fantásticas. Usando las fotos y su imaginación, hablen sobre adónde fueron y qué hicieron. En la conversación, hagan *(ask)* un mínimo de cinco preguntas.

Modelos Estudiante A: ¡Mis vacaciones fueron fantásticas!

Estudiante B: ¡Las mías también! ¿Adónde fuiste tú?

Estudiante A: Yo fui a...

Estudiante B: ¿Qué hiciste allí?

Estudiante A

Utila, Honduras

Estudiante B

Ciudad de Guatemala

Los usos del pretérito

© Cengage Learning 2016

ALAN ¿Fueron ayer al nuevo parque de diversiones?

VERO Sí. ¡Fue muy divertido! A Rafa le gustó mucho la montaña rusa *(roller coaster)*. ¡Montó en ella ocho veces! Luego por la noche, vimos un espectáculo de música y bailamos por dos horas.

Descúbrelo

- Where did Vero and Rafa go yesterday?
- How many times did Rafa ride the roller coaster?
- For how long did they dance?
- How does Vero sum up the experience at the park?

1. The preterite is one of the past tenses. You can use it to express what somebody did or what happened at a particular point in time in the past. To specify the point in time, use expressions such as the ones in the list.

    Esta mañana me desperté a las seis.   *This morning I woke up at 6:00.*

Expresiones de tiempo pasado	
esta mañana	*this morning*
ayer	*yesterday*
anoche	*last night*
anteayer	*the day before yesterday*
la semana pasada	*last week*
el fin de semana pasado	*last weekend*
el viernes pasado	*last Friday*
el mes pasado	*last month*
el año pasado	*last year*
hace tres años	*three years ago*

2. Use the preterite to say how long an action, event, or condition lasted. To specify the duration of time, use the expression **por** (+ *amount of time*).

    Vivimos allí **por muchos años**.   *We lived there **for many years**.*

3. Use the preterite to express how many times an action or event took place. To express the number of times, use expressions such as these:

una vez *once*	**cinco veces** *five times*	
dos veces *twice*	**varias veces** *several times*	

    Los chicos miraron la película **dos veces**.   *The kids watched the movie **twice**.*

4. Use the preterite to sum up an experience, especially at the beginning or end of an anecdote or story.

    ¡Mi viaje **fue** magnífico! Primero...   *My trip **was** great! First . . .*

PASO 3 GRAMÁTICA B

¡Aplícalo! 👤⟩👤 Colaborar **5-48** **Las actividades de Andrea.** Con un(a) compañero(a), miren el calendario de Andrea y completen las oraciones con el pretérito. También digan *(say)* cuándo hizo la actividad. Supongan que *(Imagine that)* hoy es viernes, 26 de febrero.

Modelo   Andrea (ir) _____ a una fiesta de cumpleaños _____.

Andrea **fue** a una fiesta de cumpleaños **el viernes pasado**.

FEBRERO

lun	mar	mié	jue	vie	sáb	dom
1	2	3	4	5 *boda de Carol y Mateo*	6	7
8	9	10	11	12 *graduación de Katia*	13	14
15	16	17 *partido de fútbol*	18	19 *cumpleaños de Gil*	20 *Copán*	21 *Copán*
22	23	24 *examen*	25 *8 p.m. teatro*	(26)	27	28

Palabras útiles

anoche
anteayer
el fin de semana pasado
el miércoles pasado
hace dos semanas
hace tres semanas

1. Andrea (tener) _____ un examen _____.

2. Andrea (asistir) _____ a una boda _____.

3. Andrea (ir) _____ al teatro _____.

4. La graduación de Katia (ser) _____ _____.

5. Andrea (viajar) _____ a Copán _____.

6. Andrea (ver) _____ un partido de fútbol _____.

👤👤 **5-49** **¿Cuántas veces?** ¿Cuántas veces hiciste las siguientes actividades la semana pasada? Con un(a) compañero(a), entrevístense *(interview each other)*.

Modelo   **Estudiante A:** La semana pasada limpié mi cuarto **dos veces**. ¿Cuántas veces limpiaste tu cuarto?

Estudiante B: La semana pasada **no** limpié mi cuarto **ni una sola vez** *(not even once)*.

La semana pasada...

1. limpié mi cuarto _____. ¿Cuántas veces limpiaste tu cuarto?

2. me quedé en cama hasta el mediodía _____. ¿Cuántas veces te quedaste tú en cama hasta el mediodía?

3. hablé con un pariente _____. ¿Cuántas veces hablaste con un pariente tuyo?

4. comí en la cafetería _____. ¿Cuántas veces comiste tú en la cafetería?

5. fui a la biblioteca _____. ¿Cuántas veces fuiste tú a la biblioteca?

6. tomé el autobús _____. ¿Cuántas veces tomaste tú el autobús?

5-50 **La última vez que...** ¿Cuándo fue la última vez *(When was the last time)* que hiciste las siguientes cosas? Con un(a) compañero(a), entrevístense *(interview each other)* con estas preguntas. Hagan *(Ask)* otras preguntas originales para continuar la entrevista.

1. ¿Cuándo fue la última vez que comiste en un restaurante chino? ¿Con quién fuiste? ¿Qué comiste? ¿Cuánto costó? ¿ ... ?

2. ¿Cuándo fue la última vez que viajaste? ¿Adónde fuiste? ¿Qué medio de transporte usaste? ¿Cuánto tiempo estuviste allí? ¿ ... ?

3. ¿Cuándo fue la última vez que fuiste al cine? ¿Qué película viste? ¿Te gustó? ¿Cómo te sentiste al final? ¿ ... ?

4. ¿Cuándo fue la última vez que tuviste una fiesta de cumpleaños? ¿Qué hicieron en la fiesta? ¿Cuántas velas apagaste? ¿Recibiste regalos? ¿ ... ?

5. ¿Cuándo fue la última vez que hiciste un brindis? ¿Cuál fue la celebración? ¿Qué dijiste en el brindis? ¿Te pusiste nervioso(a)? ¿ ... ?

5-51 **Detector de mentiras.** ¿Eres bueno(a) para detectar mentiras *(lies)*? Con un(a) compañero(a), hagan lo siguiente:

- Tomando turnos, una persona contesta la pregunta con la verdad *(truth)* o con una mentira *(lie)*. Por ejemplo: **Estudié para el último examen por cuatro horas.**
- La otra persona tiene que decir **¡Es verdad!** o **¡Es mentira!** Si acertó *(got it right)*, recibe un punto.
- El ganador *(winner)* es la persona con más puntos al final de las preguntas.

1. ¿Cuántas horas estudiaste para el último examen de español?

2. ¿A qué hora te acostaste anoche?

3. ¿Cuántas veces viste la película *Buscando a Nemo*?

4. ¿Qué hiciste el fin de semana pasado?

5. ¿Cuándo fue la última vez *(the last time)* que montaste en bicicleta?

6. ¿Adónde fuiste el verano pasado?

5-52 **Ta-Te-Ti con el pretérito.** Juega al Ta-Te-Ti *(tic-tac-toe)* con un(a) compañero(a).

- Para marcar X u O en un cuadrado, tienes que hacer una oración en el pretérito con una de las expresiones de tiempo en la tabla. Por ejemplo: **Fui al cine anoche.**
- El estudiante que tiene tres Xs o tres Os en línea vertical, horizontal o diagonal, ¡gana *(wins)* el juego!

ayer	anteayer	dos veces		tres veces	hace cinco años	anteayer
por una hora	esta mañana	hace un año		hace mucho tiempo	ayer	por tres horas
hace dos días	anoche	una vez		la semana pasada	el lunes pasado	el mes pasado

La arquitectura colonial, neoclásica y modernista

Al viajar por el mundo hispánico vemos que su arquitectura es tan variada como su geografía y sus tradiciones culturales. Sin embargo *(However)*, en casi todas las regiones podemos presenciar los siguientes tres estilos arquitectónicos.

El estilo español colonial

Este estilo dominó el continente americano desde el siglo *(century)* XVI hasta el siglo XIX. Se basó en los patrones de construcción del sur de España pero con materiales locales. Las características principales incluyen paredes de estuco, puertas y ventanas en madera y patios con arcos. Hoy en día, muchas casas se construyen en este estilo, denominado *neocolonial*. Este estilo va a persistir por su atractivo especial.

Palabras de arquitectura

el arco	*arch*
el (la) arquitecto(a)	*architect*
el edificio	*building*
la línea (recta, curva)	*(straight, curved) line*
la madera	*wood*
la piedra	*stone*

Estrategia Focusing on the time frame

You can enhance your reading comprehension by paying attention to time expressions and verb endings. These clues tell you whether a sentence refers to a past, present, or future event or action. For instance, the preterite verb ending **-ó** expresses a past action, while the expression **hoy en día** refers to a present situation, and verb phrases such as **va a** *(+ infinitive)* refer to the future. As you read the text, figure out the time frame for each sentence—present, past, or future.

5-53 **Comprensión.** Identifica los estilos de arquitectura de estos tres edificios. En cada caso, menciona dos o tres características de ese estilo. Sigue el modelo.

Modelo Este edificio es de estilo (colonial / neoclásico / modernista). El edificio tiene (arcos / columnas romanas / líneas curvas). También...

1. Casa Batló, Barcelona, España

2. Palacio de la Moneda, Santiago, Chile

3. Palacio Torre Tagle, Lima, Perú

El estilo neoclásico

En el siglo XIX, gran interés despertó por las formas clásicas grecorromanas. Los arquitectos de este estilo rechazaron *(rejected)* la decoración excesiva del barroco y buscaron belleza *(beauty)* en la simetría y la proporción. Construyeron edificios y monumentos con columnas romanas, líneas rectas y fachadas *(facades)* monumentales pero simples.

El estilo modernista

El movimiento modernista se desarrolló *(developed)* entre los siglos XIX y XX y rompió las tendencias tradicionales. Uno de los más famosos exponentes del Modernismo fue Antoni Gaudí. Este arquitecto de Barcelona, España, creó nuevas formas arquitectónicas. Usó líneas curvas, motivos inspirados en la naturaleza *(nature)* y exteriores de piedra, cerámica y hierro *(iron)*.

Antigua, Guatemala, es famosa por su arquitectura colonial.

5-54 **¿Y tú?** Imagina que tu universidad va a construir un nuevo edificio y tú eres el (la) arquitecto(a). Describe el edificio que diseñas. ¿Tiene líneas precisas o curvas? ¿Cómo son las paredes? ¿Qué materiales usas?

Composición: Un mensaje

Write a message to your Spanish instructor and tell him/her about your current job in a summer camp (**campamento de verano**) for Spanish-speaking children. Include a salutation (**Estimado(a) profesor(a):**), a greeting, an overview of your job, and a description of a typical day. Include some longer sentences by adding details. To finish, write two questions and a closing (**Cordiales saludos,** *your name*).

 **Revisión en pareja**. Exchange papers with a classmate and edit each other's work.

- Does the message include all the requested information? Write one positive comment and one suggestion for improvement.
- Are there several longer, detailed sentences? Point out any place where another detail could be added.
- Are the verbs conjugated correctly? Are reflexive pronouns placed properly? Circle any possible errors of this kind.

5-55 **Nosotros / *Share It!*** En línea, subiste *(you posted)* una foto o un video de tu residencia / apartamento / casa. También viste las publicaciones *(posts)* de varios compañeros de clase. Ahora *(Now)*, con dos o tres compañeros(as), comenten sobre estas publicaciones y contesten las preguntas.

1. ¿Dónde vive la mayoría *(majority)* de la clase: en una residencia, en un apartamento o en una casa?

2. ¿Quién tiene el cuarto más bonito? ¿Cómo es?

3. ¿Quién tiene el cuarto más limpio?

4. ¿En cuál de los lugares te gustaría vivir?

5. ¿Cuál de las fotos o de los videos te gusta más? ¿Por qué?

 5-56 **Perspectivas: Los quehaceres domésticos.** En línea, miraste un video en el que *(in which)* tres estudiantes explican quiénes hacen los quehaceres domésticos en sus respectivas casas. ¿Qué dicen los estudiantes?

- Con dos compañeros(as) de clase, comparen sus respuestas sobre el video.
- Después, entrevístense *(interview one another)* con esta pregunta: **¿Quiénes hacen los quehaceres domésticos en tu casa?**

 5-57 **Exploración: Casa vacacional en Guatemala.** En Internet, viste muchas casas vacacionales en Guatemala y seleccionaste una para pasar una semana con tus amigos. Ahora *(Now)*, formen grupos de tres o cuatro estudiantes. Tomen turnos haciendo breves presentaciones sobre las casas. Las otras personas deben escuchar y hacer preguntas. ¿Quién tiene la mejor casa?

Modelo

Mi casa está en... Es... y tiene... Es perfecta para las vacaciones porque...

 5-58 **Conectados con... la arqueología.** En línea, leíste un artículo sobre un centro arqueológico en Petén, Guatemala. Con dos o tres compañeros(as), compartan *(share)* información de sus investigaciones sobre la arqueología.

Modelo

Las líneas de Nazca están en Perú... / La pirámide de Keops tiene 139 metros...

5-59 **Buenos detectives.** Ayer, a las tres de la tarde, hubo un crimen *(a crime took place)* en el barrio La Leona. El sospechoso *(the suspect)* —Jorge Ramírez— tiene una coartada *(alibi)*; estuvo *(was)* con su novia Angélica Vidal. Tú y tu compañero(a) son detectives y tienen que determinar si Jorge Ramírez es inocente o culpable *(guilty)*.

■ Tú (**Estudiante A**) tienes fotos de las cámaras de seguridad. Tu compañero(a) (**Estudiante B**) tiene la declaración de Angélica Vidal.

■ Tomen turnos describiendo las actividades de Angélica y Jorge; tienen que usar el pretérito en sus oraciones. Por ejemplo: **Por la mañana, Jorge y Angélica fueron al gimnasio y corrieron.**

■ Hagan una lista de las discrepancias. ¿Es Jorge Ramírez inocente?

This is a pair activity for **Estudiante A** and **Estudiante B**.

If you are **Estudiante A**, use the information on this page.

If you are **Estudiante B**, turn to p. S-5 at the back of the book.

Estudiante A

© Anne Atkinson

SÍNTESIS

Colaborar

5-60 **Lavanderas.** Carlos Mérida (1891–1984) es el artista más famoso de Guatemala. Fue uno de los primeros en iniciar el movimiento del arte proindígena en las Américas y también formó parte del movimiento muralista de México. Con un(a) compañero(a) de clase, observen el siguiente cuadro y contesten las preguntas.

1. Mira el título del cuadro. ¿Hace cuántos años fue pintado?

2. ¿Cuántas lavanderas ves? ¿Qué hacen?

3. ¿Por qué lavan la ropa allí?

4. ¿Por qué crees que Carlos Mérida pintó esta escena?

5. ¿En qué cuarto de tu casa pondrías *(would you put)* este cuadro? ¿Por qué?

© Carlos Mérida 1928 painting: "Lavanderas" Colección Museo Nacional de Arte Moderno. Ministerio de Cultura y Deportes, Guatemala

Lavanderas (1928), Carlos Mérida

5-61 **Nuevos compañeros.** Tienes que buscar un(a) nuevo(a) compañero(a) para tu apartamento. ¿Qué tipo de persona buscas?

- Primero, prepara cinco preguntas sobre los aspectos más importantes para ti. Por ejemplo: **¿Con qué frecuencia limpias tu cuarto? ¿A qué hora te levantas por la mañana? ¿Fumas?** *(Do you smoke?)*

- Luego, circula por el salón de clase y haz *(ask)* tus preguntas a un mínimo de cinco personas.

- Por último, decide cuál es el (la) mejor compañero(a) para ti y explica por qué.

ii **5-62** **Mi rutina.** ¡Juega a las charadas con un(a) compañero(a) de clase! Estudiante A selecciona una situación y actúa *(acts out)* cinco actividades que normalmente hace. Estudiante B tiene que describir las acciones y luego identificar qué situación es.

Modelo   **Estudiante A:** *(pantomimes turning off alarm and getting up from bed)*
Estudiante B: Primero te levantas.
Estudiante A: *(pantomimes pouring cereal into a bowl and eating)*
Estudiante B: Después, desayunas. (etcétera)
Estudiante B: Es una típica mañana entre semana.
Estudiante A: ¡Correcto! / ¡No! Es...

Situaciones:

una típica mañana de sábado	una típica noche entre semana
una típica mañana entre semana	una típica noche de viernes

---

ii **5-63** **Se alquila.** Dramatiza esta situación con un(a) compañero(a) de clase.

Estudiante A

Situación: Quieres alquilar *(rent out)* tu cuarto / apartamento para el verano. Ahora *(Now)* estás hablando por teléfono con una persona que tiene interés en alquilarlo.

- Describe tu cuarto / apartamento.

- Incluye información sobre los muebles, el barrio, los vecinos, etcétera.

- Contesta las preguntas de una manera positiva y amable.

Estudiante B

Situación: Vas a tomar clases durante el verano y necesitas buscar casa. Ahora *(Now)* estás hablando por teléfono con una persona que quiere alquilar *(rent out)* su cuarto / apartamento.

- Empieza así: **Hola. Me llamo _____ y me interesa** *(I'm interested in)* **alquilar tu cuarto / apartamento. ¿Cómo es?**

- Haz *(Ask)* preguntas sobre las características del cuarto / apartamento, los muebles, el barrio, los vecinos, etcétera.

- Toma *(Make)* una decisión y explícala.

Pronunciación: La letra *g*

Colaborar Con un(a) compañero(a), lean estos refranes en voz alta *(aloud)* y relacionen cada uno con su equivalente en inglés. Presten atención *(Pay close attention)* a la pronunciación de la letra **g**.

_____ 1. Gato escaldado, de agua fría huye.

_____ 2. En el peligro, se conoce al amigo.

_____ 3. En la guerra y en el amor, todo es permitido.

_____ 4. Muchas manos hacen ligero el trabajo.

a. *A friend in need is a friend indeed.*

b. *Once bitten, twice shy.*

c. *Many hands make light work.*

d. *All is fair in love and war.*

VOCABULARIO

RECURSOS

Para aprender mejor
Label the rooms, the furniture, and the objects in your place of residence with sticky notes in Spanish.

Sustantivos

la alfombra *rug*
la aspiradora *vacuum*
la bañera *bathtub*
el barrio *neighborhood*
la basura *trash*
la cama *bed*
la cara *face*
el cartel *poster*
la chimenea *fireplace*
el clóset *closet*
la cocina *kitchen*
el comedor *dining room*
la cómoda *dresser*
el cuadro *(wall) picture*
el desastre *mess*
el desorden *untidyness*
los dientes *teeth*
el dormitorio *bedroom*
la ducha *shower*
la escalera *staircase*
el escritorio *desk*
el espejo *mirror*
el estante *shelf*
el estilo *style*
la estufa *stove*
el fregadero *kitchen sink*
la fuente *fountain*
la gaveta *drawer*
el horno *oven*
el inodoro *toilet*
el jardín *yard; garden*
la lámpara *lamp*
el lavamanos *bathroom sink*
el lavaplatos *dishwashing machine*
la llave *key*
las manos *hands*
la mesita (de noche) *nightstand*
el microondas *microwave oven*
los muebles *furniture*
el pasillo *hallway*

el patio *patio; courtyard*
el piso *floor; story*
la planta *plant*
el quehacer *chore*
el refrigerador *refrigerator*
el rincón *corner*
el ruido *noise*
la rutina diaria *daily routine*
la sala *living room*
el sillón *armchair*
el sofá *couch, sofa*
el (la) vecino(a) *neighbor*

Verbos

acostarse (ue) *to go to bed*
afeitarse *to shave*
arreglarse *to get oneself ready*
ayudar a *to help*
bañarse *to take a bath, to bathe*
barrer *to sweep*
buscar *to look for*
cenar *to have supper*
construir *to build*
desayunar *to have breakfast*
despertarse (ie) *to wake up*
divertirse (ie) *to have a good time*
dormirse (ue) *to fall asleep*
ducharse *to take a shower*
encontrar (ue) *to find*
enojarse *to get angry, to get mad*
guardar *to put away*
hacer la cama *to make the bed*
lavar los platos *to do the dishes*
lavarse *to wash oneself*
lavarse los dientes *to brush one's teeth*
levantarse *to get up*
maquillarse *to put on make-up*
mudarse *to move*
ordenar *to tidy up*
pasar la aspiradora *to vacuum*
peinarse *to comb one's hair*

planchar *to iron*
ponerse (+ adj.) *to get (+ adjective), to become*
ponerse (+ noun) *to put on (clothing, perfume, etc.)*
preocuparse (por) *to worry (about)*
quedarse *to stay*
regar (ie) *to water*
relajarse *to relax*
sacar *to take out*
sentirse (i) *to feel*
vestirse (i) *to get dressed*

Adjetivos

acogedor(a) *cozy*
antiguo(a) *very old*
colonial *colonial*
desordenado(a) *messy*
harto(a) *fed up*
limpio(a) *clean*
moderno(a) *modern*
nuevo(a) *new*
ordenado(a) *tidy*
seguro(a) *safe*
sucio(a) *dirty*
tranquilo(a) *quiet*

Expresiones útiles

Acabo de... *I have just . . .*
La verdad es que... *Actually, . . .*
rápido *quickly*
Todavía tengo que... *I still have to . . .*

Expressions of sequence, frequency, and time, p. 173
Complaints, p. 182
Direct object pronouns, p. 186
Welcoming a friend, p. 193
Expressions of location, p. 193
Expressions to talk about the past, p. 199

La buena comida

Conexiones a la comunidad
Eat at a restaurant with a Spanish-speaking staff and order a meal in Spanish. Try some new dishes and find out what ingredients are used in them.

In this chapter you will . . .
- explore El Salvador and Nicaragua
- talk about food, health, and nutrition
- order food at a restaurant
- talk about past events

- ask for and give advice
- make generalizations and state opinions
- learn about agricultural practices
- share information about your favorite restaurant

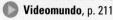

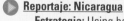

NUESTRO **MUNDO** 🌐
El Salvador y Nicaragua

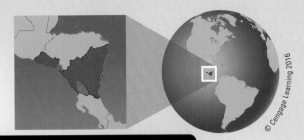

© Cengage Learning 2016

El Salvador es el país más pequeño de Centroamérica, y Nicaragua es el más grande.

República de El Salvador
Población: 6 200 000
Capital: San Salvador

Monedas: el dólar estadounidense y el colón
Exportaciones: café, azúcar *(sugar)*, textiles y ropa

República de Nicaragua
Población: 5 800 000
Capital: Managua

Moneda: el córdoba
Exportaciones: café, carne de res *(beef)*, oro *(gold)*

© John Mitchell/Alamy

En El Salvador, el segundo domingo de noviembre se celebra el "Día Nacional de las Pupusas". Las pupusas —el plato más típico salvadoreño— se preparan con harina de maíz *(corn flour)* y se sirven con curtido *(pickled cabbage slaw)*. Los restaurantes dedicados a preparar pupusas se llaman pupuserías. Donde existe una comunidad de salvadoreños fuera de El Salvador, existe una pupusería. ¿Hay una donde vives tú?

© Christian Kober/Robert Harding
World Imagery/Corbis

Demografía

El Salvador es el país más densamente poblado *(populated)* de América Latina. Es aproximadamente tan grande como Massachusetts y tiene más de 6 millones de habitantes. Más del 90% de la población es mestiza (combinación de indígena y europeo), y más del 60% vive en ciudades.

Geografía

Nicaragua es conocida *(known)* como la "tierra de lagos y volcanes". El lago de Nicaragua, o lago Cocibolca, es el lago más grande de Centroamérica. Tiene más de 400 isletas *(isles)* y varias islas *(islands)* como esta de la foto: la isla de Ometepe, formada por los volcanes Concepción y Maderas.

© Lizzie Shepherd/Getty Images

© Margie Politzer/Getty Images

Arte

En el archipiélago de Solentiname, en el lago de Nicaragua, hay pequeñas comunidades dedicadas al arte primitivista. Este movimiento artístico fue fundado *(founded)* por el poeta nicaragüense Ernesto Cardenal en 1968. Los artistas primitivistas de Solentiname pintan escenas de la vida diaria y de la espléndida flora y fauna de la región.

6-1 **¿Qué sabes?** Primero indica a qué país se refiere cada *(each)* oración: ¿El Salvador o Nicaragua? Luego contesta la pregunta.

1. Tiene más habitantes. ¿Cuántos más?

2. Tiene el lago más grande de Centroamérica. ¿Cómo se llama?

3. Tiene una comunidad importante de artistas primitivistas. ¿Quién la fundó *(established it)*?

4. Celebra el "Día Nacional de las Pupusas". ¿Qué son las pupusas?

5. Los clientes *(customers)* pagan en dólares o colones. ¿Dónde pagan en córdobas?

6. Tiene más isletas *(small isles)*. ¿Dónde están?

7. Exporta más carne *(meat)*. ¿Qué otros productos exporta?

6-2 **Videomundo.** Mira los videos de El Salvador y Nicaragua. Comenta con tus compañeros las actividades que pueden hacer si algún día visitan estos países.

Las comidas

In this *Paso*, you will . . .
- identify some foods and drinks
- use common expressions at the dinner table
- talk about past events

El desayuno

En Centroamérica, normalmente desayunamos...

café con leche

huevos

plátanos

arroz con frijoles

© 2/Alberto Coto/Ocean/Corbis

En España, por lo general, desayunamos...

mermelada

mantequilla

pan

© Digital Vision/Getty Images

En otros países, es común desayunar...

yogur

cereal

jugo (de naranja)

© mexrix/Shutterstock; © tacar/Shutterstock;
© Andrey_Kuzmin/Shutterstock

Pescado	*Fish*	**Verduras**	*Vegetables*
Mariscos	*Seafood*	el brócoli	*broccoli*
Carnes	*Meats*	las espinacas	*spinach*
el cerdo	*pork*	el maíz	*corn*
el pollo	*chicken*	la zanahoria	*carrot*
la tocineta	*bacon*	**Bebidas**	*Drinks*
Frutas	*Fruits*	la cerveza	*beer*
la banana	*banana*	el té	*tea*
las fresas	*strawberries*	el vino	*wine*
la manzana	*apple*		
la naranja	*orange*		
la piña	*pineapple*		
las uvas	*grapes*		

El almuerzo / La comida

la ensalada

las papas fritas

el bistec

La cena

la sopa de fideos

el sándwich

el queso

el jamón

el tomate

la lechuga

Otras comidas

las galletas

el helado

las tostaditas de maíz
(con salsa)

las empanadas

Condimentos	*Condiments*
el azúcar	*sugar*
la pimienta	*pepper*
la sal	*salt*

Comida rápida	*Fast food*
la hamburguesa	*hamburger*
el perro caliente	*hot dog*

Expresiones en la mesa	*Expressions at the table*
¡Buen provecho!	*Bon appetit!*
¿Me pasas (la sal), por favor?	*Could you please pass (the salt)?*
¡Qué rico(a)!	*It's really good!*
¿Quieres más sopa?	*Do you want more soup?*
No, gracias. Estoy satisfecho(a).	*No, thank you. I've had plenty / I'm full.*
Sí, gracias. Está deliciosa.	*Yes, thank you. It's delicious.*

¡Aplícalo!

6-3 **¿Cómo se llama?** Con un(a) compañero(a), lean las descripciones en voz alta e identifiquen las comidas.

1. Son frutas pequeñas y rojas (red). Se pueden comer en el cereal o con helado.

2. Viene de un animal pequeño. Lo comemos en el desayuno con tocineta.

3. Hay diferentes preparaciones: expreso, capuchino, moca.

4. Es el ingrediente principal de los sándwiches. También se come en el desayuno con mantequilla.

5. Es una bebida que viene de un animal. Se pone en el cereal.

6. Es un postre (dessert) muy frío. Hay de chocolate, fresa y vainilla.

7. Por lo general tiene lechuga, tomate y zanahorias. Se come fría.

8. Es comida rápida. Tiene pan y salchicha (sausage).

9. Son una verdura. Se pueden comer en ensalada. A Popeye le gustan mucho.

10. Son animales del mar. Muchos restaurantes en la costa los sirven.

6-4 **Ta-Te-Ti con comidas y bebidas.** Reta (Challenge) a un(a) compañero(a) a dos juegos de Ta-Te-Ti. Para poner X u O en un cuadrado (square), tienen que nombrar las comidas o bebidas indicadas. La persona con tres X o tres O en línea (in a row) ¡gana el juego!

tres bebidas	dos carnes	dos comidas rápidas		tres comidas para la merienda	dos condimentos	tres comidas para un picnic
cuatro comidas típicas para el desayuno	dos comidas del mar	tres postres (desserts)		dos ingredientes para una hamburguesa	tres ingredientes para una ensalada	dos ingredientes para un jugo de frutas
cuatro frutas	tres verduras	cuatro comidas para el almuerzo		dos productos de leche	tres ingredientes para un sándwich	tres comidas para un vegetariano

---

6-5 **Los menús.** ¡A ponerse sombreros (hats) de chef! Tú y tu compañero(a) necesitan crear menús para las siguientes personas y situaciones.

1. Su amigo Sam quiere adelgazar (lose weight). ¿Qué debe almorzar?

2. Es el aniversario de bodas de sus padres y van a dar una cena en su honor. ¿Qué van a servir?

3. Invitaron a su amiga Chantal a cenar y ella es vegetariana. ¿Qué van a preparar?

4. Trabajan en la cocina de un campamento de verano para chicos entre 8 y 10 años. ¿Qué van a preparar para la cena esta noche?

5. Su grupo estudiantil va a hacer un picnic este fin de semana. ¿Cuál es el menú?

6. Su clase va a celebrar el cumpleaños de su profesor(a) y Uds. van a traer las bebidas y la comida. ¿Qué van a traer?

Nota cultural

Meal times vary widely from country to country. In Central America, people usually eat lunch around noon and dinner around 7 p.m. However, in Spain and many Latin American countries, lunch—the main meal of the day—is eaten around 2 or 3 p.m., and dinner is eaten between 8 and 10 p.m. Table etiquette also differs from region to region. One thing that's true in all Spanish-speaking countries is that resting your hand on your lap while eating is considered rude.

¡Exprésate!

 6-6 **El desayuno.** ¿Cómo es tu desayuno típico? Con un(a) compañero(a), hagan lo siguiente:

- Primero, pregúntense *(ask each other)*: **¿Qué te gusta comer en el desayuno?**
- Luego, lean las descripciones de los desayunos en la página 212 y contesten la pregunta: **¿Qué les gusta desayunar a los centroamericanos?**
- Finalmente, comparen las respuestas usando un diagrama de Venn.

Modelo

6-7 **Mis preferencias.** ¿Qué comidas prefieres? ¿Y tu compañero(a)? Entrevístense *(Interview each other)* con estas preguntas.

1. ¿Por lo general qué almuerzas? ¿A qué hora almuerzas? ¿Dónde?
2. ¿Típicamente qué pides cuando vas a un restaurante de comida rápida? ¿Qué bebida pides?
3. ¿Cuál es tu verdura preferida? ¿Qué verdura no te gusta mucho?
4. ¿Qué bebidas tienes en el refrigerador? ¿Cuál es tu jugo preferido?
5. ¿Qué comes cuando estás enfermo(a)? ¿Y cuando tienes hambre a medianoche?
6. ¿Cuándo fue la última vez *(the last time)* que fuiste a un restaurante elegante? ¿Qué pediste?

Colaborar **6-8** **En la mesa.** Los señores Arias invitaron a Fernando a comer en su casa. Trabaja con un(a) compañero(a) de clase para crear pequeños diálogos para cada escena. Incluyan frases de **Expresiones en la mesa** de la página 213.

1.

2.

3.

Illustrations © Cengage Learning 2016

Los pronombres de complemento indirecto

NIÑOS	Abuelito, **¿nos** cuentas un chiste?
ABUELO	Claro, puedo contar**les** uno muy bueno. ¿Qué le dijo el azúcar a la leche?
NIÑOS	¿Qué?
ABUELO	"**Nos** vemos *(We'll meet up)* en el café".

■ ■ ■
Descúbrelo

- What do the children want?

- In the joke, to whom did the sugar speak? What are the two meanings of **café**?

- To whom does the pronoun **nos** refer? And **les**?

1. An indirect object **(complemento indirecto)** usually refers to a person and expresses *to whom* or *for whom* something is done. Indirect objects may be nouns *(to my guests)* or pronouns *(to me, for us)*.

> Siempre **les** sirvo flan **a mis invitados**.
> *I always serve **my guests** flan. / I always serve flan **to my guests**.*

Los pronombres de complemento indirecto			
me	*to / for me*	**nos**	*to / for us*
te	*to / for you (sing., inf.)*	**os**	*to / for you (pl., inf. in Spain)*
le	*to / for you (sing., form.)*	**les**	*to / for you (pl.; form. in Spain)*
le	*to / for him or her*	**les**	*to / for them*

2. To express phrases such as *to my guests* or *for my mother* in Spanish, you must include both the indirect object noun and its corresponding pronoun in the sentence.

   - **le**... **a** (+ singular noun / name): <u>**Le** doy una galleta **a Rosa**.</u>
   - **les**... **a** (+ plural noun / names): <u>**Les** doy refrescos **a los chicos**.</u>

3. Indirect object pronouns follow the same rules of placement as direct object pronouns.

   - In front of a single, conjugated verb: <u>**¿Nos** trae más pan?</u>
   - With verb phrases (conjugated verb + infinitive), before the conjugated verb or attached to the infinitive: <u>**¿Me** puede traer más café?</u> / <u>**¿Puede traerme** más café?</u>
   - With the present progressive tense, before the conjugated form of **estar** or attached to the end of the present participle with an added accent mark (-**ándo**-, -**iéndo**-): **El abuelo** <u>les</u> **está contando un chiste. / El abuelo está contándoles un chiste.**

4. The following verbs are commonly used with indirect objects.

contar (ue)	*to tell*	**hablar**	*to talk*	**prestar**	*to lend*
contestar	*to reply*	**mandar**	*to send*	**regalar**	*to give (as a gift)*
dar	*to give*	**mostrar (ue)**	*to show*	**servir (i)**	*to serve*
decir (i)	*to say*	**pedir (i)**	*to ask for*	**traer**	*to bring*
explicar	*to explain*	**preguntar**	*to ask*		

© Cengage Learning 2016

 6-9 ¿Qué les dices? Con un(a) compañero(a), lean las siguientes situaciones y contesten las preguntas.

Modelo Estás en la fiesta de cumpleaños de tu mejor amigo(a). ¿Qué le dices?
Estudiante A: Le digo "Feliz cumpleaños".
Estudiante B: Le digo "¡Muchas felicidades!"

1. Son las nueve de la mañana y entras en la clase de español. ¿Qué le dices al (a la) profesor(a)?

2. Yo te muestro una foto de mi nueva sobrina. ¿Qué me dices?

3. Un estudiante de intercambio *(exchange student)* acaba de llegar a tu casa. ¿Qué le dices al estudiante?

4. La fiesta formal se terminó y antes de irte *(leave)*, hablas con los anfitriones. ¿Qué les dices a los anfitriones?

5. Tus tíos van a hacer un crucero. Antes de salir, te llaman por teléfono. ¿Qué les dices a tus tíos?

6. Tu mejor amigo te cuenta que acaba de conocer a una chica fantástica. ¿Qué le dices a tu mejor amigo?

7. Estás en un restaurante y ves a dos profesores comiendo. ¿Qué les dices?

8. Tu abuela te llama y te pregunta cómo está el tiempo. ¿Qué le dices a tu abuela?

 6-10 La celebración. Aarón y Carina están haciendo los arreglos para una celebración. Con un(a) compañero(a), completen su conversación con los pronombres de complemento indirecto más lógicos. Después, lean la conversación en voz alta.

CARINA Vamos a ver si tenemos todo listo para la gran celebración del aniversario de nuestros abuelos. Ya (1. le / les) mandaste las invitaciones a todos los tíos y primos, ¿verdad?

AARÓN Sí, claro. Por lo visto *(Apparently)*, vamos a tener más de 50 invitados. Por cierto *(By the way)*, tengo buenas noticias *(news)*: Ayer hablé con el representante de la orquesta y él (2. le / nos) va a ofrecer un descuento.

CARINA ¡Magnífico! Ahora tenemos que finalizar el menú. ¿Qué (3. les / le) servimos a los invitados? El servicio de banquetes recomienda o bistec o salmón.

AARÓN Bueno, mi amiga Adriana conoce este servicio y (4. te / me) dice que el salmón es fabuloso.

CARINA Entonces pedimos el salmón. ¿Y el regalo? Cuando hablaste con mamá y papá, ¿qué (5. te / le) recomendaron?

AARÓN Mamá tuvo una idea fabulosa. Ya que *(Since)* a los abuelos (6. nos / les) gusta mucho conocer nuevos lugares, ¿por qué no (7. les / nos) regalamos un viaje?

CARINA ¡Fenomenal! Bueno, ahora voy a llamar a mamá. Quiero (8. contar(le / te) todas las noticias *(news)*.

Colaborar

6-11 **¿Cómo responden?** Trabajando con un(a) compañero(a), tomen turnos para indicar sus respuestas a las situaciones.

Modelo   Una noche llegas a casa muy tarde. ¿Qué te dicen tus padres?

Estudiante A: **Me** dicen: "¿Estás loco(a)? ¡Son casi las tres de la madrugada!" Y a ti, ¿qué **te** dicen tus padres?

Estudiante B: **Me** preguntan: "¿Lo pasaste muy bien?"

1. Una noche está lloviendo mucho y tienes un pequeño accidente con el auto. ¿Qué te dicen tus padres?

2. Un día ves a tu novio(a) con otra(o) chica(o) en un café. ¿Qué le dices a tu novio(a)?

3. Tus compañeros(as) de cuarto son buena gente pero no son muy responsables. Un día te piden dinero para comprar gasolina. ¿Qué les dices?

4. Quieres estudiar en España en el verano y les pides dinero a tus abuelos. ¿Qué te dicen tus abuelos?

6-12 **La invitación.** Rolando y Alicia invitaron a sus amigos a cenar en casa. Con un(a) compañero(a), dramaticen una pequeña conversación para cada escena. Necesitan incluir por lo menos *(at least)* un pronombre de complemento indirecto en cada diálogo: **me**, **te**, **le**, **nos**, **les**.

Verbos útiles: dar, pasar, preparar, servir

Illustrations © Cengage
Learning 2016

1.   2.   3.

6-13 **¿Qué haces?** ¿Qué haces en estas situaciones? Con un(a) compañero(a), lean los escenarios y contesten las preguntas. Comparen sus respuestas.

Modelo   El cumpleaños de tu novio(a) es la próxima semana. Quieres gastar *(spend)* $35 para su regalo. ¿Qué vas a comprar**le**?
Estudiante A: Voy a comprar**le** unas flores. ¿Y tú?
Estudiante B: Voy a dar**le** una tarjeta de regalo.

1. El aniversario de bodas de tus abuelos es el próximo mes. ¿Qué regalo vas a dar**les**?

2. Varios amigos van a tu cuarto / apartamento el próximo sábado para mirar partidos de fútbol americano. ¿Qué vas a servir**les** de comer y de beber?

3. A tu sobrino(a) de cuatro años le gusta mucho escuchar un cuento antes de acostarse. ¿Qué libro o cuento vas a leer**le**?

4. Tu mejor amigo(a) está enfermo(a) y no tiene mucho apetito. ¿Qué comida **le** vas a preparar?

5. Tu hermano y su esposa acaban de comprar una nueva casa. ¿Qué vas a comprar**les** para su fiesta de inauguración de casa *(housewarming)*?

G PASO 1 GRAMÁTICA B

El pretérito de los verbos irregulares

SRA. ALFARO ¿Estás comiendo bien en la uni, hija?

LUISA Sí, mamá, mi dieta es muy balanceada. Anteayer fuimos a KFC para comer pollo frito. Anoche una amiga vino a visitarnos y trajo una pizza de Domino's. Y hoy vamos a McDonald's para comer hamburguesas.

SRA. ALFARO ¡Ay, hija! ¿Comes solamente *(only)* comida rápida?

■ ■ ■
Descúbrelo

■ Why does Luisa think that she eats balanced meals?

■ Which three of these verbs refer to the past? **es, fuimos, vino, trajo, vamos**

■ Which past verb forms correspond to **ir, venir, traer**?

1. Many common verbs are irregular in the preterite, but a number of these do follow a pattern. One group of verbs has irregular stems (i.e., the front part of the verb) and shares the following set of endings.

El pretérito: primer grupo de verbos irregulares			
yo	-e	nosotros(as)	-imos
tú	-iste	vosotros(as)	-isteis
Ud./él/ella	-o	Uds./ellos/ellas	-ieron

estar *to be*	**estuv-**	estuve, estuviste, estuvo, estuvimos, estuvisteis, estuvieron
poder *to be able to*	**pud-**	pude, pudiste, pudo, pudimos, pudisteis, pudieron
poner *to put*	**pus-**	puse, pusiste, puso, pusimos, pusisteis, pusieron
saber *to know*	**sup-**	supe, supiste, supo, supimos, supisteis, supieron
tener *to have*	**tuv-**	tuve, tuviste, tuvo, tuvimos, tuvisteis, tuvieron
hacer *to do, to make*	**hic-**	hice, hiciste, hizo, hicimos, hicisteis, hicieron
querer *to want*	**quis-**	quise, quisiste, quiso, quisimos, quisisteis, quisieron
venir *to come*	**vin-**	vine, viniste, vino, vinimos, vinisteis, vinieron

2. Some verbs have irregular stems that always include the letter **j**. This group uses the same set of endings as the previous one, except for the **Uds./ellos/ellas** form: **-eron**.

conducir *to drive*	**conduj-**	conduje, condujiste, condujo, condujimos, condujisteis, conduj<u>eron</u>
decir *to say, to tell*	**dij-**	dije, dijiste, dijo, dijimos, dijisteis, dij<u>eron</u>
traer *to bring*	**traj-**	traje, trajiste, trajo, trajimos, trajisteis, traj<u>eron</u>

3. These four verbs have different endings from the ones previously mentioned.

dar *to give*	di, diste, dio, dimos, disteis, dieron
ver *to see*	vi, viste, vio, vimos, visteis, vieron
ser *to be*	fui, fuiste, fue, fuimos, fuisteis, fueron
ir *to go*	fui, fuiste, fue, fuimos, fuisteis, fueron

4. The preterite equivalent of **hay** is **hubo** *(there was / were)*. It is used to say that a one-time event took place: **Hubo una fiesta anoche.**

5. Some verbs have slightly different translations when they are used in the preterite.

saber *found out*	**querer** *tried to*
conocer *made one's acquaintance*	**no querer** *refused to*
poder *managed to*	

 **¡Aplícalo!**

 Colaborar

6-14 **Crucigrama.** ¿Qué hicieron todos el fin de semana pasado? Con un(a) compañero(a), completen el crucigrama con los verbos más lógicos en el pretérito.

Horizontal

3. Yo no p___ ir a la fiesta.
6. Nosotros t___ que trabajar.
8. Ingrid h_____ un viaje a la costa.
9. Yo c_____ mi auto por horas.
12. Paco y yo v_____ una película.

Vertical

1. Juan t___ cerveza a la celebración.
2. Elena f___ a un club para bailar.
4. Rita y Carmen e___ enfermas.
5. Yo no q___ hacer nada.
7. Todos mis tíos v___ a mi fiesta.
10. Los chicos d___ la verdad *(truth)*.
11. Mi amigo me d___ un regalo.

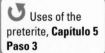 Uses of the preterite, **Capítulo 5 Paso 3**

 6-15 **La última vez.** ¿Cuándo fue la última vez *(the last time)* que hiciste estas cosas? Compara tus respuestas con las de un(a) compañero(a).

Modelo poner la mesa

    Estudiante A: ¿Cuándo fue la última vez que pusiste la mesa?

    Estudiante B: Puse la mesa ayer. ¿Y tú?

1. dar un paseo por un parque nacional
2. ver una película con subtítulos
3. tener que levantarse antes de las seis
4. traer tu computadora a la clase
5. darle un regalo a alguien
6. saber sobre un crimen

¡Exprésate!

Clase

6-16 **¿Lo hiciste tú?** Circula por el salón para hacerles preguntas en el pretérito a tus compañeros de clase. Si tu compañero(a) contesta "Sí", tiene que firmar *(sign)* y tú tienes que obtener más información. Si contesta "No", tienes que hacerle la pregunta a una persona diferente.

Modelo **Estudiante A:** ¿Viniste tarde a clase la semana pasada?
Estudiante B: ¡Sí! Vine un poco tarde.
Estudiante A: Firma *(Sign)* aquí, por favor. ¿Por qué viniste tarde?
Estudiante B: Me desperté tarde. (Y apuntas la información.)

Actividad	Persona	Más información
venir tarde a clase la semana pasada		¿Por qué?
conducir más de 300 millas en un viaje reciente		¿Adónde fuiste?
tener que ir al cajero automático hoy		¿Cuánto dinero sacaste?
estar enfermo(a) la semana pasada		¿Tuviste que ir a la clínica?
ver todas las películas de *Harry Potter*		¿Cuál te gustó más?
poder terminar toda la tarea anoche		¿A qué hora terminaste?

6-17 **Nuestras experiencias.** Con un(a) compañero(a), entrevístense con estas preguntas. Inventen otras preguntas para continuar la conversación.

1. **Ayer:** ¿Estuviste muy ocupado(a) ayer? ¿Pudiste hacer todas las cosas en tu agenda? ¿Qué tareas *(tasks)* no hiciste? (Haz una pregunta original.)

2. **Un viaje:** ¿Hiciste una excursión o un viaje el año pasado? ¿Adónde fuiste? ¿Condujiste tu auto a este lugar o tomaste un avión? ¿Cuántos días te quedaste allí? (Haz una pregunta original.)

3. **En clase:** ¿En cuál de tus clases diste una presentación la semana pasada? ¿Qué te dijo tu profesor(a) cuando terminaste? ¿Viste una película en alguna de tus clases? ¿Fue interesante? (Haz una pregunta original.)

Colaborar

6-18 **La fiesta de Gloria.** Con un(a) compañero(a), digan qué hicieron todos *(what everyone did)* en la fiesta de Gloria. Formen oraciones completas en el pretérito.

© Cengage Learning 2016

El restaurante

In this *Paso*, you will . . .
- order food at a restaurant and comment on food
- identify place settings
- talk more about past actions

El menú

Restaurante La Orquídea
Menú

Platos principales

Servidos con pan y una ensalada pequeña

Camarones empanizados
Breaded shrimp

Paella valenciana
Saffron rice dish with chicken and seafood

Churrasco a la plancha
Grilled thick-cut steak

Chuletas de cerdo
Pork chops

Espaguetis con albóndigas
Spaghetti with meatballs

Arroz con pollo
Rice dish with chicken

También le ofrecemos:

Ceviche
Raw fish marinated in lime juice

Yuca frita
Fried cassava

Tostones
Fried plantains

Postres

Flan de coco
Coconut custard

Tres leches
Cake soaked in cream

Arroz con leche
Rice pudding

Guayaba en almíbar
Guava in syrup

Bebidas

Agua mineral, limonada, refrescos, café, té

© Cengage Learning 2016. Photo: © freya-photographer/Shutterstock

---

Frases de un(a) mesero(a) / camarero(a)

¿Una mesa para cuántos?
¿Qué les traigo para beber / tomar?
¿Están listos para pedir?
Les recomiendo...
¿Quieren postre? ¿Quieren un café?
¿(Desean) Algo más?
Sí, enseguida.

Frases de un(a) cliente(a)

Al llegar a un restaurante

¿Tienen una mesa cerca de la ventana?
¿Nos trae el menú, por favor?

Preguntas sobre el menú

¿Qué nos recomienda?
¿Cuál es el plato del día?
¿Cuál es la especialidad de la casa?
¿Con qué está acompañado?

Waiter's / Waitress's phrases

A table for how many?
What can I get you to drink?
Are you ready to order?
I recommend (to you, pl.) . . .
Do you want any dessert? Do you want coffee?
Is there anything else (you want)?
Yes, right away.

Customer's Phrases

Upon arrival

Do you have a table near the window?
Can you bring us the menu, please?

Questions about the menu

What do you recommend?
What's today's special?
What's the house's specialty?
What does it come with?

En un restaurante típico

¿Están listos para pedir?

Quisiera probar el plato del día.

Para mí, la paella.

© Minerva Studio/Shutterstock

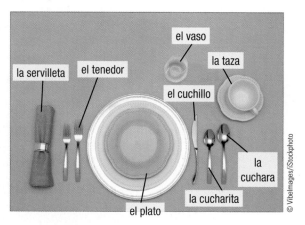

la servilleta
el tenedor
el vaso
la taza
el cuchillo
la cuchara
la cucharita
el plato

© Vibelmages/iStockphoto

¿Qué nos recomienda?

El churrasco está muy bueno.

© Minerva Studio/Shutterstock

Más preguntas sobre el menú	*More questions about the menu*
¿Me puede explicar qué es (el ceviche)?	*Can you explain what (ceviche) is?*
¿Es dulce?	*Is it sweet?*
¿Es picante?	*Is it spicy / hot?*
¿Tienen refrescos dietéticos?	*Do you have diet soda?*

Al pedir	*Ordering*
Quisiera probar (el plato del día).	*I'd like to try (today's special).*
Para mí, (la paella).	*I'll have (the paella).*
Un (agua mineral) sin hielo.	*Some (mineral water) with no ice.*

Al comer	*While eating*
El pescado está muy fresco / bueno.	*The fish is very fresh / good.*
¿Me puede traer (otra servilleta)?	*Can you bring me (another napkin)?*
¿Nos puede traer más (pan)?	*Can you bring us some more (bread)?*

Al terminar	*After eating*
Todo estuvo delicioso, gracias.	*Everything was delicious, thank you.*
La cuenta, por favor.	*The bill, please.*
¿Está incluida la propina en la cuenta?	*Is the tip included in the bill?*

PASO 2 VOCABULARIO

¡Aplícalo!

Colaborar

6-19 **¡Qué mesero más amable!** Estás comiendo con algunos amigos en un restaurante. ¿Cómo responde el mesero a tus preguntas y comentarios? Con un(a) compañero(a), relacionen las dos columnas de una manera lógica.

Tú

_____ 1. ¿Tienen una mesa para cuatro?

_____ 2. ¿Nos trae el menú, por favor?

_____ 3. ¿Qué nos recomienda?

_____ 4. ¿Me puede explicar qué es la paella?

_____ 5. ¿Nos puede traer más hielo?

_____ 6. ¿Está incluida la propina en la cuenta?

El mesero

a. El pescado está muy fresco hoy.

b. Sí, aquí lo tienen.

c. Sí, el 10%.

d. Es un plato de arroz con mariscos y pollo.

e. ¿Les gusta esta en el rincón?

f. Enseguida. ¿Quieren más agua también?

Colaborar

6-20 **En la mesa.** ¿Qué necesitas para comer estas comidas? Con un(a) compañero(a) de clase, completen las oraciones con las palabras más lógicas.

1. Para comer el churrasco a la plancha, necesito un _____ y un _____.

2. Para beber una limonada, necesito un _____.

3. Para beber el café, necesito una _____.

4. ¿Una sopa de pollo? Necesito una _____ para comerla.

5. Los camarones y el brócoli se sirven en un _____.

↻ The verb **gustar, Capítulo 3 Paso 3**

6-21 **¡Qué rico!** Tú y tu compañero(a) están en el restaurante La Orquídea. ¿Qué platos quieren Uds. probar? Usen la información de cada foto para preparar seis breves conversaciones. Sigan el modelo.

Modelo **Estudiante A:** (*Menciona el plato en la foto.*)
¿Quieres probar **la paella**?

Estudiante B: (*Explica su preferencia con* **gustar** *y la expresión debajo de la foto.*)
Sí. Me gustan mucho los platos con arroz. / No. No me gustan mucho los platos con arroz.

los platos con arroz

1. los mariscos

2. los platos italianos

3. la carne

4. el coco

5. los dulces

6. el pescado

Nota cultural

In Spanish-speaking countries, eating out is often a leisurely social occasion. People take their time selecting and enjoying the meal; afterwards, they linger in unhurried conversation, a custom known as **la sobremesa**. To avoid rushing their customers, waiters generally don't bring the check until requested.

¡Exprésate!

6-22 Nuestro mesero. Tú y tu compañero(a) piensan ir a El Salvador y quieren practicar algunas frases útiles en restaurantes. ¿Cómo pueden responder a las preguntas y los comentarios del mesero? Cada persona debe dar una respuesta diferente.

Modelo   ¿Les gusta esta mesa?
        Estudiante A: No, preferimos una mesa cerca de la ventana.
        Estudiante B: Sí, está bien.

¿Quieren una mesa en el patio?

¿Cómo quieren el café?

¿Están listos para pedir?

Las pupusas son nuestra especialidad.

¿Qué les traigo para beber?

¿Les gustó el churrasco?

¿Quieren un postre?

¿Desean algo más?

© Viktor Gladkov/Shutterstock

6-23 Unas recomendaciones. Varios clientes están en el restaurante La Orquídea. ¿Qué deben pedir? Lee las situaciones y escoge el mejor plato del menú en la página 222 para cada persona. Trabaja con un(a) compañero(a) de clase y compartan sus ideas.

1. A Gloria y a Emilio les gustan los mariscos. ¿Qué plato deben pedir?
2. A Rita le gustan mucho los postres, pero tiene alergia a la leche. ¿Qué postre le recomiendas?
3. Ricardo y Alicia prefieren un postre con frutas. ¿Cuál es el mejor postre para ellos?
4. Miguel prefiere los platos principales con arroz. ¿Cuáles de los platos le van a gustar más?
5. Javier prefiere empezar su comida con algo para picotear *(to munch on)*. ¿Qué le recomiendas?

6-24 En el restaurante. ¿Qué dicen el mesero y los clientes en estas situaciones? En grupos de tres, inventen diálogos lógicos.

¿cuenta?   ¿propina?

1.

2.

Illustrations © Cengage Learning 2016

3.

PASO 2 GRAMÁTICA A **G**

Los verbos con cambios de raíz en el pretérito

OLGA ¿Se divirtieron Uds. anoche en El Bodegón?

LINA No mucho. Jorge se sintió muy mal después de comer. Regresamos a casa enseguida y él se durmió en el sofá.

OLGA ¡Pobrecito! ¿Está mejor hoy?

LINA Sí, mucho mejor pero no quiere volver a ese restaurante.

■ ■ ■
Descúbrelo

- Why didn't Jorge and Lina have much fun last night?
- Where did Jorge fall asleep?
- What happened to the **e** in s**e**ntirse when it was conjugated in the preterite?
- What happened to the **o** in d**o**rmir when it was conjugated in the preterite?

1. A number of **-ir** verbs have stem changes when they are conjugated in the preterite. One group of verbs changes **e** to **i**; this change takes place only in the verb forms that correspond to the subjects **Ud./él/ella** and **Uds./ellos/ellas**.

Cambio en el pretérito e → i			
pedir *to ask for, to order*			
yo	pedí	nosotros(as)	pedimos
tú	pediste	vosotros(as)	pedisteis
Ud./él/ella	p**i**dió	Uds./ellos/ellas	p**i**dieron

Algunos verbos con el cambio e → i	
cons**e**guir *to get, to obtain*	rep**e**tir *to repeat*
desp**e**dirse *to say good-bye*	s**e**guir *to follow*
div**e**rtirse *to have fun*	s**e**ntirse *to feel*
p**e**dir *to ask for, to order*	s**e**rvir *to serve*
pref**e**rir *to prefer*	v**e**stirse *to get dressed*

2. Two common **-ir** verbs change **o** to **u** when conjugated in the preterite: **dormir** and **morir**. This change takes place only in the verb forms that correspond to the subjects **Ud./él/ella** and **Uds./ellos/ellas**.

Cambio en el pretérito o → u		
	dormir *to sleep*	**morir** *to die*
yo	dormí	morí
tú	dormiste	moriste
Ud./él/ella	d**u**rmió	m**u**rió
nosotros(as)	dormimos	morimos
vosotros(as)	dormisteis	moristeis
Uds./ellos/ellas	d**u**rmieron	m**u**rieron

© Cengage Learning 2016

3. Many **-ar** and **-er** verbs have stem changes in the present tense, but none of them have stem changes in the preterite. On the other hand, if an **-ir** verb has a stem change in the present, it will also have a stem change in the preterite. The kind of stem change may be different, and the stem changes take place with different subjects.

Presente (all subjects except **nosotros** and **vosotros**)	**Pretérito** (only with the subjects **Ud./él/ella** and **Uds./ellos/ellas**)
e → ie: Lisa **se divierte.**	e → i: Lisa **se divirtió.**
e → i: **Me visto** rápidamente.	e → i: **Me vestí** rápidamente.
o → ue: Los niños **duermen** bien.	o → u: Los niños **durmieron** bien.

6-25 En corto. Trabajando con un(a) compañero(a), completen las oraciones con el pretérito de los verbos. Después, lean las breves conversaciones en voz alta.

Colaborar

¡Aplícalo!

1. La fiesta

CARLOS   ¿(Divertirse) _____ Uds. mucho en la fiesta?

VANESA   ¡Muchísimo! Nosotros no (despedirse) _____ hasta las tres de la madrugada.

2. La cita *(date)*

PAULA   ¿(Divertirse) _____ mucho tu hija en su cita con Ricardo?

ANA   Creo que sí. Ricardo (conseguir) _____ boletos para el ballet, así que los dos (vestirse) _____ muy elegantemente. ¡Qué chicos más guapos!

3. Una triste noticia *(news)*

JOSÉ LUIS   ¿Es verdad que (morir) _____ el Sr. González?

PACO   Sí, es verdad. Después de cenar (sentirse) _____ un poco enfermo. El pobre *(The poor thing)* (dormirse) _____ en su sillón favorito y nunca se despertó.

6-26 Ayer. Mira las fotos y contesta las preguntas. Luego compara tus respuestas con las de un(a) compañero(a) de clase.

Colaborar

1. ¿Durmió bien anoche Marcos? ¿Y tú? ¿Dormiste bien anoche?

2. ¿Qué pidió Margarita ayer en el restaurante de comida rápida? ¿Y tú? La última vez que comiste en un restaurante de comida rápida, ¿qué pediste?

3. ¿Cómo se sintieron Jaime y Raquel anoche después de ver la película? ¿Y tú? ¿Cómo te sentiste la última vez que viste una película?

Colaborar

6-27 **El mesero despistado.** Anoche, ¡todos los clientes del restaurante Cero se quejaron *(complained)* del nuevo mesero! ¿Qué pasó? Con un(a) compañero(a) de clase, digan qué pidieron los clientes y qué les sirvió el mesero. Sigan el modelo y usen el pretérito de los verbos **pedir** y **servir**.

Modelo

un niño
Un niño **pidió** helado, pero el mesero le **sirvió** pastel.

1. nosotros   2. tú   3. la señora Chamorro   4. los señores Romero

---

Colaborar

6-28 **Una cita a ciegas.** El sábado pasado, Alba estuvo en una cita a ciegas *(blind date)* con Roberto. ¿Qué hizo Roberto esa noche?

- Con un(a) compañero(a), combinen palabras de cada columna para crear cinco oraciones. Describan las acciones de Roberto en orden cronológico.
- En todas las oraciones es necesario conjugar el verbo en el pretérito.

Después	**vestirse** rápido y...	"soy doctor"
Por último	**llegar** tarde al restaurante y...	no **ponerse** desodorante
Luego	**repetir** tres veces:	**dormirse** durante la película
Primero	la **llevar** al cine y...	ella **tener** que pagar *(pay)*
Durante la cena	**preferir** tomar un taxi pero...	no le **pedir** una disculpa *(didn't apologize)*

6-29 **Ta-Te-Ti con el pretérito.** Juega al Ta-Te-Ti con un(a) compañero(a) de clase. Antes de poner tu X u O, tienes que formar una oración completa (¡y correcta!) con el verbo en el pretérito. Por ejemplo: El mesero **sirvió** el postre.

Frases útiles

Te toca a ti. *It's your turn.*
Me toca a mí. *It's my turn.*
Correcto. *That's right.*
No, el verbo correcto es... *No, the right verb is . . .*
Ganaste tú. / Gané yo. *You won. / I won.*
Empatamos. *It's a tie.*

servir	pedir	divertirse
vestirse	dormir	repetir
preferir	morir	sentirse

Resumen del pretérito

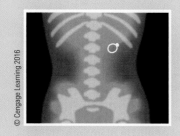

GERARDO ¡Anoche fue un fiasco! Llegué al restaurante temprano, a las siete. Le di el anillo de compromiso *(engagement ring)* al mesero y él lo puso en el flan. La cena estuvo deliciosa. Comimos y hablamos por una hora. Finalmente, el mesero trajo el postre ¡y Vicki se comió todo el flan! ¡No sintió el anillo!

1. The preterite is used in these ways:

- To express what happened on a particular occasion: **Conocimos Managua ayer / la semana pasada / en 2010 / hace dos años.**

- To say how long an action or event lasted: **Estudié por varios minutos / por una semana / por muchos años.**

- To tell how many times an action or event took place: **Fuimos al nuevo restaurante una vez / dos veces / varias veces.**

- To sum up an experience: **Ayer fue un día maravilloso.**

2. Regular verbs have the following endings in the preterite.

	lavar *to wash*	**comer** *to eat*	**vivir** *to live*
yo	lav**é**	com**í**	viv**í**
tú	lav**aste**	com**iste**	viv**iste**
Ud./él/ella	lav**ó**	com**ió**	viv**ió**
nosotros(as)	lav**amos**	com**imos**	viv**imos**
vosotros(as)	lav**asteis**	com**isteis**	viv**isteis**
Uds./ellos/ellas	lav**aron**	com**ieron**	viv**ieron**

El pretérito de los verbos regulares

3. Verbs ending in **-car**, **-gar**, and **-zar** change spelling in the **yo** form only.

-zar → -cé (almorcé, empecé, organicé, etc.)

-car → -qué (busqué, saqué, toqué, etc.)

-gar → -gué (jugué, llegué, pagué, etc.)

4. The stem changes (**e → i** and **o → u**) occur only with certain **-ir** verbs and only with the subjects **Ud., él, ella, Uds., ellos,** and **ellas.**

Common **e → i** verbs: cons**e**guir, div**e**rtirse, p**e**dir, rep**e**tir, s**e**rvir, v**e**stirse

Common **o → u** verbs: d**o**rmir, m**o**rir

5. The following verbs are irregular in the preterite: **conducir, dar, decir, estar, hacer, ir, poder, poner, querer, saber, ser, tener, traer,** and **venir.**

Descúbrelo

- What happened to the engagement ring?

- In what tense are all the verbs? When exactly did the events occur?

- Which of these verbs are regular? Stem-changing? Irregular? Have a spelling change in the **yo** form? **fue, llegué, di, puso, estuvo, comimos, hablamos, trajo, comió, sintió**

¡Aplícalo! Colaborar **6-30** **Noticias.** Con un(a) compañero(a), completen la página de Noticias *(News)* de una red social. Deben escoger los verbos más lógicos entre paréntesis y conjugarlos en el pretérito.

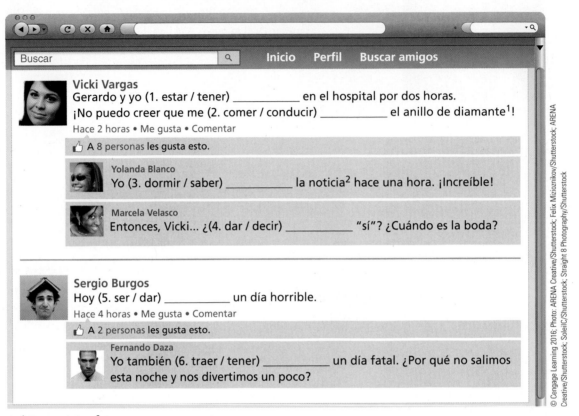

Vicki Vargas
Gerardo y yo (1. estar / tener) _____ en el hospital por dos horas.
¡No puedo creer que me (2. comer / conducir) _____ el anillo de diamante[1]!
Hace 2 horas • Me gusta • Comentar

👍 A 8 personas les gusta esto.

Yolanda Blanco
Yo (3. dormir / saber) _____ la noticia[2] hace una hora. ¡Increíble!

Marcela Velasco
Entonces, Vicki... ¿(4. dar / decir) _____ "sí"? ¿Cuándo es la boda?

Sergio Burgos
Hoy (5. ser / dar) _____ un día horrible.
Hace 4 horas • Me gusta • Comentar

👍 A 2 personas les gusta esto.

Fernando Daza
Yo también (6. traer / tener) _____ un día fatal. ¿Por qué no salimos esta noche y nos divertimos un poco?

[1]*diamond ring* [2]*news*

 6-31 **Pupusería Nana.** Lee el siguiente artículo y completa las cinco preguntas en el pretérito. Luego hazle las preguntas *(ask your questions)* a un(a) compañero(a).

Modelo   Estudiante A: ¿Cuándo **vino Ernesto Molina a Chicago**?
              Estudiante B: Vino hace...

Pupusería Nana

Hace diez años el señor Ernesto Molina se despidió de su familia en Morazán, El Salvador, vino a Chicago y abrió un restaurante pequeño. Lo llamó "Pupusería Nana" y ayer celebró un millón de pupusas servidas. Las pupusas —plato típico de El Salvador— fueron hechas por muchos años con harina *(flour)* de maíz pero hoy también hay pupusas de arroz. "Mi abuelo fue pupusero y yo, bueno, seguí la tradición de la familia" dijo Ernesto ayer, en medio de muchos clientes satisfechos *(satisfied)*, música alegre y, claro, platos de pupusas.

1. ¿Cuándo (venir)... ?   3. ¿Cómo (llamar)... ?   5. ¿Por qué (celebrar)... ?

2. ¿Qué (abrir)... ?   4. ¿Quién (ser)... ?

Clase

6-32 Cinco cosas. Vamos a ver cuántas personas hicieron las mismas (*same*) actividades ayer.

- Primero, escribe en un papel cinco cosas que hiciste ayer. Por ejemplo: **Tomé un examen difícil. Fui al cine.** Etcétera.

- Luego, circula por el salón de clase y hazles preguntas (*ask questions*) a tus compañeros. Por ejemplo: **¿Tomaste un examen difícil ayer? ¿Fuiste al cine?**

- Si un(a) compañero(a) hizo la actividad, escribe su nombre en tu papel. ¿Cuántas personas hicieron las cosas que tú hiciste?

6-33 Un día horrible. Con tres o cuatro compañeros, formen un círculo y hagan una descripción de "Un día horrible".

- Estudiante A empieza así: **Ayer fue un día horrible.**

- Estudiante B agrega (*adds*) otra oración. Por ejemplo: **Llegué tarde a clase.**

- Estudiante C agrega otra. Por ejemplo: **Saqué una nota mala en inglés.**

- Continúen así hasta que den la vuelta (*until you go around*) dos veces.

6-34 Mi viaje a Nicaragua. Tú y tus amigos fueron a Nicaragua. Aquí tienen las fotos que sacaron. Para cada foto, di (*say*) adónde fueron y qué hicieron. Tu compañero(a) tiene que reaccionar y hacerte dos preguntas adicionales.

Modelo   **Estudiante A:** Esta foto la tomé en Montelimar. Estuvimos en la playa tres días. Comimos pescado fresco todos los días.

            Estudiante B: ¡Qué divertido! ¿Hicieron surf? ¿Montaron a caballo?

Las fotos de Estudiante A:

Las fotos de Estudiante B:

6-35 ¿A qué restaurante fuiste? Conversa con tu compañero(a) de clase sobre la última vez (*the last time*) que fueron a un restaurante. Deben mencionar:

- a qué restaurante fueron
- con quiénes fueron
- cuándo fueron
- qué pidieron
- cómo estuvo la comida
- cuánto costó

Salud y nutrición

In this *Paso*, you will . . .

- talk about health and nutrition
- ask for and give advice
- make generalizations and express opinions

La rueda de los alimentos

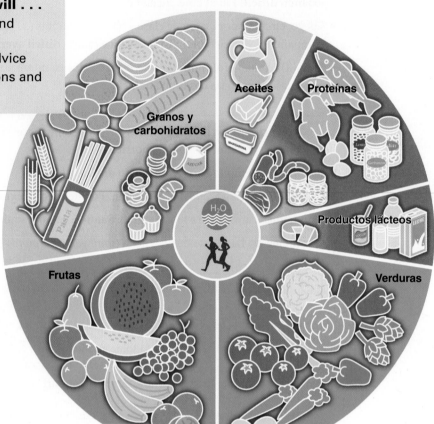

Granos y carbohidratos

Aceites

Proteínas

H₂O

Productos lácteos

Frutas

Verduras

Recomendaciones:

- ◆ Consumir principalmente frutas y verduras
- ◆ Consumir carbohidratos ricos en fibra con regularidad
- ◆ Consumir azúcares y grasas en moderación

Para hablar de un estilo de vida saludable	To talk about healthy lifestyles
Según la rueda de los alimentos, hay que...	According to the food wheel, one must . . .
comer una variedad de alimentos	eat a variety of foods
consumir muchas frutas y verduras	eat a lot of fruits and vegetables
evitar las grasas	avoid fats
También se debe...	One should also . . .
beber suficiente agua	drink plenty of water
hacer ejercicio	exercise

Hábitos malos	Bad habits
comer comida basura	to eat junk food
consumir bebidas alcohólicas en exceso	to drink alcoholic beverages in excess
fumar	to smoke
llevar una vida sedentaria	to lead a sedentary life
saltar el desayuno	to skip breakfast

Hábitos sanos

hacer ejercicio

llevar una dieta balanceada

evitar el exceso de sal

dormir suficientes horas

Pedir consejos sobre la salud y la nutrición

Quiero / Necesito...
   adelgazar
   aumentar de peso
   ponerme en forma
¿Qué debo hacer?

Dar consejos

Debes / Necesitas...
   consultar con tu médico(a) / entrenador(a)
Tienes que...
   cambiar tu dieta
   tu estilo de vida

Asking for health and nutrition advice

I want / need to . . .
   lose weight
   gain some weight
   get in shape
What should I do?

Giving advice

You should / need to . . .
   consult your doctor / trainer
You have to . . .
   change your diet
   your lifestyle

¡Aplícalo!

Colaborar

6-36 **Un programa de radio.** ¿De qué hablaron en el programa de radio Vida Sana? Con un(a) compañero(a), escojan las palabras más lógicas.

PRESENTADORA Hoy tenemos de invitada a la nutricionista Maritza Pérez; ella nos va a dar (1. consejos / estilos) sobre la salud y la (2. forma / nutrición). A ver, ¿quién llama y cuál es su problema?

ARMANDO Hola. Me llamo Armando, tengo veinte años y soy muy delgado. (3. Quiero / Hay) aumentar de (4. hábito / peso). ¿Qué debo hacer?

MARITZA Para aumentar —o (5. bajar / evitar)— de peso, hay que hacerlo de forma (6. saltar / saludable). Comer muchas papas fritas no es la solución. (7. Según / Se debe) llevar siempre una dieta (8. balanceada / alimento). Mi consejo para Armando es: empezar el día con huevos, yogur y un jugo de frutas.

GLORIA Hola. Me llamo Gloria. En mi trabajo estoy enfrente de la computadora nueve horas cada día. No tengo tiempo para ir al gimnasio.

MARITZA Gloria, llevas una (9. vida / entrenadora) sedentaria y eso no es saludable. (10. Debes / Consultas) hacer ejercicio con regularidad. Mi consejo: ir al trabajo en bicicleta.

Colaborar

6-37 **Hábitos sanos y hábitos malos.** Con un(a) compañero(a), relacionen *(match)* cada oración con un hábito de la lista.

_____ 1. Todos los días Miriam se levanta a las siete, se arregla y sale para la universidad.

_____ 2. Enrique está muy estresado cuando tiene exámenes y usa tabaco para contolar los nervios.

_____ 3. Aldo va al gimnasio todas las tardes para jugar al baloncesto.

_____ 4. Rita siempre come papas fritas, tostadas y tocineta.

_____ 5. Desde que José cumplió veintiún años, bebe cuatro cervezas todas las noches.

_____ 6. Sofía se acuesta a las once de la noche y se levanta a las siete de la mañana.

> **Hábitos**
> a. Fuma muchísimo y gasta *(spends)* bastante dinero en cigarrillos.
> b. Duerme suficientes horas y puede concentrarse en clase.
> c. Hace ejercicio para estar en forma.
> d. Salta el desayuno y a las once se está muriendo de hambre.
> e. Consume bebidas alcohólicas en exceso.
> f. Come comida basura y consume sal en exceso.

¡Exprésate!
Colaborar

6-38 **La dieta mediterránea.** ¿En qué aspectos son parecidas la dieta mediterránea y la rueda de los alimentos (página 232)? Con tu compañero(a), observen bien los dos gráficos y contesten las preguntas.

1. ¿Qué alimentos están en la base de la pirámide? ¿Y en la cima *(top)*? ¿Qué alimentos están en el segmento más grande de la rueda? ¿Y en el más pequeño?

2. ¿Cuál de los gráficos da consejos más específicos respecto a *(concerning)* la frecuencia?

3. ¿Qué recomendaciones hay respecto a la actividad física *(physical)*?

4. ¿Qué otras diferencias y semejanzas *(similarities)* observas?

5. ¿Cómo es tu dieta? ¿A cuál de las dos dietas es más parecida *(similar)*?

Dieta Mediterránea

UNA VEZ AL MES — Carnes rojas

Dulces — Huevos

UNA VEZ A LA SEMANA

Pescado — Pollo

Aceite de oliva — Vino*

Queso — Yogur

TODOS LOS DÍAS — Frutas

Verduras

Cereales — Pan — Arroz — Pastas — Patatas

* con moderación

© Cengage Learning 2016

6-39 **Año nuevo, hábitos nuevos.** ¿Qué resoluciones para el año nuevo quieres hacer para tener una dieta y estilo de vida más saludables? En grupos pequeños, tomen turnos haciendo tres o cuatro resoluciones para el año nuevo.

Modelo Para el año nuevo, voy a comer más verduras. También voy a...

6-40 **Escenas de la vida.** Con un(a) compañero(a), inventen breves conversaciones. Una persona explica su situación; la otra le da consejos: **Debes...,** **Tienes que..., Necesitas...**

Modelo Piensas correr en un maratón por primera vez.

Estudiante A: Voy a correr en un maratón en dos meses y necesito ponerme en forma. ¿Qué debo hacer?

Estudiante B: Debes consultar con un entrenador. Necesitas correr tres veces por semana y también cambiar tu dieta.

1. Llevas una vida muy sedentaria. Últimamente *(Lately)* te sientes cansado(a).

2. Estás ocupado(a) con tus clases y nunca tienes tiempo para comer bien.

3. Se va a celebrar "Míster Universo" y "Miss Olimpia" en tu campus. Quieres participar pero no tienes experiencia en fisicoculturismo *(bodybuilding)*.

Las expresiones impersonales

SARA ¡Armando! Es malo comer mucha comida frita. Se debe evitar las grasas.

ARMANDO Tranquila, Sara. La vida es corta, ¡hay que disfrutarla!

■ ■ ■
Descúbrelo

- Why doesn't Sara want Armando to eat fried chicken? Does Armando agree? What is his philosophy on life?

- Does **se debe** refer to someone specific or to people in general?

- Does an infinitive or a conjugated verb follow the expressions **es malo**, **se debe**, and **hay que**?

- Are those three expressions used to express plans for the future or to give advice?

1. Impersonal expressions (**las expresiones impersonales**) are those that do not have specific things or people as subjects. They refer to people in general and are often used to make generalizations, give advice, or express opinions.

Hay que comer una variedad de alimentos.	***One / We / You must*** eat a *variety of foods.*
Es recomendable hacer ejercicio regularmente.	***It's advisable*** *to exercise regularly.*

2. One common kind of impersonal expression follows the pattern **Es** + *adjective* + *infinitive*.

Es importante estar en forma.	***It's important to be*** *in shape.*

Expresiones impersonales: Es + *adjetivo*	
Es buena idea...	*It's a good idea . . .*
Es bueno...	*It's good . . .*
Es malo...	*It's bad . . .*
Es mejor...	*It's better . . .*
Es importante...	*It's important . . .*
Es necesario...	*It's necessary . . .*
Es preciso...	*It's necessary / essential . . .*
Es preferible...	*It's preferable . . .*
Es recomendable...	*It's advisable . . .*

3. Another kind of impersonal expression uses the pattern **Hay que** + *infinitive*. It expresses the idea that *one must do something.*

Hay que comer más fruta.	***One / You must eat*** *more fruit.*

4. A more indirect way to influence someone's behavior is to use **Se debe** + *infinitive*.

Se debe beber más agua.	***One / You should drink*** *more water.*
No se debe saltar el desayuno.	***One / You shouldn't skip*** *breakfast.*

6-41 **Un estilo de vida saludable.** ¿Qué se debe hacer para llevar un estilo de vida saludable? Tomando turnos con un(a) compañero(a), digan si **se debe** o **no se debe** hacer las siguientes cosas.

Para llevar un estilo de vida sano, se debe / no se debe...

1. fumar
2. comer una variedad de alimentos
3. consumir sal en exceso
4. beber suficiente agua
5. escoger alimentos ricos en fibra
6. llevar una vida sedentaria
7. estar estresado todo el día
8. hacer ejercicio

6-42 **Consejos para el primer año.** Tu nuevo(a) amigo(a) es estudiante de primer año y necesita tus consejos. ¿Qué le dices? Con un(a) compañero(a), una persona lee un problema de la columna A y la otra lee el consejo más lógico de la columna B.

A: Los problemas	B: Los consejos
_____ 1. Quiero sacar buenas notas en todas mis clases.	a. Es buena idea participar en un grupo estudiantil.
_____ 2. Me gustaría conocer a más personas.	b. Es mejor hablar de los pequeños problemas francamente *(frankly)*.
_____ 3. No sé qué quiero hacer en el futuro.	c. Es necesario llevar una dieta balanceada.
_____ 4. ¡No quiero aumentar de peso!	d. Es importante explorar varias opciones durante el primer año.
_____ 5. ¡Mi compañero(a) de cuarto nunca limpia el baño!	e. Es preciso completar toda la tarea y asistir a clase todos los días.

6-43 **Compartan opiniones.** ¿Cuáles son tus opiniones sobre estas situaciones comunes? Con una(a) compañero(a), expresen y compartan *(share)* sus opiniones. Usen las expresiones de la lista.

Modelo vivir con una persona desordenada

Estudiante A: En mi opinión, es muy difícil vivir con una persona desordenada. ¿Y tú? ¿Qué piensas?

Estudiante B: Estoy de acuerdo. *(I agree.)* / En mi opinión, ¡es fantástico vivir con una persona desordenada!

es difícil / fácil	es interesante / aburrido	es buena idea / mala idea
es imposible / posible	es fantástico / horrible	es bueno / malo
(no) es importante	(no) es necesario	(no) es práctico

1. tener una mascota en la residencia estudiantil
2. cenar con la familia todas las noches
3. estudiar los fines de semana
4. llevar una dieta sana en la universidad
5. seguir a una persona famosa en Twitter
6. vivir con una persona bromista
7. participar en una fraternidad o sororidad
8. hacer ejercicio todos los días

¡Exprésate!

© Dejan Stanisavljevic/Shutterstock

6-44 ***"Freshman Fifteen."*** Según un estudio reciente, el estudiante típico aumenta cinco libras (*pounds*) de peso durante el primer año de estudios universitarios. No es tanto como la leyenda urbana del "*Freshman Fifteen*", pero sí es un aumento significativo. En grupos de tres o cuatro, hagan lo siguiente:

- Exploren y comenten las causas del aumento de peso: **¿Por qué aumentan de peso los estudiantes de primer año? ¿Qué comidas sirven en el campus? ¿Hay suficiente variedad de alimentos sanos? ¿Hace suficiente ejercicio el estudiante típico?**

- Hagan un cartel para una campaña educativa con cinco consejos para los estudiantes de primer año. ¿Qué deben hacer para evitar el aumento de peso? Usen expresiones como **Es preciso..., Es importante..., Es necesario...**, etcétera.

6-45 **Opiniones.** ¿Qué piensas de estas declaraciones? En grupos pequeños, expresen sus opiniones y justifíquenlas con una o dos razones (*reasons*). Incluyan un mínimo de una expresión impersonal para cada caso.

Modelo Es malo consumir cafeína porque es un estimulante fuerte (*strong*).

> **Estudiante A:** Para mí, no es malo consumir cafeína en moderación. Es bueno consumir un poco de cafeína, como una taza de café, especialmente por la mañana. ¿Qué opinan Uds.?
>
> **Estudiante B:** Estoy de acuerdo.
>
> **Estudiante C:** No estoy de acuerdo. En mi opinión, es preferible no consumir cafeína. Es mejor evitar los estimulantes.

1. Los vegetarianos son las personas más sanas.
2. Tener que dormir ocho horas diarias es un mito (*myth*).
3. Para adelgazar es importante comer cinco comidas pequeñas diarias.
4. Una manzana al día aleja (*keeps away*) al doctor.
5. Es bueno consumir mucho yogur.
6. Es mejor tomar jugo de verduras que comer verduras.

Frases útiles

En mi opinión
  In my opinion
Para mí
  In my opinion
Pienso que
  I think (that)
(No) Estoy de acuerdo.
  I (dis)agree.
¿Qué opinan Uds.?
  What's your opinion?

6-46 **La charla.** Con un(a) compañero(a) de clase, dramaticen una escena entre las personas de las fotos. ¿Qué dice la persona sedentaria sobre sus malos hábitos? ¿Qué consejos le da el entrenador (*trainer*)?

Modelo **Estudiante A:** Quiero ponerme en forma. ¿Qué debo hacer?
Estudiante B: Primero, necesito saber tus hábitos...

© Jeff Wasserman/Shutterstock

© ruigsantos/Shutterstock

Los adverbios

SILVIA Estoy muy preocupada por Jaime. Duerme poco y fuma constantemente.

PAMELA Sí, el pobre *(the poor thing)* está completamente estresado por los exámenes.

SILVIA ¿Por qué no lo invitamos a salir? Podemos ir a cenar al nuevo restaurante orgánico.

PAMELA ¡Buena idea! Lo llamo esta tarde.

1. Adverbs are words or phrases that supply information about when, where, how, or how much something is done. They are often placed after a verb or at the end of a sentence.

Los adverbios	
How?	Juan cocina **bien**. *Juan cooks well.* **rápido** *fast, quickly* **despacio** *slowly* **bien** *well* **mal** *poorly, badly* **perfectamente** *perfectly*
When?	Le traigo más pan **enseguida**. *I'll bring you more bread right away.* **enseguida** *right away* **ahora** *now* **ya** *already* **ya no** *no longer* **todavía** *still* **pronto** *soon*
How much?	¡Uy, comí **demasiado**! *Oh, I ate too much!* **demasiado** *too much* **mucho** *a lot* **poco** *little, not much*
Where?	Siempre comemos **allí**. *We always eat there.* **aquí** *here* **allí** *there* **cerca** *close by* **lejos** *far away*

■ ■ ■
Descúbrelo

■ According to Silvia, how is stress affecting Jaime's sleeping and smoking habits?

■ Where do the two friends want to invite him out to eat?

■ When will Pamela call him with this invitation?

■ Which words are the Spanish equivalents of *completely* and *constantly*? What part of these Spanish words seems to correspond to English *-ly*?

2. Many adverbs in English end in *-ly*, such as *slowly* and *totally*. The Spanish equivalents are formed by adding **-mente** to the feminine form of the adjective. If the original adjective has an accent mark, the adverb does too.

fácil + mente → fácilmente	*easily*
lógica + mente → lógicamente	*logically*
reciente + mente → recientemente	*recently*
sola + mente → solamente	*only*
tranquila + mente → tranquilamente	*tranquilly, peacefully*

3. Adverbs can also describe adjectives or even other adverbs and express *to what extent*. An adverb used in this way is placed in front of the adjective or adverb.

> Ellos conducen **bastante** mal. | *They drive **quite** poorly.*

Adverbios de cantidad o grado			
bastante	*quite, rather, fairly*	**muy**	*very*
casi	*almost*	**un poco**	*a little*
completamente	*completely*		

¡Aplícalo! Colaborar

6-47 **Un nuevo estilo de vida.** Elena decidió cambiar su estilo de vida y escribió sobre la experiencia en un blog. Trabajando con un(a) compañero(a), lean su blog y clasifiquen los adverbios en negrita *(boldface)* según el tipo de información expresado.

¿Dónde?	¿Cuándo?	¿Cómo?	¿Hasta qué punto? *(To what extent?)*

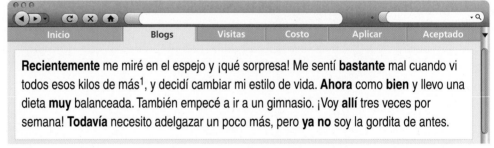

Recientemente me miré en el espejo y ¡qué sorpresa! Me sentí **bastante** mal cuando vi todos esos kilos de más[1], y decidí cambiar mi estilo de vida. **Ahora** como **bien** y llevo una dieta **muy** balanceada. También empecé a ir a un gimnasio. ¡Voy **allí** tres veces por semana! **Todavía** necesito adelgazar un poco más, pero **ya no** soy la gordita de antes.

[1]*extra*

 Colaborar

6-48 **Un estudiante excelente.** Wigberta está describiendo a su compañero de clase Javier. Con un(a) compañero(a), completen su descripción con los adverbios más lógicos. Tienen que escoger una palabra apropiada de la lista y cambiarla *(change it)* a un adverbio que termina en **-mente**.

Modelo Javier es un estudiante **realmente** excelente.

completo	constante	inmediato	personal	puntual	real	típico

1. Javier está _____ dedicado a sus estudios universitarios.

2. Asiste a clases todos los días y siempre llega a clase _____.

3. Cuando no está en clase, estudia _____.

4. Si un profesor anuncia un examen, Javier empieza a prepararse

   _____.

5. _____ Javier saca la nota más alta de la clase.

6. _____, yo pienso que Javier va a ganar el Premio Nobel algún día.

¡Exprésate!

6-49 **¿Llevas una vida sana?** Trabajando con un(a) compañero(a), entrevístense *(interview each other)* con las siguientes preguntas sobre sus hábitos. ¿Cuál de Uds. lleva una vida más sana?

1. ¿Haces ejercicio regularmente?
2. ¿Cuántas horas duermes diariamente?
3. ¿Fumas ocasionalmente?
4. ¿Aproximadamente cuánta agua tomas al día?
5. ¿Es tu vida bastante sedentaria?
6. ¿Comes rápido o despacio?
7. ¿Te sientes constantemente preocupado(a)?
8. ¿Te duermes fácilmente después de acostarte?

> ↻ Present progressive, **Capítulo 4 Paso 2**

Colaborar

6-50 **Restaurante X-ito.** ¿Qué están haciendo las personas en el restaurante X-ito? ¿Y cómo lo hacen? Trabaja con un(a) compañero(a) para crear seis oraciones.

- Usen el presente progresivo y adverbios que terminan en **-mente**.
- Usen estos adjetivos para formar los adverbios: **amable, despistado, feliz, generoso, nervioso, rápido.**

Modelo Luis está comiendo helado felizmente.

6-51 **Asesores(as) de restaurantes.** Tú y tu compañero(a) de clase son asesores(as) *(consultants)* de restaurantes. Sus clientes son dueños *(owners)* de restaurantes, y Uds. tienen que darles recomendaciones para tener éxito *(be successful)*.

- Piensen en ocho recomendaciones sobre la comida, el menú, los meseros, las horas de servicio, la decoración, etcétera.
- Usen expresiones impersonales para las recomendaciones e incluyan algunos adverbios.

Modelo Es muy importante saludar a los clientes amablemente. También...

CONECTADOS CON...
LA AGRICULTURA

El arte del cultivo

La agricultura, el arte del cultivo, es una actividad tan antigua como la civilización humana. Con los avances tecnológicos y científicos, distintos métodos agrícolas han sido *(have been)* introducidos a través de los años. Aunque ahora se practica principalmente la agricultura industrial, es interesante observar que muchas de las técnicas antiguas siguen en uso.

Las acequias

En España y en las antiguas *(former)* colonias españolas de las Américas, es común ver acequias —canales de agua— utilizadas para el riego. La palabra "acequia" es de origen árabe ya que los árabes introdujeron este sistema en España hace unos mil años. Las acequias permiten transportar agua desde un río *(river)* hasta los campos. Son parte de un complejo sistema de agua que incluye azudes *(dams to raise the water level)* y norias *(water wheels)*.

Acequia en San Fulgencio, España

Estrategia: Review of reading strategies

- Look for cognates—words similar in meaning and spelling in Spanish and English.

- Activate your background knowledge: What do you already know about the topic?

- Search for specific information by scanning—running your eyes quickly over the page.

- Identify key points of information first: Who, what, when, where, why?

- Check verb endings and time expressions: Is the information related to the past, present, or future?

Palabras de agricultura

el campo	*field*
cultivar	*to grow*
el cultivo	*farming, cultivation*
el riego	*irrigation*
sembrar (ie)	*to sow*
sostenible	*sustainable*
el suelo	*soil*
la tierra	*land*

6-52 **Comprensión.** Según el artículo, ¿son estas oraciones ciertas o falsas? Cambia las oraciones falsas para que sean verdaderas *(so that they are true)*.

1. El arte de cultivar las plantas para la alimentación empezó hace mil años.

2. Con la evolución de nuevas tecnologías agrícolas, ya no se usan las acequias, las milpas y las terrazas.

3. Un sistema de riego en España fue introducido por los árabes.

4. El maíz tiene sus orígenes en la Península Ibérica, donde los españoles lo cultivaron por primera vez.

5. El cultivo del maíz con el frijol y la calabaza es un ejemplo de un ecosistema sostenible.

6. Es imposible cultivar las áreas montañosas porque hay mucha erosión del suelo.

6-53 **¿Y tú?** Trabajando con un(a) compañero(a), comenten estas preguntas.

1. ¿Es la agricultura una actividad importante en tu estado o región? ¿Cuáles son los cultivos principales?

2. ¿Te gustaría tener un pequeño jardín? ¿Qué quieres sembrar?

El sistema de milpas

Hace miles de años, las comunidades precolombinas de México y Centroamérica domesticaron y cultivaron el maíz. Desde entonces el maíz es el cereal más plantado del mundo. Tradicionalmente, el maíz se siembra en parcelas de tierra llamadas "milpas". Las milpas son pequeños ecosistemas donde crece el maíz junto con otras plantas, típicamente el frijol y la calabaza *(pumpkin)*. El frijol mantiene el suelo fértil porque deja *(leaves)* nitrógeno. Y la calabaza se arrastra *(spreads out)* en el suelo, cortando *(cutting off)* el paso a otras plantas que puedan competir con el maíz. El resultado es un agroecosistema sostenible.

Milpa en *Sun Watch Indian Village*

Las terrazas andinas

Otra práctica de los antiguos americanos que todavía existe hoy es el sistema de terrazas, comúnmente llamadas "andenes". Este sistema fue perfeccionado por los incas en las regiones montañosas de los Andes. Las terrazas son plataformas horizontales a lo largo de las montañas que permiten cultivar la tierra en pendientes *(slopes)*. Están equipadas con canales de riego y son muy efectivas en reducir la erosión, en proporcionar drenaje y en controlar la temperatura del suelo.

Terrazas en Machu Picchu, Perú

Composición: Un blog

You write a weekly blog with advice for students. This week, you are writing about healthy dining options in your area. In the introduction, explain why it is important to eat healthy and mention two or three places where students can do that. Next, describe those places with examples and details. Finally, indicate which is your favorite and why. As you write, join related sentences with connectors.

 **Revisión en pareja**. Exchange papers with a classmate and edit each other's work.

- Does each paragraph have a topic sentence? Are the paragraphs well-developed with details and examples? Write one positive comment and one suggestion for improvement.

- Have related sentences been joined with appropriate connectors? Point out any additional place this could be done.

- Are the verbs conjugated correctly? Circle any verbs that might be incorrect.

- Do the adjectives and articles match the nouns in number and gender? Underline any that might be incorrect.

Estrategia
Review of writing strategies
- Start each paragraph with a topic sentence.
- Continue with detailed information and examples.
- Join related sentences with connectors: **y, pero, así que, porque, aunque.**
- Proofread for grammatical accuracy.

NUESTRA COMUNIDAD

6-54 Nosotros / *Share It!* En línea, subiste *(you posted)* una foto o un video de tu restaurante favorito. También viste las publicaciones *(posts)* de varios compañeros de clase. Ahora, con dos o tres compañeros, comenten sobre estas publicaciones y contesten las preguntas.

1. ¿Cuáles son los restaurantes más populares de la clase? ¿Por qué son populares?

2. ¿Qué tipos de restaurantes están representados? ¿Hay algún restaurante muy elegante? ¿Hay alguno vegetariano? ¿Y alguno de comida rápida?

3. ¿Cuál de los restaurantes es nuevo para Uds.? ¿Les gustaría comer allí? Expliquen.

4. ¿Cuál de las fotos o de los videos les gusta más? ¿Por qué?

6-55 Perspectivas: Platos típicos. En línea, miraste un video en el que *(in which)* tres estudiantes describen platos típicos de sus países. ¿Qué dicen los estudiantes? Con dos compañeros de clase, comparen sus respuestas sobre el video. Después, entrevístense *(interview one another)* con estas preguntas:

- ¿Cuál es uno de tus platos preferidos de la cocina *(cuisine)* internacional?
- ¿Qué ingredientes lleva?
- ¿Normalmente comes ese plato en casa o en un restaurante?

6-56 Exploración: Restaurantes nicas. En Internet, buscaste un restaurante en Granada, Nicaragua, para ir a almorzar con tus amigos. Ahora, formen grupos de tres o cuatro estudiantes. Tomen turnos haciendo breves presentaciones sobre los restaurantes. Las otras personas deben escuchar y hacer preguntas. En tu presentación, contesta las siguientes preguntas:

- ¿Cómo se llama el restaurante?
- ¿Cómo es?
- ¿Dónde está?
- ¿Cuál es su especialidad?
- ¿Cómo son los precios *(prices)*?
- ¿Por qué seleccionaste este restaurante?

6-57 Conectados con... las artes culinarias. En línea, leíste un artículo sobre la historia del chocolate. Con dos o tres compañeros(as), compartan *(share)* información de sus investigaciones sobre platos tradicionales del mundo hispanohablante o sobre la historia de un alimento *(food)*.

Modelo

Un plato típico de *(country)* es... / *(Name of food)* es de origen...

6-58 **La cena de gala.** ¿Quiénes están en la gran cena de gala *(banquet)*? ¿Qué están comiendo? Tú y tu compañero(a) deben compartir *(share)* la información en las imágenes para contestar estas preguntas. Usa la información en estas dos imágenes; tu compañero(a) tiene que usar la información que está en la página S-6.

This is a pair activity for Estudiante A and Estudiante B.

If you are **Estudiante A**, use the information on this page.

If you are **Estudiante B**, turn now to p. S-6 at the back of the book.

- Primero, tomen turnos para describir las características físicas *(physical)* de las personas y descubrir el nombre de cada uno. Por ejemplo, Estudiante A dice: **En mi página hay una señora delgada. Tiene el pelo rubio y los ojos azules. Usa gafas. Tiene más o menos 30 años. ¿Cómo se llama? Eh... ¿cómo se escribe su nombre?**

- Luego, pregunten sobre la comida de cada persona. Por ejemplo, Estudiante B pregunta: **¿Qué está comiendo Ramón Lerma? ¿Qué está bebiendo?**

- Anoten *(Jot down)* la información.

Estudiante A

© Cengage Learning 2016

SÍNTESIS

 Colaborar

6-59 **Budín de banana.** ¿Te gusta probar nuevos platos? Lee el siguiente blog de cocina con un(a) compañero(a) de clase. Trabajen juntos para contestar las preguntas.

1. ¿Es el budín dulce? ¿Cómo lo sabes?

2. Tienes los siguientes ingredientes para preparar el budín. ¿Qué más necesitas?

Left to right: © v.s.anandhakrishna/Shutterstock; © Maks Narodenko/Shutterstock; © foodonwhite/Shutterstock; © EM Arts/Shutterstock

3. ¿Por qué dice el artículo que el budín es saludable?

4. ¿Estás de acuerdo con que es fácil de preparar?

5. ¿Puedes preparar el budín para una persona diabética? ¿Puedes prepararlo para una persona alérgica a los mariscos? ¿Y para una persona con intolerancia a los productos lácteos? ¿Y para una persona que necesita potasio?

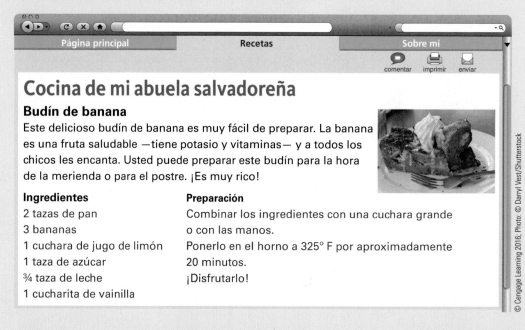

Página principal | **Recetas** | **Sobre mí**

comentar   imprimir   enviar

Cocina de mi abuela salvadoreña

Budín de banana

Este delicioso budín de banana es muy fácil de preparar. La banana es una fruta saludable —tiene potasio y vitaminas— y a todos los chicos les encanta. Usted puede preparar este budín para la hora de la merienda o para el postre. ¡Es muy rico!

Ingredientes
2 tazas de pan
3 bananas
1 cuchara de jugo de limón
1 taza de azúcar
¾ taza de leche
1 cucharita de vainilla

Preparación
Combinar los ingredientes con una cuchara grande o con las manos.
Ponerlo en el horno a 325° F por aproximadamente 20 minutos.
¡Disfrutarlo!

© Cengage Learning 2016; Photo: © Darryl Vest/Shutterstock

6-60 **Los secretos de las estrellas.** Hoy en el fabuloso programa de televisión "El secreto de las estrellas *(stars)*", el (la) presentador(a) *(host)* está hablando con una celebridad súper famosa sobre su nuevo plan para adelgazar.

- En grupos de dos, representen este segmento del show.

- Estudiante A es el (la) presentador(a) y Estudiante B es la celebridad.

© IxMaster/Shutterstock

6-61 **El restaurante El Bohemio.** Un(a) reportero(a) para un periódico *(newspaper)* muy prestigioso tiene que escribir una reseña *(review)* de un nuevo restaurante. Como parte de su investigación, decide entrevistar a varios clientes que hoy comieron allí. Dramaticen esta escena en grupos de tres.

Estudiante A	Estudiante B
Tú eres el (la) reportero(a). Tienes que:	Tú eres un(a) cliente(a) satisfecho(a) *(satisfied)*.
■ presentarte.	Tienes una impresión muy favorable del restaurante. Durante la entrevista, contestas las preguntas de forma muy positiva.
■ explicar tu trabajo y tu objetivo.	
■ pedir permiso para la entrevista.	
■ entrevistar a los clientes sobre su experiencia en el restaurante.	**Estudiante C**
Incluye preguntas en el presente y en el pretérito. Por ejemplo: **¿Qué piensan Uds. del restaurante? ¿Cómo son los precios *(prices)*? ¿Cómo es el servicio? ¿Qué pidieron? ¿Les gustó el plato principal? ¿Qué postre probó Ud.? ¿Cómo estuvo todo?** etcétera	Tú eres un(a) cliente(a) descontento(a). Tienes una mala impresión del restaurante. Durante la entrevista, te quejas *(you complain)* y contestas las preguntas de forma muy negativa.

Pronunciación: Las letras z y c

Colaborar

Con un(a) compañero(a), tomen turnos leyendo los trabalenguas *(tongue twisters)*. Presten atención *(Pay special attention)* a la pronunciación de las letras **z** y **c**.

A Rosa Rizo un reto le dijo que rezara en ruso, y aunque fue un tanto confuso, Rosa Rizo reza en ruso.	*Rosa Rizo was given a challenge to pray in Russian, and although it was a little confusing Rosa Rizo prays in Russian.*
•••	•••
El arzobispo de Constantinopla	*The archbishop of Constantinople*
se quiere desconstaninopolizar,	*wants to be deconstantinopolized,*
y el que lo desconstantinopolice	*and he who deconstantinopolizes him*
será un gran desconstantinopolizador.	*a great deconstantinopolizer will be.*

VOCABULARIO

RECURSOS

Para aprender mejor

To memorize food vocabulary, classify it in categories that are meaningful to you; for example, by meals, where foods are found in a supermarket, foods you like and dislike, etc.

Sustantivos

el alimento *food*
el almuerzo *lunch*
el (la) camarero(a) *waiter / waitress*
el carbohidrato *carbohydrate*
la cena *dinner, supper*
el (la) cliente(a) *customer*
la comida *meal; lunch; main meal of the day*
la comida basura *junk food*
la comida rápida *fast food*
el condimento *condiment*
el consejo *advice*
la cuchara *spoon*
la cucharita *teaspoon*
el cuchillo *knife*
la cuenta *bill*
el desayuno *breakfast*
la dieta *diet*
el ejercicio *exercise*
el (la) entrenador(a) *trainer*
el estilo de vida *lifestyle*
el exceso *excess*
la fibra *fiber*
el grano *grain*
la grasa *fat*
el hábito *habit*
el menú *menu*
el (la) mesero(a) *waiter / waitress*
la nutrición *nutrition*
el plato *plate; dish*
el postre *dessert*
el producto lácteo *milk product*
la propina *tip*
la proteína *protein*
la rueda *wheel*

la salud *health*
la servilleta *napkin*
la taza *cup*
el tenedor *fork*
la variedad *variety*
el vaso *drinking glass*

Verbos

adelgazar *to lose weight*
aumentar de peso *to gain weight*
cambiar *to change*
conseguir (i) *to get, to obtain*
consultar *to consult*
consumir *to eat / drink; to consume*
dar consejos *to give advice*
despedirse (i) *to say good-bye*
evitar *to avoid*
explicar *to explain*
fumar *to smoke*
hacer ejercicio *to exercise*
llevar (una vida) *to lead (a life)*
mostrar (ue) *to show*
pedir (i) *to ask for; to order*
ponerse en forma *to get in shape*
preguntar *to ask*
prestar *to lend*
regalar *to give (as a gift)*
saltar *to skip*

Adjetivos

a la plancha *grilled*
balanceado(a) *balanced*
común *common, usual*
delicioso(a) *delicious*
dietético(a) *diet*
dulce *sweet*
empanizado(a) *breaded*

fresco(a) *fresh*
frito(a) *fried*
picante *spicy / hot*
principal *main*
rico(a) *good; tasty; rich*
saludable *healthy*
sano(a) *healthy*
sedentario(a) *sedentary*
suficiente *enough; plenty*

Frases útiles

¡Buen provecho! *Bon appetit!*
con regularidad *regularly*
en exceso *too much*
en moderación *in moderation*
Estoy satisfecho(a). *I've had plenty; I'm full.*
hay que *one must*
Hubo... *There was . . . / There were . . .*
¿Me pasas..., por favor? *Could you please pass . . . ?*
¿Qué debo hacer? *What should I do?*
¡Qué rico(a)! *It's really good!*
¿Quieres más...? *Do you want more . . . ?*
se debe *one should*
según *according to*

Foods, drinks, and condiments, pp. 212–213, 222
Indirect object pronouns, p. 216
Restaurant phrases, pp. 222–223
Impersonal expressions, p. 236
Adverbs, p. 239

De compras

Conexiones a la comunidad
Visit the website of one of these popular clothing stores: Mango, Zara, or Asos. How much does your favorite garment cost there?

CAPÍTULO 7

In this chapter you will . . .
- explore Costa Rica and Panama
- talk about clothes, colors, and styles
- practice making purchases in a clothing store
- express actions that have recently taken place
- identify souvenirs and describe what they're made of
- practice bargaining in a market
- learn about the marketing strategies of three successful brands
- share information about your favorite T-shirt

NUESTRO **MUNDO**

Costa Rica y Panamá

Costa Rica y Panamá son dos países centroamericanos pequeños pero con economías fuertes. Ninguno de los dos tiene ejército *(army).*

República de Costa Rica
Población: 4 700 000
Capital: San José

Moneda: el colón
Exportaciones: bananas, piñas, café, melones

República de Panamá
Población: 3 600 000
Capital: Ciudad de Panamá

Moneda: el balboa y el dólar estadounidense
Exportaciones: oro, bananas, camarones, azúcar

Gracias al canal, Panamá es un ícono del comercio internacional. Muchos latinoamericanos van a Panamá de compras porque hay miles de artículos —televisores, relojes, perfumes, ropa— a buenos precios *(prices)*. En la Zona Libre de Colón, hay cientos de tiendas libres de impuesto *(duty-free shops)*. Es la zona franca *(tax-free zone)* más grande del hemisferio.

Arte

Muchos turistas en Panamá compran las famosas molas: coloridas piezas rectangulares cosidas a mano *(hand-sewn)* por las mujeres kunas. Los kunas son uno de siete grupos indígenas de Panamá. Viven principalmente en el archipiélago de San Blas en una comarca, o territorio autónomo.

Ecología

Dividida igualmente entre Costa Rica y Panamá, está la primera reserva binacional del mundo: el Parque Internacional La Amistad. Cubre 500 000 acres de bosque *(forest)* virgen y tiene un muy alto nivel de biodiversidad. Por su acceso remoto, el parque ha sido poco explorado.

Ciencias

Franklin Chang-Díaz, físico *(physicist)* nacido en Costa Rica, fue el primer astronauta latinoamericano de NASA. El Dr. Chang-Díaz también fundó *(founded)* Ad Astra Rocket Company. Este laboratorio está en Guanacaste, Costa Rica, y está desarrollando *(developing)* un cohete *(rocket)* de plasma para hacer el viaje Tierra–Marte *(Earth–Mars)* en 39 días.

7-1 **¿Qué sabes?** Contesta las siguientes preguntas.

1. ¿Qué tienen en común Costa Rica y Panamá?

2. ¿Por qué muchos latinoamericanos van de compras a Panamá?

3. ¿Quiénes hacen las molas?

4. ¿Dónde viven los kunas?

5. ¿Qué tiene de especial el Parque Internacional La Amistad?

6. ¿Quién es Franklin Chang-Díaz?

7-2 **Videomundo.** Mira los videos de Costa Rica y Panamá. Menciona tres cosas que aprendiste sobre estos dos países centroamericanos.

La ropa y el estilo

En el escaparate

In this *Paso*, you will . . .

- talk about clothes, colors, and styles
- point out people and things
- express what you love and what interests you, bothers you, or matters to you

la corbata

el traje

el suéter

la chaqueta

la camisa

la camiseta

los zapatos (de vestir)

los vaqueros

los zapatos (deportivos)

© Cengage Learning 2016

Los colores y los diseños *Colors and designs*

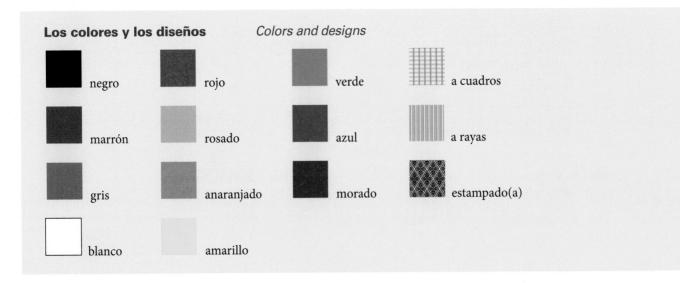

negro

rojo

verde

a cuadros

marrón

rosado

azul

a rayas

gris

anaranjado

morado

estampado(a)

blanco

amarillo

En una tienda

la falda

el traje de baño

la blusa

los pantalones

el vestido

los pantalones cortos

las sandalias

las chancletas

© Cengage Learning 2016

Ropa de invierno — *Winter clothes*

el abrigo	*coat*
las botas	*boots*
la bufanda	*scarf, muffler*
los calcetines	*socks*
la gorra	*cap*
los guantes	*gloves*
la sudadera	*sweatshirt*

Para hablar sobre el estilo de ropa — *Talking about clothing styles*

¿Qué estilo de ropa te gusta? — *What style of clothes do you like?*

   Me gusta llevar ropa cómoda. — *I like to wear comfortable clothes.*

   Me gusta vestir a la última moda. — *I like dressing in the latest fashion.*

   No me importa el estilo. — *I don't care about the style.*

   Prefiero la ropa clásica / elegante / informal. — *I prefer classic / elegant / casual clothes.*

¡Aplícalo! Colaborar

7-3 De colores. ¿Qué colores asocias con estas cosas? Trabaja con un(a) compañero(a). Tomando turnos, una persona lee cada frase en voz alta y la otra persona responde con un color.

1. las fresas y los tomates
2. la nieve y el vestido de novia
3. una noche oscura
4. el sol
5. el brócoli y las espinacas
6. un día nublado
7. el mar
8. nuestra universidad
9. el otoño
10. las uvas y las violetas

 Colaborar

7-4 De moda. ¿Cuántas personas en nuestra clase llevan esta ropa hoy? Con un(a) compañero(a), observen la ropa de sus compañeros de clase e indiquen el número de personas para cada prenda *(article of clothing)*. ¿Cuál es la prenda más popular de la clase?

1. una camiseta con el logo de nuestra universidad
2. unos zapatos deportivos
3. una camisa o una blusa a cuadros
4. una chaqueta azul o gris
5. un suéter rojo
6. unos pantalones cortos
7. unos vaqueros azules
8. unas botas marrones

 Colaborar

7-5 El estilo personal. Eduardo y Marisa están hablando de su estilo personal. Con un(a) compañero(a), lean en voz alta su conversación. Hay que escoger la palabra más lógica entre paréntesis.

MARISA ¿Qué (1. estilo / abrigo) de ropa te gusta, Eduardo?

EDUARDO En realidad, no me (2. viste / importa) mucho el estilo. Prefiero llevar ropa (3. cómoda / sucia), como vaqueros y camisetas.

MARISA ¿Siempre llevas ropa (4. informal / rubia)?

EDUARDO Bueno, no siempre. Por ejemplo, para salir a bailar me pongo algo más (5. elegante / morado).

MARISA Pues a mí sí me gusta vestir a la (6. primera / última) moda. Me encanta ir de (7. compras / invierno).

EDUARDO Ya veo. ¡Gracias a Dios que tu papá te deja usar su (8. tienda / tarjeta) de crédito!

7-6 La ropa de hoy. ¿Qué ropa llevas hoy? ¿Qué ropa lleva tu compañero(a)? Tomen turnos para describir la ropa y los colores. La otra persona tiene que decidir si la descripción es cierta o falsa.

Modelo Estudiante A: Hoy llevas una camisa verde.
Estudiante B: Falso; hoy llevo una camiseta roja. Hoy llevas...

¡Exprésate!

7-7 **¿Adónde voy?** Trabaja con un(a) compañero(a). Tomando turnos, una persona escoge un lugar de la lista y describe la ropa que lleva para ir allí. La otra persona tiene que adivinar *(guess)* el lugar adonde va.

Modelo   **Estudiante A:** Llevo un traje de baño y sandalias. ¿Adónde voy?
             Estudiante B: ¿A la playa, en verano?
             Estudiante A: ¡Sí!

Lugares	
a la playa, en verano	a un concierto
a las montañas, en invierno	a un partido de fútbol americano
a clase, en otoño	al gimnasio de tu barrio
a una boda formal	a una fiesta en tu campus

7-8 **¿Quién es?** Tomando turnos, una persona describe la ropa de un(a) estudiante en la clase y la otra persona tiene que decir quién es.

Modelo   Esta persona lleva una falda azul, una blusa blanca, un suéter rojo y chancletas. ¿Quién es?

Physical characteristics, **Capítulo 3 Paso 2**

7-9 **Súper memoria.** ¿Quién de Uds. tiene una súper memoria *(memory)*?

- Con dos o tres compañeros, miren atentamente el dibujo durante treinta segundos *(seconds)*.

- Luego, cierren los libros y saquen una hoja de papel. Trabajando individualmente, escriban oraciones con detalles del dibujo: los rasgos físicos, la ropa, los colores, el estilo, etcétera.

- Después, abran los libros y comparen notas. ¿Quién escribió la mejor descripción?

© Cengage Learning 2016

7-10 **La ropa y la moda.** Usa las siguientes preguntas para entrevistar *(interview)* a tu compañero(a). Luego él/ella te entrevista a ti.

1. ¿Qué estilo de ropa te gusta?

2. ¿Qué colores prefieres llevar? ¿Qué colores no llevas nunca?

3. ¿Qué te pones para salir con amigos?

4. ¿Cuál de tus amigos se viste a la última moda? ¿Qué se pone?

5. ¿Cuál es tu tienda de ropa preferida? Explica por qué te gusta.

6. ¿Qué ropa piensas comprar para la próxima estación? ¿Necesitas ropa elegante o informal?

Los adjetivos y los pronombres demostrativos

ELENA ¿Cómo me queda este vestido?

ROBERTA Muy bien, pero me gusta más ese. Es más elegante.

CARLA ¡Pss! ¡Elena! ¡Aquel chico te está mirando!

ELENA ¡Voy a comprar este vestido!

■ ■ ■

Descúbrelo

- Which dress does Roberta prefer? Why?

- Which one does Elena want to buy? Why?

- Which word seems to be the Spanish equivalent of *this*?

- The words **ese** and **aquel** can both mean *that* or *that one*. Which of the two words refers to something much farther away from the person speaking?

1. Demonstrative adjectives (**los adjetivos demostrativos**) are words used to point out specific persons or things, such as ***this*** shirt or ***those*** jeans. They are placed in front of nouns and, like all adjectives, match the nouns in gender and number.

¡**Esta** camisa es muy bonita! (**Camisa** *is feminine, singular.*)	***This*** *shirt is very pretty!*
Me encantan **esos** vaqueros. (**Vaqueros** *is masculine, plural.*)	*I love* ***those*** *jeans.*

2. Here are the demonstrative adjectives in Spanish. Notice that Spanish has two different words to express *that*, depending on how far away the object is from the person speaking.

Me gustan **esas** camisetas.	*I like* ***those*** *T-shirts. (near you, the person I'm talking to)*
Aquel traje es muy caro.	***That*** *suit (over there, in the back) is very expensive. (not near the person speaking nor the person spoken to)*

Los adjetivos demostrativos

	this these (close to both speakers)		that those (closer to the person being spoken to)		that those (distant from both speakers)	
masculine	este	estos	ese	esos	aquel	aquellos
feminine	esta	estas	esa	esas	aquella	aquellas

3. Demonstrative pronouns (**los pronombres demostrativos**) stand in for nouns that have already been mentioned; they use the same forms as the demonstrative adjectives.

Este vestido es más caro que **ese**.	*This dress is more expensive than* ***that one***.
Esas faldas cuestan menos que **estas**.	*Those skirts cost less than* ***these***.

4. There are two common neuter or gender-neutral demonstrative pronouns: **esto** (*this*) and **eso** (*that*). These pronouns never replace specific nouns; instead, they refer to unknown objects, ideas, or situations.

LUISA	¡He perdido mis llaves!	*I've lost my keys!*
MARCOS	¡**Eso** es terrible!	*That's terrible!*
	(**Eso** *refers to the fact that the keys have been lost.*)	

Colaborar

7-11 **En el centro comercial.** Varios chicos están de compras en un centro comercial *(shopping mall)*. Con un(a) compañero(a), lean las descripciones y decidan si la información es cierta o falsa. Cambien las oraciones falsas para que sean ciertas *(so that they are true)*.

¡Aplícalo!

© Cengage Learning 2016

1. Esta chica es alta y delgada y esa chica es baja y un poco gorda.

2. Esta chica tiene el pelo rubio y esa tiene el pelo negro.

3. Este chico lleva pantalones cortos y ese chico lleva vaqueros.

4. Estos chicos están mandando mensajes de texto y esos están mirando la ropa.

5. Esos suéteres son para mujeres y aquellos son para hombres.

6. Esas faldas son rosadas y blancas y aquellas son verdes y azules.

7-12 **Mis preferencias.** ¿Cuáles son las preferencias tuyas y las de tu compañero(a)? Entrevístense *(Interview each other)*. En los comentarios deben usar adjetivos demostrativos (**ese / esa / esos / esas**) y dar una explicación.

Modelo restaurante

Estudiante A: ¿Cuál es tu restaurante preferido?

Estudiante B: Me gusta mucho Harper's.

Estudiante A: A mí me gusta **ese** restaurante también. Los meseros son simpáticos. / A mí no me gusta **ese** restaurante; la comida es mala.

1. colores	3. desayuno	5. videojuego	7. actores
2. tienda	4. música	6. películas	8. equipo de fútbol americano

7-13 Los colores en nuestro salón de clase. ¿De qué colores son las cosas en nuestro salón de clase? Trabajando con un(a) compañero(a) de clase, tomen turnos para preguntarse sobre los colores de varios objetos. Usen palabras como **este**, **ese** y **aquel**.

Modelo   Estudiante A: ¿De qué color son **estos** bolígrafos?
Estudiante B: Son azules. ¿De qué color es **aquella** pizarra?
Estudiante A: Es blanca. ¿De qué color... ?

7-14 De compras en Panamá. Tú y tu compañero(a) de clase están de compras en Multiplaza, un gigantesco centro comercial *(shopping mall)* en Panamá. Pregúntense sobre los precios de la ropa en la tienda Tododeporte. Incluyan palabras como **este** y **ese**.

Modelo   Estudiante A: ¿Cuánto cuestan **estas** gorras?
Estudiante B: Diez dólares.
Estudiante A: ¿Y **esas**?
Estudiante B: **Esas** cuestan quince dólares.

7-15 ¿Cuáles te gustan más? ¿Qué piensas de los colores y estilos de la ropa en Tododeporte? Tomen turnos y pregúntense sobre sus preferencias. Sigan el modelo y usen adjetivos y pronombres demostrativos.

Modelo   Estudiante A: ¿Te gusta más esta gorra o esa?
Estudiante B: Me gusta más esta. ¿Cuál prefieres tú?
Estudiante A: Yo prefiero esta también. / Yo prefiero esa. El diseño es más bonito.

7-16 El presupuesto. Mira el dibujo de la actividad 7-14. Tienes un presupuesto *(budget)* de $120 para comprar ropa. ¿Qué quieres comprar en la tienda Tododeporte? Habla con un(a) compañero(a) de clase y comparen sus compras.

Modelo   Quiero comprar dos de estas camisetas. También pienso comprar esos vaqueros y...

Los verbos como *gustar*

ALEXA ¿Te gusta el traje, amor? ¿Vas a comprarlo?

MATEO Definitivamente no. Los pantalones me quedan flojos. Y la corbata me queda pequeña.

ALEXA ¿Ah sí? Pues a mí ¡me encanta el traje!

■ ■ ■
Descúbrelo

- How does the suit fit Mateo? How does it fit the mannequin?

- What word does Mateo use to describe the pants?

- What's the subject of **me quedan**? And of **me queda**? How does the verb change when the subject is plural?

- Who loves the suit? What indirect object pronoun indicates that she's referring to herself?

1. As you learned in **Capítulo 3**, the verb **gustar** follows a special sentence pattern: Just two verb forms are commonly used, and indirect object pronouns indicate *who* likes the thing or activity. Many other verbs follow the same pattern.

   INDIRECT OBJECT PRONOUN + **GUSTA** / **GUSTAN** + SUBJECT

   Me   +   gusta   +   el traje.
   I like the suit. (The suit is pleasing to me.)

	Verbos como *gustar*
encantar	*to love (a thing or an activity)*
faltar	*to be short (of something), to lack*
importar	*to matter, to be important (to somebody)*
interesar	*to be interested in*
molestar	*to bother*
parecer	*to seem, to appear*
quedar	*to fit, to have left, to remain*

2. These verbs commonly use only two forms in the present tense.

   - Use **encanta, importa, interesa**, etc. before a singular noun or an infinitive.

     Me **encanta** ir de compras.   *I love going shopping.*

   - Use **encantan, importan, interesan**, etc. before a plural noun or two singular nouns.

     Me **encantan** esos zapatos.   *I love those shoes.*

3. To specify a person with a noun *(Linda, my parents)*, use **a** + (singular noun) + **le** + (verb) for one person, and **a** + (plural noun) + **les** + (verb) for two or more people.

   A Luis le interesa diseñar ropa.   *Luis is interested in designing clothing.*

4. The verb **quedar** can mean *to have left* or *to fit*. When used to express *to fit*, another word must be added to specify how a garment or shoe fits the person.

   - The adverbs **bien** and **mal** do not change forms. For example: **Las botas te quedan <u>bien</u>.** *The boots fit you <u>well</u>.*

- Descriptive adjectives must match in gender and number the garment that is mentioned. For example: **La falda le queda floja.** *The skirt is too loose on her.*

Adjetivos que se usan con *quedar*			
apretado(a)(s)	*(too) tight, snug*	**grande(s)**	*(too) big*
flojo(a)(s)	*(too) loose, baggy*	**pequeño(a)(s)**	*(too) small*

5. The verb **parecer** *(to seem, to appear, to look)* follows a pattern similar to **quedar**; an adjective is added to express the opinion one has of the object.

OBJECT +	INDIRECT OBJECT PRONOUN +	**PARECE / PARECEN** +	ADJECTIVE
Los zapatos +	le	+ parecen	+ muy caros.
The shoes seem expensive to him/her.			

Adjetivos que se usan con *parecer*			
barato(a)(s)	*cheap, inexpensive*	**elegante(s)**	*elegant*
bonito(a)(s)	*pretty*	**feo(a)(s)**	*ugly*
caro(a)(s)	*expensive*	**informal(es)**	*casual*
cómodo(a)(s)	*comfortable*	**pasado(a)(s) de moda**	*out of style*

¡Aplícalo!

 Colaborar

7-17 **De compras.** Mientras están de compras, Eva y Clarisa ven unas blusas bonitas. Completen Uds. la conversación con las palabras correctas.

DEPENDIENTE Señoritas, ¿(1. te / les) interesa ver estas blusas?

EVA Sí, gracias. ¡Ah! Me (2. encanta / encantan) el estilo. ¿Qué dices, Clarisa?

CLARISA Las blusas me (3. parece / parecen) muy bonitas, pero el precio me (4. parece / parecen) muy alto.

EVA Pues a mí no me (5. importa / importan) los precios. Señor, me gustaría comprar esta. Aquí tiene cincuenta dólares.

DEPENDIENTE Con el impuesto *(tax)* son cincuenta y cinco, señorita. A Ud. (6. le / les) faltan cinco dólares.

EVA ¡Áyala vida! Clarisa, ¿(7. nos / te) molesta prestarme cinco dólares?

CLARISA Lo siento, Eva, pero a mí no (8. me / le) queda dinero en efectivo.

 Colaborar

7-18 **¿Cómo le queda?** ¿Qué piensas de la ropa de Susana? Con un(a) compañero(a), completen las oraciones con las palabras más lógicas.

apretado(a)(s)	flojo(a)(s)
bien	informal(es)
cómodo(a)(s)	

1. A Susana le quedan _____ los vaqueros.

2. La camiseta le queda un poco _____.

3. Los zapatos le quedan _____.

4. La ropa de Susana me parece _____ y bastante _____.

© Anna Furman/Shutterstock

¡Exprésate!

Colaborar

7-19 Problemas y soluciones. Tomando turnos con un(a) compañero(a), lean cada problema y escojan la solución más lógica. Hay que conjugar los verbos entre paréntesis en el presente; incluyan los pronombres de complemento indirecto apropiados (**le / les**).

Los problemas:

1. A Juan (quedar) largos los pantalones.
2. A Patricia (faltar) dinero en efectivo para comprar la chaqueta.
3. A Eduardo (molestar) ir de compras con su madre.
4. A Natalia (quedar) apretadas las botas.
5. A mis amigos no (interesar) estar a la última moda.

Las soluciones:

a. Tiene que pagar con tarjeta de crédito.
b. Tiene que comprar unas más grandes.
c. Debe ir a la tienda con sus amigos.
d. Necesita comprar unos más cortos.
e. Pueden comprar ropa usada.

7-20 Comentarios de ropa. ¿Qué te parecen los siguientes artículos de ropa? Comparte *(Share)* opiniones con un(a) compañero(a) de clase.

Palabras útiles: apretado, bonito, cómodo, elegante, feo, flojo, pasado de moda

© Gordana Sermek/Shutterstock

Modelo **Estudiante A:** ¿Qué te parece este vestido?
Estudiante B: Me parece muy elegante.

1.   2.   3.   4.   5.

(1) © aodaodaodaod/Shutterstock (2) © Richard Peterson/Shutterstock (3) © RTimages/Shutterstock (4) © Karkas/Shutterstock (5) © Sally Wallis/Shutterstock

7-21 Opiniones sobre las compras. En grupos de tres o cuatro, comenten estos temas y comparen sus opiniones.

1. ¿Te gusta ir de compras? Cuando vas de compras, ¿te importa más el precio o el estilo? ¿Qué otros factores son importantes para ti?
2. ¿Te interesan los programas en la tele sobre la moda? ¿Con qué frecuencia los miras?
3. ¿Qué haces cuando quieres comprar algo pero te falta dinero? ¿Cuáles son otras opciones?
4. ¿Te molesta si tu compañero(a) de cuarto usa tu ropa? ¿Cómo te sientes si tu compañero(a) usa tu ropa sin pedir permiso?
5. Si ves a un(a) amigo(a) con ropa que no le queda bien, ¿le dices algo? ¿Qué le dices?

PASO 2 VOCABULARIO

Vamos de compras

En un gran almacén

In this *Paso*, you will . . .

- practice how to make purchases in a clothing store
- use **por** and **para** to express purpose, motion, and time
- talk about actions that have recently taken place

A ver, ¿en qué piso están los zapatos?

GALERÍAS LA GLORIA

Directorio

4 CUARTO PISO Muebles – Juguetes

3 TERCER PISO Moda hombre – Servicio al cliente

2 SEGUNDO PISO Moda mujer – Zapatería

1 PRIMER PISO Moda joven – Electrónica

PB PLANTA BAJA Joyería – Perfumería – Accesorios

© Cengage Learning 2016

Los números ordinales		*Ordinal numbers*	
1° primero(a)	6° sexto(a)	*first*	*sixth*
2° segundo(a)	7° séptimo(a)	*second*	*seventh*
3° tercero(a)	8° octavo(a)	*third*	*eighth*
4° cuarto(a)	9° noveno(a)	*fourth*	*ninth*
5° quinto(a)	10° décimo(a)	*fifth*	*tenth*

Los precios	*Prices*
¿Cuánto cuesta?	*How much does it cost?*
¿Cuánto es?	*How much is it?*
Diez mil quinientos colones	*10,500 colones*
Dos millones de colones	*2,000,000 colones*

Frases de un(a) dependiente(a)	*Salesclerk's phrases*
¿En qué puedo servirle?	*How may I help you?*
¿Qué talla necesita?	*What size do you need?*
¿Busca un color en particular?	*Are you looking for a specific color?*

De compras en el centro comercial

Más frases de un(a) dependiente(a)

¿Qué le parece (esta camisa)?
¿Quiere probarse (los pantalones)?
Está rebajado(a). / Están rebajados(as).
¿Cómo desea pagar?

Frases de un(a) cliente(a)

Solo estoy mirando, gracias.
Busco (una camiseta).
Necesito talla pequeña / mediana / grande / 38.
¿Tiene uno(a) en (azul)?
¿Dónde están los probadores?
Me queda bien / mal.
Es muy caro(a). ¿Tiene uno(a) más barato(a)?
Lo / La / Los / Las compro.
Voy a pagar en efectivo / con tarjeta de crédito.

More salesclerk's phrases

What do you think about (this shirt)?
Do you want to try on (the pants)?
It's on sale. / They're on sale.
How do you want to pay?

Customer's phrases

I'm just looking, thank you.
I'm looking for (a T-shirt).
I need size small / medium / large / 38.
Do you have one in (blue)?
Where are the fitting rooms?
It fits me well / poorly.
It's very expensive. Do you have a cheaper (less expensive) one?
I'll buy it / them.
I'm going to pay cash / with a credit card.

¡Aplícalo!

Colaborar

 7-22 **El (La) dependiente(a) del mes.** Mira la gráfica de ventas *(sales)* del departamento de muebles del gran almacén Las Palmas. Trabajando con un(a) compañero(a), digan cuánto vendió cada dependiente(a) y en qué lugar está.

🔄 Large numbers, **Capítulo 4 Paso 2**

Modelo Sonia Vendelotodo está en primer lugar *(first place)*, con ventas de veinticinco millones quinientos mil colones.

Las Palmas: Departamento de Muebles			
FEBRERO			
Dependiente	**Total de ventas**	**Dependiente**	**Total de ventas**
Sonia Vendelotodo	₡25 500 000	Teófilo Tenaz	₡22 000 000
Mario Maluco	₡10 100 000	Margarita Llegatarde	₡12 600 000
Sergio Alcancía	₡24 750 000	Néstor Nifunifa	₡18 300 000
Patricia Plata	₡22 900 000	Silvia Caralarga	₡15 400 000

7-23 **El dependiente y el cliente.** ¿Quién habla: el dependiente o el cliente? Con un(a) compañero(a), tomen turnos para leer una línea *(line)* y decir si corresponde al dependiente o al cliente.

Solo estoy mirando, gracias.

¿Qué le parece aquella chaqueta?

Necesito una talla más grande.

¿Quiere probarse estas botas?

© Monkey Business Images/Shutterstock

¿En qué piso están los televisores?

Todas las camisetas están rebajadas hoy.

La tienda cierra en media hora.

¿Tiene una más barata?

7-24 **Un nuevo empleo.** Tienes un nuevo empleo *(job)*: vas a ser dependiente(a) *(salesperson)* en un almacén que tiene muchos clientes hispanos. ¿Qué necesitas decir en las siguientes situaciones? Trabajando con un(a) compañero(a), completen las frases del (de la) dependiente(a) de una manera lógica.

1. Buenos días, señora. ¿En qué _____?

2. ¿Una chaqueta? ¿Qué talla _____?

3. Tenemos suéteres en muchos colores bonitos. ¿Busca _____?

4. ¿Los probadores? Están _____.

5. La camisa no le queda bien. Pero tenemos una _____.

6. Hoy las camisas cuestan solo $20. Están _____.

7. Puede pagar en efectivo o _____.

¡Exprésate!

7-25 **El directorio.** ¿En qué pisos están estos artículos? Trabajando con un(a) compañero(a) de clase, miren el directorio de Galerías La Gloria en la página 262 y dramaticen pequeños diálogos. Sigan el modelo.

Modelo **Cliente(a):** ¿En qué piso están las faldas?

Empleado(a): Están en el segundo piso.

1. los sofás
2. las sandalias
3. las corbatas
4. los televisores

5. la colonia y los cosméticos
6. las raquetas de tenis
7. los vaqueros para chicos de 14 años
8. (Continúen con otros artículos.)

7-26 **En un gran almacén.** ¿Qué dicen el (la) cliente(a) y el (la) dependiente(a)? Trabajando con un(a) compañero(a), lean en voz alta la conversación y complétenla de una manera lógica.

Colaborar

DEPENDIENTE(A) ¿(1) _____?

CLIENTE(A) Busco una camiseta.

DEPENDIENTE(A) ¿Qué talla necesita?

CLIENTE(A) ¿(2) _____?

DEPENDIENTE(A) ¿Qué le parece esta camiseta? La tenemos en azul, gris y verde.

CLIENTE(A) (3) _____. ¿(4) _____?

DEPENDIENTE(A) Están allí, en el fondo *(in the back).*

(Unos minutos más tarde)

CLIENTE(A) Me queda apretada. ¿(5) _____?

DEPENDIENTE(A) Sí, aquí hay otra en una talla grande.

CLIENTE(A) ¡Perfecto! ¿(6) _____?

DEPENDIENTE(A) Está rebajada. (7) _____.

CLIENTE(A) Está muy bien de precio. (8) _____.

DEPENDIENTE(A) Muy bien. ¿(9) _____?

CLIENTE(A) Con tarjeta de débito.

7-27 **Por las tiendas.** Con un(a) compañero(a) de clase, dramaticen las escenas en los dibujos. Usen las expresiones de las páginas 262 y 263.

1.

2.

3.

Illustrations © Cengage Learning 2016

Por y para

ORLANDO	Caminé por tres horas por todo el centro comercial pero ¡por fin conseguí algo para mi madre!
AMANDA	¡Qué bonito!
ORLANDO	¡Y barato! Lo compré por treinta dólares.
AMANDA	Conseguiste las tres Bs: ¡bueno, bonito y barato!

■ ■ ■

Descúbrelo

- What did Orlando buy? Who is it for?
- Does Amanda think it was a good buy? Why?
- How many times is **por** used? In which instances does it mean *for*? Where does it mean *around*? With what other word does it express *finally*?
- Is **por** or **para** used to express *for my mother*?

1. The prepositions **por** and **para** are often translated as *for* in English. However, the two are not interchangeable, and they can also be used to express several different notions.

Te doy $10 **por** la camiseta.	*I'll give you $10 for (**in exchange for**) the T-shirt.*
Te doy $10 **para** la camiseta.	*I'll give you $10 for (**so you can buy**) the T-shirt.*

2. **Para** is used to express:

for (someone)	Busco un regalo **para mi sobrina**.
for (a particular use)	Esta taza es **para el café**.
in order to, to (+ infinitive)	Fui al centro comercial **para comprar botas**.
by, for (a certain time or day)	Necesito comprar el regalo de Susana **para el viernes**.

3. **Por** is used to express:

for (an amount of time)	Trabajo todos los lunes **por seis horas**.
for, in exchange for	Compré el abrigo **por ochenta dólares**.
through, by, along, around	Paseamos **por el centro comercial**.
per	Cuesta $20 **por persona**.
in / during (a time of day: **mañana / tarde / noche**)	Trabaja en esa tienda **por la tarde**.

4. **Por** is also used in certain set phrases:

por ejemplo	*for example*	**por lo general**	*generally, in general*
por eso	*for that reason, that's why*	**por lo menos**	*at least*
		por supuesto	*of course, certainly*
por favor	*please*	**por último**	*finally*
por fin	*at last*		

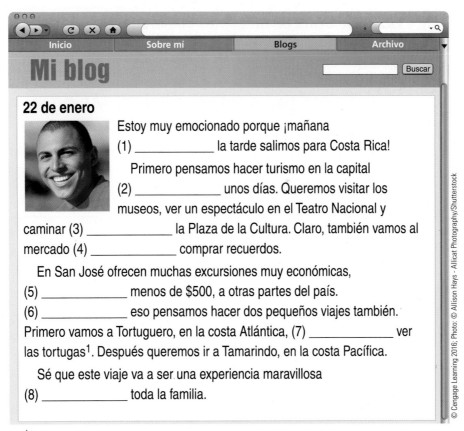

7-28 Los regalos. Carmen fue de compras ayer. Para saber qué pasó, trabaja con un(a) compañero(a) para relacionar las dos columnas. Tomando turnos, una persona lee la primera parte de cada oración y la otra persona lee la conclusión más lógica.

Colaborar

¡Aplícalo!

_____ 1. Ayer tuve que ir de compras para...

_____ 2. Di un paseo por...

_____ 3. Pasé horas buscando el regalo perfecto; por...

_____ 4. Me ofrecieron un descuento adicional del 20 por...

_____ 5. Así que (So) compré la blusa por...

_____ 6. También vi unas camisas bonitas y compré una para...

_____ 7. Al mediodía volví a casa porque por...

_____ 8. Pero mañana pienso regresar porque necesito otro regalo para...

a. el centro, donde están las tiendas más elegantes.

b. buscar un regalo para mi mamá.

c. ciento.

d. el cumpleaños de mi hermana.

e. solo $30.

f. fin, encontré una blusa muy bonita.

g. la tarde siempre cuido (babysit) a mis hermanitos.

h. papá.

7-29 Vamos de viaje. Geraldo y su familia van a Costa Rica de vacaciones. Trabajando con un(a) compañero(a), completen su blog con **por** y **para**, según el contexto. ¿Conocen algunos de los lugares mencionados?

Colaborar

| Inicio | Sobre mí | Blogs | Archivo |

Mi blog

Buscar

22 de enero

Estoy muy emocionado porque ¡mañana
(1) _____ la tarde salimos para Costa Rica!
Primero pensamos hacer turismo en la capital
(2) _____ unos días. Queremos visitar los
museos, ver un espectáculo en el Teatro Nacional y
caminar (3) _____ la Plaza de la Cultura. Claro, también vamos al
mercado (4) _____ comprar recuerdos.

En San José ofrecen muchas excursiones muy económicas,
(5) _____ menos de $500, a otras partes del país.
(6) _____ eso pensamos hacer dos pequeños viajes también.
Primero vamos a Tortuguero, en la costa Atlántica, (7) _____ ver
las tortugas[1]. Después queremos ir a Tamarindo, en la costa Pacífica.

Sé que este viaje va a ser una experiencia maravillosa
(8) _____ toda la familia.

[1]turtles

© Cengage Learning 2016. Photo: © Allison Hays - Allicat Photography/Shutterstock

PASO 2 **267**

Large numbers,
Capítulo 4 Paso 2

7-30 ¿Qué compraste? Imagina que fuiste a Costa Rica y compraste estos artículos para tus parientes. Toma turnos con tu compañero(a) para decir qué compraste, para quién y por cuántos colones.

Modelo Compré estas sandalias **para** mi hermana **por** diecinueve mil doscientos colones.

₡19.200

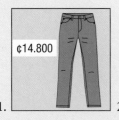
₡14.800
1.

₡16.500
2.

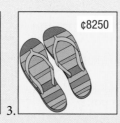
₡8250
3.

₡5500
Pura vida
4.

₡9300
5.

Illustrations: © Cengage Learning 2016

7-31 ¡Qué día! ¡Hoy tienes muchas cosas que hacer! Con tu compañero(a), tomen turnos para decir a qué hora van a los siguientes lugares y explicar para qué. Usen **para** + *infinitivo*.

Modelo a la librería
A las nueve voy a la librería **para comprar** libros de texto.

1. al almacén
2. al gimnasio
3. a la biblioteca
4. a la farmacia
5. al banco
6. al aeropuerto
7. a la clínica
8. al museo

7-32 Encuesta de un centro comercial. Con un(a) compañero(a), tomen turnos completando la encuesta *(survey)* sobre los hábitos de compra. Una persona hace las preguntas y la otra contesta con **por** o **para**.

ENCUESTA DEL CENTRO COMERCIAL GRAN PLAZA

1. ¿Para qué vino aquí hoy? _____
2. ¿Por cuáles tiendas paseó? _____
3. ¿Se compró algo para Ud.? ☐ sí ☐ no
4. ¿Cuánto pagó por eso? _____
5. ¿Cuándo prefiere ir de compras? ☐ por la mañana ☐ por la tarde

¡Gracias por su participación!

© Cengage Learning 2016

7-33 Busco un regalo. Con un(a) compañero(a), dramaticen una escena entre un(a) cliente(a) y un(a) dependiente(a). El (La) cliente(a) busca un regalo para un pariente y el (la) dependiente(a) le hace preguntas para recomendar algo. En la conversación, Uds. tienen que usar **por** y **para** cinco veces o más.

Modelo **Cliente(a):** Busco un regalo **para** mi hermana.
Dependiente(a): ¿Es **para** su cumpleaños?...

El presente perfecto de indicativo

comprar el vestido

reservar un hotel ✓

pedir las flores

© Cengage Learning 2016

MIRTA ¿Has comprado tu vestido de novia?

ALICIA No, no he tenido tiempo.

MIRTA Chica, ¡tu boda es en dos meses!

ALICIA Bueno, he reservado un hotel para la recepción. Ya es algo.
(It's a start.)

1. The present perfect tense (**el presente perfecto**) is used to express what somebody *has done* or what events *have taken place*. It is composed of two words: the present tense of the verb **haber** followed by a past participle.

    ¿**Has ido** de compras últimamente?   ***Have*** *you* ***gone*** *shopping lately?*

2. The present tense forms of **haber** are **he**, **has**, **ha**, **hemos**, **habéis**, and **han**. Past participles are formed by dropping the -**ar** of an infinitive and adding -**ado**, or by dropping the -**er** / -**ir** of the infinitive and adding -**ido**.

El presente perfecto = haber (+ *participio pasado*)		
yo	**he** *trabajado*	*I have worked*
tú	**has** *comido*	*you (inf.) have eaten*
Ud./él/ella	**ha** *vivido*	*you (form.)/he/she have lived*
nosotros(as)	**hemos** *comprado*	*we have bought*
vosotros(as)	**habéis** *estudiado*	*you (pl.) have studied*
Uds./ellos/ellas	**han** *salido*	*you (pl.)/they have left*

3. Some past participles are irregular.

    abrir: **abierto** *opened*   poner: **puesto** *placed, set*
    decir: **dicho** *said*   resolver: **resuelto** *solved, resolved*
    escribir: **escrito** *written*   romper: **roto** *broken*
    hacer: **hecho** *made, done*   ver: **visto** *seen*
    ir: **ido** *gone*   volver: **vuelto** *returned*
    morir: **muerto** *died*

4. The present perfect is often used in statements with the expressions **ya** and **todavía no**. Questions in the present perfect often include the phrase **alguna vez**.

    Ya hemos comprado el regalo.   *We've **already** bought the gift.*
    Todavía no he comprado nada.   *I **haven't** bought anything **yet**.*
    ¿Has comprado en esa tienda   *Have you **ever** shopped*
    alguna vez?   *in that store?*

■ ■ ■
Descúbrelo

- What does Alicia need to do to get ready for her wedding?

- Which of the things on her list has she already done?

- Why hasn't she done more?

- What little word is used to express *I have (done something)*? What ending is used in the verb forms immediately after this little word?

¡Aplícalo!

 7-34 **Ta-Te-Ti con los participios pasados.** Con un(a) compañero(a), jueguen al Ta-Te-Ti. Tomando turnos, cada persona tiene que decir el participio pasado correcto antes de poner su X o su O en el cuadrado *(square).*

comprar	vivir	hacer
escribir	comer	ver
poner	pagar	salir

abrir	trabajar	ir
asistir	morir	tener
romper	volver	preparar

Colaborar

7-35 **Una entrevista.** Federico quiere trabajar en una tienda durante el verano. Con un(a) compañero(a), completen la entrevista *(interview)* con los verbos más lógicos. Hay que usar el presente perfecto.

SR. GÓMEZ ¿(1. trabajar / vivir) Ud. alguna vez en una tienda?

FEDERICO No, pero yo (2. leer / tomar) clases de mercadotecnia *(marketing).*

SR. GÓMEZ Ah, muy bien. ¿(3. tener / ir) Ud. otro tipo de empleo *(employment)*?

FEDERICO Sí, yo (4. salir / conducir) un autobús para la universidad. Soy muy puntual y responsable.

SR. GÓMEZ ¡Qué bueno! ¿(5. hacer / romper) Ud. trabajo voluntario alguna vez?

FEDERICO Sí. En mi clase de informática nosotros (6. escribir / decir) varios programas educativos para niños. También hablo inglés aunque yo nunca (7. vivir / beber) en Estados Unidos.

SR. GÓMEZ Bueno, eso es todo por el momento. Vamos a estar en contacto.

Colaborar

7-36 **Inauguración de la tienda Tuanis.** Marilú y Manuel van a abrir una nueva tienda. ¿Qué no han hecho todavía? Con un(a) compañero(a) de clase, miren la siguiente lista. Tomen turnos para decir algo que ya han hecho y algo que todavía no han hecho.

Modelo Ya han sacado la basura pero todavía no han limpiado el baño.

> ## Cosas para hacer
>
> limpiar el baño
> ✓ sacar la basura
> ✓ lavar las ventanas
> ✓ vestir los maniquís
>   barrer el piso
> ✓ limpiar los estantes
>
> ✓ guardar los suéteres
>   planchar los pantalones
>   abrir las puertas
> ✓ escribir los precios
>   regar las plantas
>   guardar el dinero

Nota cultural

The name of this store—**Tuanis**—is a Central American word for *nice, awesome.* Slang words vary from region to region and across generations. For instance, instead of **tuanis**, many young people say **padre** (Mexico), **guay** (Spain), **chévere** (Venezuela), and **bacán** (Chile).

© Cengage Learning 2016

¡Exprésate!
Colaborar

7-37 **Centroamericanos famosos.** ¿Qué han hecho los siguientes centroamericanos para ser famosos? Trabaja con un(a) compañero(a) de clase para relacionar a las personas con sus logros *(achievements)*. Usen el presente perfecto.

© AFP/Getty Images

Modelo La activista de Guatemala Rigoberta Menchú ha recibido el Premio Nobel de la Paz *(Peace)*.

Centroamericanos famosos:	**Logros importantes:**
la activista de Guatemala Rigoberta Menchú	viajar al espacio siete veces
la actriz América Ferrera, de padres hondureños,	ganar seis premios Grammy
la diseñadora salvadoreña Francesca Miranda	escribir muchas novelas y poemas
la escritora nicaragüense Gioconda Belli	representar papeles *(roles)* en el cine y la televisión
el astronauta de Costa Rica Franklin Chang-Díaz	recibir el Premio Nobel de la Paz *(Peace)*
el cantante panameño Rubén Blades	hacer colecciones de ropa para hombres y mujeres

Clase

7-38 **Colección de firmas.** ¿Quiénes de Uds. han hecho las siguientes actividades? Circula por el salón de clase para entrevistar a varios compañeros. Si contestan "sí", tienen que firmar *(sign)* tu tabla.

Modelo **viajar** a Costa Rica
    Estudiante A: ¿**Has viajado** a Costa Rica alguna vez?
    Estudiante B: No, nunca **he viajado** a Costa Rica. / Sí, **he viajado** a Costa Rica dos veces.
    Estudiante A: Bueno, gracias. / Firma aquí, por favor.

Actividad	**Firma** *(signature)*
1. **trabajar** de dependiente(a)	
2. **comer** ceviche	
3. **hacer** un crucero	
4. **ver** un partido de hockey	
5. **bucear** en el mar	
6. **escribir** un poema de amor *(love)*	

7-39 **¡Increíble!** ¡Vamos a jugar! Primero, tienes que pensar en algo increíble que tú y tus amigos han hecho y en dos cosas que **no** han hecho. Después, formen círculos pequeños y tomen turnos para decir sus tres oraciones. Los compañeros tienen que decir cuál de las oraciones es verdad *(true)*.

Modelo **Estudiante A:** Mis amigos y yo hemos ido al canal de Panamá. Hemos nadado cinco millas en el océano Pacífico. Hemos conocido al presidente de Estados Unidos.
    Estudiante B: Han conocido al presidente de Estados Unidos, ¿verdad?
    Estudiante A: Sí, es verdad. Lo conocimos en el campus el año pasado.

El mercado de artesanías

Recuerdos típicos

In this *Paso*, you will . . .
- identify souvenirs and what they are made of
- learn how to bargain in a market
- avoid repetition when saying who or what is involved

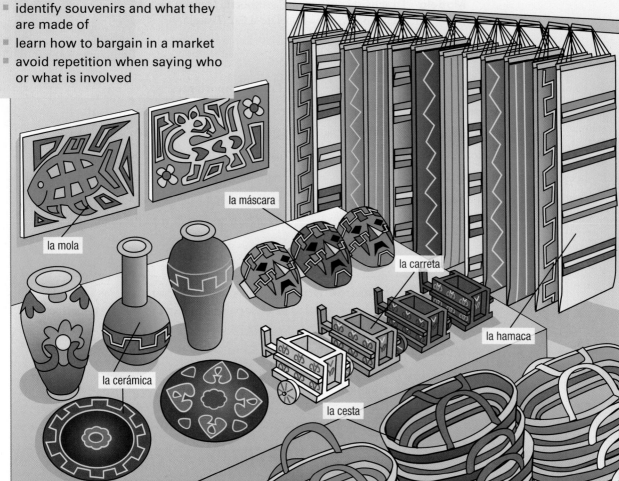

la mola

la máscara

la carreta

la hamaca

la cerámica

la cesta

Las joyas	Jewelry
el anillo	*ring*
los aretes	*earrings*
el collar	*necklace*

Los accesorios	Accessories
la billetera	*wallet*
el bolso	*purse; handbag*
el cinturón	*belt*
el llavero	*key ring*
el sombrero	*hat*

Para hablar de los materiales	Talking about materials
¿De qué está(n) hecho(a)(s)?	*What is it / are they made of?*
Está(n) hecho(a)(s) de oro / de plata / de cuero / de madera / de paja.	*It's / They're made of gold / of silver / of leather / of wood / of straw.*
Está(n) hecho(a)(s) a mano.	*It's / They're handmade.*

© Cengage Learning 2016

El regateo

Frases para regatear

¿Cuánto cuesta (ese sombrero)?
Me gusta pero no tengo mucho dinero.
Le puedo ofrecer (veinte dólares).
Gracias, pero es demasiado caro(a) para mí.
Está bien. Me lo (la) llevo.

Frases de un(a) vendedor(a)

Es de primera calidad.
Se lo (la) dejo en solo (treinta dólares).
Es mi última oferta.

Bargaining expressions

How much does (that hat) cost?
I like it, but I don't have a lot of money.
I can offer you (20 dollars).
Thank you, but it's too expensive for me.
Okay. I'll take it.

Vendor's phrases

It's top quality.
I'll give it to you for only (30 dollars).
It's my last offer.

¡Aplícalo!

Colaborar **7-40** **¿Qué es?** Kelly quiere comprar algunas cosas en el mercado de artesanías pero no recuerda las palabras exactas. Tomando turnos con un(a) compañero(a), una persona lee una descripción y la otra identifica la cosa de la lista.

un anillo	una billetera	una carreta	un collar	una hamaca
unos aretes	un bolso	un cinturón	un cuadro	una mola

1. Quiero comprar algo para mi mamá pero no recuerdo la palabra. Es un accesorio para hombres o mujeres. Está hecho de cuero normalmente. Lo llevamos con los pantalones por lo general.

2. También quiero una joya especial para mi hermana. Es un artículo muy pequeño. Está hecho de plata o de oro. Es para llevar en el dedo (*finger*).

3. Y para mis abuelos quiero un artículo de artesanías muy típico. No sé de qué está hecho, pero lo usamos para dormir en el jardín o en el patio de la casa.

4. Para mi mejor amiga quiero algo práctico. Está hecho de cuero o de paja. Es donde ponemos el dinero, el celular y otras cosas personales.

5. ¡Ay! ¡Casi me olvidé! Quiero algo para mi padre. A él le encanta el arte. ¿Cómo se llama esta cosa, el producto de un artista?

Colaborar **7-41** **En el mercado.** Trabajando con un(a) compañero(a), relacionen las dos columnas de una manera lógica. Tomando turnos, una persona lee la frase del (de la) cliente(a) y la otra lee la respuesta del (de la) vendedor(a).

El (La) cliente(a):

_____ 1. ¿Qué es algo típico de Panamá?

_____ 2. ¿Cuánto cuesta ese collar?

_____ 3. ¿Me puede hacer un descuento?

_____ 4. Le puedo ofrecer $40 por este cuadro.

_____ 5. Está bien. Me lo llevo.

El (La) vendedor(a):

a. ¿Quiere algo más?

b. Es muy poco. Se lo dejo en $50.

c. Solo $35. Está hecho de plata.

d. Si compra dos, le doy un precio especial.

e. Estas máscaras son muy típicas. Están hechas de madera.

7-42 **De compras en El Tucán.** ¡Cuántos recuerdos bonitos hay en la tienda de artesanías El Tucán! Trabaja con un(a) compañero(a) para crear diálogos sobre el precio y el material de cada objeto.

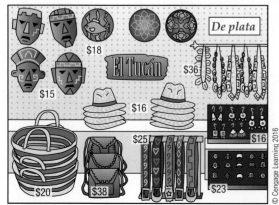

Modelo

Turista: ¿Cuánto cuesta esta máscara?

Vendedor(a): Quince dólares.

Turista: ¿De qué está hecha?

Vendedor(a): Está hecha de madera.

¡Exprésate!

👥 **7-43** **No recuerdo la palabra.** Estás de compras en San José, Costa Rica. Quieres comprar algunos recuerdos, pero ¡no recuerdas las palabras exactas para algunas de las cosas! Tomando turnos, una persona describe la cosa y la otra persona dice la palabra correcta. Sigan el modelo.

Modelo   **Cliente(a):** Disculpe, señor (señorita). Busco algo pequeño. Está hecho de cuero y es para guardar el dinero.
Vendedor(a): ¿Una billetera? Sí, tenemos muchas.

© Mike Flippo/Shutterstock;
© Liewluck/Shutterstock;
© homydesign/Shutterstock;
© cristi180884/Shutterstock;
© Cindy Shebley/Shutterstock;
© GeorgeMPhotography/Shutterstock

👥 **7-44** **A regatear.** Tienes que regatear, pero ¡por fin compras el recuerdo perfecto! Con un(a) compañero(a), lean y completen el diálogo entre tú y un(a) vendedor(a) en el mercado de artesanías. En algunos casos solo necesitan incluir una o dos palabras; en otros casos, una oración completa.

TÚ   Hola, buenos días. Estoy buscando un regalo para *(una persona)* _____. (1) ¿_____?

VENDEDOR(A)   Tenemos muchas cosas típicas y todas son de primera calidad. ¿Qué le parece(n) (2) _____? También tenemos (3) _____.

TÚ   Me gusta(n) mucho (4) _____. ¿Cuánto (5) _____?

VENDEDOR(A)   (6) _____.

TÚ   Es / Son (7) _____, pero no tengo mucho dinero. (8) ¿_____?

VENDEDOR(A)   ¿Un descuento? Bueno, si compra dos, (9) _____.

TÚ   No sé. (10) _____.

VENDEDOR(A)   Es muy poco. (11) _____. Es mi última oferta.

TÚ   Bueno, (12) _____.

👥 **7-45** **Unos recuerdos típicos.** Con un(a) compañero(a), dramaticen una escena entre un(a) cliente y un(a) vendedor(a) en el mercado de las páginas 272–273.

Estudiante A	Estudiante B
Eres el (la) cliente(a).	Eres el (la) vendedora(a).
No tienes mucho dinero, pero quieres comprar unos recuerdos para tus amigos.	Tienes muchos recuerdos bonitos y baratos. Le ofreces muchas gangas *(good buys)* a tu cliente(a).

Repaso de los pronombres de complemento directo e indirecto

© Cengage Learning 2016

CLARITA ¡Me encantan tus aretes! ¿Dónde **los** compraste?

LUPE En El Tucán. Tienen joyas bonitas y siempre me hacen un descuento.

CLARITA Mmm... el cumpleaños de mi mamá es mañana y quiero regalar**le** un collar.

LUPE ¡Vamos a El Tucán!

■ ■ ■
Descúbrelo

- What does Clarita want to know about Lupe's new earrings?

- Why are the two friends going to El Tucán?

- The first line of the conversation has a direct object pronoun: What does **los** refer to?

- The third line of the conversation has an indirect object pronoun: To whom does **le** refer?

1. A complete sentence consists of a subject, a verb, and optional elements such as direct and indirect objects. Indirect object nouns and indirect object pronouns (**los pronombres de complemento indirecto**) refer to the person(s) for whom or to whom something is done.

   Le compré una mola.   *I bought **her** a mola. / I bought a mola **for her**.*

Los pronombres de complemento indirecto			
me	*to / for me*	nos	*to / for us*
te	*to / for you (sing., inf.)*	os	*to / for you (pl., inf., Spain)*
le	*to / for you (sing., form.)*	les	*to / for you (pl.; form. in Spain)*
le	*to / for him or her*	les	*to / for them*

2. To specify a person with a noun *(to Mary, for my friend)*, the indirect object pronouns **le** and **les** are used together with the noun.

   le and **a** + *name / singular noun*   **Le** escribo **a tía Eulalia** todas las semanas.
   les and **a** + *names / plural noun*   No **les** escribo mucho **a mis primos**.

3. As you learned in **Paso 1**, indirect object pronouns are always used with verbs like **gustar**. For example: ¡**Nos** encanta ese color! *We love that color!*

4. Direct object nouns and direct object pronouns (**los pronombres de complemento directo**) answer the questions *what?* and *whom?* with respect to the verb.

   - A person: **Conozco bien a <u>María</u>. <u>La</u> conocí hace años.**

   - A thing: **Necesito un <u>vestido</u>. <u>Lo</u> voy a comprar mañana.**

Los pronombres de complemento directo			
me	*me*	nos	*us*
te	*you (sing., inf.)*	os	*you (pl., inf. in Spain)*
lo / la	*you (sing., form.)*	los / las	*you (pl.; form. in Spain)*
lo	*him, it*	los	*them (masc.)*
la	*her, it*	las	*them (fem.)*

5. Direct and indirect object pronouns follow the same rules for placement in a sentence.

- Before a conjugated verb in most verb tenses (present, present perfect, preterite): **¿Qué <u>me</u> has comprado?**

- In the present progressive tense, before the conjugated verb or attached to the end of the present participle: **¿El desfile de moda *(fashion show)*? <u>Lo</u> estamos mirando. / Estamos mirándo<u>lo</u>.**

- With verb phrases, before the conjugated verb or attached to the infinitive: **No <u>le</u> voy a dar nada. / No voy a dar<u>le</u> nada.**

¡Aplícalo!

7-46 **El viaje a la playa.** Tú y tu compañero(a) van a la playa. ¿Qué van a llevar en la maleta? Tomen turnos para preguntar si van a llevar o no van a llevar las siguientes cosas. Usen pronombres de complemento directo (**lo**, **la**, **los**, **las**) en sus respuestas.

Modelo   estas botas

      Estudiante A: ¿Vas a llevar **estas botas**?
      Estudiante B: No, no **las** voy a llevar. / No, no voy a llevar**las**.

1. este traje de baño	5. estas camisetas	8. este sombrero
2. estos pantalones cortos	6. esta chaqueta	9. este kayak
3. este iPod	7. estas chancletas	10. estas gafas de sol
4. esta hamaca		

Colaborar

7-47 **Un viaje a Costa Rica.** Marco y Rita están en San José, Costa Rica. ¿Qué hacen allí? Trabaja con un(a) compañero(a) para leer las conversaciones. Hay que escoger el pronombre de complemento correcto entre paréntesis en cada caso.

En la oficina de turismo:

    RITA   ¿Qué excursión de un día nos recomienda?

  EMPLEADO   (1. Me / Les) recomiendo el crucero Calypso a Isla Tortuga. Aquí tienen más información. ¿(2. Les / Las) interesa esta excursión?

    RITA   Sí, (3. la / los) queremos hacer mañana.

En el restaurante típico Nuestra Tierra:

  MESERO   ¿Quieren probar el flan de la casa?

  MARCO   Ya (4. lo / le) probamos ayer. Muy rico pero hoy no queremos postre. ¿Nos trae la cuenta, por favor?

  MESERO   Sí, enseguida (5. la / lo) traigo.

En el mercado La Casona:

  MARCO   A nosotros (6. le / nos) gusta esta carreta pero no tenemos mucho dinero. ¿Nos (7. la / las) puede dejar en ocho mil colones?

  VENDEDORA   Está bien, pero tienen que pagar en efectivo.

  MARCO   ¿Ocho mil colones en efectivo? Aquí (8. las / los) tiene.

¡Exprésate!

Colaborar

7-48 **¡Muchos regalos!** Mira la lista de ocasiones especiales. ¿Qué les vas a comprar a las personas indicadas? Toma turnos con un(a) compañero(a) para expresar tus planes de compras. Usen un pronombre de complemento indirecto (**le**, **les**) para indicar el destinatario *(recipient)* de cada regalo.

Modelo Para el aniversario de bodas de mis abuelos **les** voy a comprar unas flores.

1. el aniversario de bodas de tus abuelos
2. la boda de tus mejores amigos
3. el bautizo *(baptism)* de tu sobrino

4. la graduación de tu prima
5. el bar mitzvah de tu vecino
6. la jubilación *(retirement)* de tus padres

Clase

7-49 **Hacer cumplidos.** ¡Vamos a hacer cumplidos *(compliment)* a los compañeros de clase! Circula por el salón de clase y habla con varios compañeros. Menciona un artículo de ropa o un accesorio y pregunta dónde lo compró. Hay que usar pronombres de complemento directo (**lo**, **la**, **los**, **las**). Sigan el modelo.

Modelo **Estudiante A:** Me encantan tus zapatos. ¿Dónde **los** compraste?
Estudiante B: Gracias. **Los** compré en Macy's. Me gusta tu camiseta. ¿Dónde **la** compraste?

> ↻ Describing spatial relationships, **Capítulo 5 Paso 3**

7-50 **¡No lo encuentro!** Le prestaste muchas cosas a tu compañero(a) de cuarto y ahora no encuentras nada. Con un(a) compañero(a), tomen turnos preguntando dónde está algo. Usen el dibujo siguiente y pronombres de complemento. Sigan el modelo.

Modelo

Estudiante A: **Le** presté mi libro de historia a mi compañero de cuarto y ahora no **lo** encuentro. ¿Dónde **lo** dejó?
Estudiante B: Mira. **Lo** dejó encima del microondas.

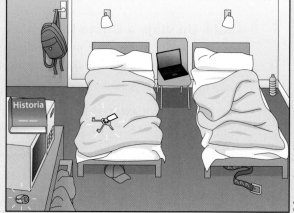
© Cengage Learning 2016

7-51 **Venta de garaje.** Entrevístense *(Interview each other)* con las preguntas sobre una venta de garaje *(garage sale)* a continuación. Usen pronombres cuando sea posible *(when possible)*.

1. ¿Cuándo fue la última vez que fuiste a una venta de garaje *(garage sale)*? ¿Quién te acompañó *(accompanied you)*?
2. ¿Qué compraste en la venta de garaje? ¿Todavía lo (la) tienes?
3. ¿Cuánto le ofreciste primero al (a la) vendedor(a)? ¿Aceptó el precio?
4. Al final, ¿cuánto le diste? ¿Te pareció el precio justo *(fair)*?
5. ¿Has hecho una venta de garaje en tu casa o apartamento? ¿Cuándo la hiciste? ¿Quién te ayudó?

G PASO 3 GRAMÁTICA B

Los pronombres de complemento directo e indirecto usados juntos

¿? ¿? ¿? ¿?

© Cengage Learning 2016

SEÑOR	Tengo un billete de mil colones. ¿Me lo cambia por tres monedas (coins) de 500, por favor?
DEPENDIENTE	¡¡Por tres monedas?! ¡No! Se lo cambio por dos monedas.
SEÑOR	¿Y entonces dónde está el favor?

1. Direct objects and indirect objects often appear together in the same sentence.

	I.O.	D.O.	
ALICIA	Marcos **me** regaló **esta chaqueta**.		*Marcos gave **me this jacket**.*

	I.O. D.O.	
ROSA	¡Qué bonita! ¿**Me la** prestas?	*How pretty! Can you lend **it to me**?*

2. When both the direct object and the indirect object are pronouns, the indirect object is placed before the direct object in Spanish. Think *I.D.* to remember the correct order.

> PRONOMBRE DE COMPLEMENTO + PRONOMBRE DE COMPLEMENTO
> INDIRECTO DIRECTO
> ¿El cuadro? Mi tía **nos lo** dio. *The painting? My aunt gave **it to us**.*

3. The indirect object pronouns **le** and **les** are replaced by the alternate form **se** whenever they occur right before a direct object pronoun.

> **le** + (lo / la / los / las) → **se** + (lo / la / los / las)
> **les** + (lo / la / los / las) → **se** + (lo / la/ los / las)

> ¿Los aretes? **Se los** regalé para su cumpleaños. *The earrings? I gave **them to her** for her birthday.*

4. Reflexive pronouns (**me**, **te**, **se**, **nos**, **os**, **se**) are placed before direct object pronouns, too.

> ¿El vestido? **Me lo** probé. *The dress? I tried **it** on **(myself)**.*

5. Double object pronouns are generally placed before the conjugated verb in the sentence. They may also be attached to the ends of present participles and infinitives; in these cases, an accent mark is added.

> ¿Y estos pantalones? ¿No quieres probár**telos**? *And these pants? Don't you want to try **them** on **(yourself)**?*

▪▪▪ Descúbrelo

- What does the man want in exchange for the thousand-colón bill? Will the clerk comply?

- In the dialogue, in which sentences are a direct and an indirect object pronoun used together? Which one comes first?

- In **Se lo cambio**, what does **lo** refer to? To whom does **se** refer?

PASO 3 GRAMÁTICA B

¡Aplícalo!

†† 7-52 **¿Qué les dio su profesor(a)?** ¿Qué información les dio su profesor(a) de español a Uds.? Tomando turnos con un(a) compañero(a) de clase, una persona pregunta si su profesor(a) de español les dio lo siguiente y la otra persona responde con dos pronombres de complemento. Sigan el modelo.

Modelo las horas de oficina

Estudiante A: ¿Nos dio las horas de oficina?

Estudiante B: Sí, nos las dio.

1. el número de su teléfono celular
2. su correo electrónico
3. la dirección de su casa

4. una lista de libros recomendados
5. las respuestas del próximo examen
6. la fecha del examen final

†† 7-53 **En el mercado de artesanías.** ¿Qué hacen las personas en el mercado de artesanías? Con un(a) compañero(a) de clase, tomen turnos haciendo las siguientes preguntas. Usen dos pronombres de complemento en cada respuesta. ¡Ojo! Hay que cambiar **le(s)** a **se** en todos los casos.

Modelo ¿A quién le vende Luis el sombrero?

Se lo vende a Vanesa.

1. ¿A quién le vende Félix las tazas de cerámica?
2. ¿A quién le pide Claudia un descuento?
3. ¿Por cuánto le vende Josefina los aretes a Claudia?

4. ¿A quién le da el dinero Vanesa?
5. ¿A quién le pone un collar Fernando?
6. ¿A quién le presta dinero Ramón?
7. ¿Quién le da dinero a Félix?
8. ¿A quién le hace Rosario una pregunta?

¡Exprésate!

 7-54 **Encuesta de satisfacción del cliente.** ¿En qué restaurante comiste recientemente? La gerencia *(management)* quiere conocer tu opinión sobre su servicio. Trabaja con un(a) compañero(a) para completar la encuesta *(survey)*.

- Estudiante A le hace las preguntas de la encuesta a Estudiante B.
- Estudiante B piensa en un restaurante donde comió recientemente y contesta las preguntas. Tiene que usar dos pronombres de complemento en cada respuesta.
- Después, cambien de papel *(exchange roles)*.

Modelo **Estudiante A:** ¿El mesero le trajo a Ud. el menú enseguida?
Estudiante B: Sí, me lo trajo enseguida.

Encuesta de satisfacción del cliente

1. ¿El mesero le trajo a Ud. el menú enseguida?
2. ¿El mesero le describió los platos del día?
3. ¿Cuántas veces le sirvieron agua?
4. ¿El chef le preparó bien la comida?
5. ¿El mesero le ofreció postre y café?
6. ¿Les va a recomendar el restaurante a sus amigos?

 7-55 **¿Quién te lo dio?** Primero necesitas darle una cosa tuya —un libro, un anillo, una gorra, etcétera— a una persona en la clase. Luego, tienes que circular por el salón de clase y preguntar a varios compañeros quién les dio el objeto.

Clase

Modelo **Estudiante A:** ¿Quién te dio ese reloj?
Estudiante B: Mark me lo dio. ¿Quién te dio... ?

 7-56 **Recuerdos de mi viaje.** Imagina que viajaste a Panamá y compraste los siguientes recuerdos. Tu compañero(a) de clase te va a preguntar a quiénes les vas a dar los recuerdos. Después, tú le haces las preguntas.

Modelo **Estudiante A:** ¿A quién le vas a dar estos aretes?
Estudiante B: Se los voy a dar a mi hermana Sara.

 1.  2.  3.   4.  5.

7-57 **Los buenos amigos.** ¿Quién es un(a) amigo(a) verdadero(a) *(true)*? Para saber, tu compañero(a) te va a hacer las siguientes preguntas. Después, tú le haces las preguntas.

1. ¿Quién te presta dinero cuando lo necesitas?
2. ¿Quién te prepara la comida cuando estás enfermo(a)?
3. ¿A quién le cuentas tus secretos?
4. ¿A quién le compras flores?
5. ¿A quién le muestras tus fotos?
6. ¿Quién te da consejos cuando tienes problemas románticos?

CONECTADOS CON...
LA MERCADOTECNIA

Tres marcas exitosas

Detrás de una marca exitosa hay una serie de estrategias de mercadotecnia excepcionales. Estas estrategias definen bien las 4 Ps: producto, precio, plaza (o distribución) y promoción. También establecen una relación con los consumidores para conseguir su preferencia y lealtad *(loyalty)*. Tres ejemplos de marcas exitosas son Juan Valdez de Colombia, Zara de España y Corona de México.

Juan Valdez: Casi todo el mundo conoce la famosa figura de Juan Valdez, el agricultor simpático de bigote y sombrero. Este personaje fue creado en la Avenida Madison (Nueva York) en 1959 para promover y diferenciar el café de Colombia. Desde entonces, tres hombres han representado a Juan Valdez, apareciendo en anuncios, películas y eventos internacionales. Juan Valdez es hoy un ícono popular, sinónimo del "mejor café del mundo". Sin duda *(Undoubtedly)*, la creación de la figura de Juan Valdez ha sido una estrategia excepcionalmente buena.

© DANIEL MUNOZ/Reuters/Corbis

Estrategia: Word families

A word family is a group of words that share the same root and therefore, similar meanings. For example, the words **vender** *(to sell)*, **vendedor(a)** *(seller)*, **venta** *(sale)*, and **vendido(a)** *(sold)* all share the root **ven-** and are related to *selling*. By determining to what word family an unfamiliar word belongs, you can deduce its meaning.

Palabras de mercadotecnia

el anuncio	*ad*
el (la) consumidor(a)	*consumer*
la estrategia	*strategy*
exitoso(a)	*successful*
la marca	*brand*
promover	*to promote*
la publicidad	*advertising*

7-58 **Comprensión.** ¿A cuál de las campañas corresponden estas estrategias de mercadotecnia? Pon una marca en la columna apropiada.

	Juan Valdez	Zara	Corona	Ninguna de las tres
1. Promover el producto con un personaje				
2. Implementar promociones diferentes para diferentes mercados				
3. Distribuir el producto exclusivamente por Internet				
4. Cambiar los productos constantemente				
5. Promover el producto en películas				
6. No hacer publicidad				

Zara: La tienda de moda española Zara vende ropa en muchos países. Esta compañía, fundada en La Coruña (España), no hace publicidad ni desfiles de moda *(fashion shows)*. Su estrategia es abrir tiendas en los mejores lugares de una ciudad, sacar rápidamente colecciones y tener una rotación de inventario constante. Cada semana las tiendas cambian sus colecciones entonces los clientes saben que si ven un artículo de ropa un día y no lo compran enseguida, la semana siguiente ya no está. Según un ejecutivo de la compañía, ese "clima de escasez *(shortage)* y de oportunidad inmediata" le da a Zara una ventaja competitiva.

Corona: La cerveza Corona es la marca líder en México y la cerveza importada número uno en Estados Unidos. La estrategia de Corona ha sido tener una campaña de publicidad diferente en el mercado local que en el mercado de exportación. En México, la campaña hace sentir orgullo *(pride)* nacional. ("En México y el mundo la cerveza es Corona.") En el extranjero, la publicidad presenta playas y relajamiento *(relaxation)*. Una mercadotecnia diferenciada parece ser clave *(key)* de su éxito.

 7-59 **¿Y tú?** En grupos pequeños, comenten estas preguntas.

1. ¿Qué otras marcas exitosas conoces? ¿Por qué crees que tienen éxito?
2. ¿Cuál es tu anuncio o promoción preferido? ¿Qué producto vende? ¿Qué anuncios te molestan? ¿Por qué?

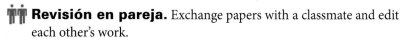

Composición: Una publicación

Imagine that you spent a whole day shopping at a mall, where you had some interesting or unusual adventures. To tell your friends all about it, you post a message on your social media page about the experience. Using the preterite, write in detail about what you did and what happened. As you write, look up at least three new words in an online dictionary, such as http://wordreference.com, and take care to choose the correct Spanish equivalents. Underline the new words.

Revisión en pareja. Exchange papers with a classmate and edit each other's work.

- Does the anecdote convey interesting information? Write one positive comment and one suggestion for improvement.
- Have the appropriate Spanish equivalents been chosen for new words? Check especially the three underlined words for accuracy.
- Are the verbs conjugated correctly? Circle any verbs that might be incorrect.

Estrategia:
Using a bilingual dictionary
- Identify the part of speech (noun, adjective, verb, etc.).
- Consider the context when selecting among various word choices.
- Watch out for set expressions and idioms.

7-60 **Nosotros /** *Share It!* En línea, subiste *(you posted)* una foto de tu camiseta favorita. También viste las publicaciones *(posts)* de varios compañeros de clase. Ahora, trabajando con dos o tres compañeros, comenten sobre estas publicaciones y contesten las preguntas.

1. ¿Quién tiene la camiseta más interesante? ¿Cómo es?

2. ¿Quién tiene la camiseta más vieja? ¿Cuántos años tiene?

3. ¿Quién lleva la camiseta porque le trae suerte *(luck)*? ¿Cuándo la lleva?

7-61 **Perspectivas: Recuerdos típicos.** En línea, miraste un video en el que *(in which)* tres estudiantes describen un recuerdo típico de su país. Con dos compañeros de clase, comparen sus respuestas sobre el video. Después, entrevístense *(interview one another)* con estas preguntas.

- ¿De dónde eres?
- ¿Cuál es un recuerdo típico de esa región?
- ¿De qué está hecho? ¿Cómo es?

7-62 **Exploración: De compras en Internet.** En Internet, "compraste" ropa para una entrevista de trabajo *(job interview)* en un gran almacén de México o España. Ahora, formen grupos de tres o cuatro estudiantes. Tomen turnos haciendo breves presentaciones sobre sus experiencias en las tiendas en Internet. Las otras personas deben escuchar y hacer preguntas.

En tu presentación, contesta las siguientes preguntas:

- ¿En qué almacén compraste tu ropa?
- ¿Qué compraste?
- ¿Cuánto pagaste?
- Basándote en la ropa que viste en Internet, ¿qué colores y estilos están de moda?
- ¿Observaste alguna diferencia entre la moda de México / España y la de Estados Unidos?

7-63 **Conectados con... la zoología.** En línea, leíste un artículo sobre el descubrimiento de un nuevo carnívoro. Con dos o tres compañeros(as), compartan *(share)* información de sus investigaciones sobre el olinguito u otro animal de América del Sur.

Modelo

El hurón y el olinguito son animales... /
El ñandú es... Vive(n) en... Come(n)...

7-64 **Diez diferencias.** Tú **(Estudiante A)** y tu compañero(a) **(Estudiante B)** tienen un dibujo de una escena en un gran almacén. A primera vista *(At first glance)* parecen idénticos, pero en realidad hay diez diferencias.

- Uds. deben compartir *(share)* la información en los dibujos para descubrir las diez diferencias, pero ¡sin mirar el dibujo de la otra persona!

- Fíjense *(Pay attention)* especialmente en las características de las personas, los estilos de ropa, los colores, el entallado *(fit)* de la ropa y la ubicación *(location)* de las cosas y las personas en el almacén. Anoten *(Jot down)* las 10 diferencias.

- Estudiante A debe empezar así: **En mi dibujo, la tienda tiene cuatro pisos.**

This is a pair activity for **Estudiante A** and **Estudiante B**.

If you are **Estudiante A**, use the information on this page.

If you are **Estudiante B**, turn to p. S-7 at the back of the book.

Estudiante A

SÍNTESIS

7-65 **De compras en el centro.** ¡Tienes muchas cosas que comprar hoy! Mira la lista y pregunta a tu compañero(a) dónde puedes comprar cada artículo. Imaginen que están delante de la fuente; hay que indicar dónde está cada lugar.

Words of location,
Capítulo 5 Paso 3

Modelo **Estudiante A:** Disculpe, ¿me podría indicar dónde puedo comprar un diccionario?

Estudiante B: Sí, claro. Puede ir a la librería Salamanca. Está en la calle Fuentes, al lado del restaurante Don Carlos.

Lista de compras

unas sandalias
un collar de oro
un sillón de cuero
dos cuadernos
unas aspirinas
una falda negra
una piña
un diccionario

© Cengage Learning 2016

Pronunciación: Combinaciones de vocales

Colaborar Con un(a) compañero(a), lean el chiste en voz alta. Presten atención a las combinaciones de vocales.

© Agung Setya Nugraha/Shutterstock

Un hombre quiere una mascota para ayudarlo con todo. Va a una tienda y el empleado le recomienda un ciempiés *(centipede)*. El hombre dice: "¿Un ciempiés? Me parece extraño *(strange)*, pero voy a comprarlo".

En casa, el hombre le dice al ciempiés: "Limpia la cocina". Treinta minutos más tarde, la cocina está completamente limpia. Entonces le dice al ciempiés: "Limpia la sala". Y en veinte minutos la sala está resplandeciente *(sparkling clean)*.

Ahora el hombre está muy contento. Le dice al ciempiés: "Ve *(Go)* a la tienda y tráeme *(bring me)* leche". El ciempiés abre la puerta y sale. Pasa una hora, pasan dos horas, pero nada.

El hombre abre la puerta y ve al ciempiés. Le dice: "¿Qué te pasa? ¿Por qué no me has traído la leche?" El ciempiés contesta: "¡Ya voy, ya voy! ¡Me estoy poniendo los zapatos!"

7-66 **Tres famosos mercados al aire libre.** Los mercados al aire libre son muy populares en España y Latinoamérica. Lee el siguiente blog sobre tres famosos mercados. Luego, formen grupos de tres personas. Cada persona debe hacer una presentación oral sobre uno de los mercados. Pueden usar este modelo.

Modelo   Nunca _____, pero me gustaría _____ algún día. Este mercado
está _____ y es _____. Cuando caminas por _____, puedes
_____. Es más _____ que _____. Me interesa ir al mercado
_____ porque _____.

Inicio   Sobre mí   Blogs   Archivo

Famosos mercados al aire libre

Lun 06 feb, 3:45 p.m.   [   ] buscar

El Rastro es el mercado al aire libre más grande y antiguo de España. Se organiza todos los domingos en el centro histórico de Madrid. Hay unos 3500 puestos[1] que venden de todo: antigüedades, libros, ropa, joyas y más.

La Feria de San Telmo, en Buenos Aires, Argentina, también se celebra todos los domingos. Alrededor de diez mil visitantes recorren el mercado para comprar o simplemente curiosear[2]. Además, en cada rincón del mercado se puede escuchar melodiosos tangos.

La Plaza de Ponchos, en Otavalo, Ecuador, es un mercado indígena de artesanías mundialmente famoso. Está abierto todos los días pero el sábado hay más actividad. Aquí se encuentran bellos ponchos, suéteres, sombreros, cuadros y objetos artesanales hechos de madera y cerámica.

Página principal   ¡Más!

[1]*stands*   [2]*browse*

7-67 **Situación: Un mercado de pulgas.** Su salón de clase es un mercado de pulgas (*flea market*). Un tercio (*one third*) de Uds. son vendedores y dos tercios (*two thirds*) son compradores.

Clase

Los vendedores tienen que...	**Los compradores deben...**
• preparar sus puestos (*stands*) con objetos personales: joyas, libros, anteojos, bolígrafos, celulares, etcétera	• pasear (*stroll*) por el mercado
• regatear con los compradores	• regatear con los vendedores
• conversar con otros vendedores, porque los mercados son lugares para socializar	• socializar con otros compradores: saludar, charlar y preguntar qué compraron y quién tiene buenos precios

VOCABULARIO

RECURSOS

Para aprender mejor
Study these vocabulary words in different settings. According to a study, students who studied a list of 40 vocabulary words in two different rooms did far better than those who studied the words twice in the same room.

Sustantivos

el abrigo *coat*
el accesorio *accessory*
el (gran) almacén *department store*
el anillo *ring*
los aretes *earrings*
la artesanía *arts and crafts*
la billetera *wallet*
la blusa *blouse*
el bolso *purse, handbag*
las botas *boots*
la bufanda *scarf, muffler*
los calcetines *socks*
la calidad *quality*
la camisa *shirt*
la camiseta *T-shirt*
la carreta *cart*
el centro comercial *mall*
la cerámica *ceramic*
la cesta *basket*
las chancletas *flip flops*
la chaqueta *jacket*
el cinturón *belt*
el collar *necklace*
la corbata *necktie*
el cuero *leather*
el (la) dependiente(a) *salesclerk*
el diseño *design*
la electrónica *electronics store / department*
el escaparate *shop window*
el estilo *style*
la falda *skirt*
la gorra *cap*
los guantes *gloves*
la hamaca *hammock*
las joyas *jewelry*
la joyería *jewelry (store / department)*
el juguete *toy*

el llavero *key ring*
la madera *wood*
la máscara *mask*
la mola *colorful appliqué panel*
el oro *gold*
la paja *straw*
los pantalones *pants*
los pantalones cortos *shorts*
la perfumería *perfume store / department*
la planta baja *ground floor*
la plata *silver*
el precio *price*
el probador *fitting room*
el regateo *bargaining*
la región *region*
las sandalias *sandals*
el servicio al cliente *customer service*
el sombrero *hat*
la sudadera *sweatshirt*
el suéter *sweater*
la talla *size*
la tienda *store*
el traje *suit*
el traje de baño *bathing suit*
los vaqueros *jeans*
el (la) vendedor(a) *vendor*
el vestido *dress*
la zapatería *shoe store / department*
los zapatos (de vestir, deportivos) *(dress, tennis) shoes*

Verbos

encantar *to love*
faltar *to be missing or lacking*
importar *to care about, to matter*
interesar *to be interested in*
molestar *to bother*
ofrecer *to offer*

parecer *to seem, to appear, to look*
probarse (ue) *to try on*
quedar *to fit; to have left, to remain*
regatear *to bargain*
resolver (ue) *to solve, to get resolved*
romper *to break*

Adjetivos

apretado(a) *(too) tight, snug*
barato(a) *cheap, inexpensive*
caro(a) *expensive*
clásico(a) *classic*
cómodo(a) *comfortable*
elegante *elegant*
estampado(a) *patterned, printed*
flojo(a) *(too) baggy, loose*
hecho(a) a mano *handmade*
informal *informal, casual*
pasado(a) de moda *out of style*
rebajado(a) *on sale*

Frases útiles

a cuadros *checkered, plaid*
a la última moda *in the latest fashion*
a rayas *striped*
alguna vez *ever*
Si compra... *If you buy . . .*
Solo estoy mirando. *I'm just looking.*
todavía no *not yet*
ya *already*

Colors, p. 252
Demonstratives, p. 256
Ordinal numbers, p. 262
Phrases used in a store, p. 262
Set phrases with *por*, p. 266
Bargaining expressions, p. 273

Nuestras tradiciones

Conexiones a la comunidad
Participate in a Hispanic or Latino celebration in your community, especially during Hispanic Heritage Month (Sept. 15–Oct. 15).

In this chapter you will . . .

- explore Colombia and Venezuela
- talk about holiday customs
- describe past, present, and future celebrations
- talk about sporting, cultural, and artistic events
- extend, accept, and decline invitations
- explore legends and myths and tell stories
- learn about the art history of Spain and Latin America
- share memories of childhood and holidays

NUESTRO **MUNDO**

Colombia y Venezuela

Colombia y Venezuela están en el norte de América del Sur. Estos dos países tienen un pasado común: fueron liberados por Simón Bolívar y formaron parte de la Gran Colombia entre 1821 y 1831.

República de Colombia
Población: 46 300 000
Capital: Bogotá
Moneda: el peso

Exportaciones: petróleo, esmeraldas, café, carbón (*coal*)

República Bolivariana de Venezuela
Población: 28 900 000
Capital: Caracas
Moneda: el bolívar fuerte

Exportaciones: petróleo, bauxita (*bauxite*), aluminio

© Daniel Munoz/Reuters/Corbis

Colombia y Venezuela, como muchos otros países, celebran el Carnaval con danzas, disfraces (*costumes*) y desfiles (*parades*). El Carnaval de Barranquilla, declarado Patrimonio de la Humanidad por la UNESCO, es único por su diversidad cultural, creatividad humana y tradiciones folclóricas. Durante cuatro días, más de un millón de personas participan en esta espectacular fiesta.

Historia

Simón Bolívar nació en Caracas, Venezuela, en 1783; y murió en Santa Marta, Colombia, en 1830. Es conocido como El Libertador porque ayudó en la lucha *(fight)* por la independencia de España de los actuales países de Bolivia, Colombia, Ecuador, Panamá, Perú y Venezuela.

Geografía

El lago de Maracaibo, en Venezuela, es el lago más grande de América del Sur. También es una zona con grandes reservas de petróleo. Se extraen más de dos millones de barriles cada día. Esto ha beneficiado la economía del país, pero también ha contaminado el lago.

Música

El vallenato es un estilo de música folclórica muy popular que se originó en Colombia. Los tres instrumentos básicos son el acordeón español, la caja *(small drum)* africana y la guacharaca *(ribbed wooden stick)* indígena.

8-1 **¿Qué sabes?** Completa las siguientes oraciones con la información que aprendiste.

1. Colombia y Venezuela tienen una historia común porque...

2. Colombia y Venezuela exportan... Hay una gran reserva de esto en...

3. En Barranquilla, Colombia, se celebra... por cuatro días. En esta fiesta, hay...

4. El personaje histórico más famoso de Colombia y Venezuela es... Libertó los actuales países de...

5. El lago más grande de América de Sur es... Está contaminado porque...

6. El vallenato es un estilo de música de... que tiene influencias...

▶ **8-2** **Videomundo.** Después de mirar los videos de Colombia y Venezuela, compara las capitales de estos dos países. Menciona los edificios, los espacios abiertos, el transporte y la población.

Los días festivos

In this *Paso*, you will . . .
- talk about holiday customs
- describe past, present, and future celebrations
- make generalizations

Día de la Independencia y Navidad

© Cengage Learning 2016

Se acostumbra celebrar el Día de la Independencia con un **desfile militar**. Siempre hay muchas **banderas** y música **patriótica**.

© Cengage Learning 2016

En la época de Navidad, muchas familias tienen **pesebres** en sus casas. **Rezan** y cantan **villancicos**.

Otros días festivos	More holidays
el Día del Amor y la Amistad	*Valentine's Day*
la Semana Santa	*Holy Week, Easter week*
el Domingo de Pascua	*Easter Sunday*
el Día del Padre	*Father's Day*
el Ramadán	*Ramadan*
el Día del Trabajo	*Labor Day*
el Yom Kipur	*Yom Kippur*
la Noche de Brujas / el Halloween	*Halloween*
el Día de Acción de Gracias	*Thanksgiving Day*
la Janucá	*Chanukah*

Año Nuevo y Día de la Madre

En muchos lugares **se recibe el Año Nuevo** con **fuegos artificiales**. Con las doce **campanadas**, se comen doce uvas.

Para **el Día de la Madre**, mostramos nuestro **cariño** con **tarjetas**, flores y regalos.

Otras costumbres

comer pavo / platos tradicionales
decorar el árbol / la casa
disfrazarse (de)
encender las velas del menorá
intercambiar regalos
ir a la iglesia / al templo / a la sinagoga / a la mezquita
regalar dulces
reunirse con amigos

Felicitaciones

¡Felices fiestas!
¡Feliz Día de (la Madre)!
¡Feliz Navidad!
¡Próspero Año Nuevo!

More customs

to eat turkey / traditional dishes
to decorate the tree / the house
to dress up in a costume (as)
to light the candles on the menorah
to exchange gifts
to go to church / to temple / to sinagogue / to mosque
to give (as a present) candy
to get together with friends

Greetings

Happy holidays!
Happy (Mother's) Day!
Merry Christmas!
Happy / Prosperous New Year!

¡Aplícalo!

🔄 Dates and months,
Capítulo 4 Paso 2

Frases útiles

Te toca a ti.   *It's your*
   turn.
Me toca a mí.   *It's my*
   turn.
Correcto.   *That's right.*
No, el día festivo
   correcto es...   *No, the*
   right holiday is . . .
Ganaste tú. / Gané yo.
   You won. / I won.
Empatamos.   *It's a tie.*

8-3   Los días festivos. ¿Sabes las fechas de los días festivos? Con un(a) compañero(a), jueguen al Súper Ta-Te-Ti. Tienen que decir qué día festivo corresponde a cada fecha antes de poner X u O. Para ganar, tienen que tener cuatro en línea horizontal, vertical o diagonal.

El primero de enero	El segundo domingo de mayo	El treinta y uno de octubre	El noveno mes del calendario musulmán *(Islamic)*
El veinticinco de diciembre	El cuatro de julio	El 15 de Nisan en el calendario hebreo *(Jewish)*	Ocho días en noviembre o diciembre
El cuarto jueves de noviembre	El catorce de febrero	Un domingo en marzo o abril, de fecha variable	El tercer domingo de junio
El tercer lunes de enero	La semana antes del Domingo de Pascua	El veintidós de febrero	El primer lunes de septiembre

Colaborar

8-4   Unas celebraciones. Vanessa, una estudiante de Estados Unidos, está en Colombia. Con un(a) compañero(a), completen su conversación en voz alta.

CAMILO   ¿Quieres venir a mi casa el 31 para celebrar el (1. Día / Año) Nuevo?

VANESSA   Sí, me encantaría. Eh, ¿cómo se (2. acostumbra / decora) celebrar ese día aquí en Colombia?

CAMILO   Normalmente las familias (3. se regalan / se reúnen) en casa y esperan las doce (4. iglesias / campanadas). Entonces todos se dan un beso *(kiss)*.

VANESSA   En mi clase de español leí que es tradicional comer doce (5. naranjas / uvas) para traer buena suerte.

CAMILO   Sí, es parte de nuestras tradiciones. ¿Cómo (6. se recibe / cantan) el Año Nuevo en Estados Unidos?

VANESSA   Por lo general (7. vamos / encendemos) a alguna fiesta y brindamos con champaña. Muchas personas celebran con (8. velas / fuegos artificiales).

CAMILO   ¡Qué divertido! Bueno, nos vemos pronto. ¡(9. Próspero / Felices) fiestas!

VANESSA   Gracias, Camilo. ¡(10. Felices / Feliz) Navidad!

8-5   Las tradiciones. Con un(a) compañero(a), tomen turnos para explicar para qué días festivos se acostumbra hacer estas cosas.

Modelo   decorar la casa

   Estudiante A: Normalmente decoramos la casa para Navidad.
   Estudiante B: Tambien, muchas personas decoran la casa para la Noche de Brujas.

1. encender velas

2. comer pavo

3. intercambiar regalos

4. rezar

5. mirar un desfile

6. escuchar música patriótica

7. encender fuegos artificiales

8. cantar villancicos

8-6 **Adivina el día festivo.** Con un(a) compañero(a), tomen turnos para describir tres tradiciones y la fecha de un día festivo. La otra persona tiene que adivinar (*guess*) el día festivo. Tienen que usar el tiempo presente en las descripciones.

Modelo **Estudiante A:** Para celebrar este día, las familias se reúnen y comen pavo. También muchas personas miran partidos de fútbol americano en la tele. La fecha es variable, pero siempre es un jueves en noviembre. ¿Qué día festivo es?

Estudiante B: Es el Día de Acción de Gracias.

8-7 **Cuatro días festivos.** ¿Qué están haciendo las personas en las fotos?
Colaborar
¿Qué días festivos están celebrando? Con un(a) compañero(a), describan las fotos usando el presente progresivo (**estar + *present participle***). Por ejemplo: **Los niños están celebrando...**

> ↻ The present progressive, **Capítulo 4 Paso 2**

1. © Lisa F. Young/Shutterstock

© Kali Nine LLC//iStockphoto

3. © Richard Levine / Alamy

4. © Anyka / Alamy

8-8 **Mi día festivo preferido.** ¿Cuál es tu día festivo preferido? ¿Cómo lo celebras? Trabajando con un(a) compañero(a), contesta estas dos preguntas con muchos detalles. Conecta la información con estas palabras: **primero, luego, después, por último.** Tu compañero(a) debe hacerte dos o tres preguntas también.

Modelo **Estudiante A:** Mi día festivo preferido es la Navidad. En mi familia, la celebramos en grande (*in a big way*). Primero, nos levantamos muy temprano y abrimos los regalos. Luego, desayunamos panqueques. Después, nos vestimos y vamos a la iglesia. Por la tarde, vamos a la casa de mis abuelos, donde comemos otros platos tradicionales. Por último, cantamos villancicos.

Estudiante B: ¿Quiénes se reúnen en la casa de tus abuelos? ¿Van muchos tíos y primos? ¿Qué platos tradicionales comen Uds.?

El *se* impersonal y el *se* pasivo

LEONARDO ¿Cómo se celebra el Día de la Independencia en Estados Unidos?

DIANA Por lo general se hace un picnic o una barbacoa por la tarde y se encienden los fuegos artificiales por la noche. Y en tu país, ¿qué se acostumbra hacer?

LEONARDO Más o menos lo mismo. En la capital también hay desfiles militares con música patriótica.

DIANA ¡Hay que celebrar la libertad *(liberty)* en grande!

Descúbrelo

- What holiday are Leonardo and Diana talking about?

- What are they comparing—their personal plans for the day or their countries' traditional celebrations?

- What word is used before the verbs **hace**, **encienden**, and **acostumbra**?

- What do you find after those three verbs? A singular noun, a plural noun, or an infinitive?

1. Sometimes the subject of a sentence is not a specific person, but *people in general*. In English, this notion can be expressed by using the subject *one*, *people*, *you*, or *we*. In Spanish, the equivalent generalizations can be made with a structure called the **se impersonal**.

> **se impersonal = SE + ÉL VERB FORM + (ADVERB / INFINITIVE)**
>
> En Navidad, **se va** a misa a la medianoche.
> *At Christmas time, **people go** to mass at midnight.*

2. Generalizations can also be made by saying that something is done without indicating who does it. In Spanish, this notion is expressed with a structure called the **se pasivo**.

- **SE + ÉL VERB FORM + (SINGULAR NOUN)**

> **Se celebra la Noche de Brujas** el 31 de octubre.
> *Halloween is celebrated on October 31.*

- **SE + ELLOS VERB FORM + (PLURAL NOUN)**

> **Se intercambian regalos** durante la época de Navidad.
> *Gifts are exchanged at Christmas time.*

3. Statements with the **se impersonal** and the **se pasivo** are made negative by adding **no** before the **se**.

> **No se fuma** en la catedral.
> *People don't smoke in the cathedral. / There's no smoking in the cathedral.*

4. The **se impersonal** and **se pasivo** structures are not used with reflexive verbs because these verbs already include **se** as part of their normal conjugation. Instead, it is common to use these patterns:

- **uno + él** *form of the reflexive verb*: En Venezuela, <u>uno se levanta</u> temprano.

- **ellos** *form of the reflexive verb*: En Venezuela, <u>se levantan</u> temprano.

- **se acostumbra +** *reflexive infinitive*: En Venezuela, <u>se acostumbra levantarse</u> temprano.

8-9 Los letreros. Con un(a) compañero(a), relacionen las oraciones a los letreros *(signs)*. Dos oraciones no se usan. Luego digan en dónde pueden estar los letreros.

Modelo El letrero significa "No se permiten perros". Puede estar en una tienda o en un parque.

a. No se aceptan tarjetas de crédito.

b. No se permite comer.

c. No se permiten perros.

d. Se busca perro.

e. Se prohíbe nadar.

f. Se vende casa.

1.   2.   3.   4.

Illustrations © Cengage Learning 2016

Colaborar

8-10 Costumbres religiosas. ¿Conoces las principales religiones del mundo? Con un(a) compañero(a), tomen turnos para leer una costumbre religiosa de la lista y decir si se hace **en la iglesia**, **en la sinagoga** o **en la mezquita**.

Modelo No se (permitir) llevar zapatos...
No se permite llevar zapatos en la mezquita.

Se (rezar) en hebreo...	Se (asistir) a una boda cristiana...
Se (celebrar) el Ramadán...	Se (aprender) sobre el islám...
Se (leer) el Nuevo Testamento...	Se (encender) velas a la Virgen...
Se (estudiar) el Toráh...	Se (celebrar) el Yom Kipur...

Colaborar

8-11 Las asignaturas. ¿Qué se hace en estas clases? Tomando turnos con un(a) compañero(a), completen las oraciones con **se** y el presente del verbo más lógico.

Academic subjects, **Capítulo 2 Paso 2**

Modelo En informática (escribir / tomar) **se escriben** programas.

1. En astronomía, (observar / pedir) _____ los planetas.

2. En inglés, (dar / leer) _____ la literatura de varios países.

3. En química, (romper / hacer) _____ experimentos científicos.

4. En psicología, (hablar / lavar) _____ de las teorías de Freud y Pavlov.

5. En ingeniería, (aprender / poner) _____ a inventar cosas útiles.

6. En antropología, (celebrar / estudiar) _____ las culturas del mundo.

8-12 **¿Qué se puede hacer?** ¿Conoces las reglas *(rules)* de tu universidad? Con un(a) compañero(a), tomen turnos preguntando si se puede hacer cada actividad de la lista. Usen esta frase: **Se puede + *infinitivo*...**

Modelo   usar celulares en clase

Estudiante A: ¿Se puede usar celulares en clase?

Estudiante B: Sí, se puede usar celulares en clase. / No, no se puede usar celulares en clase.

1. fumar en el campus
2. traer a invitados a las clases
3. conducir los automóviles por el campus
4. tener peces en las residencias
5. comer una merienda en clase
6. mover los muebles de las residencias

 8-13 **Contraste de costumbres.** Con un(a) compañero(a) de clase, comparen las tradiciones entre varios países hispanos y Estados Unidos.

- Primero, usen el **se** impersonal o pasivo y la información en la tabla para describir una costumbre de un país hispano.
- Después, usen el **se** impersonal o pasivo para describir una costumbre de Estados Unidos.

Modelo   En Navidad, **se comen hallacas** en Venezuela. En Estados Unidos, **se come pavo o jamón**.

Día festivo	País	Costumbre
Navidad	Venezuela	**comer** hallacas (tamales envueltos en hojas de banana)
Año Nuevo	Colombia	**caminar** por las calles con una maleta
Epifanía	España	**abrir** los regalos de los Reyes Magos *(Wise Men)*
el Día del Amor y la Amistad	República Dominicana	**llevar** ropa de color rojo o rosado
Semana Santa	Guatemala	**decorar** las calles con alfombras de flores
el Día de la Madre	México	**dar** una serenata *(serenade)* a las mamás

8-14 **¿Cuál es el lugar?** Trabaja con un(a) compañero(a). Tomando turnos, una persona describe qué se hace en uno de los siguientes lugares, y la otra tiene que adivinar *(guess)* el lugar.

Modelo   **Estudiante A:** En este lugar se baila, se bebe cerveza y se charla con amigos.

Estudiante B: ¿En un club?

Estudiante A: ¡Sí!

una agencia de viajes	un restaurante	la clase de español
una fiesta de cumpleaños	una biblioteca	una discoteca o un club
un gimnasio	la playa	las montañas
un gran almacén	un hotel	una ciudad grande

G PASO 1 GRAMÁTICA B

El presente, el pasado y el futuro

LILIANA ¿Qué **vas a hacer** para Semana Santa?

JAIRO No **sé**. Generalmente **voy** a la playa pero este año **quiero hacer** algo diferente.

LILIANA Pues, el año pasado mi familia y yo **asistimos** a las celebraciones religiosas en Mompox, al sur de Cartagena. ¡**Nos gustaron** mucho las procesiones!

1. Most everyday communication revolves around three time frames: the present, the past, and the future. The present tense (**el presente de indicativo**) is used to refer to ongoing actions or routines.

> Siempre **celebro** mi cumpleaños con una fiesta.
>
> *I always **celebrate** my birthday with a party.*

■ Regular verbs use the following endings.

-ar	celebr**ar**: celebr**o**, celebr**as**, celebr**a**, celebr**amos**, celebr**áis**, celebr**an**
-er	beb**er**: beb**o**, beb**es**, beb**e**, beb**emos**, beb**éis**, beb**en**
-ir	asist**ir**: asist**o**, asist**es**, asist**e**, asist**imos**, asist**ís**, asist**en**

■ Stem-changing verbs change the vowel in the stem in all persons except **nosotros** and **vosotros**. The endings are the same as for regular present-tense verbs.

e → ie	encender: enc**ie**ndo, enc**ie**ndes, enc**ie**nde, encendemos, encendéis, enc**ie**nden
o → ue	volver: v**ue**lvo, v**ue**lves, v**ue**lve, volvemos, volvéis, v**ue**lven
e → i	pedir: p**i**do, p**i**des, p**i**de, pedimos, pedís, p**i**den

■ Common irregular verbs are **estar**, **ir**, and **ser**. See the appendix for their conjugations.

■ Some verbs have irregular **yo** forms: **conduzco**, **conozco**, **digo**, **doy**, **hago**, **pongo**, **salgo**, **sé**, **tengo**, **traigo**, **vengo**, and **veo**.

2. To refer to the future (**el futuro**), it is common to use special verb phrases, consisting of *conjugated verb in the present tense + infinitive*.

> **¿Esperas ir** a la feria mañana?
>
> ***Do you expect to go** to the fair tomorrow?*

■ **ir + a + *infinitivo***   *be going to (do something)*

■ **pensar + *infinitivo***   *intend to / plan to (do something)*

■ **esperar + *infinitivo***   *expect to / hope to (do something)*

■■■ Descúbrelo

■ Where does Jairo usually spend Holy Week? Is he going there this coming one?

■ What did Liliana do last Holy Week? What did she find interesting?

■ What time frame do each of the boldfaced verbs refer to? Which ones refer to the past? The present? The future?

PASO 1 GRAMÁTICA B

3. The preterite expresses what somebody did on a particular occasion in the past.

> El año pasado **vimos** un gran desfile en el Día de la Independencia.
> *Last year we **saw** a great parade on Independence Day.*

- Regular verbs use the following endings.

-ar	mirar: mir**é**, mir**aste**, mir**ó**, mir**amos**, mir**asteis**, mir**aron**
-er / -ir	salir: sal**í**, sal**iste**, sal**ió**, sal**imos**, sal**isteis**, sal**ieron**

- Stem-changing verbs change with the subjects **Ud./él/ella/Uds./ellos/ellas**.

e → i	pedir: pedí, pediste, p**i**dió, pedimos, pedisteis, p**i**dieron
o → u	dormir: dormí, dormiste, d**u**rmió, dormimos, dormisteis, d**u**rmieron

- Common irregular verbs are: **conducir**, **decir**, **estar**, **hacer**, **poder**, **poner**, **querer**, **saber**, **ser**, **tener**, **traer**, and **venir**. See the appendix.

¡Aplícalo!

Colaborar

8-15 La rutina de mamá. Eugenio Copa describe la rutina diaria de su madre. Con un(a) compañero(a), completen su descripción en el presente.

Mi mamá (1. ser) _____ la persona más trabajadora de la familia. Normalmente mamá (2. despertarse) _____ muy temprano, antes de las seis. Todas las mañanas, ella nos (3. preparar) _____ deliciosas arepas *(corn cakes)*. Luego (4. irse) _____ a la oficina y cuando (5. volver) _____ a casa por la noche, (6. hacer) _____ los quehaceres. Nunca (7. acostarse) _____ antes de las once. ¡Yo no (8. saber) _____ cómo lo hace!

Colaborar

8-16 El Día de la Madre. ¿Cómo celebró la mamá de Eugenio el Día de la Madre? Con un(a) compañero(a), completen la narración en el pretérito.

Para celebrar el Día de la Madre, mi mamá (1. dormir) _____ hasta tarde. Mi hermano y yo (2. preparar) _____ el desayuno y se lo (3. servir) _____ en la cama. Yo le (4. regalar) _____ flores y mi hermano le (5. dar) _____ una tarjeta hecha a mano. Ella (6. ponerse) _____ muy contenta. Luego nosotros (7. ir) _____ al Parque del Este. ¡(8. Ser) _____ un día chévere *(great)*!

8-17 Los planes para el futuro. Entrevista *(Interview)* a un(a) compañero(a) para saber cuándo va a hacer las siguientes cosas. ¡Ojo! Hay que conjugar los verbos entre paréntesis en el presente.

Frases útiles: el próximo (año), este (semestre), dentro de (cinco) años, algún día

Modelo (pensar) hacer prácticas profesionales

> **Estudiante A:** ¿Cuándo piensas hacer prácticas profesionales?
> **Estudiante B:** Pienso hacer prácticas profesionales el próximo año.

1. (pensar) graduarse
2. (esperar) empezar a trabajar
3. (querer) comprar una casa
4. (ir a) terminar *Conectados*
5. (esperar) viajar por Europa
6. (ir a) visitar a tu familia

8-18 **Los propósitos de Año Nuevo.** Muy pronto llega el Año Nuevo. ¿Cuáles son tus propósitos *(resolutions)*? Con dos o tres compañeros, compartan *(share)* por lo menos un propósito para cada categoría. Usen los verbos **pensar**, **querer**, **ir** y **esperar** para expresar sus planes para el futuro.

Modelo El próximo año pienso comer menos dulces.

La dieta	Las relaciones personales
El ejercicio	Los hábitos malos
Los estudios	Otros temas

8-19 **Fechas históricas de Venezuela.** Trabaja con un(a) compañero(a) de clase para contar la historia de Venezuela en orden cronológico. Miren la línea de tiempo *(timeline)* y cambien los verbos en negrita *(boldface)* al pretérito.

Modelo En 1498, Cristóbal Colón exploró la costa de Venezuela.

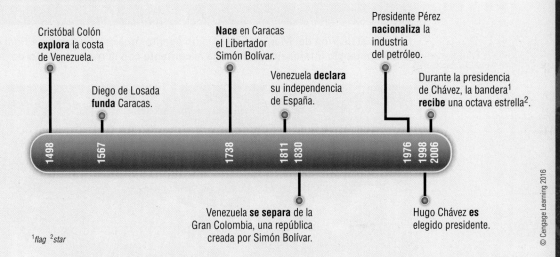

Cristóbal Colón **explora** la costa de Venezuela.

Diego de Losada **funda** Caracas.

Nace en Caracas el Libertador Simón Bolívar.

Venezuela **declara** su independencia de España.

Presidente Pérez **nacionaliza** la industria del petróleo.

Durante la presidencia de Chávez, la bandera[1] **recibe** una octava estrella[2].

1498 1567 1738 1811 1830 1976 1998 2006

Venezuela **se separa** de la Gran Colombia, una república creada por Simón Bolívar.

Hugo Chávez **es** elegido presidente.

[1] flag [2] star

© Cengage Learning 2016

8-20 **Unas fiestas inolvidables.** Tú y tu compañero(a) acaban de *(have just)* volver de Colombia, donde vivieron con una familia colombiana por un semestre. Estas son unas fotos que Uds. sacaron en la época de Navidad y Año Nuevo. Expliquen cómo celebraron esos días festivos. Usen el pretérito.

Modelo Mi familia colombiana y yo **celebramos** la Navidad en grande. Unas semanas antes, la señora **decoró** la casa con un pesebre y...

1.

© Yellow Dog Productions/Getty Images

2.

© Christian Heeb/JAI/Corbis

3.

© Pixtal/age fotostock

PASO 2 VOCABULARIO

Ferias, festivales y campeonatos

In this *Paso*, you will . . .

- talk about sporting, cultural, and artistic events
- extend, accept, and decline invitations
- describe past events and actions

Unos festivales artísticos

El Festival de Viña del Mar, en Chile, es un evento musical. En la noche final de la **Competencia Internacional**, **se elige** al **cantante** con la mejor **canción** del año.

En España, el Festival Internacional de Cine de San Sebastián **tiene lugar** cada septiembre. En este **prestigioso** evento cultural se dan **premios** a las mejores películas y a los mejores **actores**.

Para invitar	*To extend an invitation*
¿Quieres ir a (la feria) conmigo?	*Do you want to go to (the fair) with me?*
¿Te gustaría ir a (la exposición de fotografías)?	*Would you like to go to (the photography exhibit)?*
Para aceptar una invitación	*To accept*
Depende. ¿A qué hora empieza?	*It depends. What time does it start?*
Sí, me encantaría.	*Yes, I'd love to.*
Para rehusar una invitación	*To decline*
Lo siento, pero...	*I'm sorry, but . . .*
Quizás en otra ocasión.	*Maybe some other time.*

Unos eventos culturales y deportivos

El **Carnaval** de Oruro, en Bolivia, tiene **un ambiente alegre** y **festivo**. Hay **concursos** de **disfraces**, **bailes** y **teatro popular**.

Los Juegos Panamericanos **se realizan** cada cuatro años. **Atletas** de 42 países **participan** en las competencias de **eventos deportivos**, como **el atletismo**, **la natación** y **el ciclismo**.

Para pedir más información	*To ask for more information*
¿Cuánto cuesta la entrada?	*How much does the ticket cost?*
¿Qué conjunto va a tocar?	*What musical group is playing?*
¿Qué equipos juegan (en el campeonato)?	*What teams are playing (in the championship)?*
¿Qué obra de teatro van a presentar?	*What play are they showing / presenting?*
¿Dónde nos encontramos?	*Where do you want to meet?*
¿Puedes recogerme (a las siete)?	*Can you pick me up (at seven)?*

Expresiones útiles	*Useful expressions*
¡Qué emocionante!	*How exciting!*
¡Qué espectáculo!	*What a show!*

¡Aplícalo!

Colaborar

8-21 **Una invitación.** Un estudiante colombiano, José Enrique, invita a su amigo Manuel a un campeonato. Relaciona cada pregunta con la respuesta más lógica. Luego lee la conversación en voz alta con un(a) compañero(a).

Manuel:

_____ 1. ¿Vas al campeonato nacional de fútbol este sábado?

_____ 2. ¿Qué equipos juegan?

_____ 3. ¿Cuánto cuesta la entrada?

_____ 4. ¿A qué hora empieza el partido?

_____ 5. ¿Dónde nos encontramos?

José Enrique:

a. Los Millonarios y Atlético Nacional.

b. Yo puedo recogerte en tu casa.

c. Cuarenta y cinco mil pesos.

d. A las siete de la noche.

e. Sí, voy con mi padre. ¿Quieres ir con nosotros?

© Marish/Shutterstock

Colaborar

8-22 **Los Juegos Olímpicos.** ¿Te gusta ver los Juegos Olímpicos? ¿Qué sabes sobre este evento? Con un(a) compañero(a), completen el párrafo con las palabras de la lista.

atletas	deportivos	festivo	prestigiosos
competencias	espectáculo	participan	realizan

Los Juegos Olímpicos son los eventos (1) _____ más (2) _____ del mundo. (3) _____ de más de 200 países y territorios del mundo (4) _____ en estos eventos. Los Juegos Olímpicos se (5) _____ cada cuatro años y duran dos semanas. Siempre empiezan con una ceremonia de apertura (opening). Esta incluye un desfile de los atletas, un (6) _____ de música y danza, el encendido de la llama (flame) olímpica y fuegos artificiales. Es un ambiente muy (7) _____. Al día siguiente, ¡empiezan las (8) _____!

8-23 **Las preferencias.** Trabajando con un(a) compañero(a), entrevístense usando las siguientes preguntas. ¿Tienen Uds. las mismas preferencias?

1. ¿Cuál es tu campeonato favorito? ¿Qué equipos / atletas juegan? ¿Dónde tiene lugar?

2. ¿Prefieres practicar la natación o el ciclismo? ¿Dónde lo practicas?

3. En la Noche de Brujas, ¿participas en los concursos de disfraces a menudo? ¿En qué otros concursos has participado?

4. ¿Te gustan más los conciertos de música o las obras de teatro? ¿Qué conjunto musical o compañía de teatro te gusta?

5. ¿Te gusta ver los premios Óscar por televisión? En tu opinión, ¿qué actor debe ganar el próximo premio al mejor actor? ¿Y a la mejor actriz?

6. ¿Te gustan los programas de televisión de concursos entre cantantes o bailarines (dancers)? ¿Cuál prefieres mirar? ¿Por qué?

8-24 Depende. Con un(a) compañero(a), completen la conversación de una manera lógica y léanla en voz alta. ¿Acepta Claudia la invitación al final?

ANTONIO   Oye, Claudia, ¿quieres ir al festival de música conmigo?

CLAUDIA   Depende. (1) ¿_____?

ANTONIO   A las cinco de la tarde. Yo puedo recogerte a las cuatro y media.

CLAUDIA   (2) ¿_____?

ANTONIO   Tu conjunto preferido: Los Salseros.

CLAUDIA   ¡Los Salseros! (3) ¡_____!

ANTONIO   Entonces, ¿te gustaría ir?

CLAUDIA   (4) _____.

8-25 Feria de Verano. ¿Te gustaría ir a la Feria de Verano? Mira el siguiente cartel con un(a) compañero(a) de clase y contesten las preguntas. Después de contestar las preguntas, invita a tu compañero(a) a uno de los eventos.

Feria de Verano

25 DE JULIO

8 p.m.   Concierto de inauguración del conjunto Vallenato. Parque La Alameda. Entrada: 60 mil pesos.

26 DE JULIO

11 a.m.   Competencia de natación (para los niños). Piscina Municipal. Entrada: gratis.

1 p.m.   Exposición de caballos. Parque La Alameda. Entrada: 40 mil pesos.

5 p.m.   Campeonato de fútbol entre El Cóndor y Pumas. Estadio Guerrero. Entrada: 40 mil pesos.

10 p.m.   Gran espectáculo de bailes populares. Plaza de Armas. Entrada: 40 mil pesos.

27 DE JULIO

8 p.m.   Desfile de autos y disfraces en la Autopista Oriental. Entrada: gratis.

11 p.m.   Fuegos artificiales. Parque La Alameda. Entrada: gratis.

© Cengage Learning 2016

1. ¿En qué fechas se realiza la Feria de Verano? ¿Cómo termina?

2. ¿Cuál es el primer evento? ¿Cuánto cuesta la entrada?

3. ¿Para quiénes es la competencia de natación? ¿Dónde tiene lugar?

4. ¿Qué evento deportivo tiene lugar en el Estadio Guerrero? ¿Qué equipos juegan?

5. ¿Qué se va a presentar en la Plaza de Armas? ¿A qué hora empieza?

6. ¿Qué eventos no cuestan nada? ¿Dónde tiene lugar cada uno?

7. ¿Qué evento te parece más interesante? ¿Por qué?

↻ Possessive adjectives and pronouns, **Capítulo 3 Paso 1**

8-26 Nuestros preferidos. Conversa con dos o tres compañeros de clase sobre sus preferencias. Para cada categoría, di cuál es tu preferido(a) y explica por qué.

Modelo   cantante

Estudiante A: Mi cantante preferido es Juanes. ¡Es muy guapo y me encantan sus canciones! ¿Cuál es el suyo?

Estudiante B: La mía es Shakira. Su mejor canción es "Loca". ¿Cuál es el tuyo?

actor	cantante	conjunto	festival
atleta	competencia	evento deportivo	obra de teatro

PASO 2 GRAMÁTICA A

La formación del imperfecto

© Cengage Learning 2016

DANIELA Esta es una foto de mi abuelo cuando **trabajaba** en un crucero. Él **era** un músico profesional. **Cantaba** y también **tocaba** el piano, el violín y la guitarra.

KATIA ¡Qué impresionante! Yo solo sé tocar* la puerta.

*tocar (un instrumento) *to play (a musical instrument)*
tocar la puerta *to knock on the door*

■■■
Descúbrelo

- Who is the person in the photograph? What does Daniela say about him?
- Do the boldfaced verbs refer to past, present, or future events?
- What verb ending is shared by **trabajaba**, **cantaba**, and **tocaba**?

1. Spanish uses two different verb aspects to narrate and describe past events—the preterite and the imperfect. You already studied the preterite. In this **Paso** you will learn to form and use the imperfect (**el imperfecto**).

Preterite: Ayer **monté** en bicicleta por tres horas.	*Yesterday I **rode** my bike for three hours.*
Imperfect: De niño **montaba** mucho en bicicleta.	*As a child I **used to ride** my bike a lot.*

2. Most verbs in the imperfect are regular. Notice that -**ar** verbs use -**aba**- as part of the imperfect endings, while -**er** and -**ir** verbs use -**ía**-.

El imperfecto de los verbos regulares			
	-**ar** verbs	-**er** verbs	-**ir** verbs
	cantar	**comer**	**vivir**
yo	cant**aba**	com**ía**	viv**ía**
tú	cant**abas**	com**ías**	viv**ías**
Ud./él/ella	cant**aba**	com**ía**	viv**ía**
nosotros(as)	cant**ábamos**	com**íamos**	viv**íamos**
vosotros(as)	cant**abais**	com**íais**	viv**íais**
Uds./ellos/ellas	cant**aban**	com**ían**	viv**ían**

3. There are only three irregular verbs in the imperfect; there are no stem-changing verbs in this tense.

El imperfecto de los verbos irregulares			
	ir *to go*	**ser** *to be*	**ver** *to see*
yo	iba	era	veía
tú	ibas	eras	veías
Ud./él/ella	iba	era	veía
nosotros(as)	íbamos	éramos	veíamos
vosotros(as)	ibais	erais	veíais
Uds./ellos/ellas	iban	eran	veían

Colaborar

8-27 El juego de pelota. El juego de pelota *(ball)* fue un deporte-ritual común en muchas civilizaciones precolombinas en partes de México y Centroamérica. Con un(a) compañero(a), completen el siguiente párrafo sobre este juego. Hay que escoger los verbos más lógicos y conjugarlos en el imperfecto.

El juego de pelota *(ball)* se (1. jugar / tocar) _____ entre dos equipos y cada equipo (2. comer / tener) _____ de dos a siete jugadores. Los jugadores (3. vivir / deber) _____ pasar la pelota *(put the ball)* por un disco de piedra *(stone)*. Ellos no (4. poder / encender) _____ tocar *(touch)* la pelota ni con las manos ni con los pies *(feet)*. La pelota —hecha de hule *(rubber)* y látex— (5. ir / ser) _____ pesada y dura *(heavy and hard)*. Por eso, los jugadores (6. llevar / lavar) _____ protección de cuero. Generalmente el partido (7. terminar / haber) _____ cuando un equipo marcaba *(scored)* un gol. Según los arqueólogos, la pelota (8. rezar / simbolizar) _____ al Sol y los equipos, a los dioses *(gods)* del inframundo.

© espixx / Alamy

8-28 Te-Te-Ti con el imperfecto. Juega al Ta-Te-Ti dos veces con un(a) compañero(a) de clase. Tomando turnos, un(a) jugador(a) selecciona un cuadrado *(square)* y conjuga el verbo en el imperfecto. Si la conjugación es correcta, el (la) jugador(a) pone una X (o una O) en el cuadrado.

tú: querer	él: celebrar	Uds.: intercambiar	ellas: regalar	tú: recibir	tú: ser
ella: jugar	yo: ser	tú: vivir	él: ir	nosotros: ver	ella: decorar
ellos: encender	tú: ir	nosotros: disfrazarse	nosotros: reunirse	Uds.: practicar	yo: comer

8-29 A los trece años. ¿Cómo eras tú *(What were you like)* a los trece años? Completa las oraciones con un(a) compañero(a) y comparen sus experiencias.

Cuando yo tenía trece años...

1. estaba en el (séptimo / octavo / noveno) grado. ¿Y tú?

2. por lo general (me gustaba / no me gustaba) ir a la escuela. ¿Y a ti?

3. mi materia preferida era _____. ¿Y la tuya?

4. (tocaba / no tocaba) un instrumento en la orquesta o la banda de la escuela. ¿Y tú?

5. (estaba / no estaba) en un equipo deportivo. ¿Y tú?

6. hacía (muchos / pocos) quehaceres domésticos, por ejemplo _____. ¿Y tú?

7. mis héroes eran _____. ¿Cuáles eran tus héroes?

8. siempre estaba con mis amigos; nos encantaba _____. ¿Y a ti y a tus amigos?

¡Exprésate!

 8-30 **De niño(a).** ¿Con qué frecuencia hacías estas cosas cuando tenías nueve o diez años? Trabajando con un(a) compañero(a) de clase, formen preguntas en el imperfecto con las frases y entrevístense.

Expressions of frequency, **Capítulo 2 Paso 3**

Modelo   jugar al fútbol

   Estudiante A: ¿Con qué frecuencia jugabas al fútbol cuando eras niño(a)?

   Estudiante B: Lo hacía a menudo: dos o tres veces a la semana. ¿Y tú?

   Estudiante A: ¡Casi nunca jugaba! No me gustaba el fútbol.

(casi) todos los días	(casi) todas las semanas	a menudo
una o dos veces al mes	a veces	(casi) nunca

1. hacer la cama

2. mirar dibujos animados *(cartoons)*

3. contarles chistes a los amigos

4. montar en bicicleta

5. poner la mesa

6. jugar en la nieve

7. comer verduras

8. acostarse tarde

Colaborar **8-31** **Exposición de fotografía.** Fuiste a una exposición de fotos y viste esta foto de unos artistas famosos. ¿Los conoces? Con un(a) compañero(a) de clase, contesten las preguntas usando el imperfecto.

1. ¿Cómo se llamaban estos artistas? ¿De qué país eran?

2. ¿Cómo era ella? ¿Y él? En esta foto, ¿aproximadamente cuántos años tenían?

3. ¿Dónde estaban en esta foto?

4. ¿Qué tipo de ropa llevaba ella? ¿Y él?

5. ¿Parecían contentos en la foto? Explica.

Frida Kahlo y Diego Rivera en México, D.F., 1939

© Bettmann/CORBIS

8-32 **En la escuela secundaria.** ¿Cómo era tu vida en la escuela secundaria *(high school)*? Trabajando con un(a) compañero(a), entrevístense con estas preguntas y comparen sus experiencias.

1. ¿Cómo se llamaba tu escuela secundaria? ¿Era grande, pequeña o de tamaño mediano? ¿Estaba en una ciudad, en las afueras *(suburbs)* o en un área rural?

2. ¿Eras buen(a) estudiante cuando estabas en la escuela secundaria? ¿Qué clases te gustaban más? ¿Cuántas horas estudiabas en un día normal fuera de *(outside of)* clase?

3. Por lo general, ¿te gustaban tus profesores? ¿Te parecían muy estrictos algunos de ellos? ¿Qué no se podía hacer en clase? ¿Qué regla *(rule)* te molestaba más?

4. ¿En qué actividades extracurriculares participabas? Por ejemplo, ¿participabas en las obras de teatro, cantabas en el coro *(chorus)* o jugabas en algún equipo deportivo?

5. ¿Cuáles eran los eventos sociales más populares o importantes de tu escuela? ¿Qué hacían para celebrar la reunión de exalumnos *(homecoming)*? ¿Cómo era el baile de graduación *(prom)*? ¿Hacían fiestas o viajes para celebrar el final del año escolar?

G PASO 2 GRAMÁTICA B

Los usos del imperfecto

SAMUEL Abuelo, cuando tú eras pequeño, ¿qué videojuegos te gustaban más?

ABUELO No teníamos videojuegos, Samuel. Pero casi todos los días después de clase jugábamos al fútbol.

SAMUEL ¿Ganaba a menudo tu equipo?

ABUELO Sí, claro. Yo era el portero *(goalie)* y era muy rápido.

1. Both the imperfect and the preterite are used to narrate and describe past actions, but they are not interchangeable. One major use of the imperfect is to describe past traditions and routines; that is, what you *used to do* or *would do* in the past.

   These descriptions are often used with adverbs of frequency: **generalmente, normalmente, (casi) siempre, todos los días, todos los años, con frecuencia, a menudo, a veces,** etc.

De niño, yo **visitaba** a mi tía a menudo.	*As a child, I **used to visit** my aunt often.*

2. The imperfect is also used to describe people, places, and things in the past. Such descriptions often employ non-action verbs—**ser, estar, parecer,** and **tener**—and may include physical and personal characteristics, feelings, conditions, and age.

El cantante **era** muy talentoso. **Tenía** solo veinte años pero **parecía** mayor.	*The singer **was** very talented. He **was** only 20 years old but **seemed** older.*

3. The imperfect is used in storytelling to set the scene in the past: the time of day, date, location, or ongoing weather conditions.

Eran las once de la noche y **nevaba**.	*It **was** eleven o'clock at night and it **was snowing**.*

4. The imperfect is also used to describe actions that were in progress at a particular point in time in the past—the equivalent of English *was / were + -ing* form of the verb.

A las diez, los niños **miraban** el desfile.	*At 10:00, the kids **were watching** the parade.*

5. The imperfect is used with the verbs **saber, pensar,** and **creer** to express ongoing thought processes—what somebody *knew, thought,* or *believed* over a span of time.

El niño **no creía** en Papá Noel.	*The boy **didn't believe** in Santa Claus.*

■■■ Descúbrelo

- What pastimes are Samuel and his grandfather talking about?
- Does their conversation focus mostly on the present or the past?
- Does the verb **jugábamos** refer to an action that took place one time or that used to take place regularly?
- What verb does the grandfather use to describe what kind of soccer player he was?

¡Aplícalo! Colaborar

8-33 **La nostalgia.** En una página de Internet, varias personas describen los mejores recuerdos de su niñez *(childhood)*. Tomando turnos con un(a) compañero(a), lean sus descripciones. Después, usen la información de la lista para indicar por qué se usa el imperfecto para los verbos en negrita *(boldface)*.

Usos del imperfecto:

a. To describe customs, traditions, or routines in the past *(used to do / would do)*

b. To describe people, places, and things in the past: characteristics, conditions, feelings, age

c. To set the scene for a story / anecdote: time, day, location, ongoing weather conditions

d. To describe what was going on at a particular point in the past *(was / were + -ing)*

e. To express an ongoing mental process *(knew / thought / believed)*

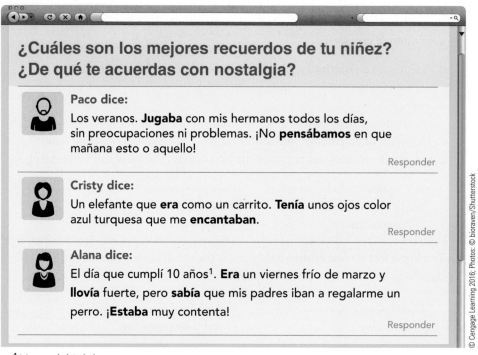

¿Cuáles son los mejores recuerdos de tu niñez?
¿De qué te acuerdas con nostalgia?

Paco dice:
Los veranos. **Jugaba** con mis hermanos todos los días, sin preocupaciones ni problemas. ¡No **pensábamos** en que mañana esto o aquello!

Responder

Cristy dice:
Un elefante que **era** como un carrito. **Tenía** unos ojos color azul turquesa que me **encantaban**.

Responder

Alana dice:
El día que cumplí 10 años[1]. **Era** un viernes frío de marzo y **llovía** fuerte, pero **sabía** que mis padres iban a regalarme un perro. ¡**Estaba** muy contenta!

Responder

[1]My tenth birthday

8-34 **Mejores amigos.** Con un(a) compañero(a), hablen de los mejores amigos de su niñez *(childhood)*.

1. ¿Quién era tu mejor amigo o amiga cuando tenías diez u once años? ¿Asistían Uds. a la misma escuela? ¿Todavía estás en contacto con él (ella)?

2. ¿Cómo era tu mejor amigo(a) en esa época *(back then)*? ¿Era extrovertido(a) o un poco tímido(a)? ¿Serio(a) o bromista? ¿Cómo es ahora? ¿Ha cambiado mucho de personalidad?

3. ¿Cómo pasaban Uds. el tiempo juntos cuando eran pequeños(as)? ¿Qué deportes practicaban? ¿Qué programas miraban en la tele o en DVD? ¿Qué más hacían?

¡Exprésate!

8-35 Las tradiciones: antes y ahora. Con un(a) compañero(a), hablen sobre los días festivos de la lista. Usen el imperfecto para describir cómo celebraban esos días cuando eran pequeños. Luego usen el presente para describir cómo celebran ahora.

tu cumpleaños	el Día de Acción de Gracias
la Noche de Brujas	el Día de la Independencia

Modelo tu cumpleaños

Estudiante A: ¿Cómo celebrabas tu cumpleaños cuando eras niño(a)?

Estudiante B: Normalmente tenía una pequeña fiesta en casa.

Estudiante A: ¿Y ahora (now)? ¿Cómo celebras tu cumpleaños por lo general?

Estudiante B: Normalmente recibo muchos mensajes de texto de mis amigos.

Colaborar

8-36 ¡Ladrón! Cuando tú y tu compañero(a) estaban en el Festival de la Calle Ocho en Miami, presenciaron (you witnessed) un crimen: un ladrón (thief) robó una billetera. Ahora la policía los está entrevistando. Usando la información en el dibujo, contesten sus preguntas.

1. ¿Precisamente dónde estaban Uds. cuando vieron el crimen?

2. ¿Qué hacían Uds.?

3. ¿Aproximadamente qué hora era?

4. ¿Cómo era el ladrón? ¿Qué ropa llevaba?

5. ¿Qué hacía la víctima cuando el robo ocurrió?

6. ¿Qué más me pueden decir sobre el crimen?

8-37 Muchas excusas. Muchas personas están enojadas contigo. ¡Necesitas muy buenas excusas para tranquilizarlos! En grupos de tres o cuatro, tomen turnos para dar excusas. Usen el imperfecto para explicar **dónde estabas** y **qué hacías**.

Modelo TU NOVIO(A) Te llamé anoche a las nueve pero no contestaste. ¿Dónde estabas? ¿Qué hacías?

Estudiante A: Lo siento mucho. Estaba en la biblioteca con algunos compañeros de clase. Estudiábamos para nuestro examen de química.

Estudiante B: Disculpa. Estaba en el consultorio del veterinario...

1. TU MAMÁ Te llamé el miércoles a las once de la noche pero no contestaste. Yo estaba muy preocupada. ¿Dónde estabas? ¿Qué hacías?

2. TU HERMANO(A) Dime (Tell me), tonto(a). ¿Dónde estabas tú el sábado a la una de la tarde? ¿Por qué no fuiste a la fiesta de cumpleaños de abuelita? Todos te esperábamos en el salón del Restaurante Fénix pero nunca llegaste. ¡Pobre abuela!

3. TU PROFESOR(A) DE ESPAÑOL ¿Por qué no viniste a clase el martes de la semana pasada? Te perdiste (You missed) el examen.

Mitos y leyendas

In this *Paso*, you will . . .
- explore legends and myths
- react to stories that others tell
- tell stories about past events

Un mito de los Andes

Las cinco águilas blancas

Este mito explica por qué las cimas de la Sierra Nevada, en Mérida, Venezuela, están siempre cubiertas de nieve.

Había una vez una mujer que se llamaba Caribay. Era hija de Zuhé (el Sol) y de Chía (la Luna). Le gustaba cantar y jugar con los árboles.

Un día, Caribay vio volar por el cielo cinco águilas blancas. Caribay quería sus hermosas plumas entonces corrió tras ellas.

© Cengage Learning 2016

Para contar una leyenda o un mito	*Storytelling*
Había una vez...	*Once upon a time . . .*
Hace muchos años...	*A long time ago . . .*
Según una leyenda / un mito...	*According to legend / myth . . .*
Por eso...	*That's why . . .*
Al final...	*At the end . . .*
el águila / las águilas	*eagle(s)*
el dios / la diosa	*god / goddess*
la pluma	*feather*
el sol / la luna / el cielo	*sun / moon / sky*
volar (ue)	*to fly*
Para comenzar una anécdota	*To begin a personal story*
Cuando tenía (diez) años...	*When I was (ten) years old . . .*
De niño(a)...	*As a child . . .*
Un día...	*One day . . .*
Una vez...	*One time . . .*

Un mito de los Andes (cont.)

Por fin, Caribay vio las cinco águilas sobre cinco cimas. Cuando quiso tocar una, vio que las águilas estaban congeladas, convertidas en hielo.

Caribay huyó aterrorizada. Las águilas blancas se despertaron furiosas y sacudieron sus alas. Las montañas se cubrieron entonces de sus plumas.

Para continuar un cuento	*To continue a story*
De repente...	*Suddenly . . .*
Entonces...	*Then . . .*
Mientras...	*While . . .*
Para saber más	*To find out more*
¿Cómo pasó?	*How did it happen?*
¿Cuándo ocurrió?	*When did it happen?*
¿Qué pasó después?	*What happened then?*
Para reaccionar	*To react*
¿De veras?	*Really?*
Menos mal.	*Thank goodness.*
No lo puedo creer.	*I can't believe it.*
¡Qué cuento más extraño / increíble / gracioso!	*What a strange / incredible / funny story!*
¡Qué horror / barbaridad!	*That's awful!*
¡Qué suerte!	*How lucky!*

¡Aplícalo!   Colaborar   **8-38** **El mito de las cinco águilas.** Trabajando con un(a) compañero(a), contesten las preguntas sobre la leyenda en las páginas 312 y 313.

1. ¿Cómo se llama la protagonista del mito?

2. ¿Quiénes eran los padres de Caribay?

3. ¿Qué vio Caribay volar por el cielo?

4. ¿Por qué corrió tras las águilas?

5. ¿Dónde encontró las águilas? ¿Cómo estaban?

6. ¿Qué hicieron las águilas cuando se despertaron?

7. ¿Qué explica este mito?

Colaborar   **8-39** **Cuéntame todo.** Trabajando con un(a) compañero(a), escojan las expresiones más lógicas y lean las conversaciones en voz alta.

1.   SAM   Mis padres me regalaron una computadora para mi cumpleaños.

     ALISA (¡Qué suerte! / ¡Qué barbaridad!)

2. MARISA Anoche me desperté a las dos de la madrugada y vi un fantasma (*ghost*) en el rincón de mi cuarto.

      JUAN (¿De veras? / Menos mal.)

3.   IVÁN ¿Recuerdas a Alicia? Este año está participando en el concurso de Miss Venezuela.

    ROBERT (¿Qué pasó después? / ¡No lo puedo creer!)

4. CARMEN Mi compañera de cuarto tuvo un accidente en su auto anoche.

    MARCOS (¿Cómo pasó? / ¿Cuándo ocurrió?)

    CARMEN No sé; creo que llovía mucho y no podía ver bien.

Colaborar   **8-40** **Una experiencia traumática.** Leticia cuenta una historia sobre su niñez. Con un(a) compañero(a), completen su historia con las expresiones más lógicas de la lista y léanla en voz alta. ¿A Uds. les ha pasado algo similar?

Cuando yo tenía 9 años	Entonces	Mientras	¡Qué horror!
De repente	Ese día	Por eso	Un día

(1) _____, tenía una maestra muy estricta en la escuela.
(2) _____, tuve una experiencia muy mala con ella a la hora de almorzar. (3) _____ servían macarrones con queso, una de mis comidas menos preferidas. (4) _____ ¿Qué podía hacer yo para no comerlos? (5) _____ tuve una idea. (6) _____ la maestra hablaba con un compañero, puse todos los macarrones en mi cartoncito de leche (*small milk carton*). Pensé que había resuelto (*I had solved*) mi problema. (7) _____ sentí una mano sobre mi hombro (*shoulder*). ¡La maestra me había visto (*had seen*)! Como castigo (*punishment*), tuve que comer los macarrones (¡con la leche de chocolate!). Fue una experiencia muy traumática para mí. (8) _____, desde ese día, nunca como macarrones con queso.

¡Exprésate! Colaborar

8-41 La leyenda de Tenochtitlán. Esta leyenda explica cómo se fundó la ciudad de Tenochtitlán.

Primera parte: Con un(a) compañero(a), pongan las cuatro partes del mito en su orden correcto.

Finalmente, en el año 1325, los aztecas llegaron al lago de Texcoco. En una roca, vieron un cactus y sobre el cactus, un águila que se comía una serpiente.	Según la leyenda, los aztecas vivían tranquilamente en Aztlán. Un día, el dios Huitzilopochtli les dijo que tenían que buscar una nueva tierra donde fundarían *(they would establish)* una gran civilización.	Allí fundaron *(they established)* Tenochtitlán, la futura capital del imperio azteca y de México. Y por eso, la imagen del águila devorando una serpiente está en la bandera *(flag)*.	Entonces los aztecas migraron. Durante trescientos años buscaron la señal *(sign)* de la tierra prometida *(promised land)*: un águila sobre un cactus devorando una serpiente.

© oculo/Shutterstock

Segunda parte: Contesten las preguntas sobre la leyenda oralmente.

1. Según la leyenda de México, ¿dónde vivían originalmente los aztecas?
2. ¿Cuál de los dioses aztecas los mandó a una nueva tierra?
3. ¿Por cuánto tiempo buscaron la señal de la tierra prometida?
4. Por fin, ¿dónde encontraron la señal? ¿Cuál era la señal?
5. ¿En qué año fundaron los aztecas la ciudad de Tenochtitlán?

8-42 Dos cuentos. ¡Vamos a contar cuentos! Primero, Estudiante A lee su cuento y Estudiante B tiene que escuchar y reaccionar a cada oración con una expresión apropiada (por ejemplo, ¿Qué pasó después?). Luego, cambien de papel *(exchange roles)*.

Expresiones útiles: ¿De veras? ¿Cómo pasó? ¿Cómo ocurrió? ¿Cómo era? ¿Qué hizo? ¡No lo puedo creer! ¡Qué barbaridad! ¡Qué extraño! ¡Menos mal!

Cuento del Estudiante A:	Cuento del Estudiante B:
1. Cuando mi hermano tenía 10 años, encontró unos cigarrillos.	1. Hace dos años, gané $1000 en la lotería.
2. Los llevó al patio de la casa y empezó a fumar uno.	2. Yo trabajaba en un café. Un día, un señor de aspecto misterioso entró.
3. Mientras fumaba, mi mamá salió de la casa. Mi hermano la vio y sintió pánico.	3. Era muy viejo, de barba blanca. Llevaba ropa morada y una mochila con flores.
4. Apagó el cigarrillo y ¡se lo comió!	4. Sí, muy extraño. Y nunca habló.
5. Sí, es verdad. Se puso muy enfermo y tuvimos que llevarlo al hospital.	5. Bueno, comió y pagó. Y de propina, me dejó *(left me)* un billete de lotería.
6. Bueno, se recuperó y lo llevamos a casa. ¡Y mi hermano nunca más fumó!	6. ¡Esa noche descubrí que había ganado *(I had won)* $1000!

El imperfecto y el pretérito: primera parte

© Cengage Learning 2016

Caperucita Roja

Había una vez una niña que se llamaba Caperucita Roja. Un día, salió de su casa con una cesta de pasteles para su abuela, quien estaba enferma. Mientras Caperucita caminaba por el bosque, se encontró con un lobo *(wolf)*. El lobo era enorme...

■■■
Descúbrelo

- What children's story is this excerpt taken from?
- Does the second sentence describe the little girl or say what she did? Is the imperfect or the preterite used?
- Find examples where two other characters are described. Is the imperfect or the preterite used?
- What was the main character doing when she encountered trouble? What verb forms are used to express this?

1. The imperfect and the preterite are used together to tell stories in the past.

Imperfecto	Pretérito
• To describe routines or customs in the past *(used to / would do something)* • To describe people, places, things, ongoing weather conditions, day, time • To describe actions that were ongoing or taking place *(was / were + ___-ing)*	• To focus on a completed action that occurred on a particular occasion • To say how long the action / event lasted or how many times the action occurred • To sum up an experience or event

2. The main actions of a story may be related to one another in three basic ways:

- **Acciones en proceso y simultáneas:** Use the **imperfecto** to describe two or more actions that were taking place (or were ongoing) at the same time.

  Patricia **miraba** el desfile en la televisión mientras yo **decoraba** la mesa.
  *Patricia **was watching** the parade on TV while **I was decorating** the table.*

- **Serie de acciones completadas:** Use the **pretérito** to express a series or sequence of completed actions.

  Primero Ana y Luisa **cenaron** en un café; luego **fueron** al cine.
  *First Ana and Luisa **had supper** in a café; then, they **went** to the movies.*

- **Una acción interrumpe otra acción:** One action may interrupt another that was already taking place. Use the **imperfecto** to describe the ongoing action. Use the **pretérito** for the action that began, ended, or interrupted the ongoing one.

  Mientras **veíamos** los fuegos artificiales, **empezó** a llover.
  *While we **were watching** the fireworks, it **started** to rain.*

3. Some verbs have different translations in the preterite.

La **conocía** *(I knew her)* bien.	BUT	La **conocí** *(I met her)* ayer.
Sabía *(She knew how)* cocinar.	BUT	**Supo** *(She found out)* la noticia.
Ella **tenía** *(had)* el pelo rubio.	BUT	Ella **tuvo** *(got into)* un accidente.

Colaborar

8-43 El 31 de octubre. James es un estudiante de Estados Unidos que estuvo un semestre en Venezuela. Con un(a) compañero(a), completen su anécdota con el imperfecto o el pretérito de los verbos, según el contexto.

¡Aplícalo!

(1. Ser) _____ el 31 de octubre: mi día festivo favorito. Joaquín me
(2. llamar) _____ y me (3. invitar) _____ a su casa. Yo
(4. escoger) _____ un disfraz en dos segundos: ¡fácil, el de siempre
(the usual)! Yo siempre (5. vestirse) _____ de Batman para Halloween.
Naturalmente, (6. sentirse: yo) _____ muy contento cuando (7. llegar: yo)
_____ a la casa de Joaquín. Pero al entrar *(upon entering)*, ¡qué horror!
Nadie (8. estar) _____ disfrazado o alegre. Mientras yo (9. pensar)
_____ en Halloween, la familia de Joaquín (10. celebrar) _____
el Día de los Angelitos *(day of remembering deceased children)*. ¡Ese día (11. ser)
_____ el más vergonzoso *(embarrassing)* de mi vida!

Colaborar

8-44 El Día de Acción de Gracias. Con un(a) compañero(a) de clase, describan la gran celebración del Día de Acción de Gracias que Uds. compartieron *(you shared)* con la familia Romero. Completen las oraciones de una manera lógica. Para los verbos, usen el imperfecto o el pretérito, según el contexto.

Modelo Mientras don Alberto cantaba, el gato (saltar) *(to jump)*…
    Mientras don Alberto cantaba, el gato **saltó encima de su cabeza.**

Serie de acciones:

1. Doña Victoria puso la mesa y (encender)…

2. Ana preparó el pavo en la cocina y lo (llevar)…

Acciones en proceso y simultáneas:

3. Mientras Miguel jugaba con el perro, Graciela (tocar)…

4. Mientras doña Victoria encendía las velas, Gustavo (servir)…

Una acción interrumpe otra:

5. Los anteojos de Miguel se rompieron cuando él (jugar)…

6. Mientras nadie miraba, José le (dar)…

© Cengage Learning 2016

¡Exprésate!

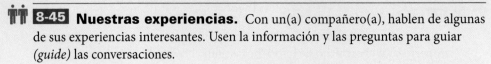

8-45 Nuestras experiencias. Con un(a) compañero(a), hablen de algunas de sus experiencias interesantes. Usen la información y las preguntas para guiar (*guide*) las conversaciones.

1. **Estudiante A:** En el año _____, mi familia y yo hicimos un viaje magnífico.

   Estudiante B: ¿Adónde fueron Uds.? ¿Cómo era el lugar? ¿Qué hicieron? ¿Conociste a muchas personas allí? (Una pregunta original)

2. **Estudiante B:** Una vez les dije una mentira (*lie*) a mis padres.

   Estudiante A: ¿Cuántos años tenías cuando les dijiste la mentira? ¿Qué les dijiste? ¿Supieron la verdad tus padres? (Una pregunta original)

3. **Estudiante A:** Un día vi un accidente de auto.

   Estudiante B: ¿Dónde ocurrió? ¿Qué tiempo hacía ese día? ¿Hubo personas heridas (*injured*)? ¿Pudiste ayudar? (Una pregunta original)

4. **Estudiante B:** Cuando tenía _____ años, recibí un regalo muy especial.

   Estudiante A: ¿Cuál fue el regalo? ¿Cómo era? ¿Quién te lo dio? ¿Era para alguna ocasión especial? (Una pregunta original)

Clase

8-46 Testigos. ¡Pronto va a pasar algo extraño en el salón de clase! Su profesor(a) va a darle algunas instrucciones a un(a) estudiante. Miren bien qué hace. Luego completen una declaración de testigo (*eyewitness report*) para la policía. En una hoja de papel, escriban una descripción del delincuente, sus acciones y el artículo que robó (*stole*).

DECLARACIÓN DE TESTIGO

Nombre: _____

Fecha: _____   Hora: _____

Lugar: _____

Descripción del delincuente: _____

_____

_____

Descripción del crimen (qué pasó): _____

_____

_____

_____

© Cengage Learning 2016

8-47 ¡Qué raro! En grupos de cuatro o cinco personas, compartan (*share*) algunas anécdotas personales. Sigan el modelo, contestando las tres preguntas: ¿Dónde estabas? ¿Qué hacías? ¿Qué pasó?

Modelo   **Estudiante A:** (¿Dónde estabas?) Esta mañana estaba en la biblioteca. (¿Qué hacías? ¿Qué pasó?) Estudiaba para un examen cuando ¡vi un gato negro!

   Estudiante B: Eso no es nada. Ayer estaba en la cafetería. Almorzaba cuando…

G PASO 3 GRAMÁTICA B

El imperfecto y el pretérito: segunda parte

Ricitos de Oro

Había una vez una niña que se llamaba Ricitos de Oro. Ella era una niña muy curiosa. Una tarde, vio una casa en medio del bosque y entró. Ella tenía mucha hambre entonces se puso contenta cuando vio tres platos de sopa sobre la mesa. Primero probó la sopa del plato grande pero le pareció muy caliente...

1. Stories often follow a familiar and predictable pattern. First, we use the **imperfecto** as we set the scene and/or give background information:

- the time, date, place and/or characters

Era una noche fría de invierno.	*It **was** a cold winter night.*
Yo **estaba** en casa con mi perrito.	*I **was** at home with my little dog.*

- the customary, habitual, or routine actions of the characters

  Normalmente, mi perrito Fifí **pasaba** la noche en su camita.
  *My dog Fifí usually **spent** the evening in his little bed.*

- what was going on at the particular moment in time

  Pero esa noche **parecía** un poco nervioso, y **se escondía** detrás del sofá.
  *But that night, he **seemed** a little nervous, and **was hiding** behind the sofa.*

2. Next, we move the story forward with the **pretérito** by telling what happened.

De repente, Fifí **corrió** a la puerta.	*Suddenly, Fifí **ran** to the door.*
Yo lo **seguí** y **abrí** la puerta.	*I **followed** him and **opened** the door.*

3. As the story moves forward, we occasionally pause and use the **imperfecto** to further describe the scene or a character.

La luna **brillaba** como el sol,	*The moon **was shining** like the sun,*
pero no **se veía** a nadie.	*but you **couldn't see** anyone.*

4. After each pause, we use the **pretérito** to move the story forward.

  Cerré la puerta y **volví** al sofá. *I **closed** the door and **returned** to the sofa.*

5. Sometimes we finish by summing up the experience with the **pretérito**.

  ¡Fue una noche muy extraña! *It **was** a very strange night!*

■ ■ ■
Descúbrelo

- What children's storybook character is **Ricitos de Oro**?

- How is **Ricitos de Oro** described in this version? Is the imperfect or the preterite used to describe her?

- When is the preterite first used in the story? When do these actions take place?

- When is the imperfect used again? Is it to describe a character or say what happened?

¡Aplícalo! **8-48** **El oso.** Con un(a) compañero(a), completen la siguiente anécdota sobre un oso *(bear)* basada en el dibujo. ¿Creen que es realista?

© Cengage Learning 2016

1. *What was the weather like?*   (Era / Fue) un día bonito. (Hacía / Hizo) mucho sol y calor.

2. *Where was the family?*   La familia Martínez (estaba / estuvo) en un parque nacional.

3. *What were they doing?*   Mientras los adultos (leían / leyeron), los niños (jugaban / jugaron) al fútbol.

4. *What interrupted the action?*   De repente, un oso (llegaba / llegó) y (daba / dio) un rugido *(growl)*.

5. *How did the family feel?*   Todos (estaban / estuvieron) inmóviles; nadie (sabía / supo) qué hacer.

6. *What happened at the end?*   Al final, el oso (se aburría / se aburrió) y (se iba / se fue).

8-49 **El gato y los ratones.** ¿Qué hace una familia de ratones *(mice)* cuando su vecino es un gato? Con un(a) compañero(a), conjuguen los verbos entre paréntesis en el imperfecto o el pretérito, según el contexto.

(1. Haber) _____ una familia de ratones que (2. vivir) _____ feliz en la pared de la cocina de los Morales. Un día, los Morales (3. conseguir) _____ una nueva mascota: ¡un gato! El gato siempre (4. dormir) _____ en la cocina. Por eso, los ratones (5. tener) _____ miedo de salir y buscar comida. Pronto, todos (6. sentir) _____ mucha hambre, entonces la mamá ratón (7. decidir) _____ salir. Ella (8. caminar) _____ cuidadosamente por el piso cuando de repente el gato (9. despertarse) _____. La mamá ratón (10. mirar) _____ al gato y ladró *(barked)*. El gato (11. salir) _____ corriendo y la mamá ratón (12. poder) _____ buscar comida. Moraleja *(Moral)*: ¡Es importante saber un segundo idioma!

¡Exprésate!

Colaborar

8-50 **La Llorona.** ¿Conoces la leyenda de la Llorona? Con un(a) compañero(a), cambien *(change)* los verbos en la leyenda del presente al imperfecto o al pretérito. Por ejemplo: Según una leyenda, la Llorona **era**...

Nota cultural

La Llorona is the best-known ghost story in Hispanic cultures. Every region has its own version, but the theme is the same: a tormented phantom searches for a lost child or love. Whenever people hear a wailing sound in the night, they say it's **la Llorona**.

La Llorona

Según una leyenda, la Llorona **es** una mujer joven y bonita. **Está** casada y **tiene** tres hijos pequeños. Un día, su esposo se **va** de la casa y **abandona** a su familia. La Llorona **se pone** furiosa y **decide** matar[1] a sus hijos porque **son** la imagen del padre. Los **lleva** a un río[2] y los **ahoga**[3]. Entonces **siente** lástima[4] pero **es** demasiado tarde: sus hijos **están** muertos. Por eso, la Llorona camina por todas partes llorando[5]: "¡Ay mis hijos! ¡Ay mis hijos!".

[1]*kill* [2]*river* [3]*drown* [4]*feels sorry* [5]*wailing*

8-51 **¿Qué pasó?** Escoge un dibujo de abajo y úsalo para contarle a tu compañero(a) un cuento original. Tienes que usar el imperfecto y el pretérito.

1. **Frases útiles:** ser Navidad, ver televisión en la sala, el novio llegar, oír a un hombre declarar su amor, no saber, romper relaciones, tener un Año Nuevo triste

2. **Frases útiles:** ser verano, hacer sol, hacer senderismo, divertirse, un águila volar, agarrar *(grab)* la mochila, buscar por horas, no encontrar la mochila

© Cengage Learning 2016

8-52 **Había una vez.** Formen grupos de cuatro estudiantes para crear cuentos originales. Cada persona necesita tener una hoja de papel y seguir estos pasos *(steps)*:

1. Individualmente, cada persona escribe en su papel el comienzo *(beginning)* de un cuento (**¿Dónde estaban las personas? ¿Qué hacían?**).

2. Todos pasan su papel a la persona a su derecha. Luego, cada persona escribe la continuación (**¿Qué pasó? Luego, ¿qué?**).

3. Todos pasan su papel a la persona a su derecha. Entonces, cada persona escribe una conclusión (**¿Qué pasó al final?**).

4. Finalmente, tomando turnos, cada persona lee el cuento. El grupo vota por el mejor cuento.

CONECTADOS CON...
LA HISTORIA DEL ARTE

La pintura contemporánea de Hispanoamérica

La pintura contemporánea de Hispanoamérica abarca una gran variedad de estilos y técnicas. Entre las diversas tendencias se destacan el muralismo, el surrealismo y el abstraccionismo.

El muralismo

El muralismo es un movimiento artístico que surgió en México después de la Revolución de 1910. Sus mayores representantes fueron Diego Rivera, José Clemente Orozco y David Alfaro Siqueiros. Estos muralistas pintaban sus obras monumentales en edificios públicos y representaban temas históricos, sociales y políticos. La figura humana es fundamental en estas idílicas escenas de la vida indígena, en los encuentros violentos de la Revolución y en las

Este panel es del mural *Creadores de la nacionalidad* (1973), de César Rengifo.

Palabras de historia del arte

la figura	figure (representation of a person or thing)
la línea	line
el movimiento artístico	artistic movement
la obra	work (of art)
pintar	to paint
la pintura	painting
la técnica	technique
el tema	theme, subject

Estrategia: Guessing meaning from context

Context refers to the words and sentences that surround an unfamiliar word. Often you will be able to approximate the meaning of a word by examining the clues from nearby text. For example, in the first paragraph you might guess that **abarca** means something like *includes* or *spans* because it is located in an introductory sentence, and immediately after the verb you see the words for *a great variety of styles and techniques*.

8-53 **Comprensión.** Aquí tienes tres obras famosas de Roberto Matta, Diego Rivera y María Luisa Pacheco. Basándote en la información del artículo, ¿quién es el (la) artista de cada obra? ¿A qué movimiento artístico corresponde? ¿Cómo lo sabes?

1. *Catavi*, 1974

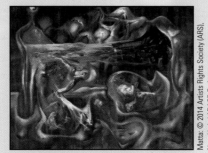

2. *Crucificción*, 1938

3. *En el Arsenal*, 1933

imágenes distintivas del socialismo o del capitalismo. El muralismo se extendió a varios países latinoamericanos. En Venezuela, por ejemplo, César Rengifo realizó varios murales que tratan de los mitos y la historia venezolanos.

El surrealismo

El surrealismo es el arte del inconsciente. Los surrealistas exploraban el mundo de los sueños y de la fantasía; pintaban escenas de la imaginación. Este movimiento nació en Francia después de la Primera Guerra *(War)* Mundial pero muy pronto se extendió a España con los célebres artistas Joan Miró, Salvador Dalí y Pablo Picasso. El pintor chileno Roberto Matta ganó gran renombre por su visión de la unidad del hombre y del cosmos y hoy se considera uno de los pintores más importantes del siglo xx. En Cuba, Wilfredo Lam dio su interpretación personal al surrealismo, creando curiosas figuras híbridas de animales, vegetales y seres humanos.

El abstraccionismo

El abstraccionismo (o pintura abstracta) es una corriente *(school, movement)* basada en el color y las líneas. En su forma más pura es el opuesto del arte figurativo; o sea *(that is)* las líneas y los colores no representan ningún objeto o persona real. Uno de los primeros y más importantes representantes en Latinoamérica fue el uruguayo Joaquín Torres García, quien incorporó elementos geométricos en sus obras. Otra pintora de fama internacional, la boliviana María Luisa Pacheco, encontraba la inspiración para sus cuadros en la luz y los colores de los glaciares y las montañas de Bolivia.

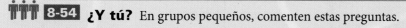 **8-54** **¿Y tú?** En grupos pequeños, comenten estas preguntas.

1. ¿Qué movimiento artístico te interesa más: el muralismo, el surrealismo o el abstraccionismo?

2. ¿Qué museo de arte has visitado recientemente? ¿Qué obra de arte te impresionó allí?

3. ¿Tienes mucho o poco talento artístico? ¿Te gusta pintar o dibujar?

 Composición: Una anécdota

We've all had our share of funny, sad, and embarrassing moments. Which one would you like to share? Choose one of your experiences (or a memorable experience of a friend or family member) and recount it in a brief story.

 **Revisión en pareja.** Exchange papers with a classmate and edit each other's work.

- Does the anecdote have a sense of beginning, middle, and end? Write one positive comment and one suggestion for improvement.

- Are the events told in chronological order? Write comments wherever the sequence isn't clear to you.

- Have the imperfect and the preterite been used correctly? Circle any verbs that might be incorrect.

Estrategia:
Creating a beginning, middle, and end

- To begin your anecdote, set the scene and give background information.

- Recount the actions in chronological order; build to a high point.

- To end, sum up the event or include a lesson you learned.

8-55 **Nosotros / *Share It!*** En línea, subiste una foto de tu niñez o de la celebración de un día festivo. También viste las publicaciones de varios compañeros de clase. Ahora, en grupos de tres o cuatro personas, comenten sobre estas publicaciones y contesten las preguntas.

Fotos de la niñez

- ¿Quiénes subieron fotos de la niñez?
- ¿Cuál es la foto más divertida? ¿Cuál es la más tierna?
- ¿Quién ha cambiado mucho de aspecto físico? ¿Cómo era de niño(a)? ¿Cómo es ahora? ¿Quién ha cambiado poco?

Fotos de los días festivos

- ¿Quiénes subieron fotos de días festivos?
- ¿Cuál es la foto más divertida? ¿Qué celebraban? ¿Qué hacían cuando se tomó la foto?
- ¿Cuál es tu foto favorita? Descríbela con muchos detalles.

 8-56 **Perspectivas: Los días festivos.** En línea, miraste un video en el que *(in which)* tres estudiantes describen la celebración de sus días festivos favoritos. ¿Qué dicen los estudiantes? Con dos compañeros(as) de clase, comparen sus apuntes sobre el video. Después, entrevístense *(interview one another)* con estas preguntas:

- ¿Cuál es tu día festivo favorito?
- ¿Cómo celebras ese día normalmente?

 8-57 **Exploración: Las ferias.** En Internet, investigaste una feria del mundo hispano. Ahora, formen círculos de tres o cuatro estudiantes. Tomen turnos haciendo pequeñas presentaciones sobre las ferias. Después, decidan en cuál de las ferias les gustaría participar a Uds.

En tu presentación, contesta estas preguntas:

- ¿Cómo se llama la feria?
- ¿Qué tipo de feria es?
- ¿Dónde tiene lugar?
- ¿Cuándo es?
- ¿Qué eventos o espectáculos hay?
- ¿Cuánto cuesta la entrada?

 8-58 **Conectados con... la historia.** En línea, leíste un artículo sobre los bucaneros. Con dos o tres compañeros(as), compartan *(share)* información de sus investigaciones sobre otro grupo o persona importante en la historia de las Américas.

Modelo

Los piratas eran... Vivían en... / Lope de Aguirre fue... Participó en...

👥 8-59 **¡Vamos al festival!** Tú y tu compañero(a) están en Colombia y quieren ir a un festival. Tú **(Estudiante A)** y tu compañero(a) **(Estudiante B)** tienen información incompleta sobre el festival.

■ Primero, tienen que hacerse *(ask each other)* preguntas para completar la información.

■ Tú empiezas con esta pregunta: **¿Cuál es el nombre completo del festival?**

■ Después, invita a tu compañero(a) a tu evento preferido.

> This is a pair activity for **Estudiante A** and **Estudiante B**.
>
> If you are **Estudiante A**, use the information on this page.
>
> If you are **Estudiante B**, turn to p. S-8 at the back of the book.

Estudiante A

PROGRAMACIÓN
Sábado 3 de abril

Festival Iberoamericano de Teatro de (1) _____

19 de (2) _____ al 4 de abril

¡Ven a este gran festival con más de (3) _____ funciones de 100 compañías internacionales! ¡Son 16 días de espectáculos inolvidables!

Entrada General
Adultos: (4) $ _____ Niños: $4000

DANZA 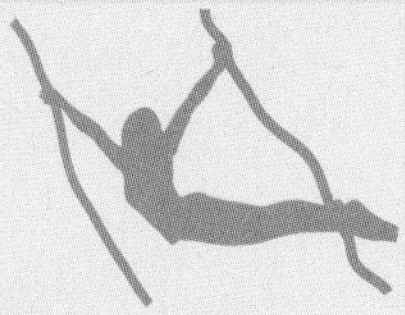
Argentina
Danza Aérea
Coliseo El Campín, 5 p.m.

España
Flamenco actual
(5) _____, 8 p.m.

TEATRO CONTEMPORÁNEO 
(6) _____

Teatro en el Blanco presenta la obra *Diciembre*
Teatro Arlequín, 6 p.m.

Estados Unidos
Corbian Visual Arts presenta
(7) _____, obra apta para todo público
Teatro Moderno, 3 y 6 p.m.

COMEDIA
Venezuela
Luis Fernández presenta un divertido espectáculo de monólogos cómicos[1]
Teatro La Castellana,
(8) ____ p.m.

TEATRO MUSICAL
(9) _____

A solas, con Margarita Rosa, combina música, video y luces
Teatro Leonardus, 5 p.m.

🎵 **GRAN CONCIERTO de** (10) _____
España
Lugar: Plaza de Toros Hora: 8 p.m. Precio: $155.000

© Cengage Learning 2016

[1]*stand-up comedy*

SÍNTESIS

Colaborar

8-60 **Bailando.** Fernando Botero (n. 1932) es el artista colombiano con más fama internacional. Ha pintado muchos cuadros caracterizados por formas voluminosas, como este.

- Con un(a) compañero(a) de clase, observen bien el cuadro y escriban un párrafo sobre la escena.
- Usen la imaginación y el tiempo imperfecto para describir la noche, el lugar, la celebración, las personas, la ropa, la música y el ambiente.
- Estén preparados para leer su párrafo a la clase.

Bailarines (2002), Fernando Botero

Clase

8-61 **¡Feliz Año Nuevo!** Tú y tus compañeros son viejos amigos. Una vez al año todos Uds. se reúnen en una fiesta para celebrar el Año Nuevo. Ahora están en esa fiesta. Tienen que hacer lo siguiente:

- Saludar a los amigos y conversar sobre lo que ha pasado *(what has happened)* durante el año. (**¿Qué hay de nuevo? ¿Qué has hecho este año?**)
- Contar sus experiencias buenas y malas. (**En febrero hice un viaje magnífico. Fui a... En abril mi novio(a) y yo rompimos nuestra relación. Estaba muy triste...**)
- Reaccionar a las noticias de sus amigos. (**¿De veras? ¡Qué suerte! ¡Qué extraño!**)
- Preguntarse sobre sus propósitos *(resolutions)* para el Año Nuevo. (**¿Cuáles son tus propósitos para el Año Nuevo? Yo voy a...**)
- A la medianoche, brindar con champaña y desearse *(wish one another)* un feliz Año Nuevo.

8-62 **El Dorado.** Muchos exploradores han buscado la mítica ciudad de El Dorado. ¿Sabes cuál es el origen de esta leyenda? Con un(a) compañero(a) de clase, lean la siguiente conversación entre un guía y un turista al norte de Bogotá.

- Conjuguen los verbos en el pretérito o el imperfecto, según el contexto.
- Completen los espacios con frases apropiadas.

© DC_Colombia/iStockphoto

GUÍA   Esta es la laguna de Guatavita. Aquí, hace muchos años, los indígenas chibchas (practicar) _____ un ritual. Cuando (haber) _____ un nuevo rey *(king)*, lo (vestir) _____ de oro y lo (poner) _____ en una balsa con cuatro compañeros.

TURISTA   ¿_____?

GUÍA   Cuando ellos (llegar) _____ al centro de la laguna, echaban *(would throw)* muchos objetos de oro al agua en honor a los dioses. Este ritual (dar) _____ origen al mito de El Dorado.

TURISTA   ¿_____?

GUÍA   Sí, es verdad. En 1580, un español (querer) _____ drenar *(drain)* la laguna de Guatavita.

TURISTA   _____. ¿_____?

GUÍA   Cientos de trabajadores indígenas (morir) _____ cuando el canal se derrumbó *(collapsed)*.

TURISTA   ¡_____!

Pronunciación: **El enlace**

Con un(a) compañero(a), lean en voz alta la primera estrofa *(stanza)* de un villancico de Navidad. Presten atención al enlace.

© Matthew Cole/Shutterstock

Arbolito

Esta noche es Nochebuena.

Vamos al monte, hermanito,

A buscar un arbolito,

Hoy que la noche es serena.

VOCABULARIO

RECURSOS

Para aprender mejor

Don't just review this vocabulary list. Every few days, go back and review the vocabulary lists from previous chapters. Incorporate reviewing old vocabulary into your study routine.

Sustantivos

el actor / la actriz *actor / actress*
el águila (f.) *eagle*
el ala (f.) *wing*
el ambiente *atmosphere*
la anécdota *personal story*
el árbol *tree*
el (la) atleta *athlete*
el atletismo *track and field*
el baile *dance*
la bandera *flag*
la campanada *(bell) stroke*
el campeonato *championship*
la canción *song*
el (la) cantante *singer*
el cariño *affection, love*
el carnaval *carnival*
el ciclismo *cycling*
el cielo *sky*
la cima *top, summit*
la competencia *competition*
el concurso *contest*
el conjunto *musical group*
la costumbre *custom*
el desfile *parade*
el día festivo *holiday*
el dios / la diosa *god / goddess*
el disfraz *costume*
los dulces *candy*
la época *time of year*
el equipo *team*
el evento *event*
la exposición *exhibition*
la feria *fair*
el festival *festival*
los fuegos artificiales *fireworks*
la iglesia *church*
la leyenda *legend*
la luna *moon*
el menorá *menorah*
la mezquita *mosque*

el mito *myth*
la natación *swimming*
la obra de teatro *(theater) play*
el pavo *turkey*
el pesebre *manger*
la pluma *feather*
el premio *prize; award*
la sinagoga *sinagogue*
el sol *sun*
la tarjeta *card*
el teatro *theater*
el templo *temple*
el villancico *carol*

Verbos

aceptar *to accept*
acostumbrar *to be accustomed to*
celebrar *to celebrate*
continuar *to continue*
convertir (ie) *to turn, to transform*
creer *to believe*
cubrir *to cover*
disfrazarse (de) *to dress up in a costume (as)*
elegir (i) *to choose*
encender (ie) *to light*
encontrarse (ue) *to meet (up)*
huir *to run away, to escape*
intercambiar regalos *to exchange gifts*
invitar *to extend an invitation*
ocurrir *to happen*
presentar *to present, to show*
reaccionar *to react*
realizar *to carry out*
recoger *to pick up*
rehusar *to decline*
reunirse *to get together*
rezar *to pray*
sacudir *to shake*

tener lugar *to take place*
volar (ue) *to fly*

Adjetivos

alegre *happy, lively*
artístico(a) *artistic*
aterrorizado(a) *terrified*
congelado(a) *frozen*
cultural *cultural*
deportivo(a) *sports related*
extraño(a) *strange, odd*
festivo(a) *festive*
furioso(a) *furious*
gracioso(a) *funny*
hermoso(a) *beautiful*
increíble *incredible*
internacional *international*
militar *military*
patriótico(a) *patriotic*
popular *popular*
prestigioso(a) *prestigious*
tradicional *traditional*

Las anécdotas

Al final... *At the end . . .*
De niño(a)... *As a child . . .*
De repente... *Suddenly . . .*
Entonces... *Then . . .*
Había una vez... *Once a upon a time . . .*
Hace muchos años... *A long time ago . . .*
Mientras... *While . . .*
Por eso... *That's why . . .*
Según... *According to . . .*
Una vez... *One time . . .*

Holidays, p. 292
Greetings, p. 293
Invitations, p. 302
To react to a story, p. 313

La salud y el bienestar

Conexiones a la comunidad
Volunteer to give health fitness classes, in Spanish, in your local community center; or shadow a medical interpreter at a local hospital.

In this chapter you will . . .
- explore Ecuador, Peru, and Bolivia
- talk about the human body
- describe symptoms of common illnesses
- say what hurts
- understand the doctor's orders
- give advice and tell others what to do
- learn about medicine in Incan times
- share a poem you wrote

NUESTRO MUNDO

Ecuador, Perú y Bolivia

Estos tres países de América del Sur se conocen como los países andinos porque la cordillera de los Andes ocupa gran parte de sus territorios. Otra parte de sus territorios incluye las junglas tropicales de la Amazonía.

República del Perú
Población: 30 200 000
Capital: Lima
Idiomas oficiales: español y quechua
Moneda: el nuevo sol
Exportaciones: cobre *(copper)*, oro, zinc, petróleo

República del Ecuador
Población: 15 600 000
Capital: Quito
Idioma oficial: español
Moneda: el dólar estadounidense
Exportaciones: petróleo, bananas, flores, camarones

Estado Plurinacional de Bolivia
Población: 10 600 000
Capitales: La Paz (administrativa), Sucre (constitucional)
Idiomas oficiales: español, quechua y aymara
Moneda: el boliviano
Exportaciones: gas, frijoles de soya, petróleo, zinc

Muchas personas practican el taichi en los países andinos. "Taichi en los parques" es un programa gratis que comenzó en la década de 1990 en Lima, Perú, como una estrategia de salud pública. El objetivo es sentir bienestar *(well-being)* físico, psicológico y social.

Perú, como una estrategia de salud pública. El objetivo es sentir bienestar *(well-being)* físico, psicológico y social.

Geografía

El lago Titicaca, entre Perú y Bolivia, es el lago navegable más alto del mundo (12 500 pies de altura). Según la mitología inca, el dios Viracocha salió de este lago para crear el Sol, la Luna y los seres humanos. Hoy, sus habitantes continúan navegando el lago en canoas de totora *(reed)*.

Arquitectura

Los antiguos incas eran grandes arquitectos. La unión de las piedras *(stones)* era tan perfecta que no necesitaban argamasa *(mortar)*. En algunas ciudades, como Cusco, Perú, se conservan paredes incas originales.

Artesanía

Desde hace mucho tiempo, los habitantes de los países andinos han usado la lana *(wool)* de llama para tejer *(weave)* hermosos ponchos, guantes, gorras y suéteres. Un lugar famoso para comprar textiles es el mercado de Otavalo, en Ecuador.

9-1 **¿Qué sabes?** Indica si cada oración es cierta o falsa. Usa la información en estas páginas para justificar tus respuestas.

1. Muchas personas en Ecuador, Perú y Bolivia viven en grandes altitudes.

2. La población de Bolivia es homogénea.

3. Perú formaba parte del Imperio inca.

4. No hay junglas en los países andinos.

5. Perú no tiene influencias chinas.

6. En partes de Ecuador hace frío.

9-2 **Videomundo.** Mira los videos de Bolivia, Ecuador y Perú. Luego trabajen en grupos pequeños para clasificar estas frases: digan si se relacionan a La Paz, Quito, Lima o las tres.

José de San Martín	iglesias	Miraflores	indígenas	mercado Mariscal
cerca de Tiahuanaco	playas	los Andes	Plaza Humboldt	arquitectura colonial

El cuerpo y la salud

In this *Paso*, you will . . .

- talk about the human body
- describe symptoms of common illnesses
- say what hurts and talk about health and injuries

Las partes del cuerpo

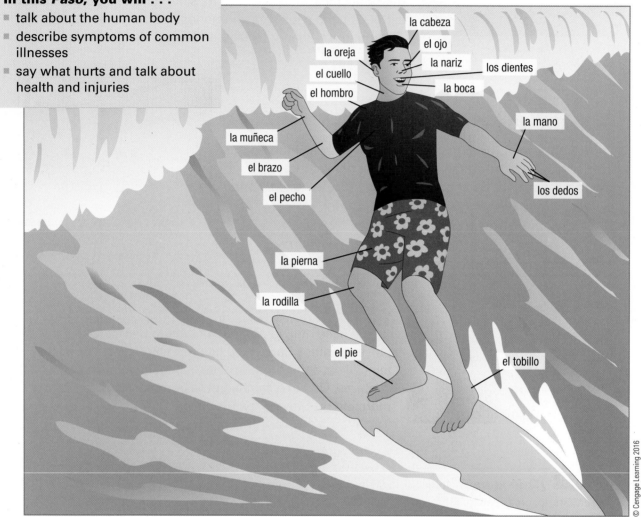

la cabeza
el ojo
la oreja
la nariz
los dientes
el cuello
la boca
el hombro
la mano
la muñeca
el brazo
el pecho
los dedos
la pierna
la rodilla
el pie
el tobillo

© Cengage Learning 2016

Los síntomas y las enfermedades	Symptoms and illnesses	Otras partes del cuerpo	Other body parts
		el corazón	heart
estar congestionado(a) / mocoso(a)	to be congested / to have a runny nose	la espalda	back
		el estómago	stomach
estornudar	to sneeze	la garganta	throat
ser alérgico(a) a...	to be allergic to . . .	el hueso	bone
tener...	to have . . .	el oído	inner ear
tos	a cough	la piel	skin
fiebre	a fever	el pulmón (los pulmones)	lung(s)
diarrea	diarrhea		
vómitos	vomiting		
gripe	the flu		
un resfriado	a cold		
una infección	an infection		
dolor de (cabeza)	a (head)ache		

La salud

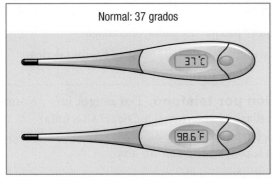

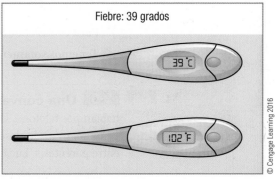

Para hablar sobre la salud

¿Cómo te sientes?
    Me siento mal / fatal / débil.
    Creo que tengo gripe.
¿Qué tienes?
    Me duele (mucho) la espalda.
    Me duelen (mucho) los oídos.
¿Qué te pasó?
    Me caí.
¡Ay!
¡Pobrecito(a)!
¡Qué lástima!
¡Que te mejores!
¡Que se mejore!

Talking about your health

How do you feel?
    I feel lousy / awful / weak.
    I think I have the flu.
What's the matter?
    My back hurts (a lot).
    My ears hurt (a lot).
What happened to you?
    I fell down.
Ow! / Ouch!
You poor thing!
That's too bad!
I hope you (inf.) feel better!; Get well!
I hope you (form.) feel better!; Get well!

¡Aplícalo!

Colaborar

9-3 **¿Qué es?** Tomando turnos con un(a) compañero(a) de clase, una persona lee la definición y la otra nombra la parte del cuerpo.

1. Los usamos para ver.

2. Es un órgano importante para la digestión.

3. Hay cinco en una mano y los usamos para escribir.

4. Tenemos dos y nos permiten tomar oxígeno.

5. Es el órgano más grande porque cubre (covers) todo nuestro cuerpo.

6. Cada uno tiene un nombre: la tibia, el fémur, la clavícula, el cóccix, etcétera.

7. La usamos para comer, beber, hablar y besar (kiss).

8. Es la unión entre el pie y la pierna.

Colaborar

9-4 **Categorías.** Trabaja con un(a) compañero(a) para leer en voz alta cada grupo de palabras y poner un círculo alrededor de la palabra que **no** corresponde a la categoría.

1. **Síntomas:** pobrecito / estornudar / estar mocoso / ser alérgico / estar congestionado

2. **Los órganos:** estómago / corazón / piel / pulmones / gripe

3. **Las articulaciones (joints):** rodilla / espalda / hombro / tobillo / muñeca

4. **La gripe:** fiebre / diarrea / tos / infección / cuello

5. **Para comer:** boca / dientes / pierna / garganta / estómago

6. **Tenemos solamente dos:** orejas / muñecas / manos / brazos / dedos

Colaborar

9-5 **Una conversación por teléfono.** Dos amigas, Inés y Norma, hablan por teléfono. Una de ellas está enferma. ¿Qué tiene? Con un(a) compañero(a) de clase, completen la conversación con las palabras más lógicas entre paréntesis. Luego, lean la conversación en voz alta.

INÉS ¡Hola, Norma! ¿Qué tal?

NORMA Me siento (1. fatal / muñeca).

INÉS ¿Por qué? ¿Qué (2. tienes / te sientes)?

NORMA Tengo tos, estoy (3. vómitos / mocosa) y me duele todo el (4. cuerpo / corazón).

INÉS ¡(5. Qué suerte / Pobrecita)! ¿También tienes (6. oído / fiebre)?

NORMA Sí, esta mañana tenía 40 (7. grados / pies).

INÉS Creo que tienes (8. diarrea / gripe). ¿Tomaste aspirina para la fiebre y el (9. dolor / dedo)?

NORMA No. Soy (10. alérgica / congestionada) a la aspirina. Tomé ibuprofeno.

INÉS Bueno, que te (11. lástima / mejores), chica. Mañana te llamo otra vez.

¡Exprésate!

Clothing and accessories, **Capítulo 7**; Double object pronouns, **Capítulo 7 Paso 3**

Colaborar

9-6 **Asociaciones.** Tomando turnos con un(a) compañero(a), una persona identifica el artículo de ropa y la otra dice en qué parte del cuerpo se lo pone.

Modelo **Estudiante A:** las chancletas

Estudiante B: Me las pongo en los pies.
(**Me** + *pronombre de complemento directo* + **pongo en** + *parte del cuerpo*)

© Jasmin Awad/ Shutterstock

1.   2.   3.   4.   5.   6.

(left to right): © cosma/Shutterstock; © elzeva/iStockphoto;
© kocetoiliev/Shutterstock; © Seregam/Shutterstock;
© Olga Popova/Shutterstock; © Jiang Hongyan/Shutterstock

9-7 **En la clínica.** Tu compañero(a) está en Ecuador y está enfermo(a). Tú estás con él/ella en la clínica y le estás completando el cuestionario *(questionnaire)* médico. Tienes que hacerle preguntas para completar el cuestionario; tu compañero(a) tiene que contestarlas. Después te toca a ti *(it's your turn)* estar enfermo(a).

CUESTIONARIO MÉDICO

Nombre _____   ☐ Hombre   ☐ Mujer

Dirección _____   Teléfono _____

¿Qué tiene?

☐ fiebre   ☐ dolor de cabeza

☐ tos   ☐ dolor de garganta

☐ dolor de estómago   ☐ dolor de pecho

☐ vómitos   ☐ diarrea

☐ naúseas   ☐ otros _____

¿Desde cuándo? _____

¿Es Ud. alérgico(a)?   ☐ no   ☐ sí   ¿A qué?   ☐ medicina   ☐ comida   ☐ otros

¿Está tomando alguna medicina?   ☐ no   ☐ sí   ¿Cuáles? _____

9-8 **Una llamada al trabajo.** Con un(a) compañero(a), imaginen que Uds. trabajan en una oficina. Dramaticen cuatro llamadas telefónicas *(telephone calls)*.

■ Una persona escoge una enfermedad de la lista. Describe sus síntomas y dice que no puede ir a trabajar.

■ La otra persona expresa empatía *(empathy)* y dice qué enfermedad es.

Modelo **Estudiante A:** Hola. Habla Jamal. No puedo ir a trabajar hoy porque tengo fiebre y dolor de garganta. Estoy muy cansado.

Estudiante B: Lo siento. Me parece que tienes mononucleosis. ¡Que te mejores!

Las enfermedades		
bronquitis	una infección intestinal	mononucleosis
gripe	una migraña *(migraine)*	un resfriado

El verbo *doler*

PACIENTE	Doctor, me duele todo el cuerpo.
DOCTOR	¿Todo el cuerpo?
PACIENTE	Sí. Me toco (*I touch*) la cabeza y me duele. Me toco los hombros y me duelen. Me duele el brazo... me duelen las piernas... me duelen los pies. ¿Qué tengo?
DOCTOR	¡Ud. tiene un dedo roto, señor!

■ ■ ■

Descúbrelo

■ What is the patient complaining about? What is the doctor's diagnosis?

■ What phrase does the patient use to say that something hurts?

■ Why does the patient sometimes say **duele** and other times **duelen**? (Hint: What follows the verb?)

1. Use the verb **doler (ue)** to say what hurts. As with the verb **gustar**, just two forms are used.

■ **Me duele + el/la +** (*singular / one body part*)

Me duele la espalda.   *My back hurts.*

■ **Me duelen + los/las +** (*plural body parts*)

Me duelen los pies.   *My feet hurt.*

2. To refer to other people, use the corresponding indirect object pronouns.

A Raúl **le** duelen los oídos.   *Raúl's ears are bothering **him** / hurt.*

El verbo *doler (ue)* *to hurt, to ache*	
me duele(n)	nos duele(n)
te duele(n)	os duele(n)
le duele(n)	les duele(n)
a + *name / singular noun* + le duele(n)	a + *names / plural noun* + les duele(n)

3. While English uses possessive adjectives such as *his throat* or *my feet* with *hurt*, Spanish uses definite articles (**el, la, los, las**) with **doler**.

¿Te duele **el** estómago?   *Does **your** stomach hurt?*

¡Aplícalo!

👤👤 **9-9** **Ta-Te-Ti con dolores.** Juega al Ta-Te-Ti con un(a) compañero(a) de clase. Para poner X u O en un cuadrado (*square*), tienen que decir correctamente **Me duele(n) +** *parte del cuerpo* en el dibujo.

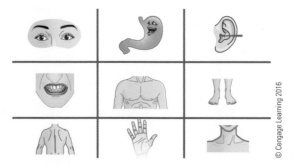

Colaborar

9-10 **¿Qué le duele?** Mientras hacía surf, este joven se cayó. Ahora le duelen muchas partes del cuerpo. Tomando turnos con un(a) compañero(a), digan qué le duele.

Modelo *(Señalando el hombro del joven)* Le duele el hombro.

Colaborar

9-11 **Un viaje a Perú.** Toda tu familia hizo un gran viaje a Perú. Pero, ¡qué lástima! Como consecuencia de sus actividades, todos están sufriendo un poco. Con un(a) compañero(a), describan los dolores de cada persona.

Modelo Tu mamá caminó por el distrito de Miraflores en Lima por seis horas. Llevaba unos zapatos que le quedaban pequeños.

Tú: ¡Pobrecita! Ahora le duelen mucho los pies.

1. Tu hermano menor tenía mucha hambre y ¡comió cinco tamales en el mercado!

2. El vuelo de tus primos llegó muy tarde, a las tres de la madrugada. Solo pudieron dormir por tres horas.

3. Tu papá quiso probar el cóctel nacional de Perú, el pisco sour. No sabía que llevaba mucho alcohol y se tomó tres.

4. Tus abuelos están un poco fuera de forma *(out of shape)* pero insistieron en explorar las ruinas de Machu Picchu todo el día.

5. La cama en tu hotel era muy dura *(hard)* e incómoda.

6. Dos de tus primos remaron *(rowed)* por el río Colca. Las corrientes *(currents)* eran muy fuertes.

7. Tu prima pidió sopa criolla en un restaurante. Cuando empezó a comerla, la sopa estaba demasiado caliente.

8. Todos Uds. caminaron por el distrito histórico por horas y horas. ¡¿Por qué no llevaron zapatos más cómodos?! ¡Qué desastre!

> **Nota cultural**
>
> Many tourists who travel to Cuzco, Peru, or La Paz, Bolivia, suffer from high altitude sickness, known as **soroche**. Symptoms include headaches, nausea, and sleep difficulties. The local remedy for **soroche** is **mate de coca**, an herbal infusion made from coca leaves. The coca leaf, which is legal in these two countries, is non-narcotic and helps promote absorption of oxygen in the blood.

9-12 La pantomima. Ayer Uds. hicieron demasiado ejercicio y hoy les duele todo. Tomando turnos con un(a) compañero(a), sigan el modelo y creen seis pequeñas conversaciones.

Modelo   **Estudiante A:** *(Indicando con el dedo una parte de su cuerpo, por ejemplo, los pies)* ¡Ay!

Estudiante B: *(Reaccionando)* ¿Qué te pasa? ¿Te duelen los pies?

Estudiante A: Sí, me duelen mucho.

9-13 Me duele todo. Tus amigos te invitan a muchas actividades, pero estás de mal humor y no quieres ir. ¿Qué excusas les das? Con un(a) compañero(a) de clase, dramaticen estas invitaciones.

- Tomando turnos, una persona lee una invitación.
- La otra persona declina la invitación y usa el verbo **doler** en su excusa.
- La primera persona reacciona.

Modelo   **Estudiante A:** Esta noche celebramos el cumpleaños de nuestra tía Julia. ¿Quieres tocar el piano en la fiesta?

Estudiante B: Lo siento, pero no puedo tocar el piano en la fiesta porque **me duelen** los dedos.

Estudiante A: ¡Qué lástima!

> **Palabras útiles**
> ¡Qué lástima!
> Quizás en otra ocasión.
> ¡Qué te mejores!

1. Vamos al karaoke mañana. ¿Quieres ir?

2. ¿Quieres ir conmigo a la clase de bicicleta fija *(spinning)* esta tarde?

3. El gimnasio en el campus tiene una nueva piscina. ¿Por qué no vamos a nadar mañana?

4. Vamos a hacer escalada en roca *(go rock climbing)* este fin de semana. ¿Tienes ganas de ir?

5. Dicen que el nuevo restaurante chino es fabuloso. ¿Vamos esta noche?

6. Voy a mudarme mañana. ¿Me ayudas con los muebles?

9-14 La buena salud. ¿Quién está en mejores condiciones físicas, tú o tu compañero(a)? Sigan el modelo y formen preguntas para entrevistarse. Después, decidan: ¿Quién necesita mejorar *(improve)* su salud?

Modelo   pecho / correr

Estudiante A: ¿Te duele el pecho cuando corres?

Estudiante B: No, no me duele. ¿Y a ti?

Estudiante A: No, no me duele. / Sí, me duele un poco.

1. dientes / comer helado

2. pies / caminar mucho

3. estómago / estar nervioso(a)

4. ojos / leer mucho

5. cabeza / estar estresado(a)

6. espalda / llevar tu mochila por el campus

7. pecho / hacer ejercicio aeróbico

Más verbos reflexivos

ELISA	Ay, Roberto, ¿qué te pasó?
ROBERTO	Juan y yo hacíamos senderismo en las montañas y me caí. No lo recuerdo bien porque me di un golpe en la cabeza.
ELISA	¡Pobrecito! Entonces te rompiste la pierna también.
ROBERTO	Sí, y me lastimé el cuello. Aparte de eso ¡nos divertimos mucho!

1. Many verbs can be used reflexively or non-reflexively.

> **Non-reflexive: Corté** el pastel de cumpleaños. *I cut the birthday cake.*
> *(The subject I performs the action and the cake receives the action.)*

> **Reflexive: Me corté** el dedo. *I cut my finger.*
> *(The subject I both performs and receives the impact of the action.)*

2. Reflexive verbs can also refer to changes in condition, such as one's health. In English these changes are expressed with *become / get* (+ adjective).

Verbos reflexivos relacionados con la salud

cortarse	*to cut oneself, to get cut*	**mejorarse**	*to get better, to improve*
darse un golpe en...	*to get hit in / on . . .*	**quemarse**	*to burn, to get burned*
enfermarse	*to get sick*	**romperse**	*to break*
lastimarse	*to get hurt,*	**sentirse (ie)**	*to feel*
	to injure oneself	**torcerse (ue)**	*to sprain, to twist*

Otros verbos reflexivos de uso común

caerse	*to fall (down)*	**olvidarse**	*to forget*

3. When a reflexive verb is conjugated, it is always accompanied by the reflexive pronoun that corresponds to the subject of the sentence.

El verbo reflexivo *sentirse (ie) to feel*

yo	**me** siento	nosotros(as)	**nos** sentimos
tú	**te** sientes	vosotros(as)	**os** sentís
Ud./él/ella	**se** siente	Uds./ellos/ellas	**se** sienten

4. Reflexive pronouns are generally placed before conjugated verbs. They can also be attached to infinitives or to present participles. When a reflexive pronoun is attached to a present participle, an accent mark is added: **-ándo-** / **-iéndo-**.

> No **me enfermo** con frecuencia.   *I don't get sick often.*
> Creo que **estás enfermándote**.   *I think that you're getting sick.*

▪▪▪ Descúbrelo

- What was Roberto doing when he fell?
- What kinds of injuries did he suffer?
- Which of these verbs are probably reflexive? **me caí, te rompiste, te pasó**
- When Roberto talks about hitting his head, does he use **la** or **mi** to refer to his head?

¡Aplícalo!

9-15 ¡Cuidado! ¿Qué les dice la Srta. Magaly a los niños en el kínder? Trabajando con un(a) compañero(a), tomen turnos para relacionar las dos partes de sus advertencias (*warnings*).

Modelo **Estudiante A:** Luci, tienes que llevar casco (*helmet*) cuando montas en bicicleta.
Estudiante B: (d) No quieres lastimarte la cabeza en el pavimento, ¿verdad?

_____ 1. Luci, tienes que llevar casco (*helmet*) cuando montas en bicicleta.

_____ 2. Jaime, ¿por qué estás jugando con los fósforos (*matches*)?

_____ 3. Miguelito, ¿quién te dio ese cuchillo?

_____ 4. Rosalinda, ¿no tienes tu colchoneta para la siesta (*sleeping mat*)?

_____ 5. Casandra, por favor, no debes comer más chocolate.

_____ 6. Álvaro, en esta clase no caminamos por encima de las mesas.

_____ 7. Beto, ¿te sientes mal?

_____ 8. Lolita, ya te he dicho tres veces que no debes tocar los peces en el acuario.

a. ¿Se olvidaron tus padres de dártela?

b. ¡Te vas a quemar!

c. Vas a enfermarte. ¿Quieres tener dolor de estómago?

d. No quieres lastimarte la cabeza en el pavimento, ¿verdad?

e. ¡Te vas a cortar!

f. Puedes romperte una pierna.

g. ¡Los vas a lastimar!

h. ¿Te duele algo? ¿Llamamos a tus padres?

9-16 Un fin de semana horrible. ¿Qué les pasó a Julieta y a Ronaldo el fin de semana pasado? Trabajando con un(a) compañero(a), escojan los verbos más lógicos, conjúguenlos en el pretérito y lean la conversación en voz alta.

> The preterite,
> **Capítulo 5 Paso 2**

JULIETA ¿Qué tal el fin de semana, Ronaldo? ¿(1. Divertirse / Sentirse) _____ mucho?

RONALDO ¡Fue horrible! El viernes mis amigos y yo almorzamos en el nuevo restaurante Clotilde y todos nosotros (2. romperse / enfermarse) _____. Yo pasé toda la noche con vómitos.

JULIETA ¡Ay, qué mala suerte! Pero ¿no tenías que jugar en el campeonato de fútbol el sábado? ¿(Tú) (3. Mejorarse / Torcerse) _____ a tiempo para jugar?

RONALDO Sí, pude jugar. Pero, imagínate, cuando yo iba a marcar un gol —¡PAF!— otro jugador chocó conmigo (*ran into me*). Yo (4. sentirse / caerse) _____ y (5. lastimarse / darse) _____ un golpe tremendo en la cabeza.

JULIETA ¡Pobrecito! Parece que los dos pasamos un fin de semana fatal. Yo fui a la playa con Alicia pero ella (6. olvidarse / levantarse) _____ de llevar protector solar y las dos (7. cortarse / quemarse) _____ la espalda.

RONALDO Bueno, por lo menos ¡nadie (8. caerse / romperse) _____ nada!

The present perfect, **Capítulo 7 Paso 2**

9-17 **¿Te ha pasado esto?** Usa las frases para formar preguntas en el presente perfecto. Circula por el salón para hacerles las preguntas a tus compañeros. Si un(a) compañero(a) contesta **Sí**, hazle la segunda pregunta y luego pídele su firma *(signature)*. ¡Ojo! Cada persona puede firmar tu papel solo dos veces.

Modelo **estar** en un hospital

Estudiante A: ¿Has estado en un hospital alguna vez?

Estudiante B: Sí.

Estudiante A: ¿Por cuántos días?

Estudiante B: Por dos días.

Estudiante A: Firma aquí, por favor.

Actividad	Una pregunta más	Firma
1. **estar** en un hospital	¿Por cuántos días?	
2. **romperse** un hueso	¿Cuál?	
3. **cortarse** con un cuchillo	¿Cuándo?	
4. **quemarse** la lengua	¿Con qué?	
5. **lastimarse** la espalda	¿Cómo?	
6. **caerse** de un caballo	¿A qué edad?	
7. **torcerse** el tobillo	¿En qué actividad?	
8. **darse** un golpe en la cabeza	¿Cuándo?	

9-18 **¡Qué mala suerte!** Estás pasando por una racha de mala suerte *(streak of bad luck)*. Imagínate en las siguientes situaciones. Con un(a) compañero(a), sigan el modelo y preparen diálogos para cada situación.

Modelo **Estudiante A:** ¿Qué te pasó?

Estudiante B: Fui de vacaciones a las montañas. Mientras esquiaba, me caí y me rompí la pierna.

Estudiante A: ¡Qué lástima! ¿Te duele mucho?

Estudiante B: No, no me duele mucho. Pero es difícil caminar.

1.

2.

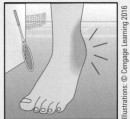
3.

Illustrations: © Cengage Learning 2016

9-19 **¡Ay!** Todos tenemos pequeños accidentes de vez en cuando. Piensa en una ocasión cuando te lastimaste y completa esta oración: **Una vez...** Dile a tu compañero(a) esta oración y contesta sus preguntas sobre la experiencia. Luego, cambien de papel *(switch roles)*.

1. ¿Dónde ocurrió el accidente?

2. ¿Cuántos años tenías?

3. ¿Con quién estabas?

4. ¿Qué hacían Uds.? ¿Qué pasó?

5. ¿Tuviste que ir al hospital? ¿Te dolía mucho?

PASO 2 VOCABULARIO

En el consultorio médico

Instrucciones de la doctora

In this *Paso*, you will . . .

- understand the doctor's orders
- give advice and tell others what to do
- say how long something has been going on or happened

© Cengage Learning 2016

Un examen médico	*A medical examination*
el (la) enfermero(a)	*nurse*
el (la) médico(a)	*doctor*
pedir cita	*to make an appointment*
Respire hondo.	*Take a deep breath.*
Tosa.	*Cough.*
Vamos a sacarle una radiografía.	*We're going to take an X-ray.*
Tratamiento	*Treatment*
Tenemos que ponerle...	*We have to put on (you) / give you . . .*
una inyección	*a shot*
unos puntos	*some stitches*
una venda	*a bandage*
un yeso	*a cast*
Vamos a darle suero intravenoso.	*We're going to give you IV fluids.*

Consejos de la doctora

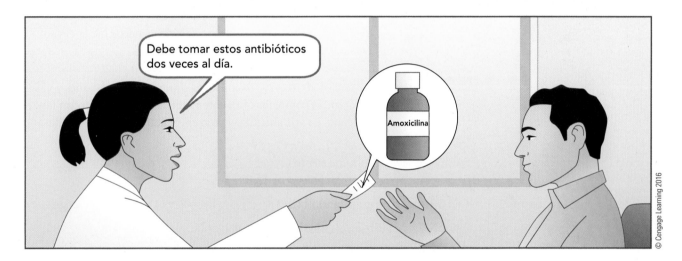

Diagnóstico	*Diagnosis*
Ud. tiene...	*You have . . .*
una fractura	*a fracture*
una intoxicación alimenticia	*food poisoning*

Consejos	*Advice*
Ud. debe / debería...	*You must / should . . .*
guardar cama	*stay in bed*
llevar una dieta líquida	*be on a liquid diet*
Ud. no debe / debería...	*You must not / shouldn't . . .*
consumir comidas altas en grasa	*eat foods high in fat*
mojar la herida	*get the wound wet*
Voy a recetarle...	*I'm going to prescribe you . . .*
unas pastillas	*some pills*
un jarabe	*a syrup*
una crema	*a lotion*
Tome este medicamento cada cuatro horas.	*Take this medicine every four hours.*

¡Aplícalo!

Colaborar

9-20 En el consultorio. ¿Qué les dice la doctora Pacheco a sus pacientes en la clínica hoy? Trabajando con un(a) compañero(a), sigan este proceso:

- Estudiante A lee un diagnóstico de la columna A.
- Estudiante B lee un tratamiento apropiado de la columna B.
- Estudiante A lee otro tratamiento lógico de la columna C.
- Estudiante B lee un diagnóstico de la columna A, y así sucesivamente.

A. El diagnóstico	B. Un tratamiento / consejo	C. Otro tratamiento / consejo
Ud. tiene una fractura de la tibia.	Voy a recetarle unos antibióticos.	Debe usar esta crema y no mojar la herida.
Ud. tiene una infección en los oídos.	No debería consumir comidas altas en grasa.	Debería llevar una dieta líquida por dos días.
Ud. se cortó el brazo pero no está roto.	Voy a recetarle unas pastillas para los vómitos.	Vamos a repetir el análisis de sangre en seis meses.
Ud. tiene una intoxicación alimenticia.	Tengo que ponerle un yeso.	Debe tomarlos dos veces al día con comida.
Ud. tiene el colesterol muy alto.	Voy a ponerle unos puntos.	¡No se olvide! No debe mojar el yeso.

Colaborar

9-21 Hablando con el doctor. Te enfermas durante tus vacaciones y vas a un centro médico. Con un(a) compañero(a), completen la conversación con las palabras más lógicas y léanla en voz alta. Consulten el vocabulario en las páginas 342 y 343.

PACIENTE   Doctor(a), me siento (1) _____. Creo que (2) _____ un resfriado o quizás (maybe) la gripe.

DOCTOR(A)   Voy a examinarlo(la). (3) _____ la boca y (4) _____ la lengua.

PACIENTE   Me (5) _____ bastante la garganta.

DOCTOR(A)   Sí, la tiene muy inflamada. Ahora, (6) _____ hondo y (7) _____.

PACIENTE   ¡Ay! Me (8) _____ el pecho también.

DOCTOR(A)   Bueno, vamos a sacarle una (9) _____, pero creo que Ud. solo tiene una (10) _____ en la garganta.

PACIENTE   ¿Qué (11) _____ hacer, doctor(a)?

DOCTOR(A)   Ud. debe tomar este (12) _____ para la tos. También, tome estas (13) _____ dos veces al día.

9-22 Encuesta de salud. Entrevista a un(a) compañero(a) con estas preguntas. Luego él/ella debe entrevistarte a ti.

1. Cuando estás enfermo(a), ¿vas a la clínica en tu campus o prefieres ir al consultorio de tu propio(a) (own) médico(a)?

2. Cuando tienes gripe, ¿guardas cama o vas a clase?

3. ¿Prefieres tomar medicamento en forma de pastillas o en jarabe?

4. En tu opinión, ¿con qué frecuencia se necesita un examen médico?

5. ¿Te interesa la carrera de medicina? ¿Por qué sí o por qué no?

¡Exprésate!

👫 **9-23 ¡Pobrecitos!** Varios turistas se enfermaron durante su viaje por Ecuador. ¿Cuál es el diagnóstico de cada uno? ¿Qué tratamientos necesitan? Tomando turnos con un(a) compañero(a), dramaticen las situaciones. Sigan el modelo.

Modelo   **Paciente:** Tengo una tos muy fuerte. Me duele mucho el pecho cuando respiro hondo.

Médico(a): *(Hace el diagnóstico y explica los tratamientos.)* Creo que Ud. tiene **bronquitis**. Vamos a **sacarle una radiografía**.

1. "Comí un sándwich delicioso de carne asada en el mercado de Otavalo, pero ahora me duele mucho el estómago. También tengo diarrea y vómitos. Me siento un poco —no sé— deshidratado(a)".

2. "La semana pasada, cuando estaba en las islas Galápagos, me caí y me torcí el tobillo. Todavía me duele mucho y no puedo caminar".

3. "Mire, doctor(a). Cuando nadaba, me entró un poco de agua por las orejas. Ahora me duelen mucho los oídos. Tengo un poco de fiebre también".

4. "¡Ay, doctor(a)! Me corté el brazo y ¡hay mucha sangre!"

👥 **Colaborar** **9-24 ¿Qué deben hacer?** ¿Qué les recomiendas a estos pacientes? Con un(a) compañero(a), tomen turnos para dar **tres** consejos a cada uno. Usen las expresiones **Ud. (no) debe...** y **Ud. debería...**

1.   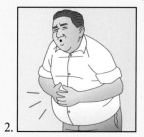
2.   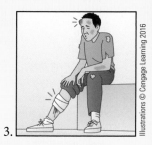
3.

Illustrations © Cengage Learning 2016

👫 **9-25 ¡Me siento fatal!** Trabajando con un(a) compañero(a), dramaticen una escena en el consultorio médico entre un(a) turista que se enferma y un(a) médico(a). El (La) paciente describe una variedad de síntomas y el (la) médico(a) le da varios tratamientos y consejos.

Modelo   **Médico(a):** Buenas tardes. ¿Cómo está Ud.?

Paciente: Para decirle la verdad, me siento...

© Alexander Raths/Shutterstock

Los mandatos formales

SR. CAMACHO	Me duele mucho la cabeza. ¿Es un tumor? ¿Una hemorragia? ¿Un implante extraterrestre?
DOCTORA	No se preocupe, Sr. Camacho. No es nada grave. Es simplemente un dolor de cabeza.
SR. CAMACHO	¿Qué debo hacer?
DOCTORA	Tome estas pastillas y llámeme en la mañana.

■ ■ ■

Descúbrelo

- What is Sr. Camacho's complaint? What does he think is causing the problem?

- What phrase does the doctor use to tell him not to worry? Is **se** placed before or after the verb?

- What other instructions does the doctor give him? What infinitives correspond to the verbs in these instructions?

1. Formal commands are used to give orders, directions, and recommendations. They are used with people you normally address with **Ud.** or **Uds.**

Sr. Calvo, **tome** Ud. estas pastillas. Ana y Susana, por favor no **corran** por la casa.	*Mr. Calvo, **take** these pills. Ana and Susana, please don't **run** in the house.*

2. Follow this process to create formal commands: First, conjugate the verb in the **yo** form of the present tense. Then drop the final **-o** and add the new ending. For a negative command, add the word **no** before the verb.

-**ar** verbs		
tom**ar**:	tom~~o~~ + **e** → tom**e** (Ud.)	**Tome** estos antibióticos.
	tom~~o~~ + **en** → tom**en** (Uds.)	**Tomen** las pastillas con agua.
-**er** verbs		
hac**er**:	hag~~o~~ + **a** → hag**a** (Ud.)	**Haga** más ejercicio.
	hag~~o~~ + **an** → hag**an** (Uds.)	No **hagan** nada por unos días.
-**ir** verbs		
dorm**ir**:	duerm~~o~~ + **a** → duerm**a** (Ud.)	**Duerma** ocho horas cada noche.
	duerm~~o~~ + **an** → duerm**an** (Uds.)	**Duerman** en un cuarto fresco.

3. Some verbs have spelling changes in the formal command forms. (The new verb **escoger** means *to choose, to pick*.)

- Verbs ending in -**gar** change to -**gue(n)**
  lle**gar**   lle**gue** (Ud.)   lle**guen** (Uds.)

- Verbs ending in -**car** change to -**que(n)**
  bus**car**   bus**que** (Ud.)   bus**quen** (Uds.)

- Verbs ending in -**zar** change to -**ce(n)**
  almor**zar**   almuer**ce** (Ud.)   almuer**cen** (Uds.)

- Verbs ending in -**ger** / -**gir** change to -**ja(n)**
  esco**ger**   esco**ja** (Ud.)   esco**jan** (Uds.)

4. Five verbs have irregular formal command forms.

Infinitivo	Ud.	Uds.
ir	**vaya**	**vayan**
saber	**sepa**	**sepan**
dar	**dé**	**den**
ser	**sea**	**sean**
estar	**esté**	**estén**

5. Commands are often used with reflexive, direct object, and indirect object pronouns.

- In a *negative* command, place the pronoun directly before the verb: **No <u>se</u> ponga esta crema en la herida.**

- In an *affirmative* command, attach the pronoun to the end of the verb; place an accent over the third-to-last syllable: **¿El jarabe? Tóme<u>lo</u> cada cuatro horas.**

Colaborar

9-26 **El examen médico.** Doña Eugenia fue a la clínica porque tiene mucha diarrea. ¿Qué le dice el doctor durante el examen médico? Tomando turnos con un(a) compañero(a), una persona cambia *(changes)* el verbo entre paréntesis a un mandato singular (**Ud.**) y la otra persona completa el consejo con la terminación más lógica.

¡Aplícalo!

1. (decirme)   a. ... estas pastillas por la mañana y por la noche.

2. (tomar)   b. ... una cita para la próxima semana.

3. (beber)   c. ... muchos líquidos.

4. (no comer)   d. ... si le duele cuando toco aquí.

5. (pedir)   e. ... dulces o grasas.

Colaborar

9-27 **Un cartel de salud pública.** ¿Cómo podemos evitar enfermarnos este invierno? Con un(a) compañero(a) de clase, creen un cartel de salud pública con cinco consejos para evitar la gripe. Usen mandatos formales plurales (**Uds.**).

¡Llega el invierno!
Sigan Uds. estas recomendaciones para no enfermarse:

Vitaminas

Direct object pronouns, **Capítulo 5 Paso 2**

Colaborar

9-28 **¿Qué debo hacer?** Después del diagnóstico, el paciente tiene muchas preguntas. Con un(a) compañero(a), tomen turnos haciendo el papel (role) del (de la) médico(a) y contestando las siguientes preguntas. En las respuestas, usen el mandato formal (**Ud.**) y los pronombres apropiados (**lo, la, los, las**).

Modelo   Paciente: ¿Con qué tomo la pastilla?
   Doctor(a): **Tómela** con un vaso de agua.

1. ¿Cuándo debo tomar los antibióticos, antes de comer o después de comer?
2. ¿Dónde puedo comprar el medicamento?
3. ¿Hasta cuándo sigo la dieta líquida?
4. ¿Hoy puedo comer papas fritas?
5. ¿Puedo beber vino?
6. ¿Para cuándo pido otra cita?

9-29 **Consulta por teléfono.** Eres enfermero(a). Tu trabajo es contestar llamadas telefónicas (telephone calls) de pacientes y darles consejos médicos. Con un(a) compañero(a) de clase, tomen turnos haciendo los papeles (playing the roles) de paciente y enfermero(a). Usen mandatos formales.

Modelo   Enfermero(a): Aló. ¿Cuál es el problema?
   Paciente: Me duele mucho la cabeza.
   Enfermero(a): No se preocupe. Tome acetaminofén o ibuprofeno y acuéstese a descansar en un cuarto oscuro.
   Paciente: Gracias. Adiós.

Problemas:

© Tyler Olson/shutterstock

1. Me duele mucho el estómago.
2. Tengo mucha tos y no puedo dormir.
3. Me corté el dedo. Hay mucha sangre.
4. Me di un golpe en la cabeza. Veo estrellas (stars).
5. Me quemé el brazo cuando sacaba algo del horno.
6. Me caí y creo que me rompí la muñeca.

9-30 **Cinco mandatos.** ¡Vamos a jugar un juego y movernos un poco!

Primera parte: Trabajando en grupos de tres, escriban en una hoja de papel cinco mandatos formales plurales (**Uds.**). Estos mandatos deben ser acciones simples que se pueden hacer en el salón de clase. Luego, den el papel a su profesor(a). Él o ella los va a redistribuir entre los diferentes grupos.

Modelo   Vayan a la puerta. Ábranla. Caminen a la pizarra. Hagan el dibujo de una hamburguesa. Digan "hola" a la clase.

Clase

Segunda parte: Cada grupo hace las acciones, en el orden en que están escritas (written) en el nuevo papel. El grupo que escribió esa lista de instrucciones debe levantar la mano.

Las expresiones de tiempo con *hacer*

SR. MEDINA Disculpe por llamar tan tarde, doctor, pero hace seis horas que mi esposa tiene un dolor muy fuerte en la parte derecha del abdomen. Creo que tiene apendicitis.

DOCTOR ¿Apendicitis? Eso es imposible. Yo ya le saqué el apéndice a su esposa.

SR. MEDINA ¿Cuánto tiempo hace que se lo sacó?

DOCTOR Hace dos años. Nadie tiene un segundo apéndice.

SR. MEDINA No, pero algunos sí tenemos una segunda esposa.

1. The verb **hacer** can be used to express an action or event that began in the past and is still going on in the present.

   ■ To ask how long something has been going on, use this question pattern:

   ¿Cuánto tiempo hace que + (presente)?
   ¿Cuánto tiempo hace que tienes fiebre?   *How long have you had a fever?*

   ■ To describe how long something has been going on, use this sentence pattern:

   hace + (time period) + que + (presente)
   Hace una semana que me siento mal.   *I've been under the weather for a week.*

2. The verb **hacer** can also be used to express how long ago something happened.

   ■ To ask how long ago something happened, use this question pattern:

   ¿Cuánto tiempo hace que + (pretérito)?
   ¿Cuánto tiempo hace que Ud.   *How long ago did you break your leg? / How*
   se rompió la pierna?   *long has it been since you broke your leg?*

   ■ To describe how long ago something happened, use either of these two patterns:

   hace + (time period) + que + (pretérito)
   Hace siete años que me lastimé la espalda.   *I injured my back seven years ago.*

   (pretérito) + hace + (time period)
   Me lastimé la espalda hace siete años.   *I injured my back seven years ago.*

■ ■ ■
Descúbrelo

■ Why does Mr. Medina think his wife has appendicitis? Why does the doctor think she doesn't?

■ What is the misunderstanding?

■ How long has Mrs. Medina been having pain? What verb is used before the number of hours?

■ How long ago has the doctor removed the appendix of a Mrs. Medina? What verb is used in front of the number of years? What question does Mr. Medina ask to find this out?

9-31 **Preguntas personales.** Completa las oraciones con expresiones de tiempo y el presente. Compara tus respuestas con las de un(a) compañero(a).

¡Aplícalo!

1. Hace _____ que (yo: estudiar) _____ español. ¿Y tú?

2. Hace _____ que (yo: vivir) _____ en esta ciudad. ¿Y tú?

3. Hace _____ que (yo: saber) _____ nadar. ¿Y tú?

4. Hace _____ que no (yo: ir) _____ al cine. ¿Y tú?

5. Hace _____ que no (yo: ver) _____ a mis abuelos. ¿Y tú?

9-32 **Sudamericanos célebres.** ¿Sabes quiénes son las personas de las fotos? ¿Cuánto tiempo hace que empezaron sus carreras profesionales? Tomando turnos con un(a) compañero(a), hagan oraciones completas con el pretérito del verbo en negrita y la expresión **hace +** **(número de años).**

Modelo   escribir su primera novela
Isabel Allende **escribió** su primera novela **hace... años.**

Isabel Allende, novelista desde 1982

1. **conducir** por primera vez en la NASCAR
2. **empezar** a jugar en las Grandes Ligas
3. **realizar** su primera exposición
4. **vender** su primer álbum
5. **aprender** a hacer surf
6. **trabajar** por primera vez como actor

Roberto Mamani Mamani, artista desde 1977

Juan Pablo Montoya, conductor de NASCAR desde 2006

Sofía Mulánovich, surfista desde 1992

John Leguizamo, actor desde 1984

Susana Baca, cantante desde 1987

Félix Hernández, beisbolista de las Grandes Ligas desde 2005

9-33 **Entrevista a una enfermera.** Con un(a) compañero(a), escriban preguntas lógicas para completar la entrevista (interview) de Elisa.

Modelo   **Supervisor:** ¿Cuánto tiempo hace que empezó Ud. su carrera?
Elisa: Hace ocho años que empecé mi carrera.

1. SUPERVISOR   ¿_____?
   ELISA   Hace tres años que soy enfermera.

2. SUPERVISOR   ¿_____?
   ELISA   Hace tres años que conseguí mi título (degree) universitario.

3. SUPERVISOR   ¿_____?
   ELISA   Hace dos meses que no le doy suero intravenoso a un paciente.

4. SUPERVISOR   ¿_____?
   ELISA   Hace un mes que no pongo inyecciones.

5. SUPERVISOR   ¿_____?
   ELISA   Hace seis meses que asistí a una conferencia sobre enfermería.

¡Exprésate!

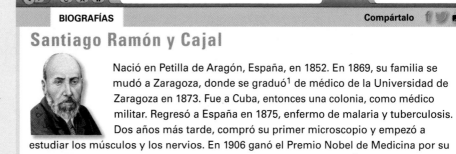

Colaborar

9-34 Santiago Ramón y Cajal. Con un(a) compañero(a) de clase, lean la información sobre este médico y contesten las preguntas.

BIOGRAFÍAS   **Compártalo**

Santiago Ramón y Cajal

Nació en Petilla de Aragón, España, en 1852. En 1869, su familia se mudó a Zaragoza, donde se graduó[1] de médico de la Universidad de Zaragoza en 1873. Fue a Cuba, entonces una colonia, como médico militar. Regresó a España en 1875, enfermo de malaria y tuberculosis. Dos años más tarde, compró su primer microscopio y empezó a estudiar los músculos y los nervios. En 1906 ganó el Premio Nobel de Medicina por su doctrina de la neurona. Ramón y Cajal también era artista y dibujó[2] muchas ilustraciones del sistema nervioso que todavía se usan hoy. Murió en Madrid en 1934.

[1]*graduated* [2]*drew*

1. ¿Cuántos años hace que nació Santiago Ramón y Cajal? ¿En qué país nació?
2. ¿Cuánto tiempo hace que se graduó? ¿Qué profesión tenía?
3. ¿En qué año compró su primer microscopio? ¿Qué partes del cuerpo estudiaba?
4. ¿Cuántos años hace que ganó el Premio Nobel de Medicina? ¿Por qué ganó?
5. ¿Cuánto tiempo hace que murió? ¿Cuántos años tenía?

9-35 Los síntomas. ¿Qué síntomas tiene el paciente y cuánto tiempo hace que los tiene? Con tu compañero(a) de clase, tomen turnos haciendo la pregunta **¿Cuánto tiempo hace que (+ síntoma)?** Contesten según esta línea del tiempo *(timeline)*.

Síntomas:

✓ sentirse enfermo

✓ tener fiebre

✓ no tener hambre

✓ estar en cama

✓ tener vómitos

✓ toser

Modelo **Estudiante A:** ¿Cuánto tiempo hace que se siente enfermo?
Estudiante B: Hace seis días que se siente enfermo.

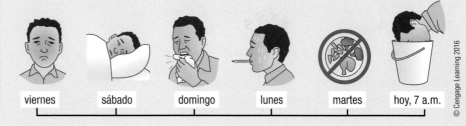

viernes   sábado   domingo   lunes   martes   hoy, 7 a.m.

9-36 El hipocondríaco. Con un(a) compañero(a), dramaticen una conversación entre un(a) hipocondríaco(a) *(hypochondriac)* y su doctor(a).

El (La) hipocondríaco(a)	El (La) médico(a)
1. Describe síntomas de enfermedades imaginarias.	2. Pregunta cuánto tiempo hace que tiene esos síntomas.
3. Di *(Say)* cuánto tiempo hace que tienes los síntomas.	4. Explica que no es nada. Pregunta si toma medicamentos y hace cuánto tiempo.
5. Contesta. Pide más pastillas.	6. Receta algo natural.

PASO 3 VOCABULARIO

El bienestar

In this *Paso*, you will . . .
- talk about well-being
- give and receive advice
- influence others

Consejos de bienestar

Secretos para el bienestar

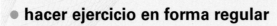

- **relajarse**

- **seguir una dieta saludable**

- **hacer ejercicio en forma regular**

- **buscar equilibrio entre el trabajo y el placer**

- **disfrutar de la vida**

Metas y maneras para mejorar la salud	Goals and ways to improve our health
compartir tus preocupaciones con un(a) amigo(a)	*to share your worries with a friend*
cuidarse	*to take care of oneself*
dejar de fumar	*to stop smoking*
desconectarse de las presiones / del trabajo	*to disconnect yourself from pressures / from work*
no dejar las cosas para más tarde	*not to procrastinate*
no preocuparse demasiado	*not to worry too much*
pedirle ayuda a alguien	*to ask someone for help*
prevenir las enfermedades	*to prevent illnesses*
reducir el estrés	*to relieve stress*
tomarse unos días libres	*to take some days off*

Consejos entre amigas

Para pedir consejos / *Asking for advice*

¿Qué me aconsejas?	*What do you advise?*
¿Qué piensas?	*What do you think?*
¿Qué debo hacer?	*What should I do?*

Para dar consejos a amigos / *Giving advice to friends*

Deberías (+ infinitivo)...	*You should . . .*
Tienes que (+ infinitivo)...	*You have to . . .*
Es importante / buena idea / mejor...	*It's important / a good idea / better to . . .*
¿Por qué no (le pides ayuda a alguien)?	*Why don't you (ask someone for help)?*
No te preocupes.	*Don't worry.*
Cuídate.	*Take care.*
Tranquilo(a). No es para tanto.	*Relax. It's no big deal.*

Para reaccionar a los consejos / *Reacting to advice*

Tienes razón.	*You're right.*
Es buena idea.	*It's a good idea.*
No sé. No estoy seguro(a).	*I don't know. I'm not sure.*

PASO 3 VOCABULARIO

¡Aplícalo! Colaborar

9-37 **Consejos entre amigos.** Hoy muchos estudiantes tienen problemas y les piden consejos a sus amigos. Con un(a) compañero(a) de clase, completen las tres conversaciones con las palabras más lógicas y léanlas en voz alta.

Conversación 1

CARLOS ¡Tengo un examen de historia mañana y estoy (1. totalmente / reducir) estresado!

RAÚL (2. Cuídate / Tranquilo), Carlos, no es para (3. razón / tanto). Es un simple examen.

CARLOS ¿Cómo puedes decir eso? ¡Tengo que sacar una B para aprobar *(pass)* la clase!

RAÚL Bueno, bueno, no te (4. fumes / preocupes). Yo te ayudo a estudiar.

Conversación 2

MARTITA Este semestre he aumentado cinco libras. ¡Necesito bajar de peso! ¿Qué me (5. aconsejas / piensas)?

PATRICIA (6. Tienes / Deja) que hacer ejercicio. (7. Deberías / Gustaría) ir al gimnasio todos los días.

MARTITA Sí, tienes (8. idea / razón). ¡Mañana voy al gimnasio!

Conversación 3

PAULINA Me preocupa mi compañera de cuarto. Creo que está deprimida *(depressed)*. ¿Qué (9. dejo / debo) hacer?

FABIÁN Nada. Es (10. mejor / regular) no molestarla.

PAULINA No sé. No estoy (11. segura / ideal)...

FABIÁN Bueno, entonces ¿(12. por / para) qué no hablas con ella?

9-38 **Tu bienestar físico y mental.** ¿Llevas una vida sana? Con un(a) compañero(a) de clase, tomen turnos para hacerse *(give each other)* la siguiente prueba *(quiz)*. ¿Qué opinan Uds. de los consejos?

🎲 Prueba: ¿Cuál es tu grado de bienestar físico y mental?

1. ¿Qué piensas de las clases de ejercicio como Pilates?
a. Ayudan a mi bienestar.
b. Son solamente una moda.

2. ¿Cómo es la dieta que sigues?
a. Es balanceada.
b. Como cuando tengo tiempo.

3. ¿Qué haces antes de acostarte?
a. Me relajo un poco.
b. Trabajo hasta dormirme.

4. ¿Te cuidas para prevenir enfermedades?
a. Sí, claro.
b. No es necesario porque soy joven.

5. ¿Qué haces cuando estás estresado(a)?
a. Comparto mis preocupaciones con alguien.
b. Fumo o bebo bebidas alcohólicas.

6. ¿Con qué frecuencia dejas las cosas para más tarde?
a. Casi nunca. Soy bastante organizado(a).
b. Casi siempre porque el placer va antes del trabajo.

Resultados y consejos

Si contestaste más "a": ¡Felicidades! Llevas una vida bastante sana. Deberías seguir así. Es muy importante cuidar la salud.

Si contestaste más "b": Tienes una mala actitud con respecto a tu bienestar. Tienes que buscar tiempo para comer bien, descansar y hacer ejercicio en forma regular.

© Cengage Learning 2016; Photo: © axanija/Shutterstock

9-39 Mente sana, cuerpo sano. Con un(a) compañero(a), entrevístense con las siguientes preguntas. ¿Eres una persona con mente sana y cuerpo sano *(sound mind and sound body)*?

1. ¿Qué causa el estrés en tu vida? ¿Qué haces para reducirlo?

2. ¿Compartes tus preocupaciones más con tus padres, con tus hermanos o con tus amigos? ¿Quién te da los mejores consejos normalmente?

3. ¿Cuidas tu salud? ¿Qué haces para prevenir enfermedades?

4. ¿Se preocupan tú y tus amigos por sacar buenas notas? ¿Qué hacen Uds. para tener equilibrio entre los estudios y el placer?

5. ¿Es fácil para ti pedirle ayuda a alguien? ¿Cuándo lo haces? ¿A quién le pides ayuda generalmente?

6. ¿Qué haces en tus días libres? ¿Cómo te desconectas de las presiones de la vida estudiantil?

9-40 Consejos y más consejos. Trabajen en grupos de tres o cuatro para completar los siguientes consejos. Para cada uno, deben llegar a un consenso o una opinión general entre los miembros del grupo. Estén preparados(as) para compartir sus oraciones con la clase.

Modelo Para disfrutar de la vida, es importante... **no preocuparse demasiado.**

1. Para reducir el estrés, es importante...

2. Para seguir una dieta saludable, es recomendable...

3. Para tener un equilibrio entre el trabajo y el placer, es necesario...

4. Para prevenir la gripe, es buena idea...

5. Para relajarnos, es mejor...

6. Para no dejar las cosas para más tarde, es preciso...

7. Para dejar de fumar, es preferible...

8. Para no estar totalmente estresado, es bueno...

9-41 Una conversación entre amigos. Mira los dibujos. ¿Qué problemas tiene Martín? ¿Qué le dice Alonso primero y qué le aconseja luego? Con un(a) compañero(a), creen una conversación lógica entre Martín y su amigo Alonso.

El presente de subjuntivo con expresiones de influencia

© Cengage Learning 2016

BOXEADOR	No puedo dormir, Memo. Tengo insomnio.
MEMO	Te recomiendo que cuentes ovejas *(sheep)* hasta dormirte.
BOXEADOR	Eso hago; pero cuando llego a nueve, siempre me levanto.
MEMO	¡Ja ja! Es mejor que consultes con el médico.

■ ■ ■
Descúbrelo

- What is the boxer's problem? What does Memo suggest first?
- Why doesn't counting sheep work? What does Memo finally advise?
- What two expressions does Memo use to preface his advice to the boxer?
- What small word links the expressions of advice with the actual instructions?

1. It's possible to influence the behavior of others in many ways, such as by persuading, making requests, giving permission, etc. To help express these ideas, the present subjunctive (**el presente de subjuntivo**) is used.

> Es importante que Ud. **deje** de fumar.   *It's important that you **stop** smoking.*

2. Sentences with the present subjunctive follow a special three-part sentence pattern. The present subjunctive is the verb form in the third part.

Main clause		Connector	Dependent Noun Clause	
Subject	Expression of Influence	*que*	New Subject	Verb in Present Subjunctive
(Yo)	Quiero	que	Ud.	**haga** más ejercicio.
I	*want*		*you*	***to exercise** more.*

3. To conjugate verbs in the present subjunctive, first conjugate the verb in the **yo** form of the present tense. Then, drop the final **o** and add the appropriate ending for the present subjunctive.

El presente subjuntivo de los verbos regulares			
	-ar	**-er**	**-ir**
	descansar (yo descanso)	**hacer** (yo hago)	**salir** (yo salgo)
que yo	descanse	haga	salga
que tú	descanses	hagas	salgas
que Ud./él/ella	descanse	haga	salga
que nosotros(as)	descansemos	hagamos	salgamos
que vosotros(as)	descanséis	hagáis	salgáis
que Uds./ellos/ellas	descansen	hagan	salgan

4. Some verbs have spelling changes in the present subjunctive.

> **g → gu** (llegar) lle**gu**e, lle**gu**es, lle**gu**e, lle**gu**emos, lle**gu**éis, lle**gu**en
>
> **c → qu** (buscar) bus**qu**e, bus**qu**es, bus**qu**e, bus**qu**emos, bus**qu**éis, bus**qu**en
>
> **z → c** (almorzar) almuer**c**e, almuer**c**es, almuer**c**e, almor**c**emos, almor**c**éis, almuer**c**en
>
> **g → j** (escoger) esco**j**a, esco**j**as, esco**j**a, esco**j**amos, esco**j**áis, esco**j**an

5. These common verbs and expressions of influence trigger the use of the subjunctive in the third part of the sentence.

Le(s) / Te aconsejo que...	Es buena idea que...
Le(s) / Te pido que...	Es importante que...
Le(s) / Te prohíbo que...	Es mejor que...
Le(s) / Te recomiendo que...	Es necesario que...
Le(s) / Te sugiero que...	Es preferible que...
Prefiero que...	Quiero que...

Colaborar

9-42 **¿Qué aconsejas?** ¿Qué le aconsejas a tu amigo Ricardo? Con un(a) compañero(a), conjuguen los verbos en el presente de subjuntivo y relacionen los problemas con los consejos.

¡Aplícalo!

Los problemas de Ricardo:

_____ 1. Tengo un poco de fiebre.

_____ 2. Siempre me duermo en clase.

_____ 3. Toso mucho cuando hago ejercicio.

_____ 4. Mi novia está totalmente estresada.

_____ 5. Mis amigos y yo bebimos mucha cerveza.

Tus consejos:

a. Le recomiendo que (hacer) _____ ejercicio para relajarse.

b. Es necesario que (dejar) _____ de fumar.

c. Les prohíbo que (conducir) _____ con alcohol en la sangre.

d. Es mejor que (tomar) _____ acetaminofén.

e. Te sugiero que (beber) _____ un poco de café.

Colaborar

9-43 **Trekking en Perú.** ¿Qué les aconseja el guía *(guide)* a un grupo de turistas? Con un(a) compañero(a), completen las oraciones con los consejos más lógicos de la lista. Usen el presente de subjuntivo.

Modelo Para prevenir problemas por la altura *(altitude)*, les recomiendo a Uds. que... **suban lenta y progresivamente**.

Consejos para el trekking	
beber un poco de agua cada hora	no hacer esfuerzos violentos
comer un buen desayuno	purificar el agua antes de beberla
subir *(ascend)* lenta y progresivamente	consumir alimentos altos en calorías
mantener una actitud positiva	

1. Para hidratarse suficientemente, es recomendable que Uds....

2. Para evitar enfermedades gastrointestinales, es necesario que Uds....

3. Para tener suficiente energía para todo el día, es esencial que Uds....

4. Tienen que comer bien durante nuestros paseos, también. Es preferible que Uds....

5. Hay menos oxígeno a estas alturas. Por eso, les aconsejo que Uds....

6. Finalmente, recuerden que el trekking requiere *(requires)* un gran esfuerzo físico y mental. Es esencial que Uds....

👥👥👥 **9-44** **¿Qué quieres?** En grupos de tres, combinen la información de las columnas para formar oraciones y expresar sus preferencias. Sigan el modelo.

Modelo   **Estudiante A:** *(Escoge una frase de la Columna A.)* **Prefiero que**...

Estudiante B: *(Escoge a una persona de la Columna B.)* Prefiero que **mi compañero(a) de cuarto**...

Estudiante C: *(Escoge una frase de la Columna C y conjuga el verbo en el presente de subjuntivo.)* Prefiero que mi compañero(a) de cuarto **no use mi computadora**.

A	B	C
Quiero que	mis padres	no **usar** (mi ropa, mi computadora, etcétera)
Prefiero que	mi compañero(a) de cuarto	**tener** (muchos amigos, una casa elegante, etcétera)
Es buena idea que	mis abuelos	**comprarme** (un auto, ropa, flores, etcétera)
Es importante que	yo	**hacer** (más ejercicio, muchos viajes, la tarea, etcétera)
Es mejor que	tú	**dejar** de (fumar, comer comida basura, etcétera)

👥👥 **9-45** **Consejos prácticos.** ¿Qué les dices a tus amigos en estos casos? Con un(a) compañero(a), dramaticen cada situación.

1. MARCOS ¿Qué debo hacer para mejorar la función del corazón?

   TÚ Tienes que hacer ejercicio aeróbico. Te recomiendo que _____ o que _____. Si te gusta más hacer ejercicio en grupo, te aconsejo que _____.

2. ANA Siempre nos dicen que tenemos que comer bien. Pero en realidad no sé mucho sobre la nutrición. ¿Qué me aconsejas?

   TÚ Primero, es importante que (tú) _____. También, es preferible que (tú) no _____. Y por último, te aconsejo que (tú) _____.

3. JAVIER Desde que llegué al campus, me he sentido bastante aislado *(isolated)*. ¿Qué piensas? ¿Qué debo hacer?

   TÚ Depende. Si te gusta el deporte, es buena idea que (tú) _____. Si te gusta la música, te aconsejo que _____. Y si quieres aprender sobre un tema fascinante, te recomiendo que _____.

👤↔👤 **9-46** **Los remedios caseros.** ¿Qué consejos les das
Colaborar a estas personas? Con un(a) compañero(a), tomen turnos para describir el problema y ofrecer unos remedios caseros *(home remedies)*.

Dulce María

Modelo   **Estudiante A:** Dulce María tiene dolor de cabeza.

Estudiante B: Le aconsejo que beba una taza de café. La cafeína alivia *(alleviates)* los dolores de cabeza.

1. Luis

2. Lucía

3. Aurora

4. Enrique

El presente de subjuntivo: verbos con cambios de raíz y verbos irregulares

HERNÁN Doctora Martini, ¡me siento fatal! No tengo energía para nada. ¿Qué me aconseja Ud.?

DOCTORA Primero, es importante que Ud. siga una dieta equilibrada. Segundo, es esencial que empiece un programa de ejercicio. Le recomiendo que vaya al gimnasio tres veces por semana. Tercero...

HERNÁN ¡Un momento, doctora! ¡Es un milagro (*miracle*)! ¡De repente me siento completamente bien!

1. Verbs that have stem changes when they are conjugated in the present indicative also have stem changes when they are conjugated in the present subjunctive. With **-ar** and **-er** verbs, stem changes occur in every person except **nosotros** and **vosotros**. Keep in mind that **-ar** and **-er** stem-changing verbs use the same verb endings as regular verbs.

> **Presente de indicativo:** Normalmente **vuelvo** a casa a las diez.
> **Presente de subjuntivo:** Esta noche es importante que yo **vuelva** a las ocho.

Cambios de raíz en verbos *-ar* y *-er*:	e → ie	o → ue
	entender *to understand*	**acostarse** *to go to bed*
que yo	entienda	me acueste
que tú	entiendas	te acuestes
que Ud./él/ella	entienda	se acueste
que nosotros(as)	entendamos	nos acostemos
que vosotros(as)	entendáis	os acostéis
que Uds./ellos/ellas	entiendan	se acuesten

2. Verbs that end in **-ir** also undergo changes in the present subjunctive. However, these stem changes take place in *all* persons, including **nosotros** and **vosotros**. Stem-changing **-ir** verbs use the same verb endings as regular **-ir** verbs.

Cambios de raíz en verbos *-ir*:	e → ie, i	o → ue, u	e → i, i
	sentirse *to feel*	**dormir** *to sleep*	**servir** *to serve*
que yo	me sienta	duerma	sirva
que tú	te sientas	duermas	sirvas
que Ud./él/ella	se sienta	duerma	sirva
que nosotros(as)	nos sintamos	durmamos	sirvamos
que vosotros(as)	os sintáis	durmáis	sirváis
que Uds./ellos/ellas	se sientan	duerman	sirvan

■ ■ ■
Descúbrelo

■ Why does Hernán ask the doctor for advice?

■ What does the doctor recommend that he do? How does he react to the advice?

■ What infinitives correspond to the verb forms **siga** and **empiece**? What happens to the **e** in the stem of the infinitive in each case?

■ Which verb form in the conversation corresponds to the infinitive **ir**?

PASO 3 GRAMÁTICA B

3. In addition to stem-changing verbs, there are five irregular verbs in the present subjunctive. These are the same five verbs that have irregular command forms.

	ir *to go*	**ser** *to be*	**estar** *to be*	**saber** *to know*	**dar** *to give*
que yo	vaya	sea	esté	sepa	dé
que tú	vayas	seas	estés	sepas	des
que Ud./él/ella	vaya	sea	esté	sepa	dé
que nosotros(as)	vayamos	seamos	estemos	sepamos	demos
que vosotros(as)	vayáis	seáis	estéis	sepáis	deis
que Uds./ellos/ellas	vayan	sean	estén	sepan	den

4. The expression **hay** *(there is / there are)* uses the form **haya** *(there be)* in the present subjunctive: **Espero que haya más opciones.**

¡Aplícalo!

Colaborar

9-47 **Las recomendaciones.** Tomás es un nuevo estudiante en tu universidad. ¿Qué recomendaciones le das? Con un(a) compañero(a), completen las oraciones con el presente de subjuntivo del verbo y una recomendación lógica.

Modelo Tomás: Quiero seguir una dieta saludable. ¿Dónde puedo almorzar en el campus?

Tú: Te recomiendo que (**tú: almorzar**) **almuerces** en... **el nuevo café orgánico en el centro estudiantil.**

1. TOMÁS Me gusta acostarme después de la medianoche, pero este semestre mi primera clase empieza a las ocho y me siento fatal en la mañana.

   TÚ Para estar alerta en la mañana, es mejor que (**tú: acostarse**) a las... Y para no saltar el desayuno, es esencial que (**tú: despertarse**) antes de las...

2. TOMÁS Quiero invitar a mi novia a cenar en un restaurante especial. ¿Dónde debemos comer? ¿Qué platos nos recomiendas?

   TÚ Les recomiendo que (**Uds.: ir**) a... Sirven muchos platos buenos, pero sugiero que (**Uds.: pedir**)...

3. TOMÁS Tengo que hacer una presentación para mi clase de historia y no soy muy organizado.

   TÚ No es bueno dejar las cosas para más tarde. Es mejor que (**tú: empezar**) el proyecto... Y los profesores siempre recomiendan que (**nosotros: tener**) un mínimo de... fuentes *(sources)* de información.

4. TOMÁS Quiero ir a mi casa durante las vacaciones. ¿Cuántos días antes del inicio *(beginning)* del nuevo semestre debo regresar al campus?

   TÚ La administración recomienda que nosotros (**volver**) al campus... Pero si quieres divertirte un poco, es buena idea que (**tú: volver**)...

5. TOMÁS Para el Día de Servicio a la Comunidad *(Community)*, voy a trabajar en una guardería *(daycare)* con un grupo de niños. Creo que van a tener entre seis y ocho años. ¿Qué podemos hacer para divertirnos un poco?

   TÚ A los niños de esa edad les encantan los deportes y los juegos activos. Es buena idea que (**Uds.: jugar**) a... O, si hace mal tiempo ese día, sugiero que (**Uds.: jugar**) a...

¡Exprésate!

Colaborar

9-48 **De niñero(a).** Estás trabajando de niñero(a) *(babysitter)* para Santiago, un niño de siete años que es un poco desobediente. Con tu compañero(a), dramaticen las situaciones. Conjuguen los verbos en el presente de subjuntivo y añadan *(add)* otra oración original.

Modelo   **Santiago:** ¡Mira! Acabo de pintar un mural en la pared de la sala. Es muy bonito, ¿no?

Tú: Quiero que (**tú: ir**) a tu cuarto inmediatamente. → Quiero que **vayas** a tu cuarto inmediatamente. **Tienes que pensar en lo que *(what)* has hecho.**

1. **SANTIAGO** Estos vegetales son asquerosos *(disgusting)*. Voy a dárselos a nuestra perra, Fifí.

   TÚ Prefiero que (tú) no le (**dar**) comida a Fifí. (+ más información)

2. **SANTIAGO** ¡Chao! Voy a jugar videojuegos en la casa de Javi. ¡Vuelvo esta noche a las diez!

   TÚ Puedes jugar videojuegos con Javi por una hora, pero quiero que (**tú: estar**) en casa a las seis en punto. (+ más información)

3. **SANTIAGO** ¡Uf! Estoy aburrido. No hay nada bueno en la tele hoy.

   TÚ ¿Por qué no jugamos al fútbol? Es importante que (**tú: ser**) más activo. (+ más información)

4. **SANTIAGO** ¡Ay! ¡Me he cortado la cabeza! ¡Mira cuánta sangre! ¡Quiero a mi mamá!

   TÚ Eso no es sangre, ¡es el cátsup de tus papas fritas! Quiero que (**tú: ir**) al baño para lavarte el pelo. (+ más información)

5. **SANTIAGO** Paco está llorando *(crying)* porque se rompió su nuevo robot. ¡Pero la culpa *(fault)* no fue mía! Yo jugaba con el robot en la piscina cuando...

   TÚ ¿En la piscina? ¡Basta ya! *(That's enough!)* Quiero que le (**tú: pedir**) perdón a Paco. (+ más información)

9-49 **¡Cuánto estrés!** A veces las relaciones personales nos causan mucho estrés. Con un(a) compañero(a), dramaticen estas situaciones. Una persona explica su problema y la otra persona da consejos usando el presente de subjuntivo.

9-50 **Nuestros problemas.** ¿Qué causa el estrés en tu vida? Con un(a) compañero(a), sigan estas instrucciones.

■ En papel, describan un pequeño problema real o inventado *(imaginary)*.

■ Su profesor(a) va a recoger *(collect)* todos los papeles y repartírselos *(hand them out)* a diferentes personas en la clase.

■ Con tu compañero(a), dramaticen una conversación entre dos amigos. Una persona explica el problema y la otra da consejos usando el presente de subjuntivo: **Te recomiendo que...**

LA MEDICINA

La cirugía cerebral de los incas

Muchas civilizaciones antiguas practicaron la cirugía cerebral pero los incas de Cusco, Perú, la perfeccionaron. Los cirujanos incas, expertos en el campo *(field)* de la medicina, hicieron cientos de cirugías de cráneo con éxito *(successfully)*. Los arqueólogos han descubierto que, entre los habitantes de Cusco del siglo xv, el 90 por ciento de los pacientes sobrevivieron. Es un número admirable dado que *(given that)* no existían los antibióticos, la anestesia moderna o los instrumentos quirúrgicos *(surgical)* de hoy.

La trepanación

La cirugía cerebral que practicaban los incas se llama trepanación. Esta operación consiste en perforar *(bore a hole in)* el cráneo con fines curativos. En tiempos modernos esta intervención se conoce como craneotomía y se practica para tratar aneurismas, tumores y lesiones. En los tiempos del Imperio inca, la trepanación se practicaba principalmente pare tratar heridas de combate. Por

Este cráneo inca muestra tres trepanaciones.

Estrategia: Understanding complex sentences

In order to understand a complex sentence, it's helpful to break it down and identify its main parts: subject, verb, and objects.

- First, find the main verb—the word that indicates action or state of being.
- Then, ask who is performing the action; the answer is the subject. Remember that word order is flexible in Spanish: The subject usually comes before the verb but it can also come after it.
- Don't confuse the subject with a direct or indirect object pronoun, which may also be placed before the verb.

Here's an example. In the sentence **Me recomienda el médico que tome las vitaminas por la noche**, **me** is the object, **recomienda** is the verb, and **el médico** is the subject.

Palabras de medicina

la cirugía	*surgery*
el (la) cirujano(a)	*surgeon*
el cráneo	*skull*
el fin curativo	*healing purpose*
la hemorragia	*bleeding, hemorrhage*
el sedante	*sedative*
sobrevivir	*to survive*

9-51 Comprensión. Contesta las siguientes preguntas según el artículo que leíste.

1. ¿Qué tipo de cirugía cerebral practicaban los incas? ¿Cuál era su principal tratamiento?

2. ¿Aproximadamente cuántos pacientes sobrevivieron a estas cirugías? ¿Por qué sorprende a los científicos modernos?

3. ¿Cómo se llama el instrumento que usaban los cirujanos incas para cortar el cuero cabelludo *(scalp)*? ¿Qué organización moderna usa ese instrumento como su símbolo?

4. ¿Cómo reducían el dolor a los pacientes? ¿Qué conocimientos demuestra *(shows)* esto?

5. ¿Crees que las actividades militares del Imperio inca resultaron en la perfección de la cirugía cerebral? Explica.

ejemplo, se usaba este método para sacar fragmentos de huesos o para aliviar la presión intracraneal después de un trauma de combate.

El cuchillo Tumi y las plantas medicinales

No se sabe con seguridad *(with certainty)* todos los detalles sobre la cirugía inca, pero sí se sabe que uno de sus instrumentos era el cuchillo Tumi. Este cuchillo de metal en forma de T se usaba para cortar el cuero cabelludo *(scalp)*. Luego, lentamente y con mucha precisión, el cirujano raspaba *(scraped)* el cráneo hasta obtener un hueco *(hole)* circular. Para hacer esto con éxito *(successfully)*, los incas tenían que conocer bien la anatomía cerebral y saber cómo controlar las hemorragias.

Aunque los incas no tenían fármacos *(drugs)* modernos, usaban plantas medicinales como la coca y el tabaco como sedantes. También le servían al paciente una cerveza de maíz que ayudaba a reducir el dolor. Para evitar infecciones, los incas también usaban plantas medicinales con propiedades antisépticas. Así, con sus conocimientos de anatomía y plantas medicinales, los incas pudieron hacer cirugías complejas y sofisticadas.

El cuchillo Tumi —el instrumento de los cirujanos incas— es hoy el símbolo del Colegio Médico de Perú.

 9-52 **¿Y tú?** En grupos pequeños, conversen sobre los siguientes temas.

1. ¿Te interesa a ti el campo *(field)* de la medicina? ¿Por qué sí o por qué no?
2. ¿Qué más sabes sobre los incas? ¿En qué otros campos eran expertos?

Composición: Un artículo

Your university is publishing a newsletter in Spanish for incoming students and you've been asked to contribute an article on healthy lifestyles. In the first paragraph, state your topic and pique the readers' interest. In the main body, provide detailed information, examples, and advice; develop cohesion by using connecting words. To end, offer some words of encouragement.

Revisión en pareja. Exchange papers with a classmate and edit each other's work.

- Does the article have a sense of beginning, middle, and end? Write one positive comment and one suggestion for improvement on the content and organization.
- Are connectors used to develop cohesion in the body of the article? Point out any place where another connector could be added.
- Is there a variety of tenses? Are the verbs conjugated correctly? Circle any possible errors of this kind.

Estrategia
Developing cohesion

Use connecting words to develop cohesion.

- To elaborate and give examples: **por ejemplo, además, también**
- To sequence the information: **para empezar, primero, por último**
- To summarize and conclude: **para resumir, en conclusión**

9-53 Nosotros / *Share It!* En línea, publicaste un poema o un video en el que recitas un poema. También viste las publicaciones de varios compañeros de clase. Ahora, formen grupos de dos o tres personas. Comenten sobre estas publicaciones y contesten las preguntas.

1. ¿Cuáles son algunos de los temas de los poemas?

2. ¿Quiénes escribieron poemas cómicos? ¿Quiénes escribieron poemas más serios?

3. ¿Cuál de los poemas te gusta más? ¿De qué se trata? *(What does it deal with?)*

4. ¿Quiénes recitaron sus poemas en video? ¿Cuál de los videos te gusta más? ¿Por qué?

9-54 Perspectivas: Los remedios caseros. En línea, miraste un video en el que tres estudiantes describen remedios caseros *(home remedies)* típicos de sus países. Con dos o tres compañeros de clase, comparen sus respuestas sobre el video. Después, entrevístense con estas preguntas:

- ¿Qué remedios caseros usas tú?
- ¿Para qué sirven?

9-55 Exploración: Los balnearios. En Internet, investigaste los balnearios *(resorts)* y los spas de los países andinos. Ahora, formen círculos de cuatro o cinco estudiantes. Tomen turnos haciendo breves presentaciones de balnearios que quieren visitar. Las otras personas deben escuchar y hacer preguntas.

En tu presentación, contesta las siguientes preguntas:

- ¿Qué balneario quieres visitar?
- ¿Dónde está?
- ¿Tiene baños termales? ¿Cuál es la temperatura del agua?
- ¿Qué otros tratamientos ofrece?
- ¿Qué otros atractivos hay para turistas?
- ¿Qué quieres hacer tú en este balneario?

9-56 Conectados con... la antropología. En línea, leíste sobre la práctica del sacrificio humano entre los incas. Con dos o tres compañeros, compartan información de sus investigaciones sobre el sacrificio humano u otros rituales.

Modelo

En el antiguo Egipto se sacrificaban a... /
Los hopis celebraban...

9-57 **En el consultorio médico.** Tú y tu compañero(a) van a dramatizar una escena en un consultorio médico. **Estudiante A** va a ser el (la) paciente y **Estudiante B** va a ser el (la) médico(a). Sigan las instrucciones.

Estudiante A: El (La) paciente

Tienes que:

- escoger **una** de las personas del dibujo y describir tus síntomas.
- hacer y contestar las preguntas.
- tomar apuntes *(notes)* sobre los consejos de tu médico.

Opción 1: **Opción 2:**

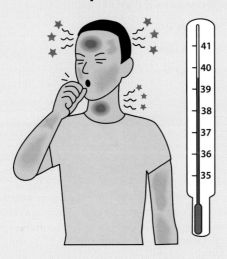 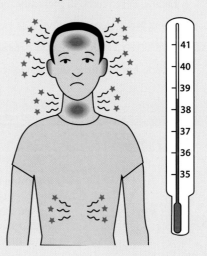

¿Qué tengo?

¿Necesito guardar cama?

¿Tengo que tomar antibióticos?

¿Qué más debo hacer?

This is a pair activity for **Estudiante A** and **Estudiante B**.

If you are **Estudiante A**, use the information on this page.

If you are **Estudiante B**, turn to p. S-9 at the back of the book.

ĬĬ 9-58 **La buena nutrición.** Con un(a) compañero(a) de clase, lean la página web sobre las vitaminas. Usen la información para explicar qué debe almorzar cada persona. Usen expresiones de influencia.

Modelo A la Srta. Blanco le falta energía y también se siente nerviosa.

La Srta. Blanco necesita más vitamina B. Le aconsejamos a la Srta. Blanco que almuerce bien. Queremos que se prepare un bistec con un huevo encima. De postre, le recomendamos que pruebe una barra de cereal.

Los pacientes:

1. El Sr. Vegas siempre está resfriado.
2. Don Gregorio se cortó el pie. Tuvieron que ponerle puntos porque no dejaba de sangrar *(bleed)*.
3. La Sra. Pérez tiene la piel muy seca. Tampoco ve muy bien de noche.
4. Doña Nelly tiene osteoporosis y casi nunca sale de su casa.
5. Don Federico siempre está cansado y se siente débil.
6. La Sra. León quiere verse joven y prevenir enfermedades.

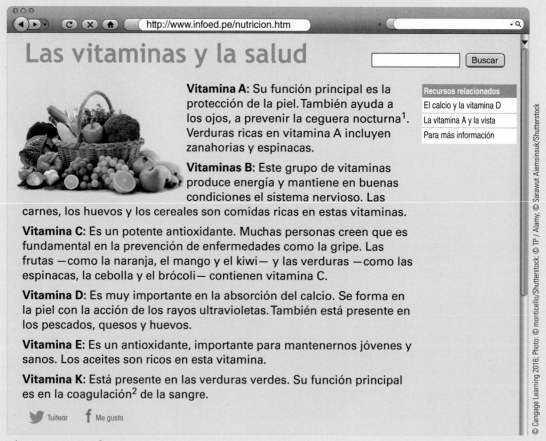

http://www.infoed.pe/nutricion.htm

Las vitaminas y la salud

Buscar

Vitamina A: Su función principal es la protección de la piel. También ayuda a los ojos, a prevenir la ceguera nocturna[1]. Verduras ricas en vitamina A incluyen zanahorias y espinacas.

Recursos relacionados
El calcio y la vitamina D
La vitamina A y la vista
Para más información

Vitaminas B: Este grupo de vitaminas produce energía y mantiene en buenas condiciones el sistema nervioso. Las carnes, los huevos y los cereales son comidas ricas en estas vitaminas.

Vitamina C: Es un potente antioxidante. Muchas personas creen que es fundamental en la prevención de enfermedades como la gripe. Las frutas —como la naranja, el mango y el kiwi— y las verduras —como las espinacas, la cebolla y el brócoli— contienen vitamina C.

Vitamina D: Es muy importante en la absorción del calcio. Se forma en la piel con la acción de los rayos ultravioletas. También está presente en los pescados, quesos y huevos.

Vitamina E: Es un antioxidante, importante para mantenernos jóvenes y sanos. Los aceites son ricos en esta vitamina.

Vitamina K: Está presente en las verduras verdes. Su función principal es en la coagulación[2] de la sangre.

Tuitear   Me gusta

[1]*night blindness* [2]*clotting*

9-59 **Haciendo ecoturismo en Ecuador.** Uds. hicieron ecoturismo en Ecuador y tuvieron muchas aventuras. Hagan esta actividad en grupos de tres o cuatro.

■ Usen el siguiente mapa como inspiración.

■ Tomen turnos para contar adónde fueron, qué hicieron y cómo se lastimaron. Usen el imperfecto y el pretérito.

■ Los demás deben reaccionar con frases apropiadas, como **¿De veras?**, **¡Qué horror!** y **¡Pobrecito(a)!**

■ Al final, ¿quién contó el cuento más increíble?

Modelo El verano pasado fui a Baños, Ecuador. Un día montaba en bicicleta cuando de repente…

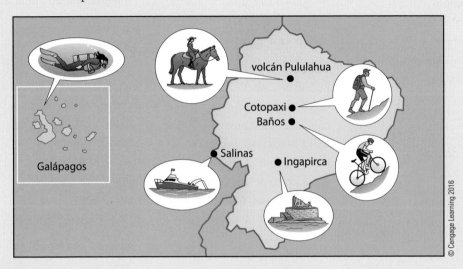

© Cengage Learning 2016

 9-60 **Situación: De intérprete en una clínica.** Trabaja con dos compañeros(as) para hacer los papeles (*play the roles*) de las siguientes personas y dramatizar una escena.

■ **Paciente:** Es un(a) turista estadounidense que está de vacaciones en Bolivia. No habla español. Está enfermo(a) o tuvo un pequeño accidente. Ahora está en una clínica y tiene que comunicarse con el (la) médico(a).

■ **Estudiante:** Es estudiante de una universidad en Estados Unidos. Durante este semestre, está trabajando de intérprete en una clínica de Bolivia. Tiene que traducir (*translate*) las cosas que dicen el (la) paciente y el (la) médico(a).

■ **Médico(a):** Trabaja en una clínica en Bolivia. No habla inglés, y por eso depende de los servicios del estudiante.

Pronunciación: Las letras *b*, *v* y *x*

Colaborar Con un(a) compañero(a), lean estos trabalenguas (*tongue twisters*) en voz alta para practicar la pronunciación de las letras **b**, **v** y **x**.

1. Pablito clavó un clavito. ¿Qué clavito clavó Pablito?

2. Una bruja tiene una brújula en una burbuja. Y con la aguja embrujada te embruja.

3. Maximiliano, el expresidente, era extraordinario y muy exigente.

VOCABULARIO

RECURSOS

Para aprender mejor

Use picture flashcards to memorize parts of the human body. These flashcards are available online, or you can make your own.

Sustantivos

el análisis de sangre *blood test*

el antibiótico *antibiotic*

el bienestar *well-being*

el consejo *advice*

el consultorio *(medical) office*

la crema *lotion*

el diagnóstico *diagnosis*

la diarrea *diarrhea*

el dolor de... *. . . ache*

la enfermedad *illness*

el (la) enfermero(a) *nurse*

el equilibrio *balance*

el estrés *stress*

el examen médico *medical exam*

la fiebre *fever*

la fractura *fracture*

el grado *degree*

la gripe *flu*

la herida *wound*

la infección *infection*

la instrucción *instruction*

la intoxicación alimenticia *food poisoning*

la inyección *shot*

el jarabe *syrup*

la manera *way, method*

el medicamento *medicine*

el (la) médico(a) *doctor*

la meta *goal*

la obligación *obligation*

la parte *part*

la pastilla *pill*

el placer *pleasure*

la preocupación *worry*

la presión *pressure*

el punto *stitch*

la radiografía *X-ray*

el resfriado *cold*

el secreto *secret*

el síntoma *symptom*

el suero intravenoso *IV fluids*

la tos *cough*

el trabajo *work*

el tratamiento *treatment*

la venda *bandage*

el vómito *vomit*

el yeso *cast*

Verbos

buscar *to seek*

caerse *to fall (down)*

compartir *to share*

cortar(se) *to cut, to get cut*

cuidarse *to take care of oneself*

darse un golpe *to get hit*

dejar de *to stop (doing something)*

desconectarse *to disconnect oneself*

disfrutar de la vida *to enjoy life*

doler *to hurt, to ache*

enfermarse *to get sick*

escoger *to choose, to pick*

estornudar *to sneeze*

guardar cama *to stay in bed*

lastimarse *to get hurt, to injure oneself*

mejorarse *to get better, to improve*

mojar *to get wet*

olvidarse *to forget*

pedir ayuda *to ask for help*

pedir cita *to make an appointment*

preocuparse *to worry*

prevenir (ie) *to prevent*

quemarse *to burn, to get burned*

reaccionar *to react*

recetar *to prescribe*

reducir *to relieve*

relajarse *to relax*

respirar (hondo) *to breathe (deeply)*

romperse *to break*

sentirse (ie) *to feel*

tomarse unos días libres *to take some days off*

torcerse (ue) *to sprain, to twist*

toser *to cough*

Adjetivos

alérgico(a) *allergic*

alto(a) en grasa *high in fat, fatty*

congestionado(a) *congested*

débil *weak*

fatal *awful*

ideal *ideal, perfect*

líquido(a) *liquid*

mal *lousy*

mocoso(a) *having a runny nose*

Frases útiles

¡Ay! *Ow!, Ouch!*

Cuídate. *Take care.*

no dejar las cosas para más tarde *not to procrastinate*

No es para tanto. *It's no big deal.*

No estoy seguro(a). *I'm not sure.*

No te preocupes. *Don't worry.*

¡Pobrecito(a)! *You poor thing!*

¡Qué lástima! *That's too bad!*

¡Que se mejore! *I hope you (formal) feel better!*

¡Que te mejores! *I hope you (informal) feel better!*

Sí, entiendo. *Yes, I understand.*

Tranquilo(a). *Relax.*

Parts of the body, p. 332

Time expressions with *hacer*, p. 349

Advice, p. 353

Verbs and expressions of influence, p. 357

El mundo laboral

CAPÍTULO 10

Conexiones a la comunidad
Visit your school's career center and find out what fields need professionals who are bilingual in English and Spanish.

In this chapter you will . . .

- explore Argentina, Uruguay, and Paraguay
- talk about professions and jobs
- say what you have and had done
- discuss your plans and goals for the future
- practice interviewing for a job
- express emotion, doubt, denial, and certainty
- learn about video game design in Spain and South America
- share information about interesting jobs

NUESTRO MUNDO
Argentina, Uruguay y Paraguay

Estos países están en el Cono Sur, el área más al sur del continente americano. Es una región de grandes ríos y de tradiciones europeas.

República del Paraguay
Población: 6 700 000
Capital: Asunción
Idiomas oficiales: español y guaraní
Moneda: el guaraní
Exportaciones: soja *(soybeans)*, comida para animales, algodón

República Argentina
Población: 43 000 000
Capital: Buenos Aires
Idioma oficial: español
Moneda: el peso
Exportaciones: soja *(soybeans)*, petróleo, gas, vehículos

República Oriental del Uruguay
Población: 3 300 000
Capital: Montevideo
Idioma oficial: español
Moneda: el peso
Exportaciones: carne, arroz, productos de cuero

Una de las ocupaciones idealizadas en las culturas de Argentina, Uruguay y partes de Paraguay es la del gaucho *(cowboy)*. Desde 1600, los gauchos han vivido y trabajado en las extensas llanuras ganaderas *(cattle-raising plains)*. El gaucho es experto en caballos y es admirado por su carácter heroico, corazón noble y espíritu independiente.

Gastronomía

El mate es una infusión estimulante preparada con hojas *(leaves)* secas de yerba mate. Se bebe a toda hora del día en Argentina, Uruguay y Paraguay. Esta bebida se prepara tradicionalmente en una calabaza *(gourd)* y se toma con una bombilla *(straw)* de plata.

Música

El tango es sinónimo del Río de la Plata. Esta música y baile sensual se originó en los barrios pobres de Buenos Aires y Montevideo hace 200 años. Hoy, el tango se baila en todo el mundo. También se escucha el electrotango: fusión de tango y música electrónica.

Geografía

Debajo de la superficie de parte de Argentina, Uruguay y Paraguay, está uno de los reservorios de agua más grandes del mundo: el Acuífero Guaraní. Este acuífero puede abastecer *(supply)* agua a seis millones de personas durante 200 años.

10-1 **¿Qué sabes?** Explica los significados de las siguientes palabras.

1. Cono Sur
2. guaraní
3. mate
4. tango
5. gaucho
6. peso

10-2 **Videomundo.** Mira los tres videos de Argentina, Paraguay y Uruguay. Con base en las imágenes y la información presentada, explica lo siguiente:

1. ¿Por qué se dice que Buenos Aires es el París de Sudamérica?
2. ¿Por qué se dice que Paraguay es el país del guaraní?
3. ¿Por qué se dice que Montevideo es la tacita de plata *(small silver teacup)*?

Profesiones y vocaciones

En el centro de orientación vocacional

In this *Paso*, you will . . .
- talk about professions
- describe your strengths and abilities
- talk about what you have and had done

No sé qué profesión elegir.

A ver... dime. ¿Cuáles son tus puntos fuertes?

© Marmaduke St. John / Alamy

© Konstantin Chagin/Shutterstock

Tengo la capacidad de trabajar en equipo.

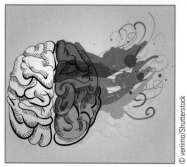

© venimo/Shutterstock

Soy creativo(a).

© Sergey Nivens/Shutterstock

Soy bueno(a) en tecnología.

Puntos fuertes	*Strengths*
Soy...	*I'm . . .*
emprendedor(a)	*enterprising*
flexible	*flexible*
paciente	*patient*
Soy bueno(a)...	*I'm good . . .*
con las manos	*with my hands*
en matemáticas	*at math*
Tengo la capacidad de...	*I have the ability to . . .*
convencer a la gente	*persuade people*
resolver (ue) problemas	*solve problems*

¿En qué consiste su trabajo?

La abogada (El abogado) ayuda a los clientes con asuntos legales.

El técnico (La técnica) analiza datos.

El arquitecto (La arquitecta) diseña edificios.

El científico (La científica) hace investigaciones.

La periodista (El periodista) informa al público.

La maestra (El maestro) enseña a los niños en una escuela.

Otras profesiones — *More professions*

el (la) agente de bolsa / de bienes raíces	*stockbroker / real estate agent*
el (la) artista	*artist*
el (la) cirujano(a)	*surgeon*
el (la) contador(a)	*accountant*
el hombre (la mujer) de negocios	*businessman, businesswoman*
el (la) ingeniero(a)	*engineer*
el (la) psicólogo(a)	*psychologist*
el (la) trabajador(a) social	*social worker*

Más responsabilidades — *More responsibilities*

arreglar (computadoras)	*to fix (computers)*
atender (ie) (al cliente)	*to look after, to attend to (the customer)*
manejar (proyectos)	*to manage (projects)*
vender (casas)	*to sell (houses)*

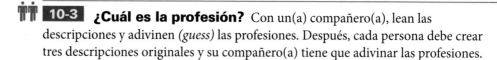
¡Aplícalo!

 10-3 **¿Cuál es la profesión?** Con un(a) compañero(a), lean las descripciones y adivinen (*guess*) las profesiones. Después, cada persona debe crear tres descripciones originales y su compañero(a) tiene que adivinar las profesiones.

1. Atiende a los pacientes en un hospital o en un consultorio médico. Por ejemplo, les toma la temperatura. Pero no les puede recetar medicamentos.

2. Trabaja con niños en una escuela primaria. Por ejemplo, les enseña a leer.

3. Es bueno en matemáticas. Trabaja con clientes privados o en una compañía. Analiza datos financieros y produce informes sobre el dinero.

4. Ayuda a la gente con sus problemas personales y emocionales. Da consejos sobre conflictos familiares. Recomienda alternativas para resolver problemas.

Colaborar
10-4 **En el centro de orientación vocacional.** Carola está hablando con un consejero sobre sus opciones para una carrera. Trabajando con un(a) compañero(a), escojan las palabras más lógicas entre paréntesis y lean la conversación en voz alta.

CAROLA   No sé qué (1. profesión / público) elegir y quisiera explorar las opciones. ¿Me puede ayudar?

SR. BRAVO   Sí, claro. A ver... ¿Cuáles son tus (2. problemas / puntos fuertes)?

CAROLA   Soy (3. creativa / perezosa) y tengo (4. la capacidad / el público) de trabajar en equipo.

SR. BRAVO   ¿Te gusta más trabajar con otras personas o analizar (5. edificios / datos)?

CAROLA   Soy (6. buena / flexible), pero me interesa más ayudar a los niños.

SR. BRAVO   Entonces tienes muchas opciones buenas. Por ejemplo, puedes ser maestra y (7. convencer / enseñar) a los niños. ¿Por qué no observas a varios profesionales? Yo te (8. ayudo / vendo) a convocar una reunión (*set up a meeting*).

Colaborar
10-5 **Las actividades de los profesionales.** ¿En qué consiste el trabajo de estos profesionales? Con un(a) compañero(a), escojan un verbo lógico para completar cada descripción. Usen el tiempo presente o el infinitivo, según el contexto.

analizar	atender	hacer	resolver	tener
arreglar	convencer	manejar	ser	vender

1. Los agentes de bienes raíces _____ casas. Necesitan tener la capacidad de _____ a la gente.

2. A menudo los hombres y las mujeres de negocios _____ proyectos con valor (*worth*) de millones de dólares. Necesitan _____ emprendedores.

3. Los abogados _____ problemas legales. Tienen que _____ las necesidades (*needs*) de sus clientes.

4. Los técnicos pueden tener varias responsabilidades. Algunos _____ computadoras; otros _____ datos.

5. Los científicos _____ investigaciones. Por lo general ellos _____ que ser buenos en tecnología.

¡Exprésate!

 10-6 **Opiniones sobre las profesiones.** ¿Qué profesiones asocias

Colaborar

con las características de la lista? Con un(a) compañero(a), escriban dos o tres profesiones para cada característica. Expliquen sus respuestas.

> convencer a la gente
> creativo e imaginativo
> horario de 9 a 5
> mucha responsabilidad
>
> resolver problemas
> rutinario
> salario alto
> salario bajo

 10-7 **La mejor profesión.** ¿Cuáles son las mejores profesiones

Colaborar

para estas personas? Con un(a) compañero(a), lean la información y den sus recomendaciones para cada persona.

Modelo Susana debería ser maestra. Si es buena en ciencias, también puede ser médica o enfermera.

> **Susana**
> Es paciente y organizada.
> Tiene la capacidad de trabajar en equipo.
> Es buena con niños.

1. **Álvaro**
   Es emprendedor y sociable.
   Tiene la capacidad de convencer a la gente.
   Le gusta trabajar en equipo.

3. **Víctor**
   Es serio y muy responsable.
   Tiene la capacidad de manejar proyectos.
   Es bueno en tecnología.

2. **Rosaura**
   Es creativa y tiene imaginación.
   Tiene la capacidad de expresar sus ideas claramente.
   Es buena con las manos.

4. **Julieta**
   Es analítica y tiene disciplina.
   Tiene la capacidad de resolver problemas.
   Prefiere trabajar con datos y no con personas.

 10-8 **La profesión perfecta para ti.** Entrevista a un(a) compañero(a) de clase con las preguntas sobre sus cualidades (*qualities*) y capacidades. ¿Cuál es la profesión perfecta para tu compañero(a)? Dale una o dos recomendaciones.

1. ¿Cuáles son tus puntos fuertes?
2. ¿En qué asignatura eres bueno(a)?
3. ¿Cómo es tu personalidad?
4. ¿Prefieres trabajar en equipo o individualmente?
5. ¿Te gusta más trabajar con personas, con datos o con cosas?
6. ¿Qué te gusta hacer en tu tiempo libre?
7. (Otra pregunta original)

© Andresr/Shutterstock

Repaso del presente perfecto

DIRECTOR Necesitamos una persona con mucha experiencia. ¿Ha manejado Ud. proyectos? ¿Ha resuelto problemas técnicos? ¿Ha hecho investigación original?

SR. FLOJO Sí, señor. Yo he hecho un poco de todo. ¡En los cuatro últimos meses he tenido diez empleos *(jobs)* diferentes!

Descúbrelo

- What does the personnel director want to know about the job candidate?
- According to the job candidate, what proves that he has had lots of experience?
- What words in Spanish correspond to *Have you managed . . .*? And to *I have had . . .*?
- In those two expressions, which part corresponds to the verb **haber**? Which is the past participle?

1. The present perfect (**el presente perfecto**) is used to express what has happened or what people have done.

> Siempre **he trabajado** para esta empresa.   *I've always **worked** for this firm.*

2. To form the present perfect, conjugate **haber** in the present tense and add a past participle.

El presente perfecto			
haber (+ *participio pasado*)			
yo	**he** *trabajado*	nosotros(as)	**hemos** *analizado*
tú	**has** *aprendido*	vosotros(as)	**habéis** *vendido*
Ud./él/ella	**ha** *vivido*	Uds./ellos/ellas	**han** *atendido*

3. To form the past participle of a regular verb, drop the last two letters of the infinitive and add the appropriate ending.

> **-ar** verbs: trabajar + **-ado** → trabaj**ado** *worked*
> **-er** verbs: aprender + **-ido** → aprend**ido** *learned*
> **-ir** verbs: vivir + **-ido** → viv**ido** *lived*

4. Some verbs have irregular past participles.

Participios pasados irregulares			
Infinitive	Past participle	Infinitive	Past participle
abrir	**abierto**	poner	**puesto**
decir	**dicho**	resolver	**resuelto**
escribir	**escrito**	romper	**roto**
hacer	**hecho**	ver	**visto**
morir	**muerto**	volver	**vuelto**

Colaborar

10-9 **Esta semana.** Según estos profesionales, ¿qué han hecho esta semana? Tomando turnos con un(a) compañero(a), una persona conjuga el verbo en el presente perfecto y lee la oración. La otra persona identifica la profesión.

Modelo Miguel: "Yo (vender) tres casas esta semana".
Estudiante A: Yo he vendido tres casas esta semana.
Estudiante B: Miguel es agente de bienes raíces.

1. Lidia: "Yo (hacer) cinco operaciones cardíacas esta semana".

2. Cándido: "Mi compañero de trabajo y yo (arreglar) más de 100 computadoras".

3. Maya: "Mis colegas y yo (escribir) un artículo sobre la corrupción".

4. Simón: "Yo (atender) a más de cien clientes en mi boutique".

5. Rosa Anita: "Yo (ayudar) a varios niños con sus problemas emocionales".

6. Juan: "Mi equipo (resolver) el problema con el diseño del edificio".

10-10 **¿Qué han hecho estos profesionales?** Con un(a) compañero(a), tomen turnos haciendo la pregunta: **¿Qué ha hecho _(nombre de la persona)_?** La otra persona elige una frase lógica de la lista y conjuga el verbo en el presente perfecto.

Modelo **Estudiante A:** ¿Qué ha hecho Harald Andrés Helfgott?
Estudiante B: Ha encontrado...

> **poner** al mundo en contacto con Cuba con su blog llamado Generación Y
> **participar** en cuatro misiones al espacio
> **diseñar** muchos puentes _(bridges)_, entre ellos, el Puente de la Mujer en Buenos Aires
> **comprar** muchas compañías, entre ellas, Anheuser-Busch
> **encontrar** la solución de los números primos de Goldbach
> **ganar** medallas en taekwondo

1. Harald Andrés Helfgott, matemático (n. 1977, Perú)

2. Santiago Calatrava, arquitecto (n. 1951, España)

3. María Asunción Aramburuzabala, mujer de negocios (n. 1963, México)

4. Sebastián Crismanich, atleta (n. 1986, Argentina)

5. Yoani Sánchez, periodista (n. 1975, Cuba)

6. Ellen Ochoa, ex astronauta (n. 1958, Estados Unidos)

10-11 ¿Qué has hecho este semestre? ¿Qué han hecho tú y tu compañero(a) este semestre? Conjuguen los verbos en el presente perfecto y entrevístense.

Modelo analizar datos

Estudiante A: ¿Has analizado datos en alguna clase este semestre?

Estudiante B: Sí, he analizado datos en mi clase de química. ¿Y tú?

1. hacer investigaciones científicas
2. escribir un informe de 5 páginas
3. ayudar a la comunidad
4. diseñar algo
5. resolver problemas matemáticos
6. trabajar en equipo en algún proyecto

10-12 Anuncios de empleo. Tú y tu compañero(a) necesitan trabajo. ¿Cuáles son los mejores puestos para Uds.? Entrevístense usando preguntas en el presente perfecto.

Modelo **Estudiante A:** A ver... ¿Has trabajado alguna vez en un restaurante?

Estudiante B: No, nunca he trabajado en un restaurante.

Estudiante A: Entonces no puedes ser camarero(a). ¿Has... ?

Diseñador(a) Web
Buscamos DISEÑADOR(A) WEB para realizar tareas de edición web. Es necesario ser competente en Flash y Photoshop. Interesados enviar CV a empleo@MSP.com.uy

Se buscan chicos(as)
Se buscan chicos(as) entre 18 y 25 años para animar cumpleaños infantiles. Deben ser pacientes y tener experiencia con niños. Llamar al 02 902 0111.

Camareros(as)
Necesitamos CAMAREROS(AS) con experiencia para nuevo restaurante. Buena presencia, con capacidad para atender grupos grandes. Llamar al 04 432 0987.

Bloguero(a)
Se busca BLOGUERO(A) serio(a) con experiencia. Es indispensable saber jugar al póker y hablar inglés. Ingresar a www.abcd.com

Recepcionista
Se necesita recepcionista con experiencia. Excelente manejo de computadora. Buena relación con los clientes. Favor enviar referencias a mendez@jobs.com.uy

Vendedores(as)
Se buscan VENDEDORES(AS) para tienda en Montevideo. Buscamos personas dinámicas con experiencia en ventas, buena presencia y flexibilidad de horario. Llamar al 05 325 0887.

© Cengage Learning 2016

10-13 Situaciones del mundo laboral. Con un(a) compañero(a), dramaticen la situación entre dos empleados de Novotec.

Estudiante A	Estudiante B
Eres técnico(a) de informática. Hoy, ya has hecho estas tareas: **resolver** el problema del virus y **arreglar** el circuito de la computadora del gerente (*manager*) de la compañía.	Eres gerente (*manager*) de la compañía. Quieres saber si el (la) técnico(a) ya ha hecho lo siguiente: **instalar** el nuevo sistema, **arreglar** tu computadora, **resolver** el problema del virus y **diseñar** la nueva página web.

El pluscuamperfecto

Un taxista conducía a un ingeniero eléctrico, un ingeniero mecánico y un ingeniero en informática. Ya habían recorrido varios kilómetros cuando el vehículo dejó de funcionar. Enseguida, el ingeniero eléctrico dijo que probablemente había sido un circuito. El mecánico dijo que seguramente había sido el motor. Finalmente el de informática dijo: "¿Por qué no salimos y entramos otra vez?"

1. The past perfect (**el pluscuamperfecto**) is used to express what had happened or what somebody had done *before* another past event took place.

> Cuando llegué a la oficina, la secretaria **había terminado** su trabajo.
> *By the time I got to the office, the secretary **had finished** her work.*

2. The past perfect consists of two parts: the verb **haber** and a past participle. Only the forms of **haber** change to match the subject; the past participle always has the same form.

El pluscuamperfecto			
haber (+ *participio pasado*)			
yo	había *trabajado*	nosotros(as)	habíamos *vendido*
tú	habías *analizado*	vosotros(as)	habíais *vivido*
Ud./él/ella	había *aprendido*	Uds./ellos/ellas	habían *atendido*

3. Recall how to form past participles: -**ar** verbs drop the -**ar** and add -**ado**; -**er** and -**ir** verbs drop their endings and add -**ido**. Common irregular past participles include **abierto, dicho, escrito, hecho, puesto, roto, visto,** and **vuelto.**

4. The past perfect is often accompanied by the time expression **ya** *(already)*. This expression is always placed before the conjugated form of **haber**.

> <u>**Ya**</u> **habíamos atendido** a cinco clientes cuando nos llamó José.
> *We **had** <u>**already**</u> **taken care** of five clients when José called us.*

5. The past perfect is also often used to report what somebody said.

> **Direct quote:** El arquitecto dijo: "Diseñé el museo en 1999".
> *The architect said: "I designed the museum in 1999."*

> **Reported quote:** El arquitecto dijo que **había diseñado** el museo en 1999.
> *The architect said that he **had designed** the museum in 1999.*

Descúbrelo

- In the joke, who had the taxi driver picked up before the car broke down?
- What did each engineer think had happened?
- Did the action **habían recorrido** happen before or after the action **dejó de funcionar**?
- What is the infinitive of **habían**? And of **recorrido**?

PASO 1 GRAMÁTICA B

¡Aplícalo! Colaborar **10-14** **Un currículum vitae.** Trabaja con un(a) compañero(a) de clase para contestar las preguntas sobre Jorge Pérez en oraciones completas.

1. ¿En qué ciudad había vivido antes de ir a la Universidad de Buenos Aires?

2. ¿Qué premio había ganado antes de empezar su carrera?

3. ¿Ya había aprendido inglés cuando entró a la universidad?

4. ¿Dónde había trabajado antes de ser diseñador gráfico?

5. ¿Ya manejaba Macromedia cuando empezó a trabajar en la Editorial Zulia?

6. ¿Es Jorge un buen candidato para maestro de arte? ¿Por qué?

PÉREZ ALBA, Jorge Enrique

Av. Esmeralda 766   Ciudad de Buenos Aires   Tel. 4327-1165   jeperez@email.com

Estudios
2007–2011 Licenciado en Diseño Gráfico, Universidad de Buenos Aires
2004–2006 Colegio San Ignacio de Córdoba

Otros cursos
2010 Manejo de Adobe y Macromedia, Centro de Formación
2008 Curso de inglés, Sarasota Community College

Experiencia laboral
2012–actualmente Diseñador Gráfico, Mercatel, S.A.
2009 Coordinador de proyecto, Editorial Zulia

Premios
2009 Finalista en concurso de logotipos
2005 1er premio en concurso de fotografía, Casa de Cultura

© Cengage Learning 2016. Photo: © Sireonio/Dreamstime.com

 Colaborar **10-15** **¿Qué les dijo Alejandro?** Graciela, la niñera *(babysitter)* de Alejandro, perdió su trabajo. ¿Qué les dijo Alejandro a sus padres para que la despidieran *(that caused them to fire her)*? Tomando turnos con un(a) compañero(a) de clase, digan qué les dijo Alejandro a sus padres.

Modelo   "Trajo a su novio".
             Alejandro les dijo que Graciela había traído a su novio.

1. "Se comió todas las galletas".

2. "No me leyó un cuento".

3. "Perdió la llave de la casa".

4. "No le dio de comer al perro".

5. "Rompió la lámpara de la sala".

6. "Vio una película clasificada para mayores de 18 años".

© auremar/Shutterstock

¡Exprésate!

 Colaborar

10-16 **La oficina de Urutex.** ¿Qué había ocurrido en la oficina de Urutex antes de que los empleados llegaran hoy? Con un(a) compañero(a), miren los dibujos y escriban cinco cosas que habían ocurrido.

Modelo Alguien había abierto la ventana.

Ayer, 5:00 p.m.   **Hoy, 8:00 a.m.**

© Cengage Learning 2016

10-17 **Antes de la universidad.** ¿Quiénes de Uds. habían hecho las siguientes cosas antes de ingresar *(enter)* a la universidad? Circula por el salón para entrevistar a tus compañeros de clase. Cuando un(a) compañero(a) contesta "sí", tiene que firmar *(sign)* su nombre. ¡Ojo! No puedes coleccionar más de dos firmas por persona.

Clase

Modelo **lavar** tu propia *(own)* ropa
Estudiante A: Antes de venir a la universidad, ¿**habías lavado** tu propia ropa?
Estudiante B: Sí, claro, la **había lavado** muchas veces. / No, no la **había lavado**.
Estudiante A: Bueno, firma aquí, por favor. / Gracias.

Actividad	Firma
1. **lavar** tu propia *(own)* ropa	
2. **compartir** un dormitorio con alguien	
3. **hacer** una investigación científica	
4. **leer** libros sobre filosofía o religión	
5. **estudiar** español	
6. **vivir** lejos de tu familia	
7. **estar** despierto(a) toda la noche	

Nota cultural

A common profession in Argentina is that of psychologist. There are approximately 154 psychologists per 100,000 residents, making Argentina the country in the world with the most psychologists per capita. About 85% of them are women and about half reside in Buenos Aires.

 10-18 **¿Cuál es mi profesión?** Formen grupos pequeños para jugar este juego: Tomando turnos, una persona piensa en una profesión y los demás tienen que adivinar *(guess)* cuál es. Para dar una pista *(clue)*, la persona dice lo que *(what)* había hecho en su trabajo cuando fue a almorzar.

Modelo **Estudiante A:** Cuando fui a almorzar, ya había vendido dos casas.
Estudiante B: ¿Eres agente de bienes raíces?
Estudiante A: ¡Sí! Ahora te toca a ti *(Now it's your turn)*.
Estudiante B: Cuando fui a almorzar, ya había...

Metas y aspiraciones

In this *Paso*, you will . . .
- ask others about their dreams and aspirations
- talk about your plans and goals for the future
- express your feelings about current or future events

Los planes para el futuro

Preguntas sobre el futuro	Questions about the future
¿Qué quieres ser?	*What do you want to be?*
¿A qué quieres dedicarte?	*What do you want to do for a living?*
¿Cuál es tu sueño?	*What's your dream?*
¿Cuáles son tus aspiraciones en la vida?	*What are your aspirations in life?*
¿Cómo piensas realizar tus sueños / tu meta?	*How do you plan to achieve your dreams / your goal?*

Metas a corto plazo	*Short-term goals*
conseguir una beca	*to get a scholarship*
estudiar en el extranjero	*to study abroad*
hacer una pasantía	*to do an internship*
conseguir un buen empleo	*to find a good job*

Las aspiraciones

Me gustaría hacer un postgrado.

Sueño con tener mi propio negocio.

Pienso casarme dentro de unos años.

Quiero ser rico(a).

Espero conocer el mundo.

Mi meta es ser un(a) gran empresario(a) algún día.

Metas a largo plazo	Long-term goals
ayudar al prójimo	to help others
dedicarse a la investigación / al servicio público	to dedicate oneself to research / to public service
ganar (mucho) dinero	to make (a lot of) money
ser... de una empresa grande	to be . . . at a large firm
jefe(a)	the boss
empleado(a)	an employee
gerente	a manager
tener éxito	to succeed, to be successful
trabajar para...	to work for . . .
un banco	a bank
el gobierno	the government

¡Aplícalo!

Colaborar **10-19** **¿Lógica o ilógica?** Tomando turnos con un(a) compañero(a) de clase, una persona lee la oración y la otra dice si es lógica *(logical)* o ilógica *(illogical)*.

1. Mi sueño es ser doctor: por eso voy a hacer un postgrado.

2. Quiero ser rico, entonces pienso ganar mucho dinero.

3. Pienso ser soltero entonces voy a casarme con mi novia.

4. Mi meta es tener mi propio negocio: por eso voy a ser empleado de un banco.

5. No me gusta viajar, entonces quiero ir al extranjero.

6. Me gustaría hacer un postgrado: por eso voy a conseguir una beca.

7. Quiero dedicarme al servicio público: por eso voy a trabajar para el gobierno.

8. Mi aspiración es ser un gran empresario: por eso voy a trabajar con las manos.

9. (Cada persona debe hacer dos oraciones originales.)

Colaborar **10-20** **Distintas aspiraciones.** ¿Qué aspiraciones tenía el abuelo y qué aspiraciones tiene el nieto? Con un(a) compañero(a), escojan las palabras correctas entre paréntesis y lean la conversación en voz alta.

ABUELO   Cuando era joven yo tenía muchas (1. aspiraciones / investigaciones) en la vida.

SEBASTIÁN   Cuéntame, abuelo, ¿con qué (2. soñabas / ganabas)?

ABUELO   Uno de mis (3. negocios / sueños) era conocer el mundo. Pero, ya sabes. Tuve que quedarme y trabajar para la (4. beca / empresa) de mi padre. Él fue un gran (5. empresario / postgrado) que tuvo mucho (6. rico / éxito). Pero tú eres joven. ¿Por qué no viajas y estudias en el (7. gerente / extranjero)?

SEBASTIÁN   ¿Yo? No, no. Mi (8. meta / banco) es trabajar para el gobierno local. Quiero (9. casarme / dedicarme) al servicio público.

ABUELO   Ayudar al (10. prójimo / empleo), ¿eh? ¡Tengo un nieto idealista!

10-21 **¿Qué es más importante para ti?** Entre las dos actividades, ¿cuál es más importante o más interesante? Comparte tus pensamientos *(thoughts)* con un(a) compañero(a) de clase. ¿Tienen Uds. opiniones parecidas o diferentes?

Modelo   ser jefe(a) / dedicarme a la investigación

> **Estudiante A:** Para mí, es más importante ser jefe. ¿Y para ti?
> **Estudiante B:** Para mí, es más interesante dedicarme a la investigación.

1. trabajar para una empresa grande / tener mi propio negocio

2. conocer el mundo / ser rico(a)

3. graduarme en cuatro años / encontrar la carrera perfecta

4. ganar mucho dinero / ayudar al prójimo

5. hacer un postgrado / hacer una pasantía

6. trabajar con las manos / dedicarme a la atención al cliente

¡Exprésate!

ooo 10-22 Planes y aspiraciones. En grupos de tres o cuatro, completen las oraciones y comparen sus planes y aspiraciones. Al final, informen a su profesor(a) sobre (1) las aspiraciones que tienen en común y (2) los planes más interesantes.

1. Antes de graduarme de la universidad, voy a _____. Además, me gustaría _____.

2. Después de graduarme, pienso _____. Además, me gustaría _____.

3. Antes de cumplir 30 años de edad, espero _____. También me gustaría _____.

4. Sueño con _____ algún día. Mi meta es _____.

↻ Giving advice, **Capítulo 9 Pasos 2 y 3**

⋔×⋔ 10-23 ¿Qué aconsejan? Con un(a) compañero(a) de clase, lean el siguiente
Colaborar foro (*forum*); sigan el modelo para escribir una respuesta para cada persona.

Modelo (Rubén), si tu sueño es (ser actor), te sugiero que....

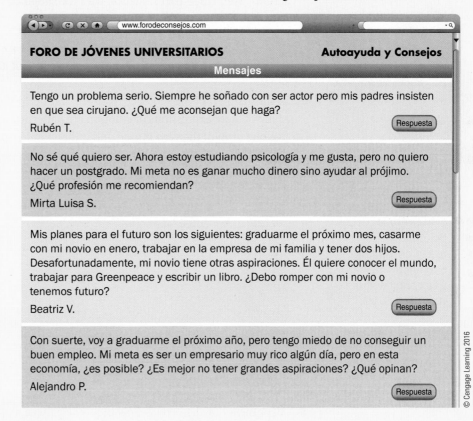

FORO DE JÓVENES UNIVERSITARIOS — **Autoayuda y Consejos**

Mensajes

Tengo un problema serio. Siempre he soñado con ser actor pero mis padres insisten en que sea cirujano. ¿Qué me aconsejan que haga?
Rubén T.
[Respuesta]

No sé qué quiero ser. Ahora estoy estudiando psicología y me gusta, pero no quiero hacer un postgrado. Mi meta no es ganar mucho dinero sino ayudar al prójimo. ¿Qué profesión me recomiendan?
Mirta Luisa S.
[Respuesta]

Mis planes para el futuro son los siguientes: graduarme el próximo mes, casarme con mi novio en enero, trabajar en la empresa de mi familia y tener dos hijos. Desafortunadamente, mi novio tiene otras aspiraciones. Él quiere conocer el mundo, trabajar para Greenpeace y escribir un libro. ¿Debo romper con mi novio o tenemos futuro?
Beatriz V.
[Respuesta]

Con suerte, voy a graduarme el próximo año, pero tengo miedo de no conseguir un buen empleo. Mi meta es ser un empresario muy rico algún día, pero en esta economía, ¿es posible? ¿Es mejor no tener grandes aspiraciones? ¿Qué opinan?
Alejandro P.
[Respuesta]

© Cengage Learning 2016

⋔⋔ 10-24 Entrevista personal. Usa las siguientes preguntas (¡y otras originales!) para entrevistar (*interview*) a tu compañero(a). Luego él/ella te entrevista a ti.

1. ¿Te gustaría estudiar en el extranjero? ¿En qué país? ¿Por qué?

2. ¿Qué profesiones o empleos te interesan más? ¿Qué soñabas ser cuando tenías 10 años? ¿Cómo han cambiado tus aspiraciones y sueños?

3. ¿Cuándo piensas graduarte? Después de graduarte, ¿piensas conseguir un empleo o hacer un postgrado?

4. Para ti, ¿qué significa tener éxito? ¿Quieres ser rico(a)? ¿Ser famoso(a)? ¿Casarte y tener hijos? ¿Tener tu propio negocio?

El presente de subjuntivo con expresiones de emoción (Parte I)

JULIO CÉSAR   Papá, mamá, quiero ser cirujano.

MAMÁ   Me sorprende que quieras ser cirujano. ¡A ti no te gusta ver sangre!

PAPÁ   A mí me encanta que quieras ser cirujano, hijo. ¡Vas a ganar mucho dinero!

■ ■ ■

Descúbrelo

- What does Julio César want to do for a living?

- How do his parents feel about it? Why?

- What phrase does the mother use to express her surprise?

- What phrase does the father use to express his pleasure?

- What verb in the dialogue is in the present subjunctive? After what small word does it appear?

1. To express how you feel about a current or future event or another person's actions, use a three-part sentence, with the subjunctive in the third part.

EXPRESSION OF EMOTION + **QUE** + (NEW SUBJECT) PRESENT SUBJUNCTIVE
Me preocupa   que   mi novio no **tenga** ninguna entrevista.
*It worries me (I'm worried) that   my boyfriend doesn't **have** a single interview.*

2. In the first part of the sentence, your (or another person's) feelings are expressed. Many of these expressions of emotion are patterned much like the verb **gustar**. Just one form of the verb is used and indirect object pronouns indicate who feels that particular way.

A mis padres **les sorprende** que yo quiera casarme.
It surprises my parents that I want to get married.

sorprender to surprise; to be surprised	
me sorprende	nos sorprende
te sorprende	os sorprende
le sorprende	les sorprende
a + *singular noun* + le sorprende	a + *plural noun / multiple nouns* + les sorprende

3. All of the following verbs follow the same pattern as **sorprender**.

Expresiones de emoción	
Me alegra que...	*It makes me happy that . . . / I'm happy that . . .*
Me encanta que...	*I'm delighted that . . . / It delights me that . . .*
Me enfada que...	*It angers me that . . . / I'm angry that . . .*
Me gusta que...	*I like the fact that . . .*
Me molesta que...	*It bothers me that . . .*
Me preocupa que...	*It worries (concerns) me that . . .*

4. To express hopes and wishes, use this special expression:

> **Ojalá que** (+ *present subjunctive*)
> ¡**Ojalá que** consigas un puesto pronto!   *I hope that you get a job soon!*

5. To form the present subjunctive of most verbs, you must conjugate the verb in the **yo** form of the present tense, drop the **-o**, and add the endings shown below. To review irregular and stem-changing verbs, see pages 359–360.

-ar verbs	habl**ar**: habl**e**, habl**es**, habl**e**, habl**emos**, habl**éis**, habl**en**
-er verbs	com**er**: com**a**, com**as**, com**a**, com**amos**, com**áis**, com**an**
-ir verbs	sal**ir**: sal**ga**, sal**gas**, sal**ga**, sal**gamos**, sal**gáis**, sal**gan**

Colaborar

10-25 **Los chismes.** ¿Qué chismes (*gossip*) cuentan Valentina y Florencia? Con un(a) compañero(a), lean la conversación en voz alta. Tienen que conjugar los verbos más lógicos en el presente de indicativo (por ejemplo, **sorprende**, **gusta**, etcétera).

VALENTINA ¿Sabes una cosa? Martín va a casarse el próximo fin de semana.

FLORENCIA ¡Eso es increíble! Me (1. sorprender / gustar) que se case tan pronto. Tiene solo 19 años. ¿Has oído la noticia sobre Ana Laura? Se rompió el tobillo.

VALENTINA ¡Ay! Lo siento mucho. Me (2. preocupar / encantar) que ella no pueda participar en el festival de baile. Por lo menos tengo buenas noticias sobre Juan Carlos. ¡Le dieron una beca para estudiar en Japón!

FLORENCIA ¡Qué buena suerte! Me (3. alegrar / molestar) mucho que él pueda ir al extranjero. ¿Sabes quiénes viajan al extranjero también? Lucía y Gonzalo. Salen mañana.

VALENTINA No me dijeron nada. ¡Me (4. gustar / enfadar) que ellos nunca me dicen nada! Bueno, esta noche voy a olvidarme de aquellos dos.

FLORENCIA Sí, me (5. encantar / sorprender) que haya fiesta esta noche. ¡Va a ser muy divertida! Oí que Santiago va a ser el *dee jay*.

VALENTINA Oíste mal. Santiago es mi nuevo novio y él no va a ser el *dee jay* porque a mí me (6. gustar / molestar) que él trabaje en nuestras fiestas.

10-26 **¡Me molesta!** Con un(a) compañero(a), completen las oraciones para expresar algunas de sus frustraciones. Usen el presente de subjuntivo.

Modelo Me molesta que los profesores...
> **Estudiante A:** Me molesta que los profesores no nos permitan beber café en clase.
> **Estudiante B:** Eso no me molesta mucho. Me molesta más que...

1. Me molesta que los profesores...

2. Me molesta que mi hermano(a)...

3. Me molesta que mis padres...

4. Me molesta que mi compañero(a) de cuarto...

5. Me molesta que mi novio(a) / amigo(a)...

6. Me molesta que nuestra universidad...

PASO 2   **387**

¡Aplícalo!

10-27 **¡Ojalá!** En grupos de tres o cuatro personas, tomen turnos para expresar sus esperanzas *(hopes)* sobre cada uno de los temas. Usen la expresión **ojalá que** (+ *presente de subjuntivo*).

Modelo las clases el próximo semestre
> **Estudiante A:** ¡Ojalá que mis clases sean fáciles el próximo semestre!
> **Estudiante B:** ¡Ojalá que yo no tenga una clase a las ocho de la mañana!
> **Estudiante C:** ¡Ojalá que mis profesores no me den mucha tarea!

Temas:

1. las clases el próximo semestre

2. la vida social y las actividades extracurriculares

3. mi mejor amigo(a) / mi novio(a) / mi compañero(a) de cuarto

4. nuestro equipo de fútbol americano / béisbol / fútbol / baloncesto

5. el gobierno estudiantil / el gobierno de nuestro país

10-28 **¿Cómo se sienten?** ¿Cómo se sienten tus familiares y tus amigos sobre diferentes aspectos de tu vida? Completa cada oración con tu información personal; compara tus respuestas con las de un(a) compañero(a). ¡Ojo! Tienes que hablar sobre eventos futuros o actuales *(present; ongoing)*.

Modelo A mi papá le preocupa que... **yo viva solo(a) en un apartamento**.

1. A mis padres les preocupa un poco que...

2. A mi abuela le alegra que...

3. A mi mejor amigo(a) le sorprende un poco que...

4. A mi mamá le molesta que...

5. A mi(s) hermano(s) / hermana(s) le(s) encanta que...

6. A mis amigos(as) les gusta que...

10-29 **El matrimonio de Sarita.** ¿Qué piensan todos del próximo matrimonio de Sarita? Con un(a) compañero(a), tomen turnos para describir los sentimientos de todos. Verbos útiles: **alegrar, encantar, enfadar, molestar, preocupar, sorprender**.

Modelo Al perro le enfada que...

© Cengage Learning 2016

El presente de subjuntivo con expresiones de emoción (Parte II)

© Cengage Learning 2016

MARCOS	Papá, me gustaría estudiar en el extranjero el próximo verano. ¿Puedo ir?
SEÑOR RUBIO	Hijo, es bueno que quieras conocer el mundo, pero francamente, no tenemos dinero para eso.
MARCOS	¡No te preocupes, papá! Hay muchas becas para estudiar en otros países.
SEÑOR RUBIO	Entonces tienes mi permiso. Espero que consigas suficiente dinero para realizar tus sueños.

1. As you have seen earlier in this chapter, a three-part sentence is used to express how someone feels about a current or future event or another person's actions. The subjunctive is used in the third part of the sentence.

> EXPRESSION OF EMOTION + **QUE** + (NEW SUBJECT) PRESENT SUBJUNCTIVE
> Siento mucho que (tú) no **puedas** ir al extranjero.
> *I'm very sorry* *that* *you **can't** go abroad.*

2. In the first part of the sentence, you must conjugate the verb in the present indicative (the present tense introduced in **Capítulo 1**). Choose the verb ending that matches the subject of the sentence—the person who feels a particular way.

> **Sentimos** que Elena ya no quiera trabajar para nuestra empresa.
> *We regret that Elena no longer wishes to work for our company.*

Verbos de emoción	
sentir	*to regret, to be sorry*
tener miedo de	*to be afraid*
esperar	*to hope*

3. Many expressions of emotion consist of the phrase **Es** (+ *adjective*). These phrases are used in the first part of a sentence to describe a wide variety of feelings.

> EXPRESSION OF EMOTION + **QUE** + PRESENT SUBJUNCTIVE
> **Es triste** que no haya muchas ofertas de empleo.
> *It's sad* *that* *there aren't many job offers out there.*

Expresiones impersonales de emoción	
Es bueno / malo que...	*It's good / bad that . . .*
Es curioso que...	*It's odd that . . .*
Es estupendo que...	*It's great / wonderful that . . .*
Es extraño que...	*It's strange that . . .*
Es fantástico que...	*It's fantastic that . . .*
Es una lástima que...	*It's a shame / too bad that . . .*
Es ridículo que...	*It's ridiculous that . . .*
Es triste que...	*It's sad that . . .*

■ ■ ■
Descúbrelo
■ What does Marcos want to do next summer?
■ What does Mr. Rubio feel is a positive aspect of his son's dream?
■ What is an obstacle to this dream?
■ What phrase does Mr. Rubio use to express his hope for his son? Is the present indicative or the present subjunctive used after this phrase?

¡Aplícalo!

Colaborar

10-30 **La vida de Marcos.** Marcos está lamentando las vicisitudes *(difficulties)* de la vida. Con un(a) compañero(a), completen las oraciones. Hay que conjugar el primer verbo en el presente de indicativo y el segundo en el presente de subjuntivo.

1. No tengo ganas de estudiar este fin de semana, pero (yo: tener) _____ miedo de que el profesor de química nos (dar) _____ un examen el lunes.

2. Mi nuevo compañero de cuarto no es muy responsable. (Yo: esperar) _____ que él no (usar) _____ mis cosas sin pedir permiso.

3. Tengo muchas ganas de ver a mi hermano. (Yo: sentir) _____ mucho que él no (poder) _____ venir al campus para visitarme el próximo fin de semana.

4. (Ser) _____ ridículo que mis padres no me (permitir) _____ estudiar en el extranjero. ¿Cómo voy a aprender a hablar francés si no puedo ir a Francia?

Colaborar

10-31 **Por el campus.** Con un(a) compañero(a), expresen sus opiniones sobre estas situaciones en el campus. Usen frases de la lista y cambien los verbos al presente de subjuntivo.

Modelo La biblioteca **cierra** a medianoche.
Es ridículo que la biblioteca **cierre** a medianoche.

Es bueno	**Es estupendo**	**Es fantástico**	**Es malo**
Es curioso	**Es extraño**	**Es una lástima**	**Es ridículo**

1. No se **permite** usar celulares en clase.
2. Los libros de texto **cuestan** mucho.
3. **Dan** muchas becas a los atletas.
4. No **hay** suficiente aparcamiento *(parking)*.
5. Todos los estudiantes **tienen** que estudiar idiomas para graduarse.

Rosa Villareal

el profesor Pérez

Colaborar

10-32 **¿Quién lo dice?** Con un(a) compañero(a), cambien los verbos al presente de subjuntivo. Después, indiquen quién está hablando: el profesor o su estudiante, Rosa.

1. Espero que todos mis estudiantes (hacer) la tarea.
2. Siento que mi novio no (venir) a visitarme este fin de semana.
3. Tengo miedo de que mi amiga (pensar) abandonar sus estudios.
4. Es curioso que mis estudiantes (ganar) más dinero que yo.
5. Espero que mis compañeros y yo (conseguir) becas.
6. Es ridículo que yo no (poder) hacer una pasantía.
7. Es triste que algunos estudiantes no (tener) éxito en mis clases.
8. Es bueno que mis compañeros y yo (poder) realizar nuestros sueños.

¡Exprésate!

10-33 ¡Así es la vida! Con un(a) compañero(a), hablen de los altibajos *(ups and downs)* de la vida.

- Tomando turnos, una persona usa el presente de indicativo para describir una preocupación, un plan, etcétera. ¡Ojo! No deben hablar de eventos pasados. Tienen que hablar de situaciones actuales *(current)* o de situaciones futuras.
- La otra persona usa una expresión de la lista y el presente de subjuntivo para reaccionar.

Modelo **Estudiante A:** Mi hermana piensa estudiar en Francia el próximo verano.
Estudiante B: ¡Es estupendo que tu hermana pueda estudiar en el extranjero!

Para reaccionar:

Es bueno / malo que...	Es ridículo que...	Espero que...
Es estupendo que...	Es triste que...	Siento que...
Es extraño que...	Es una lástima que...	

Subjunctive with expressions of influence, **Capítulo 9 Paso 3**

10-34 Los planes para el futuro. En grupos de tres personas, hablen de sus planes para el futuro. Sigan el modelo.

Modelo ¿Qué sueñas hacer después de graduarte?
Estudiante A: *(Contesta la pregunta.)* Sueño con trabajar para una multinacional.
Estudiante B: *(Reacciona de forma positiva al plan.)* Es estupendo que pienses trabajar para una multinacional.
Estudiante C: *(Da una recomendación o consejo.)* Recomiendo que hagas un postgrado en administración de empresas primero.

1. ¿Qué sueñas hacer después de graduarte?
2. ¿Dónde te gustaría vivir en el futuro?
3. ¿Cuál es tu meta principal, respecto a *(with respect to)* una carrera o profesión?
4. ¿Cuál es tu meta principal, respecto a tu vida personal?
5. ¿Qué esperas lograr *(achieve)* antes del final de este año?

10-35 Una discusión familiar. Con un(a) compañero(a), creen un diálogo para cada dibujo. Estudiante A es el padre (la madre) y Estudiante B es el hijo. Incluyan oraciones con el presente de subjuntivo.

1. El hijo le cuenta sus planes a su padre (madre).

2. El padre o la madre reacciona a los planes. Luego discuten los planes. El padre (La madre) le da unas recomendaciones.

3. Resuelven el problema y todos expresan sus sentimientos.

Illustrations © Cengage Learning 2016

Buscando empleo

In this *Paso*, you will . . .

- practice interviewing for a job
- discuss job requirements and benefits
- express doubt, denial, and certainty

Una oferta de empleo

TUTORES DE INGLÉS

Centro de Idiomas Chaco necesita
TUTORES DE INGLÉS

Requisitos: excelente nivel de inglés, estudios universitarios

Horario flexible y salario competitivo

Interesados favor presentarse en horario de oficina en Ayolas 560, Asunción

© Cengage Learning 2016

Frases del (de la) entrevistado(a)

Me interesa mucho este puesto porque...
¿Cuáles son los requisitos?
Estoy disponible (todas las tardes).
¿Cuánto es el salario?
¿Qué beneficios ofrecen?
¿Cuándo puedo empezar?

Interviewee's phrases

I'm very interested in this position because . . .
What are the requirements?
I'm available (every afternoon).
What's the salary?
What benefits are offered?
When can I start?

La entrevista de trabajo

Frases del (de la) entrevistador(a)	*Interviewer's phrases*
¿Dónde hizo sus estudios?	*Where did you get your degree?*
¿Tiene referencias / una carta de recomendación?	*Do you have references / a letter of recommendation?*
¿Por qué lo (la) debemos contratar?	*Why should we hire you?*
Ofrecemos seguro médico y vacaciones pagadas.	*We offer health insurance and paid vacations.*
Hay posibilidad de aumento de sueldo cada año.	*There's a possibility of yearly salary increases.*
Le vamos a avisar dentro de (una semana).	*We'll let you know in (a week).*
El puesto es suyo.	*The job is yours.*

¡Aplícalo! **10-36** **Buscando trabajo.** Carlos Alberto está hablando con el asistente administrativo de una escuela de idiomas sobre el puesto de tutor. Trabajando con un(a) compañero(a), relacionen las preguntas de Carlos Alberto con las respuestas del asistente. Tomando turnos, una persona lee la pregunta y la otra lee la respuesta.

Carlos Alberto:

_____ 1. ¿Cuáles son los requisitos?

_____ 2. ¿Cuánto es el salario?

_____ 3. ¿Qué beneficios ofrecen?

_____ 4. ¿Cómo es el horario de trabajo?

_____ 5. ¿Quiere una copia de mi currículum?

_____ 6. ¿Cuándo van a avisar a los candidatos?

El asistente administrativo:

a. Sí. También necesitamos dos cartas de recomendación.

b. Es flexible pero tiene que trabajar tres días por semana.

c. Es competitivo y hay posibilidad de aumento cada año.

d. Ofrecemos seguro médico.

e. Lo llamaremos para una entrevista dentro de una semana.

f. Hay que tener título universitario y un año de experiencia.

 10-37 **La entrevista.** María José tiene una entrevista para un puesto en un campamento *(camp)* para niños. Trabajando con un(a) compañero(a), completen la conversación entre María José y el director con las palabras más lógicas de la lista. Después, lean el diálogo en voz alta.

capacidad	Dónde	medio	puesto	suyo
cartas	estudios	placer	Quién	tercer
contratar	experiencia	Por qué	referencias	voluntaria

DIRECTOR ¿(1) _____ quiere trabajar en nuestro campamento?

MARÍA JOSÉ Me interesa mucho este (2) _____ porque me encanta trabajar con niños.

DIRECTOR ¿Qué (3) _____ tiene en este campo?

MARÍA JOSÉ Hace dos años que trabajo de (4) _____ en una escuela.

DIRECTOR ¿(5) _____ hizo sus estudios?

MARÍA JOSÉ Este es mi (6) _____ año en la Universidad de Belgrano, donde estudio para maestra.

DIRECTOR Ud. tiene (7) _____, ¿verdad?

MARÍA JOSÉ Sí, tengo varias (8) _____ de recomendación de mis profesores.

DIRECTOR ¿Por qué la debemos (9) _____?

MARÍA JOSÉ Soy una persona responsable y tengo la (10) _____ de trabajar en equipo. Además, mis (11) _____ me han preparado para este tipo de trabajo.

DIRECTOR De momento solo tenemos puestos a (12) _____ tiempo. Pero si lo quiere, el puesto es (13) _____.

MARÍA JOSÉ ¡Sí, acepto con gran (14) _____! Muchas gracias.

¡Exprésate!

10-38 Mi experiencia. ¿Qué experiencia laboral tienes? Con un(a) compañero(a), tomen turnos para describir un puesto de trabajo que han tenido en el pasado. Completa las oraciones con los detalles sobre tu empleo.

1. (El año pasado / El verano pasado / ¿?) trabajé en...

2. Era un trabajo (a tiempo completo / a medio tiempo).

3. Mis beneficios incluían...

4. Mi trabajo consistía en...

5. (No) Me gustó el trabajo porque...

10-39 Una oferta de empleo.

Colaborar

Estás estudiando en Argentina y quieres buscar un puesto a medio tiempo para ganar un poco de dinero. Con un(a) compañero(a), lean el anuncio y contesten las preguntas.

1. ¿Qué puestos están disponibles?

2. ¿Cuáles son los requisitos?

3. ¿Qué beneficios ofrece el puesto?

4. ¿Son los puestos a tiempo completo o a medio tiempo?

5. ¿Te interesa uno de los puestos? ¿Por qué?

Nuevo restaurante en zona turística busca camareros y ayudantes[1] de pizzero. Puestos a tiempo completo y a medio tiempo. Salario competitivo, vacaciones pagadas.

Requisitos: Buscamos gente puntual[2] y con buena predisposición al trabajo en equipo.

• Buena presencia
• Edad de 20 a 30 años
• Secundaria completa
• Conocimiento de inglés, preferible

Interesados llamar al 4613-6654

© Cengage Learning 2016

[1]assistants [2]punctual

10-40 Una entrevista. Con tu compañero(a), dramaticen una entrevista para el puesto del anuncio de la Actividad 10-39.

El (La) candidato(a)	El (La) jefe(a) de personal
1. Saluda al jefe (a la jefa) y preséntate (**Buenos días. Me llamo... y estoy aquí para...**)	2. Saluda al candidato (a la candidata) y pregúntale por qué quiere este puesto. (**¿Por qué le interesa... ?**)
3. Explica por qué quieres el puesto. (**Me interesa mucho porque...**)	4. Haz preguntas sobre la experiencia. (**¿Qué experiencia... ?**)
5. Contesta las preguntas del jefe (de la jefa) sobre tu experiencia.	6. Haz preguntas sobre el horario de trabajo. (**¿Está dispuesto(a) a... ?**)
7. Contesta las preguntas. Haz preguntas sobre el salario y los beneficios.	8. Contesta las preguntas. Indica cuándo vas a contactarlo(la) con una decisión.

El presente de subjuntivo con expresiones de duda y de negación

MARITZA	¿Cómo te fue en la entrevista con Compu-Plus, Bruno?
BRUNO	No muy bien. Dudo que me ofrezcan el puesto.
MARITZA	Pero ¿por qué? Ya tienes tu maestría en computación.
BRUNO	Sí, pero el director no cree que yo tenga suficiente experiencia.

■ ■ ■
Descúbrelo

- Is Bruno feeling certain or doubtful that he'll be offered the job he wants?
- What is the director's opinion about Bruno's qualifications?
- What are the Spanish equivalents of *I doubt* and *he doesn't think*?
- Are the verbs **ofrezcan** and **tenga** in the present indicative or the present subjunctive?

1. To express feelings of doubt about current and future events, a three-part sentence pattern is used. The present subjunctive is used in the third part, in which the current or future event is described.

EXPRESSION OF DOUBT +	QUE	+ PRESENT SUBJUNCTIVE
Dudo	que	le **den** el puesto a Javier.
I doubt	*that*	*they'll **give** the job to Javier.*

2. To deny that something is so or that something will take place, the same three-part pattern is used.

EXPRESSION OF DENIAL +	QUE	+ PRESENT SUBJUNCTIVE
No es verdad	que	Javier **tenga** buenas referencias.
It's not true	*that*	*Javier **has** good references.*

3. Here are some of the most common expressions of doubt, uncertainty, and denial.

Verbos de duda y negación
dudar   *to doubt*
no creer   *not to believe*
no pensar   *not to think*
no estar seguro(a) de   *not to be sure*

4. Many impersonal expressions—phrases with *it* as the subject—can be used to indicate doubt, uncertainty, and denial.

No es posible que ella haga estudios de postgrado.
It's not possible for her to do graduate work.

Expresiones de duda y negación	
Es imposible que...	*It's impossible that / for . . .*
(No) Es posible...	*It's (not) possible that . . .*
(No) Es probable que...	*It's (not) likely that . . .*
No es cierto que...	*It's not true that . . .*
No es verdad que...	*It's not true that . . .*

Colaborar

10-41 **¡No es verdad!** Tu compañero(a) de cuarto te acusa de hacer muchas cosas pero tú niegas *(denies)* todo. Tomando turnos con un(a) compañero(a), una persona lee la oración y la otra lo niega *(denies it)*. Sigan el modelo.

Modelo "Siempre haces ruido cuando yo quiero estudiar".
No es verdad que yo haga mucho ruido.

1. "Nunca me ayudas a limpiar el cuarto".
2. "Siempre llevas mi chaqueta sin pedir permiso".
3. "Todos tus amigos me odian".
4. "Nunca me invitas cuando hay una fiesta".
5. "Siempre pierdes la llave del cuarto".
6. "Tus calcetines sucios siempre están sobre mi cama".

Colaborar

10-42 **El pesimista.** Matías se siente muy pesimista hoy. ¿Qué dice él? Trabajando con un(a) compañero(a), combinen la información de las tres columnas para crear cinco oraciones lógicas y ¡pesimistas! Sigan el modelo.

Modelo **Estudiante A:** *(Begins with a phrase from column A)* Es imposible...
Estudiante B: *(Adds a new subject from column B)* Es imposible que yo...
Estudiante A: *(Finishes with a phrase from column C)* Es imposible que yo saque A en física.

A	B	C
Dudo	yo	**ganar** muchos partidos este año
Es imposible	nuestro equipo	**ir** a Europa en las próximas vacaciones
No es probable	mis padres	**sacar** A en física
No es posible	mis hermanos y yo	**poder** conseguir un buen empleo
No creo	mi mejor amigo(a)	**hacer** una pasantía en Europa

Colaborar

10-43 **En un jardín infantil.** Tú y tu compañero(a) trabajan en un jardín infantil *(preschool)*. Tomen turnos respondiendo a cada pregunta o comentario con una expresión de negación.

Modelo **Nina:** Me gusta el chocolate. Tiene mucha vitamina C, ¿verdad?
Tú: No, Nina, no es verdad que el chocolate tenga mucha vitamina C.

Colaborar

10-44 **Una solicitud de empleo.** Los gerentes de la empresa Grupo Uno están haciendo comentarios sobre la candidata Marina Prado. Con un(a) compañero(a), tomen turnos para reaccionar a cada comentario. Usen una expresión de duda y justifiquen sus opiniones.

Modelo "Un señor Prado trabaja para nosotros. Probablemente es el esposo de Marina, ¿no cree?"

No pienso que sea el esposo de Marina porque ella es soltera.

1. "Marina tiene mucha experiencia en la administración de empleados".

2. "Marina sabe muchos idiomas".

3. "A Marina le importa más ayudar al prójimo que ganar dinero".

4. "Marina puede conducir a nuestras oficinas por toda Argentina".

5. "¿Puede Marina hablar con nuestros clientes en Estados Unidos?"

6. "¿Creen que Marina acepte un salario de $2000 pesos?"

Información Personal

Nacionalidad: __argentina__

Estado civil: __soltera__

¿Tiene automóvil? ☐ sí ☒ no

Formación Educativa

Título: __Licenciada en Psicología (2011)__

Antecedentes de Empleo

Empresa: __Instituto Mayor de Salud__

Posición: __Asistente de psicólogo__

Salario: __$2000 pesos__

Razón de salida: __Me gustaría__
__conseguir un puesto con mejor salario.__

Idiomas

Inglés: ☒ básico ☐ avanzado

Otro: _____

Posición a la que aspira:

__Administradora de empleados__

Salario al que aspira: __$3500 pesos__

10-45 **Especulaciones.** Completa las siguientes oraciones de una manera original. Luego, comparte tus respuestas con dos o tres compañeros(as). ¡Ojo! Hay que usar el presente de subjuntivo.

Modelo Respecto a mi mejor amigo(a), dudo que él (ella)... **pueda graduarse en mayo.**

1. Respecto a mis notas este semestre, es posible que yo...

2. Sobre mi profesor(a) preferido(a), no pienso que él (ella)...

3. Hablando de las vacaciones, dudo que mis amigos y yo...

4. Respecto al dinero, no es probable que mis amigos y yo...

5. En cuanto al estrés, es probable que...

6. En cuanto a mi familia, no estoy seguro(a) de que mis padres (abuelos / hermanos)...

10-46 **Rompiendo estereotipos.** Hay muchos estereotipos *(stereotypes)* falsos sobre varias profesiones. ¿Conoces algunos? En grupos de tres o cuatro, tomen turnos para describir un estereotipo de una profesión de la lista. Después, rompan el estereotipo con una expresión de duda o negación.

Modelo Estudiante A: Un estereotipo de los políticos es que todos son corruptos, pero yo no pienso que todos sean corruptos.

Estudiante B: Un estereotipo de los escritores es que fuman mucho, pero dudo que muchos escritores fumen.

los abogados	los enfermeros	los políticos
los artistas	los escritores	los profesores
los contadores	las gerentes mujeres	(otra profesión)

El presente de indicativo con expresiones de certeza y afirmación

MANUEL   Estoy seguro de que me van a dar el puesto. No hay duda de que soy el mejor candidato.

RODRIGO   ¿Por qué estás tan seguro?

MANUEL   El anuncio dice "Buscamos persona responsable". Sé que tengo experiencia en eso porque en mi trabajo anterior siempre me decían que ¡yo era el responsable de todas las cosas que ocurrían!

1. To express a strong belief or certainty about current and future events, a three-part sentence is used. The verb in the third part must be conjugated in the present indicative, *not* in the present subjunctive.

> EXPRESSION OF BELIEF / CERTAINTY + **QUE** + INDICATIVE
>
> Creo   que   este puesto **es** magnífico.
> *I think*   *that* *this job **is** great.*

2. Here are some common verbs used to express belief and certainty:

creer	*to believe, to think*	**saber**	*to know*
pensar	*to think*	**estar seguro(a)(s) de**	*to be sure*

3. The present indicative is also used after set phrases of belief and certainty.

Es verdad que ofrecen beneficios.   ***It's true that*** *they offer benefits.*

Expresiones de afirmación y certeza	
No hay duda de que...	*There's no doubt that . . .*
Es verdad que...	*It's true that . . .*
Es cierto que...	*It's true that . . .*

4. The uses of the indicative and subjunctive are summarized in the chart.

Indicative: Strong belief, certainty, affirmation	Subjunctive: Disbelief, doubt, uncertainty, denial
creer que...	no creer que...
pensar que...	no pensar que...
estar seguro(a)(s) de que...	no estar seguro(a)(s) de que...
Es verdad que...	No es verdad que...
Es cierto que...	No es cierto que...
No hay duda de que...	dudar que...
saber que...	(No) es posible que...
	Es imposible que...

■ ■ ■
Descúbrelo

- What is Manuel so sure of? What kind of employee are they looking for?

- Why does Manuel think that he's the best person for the job?

- What three phrases does Manuel use to express certainty?

- After the expressions of certainty, is the indicative or subjunctive used?

PASO 3 **GRAMÁTICA B**

¡Aplícalo!   👤×👤   **10-47**   **Padres preocupados.** Los padres de Daniel se preocupan por
Colaborar   su futuro. ¿Qué dicen? Trabaja con un(a) compañero(a) de clase para escoger las
expresiones correctas.

PADRE   Nuestro hijo va a graduarse en noviembre, ¿verdad?

MADRE   Sí, tranquilo. (1. Dudo / Estoy segura de) que Daniel se gradúa en
noviembre; ya casi termina. Pero después, ¿qué va a hacer? ¿Estudios
de postgrado?

PADRE   (2. No creo / No hay duda de) que haga estudios de postgrado. Él quiere
conseguir un empleo inmediatamente.

MADRE   ¡Ay, pero en esta economía! No hay muchos empleos.
(3. No es verdad / Pienso) que nadie lo va a contratar.

PADRE   No seas pesimista, Isa. Daniel es muy inteligente y preparado.
(4. No es posible / Creo) que puede conseguir un puesto.

MADRE   ¡Ojalá! Y luego, que se case con Valentina. (5. Es probable / Sé) que ella
quiere casarse pronto.

PADRE   Pues, a nuestro hijo le gusta estar soltero. (6. No pienso / Es cierto) que
quiera casarse.

MADRE   Ya veremos *(We'll see)...*

👤×👤   **10-48**   **Una oferta de empleo.** Zunilda solicitó un puesto de contadora
Colaborar   y ahora está especulando *(speculating)* sobre el puesto. Con un(a) compañero(a),
completen las oraciones con las formas correctas de los verbos en el presente de
indicativo o en el presente de subjuntivo.

1. ¿El horario? Estoy segura de que el puesto
(ser) _____ de tiempo completo. Es
posible que la oficina (abrir) _____ a
las diez de la mañana y (cerrar) _____ a
las ocho de la noche. No es probable que los
empleados (tener) _____ que trabajar los
fines de semana.

2. ¿Los beneficios? Creo que la empresa
(ofrecer) _____ buenos beneficios. Es
muy probable que ellos (ofrecer) _____
seguro médico y vacaciones pagadas. Dudo
que (haber) _____ un gimnasio para los empleados. Y no creo que les
(dar) _____ a los nuevos empleados tarjetas de transporte.

3. ¿Los compañeros de trabajo? Sé que (haber) _____ veinte empleados. No
estoy segura de que muchos empleados (ser) _____ mujeres pero pienso que
todos los contadores (ser) _____ muy simpáticos. No hay duda de que yo
(ir) _____ a hacer nuevos amigos.

© kurhan/Shutterstock

¡Exprésate!

 10-49 **Seguro(a) en la entrevista.** Imagina que estás en una entrevista para un puesto de vendedor(a) de paneles solares. ¿Cómo respondes para dar la impresión de ser una persona segura de sí misma *(self-confident)*? Tomando turnos con un(a) compañero(a), contesta las preguntas con expresiones de certeza y afirmación.

Modelo **Estudiante A:** ¿Trabaja Ud. bien en equipo?

Estudiante B: No hay duda de que trabajo bien en equipo. En la universidad hice muchos proyectos con otros compañeros.

1. El puesto requiere viajar mucho por avión. ¿Es esto un problema?
2. ¿Puede Ud. trabajar bajo presión?
3. Nuestra empresa es bastante pequeña. ¿No prefiere trabajar en una empresa más grande?
4. Ud. no tiene mucha experiencia como vendedor(a). ¿Por qué debemos contratarlo(la)?
5. ¿Cree Ud. que va a tener éxito en esta empresa?
6. (Otra pregunta original)

 10-50 **La bola de cristal.** Tú y tu compañero(a) de clase consultaron a una adivina *(fortune teller)* simplemente para divertirse. Una persona debe leer las predicciones de la adivina, y la otra debe reaccionar con certeza o duda.

Modelo **Estudiante A:** La adivina me dijo: "Veo una boda: ¡la tuya!"

Estudiante B: Sí, es posible que te cases algún día.

Predicciones para Estudiante A:

"Vas a tener cinco hijos".

"Te veo en el extranjero".

"Te gusta la política".

"En el futuro trabajas con animales".

© Cora Reed/Shutterstock

Predicciones para Estudiante B:

"Te veo en una gran mansión".

"Vas a ganar un premio".

"Estarás en televisión".

"Te veo mayor y triste".

10-51 **¿Conoces a tu compañero(a)?** Primero, contesta por escrito las siguientes preguntas sobre tu compañero(a) de clase con expresiones de certeza o de duda. Luego, lee tus respuestas en voz alta y tu compañero(a) dice si acertaste *(whether you were right)*.

Modelo ¿Practica tu compañero(a) deportes en forma regular?

Estudiante A: Mi compañero(a) practica deportes en forma regular.

Estudiante B: Es cierto que practico deportes en forma regular. / No es cierto que practique deportes en forma regular.

1. ¿Hace tu compañero(a) la tarea todos los días?
2. ¿Lee revistas de chisme *(gossip)* como *People*?
3. ¿Sabe preparar arroz?
4. ¿Estudia español todos los días?
5. ¿Come en McDonald's?
6. ¿Mira programas de ciencia ficción?

CONECTADOS CON...
EL DISEÑO DE VIDEOJUEGOS

Diseñadores de videojuegos

Regnum Online

Cada enero, durante dos días, miles de profesionales y aficionados *(enthusiasts)* del diseño de videojuegos participan en el Global Game Jam. Este evento mundial tiene lugar en forma simultánea en más de 60 países del mundo, entre ellos, España, México, Colombia, Venezuela y Argentina.

Al comienzo de este maratón, los organizadores del evento anuncian un tema *(theme)*. Pocos minutos después, los participantes forman equipos de trabajo y durante las próximas 48 horas, cada equipo crea un videojuego sobre el tema dado (por ejemplo, la extinción). Primero tienen que definir el argumento y la mecánica —o reglas— del juego. Después deben crear una interfaz, programar, hacer los gráficos, ponerle efectos de sonido y probar la presencia de errores. Al final de este gran experimento de creatividad global, todos los videojuegos diseñados se suben al sitio oficial y se comparten con el resto del mundo.

Estrategia: Summarizing

Summarizing is an effective technique to check your comprehension of news articles and stories. To summarize, restate and synthesize the information in your own words. Include the main ideas, important supporting details, and the connections among the major points of information.

Palabras del diseño de videojuegos

el argumento	*plot, story*
la consola	*(game) console*
el (la) diseñador(a)	*designer*
los efectos de sonido	*sound effects*
la interfaz	*interface*
probar	*to test*
las reglas	*rules*
el (la) usuario(a)	*user*
el videojuego de rol (multijugador)	*(multiplayer) role-playing videogame*

10-52 Comprensión. Para resumir *(summarize)* el artículo, completa las oraciones de una manera lógica.

1. El diseño de los videojuegos es una pasión internacional. En el Global Game Jam, los participantes de más de 60 países...

2. Como parte del evento, los participantes tienen que...

3. El diseño de los videojuegos no es solamente un acto de creatividad. También es una industria que...

4. La industria de los videojuegos incluye a varios países hispanos. Por ejemplo...

5. El negocio también incluye a países más pequeños, como Uruguay. Allí...

6. En conclusión, aunque muchos videojuegos tienen nombres en inglés, ...

10-53 ¿Y tú? Trabajando con un(a) compañero(a), comenten estas preguntas.

1. ¿Te gusta jugar a los videojuegos? En un día normal, ¿cuánto tiempo pasas jugando con ellos? ¿Cuál te gusta más? ¿Para ti, cuál es el atractivo *(attraction)* de ese videojuego?

2. ¿Qué aspecto del diseño de los videojuegos te interesa más: la creación del argumento y de las reglas; el diseño de los gráficos y los sonidos; o los aspectos tecnológicos? ¿Te gustaría participar en el Global Game Jam?

Un negocio serio

El diseño de videojuegos no es solamente una actividad creativa sino también un negocio serio. Las diversas plataformas de distribución —consolas, teléfonos inteligentes, redes sociales, tabletas— han llevado a los videojuegos a ser un producto de consumo masivo. A nivel mundial, la industria de videojuegos genera más dinero que el cine o la música.

Hecho en Iberoamérica

Desde hace más de una década, existen muchas empresas en España y en Argentina que desarrollan videojuegos. Pyro Studios y Novarama son dos ejemplos de empresas españolas que diseñan videojuegos para las grandes compañías de Estados Unidos y Japón. En Argentina, NGD Studios creó Regnum Online, un videojuego de fantasía de rol multijugador con usuarios en 150 países.

Países más pequeños como Uruguay también tienen estudios de videojuegos. En Montevideo, el investigador y diseñador de videojuegos Gonzalo Frasca tiene una empresa llamada Powerful Robot Games. Sus clientes incluyen Cartoon Network, Disney y Lucasfilm. Según Gonzalo Frasca, los buenos videojuegos "sirven para descubrir *(discover)* el mundo, explorar sus límites y ver qué pasa".

Es muy posible que tú o tus amigos hayan jugado un videojuego hecho por un diseñador hispanohablante. Los nombres de las empresas generalmente son en inglés —el idioma de la industria— pero a menudo sus creadores tienen apellidos *(last names)* como Suárez, Sánchez Crespo, Gálvez y Campelo.

Composición: Una carta de solicitud

Two job ads have caught your eye. In one, Roberto González is looking for a math tutor for his 12-year-old son. In another, Carla Aguado is looking for bilingual sales clerks to work at her souvenir shop next summer. Choose one of these positions and write a letter to apply for the job. Begin with the salutation **Estimado(a) señor(a)** *(surname):* and express your interest. In the main body, describe your experience, personal qualities, and strong points. Ask two or three questions about the position. To close, state how the employer may contact you and express optimism about being the right person for the job.

Colaborar

Revisión en pareja. Exchange papers with a classmate and edit each other's work.

- Does the letter have a sense of beginning, middle, and end? Does it contain convincing information about the candidate's qualifications? Write one positive comment and one suggestion for improvement.

- Are the verbs conjugated correctly? Are adjectives used in the correct form? Circle any that might be incorrect.

- Are capitalization, spelling, and punctuation correct? Underline any mistakes you see.

Estrategia
Proofreading

- Check for subject-verb agreement, correct verb forms, and appropriate tense.
- Look for noun-adjective agreement and adjective placement.
- Double-check the use of **ser** and **estar**.
- Recall that days of the week and months of the year are not capitalized.
- Check for accent marks and punctuation.

10-54 **Nosotros / *Share It!*** En línea, subiste una descripción o un video sobre una persona con un trabajo interesante. También viste las publicaciones de varios compañeros de clase. Ahora, formen grupos de tres o cuatro estudiantes. Comenten sobre las publicaciones y contesten las preguntas.

1. ¿Cuáles son algunos de los trabajos mencionados?

2. ¿Qué campos están representados? ¿Predomina un campo en particular?

3. En tu opinión, ¿cuáles son los tres trabajos más interesantes? ¿En qué consiste cada uno?

4. ¿Te gustaría tener alguno de los trabajos? ¿Cuál? ¿Por qué?

 10-55 **Perspectivas: Mi carrera.** En línea, miraste un video en el que tres estudiantes hablan de sus carreras y planes para el futuro. ¿Qué dicen los estudiantes? Con dos compañeros(as) de clase, comparen sus respuestas sobre el video. Después, entrevístense *(interview one another)* con estas preguntas.

- ¿Qué carrera estudias?
- ¿Por qué decidiste seguir esa carrera?
- ¿Dónde te gustaría trabajar después de graduarte?

 10-56 **Exploración: Los anuncios.** En Internet, investigaste las ofertas de trabajo en Paraguay. Ahora, formen círculos de tres o cuatro estudiantes. Tomen turnos describiendo con detalles los puestos que les interesan. En tu presentación, incluye las respuestas a estas preguntas:

- ¿Qué tipo de puesto es?
- ¿Dónde está ubicada la empresa?
- ¿Cuáles son los requisitos?
- ¿Qué salario ofrecen?
- ¿Qué beneficios ofrecen?
- ¿Por qué te interesa?

  10-57 **Conectados con... la música.** En línea, leíste un artículo sobre el candombe en Uruguay. Con dos o tres compañeros(as), compartan *(share)* información de sus investigaciones sobre otros estilos de música.

> **Modelo**
>
> La cumbia nació en la costa del Caribe de Colombia... /
> El origen de la música *country* de Estados Unidos es...

10-58 **La biografía de una presidenta.** Tú y tu compañero(a) van a intercambiar información sobre una mujer muy importante: la primera en ser elegida *(elected)* a la presidencia de Argentina. Para completar la tabla, Uds. necesitan hacerse preguntas como las siguientes. **Estudiante B** tiene que empezar el intercambio con la primera pregunta.

This is a pair activity for **Estudiante A** and **Estudiante B**.

If you are **Estudiante A**, use the information on this page.

If you are **Estudiante B**, turn to page S-10 at the back of the book.

- **¿Cuál es el nombre completo de... ? / ¿Cómo se llama... ?**
- **¿Dónde / Cuándo nació... ?**
- **¿En qué año se casó / se graduó / ... ?**
- **¿Qué pasó / hizo en el año... ?**
- **¿Qué había sido antes de ser elegida presidenta?**
- **(Otras preguntas originales)**

© AFP/Getty Images

Estudiante A

Nombre completo	Cristina Elisabet Fernández de Kirchner
Fecha y lugar de nacimiento	_____ de febrero de _____ _____, Argentina
Profesión	Abogada y política
Datos personales	1975: _____ con Néstor Kirchner, un compañero de la universidad. 1977: Nació su hijo Máximo. 1990: Nació su hija _____. 2003–2007: Su esposo Néstor fue presidente de Argentina. _____: Su esposo se murió y Cristina quedó viuda *(widow)*.
Estudios y carrera profesional	1973: Empezó sus estudios en la Universidad Nacional de La Plata (UNLP). Fue muy activa en asociaciones estudiantiles políticas. _____: Se graduó de la Facultad de Derecho de la UNLP. 1979–1985: Con su esposo, se dedicó a la práctica privada como abogada. 1985: Empezó a ser muy activa en el Partido *(Party)* _____. 1995–2007: Tuvo varios puestos nacionales, tales como Senadora Nacional y Diputada Nacional. 2007: _____.

SÍNTESIS

10-59 **Manifestación.** Con un(a) compañero(a), observen el cuadro *Manifestación* del artista argentino Antonio Berni (1905–1981). Fue pintado en 1934, año de crisis económica y conflictos laborales. Observen las caras de los trabajadores. ¿Qué pensaban? Completen el párrafo con sus ideas; usen el indicativo o el subjuntivo, según sea necesario.

Colaborar

© Antonio Berni. Manifestación, 1934 Collection Malba – Fundación Costantini, Buenos Aires

Manifestación es una obra de realismo social. En ella, los trabajadores piden "pan y trabajo" en un pueblo de Argentina. Es probable que estén manifestando (*demonstrating*) porque (1) _____.

Las caras de las personas son muy expresivas. Pienso que el señor mayor con sombrero está triste porque (2) _____. Al señor con la gorra roja le enfada que (3) _____. Al señor de barba blanca le preocupa que (4) _____.

Es curioso que dos señores miren hacia arriba. Yo creo que ellos (5) _____. Muy pronto la policía va a poner fin a la manifestación.

Pronunciación: Las letras *d* y *q*

Colaborar

¿Sabes pronunciar las letras **d** y **q**? Con un(a) compañero(a), lean en voz alta estos refranes. Relacionen cada uno con su equivalente en inglés.

1. Quien tarde se levanta, todo el día trota.

2. Suegra, abogado y médico... cuánto más lejos mejor.

3. En cualquier trabajo u obra, el que no ayuda estorba.

a. *In any kind of work or undertaking, he who doesn't help is in the way.*

b. *Mothers-in-law, lawyers, and doctors: The farther away they are, the better.*

c. *He who rises late spends the whole day running.*

406 Capítulo 10

Colaborar

10-60 **¡Prepárese para la entrevista!** Tú y tu compañero(a) de clase trabajan en el centro de orientación vocacional. Su jefe les ha pedido que terminen de escribir la siguiente hoja informativa. Completen los últimos cuatro consejos con el mandato formal. Luego compartan sus oraciones con otros estudiantes.

¡Prepárese para la entrevista!

La entrevista es un paso fundamental para hacer saber que Ud. es el candidato ideal para el puesto. Aquí tiene Ud. algunos consejos importantes.

Lo que debe hacer:

- Lea sobre la empresa que lo (la) está entrevistando. Aprenda el nombre de la persona que lo (la) va a entrevistar y cómo pronunciarlo correctamente.

- Es muy importante proyectar una imagen de profesionalismo. Vístase bien. Si es hombre, aféitese; y si es mujer, péinese el pelo hacia atrás.

- _____

Lo que no debe hacer:

- _____
- _____
- _____

© Cengage Learning 2016

Clase

10-61 **Una reunión de exalumnos.** Es el año 2025 y Uds. están en una reunión de exalumnos. Circulen por el salón para conversar con sus viejos compañeros de clase. Deben hacer lo siguiente:

- Saludar a los viejos compañeros. (**Hola, Sammy. ¡Hace muchos años que no nos vemos! ¿Qué hay de nuevo en tu vida?**)

- Intercambiar información sobre el trabajo. (**¿Dónde trabajas ahora? ¿En qué consiste tu trabajo? ¿Te gusta? etcétera**)

- Decirle una buena o mala noticia a por lo menos dos personas. (**Mi esposa va a tener un bebé en abril; Me van a dar un aumento de sueldo el próximo año; Mi papá está muy enfermo; etcétera**)

- Decirle un chisme _(piece of gossip)_ sobre un(a) compañero(a) a por lo menos una persona. (**¿Has oído la noticia? La esposa de Sammy va a tener un bebé.**)

- Reaccionar a las noticias de tus compañeros. (**Es triste que..., Es estupendo que..., Estoy seguro(a) de que..., Dudo que...**)

VOCABULARIO

RECURSOS

Para aprender mejor
One of the best ways to learn new words is to use them in sentences, because this gives them context. As you study the following words, put each one in a sentence. For example: **Mi mayor aspiración es ser cirujano**.

Sustantivos

la aspiración *aspiration, wish*
el asunto (legal) *(legal) issue*
el aumento (de sueldo) *(salary) increase*
la beca *scholarship*
el beneficio *benefit*
el campo *field*
la capacidad *ability*
la carta de recomendación *letter of recommendation*
el centro de orientación vocacional *career center*
la copia *copy*
el currículum *curriculum vitae*
los datos *data*
el edificio *building*
el (la) empleado(a) *employee*
el empleo *employment*
la empresa *firm*
el (la) empresario(a) *entrepreneur*
la entrevista *interview*
la escuela *school*
el éxito *success*
la experiencia *experience*
el extranjero *abroad*
el (la) gerente *manager*
el gobierno *government*
la investigación *research*
el (la) jefe(a) *boss*
el negocio *business*
el nivel *level*
la oferta *offer*
la pasantía *internship*
la posibilidad *possibility*
el postgrado *graduate degree*
la profesión *profession*
el proyecto *project*
el público *public; audience*

el puesto *position; job*
el punto fuerte *strength*
la referencia *reference*
las relaciones internacionales *international relations*
el requisito *requirement*
la responsabilidad *responsibility*
el salario *salary*
el seguro médico *health insurance*
el servicio público *public service*
la solicitud *application*
el sueño *dream*
la tecnología *technology*
la vocación *vocation*
el (la) voluntario(a) *volunteer*

Verbos

analizar *to analyze*
arreglar *to fix*
atender (ie) *to look after, to attend to*
avisar *to let know*
ayudar al prójimo *to help others*
casarse *to get married*
conseguir (i) *to get*
contratar *to hire*
convencer *to persuade*
dedicarse *to dedicate oneself to; to do*
diseñar *to design*
dudar *to doubt*
enseñar *to teach*
ganar dinero *to make / to earn money*
graduarse *to graduate*
hacer investigaciones *to research*
informar *to inform*
llenar *to fill (out)*

manejar *to manage*
realizar *to achieve*
resolver (ue) *to solve*
solicitar *to apply for*
soñar (ue) con *to dream about*
sorprender *to surprise; to be surprised*
tener éxito *to succeed, to be successful*
vender *to sell*

Adjetivos

a corto plazo *short-term*
a largo plazo *long-term*
competitivo(a) *competitive*
creativo(a) *creative*
disponible *available*
dispuesto(a) *willing*
emprendedor(a) *enterprising*
flexible *flexible*
interesado(a) *interested*
medio tiempo *half-time*
paciente *patient*
propio(a) *own*
rico(a) *rich, wealthy*
tiempo completo *full-time*
universitario(a) *university*

Frases útiles

Cómo no. *Of course.*
con suerte *with luck*
Ojalá que... *I hope that . . . , May . . .*

Professions, p. 373
Phrases to express feelings, pp. 386–387, 389
Phrases to express doubt and denial, p. 396
Phrases to express certainty, p. 399

Hacer turismo

Conexiones a la comunidad
Take virtual tours at sites such as **La Sagrada Familia visita virtual, Museo de Historia Mexicana recorrido virtual,** and **Chile turístico en 360**.

In this chapter you will . . .

- explore Chile
- talk about tourist destinations and activities
- describe hypothetical people, places, and things
- handle airport and car rental transactions

- talk about future events
- ask for and give directions
- learn about Pablo Neruda's poetry
- share information about a tourist attraction

NUESTRO MUNDO
Chile

Chile es un país de América del Sur. Es muy largo y estrecho *(narrow)*: tiene más de 4000 kilómetros de costa pero menos de 180 kilómetros de ancho *(wide)*.

República de Chile
Población: 17 400 000
Capital: Santiago
Moneda: el peso
Exportaciones: cobre *(copper)*, litio *(lithium)*, fruta, pescado

En el extremo sur de Chile, donde las temperaturas son muy bajas y la precipitación bastante alta, hay un gran número de glaciares. El glaciar más grande se llama Pío XI. Es tan grande como la ciudad de Santiago y tiene una característica única: cada día crece *(it grows)* aproximadamente 50 metros. Su atracción turística es obvia: ¡es espectacular!

Sociología

Los mapuches son el grupo indígena más grande de Chile. También son los que ofrecieron mayor resistencia a los conquistadores españoles. Hasta el día de hoy, los mapuches participan en demostraciones para demandar su autonomía.

Economía

Chile es uno de los mayores productores de uvas del mundo. Cuando es invierno en Estados Unidos, es verano en Chile. Durante esa época Chile exporta uvas y otras frutas como manzanas, nectarinas y arándanos *(blueberries)*. Chile también exporta un producto hecho de las uvas: el vino.

Ciencias

Científicos de Chile y otros países construyeron un Centro de Investigación Luna-Marte en el desierto de Atacama para simular una colonia en el planeta Marte *(Mars)*. El desierto de Atacama es el lugar ideal para esta base porque tiene condiciones similares a las de Marte: temperaturas extremas, cero precipitación y vientos fuertes.

11-1 **¿Qué sabes?** Contesta las preguntas con la información correcta.

1. ¿Cuál es la población de Chile? ¿Cuál es la capital?

2. ¿Qué productos exporta Chile? ¿Por qué los países en el hemisferio norte importan frutas de Chile?

3. ¿Dónde está el Glaciar Pío XI? ¿Qué tiene de especial?

4. ¿Cuál es la comunidad indígena más grande de Chile? ¿Crees que muchos de ellos quieren asimilarse a la sociedad de Chile o no? ¿Por qué?

5. ¿Dónde está el Centro de Investigación Luna–Marte? ¿Por qué los científicos escogieron este lugar?

6. Al observar las fotos en estas páginas, ¿cómo describes la geografía de Chile?

11-2 **Videomundo.** Después de ver el video sobre Santiago, describe los siguientes lugares: la Alameda, la Plaza de Armas, el Mercado Central, el Parque Metropolitano.

Destinos turísticos

Explorando el país

Al **norte** de Chile, **se encuentra** el **desierto** de Atacama, el más **seco** del mundo. Aquí, el cielo es muy **claro** y por eso es un lugar perfecto para **observar las estrellas**.

Santiago, **ubicado** en el **valle central** del **país**, es la **sede del gobierno**. Los **cerros** del Parque Metropolitano ofrecen una **vista panorámica** de esta ciudad.

In this *Paso*, you will . . .

- describe the geography of various regions
- exchange information about tourist destinations
- describe hypothetical people, places, and things

Los puntos cardinales	*Cardinal directions*
el norte	*north*
el sur	*south*
el este	*east*
el oeste	*west*

La geografía	*Geography*
el bosque tropical / lluvioso	*tropical forest / rainforest*
el campo	*country (rural area)*
el cañón	*canyon*
la cordillera	*(mountain) range*
el glaciar	*glacier*
el río	*river*

El clima	*Climate*
El clima es...	*The climate is . . .*
cálido / frío	*hot / cold*
seco / húmedo	*dry / humid*
templado	*mild*

Explorando el país (cont.)

El **sur** de Chile se caracteriza por **bosques**, **volcanes** y **lagos**. Sus **magníficos paisajes atraen** a turistas que disfrutan de la **naturaleza**.

Rapa Nui es una **isla** pequeña en medio del **océano** Pacífico. Es conocida por sus **enigmáticas estatuas** o *moáis*.

Actividades	*Activities*
hacer caminatas	*to hike, to go hiking*
hacer escalada en roca	*to go rock climbing*
hacer rafting	*to go (white-water) rafting*
hacer snowboard	*to snowboard, to go snowboarding*
observar las ballenas	*to go whale-watching*
visitar...	*to visit . . .*
el acuario	*the aquarium*
el barrio histórico	*the historical neighborhood*
el castillo	*the castle*
el observatorio	*the observatory*
el parque zoológico	*the zoo*
las ruinas	*the ruins*

Preguntas sobre un destino turístico	*Questions about a tourist destination*
¿Dónde está ubicado?	*Where is it located?*
¿Cómo son la geografía y el clima?	*What are the geography and climate like?*
¿Cuáles son los atractivos principales?	*What are the main attractions?*
¿Cuándo es la temporada alta?	*When is peak season?*

PASO 1 VOCABULARIO

¡Aplícalo!

Colaborar

11-3 **La geografía.** ¿A qué categorías pertenecen *(belong)* estos lugares? Con un(a) compañero(a), escriban los términos geográficos en las columnas apropiadas.

cordillera   desierto   isla   lago   río   volcán

Misisipí	Andes	Galápagos	Sahara	Superior	Vesubio
Amazonas	Alpes	Hawái	Atacama	Erie	Etna
Nilo	Rocosas *(Rocky)*	Bora Bora	Mojave	Titicaca	Mauna Loa

Colaborar

11-4 **El Alcázar de Segovia.** Con un(a) compañero(a), lean el siguiente párrafo sobre el lugar en la foto. Hay que escoger las palabras correctas.

© Neirfy/Shutterstock

El edificio de la foto parece un auténtico (1. castillo / campo) de las películas de Disney. Se llama el Alcázar de Segovia y está (2. escalada / ubicado) sobre un (3. barrio / cerro) en la confluencia de los (4. ríos / paisajes) Eresma y Clamores. Fue residencia de los Reyes Católicos y ahora es (5. sede / caminata) del Archivo General Militar. Por supuesto, (6. oeste / atrae) a miles de turistas de todas partes del (7. mundo / bosque). Los turistas pueden subir a la Torre de Juan II y disfrutar de la (8. vista / estatua) panorámica de Segovia, una de las ciudades más bonitas y monumentales de España.

↻ Present perfect, **Capítulo 7 Paso 2**

Clase

11-5 **Colección de firmas.** Circula por el salón de clase para preguntar a tus compañeros si han hecho las siguientes actividades. Si alguien contesta "sí", pregunta "¿dónde?". Escribe la información y pide a la persona que firme. ¡Ojo! Tienes que conjugar el verbo en la forma **tú** del presente perfecto.

Modelo   **hacer** snowboard
    Estudiante A: ¿Has hecho snowboard alguna vez?
    Estudiante B: No, nunca he hecho snowboard. / Sí, he hecho snowboard varias veces.
    Estudiante A: Bueno, gracias. / ¿Ah sí? ¿Dónde lo has hecho?
    Estudiante B: En Aspen, Colorado.

Actividad	Lugar (¿Dónde?)	Firma
1. **hacer** rafting		
2. **visitar** un castillo		
3. **ir** a un acuario		
4. **ver** las estrellas desde un observatorio		
5. **dar** un paseo por un barrio histórico		
6. **observar** las ballenas		

11-6 **Mi lugar de nacimiento.** Usa las preguntas a continuación para entrevistar a tu compañero(a) de clase sobre su lugar de nacimiento *(birthplace)*.

1. ¿Dónde naciste *(were you born)*? ¿Dónde está ubicado?

2. ¿Cómo es el clima allí en primavera? ¿Y en otoño?

3. ¿Cómo es la geografía de tu ciudad natal *(hometown)*? ¿Hay un río cerca? ¿Cómo se llama?

4. ¿Cuál es el atractivo principal de ese lugar? ¿Qué más se puede visitar?

5. ¿Desde dónde se tiene una vista panorámica de la ciudad?

6. ¿Llegan turistas a tu ciudad natal *(hometown)*? ¿Cuál es la mejor temporada para visitar?

↻ Vacation activities, **Capítulo 4 Paso 1**

 11-7 **Mis experiencias turísticas.** Para cada actividad, recomienda a tu compañero(a) un lugar que conoces. Describe el lugar con muchos detalles.

Modelo visitar el barrio histórico

Te recomiendo que visites el barrio histórico de Charleston, Carolina del Sur. Tiene hermosas casas históricas del siglo *(century)* diecinueve. También hay un mercado al aire libre y muchos restaurantes con comida típica.

1. ir en lancha	5. visitar el parque zoológico
2. pescar	6. montar a caballo
3. observar las estrellas	7. explorar las ruinas arqueológicas
4. hacer caminatas	8. esquiar (en el agua o en la nieve)

11-8 **Juego de adivinanzas.** Con un(a) compañero(a), jueguen este juego de adivinanzas *(guessing game)*. **Estudiante A** describe un destino turístico, ¡sin decir el nombre del lugar! **Estudiante B** hace unas preguntas y luego adivina qué lugar es. Usen los destinos en las fotos y otros originales.

Modelo **Estudiante A:** Este destino turístico está en el oeste de Estados Unidos. Es famoso por su géiser. Se puede hacer rafting y caminatas en el verano.

Estudiante B: ¿Es un parque nacional famoso?

Estudiante A: Sí.

Estudiante B: ¿Es el parque Yellowstone?

Estudiante A: ¡Correcto!

Machu Picchu, Perú

Cozumel, México

Gran Cañón, Estados Unidos

El Yunque, Puerto Rico

Las cláusulas adjetivales

PAUL	¿Adónde piensas ir en tus vacaciones, Selma?
SELMA	Voy a Iquique, donde viven mis tíos.
PAUL	Ah, sí. He oído hablar de Iquique. Es la ciudad que está cerca de los famosos géiseres, ¿verdad?
SELMA	Sí. Y también está cerca de los geoglifos, que son enormes dibujos de animales en los cerros.

■ ■ ■

Descúbrelo

■ Where is Selma going on vacation?

■ What can tourists do in that area of Chile?

■ When Selma first mentions Iquique, what extra information does she provide about the city? What word does she use to connect that information to the rest of the sentence?

■ How does Paul identify or describe the city of Iquique? What word does he use to connect that information to the rest of the sentence?

1. Adjectives such as **pequeño**, **inteligente**, and **lluvioso** are used to describe nouns (the names for people, places, and things). A noun can also be described by a clause—a group of words with a subject and a verb. When a clause functions as an adjective, it is known as a relative clause or an adjective clause (**cláusula adjetival**).

Adjective:	Rapa Nui es una isla **pequeña**.
	*Rapa Nui is a **small** island.*
Adjective clause:	Rapa Nui es una isla **que está ubicada en el océano Pacífico**.
	*Rapa Nui is an island **that is located in the Pacific Ocean**.*

2. An adjective (or relative) clause is linked to the main part of a sentence with a relative pronoun (**pronombre relativo**). In Spanish, **que** is the most common relative pronoun. The relative pronoun **que** can refer to people, places, and things; it is the Spanish equivalent of *who*, *that*, and *which*.

> José de San Martín es el líder militar **que luchó por la independencia de Chile**.
> *José de San Martín is the military leader **who fought for Chile's independence**.*

> Los vinos **que se producen en Chile** son mundialmente famosos.
> *The wines **that are produced in Chile** are world famous.*

3. The relative pronoun **quien(es)** refers only to people. It is used in two cases:

■ As an alternative to **que**, when the relative clause is set off by commas because it introduces parenthetical or non-essential information.

> Nuestro guía, **quien / que es de Santiago**, conoce Chile muy bien.
> *Our guide, **who is from Santiago**, knows Chile really well.*

■ After prepositions (**de**, **con**, **para**, **por**, **a**, etc.) (**Que** is not used in this case.)

> La persona **con quien debes hablar** es el Sr. Bernal.
> *The person **(whom) you should speak with** is Mr. Bernal. / The person **with whom you should speak** is Mr. Bernal.*

4. To refer to places, the relative pronoun **donde** is used to express *where*.

> La Zona Austral es una región **donde se puede hacer turismo de aventura**.
> *The Zona Austral is a region **where you can engage in adventure tourism**.*

11-9 **¿Cómo se llaman?** ¿Cómo se llaman los lugares, los objetos y las personas mencionadas en el artículo? Con un(a) compañero(a) de clase, lean el artículo y luego contesten las preguntas.

1. ¿Qué nombres tiene la isla de Chile que está en la Polinesia?

2. ¿Cómo se llama la persona europea que hizo el primer contacto con la isla en 1722?

3. ¿Cómo se llaman las estatuas que se encuentran en la isla?

4. ¿Cómo se llaman las plataformas donde descansan las estatuas?

5. ¿Cómo se llama el festival que celebra las tradiciones ancestrales?

Un museo al aire libre

Uno de los museos al aire libre más fascinantes del mundo es la Isla de Pascua. Ubicado a unos 3700 km de Chile, en la Polinesia, este territorio chileno se considera la isla habitada más remota del planeta. Su antiguo nombre polinesio era Te Pito O Te Henua, que significa *el centro del mundo*. Hoy se conoce como Rapa Nui y también como Isla de Pascua: nombre que le dio el explorador Jacob Roggeveen cuando llegó a la isla el Domingo de Pascua del año 1722.

Los objetos arqueológicos más famosos de la isla son los moáis, unas figuras gigantes hechas de roca volcánica. Hay cientos de estas estatuas sobre plataformas ceremoniales llamadas ahus. La isla también cuenta con ruinas y petroglifos que hablan de una antigua y compleja cultura.

Otra atracción es el festival Tapati Rapa Nui, que se celebra cada febrero. Durante esta fiesta, se realizan ceremonias, danzas y la tradicional Haka Pei, una competencia en que unos hombres se deslizan[1] sobre los troncos[2] del árbol del banano desde el cerro Pu'i. ¡Es muy emocionante!

[1]*slide* [2]*trunks*

11-10 **El verano pasado.** Con un(a) compañero(a) de clase, combinen las oraciones usando un pronombre relativo apropiado: **que**, **quien(es)** o **donde**.

Modelo El verano pasado hicimos un recorrido. El recorrido duró dos semanas.
        El verano pasado hicimos un recorrido que duró dos semanas.

1. Empezamos el recorrido en la capital. En la capital hay un famoso barrio histórico.

2. Nos gustó mucho el barrio histórico. En el barrio histórico viven muchos artistas.

3. Luego fuimos a una playa. La playa está ubicada al sur del país.

4. Esta foto es de Ricardo y Alba. Conocimos a Ricardo y a Alba en un crucero.

5. El crucero nos llevó a una isla. En la isla hay muchos animales marinos.

6. Por último conocimos una zona arqueológica. La zona arqueológica es conocida por sus enigmáticas estatuas.

11-11 **En la playa.** Con un(a) compañero(a), observen este dibujo. Tomando turnos, una persona pide a la otra que señale *(point out)* a alguien en el dibujo, y la otra responde. Usen cláusulas adjetivales en las preguntas, como en el modelo.

Modelo **Estudiante A:** ¿Dónde está la chica que está pescando?

Estudiante B: *(señalando con el dedo)* Aquí está, en el velero. ¿Dónde está... ?

© Cengage Learning 2016

11-12 **Ciudades famosas.** En grupos de tres o cuatro personas, tomen turnos para describir una ciudad famosa. Los demás tienen que adivinar *(guess)* la ciudad. Usen pronombres relativos, como en el modelo.

Modelo **Estudiante A:** Es una ciudad donde se puede visitar el acuario más grande del mundo.

Estudiante B: No sé. Danos otra pista *(Give us another clue)*.

Estudiante A: Es una ciudad que está en el sur de Estados Unidos.

Estudiante C: ¿Atlanta?

11-13 **Circunlocución.** Con un(a) compañero(a), dramaticen escenas entre un(a) turista y un(a) dependiente(a) en una tienda. El (La) turista quiere comprar algo, pero no sabe el nombre del objeto; lo describe hasta que el (la) dependiente(a) lo identifica correctamente. ¡Ojo! El (La) turista tiene que usar una cláusula adjetival en cada descripción.

Modelo **Dependiente:** Buenas tardes. ¿En qué puedo servirle?

Turista: Quiero comprar algo pero no sé cómo se llama. Es una joya **que se pone en el dedo**.

Dependiente: ¿Un anillo?

> **Algunas cosas que hay en la tienda:** anteojos, billeteras, bolígrafos, calcetines, calendarios, carteles, cinturones, corbatas, cremas, cuchillos, espejos, globos, gorras, jarabes, joyas, lámparas, llaveros, memorias USB, relojes, servilletas, sudaderas, tarjetas

G PASO 1 GRAMÁTICA B

El presente de subjuntivo y las cláusulas adjetivales

FRANCISCA ¿Adónde quieres ir de vacaciones este año?

MIGUEL No sé. Prefiero ir a algún lugar donde yo pueda dormir mucho y relajarme. ¿Y tú?

FRANCISCA Yo quiero ir a una ciudad que tenga muchas actividades culturales, como la ópera.

MIGUEL ¡Buena idea! ¡La ópera siempre me da sueño *(makes me sleepy)*!

1. Adjective clauses, like adjectives, are used to describe people, places, and things. An adjective clause is connected to the main part of a sentence with the relative pronoun **que**, or sometimes with **quien(es)** or **donde**.

> El Valle Central es la región **que produce los vinos más famosos de Chile**.
> *The Central Valley is the region **that produces the most famous wines of Chile**.*

2. When an adjective clause describes people, places, or things that are specific or known to the speaker, the verb in the adjective clause is conjugated in the *present indicative*.

> ¡El guía **que trabaja para Turichile** habla tres lenguas!
> *The guide **that works for Turichile** speaks three languages!*

> El desierto de Atacama es el lugar **donde mejor se puede ver las estrellas**.
> *The Atacama Desert is the place **where you can best see the stars**.*

3. However, the *present subjunctive* must be used when the adjective clause refers to people, places, or things that are:

■ non-specific or hypothetical

> Queremos un guía **que hable inglés o francés**.
> *We want a guide **who speaks English or French**.*
> *(We don't have a particular person in mind; anyone who can speak these languages will do.)*

■ non-existent

> En esta agencia, no hay ningún guía **que hable japonés**.
> *In this agency there are no guides **who speak Japanese**.*
> *(Nobody with this skill works at the agency; the person does not exist.)*

■ ■ ■
Descúbrelo

■ What kind of place does Miguel want to visit for his vacation?

■ What kind of city does his wife want to go to?

■ Do Francisca and Miguel mention specific places that offer these activities?

■ When Miguel and Francisca describe these places, do they use the present indicative or the present subjunctive?

¡Aplícalo! Colaborar **11-14** **¿Adónde vamos?** Marisa y Lucía quieren ir a Chile de vacaciones pero ¿qué parte del país deben visitar? Con un(a) compañero(a), completen su conversación con el presente de indicativo o el presente de subjuntivo, según el contexto.

> **Nota cultural**
>
> In Chile, **hostales**, or hostels, are affordable alternatives to hotels. Some offer private rooms and others have shared rooms with bunk beds, but they all have shared common spaces, where travelers are encouraged to interact with one other.

LUCÍA ¿Por qué no vamos al norte de Chile para nuestras vacaciones? En el pueblo de La Serena hay un observatorio donde (1. se puede / se pueda) observar las estrellas. ¡Todos dicen que la vista es espectacular!

MARISA Y cerca de allí hay un museo de arqueología donde (2. se encuentran / se encuentren) unas de las momias *(mummies)* más antiguas del mundo. ¡Me encanta la idea de ir al norte!

LUCÍA Bueno, antes de decidir, tenemos que explorar las opciones. Tengo un amigo que (3. recomienda / recomiende) un viaje a la Patagonia.

MARISA ¿A la Patagonia? ¿Cómo es el clima allí? La verdad, no quiero ir a ningún lugar donde (4. hace / haga) mucho frío.

LUCÍA Bueno, según mi amigo, la Patagonia es la zona de Chile que (5. recibe / reciba) más nieve.

MARISA ¡Entonces no vamos a la Patagonia! Mira, francamente, no tengo mucho dinero. Quiero ir a algún lugar que (6. tiene / tenga) hoteles económicos.

LUCÍA Y yo prefiero un destino donde (7. hay / haya) también un poco de vida nocturna: clubs, restaurantes, cines.

MARISA Bueno, tenemos que seguir investigando. Quizás *(Perhaps)* podemos encontrar un tour que (8. ofrece / ofrezca) un poco de todo.

LUCÍA ¡Buena idea!

 11-15 **En mi próximo viaje.** ¿Con qué tipo de viaje sueñas tú? Trabaja con un(a) compañero(a) de clase para completar las oraciones con el presente de subjuntivo. Comparen sus respuestas.

Modelo Prefiero viajar con una persona que (**saber** hablar varios idiomas / **ser** divertida / **tener** mucho dinero).

Estudiante A: Prefiero viajar con una persona que **sepa** hablar varios idiomas. ¿Y tú?

Estudiante B: Yo prefiero viajar con una persona que **tenga** mucho dinero.

1. Quiero ir a algún lugar que (**ofrecer** turismo de aventura / **tener** museos y barrios históricos / **estar** cerca del mar).

2. Quiero viajar con una persona que (**ser** responsable / **ser** flexible / no **tener** miedo de las cosas nuevas).

3. Me interesa usar los medios de transporte que nos (**permitir** ver el paisaje / **ser** económicos / **poner** en contacto con la gente).

4. Prefiero los hoteles que (no **costar** mucho / **tener** piscina y gimnasio / **estar** en el corazón de la ciudad).

5. Quiero comer en restaurantes que (**servir** comida típica / **ofrecer** un buffet / **tener** música o karaoke).

¡Exprésate!

 11-16 **Pensando en el futuro.** ¿Cómo es tu vida ahora? ¿Qué sueños tienes para el futuro? Con un(a) compañero(a), completen las oraciones con el presente de indicativo o el presente de subjuntivo, según el contexto. Comparen sus respuestas.

Modelo Ahora tengo un(a) novio(a) que... **es divertido(a) pero poco responsable.** Quiero tener un(a) novio(a) que... **piense más en el futuro.** ¿Y tú?

1. Este semestre, vivo en (una residencia / un apartamento / una casa) que... El próximo año, quiero vivir en (una residencia / un apartamento / una casa) que...

2. Este semestre, vivo con un(a) compañero(a) que... El próximo año, espero vivir con un(a) compañero(a) que...

3. Ahora, sigo una dieta que... En el futuro, espero seguir una dieta que...

4. Ahora, mi familia y yo vivimos en una región donde... Algún día, espero vivir en una región donde...

5. Respecto al trabajo, algún día quiero un puesto que... No quiero ningún puesto que...

 11-17 **Nuestras sugerencias.** Tu universidad es muy buena pero... ¿qué sugerencias tienes para mejorar la vida académica y social de los estudiantes? Trabaja con un(a) compañero(a) para completar estas oraciones con el presente de subjuntivo y otras palabras lógicas. Comparen sus ideas.

1. Nuestra universidad debe ofrecer más clases que...

2. También es esencial tener más profesores que...

3. Nuestra biblioteca debe tener espacios *(spaces)* especiales donde...

4. También, necesitamos más restaurantes que...

5. En cuanto a los libros de texto, es importante tener una librería que...

 Colaborar **11-18** **Se busca.** Tú y tu compañero(a) son dueños *(owners)* de una agencia de viajes que organiza tours a Europa. Uds. necesitan contratar dos nuevos guías *(tour guides)*. ¿Qué tipo de persona buscan? ¿Qué características, conocimientos *(knowledge)* y destrezas *(skills)* deben tener los guías? Trabajen juntos para completar el anuncio en el presente de subjuntivo.

SE BUSCAN GUÍAS	
Empresa:	Eurotour
Puesto:	Guía Turístico Cultural
Descripción:	Los guías de Eurotour son responsables de organizar y llevar tours a Europa.
	Buscamos personas que _____
	También queremos contratar personas que _____
	_____
	y que _____

© Cengage Learning 2016

En el aeropuerto

In this *Paso*, you will . . .
- handle routine airport and car rental transactions
- talk about future events

En el mostrador de la aerolínea

¿Cuántas maletas quiere facturar?

Solo esta. También tengo un equipaje de mano.

Está bien. Se permite llevar a bordo dos piezas.

© imageBROKER / Alamy

Frases del (de la) pasajero(a)

Quisiera un asiento de pasillo / de ventanilla.
¿De qué puerta sale el vuelo (641)?
¿Cuánto se va a demorar el vuelo?
¿Dónde está el reclamo de equipaje?

Frases del (de la) agente

Aquí tiene la tarjeta de embarque.
Pase por el control de seguridad.
Necesita mostrar el documento de identidad / el pasaporte.
Después de recoger el equipaje, pase por la aduana.

Passenger's phrases

I'd like an aisle / a window seat.
Which gate does flight (641) leave from?
How long will the flight be delayed?
Where's baggage claim?

Airline representative's phrases

Here's your boarding pass.
Proceed through the security check.
You need to show your I.D. / passport.
After you pick up your luggage, proceed through customs.

En el alquiler de autos

Frases del (de la) cliente(a)

¿Cuáles son las tarifas?
¿Está incluido el seguro?
¿Dónde hay una gasolinera?
¿Cuál es el límite de velocidad en carretera?

Frases del (de la) agente

¿Me permite ver su permiso de conducir?
En caso de avería, llame a este número.
Aquí tiene la llave.
No se olvide de llenar el tanque de gasolina.

Customer's phrases

What are the rates?
Is the insurance included?
Where's a gas station?
What's the highway speed limit?

Agent's phrases

May I see your driver's license?
In case of a breakdown, call this number.
Here's the key.
Don't forget to fill the gas tank.

PASO 2 VOCABULARIO

¡Aplícalo!

👤><👤
Colaborar

11-19 **Paso por paso.** Piensas hacer un viaje por avión a otro país. ¿En qué orden haces estas cosas? Con un(a) compañero(a), escriban los números del 1 al 10 para poner las actividades en el orden más lógico.

_____ Ir al reclamo de equipaje.

_____ Tomar un taxi de tu casa al aeropuerto.

_____ Leer durante el vuelo.

_____ Ir al mostrador de la aerolínea.

_____ Facturar el equipaje.

_____ Esperar el vuelo en la puerta.

_____ Pasar por la aduana.

_____ Salir del avión.

_____ Entrar al avión.

_____ Pasar por el control de seguridad.

👤><👤
Colaborar

11-20 **En el alquiler de autos.** Estás en un alquiler de autos. ¿Cómo responde el agente a tus preguntas? Con un(a) compañero(a), relacionen las dos columnas de una manera lógica.

Tú:

_____ 1. ¿Tienen Uds. un auto con cambio automático?

_____ 2. ¿Cuáles son las tarifas?

_____ 3. ¿Está incluido el seguro?

_____ 4. ¿Cuál es el límite de velocidad?

_____ 5. ¿Dónde hay una gasolinera?

El agente:

a. Hay una en la esquina.

b. Sí, pero es más caro que uno con cambio manual.

c. Sí, está incluido en la tarifa.

d. Depende del modelo. El económico se alquila por $50 por día.

e. En la ciudad, se puede conducir a 50 kilómetros (30 millas) por hora.

Telling time, **Capítulo 2 Paso 2**

👤👤

11-21 **¿Salimos a tiempo?** La preocupación universal de todos los pasajeros es esta: ¿Vamos a salir a tiempo? Con un(a) compañero(a), sigan el modelo y preparen cuatro conversaciones.

Modelo

Pasajero(a): Disculpe, ¿de qué puerta sale el vuelo (616)?

Agente: De la puerta (22).

Pasajero(a): ¿El vuelo va a salir a tiempo?

Agente: Sí, el vuelo va a salir a las (9:15). / Lo siento, pero se va a demorar. Va a salir a las (10:15).

SALIDAS ✈		ALFALÍNEAS		
VUELO	DESTINO	HORA	PUERTA	ESTADO
216	CONCEPCIÓN	09:55	30	A TIEMPO
306	PUNTA ARENAS	10:45	27	DEMORADO 11:20
875	ARICA	11:15	35	DEMORADO 13:30
735	LA SERENA	12:30	31	A TIEMPO
562	ANTOFAGASTA	13:05	23	DEMORADO 14:15
416	CONCEPCIÓN	14:20	29	DEMORADO 14:45

© Cengage Learning 2016

¡Exprésate!

👤×👤
Colaborar

11-22 **Para alquilar un auto.** Acabas de llegar al aeropuerto y ahora necesitas alquilar un auto por una semana. Trabaja con un(a) compañero(a) para completar esta conversación con palabras, frases y oraciones lógicas.

CLIENTE Buenas tardes. Quisiera (1) _____.

AGENTE Muy bien, señor (señorita). ¿Qué tipo de auto prefiere Ud.? ¿Con cambio (2) _____?

CLIENTE Bueno, quiero (3) _____. ¿Cuál es la tarifa?

AGENTE Para un auto con / de (4) _____, la tarifa es de $300 por semana.

CLIENTE ¿Está incluido (5) _____?

AGENTE Sí, está incluido. ¿Me permite (6) _____?

CLIENTE Aquí lo tiene. Eh... ¿Cuál es (7) _____?

AGENTE En la carretera, 120 kilómetros por hora. A propósito *(By the way)*, ofrecemos un servicio especial con todos nuestros autos. Llame a este número (8) _____.

CLIENTE Gracias. Tengo una pregunta más. Antes de devolver el auto, quiero llenar el tanque. (9) ¿_____?

AGENTE Hay una a la entrada del aeropuerto. ¡Que tenga buen viaje!

👤👤 **11-23** **En el aeropuerto.** Estás estudiando en Chile y decides hacer un viaje por avión a Argentina. Con tu compañero(a), dramaticen estas escenas en el aeropuerto.

1. en el mostrador

2. en la puerta

3. al llegar

👤×👤
Colaborar

11-24 **Consejos.** Julia, una amiga chilena, viene a Estados Unidos para conocer el país. Es su primer viaje al extranjero y tiene muchas preguntas. Con un(a) compañero(a), contesten sus preguntas con información detallada.

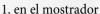

¿Cuántas maletas debo llevar?

¿Qué documentos necesito?

¿Cuál es la tarifa para alquilar un auto pequeño?

¿Puedo llevar mi computadora portátil a bordo?

¿Es mejor viajar por tren o alquilar un auto?

¿Cuál es el límite de velocidad en la carretera?

¿Cómo es el control de seguridad en el aeropuerto?

¿Tengo que pasar por la aduana?

PASO 2 GRAMÁTICA A

El futuro: los verbos regulares

TURISTA ¿Qué está programado para mañana?

GUÍA El tour a Valdivia. Por la mañana visitaremos el Barrio Histórico y el Mercado Municipal. Luego comeremos en uno de los restaurantes cerca del mercado. Después de almorzar, Uds. estarán libres *(free)* para hacer lo que quieran *(whatever you want)*.

TURISTA ¡Maravilloso!

■■■ Descúbrelo

- What will the tourists do tomorrow morning? And in the afternoon?

- In the tour guide's description of Valdivia, which Spanish verb forms correspond to *we will visit* and *we will eat*? Is there any difference in the endings for these **-ar** and **-er** verbs?

- Look at the verb forms **vistaremos**, **comeremos**, and **estarán**. What part of the infinitive are these endings attached to?

1. The future tense (**el futuro**) describes what somebody will do or what will take place in the future. As you see in the examples, the English word *will* is not translated; instead, the idea of future time is expressed through the future tense verb endings.

> Su tour **empezará** con una visita a la Plaza Mayor. Luego, **visitaremos** un museo de arte.
> *Your tour **will begin** with a visit to the Plaza Mayor. Next, **we will visit** the art museum.*

2. To form the future tense of regular verbs, add the endings to the entire infinitive. Notice that the same set of endings is used for **-ar**, **-er**, and **-ir** verbs.

> TURISTA ¿Cómo **viajaremos** a la isla de Chiloé?
> *How **will we travel** to Chiloé Island?*
> GUÍA **Iremos** en avión porque está muy lejos.
> *We'll go by plane because it is very far away.*

El futuro de los verbos regulares				
		viajar *to travel*	volver *to return*	ir *to go*
yo	-é	viajaré	volveré	iré
tú	-ás	viajarás	volverás	irás
Ud./él/ella	-á	viajará	volverá	irá
nosotros(as)	-emos	viajaremos	volveremos	iremos
vosotros(as)	-éis	viajaréis	volveréis	iréis
Uds./ellos/ellas	-án	viajarán	volverán	irán

👤×👤 **11-25** **El blog de Amanda.** Con un(a) compañero(a), completen el blog de
Colaborar Amanda con el futuro de los verbos más lógicos entre paréntesis.

```
◀▶ ⊙ C ✕ ⌂        www.uni.cl/blogs/amanda              ▾ ⌕
      Inicio            Sobre mí           Blogs            Archivo        ▾
                                            [            ] [Buscar]
```

Estoy muy emocionada porque mi amigo Santiago y yo vamos de excursión. Primero,
Santiago (1. pasar / volver) _____ por mi casa temprano por la mañana. Nosotros
(2. tomar / conducir) _____ por la carretera A76 hacia el norte. Después de dos
horas, mi amigo y yo (3. alquilar / llegar) _____ a nuestro destino en la cordillera.
Allí nosotros (4. dar / caminar) _____ un paseo por el centro del pueblo para
explorar un poco ese lugar. Más tarde, nosotros (5. comer / beber) _____ en uno
de los restaurantes típicos. A Santiago le interesan los museos más que a mí. Así que, por
la tarde, él (6. comprar / visitar) _____ el pequeño museo del pueblo. Pero yo
(7. acostarme / sentarse) _____ en un café y (8. ver / oír) _____ pasar
a la gente. Más tarde, Santiago y yo (9. ir / ser) _____ de compras a las tiendas de
artesanía. Por último, nosotros (10. volver / mostrar) _____ a casa.

👤👤👤 **11-26** **¡Hay mucho que hacer!** ¿Qué piensan hacer todos durante las
vacaciones? Trabaja con dos o tres compañeros(as) para describir los planes con la
información en las columnas. Hay que usar el futuro y seguir el modelo.

Modelo **Estudiante A:** *(Escoge un sujeto de la columna A)* Mis amigos y yo...

Estudiante B: *(Escoge y conjuga un verbo de la columna B)* Mis amigos y yo
observaremos...

Estudiante C: *(Escoge una expresión lógica de la columna C)* Mis amigos y yo
observaremos las ballenas...

Estudiante D/A: *(Escoge un lugar lógico de la columna D)* Mis amigos y yo
observaremos las ballenas en el mar.

A	B	C	D
yo	observar	las ruinas	en el mar
mis padres	visitar	la antigua catedral	en el barrio histórico
mis amigos y yo	explorar	las estrellas	en el acuario
mi mejor amigo(a)	recorrer	las ballenas	en el observatorio
tú	ver	el barrio histórico	de la capital
Uds.	conocer	los peces y los delfines	en la zona arqueológica

👤👤 **11-27** **¿Cómo será el día?** ¿Qué piensas hacer el resto del día? Trabaja con
un(a) compañero(a) y entrevístense con estas preguntas.

1. ¿Adónde irás después de la clase de español?

2. ¿Cuánto tiempo estudiarás esta noche?

3. ¿Verás televisión para relajarte? ¿Qué programas?

4. ¿Escribirás en Facebook antes de acostarte?

5. ¿Dónde comerás? ¿Con quiénes?

6. ¿Jugarás algún deporte? ¿Cuál?

7. ¿Hablarás con tu familia? ¿Con tu novio(a)?

8. ¿A qué hora te acostarás?

¡Exprésate!

Colaborar

11-28 **El viaje de Claudia.** Con un(a) compañero(a), tomen turnos para describir los planes de Lisa para el próximo fin de semana largo.

Modelo **Estudiante A:** El viernes por la mañana, Lisa **dará un paseo en velero y...**

	el viernes	el sábado	el domingo
por la mañana			
por la tarde			
por la noche			

Illustrations © Cengage Learning 2016

11-29 **¿Cómo será diferente?** Tú y tu compañero(a) tienen que hacer predicciones para el futuro. ¿Cómo será diferente la vida en 25 años? Completen las oraciones en el tiempo futuro y comparen sus ideas.

1. Ahora mucha gente viaja por avión. En el futuro...
2. Ahora muchas personas conducen sus autos para llegar al trabajo. En el futuro...
3. Ahora muchas tiendas abren a las 10 y cierran a las 9. En el futuro...
4. Ahora el año escolar *(school year)* empieza en agosto o septiembre y termina en mayo o junio. En el futuro...
5. Ahora muchas personas mueren de cáncer o problemas cardíacos. En el futuro...

Colaborar

11-30 **El itinerario.** Imaginen que tú y tu compañero(a) trabajan para la Agencia Viaje y Sol. Contesten las preguntas de los señores Trotamundos con la información del anuncio. Usen el futuro en sus respuestas lo más posible.

Gran Tour de Guatemala
26 de junio – 2 de julio

Paquete incluye
- Boleto de ida y vuelta en Aerolíneas Avianca
- 7 días/6 noches de alojamiento en el Hotel Galgos (tres estrellas)
- Todas las habitaciones tienen aire acondicionado y baño privado; desayuno diario
- Visita de la ciudad con servicio de un guía profesional: Plaza Mayor, Palacio Nacional de la Cultura, Mercado de Artesanía, Jardín Botánico y más

Desde $1500
¡Hagan sus reservaciones hoy!

© Cengage Learning 2016

1. ¿Cuántos días pasaremos en Guatemala?
2. ¿Qué aerolínea tomaremos?
3. ¿Qué sitios de interés conoceremos en la ciudad?
4. ¿Quién nos llevará a los sitios de interés?
5. ¿De qué categoría será el hotel?
6. ¿Dónde desayunaremos?

El tiempo futuro: los verbos irregulares

MAMÁ	¡Está nevando mucho! ¿Qué harás si cancelan tu vuelo?
GONZALO	Tendré que alquilar un auto.
MAMÁ	Pero con esta nieve ¿podrás pasar por las montañas?
GONZALO	Sí, alquilaré un auto de doble tracción. No te preocupes, mamá.

1. As you have seen, the future tense (**el futuro**) describes what somebody will do or what will take place in the future.

> El vuelo **saldrá** a las nueve y **llegará** a las once y cuarto.
> *The flight **will leave** at 9 and (**will**) **arrive** at 11:15.*

2. A number of common verbs are irregular in the future tense. These verbs use the *same endings* as regular verbs, but the *stem* (or front part of the verb) is irregular.

> ¿Qué **harán** Uds. durante las próximas vacaciones?
> *What **will** you **do** on your next vacation?*

Infinitivo	Raíz *(Stem)*	Infinitivo	Raíz *(Stem)*
decir	**dir-**	salir	**saldr-**
hacer	**har-**	saber	**sabr-**
tener	**tendr-**	querer	**querr-**
poner	**pondr-**	poder	**podr-**
venir	**vendr-**		

El futuro de los verbos irregulares			
decir *to say, to tell*			
yo	dir**é**	nosotros(as)	dir**emos**
tú	dir**ás**	vosotros(as)	dir**éis**
Ud./él/ella	dir**á**	Uds./ellos/ellas	dir**án**

3. The future of **hay** *(there is / there are)* is **habrá** *(there will be)*. Both of these forms are derived from the infinitive **haber**.

> ¿**Habrá** una excursión por la mañana?
> *Will there be an excursion in the morning?*
>
> No, pero **habrá** una por la tarde.
> *No, but there will be one in the afternoon.*

Descúbrelo

- Why is Gonzalo's mother worried?
- What will Gonzalo have to do if the flight is canceled?
- What will he do to make sure he can drive through the mountains?
- What future tense verb forms in the conversation correspond to the infinitives **hacer**, **tener**, and **poder**? Are the future tense verb endings added to the infinitive in these cases?

PASO 2 GRAMÁTICA B

¡Aplícalo! Colaborar **11-31** **Agencia Eco-Cultural.** Tú y tu compañero(a) piensan hacer una excursión con la Agencia Eco-Cultural.

- Primero, identifiquen los verbos en el tiempo futuro en el artículo; den el infinitivo de cada uno. Por ejemplo: vendrá → venir.
- Luego, contesten las preguntas.

1. ¿Qué explica esta página web? ¿Qué se debe hacer después de salir del avión?
2. ¿Dónde estará el agente esperando? ¿Qué tendrá en su mano?
3. ¿Querrán Uds. hacer una excursión con Agencia Eco-Cultural? ¿Por qué?

http://www.ecocultural.com/es

| ¿Quiénes somos? | Bienvenida | Tours | Reserva en línea | Contacto |

¡Agencia Eco-Cultural le da la bienvenida!

Nuestro servicio empieza antes de que Ud. llegue al aeropuerto. Un miembro de nuestra agencia vendrá al aeropuerto temprano y confirmará el estado de su vuelo. Así usted podrá estar tranquilo: aun si el vuelo llega temprano, habrá alguien para recibirlo.

Cuando Ud. salga del avión, tendrá que pasar por migración y luego el reclamo de equipaje. Por último Ud. hará aduana. Esto tomará entre 30 y 45 minutos.

Después de pasar por la aduana, Ud. saldrá por una puerta grande a mano izquierda. Nuestro agente estará allí esperándolo. Ud. sabrá quién es porque tendrá un cartel con su nombre escrito. Muéstrele un documento de identidad y él lo llevará al hotel.

Agencia Eco-Cultural tiene más de 10 años de experiencia. Con nosotros, su llegada será fácil y tranquila.

 Colaborar **11-32** **Será diferente.** La familia Fujimoto fue de vacaciones a Puerto Rico pero no hizo muchas cosas. ¡El próximo año será diferente! Con tu compañero(a), digan qué harán diferente. Usen la forma del tiempo futuro para los verbos.

Modelo Los Fujimoto no compraron nada en Plaza Las Américas, pero el próximo año... **comprarán muchas cosas**.

1. La familia Fujimoto no quiso ir a la Bahía Bioluminiscente, pero el próximo año...
2. Midori y Keiko no vieron pájaros en el bosque lluvioso El Yunque, pero el próximo año...
3. Los padres no salieron de noche porque tenían miedo, pero el próximo año...
4. Doña Sumiko no hizo rafting en el río Guabo, pero el próximo año...
5. Nadie en la familia sabía bucear, pero el próximo año...
6. Keiko casi no fue a la playa porque no quería quemarse, pero el próximo año...
7. La familia no tenía ganas de visitar el Observatorio de Arecibo, pero el próximo año...

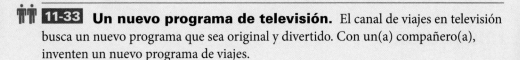

¡Exprésate!

© Radu Razvan/Shutterstock

11-33 **Un nuevo programa de televisión.** El canal de viajes en televisión busca un nuevo programa que sea original y divertido. Con un(a) compañero(a), inventen un nuevo programa de viajes.

- Usen las siguientes oraciones como guía para describir su programa.
- Luego, presenten su idea al resto de la clase. Sus compañeros votarán por el mejor programa.

Un nuevo programa de televisión para el canal de viajes

Nuestro programa se llamará...

El anfitrión (La anfitriona) será...

Cada semana, el anfitrión (la anfitriona) irá a... y...

Los televidentes[1] podrán...

Al final del show, el anfitrión (la anfitriona) dirá...

Para tener éxito, tendremos que...

Las personas querrán ver este programa porque...

---

[1]*TV viewers*

11-34 **¿Qué harán en el futuro?** Formen grupos pequeños y tomen turnos diciendo dos cosas que harán en el futuro y dos cosas que nunca harán en el futuro. Usen los verbos de la siguiente lista. Al final de cada turno, los compañeros deben expresar sus reacciones.

Modelo **Estudiante A:** En el futuro, yo tendré mi propio negocio y seré rico. Nunca me casaré y nunca tendré hijos.

Estudiante B: Yo también espero tener mi propio negocio.

Estudiante C: Yo dudo que nunca te cases.

casarse	dar	ir	salir	trabajar
conocer	estar	poder	ser	venir
conseguir	ganar	querer	tener	vivir
construir	hacer	saber		

11-35 **La visita.** Tu buen(a) amigo(a) viene a visitarte por tres días. Es la primera vez que viene a esta región del país. ¿Qué harán para divertirse? Cuéntale a tu compañero(a) de clase tus planes para cada día. Usa el tiempo futuro.

Modelo El primer día haremos un pequeño tour del campus por la mañana. Por la tarde, iremos al nuevo gimnasio y nadaremos. Por la noche...

1. El primer día...
2. El segundo día...
3. El tercer día...

Palabras útiles

hacer caminatas
salir a bailar
tener una fiesta
ir de compras
salir a comer

Indicaciones

In this *Paso*, you will . . .
- ask for and give directions in a city and in a rural area
- give instructions to others
- suggest group activities

En la ciudad

> Disculpe. ¿Cómo llego al Mercado Central?

> Tome la primera calle a la izquierda y camine tres cuadras.

© Michael Blann/Getty Images

Plano de Santiago

PUENTE PADRE HURTADO
PUENTE LA PAZ
PUENTE RECOLETA
RÍO MAPOCHO
PUENTE PATRONATO
PUENTE LORETO
CAL Y CANTO
SAN PABLO
MORANDÉ
BANDERA
ROSAS
DIAG. CERVANTES
ESMERALDA
STO. DOMINGO
SAN ANTONIO
MAC IVER
TEATINOS
CATEDRAL
MONJITAS
COMPAÑÍA
MIRAFLORES
AHUMADA
ESTADO
MERCED
SANTA LUCÍA
HUÉRFANOS

1. Estación Mapocho
2. Mercado Central
3. Mall del Centro
4. Iglesia de Santo Domingo
5. Casa de los Velasco
6. Museo de Bellas Artes
7. Parque Forestal
8. Palacio Edwards
9. Edificio ex Congreso Nacional
10. Catedral Metropolitana y Museo Arte Sagrado
11. Correo Central
12. Museo Histórico Nacional
13. Municipalidad de Santiago
14. Tribunales de Justicia
15. Museo Chileno de Arte Precolombino
16. Plaza de Armas
17. Casa Colorada
18. Basílica y Museo de la Merced
19. Cerro Santa Lucía

Para pedir indicaciones

¿Puede Ud. ayudarme? Busco...
Perdone. / Disculpe. ¿Dónde está... ?
¿Se puede ir a pie?
¿Pasa el autobús cerca de... ?

Para dar indicaciones

Siga derecho hasta llegar a...
Doble a la izquierda / a la derecha.
Tome la primera (segunda) calle a la izquierda.
Cruce la calle / la plaza.
Vaya a la esquina / unos cien metros.
No se puede perder.

To ask for directions

Can you help me? I'm looking for . . .
Excuse me. Where is . . . ?
Can I walk there (go on foot)?
Does the bus go near the . . . ?

To give directions

Go straight until you reach . . .
Turn left / right.
Take the first (second) street on your left.
Cross the street / the plaza (square).
Go to the corner / about 100 meters.
You can't get lost; You can't miss it.

En la carretera

¿Es este el camino a San Antonio?

Sí, va bien. Siga por esta ruta hacia el sur.

© Cultura/Seb Oliver/Getty Images

© Cengage Learning 2016

Preguntas del (de la) conductor(a)	Driver's questions
¿Por dónde se va para llegar a... ?	*How does one get to . . . ?*
¿A qué distancia está... ?	*How far away is . . . ?*
¿Cuánto se tarda en llegar?	*How long does it take to get there?*
¿Hay que pagar peaje?	*Does one have to pay a toll? / Is it a toll road?*
¿Dónde se puede estacionar?	*Where can one park?*

Para dar indicaciones	*To give directions*
Tome la ruta / la carretera (5) hacia (el norte).	*Take route / highway (5) heading (north).*
Siga los letreros.	*Follow the signs.*
Hay que tomar la salida (San Bernardo).	*You need to take the (San Bernardo) exit.*
Pasará por el puerto / un pueblo.	*You'll go by the port / a small town.*
Continúe hasta el semáforo / el puente.	*Continue until you reach the traffic light / the bridge.*
Está a unos (diez) kilómetros.	*It's about (ten) kilometers from here.*

¡Aplícalo!

© imageBROKER / Alamy

Colaborar **11-36** **Una excursión en auto.** Piensas hacer una excursión y pides indicaciones en el alquiler de autos. Trabajando con un(a) compañero(a), escojan las expresiones más lógicas entre paréntesis y lean la conversación en voz alta.

CLIENTE	¿Por dónde se va para (1. salir / llegar) al Parque Nacional?
AGENTE	Tome (2. el semáforo / la ruta) F-370 hacia el este y siga (3. los letreros / el peaje).
CLIENTE	¿A qué (4. carretera / distancia) está?
AGENTE	Está a unos 50 (5. kilómetros / centígrados).
CLIENTE	¿Cuánto (6. se tarda / se va) en llegar?
AGENTE	Más o menos una hora. No se puede (7. ver / perder).
CLIENTE	¿Qué (8. ciudad / salida) tengo que tomar?
AGENTE	La de San Antonio. Primero, pasará por (9. un puente / una esquina). Justo después, verá la salida.

11-37 **¿Cuál es el destino?** Tú y tu compañero(a) están en la esquina de la calle Huérfanos y el Paseo Ahumada en Santiago. Individualmente, tienen que leer y seguir las indicaciones. Hay que mirar el plano en la página 432 y empezar en la X. Escriban el destino en la tabla. ¿Quién llega a los destinos primero?

Destino #1: _____	**Destino #2:** _____	**Destino #3:** _____
Siga derecho por una cuadra y doble a la izquierda.	Siga derecho hasta llegar a la Plaza de Armas.	Siga por Ahumada y tome la segunda calle a la derecha.
Siga por esta calle y tome la primera calle a la derecha.	Cruce la plaza.	Camine cuatro cuadras y luego doble a la izquierda.
Vaya una cuadra más.	Ud. verá dos edificios grandes.	Continúe por esa calle hasta el final.
Está en la esquina.	El lugar que Ud. busca está a la derecha.	Está un poco lejos. Quizás debe tomar un taxi.

Colaborar **11-38** **¿Cómo llego?** Con un(a) compañero(a), completa las conversaciones entre un policía y varios turistas en Santiago.

1. TURISTA ¿_____?

   POLICÍA Sí, tome el bus 52. El acuario está en la quinta parada *(stop)*.

2. TURISTA ¿_____?

   POLICÍA ¿El Museo de Arte Precolombino? Está un poco lejos. Mejor tome un taxi.

3. TURISTA ¿_____?

   POLICÍA ¿A San Antonio? Tiene que tomar la ruta 5 hacia el sur y seguir los letreros.

4. TURISTA ¡Estoy perdido(a)! ¿_____?

   POLICÍA ¿A San Felipe? No, Ud. va mal. Hay que tomar la carretera F-68.

11-39 **Unas recomendaciones.** Tú y tu compañero(a) están estudiando en Santiago, Chile, y conocen la ciudad muy bien. Un día, mientras están en el centro, varios turistas les piden su ayuda. En cada caso, Uds. tienen que darles una recomendación y explicarles cómo llegar. Están en la X en el plano en la página 432.

Modelo Me interesa mucho la historia. ¿Qué museo debo visitar?

Ud. debe visitar el Museo Histórico Nacional. ¡Es un lugar fascinante! Siga derecho por Ahumada y camine unas dos cuadras. El museo está a la derecha, cerca del Correo Central.

1. Me encanta el arte, especialmente el arte precolombino. ¿Qué museo debo visitar?

2. Me interesa la arquitectura. ¿Hay iglesias de estilo colonial por aquí?

3. Quiero comprar algunos recuerdos de Chile. ¿Hay algún mercado por aquí?

11-40 **Por nuestro estado.** ¿Cuáles son algunos destinos populares en tu estado para pasar el fin de semana? Trabajando con un(a) compañero(a), contesten las preguntas de sus amigos Daniel y Carlos. Para las indicaciones, incluyan:

- la(s) carretera(s)
- uno o dos puntos de referencia *(landmarks)*, como puentes, pueblos, etcétera
- la salida de la carretera

Daniel y Carlos

11-41 **¡Estoy perdida!** Trabaja con un(a) compañero(a) para crear y dramatizar diálogos para las escenas.

1.

2.

3.

Los mandatos informales de *tú*

MARTA	No quiero enfermarme durante mi viaje. ¿Qué me aconsejas?
CAROLINA	Hay que tener mucho cuidado con las comidas. Come en restaurantes de aspecto limpio. Y no comas la comida de la calle.
MARTA	¿Y si me enfermo?
CAROLINA	En ese caso, ve a una farmacia y pídele consejos al farmacéutico.

■ ■ ■

Descúbrelo

- What is Marta worried about?

- According to Carolina, what should Marta be careful with?

- What verb form does Carolina use to tell her where to eat? To tell her where *not* to eat?

- How does Carolina phrase the advice to go to a pharmacy if she gets sick?

1. Informal commands are used to give instructions, directions, and advice to people whom you address as **tú**. This type of command has different forms for affirmative *(Do this)* and negative *(Don't do this)* commands.

To form the affirmative **tú** command of regular verbs, drop the **-s** from the **tú** form of the present indicative tense.

visitar →	visita~~s~~ →	**Visita** la catedral.	*Visit* the cathedral.
volver →	vuelve~~s~~ →	**Vuelve** enseguida.	*Come* right back.
pedir →	pide~~s~~ →	**Pide** un descuento.	*Ask for* a discount.

2. Many common verbs have irregular affirmative **tú** commands.

Infinitivo	Mandato *tú*	Infinitivo	Mandato *tú*
decir	**di**	salir	**sal**
hacer	**haz**	ser	**sé**
ir	**ve**	tener	**ten**
poner	**pon**	venir	**ven**

3. The negative **tú** command is identical to the **tú** form of the present subjunctive.

Present subjunctive:	No quiero que tú **conduzcas** por ese camino.
Negative *tú* command:	No **conduzcas** por ese camino.

4. The same irregular forms of the present subjunctive are used in the negative **tú** commands.

Infinitivo	Mandato negativo *tú*
dar	**no des**
estar	**no estés**
ir	**no vayas**
saber	**no sepas**
ser	**no seas**

5. Commands are often used with various kinds of pronouns, such as reflexive, direct object, or indirect object pronouns.

- Pronouns are attached to the ends of the affirmative commands. An accent mark is added to the stressed vowel when the new expression has more than two syllables: **¡Levántate!** *Get up!*

- Pronouns are placed in front of negative **tú** commands, between the **no** and the verb form: **No les des los boletos.** *Don't give them the tickets.*

Colaborar

11-42 **La seguridad.** ¿Qué precauciones necesitamos tomar para disfrutar de un viaje seguro *(safe)*? Con un(a) compañero(a), completen los consejos con los verbos más lógicos de la lista. Usen los mandatos informales de **tú**.

¡Aplícalo!

aprender	hacer	saber	tomar
cerrar	llevar	salir	usar
dejar	poner	tener	

¡(1) _____ precauciones para tener un viaje feliz!

En general, Chile es un país muy seguro para viajar. (2) _____ tu sentido común y no vas a tener ningún problema grave de seguridad.

- (3) _____ una fotocopia de tu pasaporte y (4) _____ el original en un lugar seguro.
- Al pasar por la aduana, (5) _____ cuidado con el equipaje.
- Siempre (6) _____ la habitación del hotel con llave cuando salgas.
- Si alquilas un auto, (7) _____ las normas de tráfico del país.
- Al estacionar el auto, no (8) _____ nada visible en el interior.
- No (9) _____ a caminar solo(a) por el centro de la ciudad en la noche.
- No (10) _____ cosas de valor en las excursiones a la playa.

Colaborar

11-43 **El primer viaje.** Tu amigo(a) va a hacer su primer viaje al extranjero y necesita tu ayuda. Con un(a) compañero(a), respondan a sus preguntas con consejos lógicos. Una persona debe usar un mandato afirmativo y la otra persona debe usar un mandato negativo.

Direct object pronouns, Capítulo 5 Paso 2

Modelo ¿Dónde pongo el pasaporte? ¿En la maleta?
Estudiante A: No, **no lo pongas** en la maleta.
Estudiante B: **Ponlo** en el equipaje de mano.

1. ¿Cuándo hago la reservación para el vuelo? ¿La semana antes del viaje?
2. ¿Dónde cambio el dinero? ¿En el aeropuerto?
3. ¿Cuánto les doy de propina a los camareros en los restaurantes? ¿El 5%?
4. ¿Cuándo visito los museos? ¿A mediodía?
5. ¿Dónde compro los recuerdos? ¿En la tienda del hotel?

11-44 **El ángel y el diablo.** Trabaja con dos compañeros(as). Tomando turnos, una persona lee una declaración (**No quiero estudiar esta noche.**); otra persona da un mandato informal del ángel (**¡Estudia mucho!**); y otra persona diferente da un mandato informal del diablo *(devil)* (**¡No estudies!**).

1. No quiero ir al dentista.
2. Tengo ganas de salir esta noche.
3. No quiero limpiar mi cuarto.
4. No quiero hacer la tarea de español.
5. Mañana quiero dormir hasta tarde.
6. Quiero mandar mensajes de texto durante clase.

11-45 **Consejos turísticos.** Un amigo de Chile hace turismo en tu estado. ¿Qué consejos le das? Con un(a) compañero(a) de clase, ofrezcan consejos turísticos con los mandatos informales de **tú**. Incluyan explicaciones para justificar sus consejos.

Modelo Me gustaría probar la comida típica de esta región.
Come en el restaurante Lizard's Thicket. Sirven comida muy típica de Carolina del Sur.

11-46 **Cuatro situaciones.** Trabaja con un(a) compañero(a) de clase. Para cada situación, escriban tres mandatos informales —dos afirmativos y uno negativo— que la persona en esa situación diría *(might say)*. Después, escojan **una** de las series de mandatos y léanla a la clase. La clase debe identificar a qué situación corresponde.

Situación 1: Un estudiante que se va de viaje por dos semanas le da instrucciones a su compañero de cuarto.

Situación 2: Un padre le da consejos a su hija, quien quiere viajar a Argentina pero no tiene dinero.

Situación 3: Un taxista le da instrucciones a un nuevo compañero de trabajo antes de prestarle el auto.

Situación 4: Una profesora de español le da consejos a un estudiante que viajará a México.

Los mandatos de *nosotros*

© Cengage Learning 2016

MAMÁ	¿Qué hacemos primero?
MIGUEL	¡Hagamos castillos en la arena *(sand)*!
ROSITA	¡Nademos en el mar!
ANA	¡Vamos al acuario!

1. The first person plural commands (**mandatos de *nosotros***) are used to express the notion *Let's do something.* They are created by using the **nosotros** form of the present subjunctive. Both the affirmative (*Let's . . .*) and the negative (*Let's not . . .*) command use the same form.

Affirmative:	**Comamos** en ese nuevo restaurante.	*Let's eat at that new restaurant.*
Negative:	**No comamos** en casa esta noche.	*Let's not eat at home tonight.*

2. The verb **ir** is the only exception to the previous rule. This verb has different forms for the affirmative and negative.

¡Vamos!	*Let's go!*	**¡No vayamos!** *Let's not go!*

3. When used with pronouns, **nosotros** commands follow the same general rules of placement as do other kinds of commands.

- Attach the pronoun to the end of an affirmative command. Add an accent mark to the ending: -**ámos** + *pronoun* or -**émos** + *pronoun.* For example: **¿El recuerdo? ¡Comprémos̱lo!**

- Place the pronoun in front of the verb in a negative command. For example: **¿El recuerdo? No ̱lo compremos.**

4. The pronouns **nos** and **se** follow special rules when used with affirmative **nosotros** commands.

- Drop the final -**s** of the command before attaching the reflexive pronoun **nos**.

  Levantemo~~s~~ + **nos** → ¡Levantémo**nos** temprano!   *Let's get up early!*

- Delete the final -**s** of the command before attaching **se**. This avoids creating a double *s*.

  Demo~~s~~ + **se** + lo   →   ¡Démo**se**lo!   *Let's give it to him!*

5. Another way to give a *let's* command is to use **Vamos + a + *infinitive*.** This alternate expression is used only for affirmative commands. For example: **¡Vamos a tomar el tour!** *(Let's take the tour!)*

■ ■ ■
Descúbrelo
- What does the mother want to know?
- What suggestions do the children offer?
- What verb forms do the children use to offer their ideas? What infinitive corresponds to each one?

PASO 3 GRAMÁTICA B

¡Aplícalo! Colaborar **11-47** **En el Zoológico Nacional.** En tu semestre en Santiago de Chile, trabajas de medio tiempo en un jardín infantil *(preschool)*. Hoy, los niños van de excursión al Zoológico Nacional. ¿Qué les dices? Trabaja con un(a) compañero(a) para completar los mandatos de **nosotros** con los verbos más lógicos de la lista.

| cruzar | decir | hacer | ir | lavarse | olvidarse | sentirse | tocar |

1. ¡_____ la calle con mucho cuidado!

2. _____ primero a la exhibición de flamingos.

3. No _____ de ver los animales nativos.

4. ¡No _____ los animales peligrosos *(dangerous)*!

5. _____ las manos antes de comer.

6. _____ adiós a los animales: ¡es hora de irnos!

↻ Direct object pronouns, **Capítulo 5 Paso 2**

 Colaborar **11-48** **Compañeros de viaje.** Tú y tu compañero(a) alquilaron un auto en Santiago de Chile. Tomen turnos haciendo y contestando las siguientes preguntas. En sus respuestas, usen los mandatos de **nosotros** y los pronombres apropiados.

Modelo **Estudiante A:** ¿Compramos un mapa de Chile?
Estudiante B: Sí, comprémoslo.

1. ¿Llenamos el tanque de gasolina ahora o después?
2. Hace calor. ¿Abrimos las ventanas?
3. ¿Tomamos la autopista para ir más rápido?
4. ¿Pagamos el peaje con monedas *(coins)*?
5. ¿A quién le pedimos direcciones?
6. Oye, ¿vamos a visitar el puerto?
7. Mira, esa persona hace dedo *(is hitchhiking)*. ¿La llevamos?

11-49 **¡Hagamos turismo en Chile!** ¿Qué quieren hacer tú y tus amigos en Chile? Con un(a) compañero(a) de clase, miren el mapa y tomen turnos haciendo sugerencias. Usen los mandatos de **nosotros**; sigan el modelo.

Frases útiles

¡Claro que sí! *Of course!*
Como quieras. *Whatever you want.*
De acuerdo. *Okay.*
¡Ni loco(a)! *No way!*

Modelo **Estudiante A:** Observemos las estrellas en el desierto de Atacama.
Estudiante B: ¡Buena idea!

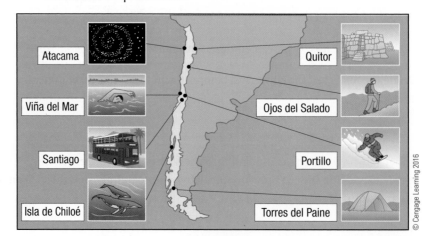

¡Exprésate!

 11-50 **Planes para el fin de semana.** Tomando turnos, una persona lee una pregunta, y la otra hace una sugerencia con un mandato de **nosotros.** Luego la primera persona reacciona de manera negativa.

Modelo   **Estudiante A:** ¿Dónde quieres comer esta noche?

Estudiante B: Comamos en Casa Linda.

Estudiante A: No tengo ganas de comer comida mexicana esta noche.

1. ¿Qué película quieres ver?
2. ¿Dónde quieres almorzar mañana?
3. ¿Dónde quieres ir de compras?
4. ¿Qué deporte quieres hacer el domingo?
5. ¿A quién quieres invitar a jugar Wii?
6. ¿Cuándo quieres estudiar?

11-51 **¿Qué hacemos?** Tú y tu compañero(a) van a pasar el día en Madrid, España. Lean la guía y usen mandatos de **nosotros** para dramatizar cinco breves conversaciones:

- Tomando turnos, una persona hace una sugerencia. Por ejemplo: **Visitemos el Museo del Prado.**

- La otra persona puede responder de forma positiva (**¡Buena idea!**) o puede ofrecer una alternativa (**No visitemos el Prado; es muy caro. Vamos al Parque del Retiro.**).

GUÍA TURÍSTICA DE MADRID

Palacio Real
Residencia oficial de la Familia Real Española
Abierto de 9:30 a 18:00
8,00 euros

Museo del Prado
Famoso museo de arte
Abierto de 9:00 a 20:00
8,00 euros

Parque del Retiro
Contiene un lago donde se puede pasear en bote, también hay cafeterías y músicos callejeros
Abierto de 6:00 a 22:00
Alquiler de botes:
4,55 euros

Estadio Santiago Bernabeu
Visita guiada del estadio de fútbol
Horario: 10:30 a 18:30
20,34 euros

Madrid Snowzone
Pista de esquí cubierta con nieve artifical
Abierto de 10:00 a 22:00
1 hora: 19 euros

Parque de Atracciones
Atracciones mecánicas como el Abismo y el Tornado
Horario varía
Entrada: 29,90 euros

Sala Contraclub
Espectáculo de flamenco
A las 22:30
10 euros

Teatro Kapital
Discoteca de siete pisos
Abierto de 24:00 a 7:00
12 euros

La Paella de la Reina
Restaurante estilo mediterráneo
Abierto de 13:30 a 16:00 y de 20:30 a 23:30
Precio aproximado:
30 euros

De Pata Negra
Restaurante de tapas
Abierto de 18:00 a 24:00
Precio menos de 15 euros

Pizzerría La Reginella
Pizzas y comida italiana
Abierto de 13:00 a 24:00
Entre 10 y 15 euros

© Cengage Learning 2016; Photo: © Rob Wilson/Shutterstock

11-52 **¿Quién es?** ¿Qué dicen las personas de la lista mientras hacen una excursión por la ciudad? Tomando turnos con dos o tres compañeros(as), un(a) estudiante escoge una persona de la lista y dice un mandato de **nosotros** afirmativo y uno negativo. Los miembros del grupo tienen que adivinar *(guess)* quién es.

Modelo   **Estudiante A:** No caminemos tan lejos. Regresemos al hotel.

Estudiante B: ¿Lo dice el padre cansado?

Estudiante A: ¡Sí!

Personas en la excursión

niña mimada	padre cansado	joven aventurera
guía estricto	conductor despistado	estudiante intelectual

CONECTADOS CON...

LA LITERATURA: POESÍA

Las odas de Neruda

Valparaíso, Chile

La cebolla, el gato, Walt Whitman, el color verde... estas son algunas de las temáticas de las odas del poeta Pablo Neruda (1904–1973). Las odas son composiciones poéticas en las cuales se expresa admiración por algo o alguien. Este gran poeta chileno escribió cientos de ellas.

Aunque escritas en forma sencilla, las odas de Neruda transmiten imágenes inesperadas *(unexpected)*. Su uso de metáforas, símiles y la personificación crea descripciones excepcionales. En "Oda a Valparaíso", por ejemplo, Neruda da características humanas a una ciudad muy querida *(beloved)* de Chile.

Estrategia: Keys to understanding poetry

Poems are better appreciated and understood if you use visualization. Poets use imagery, metaphors, similes, and personification to transmit meaning. As you read a poem, create a picture in your mind. Imagine what sights, sounds, and feelings are expressed through the various poetic techniques.

Palabras de poesía

la imagen	*image*
la metáfora	*metaphor*
la personificación	*personification*
la poesía	*poetry*
el símil	*simile*
la temática	*subject matter*
el verso	*line, verse*

11-53 Comprensión. ¿Comprendiste la oda de Neruda? Completa las oraciones.

1. Valparaíso es un (volcán / puerto / desierto).

2. Neruda compara los cerros de Valparaíso con (el pelo / el pecho / los pies) de una persona.

3. Para el poeta, Valparaíso es un (marinero *(sailor)* / cantante de ópera / hombre serio de negocios).

4. Para dar la impresión de que Valparaíso es una ciudad enérgica *(energetic)*, el poeta no usa (metáforas / oraciones / versos).

5. Después de leer el poema, sabemos que hubo (un tornado / una erupción volcánica / un terremoto *(earthquake)*) en Valparaíso.

6. El poeta indica que Valparaíso (queda destruido / sigue fuerte / sufrió mucho) después de ese desastre natural.

11-54 ¿Y tú? Trabajando en grupos pequeños, comenten estas preguntas.

1. ¿Les gusta la poesía? ¿Por qué sí o por qué no?

2. ¿Han leído antes un poema de Pablo Neruda? ¿Cuál?

3. ¿Por qué creen que Neruda escribió una oda a Valparaíso? ¿A qué lugar, objeto o persona escribirían Uds. una oda? Expliquen.

Oda a Valparaíso (extracto)

Valparaíso,
qué disparate[1]
eres,
qué loco,
puerto loco,
qué cabeza
con cerros,
desgreñada[2],
no acabas
de peinarte,
nunca
tuviste
tiempo de vestirte,
siempre
te sorprendió

la vida,
te despertó la muerte,
en camisa,
en largos calzoncillos[3]
con flecos[4] de colores,
desnudo[5]
con un nombre
tatuado en la barriga[6],
y con sombrero,
te agarró el terremoto[7],

[...]

el beso
del ancho mar colérico
que con toda su fuerza[8]

golpeándose[9] en tu piedra
no pudo
derribarte[10],
porque en tu pecho austral
están tatuadas
la lucha,
la esperanza,
la solidaridad
y la alegría
como anclas[11]
que resisten
las olas[12] de la tierra.

[1]*ridiculous* [2]*uncombed* [3]*underwear* [4]*fringes* [5]*naked* [6]*tattooed on your belly* [7]*the earthquake caught you off guard*
[8]*strength* [9]*striking, beating* [10]*knock you down* [11]*anchors* [12]*waves*

Pablo Neruda. Excerpt from "Oda a Valparaíso", ODAS ELEMENTALES. © Fundación Pablo Neruda, 2014. Used with permission.

Composición: Un blog

You regularly write a blog with suggestions and reflections on student life. In this week's entry you want to write about the perfect tourist destination for spring break (**las vacaciones de primavera**). Include information about its location, geography, climate, attractions, and activities. To end the blog, invite your readers to comment.

Revisión en pareja. Exchange papers with a classmate and edit each other's work.

- Does the blog contain interesting and detailed information? Write one positive comment and one suggestion for improvement.

- Are a variety of sentence types used? Indicate where related ideas could be combined to create more complex sentences.

- Are the verbs conjugated correctly? Circle any verbs that might be incorrect.

Estrategia
Using a variety of sentence types

- Simple sentence: Subject + (**no**) conjugated verb + other elements.

- Compound sentence: Simple sentence + **y** / **o** / **pero** / **porque** + simple sentence.

- Complex sentence: Simple sentence + **que** / **donde** / **quien** + simple sentence.

NUESTRA COMUNIDAD

11-55 **Nosotros / *Share It!*** En línea, subiste una descripción o un video sobre una atracción turística interesante. También viste las publicaciones de varios compañeros de clase. Ahora, trabaja con dos o tres compañeros(as); comenten sobre esas publicaciones y contesten las preguntas.

1. ¿Cuáles son algunas de las atracciones turísticas? ¿Dónde están ubicadas?
2. Describe la variedad de actividades representadas en las atracciones.
3. ¿Cuáles de las atracciones te gustaría visitar? ¿Qué te gustaría hacer allí?
4. ¿Quién hizo el video más atractivo? ¿Por qué te gusta?

11-56 **Perspectivas: Mi tierra.** En línea, miraste un video en el que tres estudiantes hablan de dónde nacieron y cómo es ese pueblo (esa región). ¿Qué dicen los estudiantes? Con tus compañeros de clase, comparen sus respuestas sobre el video. Después, entrevístense y contesten estas preguntas.

- ¿Dónde naciste *(were you born)*?
- ¿Dónde está ubicado ese lugar?
- ¿Cómo es la geografía allí?
- ¿Cómo es el clima allí?

11-57 **Exploración: El alquiler de autos.** En Internet, investigaste la posibilidad de alquilar un auto en Chile. Ahora, formen círculos de cuatro o cinco estudiantes. Tomen turnos describiendo con detalles los autos que quieren alquilar. Incluyan:

- Nombre de la agencia
- Modelo de auto
- Tarifa
- Otra información

11-58 **Conectados con... la literatura: poesía.** En línea, leíste un poema de Roque Dalton. Con dos o tres compañeros(as), compartan información de sus investigaciones sobre el poema de Whitman o sobre un(a) poeta hispanohablante, o compartan sus poemas originales.

> **Modelo**
>
> El poema de Whitman es una celebración... /
> Pablo Neruda fue un poeta chileno...

11-59 **¿Qué llevamos a la isla Robinson Crusoe?** Tú y tu compañero(a) van a hacer turismo en la isla Robinson Crusoe en el mes de diciembre. Tú (**Estudiante A**) y tu compañero(a) (**Estudiante B**) tienen dos páginas diferentes de una guía turística y dos listas diferentes. Hagan lo siguiente:

- Tomando turnos, una persona pregunta si necesita llevar algo de su lista.
- La otra persona consulta la información de la guía turística, responde a la pregunta y da una explicación.
- Continúen intercambiando información sobre todas las cosas en las listas. Pongan una ✓ al lado de cada cosa que deben llevar.

This is a pair activity for **Estudiante A** and **Estudiante B**.

If you are **Estudiante A**, use the information on this page.

If you are **Estudiante B**, turn to p. S-11 at the back of the book.

Modelo **Estudiante B:** ¿Tenemos que llevar pasaporte?

Estudiante A: ¡Sí! La isla Robinson Crusoe es parte de Chile y por eso necesitamos pasaporte. ¿Tenemos que llevar... ?

Estudiante A

Mi lista:

zapatos de vestir ☐   snowboard ☐   máscara y snórkel ☐
traje de baño ☐   palos de golf ☐   binoculares ☐

Isla Robinson Crusoe

DATOS GENERALES
La isla Robinson Crusoe forma parte del archipiélago Juan Fernández. Como indica su nombre, aquí vivió cuatro años el marinero Selkirk que inspiró la famosa novela. Hoy, hay cerca de 600 habitantes que viven de la pesca y el turismo.

Acceso: La isla Robinson Crusoe está ubicada a 400 millas de la costa de Chile. Durante los meses de enero y febrero hay vuelos diarios desde el aeropuerto de Santiago de Chile. El vuelo dura 2 o 3 horas. También se puede llegar por barco[1] desde el puerto de Valparaíso. El barco hace este viaje aproximadamente una vez por mes y tarda unas 40 horas.

Clima: El clima es subtropical húmedo. La temperatura media en las estaciones de primavera y verano es de 66ºF. En las estaciones de otoño e invierno llueve mucho y las temperaturas bajan a aproximadamente 45ºF. Es por eso que la temporada turística es entre octubre y abril.

Servicios: La isla tiene correo, teléfonos públicos, internet y televisión. No hay bancos ni cajeros automáticos ni tampoco se recibe pago con tarjeta de crédito. Tampoco hay farmacias pero en caso de emergencia hay una posta de salud.

[1]*boat*

© Cengage Learning 2016; Photo: © Svea Pietschmann / Alamy

SÍNTESIS

11-60 **Unas vacaciones magníficas.** Tú y tu compañero(a) acaban de volver de sus vacaciones. Usando las fotos y su imaginación, hablen de sus vacaciones. Incluyan la siguiente información:

- ¿Adónde fuiste? ¿Con quién?
- ¿Cuántos días pasaste allí?
- ¿Qué lugares visitaste? ¿Cómo eran?

- ¿Qué hiciste allí?
- ¿Pasó algo inesperado *(unexpected)*?
- ¿Te gustaría volver algún día? ¿Por qué?

Estudiante A:

México, D.F.

Estado de Hidalgo, México

Tula, México

Estudiante B:

El Chaltén, Argentina

La Hoya, Argentina

Buenos Aires, Argentina

11-61 **Situación: ¡Vamos de viaje!** ¿Estás preparado(a) para visitar un país donde se habla español? Con un(a) compañero(a), practiquen todas las situaciones básicas de un viaje. Primero, dramaticen cada situación. Más tarde, Uds. tendrán que

Clase representar una de las escenas para la clase; la clase va a adivinar *(guess)* cuál es.

Situaciones	Estudiante A	Estudiante B
1. En un hotel: conseguir una habitación	turista	recepcionista
2. En el alquiler de autos: conseguir un auto	empleado(a)	cliente(a)
3. En un restaurante: pedir una comida	cliente(a)	mesero(a)
4. En el mercado: regatear por unos recuerdos	vendedor(a)	turista
5. En el mostrador de la aerolínea: facturar el equipaje y escoger el asiento	pasajero(a)	agente

11-62 **Club de Viajes.** Tú y tus compañeros son socios *(members)* del Club de Viajes. En sus reuniones, los socios toman turnos para hacer pequeñas presentaciones, cada una sobre un destino turístico. ¡Hoy es día de reunión! Formen grupos de tres o cuatro personas. Cada persona tiene que hablar sobre un destino especial y el resto del grupo tiene que hacerle preguntas.

Incluyan esta información en las presentaciones:

- ¿Cuál es el destino?
- ¿Dónde está ubicado?
- ¿Cómo es la geografía?
- ¿Cómo es el clima?
- ¿Qué se puede hacer allí?
- ¿Por qué te gusta?

Pronunciación: El acento tónico

Colaborar Con un(a) compañero(a), presten atención al acento tónico *(stress)* y lean el chiste en voz alta.

© Motimo/Shutterstock

Una noche, el autobús iba por la carretera a toda velocidad. El chófer conducía de una forma realmente loca. Uno de los pasajeros tenía miedo y le dijo al ayudante *(assistant)*: "Por favor. Dígale al chófer que vaya más despacio. No tenemos prisa". Y el ayudante contestó: "¡Uy! ¡No, señor! Si lo despierto, ¡me mata *(he'll kill me)*!"

VOCABULARIO

RECURSOS

Sustantivos

el acuario *aquarium*

la aduana *customs*

la aerolínea *airline*

el (la) agente *(airline) representative*

el alquiler *rental*

el asiento de pasillo / de ventanilla *aisle / window seat*

el atractivo *attraction*

el auto *car*

la avería *breakdown*

el barrio histórico *historical neighborhood*

el bosque (tropical / lluvioso) *(tropical / rain) forest*

el cambio automático / manual *automatic / manual shift*

el camino *way*

el campo *country (rural area)*

el cañón *canyon*

la carretera *highway*

el castillo *castle*

el cerro *hill*

el clima *climate*

el (la) conductor(a) *driver*

el control de seguridad *security check*

la cordillera *(mountain) range*

el desierto *desert*

el destino turístico *tourist destination*

la doble tracción *four-wheel drive*

el documento de identidad *ID*

el equipaje (de mano) *(carry-on) luggage*

la esquina *corner*

la estatua *statue*

el este *east*

la estrella *star*

la gasolinera *gas station*

el glaciar *glacier*

las indicaciones *directions*

la isla *island*

el kilómetro *kilometer*

el lago *lake*

el letrero *sign*

el límite de velocidad *speed limit*

el metro *meter*

el mostrador *counter*

la naturaleza *nature*

el norte *north*

el observatorio *observatory*

el océano *ocean*

el oeste *west*

el país *country*

el paisaje *landscape, scenery*

el parque zoológico *zoo*

el (la) pasajero(a) *passenger*

el pasaporte *passport*

el peaje *toll*

el permiso de conducir *driver's license*

la pieza *piece; item*

el pueblo *small town*

el puente *bridge*

la puerta *gate*

el puerto *port*

el punto cardinal *cardinal direction*

el reclamo de equipaje *baggage claim*

el río *river*

las ruinas *ruins*

la ruta *route*

la salida *exit*

la sede *seat*

el seguro *insurance*

el semáforo *traffic light*

el sur *south*

el tanque de gasolina *gas tank*

la tarifa *rate*

la tarjeta de embarque *boarding pass*

la temporada alta *peak season*

el valle *valley*

la vista *view*

el volcán *volcano*

el vuelo *flight*

Verbos

alquilar *to rent*

atraer *to attract*

cruzar *to cross*

demorarse *to be delayed*

doblar *to turn*

encontrarse *to be located*

estacionar *to park*

facturar *check in*

hacer caminatas *to go hiking*

hacer escalada en roca *to go rock climbing*

hacer rafting *to go (white-water) rafting*

hacer snowboard *to snowboard*

observar las ballenas *to go whale-watching*

pasar *to pass; to proceed*

pasar cerca de / por *to go near / by*

perderse *to get lost*

seguir derecho *to go straight*

tardarse *to take long*

Adjetivos

cálido(a) *hot*

claro(a) *clear*

enigmático(a) *enigmatic*

húmedo(a) *humid*

incluído(a) *included*

magnífico(a) *magnificent*

panorámico(a) *panoramic*

principal *main*

seco(a) *dry*

templado(a) *mild*

ubicado(a) *located*

Frases útiles

a bordo *on board*

¿A qué distancia está(n)... ? *How far is (are) . . . ?*

en caso de *in case of*

¿Me permite... ? *May I . . . ?*

Relative pronouns, p. 416

¡Adelante!

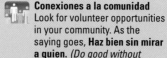

Conexiones a la comunidad
Look for volunteer opportunities in your community. As the saying goes, **Haz bien sin mirar a quien.** *(Do good without looking at whom.)*

In this chapter you will . . .

- explore the United States
- discuss study abroad and volunteer work
- talk about the news
- describe possible outcomes

- express emotion, doubt, and uncertainty
- discuss hypothetical and contrary-to-fact situations
- read a short story about migrant farm workers
- share past volunteer experiences

NUESTRO MUNDO

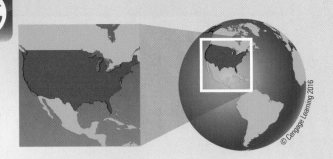

Estados Unidos

Estados Unidos es el segundo país del mundo con más hispanohablantes. Se prevé que para el año 2060, uno de cada tres residentes será hispano.

© Cengage Learning 2016

Estados Unidos de América (EE.UU.)
Población total: 316 000 000
Capital: Washington, D.C.
Moneda: el dólar
Exportaciones: productos agrícolas, químicos, automóviles, computadoras

Población hispana: 54 000 000
64% mexicanos
9% puertorriqueños
3,5% cubanos
3% dominicanos
20,5% otros

© Luis M. Alvarez/AI Images

Univisión es la principal cadena de televisión en español de Estados Unidos. Los programas más vistos son las telenovelas *(soap operas)*, los partidos de fútbol y las noticias *(news)*. En esta foto están Jorge Ramos y María Elena Salinas —dos de los hispanos más influyentes de Estados Unidos— que han presentado Noticiero Univisión desde 1987. Muchos hispanos miran este noticiero *(news program)* porque da muchas noticias de Latinoamérica y también presenta temas que afectan a la comunidad hispana, como la inmigración.

Historia

Cincuenta y cinco años antes de la llegada de los peregrinos *(pilgrims)* —en 1565— los españoles fundaron San Agustín, en Florida. Es la ciudad más antigua de Estados Unidos. Su mayor símbolo es el castillo San Marcos, construido para defender la ciudad contra los piratas como Sir Francis Drake.

Sociología

En la década de 1970 el gobierno de Estados Unidos empezó a usar el término **hispano** para referirse a las personas de origen de países de habla española. Muchas personas conocidas como **hispanas** —un grupo grande, diverso y multiétnico— prefieren llamarse mexicanos, salvadoreños, colombianos, etcétera. A otras les gusta llamarse **hispano** o **latino** porque promueve la unidad y ayuda a ganar poder político.

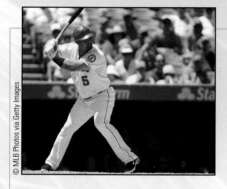

Deportes

El béisbol, pasatiempo nacional de Estados Unidos, refleja el cambio demográfico del país. Alrededor del 30% de los jugadores profesionales son de origen latinoamericano, la mayoría de República Dominicana y de Venezuela. Entre las superestrellas están Albert Pujols, Carlos González, Hanley Ramírez y Miguel Cabrera.

12-1 **¿Qué sabes?** Contesta las siguientes preguntas con tus opiniones y la información correcta.

1. ¿Crees que Estados Unidos es un país hispano? Explica.

2. ¿Quiénes presentan Noticiero Univisión? ¿Por qué es tan popular entre la comunidad latina?

3. ¿Cuál es la ciudad más antigua de EE.UU.? ¿Quiénes la fundaron? ¿Cuándo?

4. ¿Quién es **hispano**? ¿Qué otros términos se usan y por qué?

5. ¿Qué deporte de Estados Unidos tiene un porcentaje grande de jugadores latinos? ¿Cuáles son los países que producen más jugadores en las ligas americanas?

▶ **12-2** **Videomundo.** Después de mirar los videos de Nueva York, Miami y San Antonio, haz tres generalizaciones sobre la población latina en estas ciudades.

Estudiar en el extranjero

In this *Paso*, you will . . .
- discuss study abroad programs
- talk about indefinite or uncertain events

Un folleto

Centro de Idiomas A.C.E.
¡Aprende español en el extranjero!
• España   • Costa Rica   • Argentina

Cursos

- Español intensivo
- Lengua y cultura
- Música y danza
- Historia y arte

Alojamiento

- Familias anfitrionas
- Pisos compartidos
- Hostales y apartamentos
- Residencias estudiantiles

Ofrecemos instrucción personalizada en grupos con un máximo de 8 estudiantes.

Nuestras clases te dan la oportunidad de sumergirte en la cultura.

© Cengage Learning 2016. Photos: © Rido/Shutterstock; © tandem/Shutterstock

Para hablar de programas en el extranjero

Para elegir el mejor programa, es importante...
    comparar precios
    consultar con tu consejero(a) académico(a)
    tener en cuenta tus prioridades
Antes de viajar, es aconsejable...
    conseguir una visa estudiantil
    hacer un presupuesto
    informarse sobre las costumbres

To talk about study abroad programs

To choose the best program, it's important . . .
    to compare prices
    to consult with your academic advisor
    to take into account your priorities
Before traveling, it's advisable . . .
    to get a student visa
    to prepare a budget
    to find out about the customs

Durante la estadía

Para vivir la experiencia al máximo, intégrate a la rutina de la familia.

Para ser un(a) huésped considerado(a), conserva el agua y la electricidad.

Para hacer nuevas amistades, sé amable y cortés con todos.

Otros consejos

Es importante...
    evitar malentendidos culturales
    guardar los documentos en un lugar seguro
    respetar las normas de conducta
    saber dónde está la embajada / el consulado
    tener la mente abierta

Sentimientos comunes

Extraño mucho a (mi familia).
Me siento abrumado(a) / muy a gusto.
No me acostumbro a (la vida de aquí).

Other advice

It's important . . .
    to avoid cultural misunderstandings
    to keep your documents in a safe place
    to respect the norms of personal conduct
    to know where the embassy / consulate is
    to have an open mind

Common feelings

I miss (my family) very much.
I feel overwhelmed / at home.
I can't get used to (life here).

¡Aplícalo!

12-3 **Con el consejero académico.** Emilio está hablando con su consejero académico sobre la posibilidad de estudiar en el extranjero. Con un(a) compañero(a), completen la conversación con las palabras más lógicas.

EMILIO Profesor Darío, me encantaría estudiar en el (1. hostal / extranjero), pero no sé cómo (2. elegir / compartir) el mejor programa.

PROF. DARÍO Primero, hay que tener en cuenta tus (3. residencias / prioridades) respecto al destino, los cursos y el (4. visa / alojamiento).

EMILIO Siempre he soñado con estudiar en España. Me interesa un curso (5. intensivo / máximo) y prefiero vivir con una familia (6. anfitriona / estudiantil) para sumergirme en la cultura.

PROF. DARÍO En ese caso, ¿por qué no investigas el programa del Centro de Idiomas A.C.E.? Ofrecen instrucción (7. considerada / personalizada) con grupos pequeños. Y (8. el precio / la danza) por el curso intensivo es muy competitivo.

EMILIO Suena perfecto. Profesor, esta va a ser mi primera (9. embajada / experiencia) en el extranjero y quiero (10. evitar / acostumbrarse) malentendidos culturales. ¿Qué me aconseja?

PROF. DARÍO Lo más importante es tener la mente (11. considerada / abierta) y (12. respetar / conservar) las normas de conducta.

EMILIO ¿Me puede dar un ejemplo de una norma de conducta?

PROF. DARÍO Cómo no. Para ser un (13. consulado / huésped) considerado, no camines por la casa sin zapatos. Es (14. abrumado / aconsejable) que siempre observes e imites a los demás.

EMILIO Gracias, profesor. Creo que voy a sentirme muy (15. a gusto / a la vida).

12-4 **Las preferencias.** ¿A ti y a tu compañero(a) les gustaría estudiar en el extranjero? Tomando turnos, completen las oraciones oralmente para comparar sus preferencias.

1. Quiero estudiar en (España / Costa Rica / Argentina / ¿?). ¿Dónde quieres estudiar tú?

2. Prefiero tomar un curso (intensivo / de lengua y cultura / de música y danza / de historia y arte / ¿?). ¿Qué tipo de curso prefieres tú?

3. Me interesa vivir (con una familia anfitriona / en un hostal / en un piso compartido / en una residencia estudiantil). ¿Qué tipo de alojamiento prefieres tú?

4. Respecto a mis prioridades, para mí es importante encontrar un programa que (no sea muy caro / ofrezca la oportunidad de sumergirme en la cultura / esté en una ciudad grande / ¿?). ¿Qué es más importante para ti?

5. En cuanto a los documentos, (ya tengo / necesito conseguir) un pasaporte. ¿Y tú? ¿Ya tienes pasaporte?

¡Exprésate!

 Colaborar

12-5 **En Estados Unidos.** Tomás, un estudiante de España, quiere estudiar inglés en tu campus. ¿Qué debe saber él? Con un(a) compañero(a), hagan un resumen oral *(make an oral summary)* de la información esencial sobre cada punto.

- **El alojamiento:** ¿Qué opciones hay en su campus o cerca de su campus? ¿Cuál le recomiendan Uds. a Tomás?

- **El presupuesto:** ¿Cuánto dinero necesita para el alojamiento? ¿Para las comidas? ¿Para divertirse?

- **Para vivir la experiencia al máximo:** ¿Qué debe hacer para hacer nuevas amistades en su campus? ¿Adónde debe ir para conocer el estado? ¿Qué puede hacer para practicar el inglés?

> ↻ Giving advice,
> **Capítulo 6 Paso 3,**
> **Capítulo 9 Paso 1**

12-6 **¡Necesito tus consejos!** Estás estudiando en España y un(a) amigo(a) no se está acostumbrando a la vida del país. ¿Qué le dices? Con un(a) compañero(a), completen las conversaciones con sus recomendaciones.

Modelo **Estudiante A:** Mi mamá anfitriona insiste en que yo vuelva a casa a la una para almorzar, pero francamente, me gustaría quedarme en el instituto con mis amigos. ¿Qué hago?

Estudiante B: Para sumergirte en la cultura, tienes que integrarte a la rutina de tu familia anfitriona. Creo que debes volver a casa para almorzar con ellos, como la señora te pide.

1. Ayer, cuando miraba la tele en casa con mi familia, puse los pies encima de la mesita. Mi mamá anfitriona no me dijo nada, pero me miró de una manera rara *(strange)*. ¿Qué piensas tú? ¿Hice algo malo?

2. Mi hermano anfitrión me dijo que para recibir el Año Nuevo, todos comen doce uvas a la medianoche. ¡Qué locura! *(That's crazy!)*

3. ¡Extraño mucho a mi familia! Todas las noches paso horas hablando con ellos por Internet. Es que no tengo muchos amigos aquí. Es muy difícil hacer nuevas amistades. ¿Qué me aconsejas?

4. Esta mañana me duché y cuando salí del baño, 30 minutos más tarde, mis hermanos anfitriones parecían un poco enojados conmigo. ¿Qué pasa con ellos?

12-7 **Experiencias comunes.** Es difícil para muchos estudiantes acostumbrarse a la vida de otro país. Con un(a) compañero(a), dramaticen estas escenas de experiencias típicas. Una persona representa a la persona en el dibujo; la otra persona le da consejos para integrarse a la vida del país.

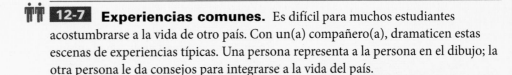

1. Daniel, con su familia mexicana

2. Elizabeth, en su residencia en Perú

3. Ty, en un club en España

Illustrations © Cengage Learning 2016

PASO 1 GRAMÁTICA A

El subjuntivo en las cláusulas adverbiales

MANUEL Hola, Rosario. ¿Adónde vas con tanta prisa?

ROSARIO ¡Hola, Manuel! Es que tengo una cita con mi consejero académico. Necesito hablar con él **para que** me explique las opciones para estudiar en el extranjero.

MANUEL ¿Estudiar en el extranjero? ¡Qué buena idea! Oye, **después de que** hables con él, ¿vamos al café **para** conversar? Me gustaría saber más sobre estas oportunidades.

■■■
Descúbrelo

- Why does Rosario need to meet with her advisor?

- What expression does Rosario use to introduce the reason for this meeting? Is this expression followed by the indicative or the subjunctive?

- When does Manuel want to meet with Rosario for coffee? Is the indicative or the subjunctive used following the phrase **después de que**?

1. Adverbial clauses (**las cláusulas adverbiales**) provide information about how, why, and when actions take place. These dependent clauses are introduced by special connectors called conjunctions (**las conjunciones**).

   > **Después de que** hables con tu consejero, ¿tomamos un café?
   > *After you talk with your advisor, why don't we go get some coffee?*

2. Some conjunctions always require the subjunctive in the adverbial clause.

   > Pienso estudiar en el extranjero **con tal de que me** <u>ofrezcan</u> **una beca**.
   > *I plan to study abroad **provided that I'm** <u>offered</u> (they offer me) a scholarship.*

Conjunciones que siempre se usan con el subjuntivo			
a menos que	*unless*	**en caso de que**	*in case*
antes de que	*before*	**para que**	*so that*
con tal (de) que	*provided that*	**sin que**	*without*

3. Other conjunctions, which refer to time, require the subjunctive in the adverbial clause only to refer to future actions or events.

   > Vas a aprender mucho **cuando** <u>estudies</u> **en Chile el próximo verano**.
   > *You're going to learn a lot **when you** <u>study</u> **in Chile next summer**.*

Conjunciones que se usan con el subjuntivo para hablar del futuro			
cuando	*when*	**hasta que**	*until*
después de que	*after*	**mientras**	*while*
en cuanto	*as soon as*	**tan pronto como**	*as soon as*

4. With a few conjunctions, the subjunctive is used only when the subjects in the main and dependent clauses are different. When the subjects are the same, the infinitive is used.

Two different subjects: Use the subjunctive	One subject: Drop *que* and use the infinitive
antes de que	**antes de**
Antes de que vayas a casa, ¿almorzamos?	**Antes de** ir a casa, quiero almorzar.
después de que	**después de**
Te llamaré **después de que** hables con ellos.	Te llamaré **después de** hablar con ellos.
para que	**para**
Ofrecen cursos virtuales **para que** todos tengan más flexibilidad de horario.	Prefiero tomar un curso virtual **para** tener más flexibilidad de horario.
sin que	**sin**
No debes estudiar en el extranjero **sin que** tu consejero apruebe tu plan de estudios.	No debes salir de casa **sin** llevar una copia de tu pasaporte.

Colaborar

12-8 **Estudiando en el extranjero.** Con un(a) compañero(a), lean cada comentario e identifiquen lo siguiente:

¡Aplícalo!

- la persona de la lista que está hablando
- la cláusula adverbial
- si el verbo de la cláusula adverbial está en el indicativo o el subjuntivo

Modelo   "Empecé a extrañar a mi familia en cuanto entré al avión".
la persona = Alan, el estudiante; la cláusula adverbial = en cuanto entré al avión; el verbo = indicativo

Alan, el estudiante	la consejera	el profesor
la madre de Alan	la novia de Alan	de español

1. "Saca el certificado del curso de español intensivo para que recibas crédito en la universidad".
2. "Me sentí un poco abrumado hasta que me acostumbré a la vida de aquí".
3. "Mañana practicaremos el subjuntivo en cuanto repasemos los mandatos".
4. "No te voy a mandar dinero hasta que hagas un presupuesto".
5. "Voy a enfadarme a menos que me llames todos los días durante tu viaje".

Colaborar

12-9 **La rutina de Alejandro.** Alejandro está estudiando en Costa Rica. Con un(a) compañero(a), completen las oraciones sobre su rutina con los verbos más lógicos de la lista. Escríbanlos en el presente de indicativo o subjuntivo.

comer	ir	llegar	necesitar	terminar	ver

1. Todos los días Alejandro se levanta temprano. Prefiere ducharse antes de que sus hermanos anfitriones _____ usar el baño.
2. Su mamá anfitriona siempre le prepara gallo pinto para que _____ un buen desayuno antes de ir al Centro de Idiomas.
3. Sale de casa a las ocho y media a menos que su clase _____ de excursión.
4. Siempre vuelve a casa a la una de la tarde, después de que _____ las clases.
5. Todos los días, en cuanto Alejandro _____ a casa, almuerza con su familia.

PASO 1   **457**

12-10 **Seis consejos.** Trabaja con un(a) compañero(a) para terminar de escribir el siguiente cartel. Escojan las frases más lógicas de la lista y conjuguen los verbos en negrita en la forma **tú**. Para los últimos dos consejos, complétenlos de manera original.

saber cuánto dinero necesitas	**perder** tu pasaporte
elegir un programa	**decidir** estudiar en el extranjero

¿Piensas estudiar en el extranjero?

Sigue estos seis consejos:

- Es mejor consultar con tu consejero(a) académico(a) en cuanto _____
- Es importante comparar precios antes de que _____
- Es esencial hacer un presupuesto para que _____
- Es aconsejable saber dónde está el consulado en caso de que _____
- Es recomendable vivir con una familia anfitriona para que _____
- Es buena idea _____

 12-11 **Durante las vacaciones.** ¿Qué piensas hacer cuando termine este semestre? Compara planes con un(a) compañero(a). Tienen que completar cada oración con un sujeto diferente y el presente de subjuntivo.

Modelo Compraré ropa nueva después de que... **me paguen en mi nuevo trabajo.**

1. No pienso abrir un libro de texto hasta que...
2. Haré un viaje con tal de que...
3. Voy a dormir hasta tarde todos los días a menos que...
4. Visitaré a mi familia tan pronto como...
5. Conseguiré un empleo después de que...
6. Me divertiré mucho antes de que...

 12-12 **Sí... pero hay una condición.** Cuando le pides un favor a tu amigo José, él siempre está dispuesto *(willing)* a ayudarte, pero ¡con algunas condiciones! Tomando turnos con un(a) compañero(a), completen las conversaciones entre tú y José. Necesitan incluir los adverbios **con tal de que** o **a menos que** en las respuestas de José.

Modelo Estudiante A (Tú): ¿Puedes llevarme al centro comercial?
Estudiante B (José): Te llevo **con tal de que me invites a almorzar.** / No te llevo **a menos que pagues la gasolina para el auto.**

1. ¿Me prestas *(lend)* un poco de dinero? Tengo que comprar un regalo de cumpleaños para mi abuela.
2. ¿Me puedes explicar este problema de cálculo? Tengo un examen mañana y no comprendo nada.
3. ¿Puedo usar tu computadora? La mía tiene algún virus y no está funcionando.
4. ¿Me presentas a tu primo(a)? ¡Qué guapo(a) es!
5. ¿Me puedes llevar al aeropuerto? Voy a Florida para el fin de semana.
6. ¿Puedo dormir en tu apartamento esta noche? He perdido la llave de mi cuarto.

G PASO 1 **GRAMÁTICA B**

Repaso de los usos del presente de subjuntivo

© Cengage Learning 2016

MANUEL	Bueno, Rosario, ¿cómo van tus planes para estudiar en el extranjero?
ROSARIO	Muy mal. Mis padres no quieren que yo vaya a otro país para estudiar. Papi dice que no tienen dinero para lujos *(luxuries)* de ese tipo.
MANUEL	¿No hay nadie que te pueda ayudar? ¿Un tío rico? ¿Una abuela?
ROSARIO	¡Claro! ¡Mi abuela! Es posible que ella me preste *(lend)* el dinero.

1. The present subjunctive is used in dependent noun clauses after expressions of influence, emotion, doubt, and denial.

	MAIN CLAUSE	**QUE**	DEPENDENT CLAUSE WITH SUBJUNCTIVE
Influence	Papá no quiere	que	yo **estudie** en el extranjero.
	Dad doesn't want		*me to study* abroad.
Emotion	Siento	que	no **puedas** estudiar en Chile.
	I'm sorry	*that*	*you can't* study in Chile.
Doubt	Es posible	que	mi tía me **preste** el dinero.
	It's possible	*that*	*my aunt **will lend** me the money.*
Denial	No es verdad	que	este programa **sea** caro.
	It's not true	*that*	*this program **is** expensive.*

2. The indicative, not the subjunctive, is used after **que** when the main clause expresses belief or certainty.

Belief	Creo	que	**ofrecen** alojamiento con familias.
	I think	*(that)*	*they **offer** lodging with families.*
Certainty	No hay duda de	que	A.C.E. **tiene** el mejor programa.
	There's no doubt	*that*	*A.C.E. **has** the best program.*

3. The subjunctive is used in an adjective clause to refer to a non-specific, hypothetical, or non-existent person, place, or thing. The dependent clause is linked to the main clause with **que** *(that, who)*, **quien** *(who)*, or **donde** *(where)*.

	MAIN CLAUSE	CONNECTOR	DEPENDENT ADJECTIVE CLAUSE
Hypothetical /	Quiero un programa	que	**tenga** buena reputación.
Non-specific	*I want a program*	*that*	***has** a good reputation.*
Non-existent	No hay nadie	que	me **pueda** ayudar.
	There's nobody	*who*	*can help me.*

■ ■ ■
Descúbrelo

■ Why is Rosario feeling sad at the beginning of the conversation?

■ How does Manuel suggest that she solve her problem?

■ In which sentence is the subjunctive used after an expression of influence? After an expression of doubt?

■ Why is the subjunctive used after the word **nadie** in the conversation?

4. The indicative is used in dependent adjective clauses when they refer to known or specific people, places, and things.

Known / Specific	Vivo con una familia	que	**tiene** tres hijos.
	I live with a family	*that*	***has** three children.*

5. The present subjunctive is used in adverbial clauses to express when, why, and how actions take place. These conjuctions always require the subjunctive: **a menos que, con tal (de) que, en caso de que, antes de que, para que,** and **sin que.**

> Ten un pasaporte **en caso de que** <u>estudies</u> en el extranjero.
> *Have a passport **in case** <u>you study</u> abroad.*

6. These conjunctions use the subjunctive when the adverbial clause refers to an action that has not been completed: **cuando, después de que, en cuanto, hasta que, mientras,** and **tan pronto como.**

> **En cuanto** <u>lleguemos</u> a Cusco, conoceremos a las familias anfitrionas.
> *As soon as <u>we arrive</u> in Cusco, we will meet the host families.*

¡Aplícalo!

Colaborar

12-13 **¡A estudiar!** ¿Cómo reaccionan todos cuando les dices que vas a estudiar en el extranjero? Con un(a) compañero(a), completen cada oración con una expresión apropiada: **Me alegra, Me preocupa, Ojalá, Espero, Es una lástima, Es posible,** etcétera.

1. Tu profesor(a) de español: ¡_____ que vayas a estudiar español en el extranjero!

2. Tu papá: _____ que el programa cueste mucho dinero.

3. Tu novio(a): No sé. _____ que nuestra relación sufra.

4. Tu familia anfitriona: _____ que estés a gusto con nosotros.

5. Tus amigos: _____ que tengas una experiencia fantástica.

Colaborar

12-14 **Hablando con el consejero.** Un estudiante tiene muchas preguntas sobre el programa para estudiar en el extranjero. Con un(a) compañero(a), lean las preguntas y completen las respuestas; usen el subjuntivo.

1. ESTUDIANTE ¿Le llevo un regalo a mi familia anfitriona?
   CONSEJERO Es buena idea que _____.

2. ESTUDIANTE ¿Puedo llevar mi computadora portátil?
   CONSEJERO Sí, pero es mejor que _____.

3. ESTUDIANTE ¿Podré hacer escalada en roca?
   CONSEJERO No estoy seguro de que _____.

4. ESTUDIANTE ¿Qué hago si extraño a mi familia?
   CONSEJERO Te recomiendo que _____.

5. ESTUDIANTE ¿Y qué hago si me siento muy estresado?
   CONSEJERO Busca a alguien que _____.

Colaborar

12-15 El choque cultural. ¿Has experimentado alguna vez un choque cultural *(culture shock)*? Con un(a) compañero(a), lean el siguiente artículo sobre este tema. Luego contesten las preguntas con oraciones completas.

1. ¿Cuándo se experimenta el choque cultural? ¿Es verdad que es una experiencia permanente?

2. ¿Qué factores contribuyen al choque cultural? En tu opinión, ¿cuáles son otros factores que puedan influir?

3. ¿Cuáles de los síntomas les sorprende que el choque cultural produzca?

4. ¿Qué recomienda el artículo que hagamos para minimizar el choque cultural? ¿Qué más aconseja?

5. ¿Conocen a alguien que sufra de choque cultural? ¿De dónde es? ¿Qué es importante que sepa?

El choque cultural

¿Qué es?

El choque cultural es una experiencia totalmente normal cuando uno empieza a vivir en un país extranjero. La comida, el clima, las normas de conducta, todo es diferente. Algunos síntomas de choque cultural son ansiedad, confusión, nostalgia y, a veces, depresión y problemas de salud.

¿Cómo podemos minimizarlo?

- tener una mente abierta y una actitud positiva
- participar en actividades de la escuela y la comunidad
- tener una buena relación con la familia anfitriona
- hacer nuevas amistades y mantener contacto con las viejas

Cochinillo asado, plato típico de Segovia

¿Algo más?

Es importante tener en cuenta que el choque cultural es una fase temporal. Con el tiempo, uno se adapta y empieza a apreciar la nueva cultura. Al final, el choque cultural nos ayuda a tener diferentes perspectivas y crecer[1] como personas.

[1]*grow*

12-16 Los criterios. ¿Cuáles son tus criterios para elegir un programa de estudio en el extranjero? Formen grupos de tres o cuatro personas y miren los siguientes criterios. Para cada uno, expresen sus opiniones y compartan sus ideas. Usen oraciones con el subjuntivo.

Modelo dónde está ubicado

Estudiante A: Para mí, es muy importante que el programa **esté** ubicado en una ciudad grande, donde **haya** muchos museos, restaurantes, tiendas y clubs.

Estudiante B: Pues, yo prefiero que **esté** en un pueblo pequeño y tranquilo.

Estudiante C: En mi opinión...

1. dónde está ubicado

2. el tamaño de las clases

3. el tipo de alojamiento

4. el precio del programa

5. las actividades culturales que ofrecen

6. la duración del programa

El voluntariado

Oportunidades de voluntariado

Casa Hispana
Una organización sin fines de lucro

OPORTUNIDADES DE VOLUNTARIADO:

Mentores para escuela primaria
¡Haz la diferencia en la vida de un niño!

Responsabilidades:
- reunirse con un alumno de primaria
- compartir actividades divertidas
- ayudar con las tareas escolares

Asistente de publicidad
¡Utiliza tus habilidades de computación y de organización!

Responsabilidades:
- crear carteles y folletos
- coordinar y organizar eventos
- colaborar con otras organizaciones

© Cengage Learning 2016; Photos: © iofoto/Shutterstock; © Inga Ivanova/Shutterstock

Otras oportunidades	*Other opportunities*
ayudar a...	*to help . . .*
familias de bajos ingresos	*low-income families*
personas discapacitadas	*handicapped people*
personas sin hogar	*homeless people*
recoger basura	*to pick up trash*
repartir a domicilio comida caliente	*to home-deliver hot meals*
solicitar donativos / dinero	*to ask for donations / money*
trabajar en la conservación de la naturaleza	*to work in nature conservation*

Oportunidades de voluntariado (cont.)

Servimos a la comunidad hispana desde 1985

Aprendizaje de inglés

¿Quieres ayudar a los inmigrantes a aprender inglés?

Responsabilidades:

- impartir clases de inglés como segundo idioma
- participar en grupos de conversación

Reconstrucción de viviendas

¡Pongamos manos a la obra para reparar casas!

Responsabilidades:

- pintar paredes
- arreglar techos
- construir rampas

Los voluntarios no necesitan tener experiencia previa porque reciben un entrenamiento. Es necesario un nivel de español intermedio y la edad mínima de 18 años.

Otros tipos de voluntariado

¿Has trabajado de voluntario(a) alguna vez?
Sí, el año pasado trabajé en...
    un comedor de caridad
    una guardería
    un hogar para ancianos
    un refugio de animales

Other volunteer work

Have you ever done volunteer work?
Yes, last year I worked in . . .
    a soup kitchen
    a day-care center
    a nursing home
    an animal shelter

PASO 2 VOCABULARIO

Colaborar

¡Aplícalo!

12-17 **Organizaciones sin fines de lucro.** Con un(a) compañero(a), relacionen el nombre de cada organización de voluntariado con el trabajo que realiza.

¿Qué hacen los voluntarios?

_____ 1. Trabajan en la conservación de la naturaleza.

_____ 2. Son mentores de niños y jóvenes.

_____ 3. Construyen viviendas para familias de bajos ingresos.

_____ 4. Ayudan a los enfermos y a las víctimas de catástrofes.

_____ 5. Reparten comida a las casas de ancianos y personas discapacitadas.

¿Cómo se llama la organización?

a. Hábitat para la Humanidad

b. Meals-on-Wheels

c. Sierra Club

d. Hermano Mayor Hermana Mayor

e. Médicos Sin Fronteras

12-18 **En la Casa Hispana.** Con un(a) compañero(a), lean la conversación y escojan las palabras más lógicas.

VOLUNTARIO Me gustaría trabajar de (1. donativo / voluntario) para la Casa Hispana porque quiero ayudar a los (2. voluntariados / inmigrantes) latinos; pero no sé en qué capacidad.

COORDINADORA Pues, necesitamos un (3. asistente / anciano) de publicidad para crear (4. folletos / ingresos) informativos.

VOLUNTARIO Para ser sincero, prefiero no trabajar en una oficina.

COORDINADORA ¿Te gustaría reparar las (5. viviendas / caridades) de familias inmigrantes?

VOLUNTARIO Sí, ¡me encantaría!, pero no tengo experiencia (6. compartida / previa) en construcción.

COORDINADORA Eso no importa. Nosotros ofrecemos (7. guardería / entrenamiento). El único requisito es una actitud positiva.

VOLUNTARIO Entonces estoy listo para empezar. ¡Manos a la (8. obra / tarea)!

Colaborar

12-19 **Puestos de voluntariado.** Como asistentes de publicidad, tú y tu compañero(a) necesitan completar los siguientes anuncios para puestos de voluntariado. Escriban terminaciones lógicas para cada uno.

1. Escuela primaria busca voluntarios para ayudar a los...

2. Ven al parque central este viernes a las 6 p.m. para repartir ropa y comida a las...

3. Iglesia San Marcos busca tutores para clases gratis de inglés como...

4. Constructora Ibiza, Inc. te invita a poner manos a la obra. Este domingo vamos a construir...

5. Grupo Eco necesita voluntarios para repartir folletos sobre la conservación de...

Illustrations © Cengage Learning 2016

¡Exprésate!

Colaborar **12-20** **Voluntariado en Ecuador.** Con un(a) compañero(a) de clase, lean esta publicidad para un programa de voluntariado y contesten las preguntas.

1. ¿Dónde y cuándo toma lugar el programa de voluntariado?
2. ¿Qué tipo de tareas realizan los voluntarios? ¿Dónde trabajan?
3. ¿Cuántos años tienen que tener los voluntarios? ¿Qué nivel de español deben tener?
4. ¿Cuánto cuesta participar en el programa? ¿Está incluido el boleto de avión?
5. ¿Les interesa este programa de voluntariado? ¿Por qué sí o por qué no?

VOLUNTARIADO EN PUNTA BLANCA, ECUADOR
27 DE JULIO – 12 DE AGOSTO

Actividades de voluntariado

- **Limpiar playas.** Tres veces por semana vamos a la playa para recoger la basura.
- **Ayudar a los animales de mar.** Observamos las ballenas que visitan nuestras costas y ayudamos a que las tortugas lleguen a la playa para poner sus huevos.
- **Trabajar con niños.** Visitamos escuelas primarias y guarderías. Organizamos actividades para que los niños aprendan sobre la conservación de la naturaleza.

Requisitos

Edad mínima de 16 años; nivel intermedio de español.

Costo

$200 USD. Esto incluye vivienda y comida. No incluye transporte o gastos personales.

Visita nuestra página web www.nuestratierra.org

© Cengage Learning 2016

12-21 **Un puesto de voluntario.** Imagina que eres coordinador(a) de voluntarios; tu compañero(a) quiere trabajar de voluntario(a). Entrevista a tu compañero(a) con las preguntas siguientes. Después, explica para qué puesto vas a contratarlo(la). Cuando terminen, cambien de papel *(change roles)*.

1. ¿Has trabajado de voluntario(a) alguna vez? ¿Qué actividades realizabas?
2. ¿Por qué quieres hacer trabajo voluntario ahora? ¿A quiénes te gustaría ayudar?
3. ¿Qué tipo de trabajo no te interesa hacer? ¿Por qué?
4. ¿Cuáles son tus puntos fuertes? ¿Y tus puntos débiles?
5. ¿Cuántas horas por semana estás disponible? ¿Tienes tu propio auto?

 The imperfect and the preterite, **Capítulo 8 Paso 3**

Colaborar **12-22** **Pasando el verano como voluntarios.** ¿Qué hicieron estos estudiantes el verano pasado? Con un(a) compañero(a), escriban tres oraciones sobre cada foto. Digan dónde trabajaron y qué hicieron.

1. Jacobo

2. Maya

3. David

4. Norma

El imperfecto de subjuntivo

SOFÍA ¿Qué tipo de voluntariado hiciste para el Día de Servicio a la Comunidad?

JOSÉ Pasé el día en una escuela primaria donde ayudé a los niños con su tarea.

SOFÍA Pero, ¿no me dijiste que querías construir rampas para personas discapacitadas?

JOSÉ Sí, pero **ese grupo necesitaba voluntarios que tuvieran experiencia.** Entonces **la coordinadora me recomendó que trabajara en la escuela.** ¡Me gustó mucho! Creo que voy a cambiar mi carrera a la educación.

■ ■ ■
Descúbrelo

- What did José end up doing for Community Service Day?

- Why wasn't he able to participate in his first-choice activity?

- Do the phrases in boldface in the dialogue refer to the present, the past, or the future?

1. The past subjunctive, also called the imperfect subjunctive (**el imperfecto de subjuntivo**), is used in sentences that refer to the past.

> La coordinadora me sugirió que **trabajara** en una escuela.
> *The coordinator suggested that **I work** in a school.*

2. The forms of the past subjunctive are based on the **ellos** form of the preterite. After conjugating the verb in the preterite, remove the **-on** and add the new endings. Notice that an accent mark must be added to the **nosotros** form.

El imperfecto de subjuntivo			
	-ar	**-er**	**-ir**
	trabajar (trabajar~~on~~)	volver (volvier~~on~~)	salir (salier~~on~~)
que yo	trabaj**ara**	volv**iera**	sal**iera**
que tú	trabaj**aras**	volv**ieras**	sal**ieras**
que Ud./él/ella	trabaj**ara**	volv**iera**	sal**iera**
que nosotros(as)	trabaj**áramos**	volv**iéramos**	sal**iéramos**
que vosotros(as)	trabaj**arais**	volv**ierais**	sal**ierais**
que Uds./ellos/ellas	trabaj**aran**	volv**ieran**	sal**ieran**

3. The past subjunctive uses the same irregular stems as the preterite.

> ir → fuer~~on~~ → yo fuera
> Mamá no quería que **yo fuera** a Chile para estudiar.
> *Mom didn't want **me to go** to Chile to study.*

> hacer → hicier~~on~~ → nosotros hiciéramos
> El director nos pidió que **hiciéramos** unos folletos.
> *The director asked **us to make** some brochures.*

The past subjunctive of **hay**, from the verb **haber**, is **hubiera**.

12-23 **Cuatro en línea.** Practica las formas del imperfecto de subjuntivo jugando "cuatro en línea" con un(a) compañero(a). Tomando turnos, escojan un sujeto y un verbo y conjúguenlo en el imperfecto de subjuntivo. Si la forma es correcta, pongan X u O en el cuadrado. La primera persona con cuatro X (u O) en línea, ¡gana!

	ser	vivir	conocer	decir	hacer	trabajar
yo						
el asistente						
los voluntarios						
tú						
mis amigos y yo						
Uds.						

Colaborar

12-24 **En la última reunión.** ¿Qué dijo el coordinador de voluntarios en la última reunión? Con un(a) compañero(a), completen las oraciones; tienen que conjugar los verbos más lógicos en el imperfecto de subjuntivo.

1. Hábitat para la Humanidad quería un voluntario que (tener / ir) _____ experiencia en la construcción.

2. Adopt-a-Highway buscaba personas que (conducir / poder) _____ recoger basura.

3. La Guardería ABC hizo un entrenamiento para que nosotros (aprender / salir) _____ primeros auxilios (*first aid*).

4. El comedor de caridad solicitó más comida en caso de que (pintar / venir) _____ más personas con hambre.

5. El parque nacional buscaba un diseñador gráfico para que (crear / salir) _____ letreros.

6. El Museo de Arte no quería más voluntarios a menos que (saber / construir) _____ de arte chicano.

Colaborar

12-25 **Antes de ir al extranjero.** ¿Qué te dijeron todos antes de que te fueras a estudiar a España? Con un(a) compañero(a), completen cada oración con una frase de la lista. Cambien el verbo en negrita al imperfecto de subjuntivo.

comer bien en la cafetería	no **estar** para su cumpleaños
escribir o **llamar** a menudo	no **salir** con otros(as) chicos(as)
hacer la tarea todos los días	**poder** sobrevivir (*survive*)

1. Antes de ir a España, mis padres me pidieron que...

2. Mi novio(a) me pidió que...

3. A mi mamá le preocupaba que...

4. Mis amigos no creían que yo...

5. Mi hermanito(a) estaba triste de que...

6. Mi profesor(a) de español quería que...

¡Exprésate!

Colaborar

12-26 **¡Ojalá!** Tú y tu compañero(a) están organizando un Día de Servicio, pero no tienen suficientes voluntarios y recursos. Usen **ojalá + el imperfecto de subjuntivo** para expresar sus esperanzas frustradas *(unfulfilled hopes).*

Modelo   El refugio de animales no tiene comida para gatos.
    ¡Ojalá que tuviéramos comida para gatos!

1. El comedor de caridad necesita más voluntarios para preparar sándwiches.

2. El hogar para ancianos quiere establecer una biblioteca para sus residentes.

3. Los niños no pueden jugar en el parque porque está cubierto de basura.

4. Un tornado destruyó el techo de la casa de una familia de bajos ingresos.

5. Una iglesia quiere ayudar a los inmigrantes a aprender inglés.

12-27 **En la escuela secundaria.** ¿Cómo era la vida cuando estabas en la escuela secundaria? Con un(a) compañero(a), completen las oraciones. ¿Cuál de Uds. tenía los padres más estrictos? ¿Y la escuela más estricta?

1. Por lo general, los profesores de mi escuela secundaria pedían que nosotros...

2. En muchas clases, los profesores prohibían que nosotros...

3. El (La) director(a) de la escuela insistía en que los estudiantes...

4. Respecto a la tarea, mis padres preferían que yo...

5. También esperaban que yo... después de graduarme de la escuela secundaria.

12-28 **El campamento Nuevos Amigos.** Con un(a) compañero(a), dramaticen una entrevista entre un(a) voluntario(a) y un(a) periodista.

- **Estudiante A:** Fuiste voluntario(a) en el campamento el año pasado.
- **Estudiante B:** Eres periodista y quieres aprender más sobre el campamento.

Preguntas para la entrevista:

1. ¿Cuándo participaste en el campamento Nuevos Amigos?

2. ¿Era necesario que los voluntarios tuvieran experiencia previa?

3. ¿Qué cualidades personales quería el Centro que los voluntarios tuvieran?

4. ¿Qué tipo de entrenamiento ofreció el Centro antes de que los voluntarios conocieran a sus nuevos amigos?

5. ¿Qué aspecto del campamento te gustó más?

Nota cultural

Voluntariado Juvenil is a volunteer program for young people sponsored by the Peruvian government. Volunteers and organizations are matched according to interests and needs. Some areas of work are natural disaster relief, AIDS education, and the fight against poverty.

Campamento Nuevos Amigos

Objetivos
- integrar socialmente a los niños y jóvenes discapacitados
- compartir actividades divertidas

¿Cómo funciona?
Los voluntarios se reunirán con sus nuevos amigos durante cuatro sábados en el mes de julio para compartir actividades en lugares públicos como museos y parques.

Requisitos:
- tener entre 15 y 28 años
- asistir a un entrenamiento de cuatro horas
- participar en todos los sábados del programa
- tener un corazón grande y los brazos abiertos

© Cengage Learning 2016; Photo: © Jaren Wicklund/age fotostock

G PASO 2 GRAMÁTICA B

Los usos del imperfecto de subjuntivo

© Cengage Learning 2016

JUAN	¿Trabajaste de voluntario en el Día de Servicio a la Comunidad?
MARGARITA	Sí. El coordinador me pidió que trabajara en el comedor de caridad.
JUAN	¿Cómo te fue?
MARGARITA	Bueno, no había nadie que supiera cocinar muy bien, pero preparamos un almuerzo sencillo para más de 200 personas. Después, repartimos camisas y pantalones para que todos tuvieran ropa limpia.

1. The past subjunctive is used in the same ways and for the same reasons as the present subjunctive. The present subjunctive is used when the verb in the main clause refers to the present or the future. The past subjunctive is used when the verb in the main clause refers to the past.

> **Present:** El director prefiere que yo **trabaje** en el comedor de caridad.
> *The director prefers that **I work** in the soup kitchen.*
> **Past:** La coordinadora quería que yo **trabajara** en el comedor de caridad.
> *The coordinator wanted **me to work** in the soup kitchen.*

2. The past subjunctive is used in dependent noun clauses after past expressions of influence, emotion, doubt, and denial. The word **que** connects the two parts of the sentences.

MAIN CLAUSE	QUE	DEPENDENT NOUN CLAUSE
Sentía mucho	que	no **pudieras** estudiar en Chile.
I was very sorry	*that*	*you **were** unable to study in Chile.*

3. The past subjunctive is used in adjective clauses to refer to a non-specific, hypothetical, or non-existent person, place, or thing when the main clause refers to the past. The dependent clause is linked to the main clause with **que** (that, who), **quien** (who), or **donde** (where).

MAIN CLAUSE	CONNECTOR	DEPENDENT ADJECTIVE CLAUSE
Buscaba un programa	que	**tuviera** una buena reputación.
I was looking for a program	*that*	***had** a good reputation.*

4. The past subjunctive is used with adverbial clauses when the main clauses refer to the past. Common conjunctions that require the subjunctive are **a menos que** *(unless)*, **antes de que** *(before)*, **con tal (de) que** *(provided that)*, **en caso de que** *(in case that)*, **para que** *(so that, in order)*, and **sin que** *(without)*.

MAIN CLAUSE	CONNECTOR	DEPENDENT ADVERBIAL CLAUSE
Dos chicos entraron en la guardería	sin que	yo los **viera**.
Two kids went into the day care center	*without*	***my seeing** them.*

■ ■ ■
Descúbrelo
- Where did Margarita work on Community Service Day?
- What did she do there? Mention two activities.
- In which three sentences is the past subjunctive used?

¡Aplícalo!

Colaborar

12-29 **Las reacciones de Rachel.** Cuando Rachel fue a España para estudiar, sus amigos siguieron su estado *(status)* en una red social. Con un(a) compañero(a), lean los estados de Rachel y después escojan una expresión lógica para describir las reacciones de Rachel a cada situación.

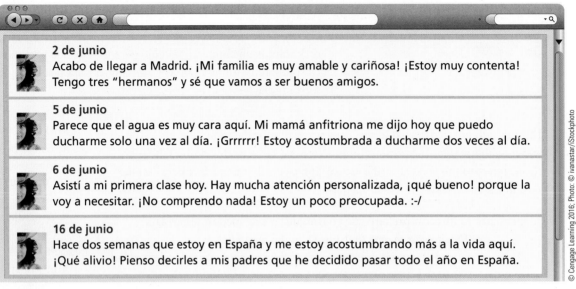

2 de junio
Acabo de llegar a Madrid. ¡Mi familia es muy amable y cariñosa! ¡Estoy muy contenta! Tengo tres "hermanos" y sé que vamos a ser buenos amigos.

5 de junio
Parece que el agua es muy cara aquí. Mi mamá anfitriona me dijo hoy que puedo ducharme solo una vez al día. ¡Grrrrrr! Estoy acostumbrada a ducharme dos veces al día.

6 de junio
Asistí a mi primera clase hoy. Hay mucha atención personalizada, ¡qué bueno! porque la voy a necesitar. ¡No comprendo nada! Estoy un poco preocupada. :-/

16 de junio
Hace dos semanas que estoy en España y me estoy acostumbrando más a la vida aquí. ¡Qué alivio! Pienso decirles a mis padres que he decidido pasar todo el año en España.

1. El primer día de su estadía, a Rachel (le alegró que / le enfadó que) su familia fuera muy amable. (Dudaba que / Sabía que) ella y sus nuevos hermanos serían buenos amigos.

2. Unos días más tarde, a Rachel (le encantó que / le enfadó que) no pudiera ducharse varias veces al día. (Le encantó que / No había duda de que) tenía un poco de choque cultural.

3. El 6 de junio fue un día de emociones contradictorias. Por un lado, (le pareció estupendo que / le enfadó que) hubiera atención personalizada en las clases. Pero (le preocupaba que / le encantó que) no comprendiera bien a sus profesores.

4. Antes, Rachel (creía que / le alegró que) sería difícil acostumbrarse a la vida en el extranjero. Pero después de dos semanas, (estaba segura de que / le enfadó que) quería pasar todo un año en España.

Colaborar

12-30 **¿Qué te dijeron?** El año pasado estudiaste en España. Antes de tu viaje, ¿cómo reaccionaron a tus planes tus amigos y familiares? Con un(a) compañero(a), relacionen las dos columnas y conjuguen los verbos en el imperfecto de subjuntivo.

1. Mis padres me recomendaron que...

2. Mi novio(a) me pidió que...

3. Mi abuela quería que...

4. Mi profesor de español me aconsejó que...

5. Mis amigos creían que yo...

a. (estudiar) todos los días

b. (hacer) siempre mi tarea

c. (llamar) a menudo

d. no (poder) sobrevivir *(survive)* en una cultura diferente

e. no (salir) con otros(as) chicos(as)

¡Exprésate!

12-31 Los compañeros consejeros. ¿Qué les aconsejas a los estudiantes en estas situaciones? Trabajen en grupos de tres personas y sigan el modelo. Tomen turnos para dar consejos y reportar la información.

Modelo **Estudiante A:** *(Lee la situación)* "Me gustaría estudiar en el extranjero pero no sé adónde quiero ir".

Estudiante B: *(Da consejos)* Debes hablar con tu profesor de español. Él te puede dar información sobre diferentes programas.

Estudiante C: *(Reporta la información)* Keesha le recomendó que hablara con su profesor de español.

1. "Quiero trabajar de voluntario(a) el próximo verano. No tengo experiencia en la construcción pero estoy dispuesto(a) a aprender. Prefiero trabajar al aire libre. ¿Con qué organización debo buscar trabajo?"

2. "El aniversario de mis abuelos es en julio y mis padres han organizado una gran fiesta para toda la familia. Mi novio(a) me ha invitado a pasar dos semanas en Europa con su familia y las fechas coinciden con la fiesta. ¿Qué hago?"

3. "Hay una chica en mi clase de química que hace trampa *(cheats)* en todos los exámenes. La clase tiene más de 100 personas y por eso el profesor y los monitores no han observado lo que ella está haciendo. ¿Qué debo hacer?"

4. "Hace un año que mi mejor amiga sale con su novio, Joe. El otro día, vi a Joe en un club y ¡él estaba besando *(kissing)* a otra chica! Él no me vio".

12-32 Experiencias con el voluntariado. ¿Has trabajado de voluntario(a) alguna vez? Pensando en esa experiencia, completa las oraciones con el imperfecto de subjuntivo. Luego, comparte tus experiencias con un(a) compañero(a).

1. Una vez, trabajé de voluntario(a) en...   4. Me molestó un poco que...

2. Me gustó que...   5. Era bueno que yo...

3. Me sorpendió que...   6. Era una lástima que yo...

↻ Numbers, **Capítulo 1 Paso 1**

12-33 Los hispanos en Estados Unidos. Aquí tienes algunos datos sobre los hispanos en Estados Unidos. Con un(a) compañero(a), comparen sus reacciones a la información. Usen las expresiones de la lista.

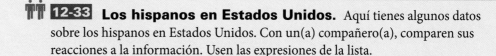

No pensaba que (+ imperfecto de subjuntivo)   Sabía que (+ imperfecto de indicativo)
No creía que (+ imperfecto de subjuntivo)   No sabía que (+ imperfecto de indicativo)

Modelo El 75% de la población hispana vive en California, Texas, Florida, Nueva York e Illinois.

Estudiante A: No pensaba que el 75% de la población viviera en esos estados.

Estudiante B: Yo no sabía que había muchos hispanos en Illinois.

- El 94% de los hispanos entre 18 y 34 años tiene acceso a Internet en casa.
- Hay 16 estados con por lo menos medio millón de habitantes hispanos.
- El 79% de los hispanos entre 18 y 34 años prefiere hablar inglés en el trabajo.

- El 70% de los niños hispanos vive con padres casados.
- El 50% de los hispanos tiene menos de 26 años.
- El 47% de la población de Nuevo México es hispana.

Las noticias

In this Paso, you will . . .
- talk about the news
- say what would happen under certain circumstances
- discuss contrary-to-fact situations

Noticias en línea

Miles de habitantes del Caribe se preparan para la llegada de un fuerte huracán

El servicio meteorológico informó que un huracán de categoría 4 avanza hacia la costa de Florida a una velocidad de 220 kilómetros por hora. Se prevé que tocará tierra el viernes a la medianoche.

El huracán atravesó Cuba hoy, provocando muchas inundaciones y dejando dos personas muertas. Las autoridades pidieron a cerca de 1,5 millones de personas que evacuaran la bahía de Tampa.

Hablar sobre las noticias	*Talking about the news*
¿Te enteraste de lo que pasó?	*Did you hear about what happened?*
Acabo de leer / oír que...	*I've just read / heard that . . .*
Hubo un ataque terrorista.	*There has been a terrorist attack.*
Hubo un asesinato.	*There has been a murder.*
¡No lo puedo creer!	*I can't believe it!*
¡No me digas!	*No way! / You're kidding!*
¿Dónde ocurrió?	*Where did it happen?*
¿Cuándo ocurrió?	*When did it happen?*

Noticias en línea (cont.)

MUNDI NOTICIAS

Tu portal a las noticias internacionales

| ECONOMÍA | DEPORTES | ÚLTIMAS NOTICIAS | ENTRETENIMIENTO | OPINIÓN |

Últimas noticias

Un choque de trenes en el noreste deja 30 heridos.

El candidato de la oposición denuncia corrupción en el gobierno.

La huelga de taxistas paraliza la capital.

Científicos británicos descubren nuevo planeta.

Síguenos

Twitter   Facebook   Google+

Buscar

Los desastres naturales	*Natural disasters*
la erupción volcánica	*volcanic eruption*
el incendio (forestal)	*(forest) fire*
el terremoto	*earthquake*

La política	*Politics*
la guerra	*war*
la paz	*peace*
la manifestación para protestar...	*demonstration to protest . . .*
luchar por la libertad / los derechos	*to fight for freedom / rights*
mejorar (las condiciones)	*to improve (conditions)*
votar en las elecciones	*to vote in the elections*

¡Aplícalo!

Colaborar

12-34 **Los desastres naturales.** ¿Cuál es el mejor titular *(headline)* para cada artículo? Con un(a) compañero(a), lean las noticias y escojan sus respuestas.

Terremoto sacude las costas del país

País se prepara para más agua

Altas temperaturas contribuyen al desastre

Presidente conmemora primer aniversario del terremoto

Incendios en los bosques se intensifican

© Cengage Learning 2016

1. Titular: _____	2. Titular: _____	3. Titular: _____
Varias provincias del oeste del país fueron afectadas el domingo por un fuerte sismo, registrado de magnitud 6, sin que reportaran víctimas o heridos. Una fuente *(source)* de la policía dijo que había muchas casas con problemas en sus estructuras en algunos pueblos andinos.	Según informaron las autoridades, cerca de 50 pueblos están en estado de emergencia a causa de incendios forestales. Un funcionario ha confirmado que 4 personas han muerto mientras que los bomberos han evacuado a 85 000 personas de la zona afectada.	Un día después que el primer ministro prometió ayuda para los pueblos devastados por las inundaciones, los residentes de otras 80 comunidades siguen en estado de alerta. Según los meteorólogos, las fuertes lluvias continuarían durante las próximas 24 horas.

Colaborar

12-35 **El huracán.** Con un(a) compañero(a), lean el artículo sobre el huracán en la página 472 y contesten las preguntas.

1. ¿Qué área geográfica afectará el huracán?

2. ¿De qué categoría es el huracán? ¿A qué velocidad avanza?

3. Según el servicio meteorológico, ¿cuándo llegará el huracán a la costa de Florida?

4. ¿Cuántas personas ya han muerto? ¿Qué otros desastres ha causado?

5. ¿Qué precauciones están tomando los habitantes del estado de Florida?

Colaborar

12-36 **¡No me digas!** Con un(a) compañero(a), completen la conversación.

DANIEL   Oye, Aracely. ¿Te (1. enteraste / escuchaste) de lo que pasó?

ARACELY   No. ¿(2. Cómo / Qué) pasó?

DANIEL   Acabo de oír que hubo (3. un ataque / una huelga) terrorista.

ARACELY   ¡No me digas! ¿(4. Dónde / Cuándo) ocurrió?

DANIEL   En la embajada. Un vehículo explotó durante una manifestación contra la (5. guerra / libertad).

ARACELY   ¡No lo puedo (6. votar / creer)!

DANIEL   Sí, es verdad. La explosión ha (7. luchado / dejado) 45 heridos.

ARACELY   Pon la tele. Quiero ver las últimas (8. erupciones / noticias).

12-37 **Nuevo planeta.** Con un(a) compañero(a), lean el artículo sobre un nuevo planeta y completen el diálogo de una manera lógica; tienen que incorporar información del artículo.

ESTUDIANTE A Acabo de leer que _____.

ESTUDIANTE B ¿Un nuevo planeta? ¡_____! ¿Quiénes lo descubrieron?

ESTUDIANTE A _____.

ESTUDIANTE B ¡Imagínate! ¿_____?

ESTUDIANTE A En la Vía Láctea, a una distancia de _____.

ESTUDIANTE B ¡_____! ¡Está muy lejos! ¿Cómo pudieron detectarlo?

ESTUDIANTE A _____.

ESTUDIANTE B ¿Qué más saben del planeta?

ESTUDIANTE A _____.

ESTUDIANTE B ¡Fascinante! Me gustaría _____.

Primer planeta de origen extragaláctico

El nuevo planeta cuenta con una masa de 1,25 veces la de Júpiter.

Un equipo de astrónomos europeos, empleando el telescopio del Observatorio La Silla en Chile, ha detectado el primer planeta extra galáctico. Según los científicos, el nuevo planeta es parecido[1] a Júpiter y orbita una estrella que entró en la Vía Láctea[2] desde otra galaxia.

Hace millones de años, la estrella formaba parte de una galaxia enana[3], la cual fue devorada por la Vía Láctea. Esta fusión cósmica ha puesto el planeta al alcance[4] de los telescopios. El planeta, conocido como HIP 13044 b, está a unos 2000 años luz de la Tierra. El equipo ha calificado el descubrimiento de "muy apasionante".

[1]similar [2]Milky Way [3]dwarf [4]within reach

↻ Present progressive, Capítulo 4 Paso 2

 **12-38** **Charadas: Las noticias en vivo.** Trabajando con dos o tres compañeros(as), dramaticen una escena de las noticias, ¡pero sin hablar! Presenten la escena al resto de la clase. La clase debe describir la escena con una oración en el presente progresivo.

Modelo *(Tres estudiantes hacen una pantomima de una huelga.)* "Uds. están participando en una huelga".

12-39 **Mi experiencia.** ¿Has experimentado alguna vez un desastre natural? ¿Leíste de algún desastre que te afectara *(affected you)* mucho? Tomando turnos, describan esta experiencia a dos o tres compañeros(as). Mencionen toda la información de abajo. Sus compañeros(as) tienen que hacer otras preguntas originales sobre la experiencia.

Frases útiles

un deslizamiento de tierra *mudslide*
una granizada *hail storm*
una tormenta de nieve *snowstorm*
un tornado *tornado*

- ¿Qué tipo de desastre experimentaste?
- ¿Dónde ocurrió?
- ¿Cuántos años tenías?
- ¿Con quién estabas?

- ¿Qué hacías cuando ocurrió?
- ¿Qué pasó?
- ¿Cómo te sentiste?
- ¿Estuvo en las noticias?

El condicional

PERIODISTA	Como presidenta, ¿qué haría Ud. durante el primer año de su mandato *(term)*?
CANDIDATA	Yo mejoraría las condiciones económicas para todos.
PERIODISTA	¿Qué haría para combatir la corrupción?
CANDIDATA	Trabajaría con el Congreso para crear más transparencia en el gobierno.

■ ■ ■
Descúbrelo

- What would the presidential candidate do during her first year in office?
- How would she fight corruption?
- What verb ending conveys the information *I would . . . ?*
- What infinitive do you think corresponds to the verb form **haría**?

1. The conditional tense (**el condicional**) is used to say what somebody *would do* or what *would happen* under certain conditions.

> Como presidente, yo **mejoraría** las condiciones económicas para todos.
> *As president, **I would improve** economic conditions for everyone.*

2. The conditional tense of regular verbs is formed by adding the following endings to the *whole infinitive*. The same set of endings is used for **-ar**, **-er**, and **-ir** verbs.

El condicional de verbos regulares			
	luchar *to fight*	**comer** *to eat*	**vivir** *to live*
yo	lucharía	comería	viviría
tú	lucharías	comerías	vivirías
Ud./él/ella	lucharía	comería	viviría
nosotros(as)	lucharíamos	comeríamos	viviríamos
vosotros(as)	lucharíais	comeríais	viviríais
Uds./ellos/ellas	lucharían	comerían	vivirían

3. The conditional tense of irregular verbs is formed by adding the same endings to an irregular stem. These irregular stems are used for the future tense, too.

Infinitivo	Raíz *(Stem)*	Infinitivo	Raíz *(Stem)*
decir	**dir-**	salir	**saldr-**
hacer	**har-**	saber	**sabr-**
tener	**tendr-**	querer	**querr-**
poner	**pondr-**	poder	**podr-**
venir	**vendr-**		

El condicional de los verbos irregulares			
hacer *to do*			
yo	haría	nosotros(as)	haríamos
tú	harías	vosotros(as)	haríais
Ud./él/ella	haría	Uds./ellos/ellas	harían

© Cengage Learning 2016

4. The conditional of **hay**, from the verb **haber**, is **habría** *(there would be)*.

5. The conditional is often used with the verbs **deber**, **poder**, and **querer** to indicate politeness, as a softened way to express wishes or make suggestions.

> **¿Podrías** pasar por mí a las ocho? ***Could you*** *come by for me at eight o'clock?*

6. The conditional can be used for reported speech, to express what somebody said.

> **Statement:** "Combatiré la corrupción".
> *"I will fight against corruption."*
> **Reported speech:** El presidente dijo que **combatiría** la corrupción.
> *The president said that **he would fight** corruption.*

12-40 Muchas excusas. Te gustaría hacer muchas cosas, pero también existen varios obstáculos. ¿Por qué **no** puedes hacer estas cosas? Con un(a) compañero(a), completen las oraciones. Den excusas diferentes para cada situación.

¡Aplícalo!

Modelo Iría al gimnasio todos los días pero...

> **Estudiante A:** Iría al gimnasio todos los días pero está bastante lejos de mi residencia.

> **Estudiante B:** Iría al gimnasio todos los días pero me lastimé la rodilla.

1. Trabajaría de voluntario(a) pero...

2. Vería las noticias en español pero...

3. Comería más frutas y verduras pero...

4. Hablaría más a menudo con mis abuelos pero...

5. Limpiaría mi cuarto pero...

6. Participaría en más grupos estudiantiles pero...

7. Estudiaría en el extranjero pero...

8. Buscaría trabajo para el verano pero...

12-41 Propósitos de Año Nuevo. ¿Qué propósitos *(resolutions)* de Año Nuevo hicieron las siguientes personas? Trabajando con un(a) compañero(a), reporten qué dijeron. Sigan el modelo.

Modelo Tania dijo que haría más ejercicio.

Clase

12-42 **Situaciones hipotéticas.** ¿Qué harían tú y tus compañeros de clase en diferentes situaciones hipotéticas?

Primera parte: Para cada situación, decide si tú lo harías o no. Encierra en un círculo *(Circle)* Sí o No. ¡Contesta honestamente!

Situación hipotética	Primera parte: Tu respuesta	Segunda parte: Firma de estudiante
1. **comer** un plato de insectos por 10 mil dólares	Sí No	
2. **afeitarse** la cabeza para caridad	Sí No	
3. no **bañarse** durante un año por un millón de dólares	Sí No	
4. **donar** tu cadáver a la Facultad de Medicina	Sí No	
5. **ser** parte de una colonia permanente en Marte *(Mars)*	Sí No	

Segunda parte: Circula por el salón para entrevistar a varios compañeros; usa la forma **tú** del condicional. Si alguien contesta igual que tú, pídele que firme *(sign)*.

Modelo **Estudiante A:** ¿Comerías un plato de insectos por 10 mil dólares?

Estudiante B: Por diez mil dólares, sí, lo comería. / No, ¡nunca comería un plato de insectos!

Estudiante A: Yo también (tampoco). Firma aquí, por favor. / Yo sí (no) lo comería.

12-43 **¡Un millón de dólares!** ¿Qué harías con un millón de dólares? Formen un círculo de cuatro o cinco estudiantes; tomando turnos, digan lo que harían. No pueden repetir la idea de otra persona.

Modelo **Estudiante A:** Construiría viviendas para personas sin hogar.

Estudiante B: Me compraría diez autos nuevos.

12-44 **Las últimas noticias.** Imagina que estas últimas noticias son reales. ¿Cómo reaccionarías? ¿Qué harías? Comparte tus reacciones con un(a) compañero(a) de clase; usen el condicional.

Modelo Descubren vida inteligente en otro planeta.

Estudiante A: Sería muy interesante aprender sobre sus costumbres. Querría saber si tienen una cura para el cáncer.

Estudiante B: Pues, yo tendría miedo de que nos invadieran. ¡Me iría a vivir al bosque donde no me pudieran encontrar!

HAY PAZ EN TODOS LOS PAÍSES DEL MUNDO

TODOS LOS COCINEROS DE LA CIUDAD ESTÁN EN HUELGA

NO HAY MÁS PETRÓLEO EN EL MUNDO

EL PRESIDENTE ANUNCIA QUE LAS UNIVERSIDADES PÚBLICAS SERÁN GRATIS

¡UN COMETA SE ESTRELLARÁ[1] EN NUESTRO CAMPUS EN DOS HORAS!

[1]*will crash*

El imperfecto de subjuntivo con cláusulas de *si*

© Cengage Learning 2016

PROF. Vamos a examinar algunas situaciones hipotéticas respecto a la economía.

(Mientras el profesor habla, los estudiantes sueñan despiertos.)

GONZALO Si tuviera más dinero, iría a Florida para las próximas vacaciones.

JUANA Si yo fuera profesora, no tendríamos clases los viernes.

ANITA Si el profesor cancelara la clase, podría tomar el sol esta tarde.

1. To express what somebody would do (or what would happen) under certain conditions, a two-part sentence is often used.

THE CONDITION	THE RESULT / CONSEQUENCE
Si yo tuviera más dinero,	iría de vacaciones a Florida.
If I had more money,	*I'd take a vacation to Florida.*

2. These kinds of sentences are called *contrary-to-fact* because the conditions are very unlikely or not real. The past subjunctive is used after the conjunction **si** *(if)* to express these unreal conditions.

Si el profesor **cancelara** la clase, yo podría tomar el sol esta tarde.
*If the professor **cancelled** class (but he isn't going to), I could sunbathe this afternoon.*

3. The conditional tense is used to express what somebody would do under contrary-to-fact conditions. The part of the sentence with the conditional tense can be placed before or after the **si** clause.

<u>Si yo fuera profe</u>, no **tendríamos** clase los viernes.
*<u>If I were a prof</u>, **we wouldn't have** class on Fridays.*

No **tendríamos** clase los viernes <u>si yo fuera profe</u>.
***We wouldn't have** class on Fridays <u>if I were a prof</u>.*

■ ■ ■
Descúbrelo

■ Under what conditions would Gonzalo go to Florida?

■ What would Juana do if she were a professor?

■ What circumstances would allow Anita to soak up some sun?

■ What tense is used to express the conditions that would make another action possible?

Colaborar

12-45 **Relacionar.** ¿Qué piensan los voluntarios de la Cruz Roja? Con un(a) compañero(a), relacionen las dos columnas para formas oraciones lógicas.

¡Aplícalo!

_____ 1. No habría inundaciones...

_____ 2. Sabrían que hay una alerta de huracán...

_____ 3. Si el incendio forestal avanzara hacia el sur...

_____ 4. Necesitaríamos más medicina...

_____ 5. Si hubiera una erupción volcánica...

_____ 6. La Cruz Roja no existiría...

a. si dejara de llover.

b. llovería cenizas *(ashes)*.

c. muchas casas se quemarían.

d. si no fuera por los voluntarios.

e. si la gripe se convirtiera en pandemia.

f. si escucharan el servicio meteorológico.

Colaborar
12-46 **Noticias de Santa Ana.** Con un(a) compañero(a) de clase, lean estas noticias sobre las inundaciones. Luego contesten las preguntas usando oraciones completas.

1. ¿Qué le ocurriría a tu casa si vivieras en Santa Ana?
2. ¿Dónde tendrías que dormir si fueras residente de Santa Ana?
3. ¿Qué transporte usarías si ayudaras en la evacuación?
4. ¿A qué número llamarías si quisieras hacer un donativo?
5. En una evacuación, si pudieras llevar solamente una cosa de tu casa, ¿qué llevarías? ¿Por qué?

Inundaciones en Santa Ana

Fuertes lluvias en Santa Ana provocaron graves inundaciones y dejaron tres personas muertas. La evacuación se llevó a cabo por medio de lanchas, el único medio de transporte posible en las calles que se han convertido en verdaderos[1] ríos. Los residentes duermen en el gimnasio de la escuela primaria José Martí.

La escuela está aceptando donativos; llamen al 614-9608 para más información.

[1]*real*

Colaborar
12-47 **Condiciones para casarse.** Alejandro quiere casarse con Carlita, pero Carlita solamente se casaría con él bajo ciertas condiciones. ¿Cuáles son? Con un(a) compañero(a) de clase, escriban seis condiciones según el dibujo.

Modelo Carlita se casaría con Alejandro si él fuera más alto.

© Cengage Learning 2016

¡Exprésate!

††† 12-48 Ta-Te-Ti con cláusulas de *si*. Juega al Ta-Te-Ti con un(a) compañero(a) de clase. Tomando turnos, escojan un cuadro, terminen la oración y si es correcta, pongan X u O. La persona que tiene tres en línea ¡gana!

Si yo fuera tú...	Yo no estudiaría español si...	Si nuestros profesores estuvieran en huelga...
Si leyeras las noticias...	Sería candidato(a) para presidente si...	Si tuviera dinero...
Iría a México si...	Si hubiera un terremoto ahora...	No vendría a clase si...

††† 12-49 Preguntas que te hacen pensar. Entrevista a un(a) compañero(a) de clase con las preguntas siguientes. Comparen sus respuestas.

1. ¿Qué harías si encontraras en la calle una billetera con mil dólares?

2. Si pudieras pasar una semana en cualquier *(any)* ciudad del mundo, ¿adónde irías?

3. Si aceptara tu invitación a cenar contigo, ¿a qué actor o actriz invitarías?

4. ¿Cuántos años te gustaría tener si pudieras tener cualquier *(any)* edad por una semana?

5. Si te convirtieras en un animal, ¿preferirías ser un pájaro, una ballena o un perro?

6. Si tu vida fuera un libro o una película, ¿qué personaje querrías ser?

7. Si fueras atleta profesional, ¿qué deporte practicarías?

8. Si alguien te regalara un velero, ¿qué nombre le pondrías?

††† 12-50 Actividad en cadena. Formen círculos de 4 o 5 estudiantes. Un(a) estudiante empieza la cadena *(chain)* completando la primera situación hipotética. Los otros estudiantes, por turnos, añaden oraciones lógicas. Repitan el proceso con las otras situaciones hipotéticas.

Modelo Si pudiera visitar un país hispanohablante, iría a...

Estudiante A	Estudiante B	Estudiante C	Estudiante D
Si pudiera visitar un país hispanohablante, iría a España.	Si fuera a España, haría una excursión a la playa.	Si hiciera una excursión a la playa, nadaría y tomaría el sol.	Si tomara mucho sol, tendría que beber mucha agua.

1. Si pudiera visitar un país hispanohablante, iría a...

2. Si no tuviéramos clase hoy, yo...

3. Si todos mis amigos fueran estrellas de cine, nosotros...

4. Si una guerra empezara mañana, yo...

5. Si mis abuelos me regalaran un auto nuevo, yo...

CONECTADOS CON...
LA LITERATURA: CUENTOS

Un cuento de Francisco Jiménez

Francisco Jiménez nació en México en 1943 y emigró con su familia a Estados Unidos cuando tenía seis años. De niño, trabajaba en los campos de California para ayudar a su familia. Más tarde, hizo estudios universitarios y obtuvo su doctorado en Literatura en la Universidad de Columbia. Aquí tienes una selección de su cuento autobiográfico "Cajas de cartón", en el cual leemos la historia de una familia, vista por los ojos de un niño. Esta selección empieza en los campos (fields) de California durante la cosecha (harvest time).

Cajas de cartón (fragmento)

Después del almuerzo volvimos a trabajar. El calor oliente y pesado, el zumbido de los insectos, el sudor y el polvo hicieron que la tarde pareciera una eternidad. Al fin las montañas que rodeaban el valle se tragaron° el sol. Una hora después estaba demasiado oscuro para seguir trabajando. Las parras° tapaban las uvas y era muy difícil ver los racimos°. "Vámonos", dijo Papá señalándonos que era hora de irnos.

swallowed up

vines

bunches of grapes

Estrategia: Keys to understanding short stories

Short stories are short narrative works of fiction. To understand and appreciate them, identify these five key elements as you read.

- Characters: Who is the protagonist, or main character?
- Setting: Where and when does the story take place?
- Plot: What series of events occurs?
- Conflict: What kind of struggle is the main character engaged in?
- Theme: What is the central idea of the story?

Palabras para analizar los cuentos

el conflicto	*conflict*
el cuento	*short story*
el escenario	*setting*
la novela	*novel*
el personaje	*character*
el tema	*theme*
tener lugar	*to take place*
la trama	*plot*

12-51 **Comprensión.** ¿Comprendiste el cuento? Contesta las preguntas.

1. ¿Quién es el personaje principal?

2. ¿Dónde tiene lugar el cuento?

3. ¿Es el ambiente *(mood)* festivo u opresivo?

4. Al final de la selección, ¿por qué está el narrador feliz?

5. ¿Cuál es uno de los temas del cuento?

12-52 **¿Y tú?** Trabajando en grupos pequeños, comenten estas preguntas.

1. ¿Cuál es uno de tus cuentos preferidos? ¿Quién es el personaje principal? ¿Cuál es el tema?

2. ¿Conoces a alguna familia de inmigrantes? ¿Por qué inmigraron a Estados Unidos? ¿En qué empezaron a trabajar cuando llegaron?

Entonces tomó un lápiz y comenzó a calcular cuánto habíamos ganado ese primer día. Apuntó números, borró algunos, escribió más. Alzó la cabeza sin decir nada. Sus tristes ojos sumidos° estaban humedecidos°.

lost in thought; wet (with tears)

Cuando regresamos del trabajo, nos bañamos afuera con el agua fría bajo una manguera°. Luego nos sentamos a la mesa hecha de cajones de madera° y comimos con hambre la sopa de fideos, las papas y tortillas de harina blanca recién hechas. Después de cenar nos acostamos a dormir, listos para empezar a trabajar a la salida del sol°.

hose
wooden boxes

sunrise

Al día siguiente, cuando me desperté, me sentía magullado°, me dolía todo el cuerpo. Apenas° podía mover los brazos y las piernas. Todas las mañanas cuando me levantaba me pasaba lo mismo hasta que mis músculos se acostumbraron° a ese trabajo.

bruised
Hardly

got used to

Era lunes, la primera semana de noviembre. La temporada de uvas había terminado y yo podía ir a la escuela. Me desperté temprano esa mañana y me quedé acostado mirando las estrellas y saboreando° el pensamiento° de no ir a trabajar y de empezar el sexto grado por primera vez ese año.

savoring
thought

Composición: Un artículo

Write an article for a class newspaper, with a special focus on your class, campus, and city. For example: volunteer opportunities, study abroad options, university sports news, campus elections, upcoming events, a review of a recent event or new restaurant, etc.

Revisión en pareja. Exchange papers with a classmate and edit each other's work.

- Does the article contain interesting content? Is it well organized? Write one positive comment and one suggestion for improvement.

- Are several types of sentences included? Point out where sentences may be effectively joined.

- How accurate is the grammar? Circle any verbs or adjectives that may be incorrect. Underline words that may be misspelled or missing accent marks.

Estrategia
Review of key writing strategies (Capítulos 7–11)

- Create a clear beginning, middle, and end.
- Organize the information and provide examples.
- Use a variety of sentence types.
- Edit for content and organization.
- Proofread for errors in grammar, spelling, and punctuation.

12-53 **Nosotros / *Share It!*** En línea, subiste una descripción o un video sobre una experiencia que tuviste con el trabajo voluntario. También viste las publicaciones de varios compañeros de clase. Ahora, comenta sobre estas publicaciones y contesta las preguntas con un(a) compañero(a).

1. ¿En qué tipos de trabajo voluntario han participado tus compañeros de clase?

2. ¿Quién tuvo la experiencia más gratificante? ¿Y la más interesante?

3. ¿Te gustaría trabajar de voluntario(a) en uno de los lugares mencionados? ¿En cuál?

12-54 **Perspectivas: Estudiar en el extranjero.** En línea, miraste un video en el que tres estudiantes hablan de dónde les gustaría estudiar. ¿Qué dicen los estudiantes? Con dos compañeros(as) de clase, comparen sus respuestas sobre el video. Después, conversen sobre sus propias respuestas a las preguntas:

- Si pudieras estudiar en un país extranjero, ¿en cuál sería?

- ¿Por qué te gustaría estudiar allí?

12-55 **Exploración: El mundo de las noticias.** En Internet, leíste un artículo en un sitio de noticias. Ahora, formen círculos de tres o cuatro estudiantes. Tomen turnos haciendo breves presentaciones sobre los artículos. Las otras personas deben escuchar y hacer preguntas.

Yo leí un artículo sobre _____.

Encontré este artículo en un sitio de noticias en (país) _____.

Según el artículo, _____. También, _____. Otra idea importante es que _____.

Para mí, el artículo (no) fue interesante porque _____.

  12-56 **Conectados con... la literatura: cuentos.** En línea, leíste el fragmento de un cuento escrito por Julia Álvarez. Con dos o tres compañeros(as), compartan información de sus investigaciones sobre algunas diferencias culturales o sobre un(a) autor(a) latino(a).

Modelo

En Estados Unidos hay mucha gente que toma café... En Uruguay... / Julia Álvarez ha vivido en República Dominicana y en Estados Unidos...

12-57 **¡A estudiar en el extranjero!** Tú y tu compañero(a) van a dramatizar una escena entre un(a) consejero(a) académico(a) y un(a) estudiante que quiere ir al extranjero el próximo verano para estudiar español.

Estudiante A: el (la) consejero(a)
Tienes que:

- hacerle preguntas sobre las prioridades y las preferencias del (de la) estudiante

- usar la información sobre los dos programas para contestar las preguntas

- ayudar al (a la) estudiante a tomar una decisión (**Recomiendo que...**)

Estudiante B: el (la) estudiante
Tienes que:

- empezar la conversación: **Quisiera estudiar en el extranjero el próximo verano. ¿Qué programas me recomienda Ud.?**

- hacer preguntas y tomar apuntes

- elegir un programa

> This is a pair activity for **Estudiante A** and **Estudiante B**.
>
> If you are **Estudiante A**, use the information on this page.
>
> If you are **Estudiante B**, turn to p. S-12 at the back of the book.

Estudiante A

CURSOS DE VERANO EN LINGUACENTRO
Los mejores cursos a los mejores precios

Santiago, República Dominicana
8 de junio – 15 de julio

Cursos
- Español intensivo
- Gramática y composición
- Cultura afro-caribeña

Alojamiento
- residencias estudiantiles (con comedor)
- familias anfitrionas (cuartos compartidos)

Excursiones y visitas culturales
- tour de una fábrica de cigarros puros
- asistencia a un partido de béisbol
- visita guiada de la capital
- día libre en las playas de Cayo Levantado

Solo $4000, todo incluido*
*Excepto transporte EE.UU.—República Dominicana—EE.UU.

Lima, Perú
29 de junio – 4 de agosto

Cursos
- Español intensivo
- Conversación y cultura
- Política de Perú

Alojamiento
- residencias estudiantiles (no incluye comidas)
- familias anfitrionas (cuartos individuales)

Excursiones y visitas culturales
- tour de la capital
- excursión de 3 días a Cusco y Machu Picchu
- visita opcional a Iquitos y río Amazonas

Solo $4500, todo incluido*
*Excepto transporte aéreo EE.UU.—Perú—EE.UU. y la visita a Iquitos

SÍNTESIS

12-58 **Baldo.** Baldo es una tira cómica creada por Héctor Cantú y Carlos Castellanos; se basa en una familia latina de Estados Unidos. Con un(a) compañero(a) de clase, lean esta tira cómica y contesten las preguntas.

1. ¿Qué le pregunta Gracie a su padre? ¿Por qué él contesta que no?

2. Para el padre, ¿qué cualidades son importantes en un candidato político? ¿Por qué le gustaría que su apellido terminara en **z**?

3. ¿Qué opina la tía Carmen? ¿Es ella más honesta que el padre? Explica.

4. ¿Cómo contestarías tú la pregunta de Gracie? ¿Por quién votarías en las elecciones? ¿Es importante que esa persona comparta tus tradiciones?

BALDO © 2008 Baldo Partnership. Dist. By UNIVERSAL UCLICK. Reprinted with permission. All rights reserved.

Pronunciación: Repaso

¿Sabes pronunciar bien las consonantes y las vocales en español? Con un(a) compañero(a), lean en voz alta el chiste para practicar la pronunciación.

Un día, el presidente del país tiene una conferencia de prensa y un periodista le pregunta: Señor presidente, ¿es verdad que hay crisis económica en nuestro país?

El presidente le contesta: La verdad, según un estudio reciente, realmente hay solo seis personas que sufren de crisis económica.

Entonces otro periodista le pregunta: Por favor, díganos, ¿quiénes son esas seis personas?

El presidente contesta: Tú, él, ella, ustedes, ellos, ellas.

TT **12-59** **La cápsula del tiempo.** Tu universidad va a preparar una cápsula del tiempo para las futuras generaciones de estudiantes. Un comité va a decidir qué objetos serán incluidos. Si tú y tu compañero(a) estuvieran en el comité, ¿qué pondrían en la cápsula?

- Hagan una lista de 6 a 10 objetos.
- Expliquen por qué los objetos serían representativos de la presente generación de estudiantes.

Modelo Nosotros pondríamos un iPod en la cápsula, porque la música es importante en la vida de los estudiantes y el iPod es una manera común de escucharla.

TTT **12-60** **El noticiero.** Trabajando en grupos de cuatro o cinco personas, preparen un noticiero *(newscast)* y preséntenselo a la clase. Cada persona en el grupo tiene que preparar uno de los componentes de la lista. Cada segmento debe durar aproximadamente un minuto.

- la noticia más importante del día
- el pronóstico del tiempo
- una entrevista con el (la) Voluntario(a) del Año
- la reseña *(review)* de una película
- un informe sobre los deportes

© Glovatskiy/Shutterstock

12-61 **La fiesta de despedida.** ¡Qué rápido ha pasado el tiempo! Es el fin del semestre y todos Uds. deciden tener una fiesta para despedirse *(say good-bye)* de los compañeros de clase. En la fiesta, tienen que hacer lo siguiente:

Clase

- hablar de los planes para las próximas vacaciones o el próximo semestre (**¿Qué vas a hacer... ?** / **¿Piensas estudiar español el próximo semestre?** / **Espero que...**)
- recordar y comentar las cosas que han ocurrido durante el semestre (**¿Recuerdas el día cuando... ?** / **Nunca voy a olvidar el día que...** / **Sí, fue muy divertido.**)
- despedirse de los compañeros y el (la) profesor(a) (**Fue un placer trabajar contigo.** / **Me gustó mucho esta clase.** / **He aprendido mucho.**)
- hacer un brindis (**¡Brindemos por el (la) profesor(a)!** / **Brindo por...**)

VOCABULARIO

RECURSOS

Para aprender mejor
Watch a Spanish newscast on YouTube and while you listen, put a check mark next to each vocabulary word you hear.

Sustantivos
el alojamiento *lodging*
el (la) alumno(a) *student*
la amistad *friendship*
el aprendizaje *learning*
el asesinato *murder*
el (la) asistente *assistant*
el ataque terrorista *terrorist attack*
la autoridad *authority*
el (la) candidato(a) *candidate*
el choque *crash, collision*
el comedor de caridad *soup kitchen*
el (la) consejero(a) *advisor*
el consulado *consulate*
la corrupción *corruption*
el curso *course*
los derechos *rights*
el desastre natural *natural disaster*
el donativo *donation*
las elecciones *elections*
la electricidad *electricity*
la embajada *embassy*
el entrenamiento *training*
el entretenimiento *entertainment*
la erupción volcánica *volcanic eruption*
la escuela primaria *elementary school*
la estadía *stay*
el folleto *brochure*
la guardería *day-care center*
la guerra *war*
la habilidad *skill*
el (la) herido(a) *wounded (person)*
el hogar para ancianos *nursing home*
el hostal *guesthouse*
la huelga *strike*
el (la) huésped *guest*

el huracán *hurricane*
el idioma *language*
el incendio (forestal) *(forest) fire*
el (la) inmigrante *immigrant*
la inundación *flooding*
la libertad *freedom*
el malentendido *misunderstanding*
la manifestación *demonstration*
el máximo *maximum*
la mente abierta *an open mind*
las normas de conducta *norms of personal conduct*
las noticias *news*
la oportunidad *opportunity*
la oposición *opposition*
la organización *organization*
la paz *peace*
la persona sin hogar *homeless person*
el piso *apartment (Spain)*
el planeta *planet*
el presupuesto *budget*
la prioridad *priority*
la publicidad *publicity, advertising*
la reconstrucción *rebuilding*
el refugio de animales *animal shelter*
la tarea escolar *schoolwork*
el techo *roof*
el terremoto *earthquake*
la visa estudiantil *student visa*
la vivienda *housing*
el voluntariado *volunteering*

Verbos
acostumbrarse *to get used to*
avanzar *to move forward*
conservar *to save*
crear *to create*
denunciar *to denounce, to condemn*

descubrir *to discover*
enterarse *to find out*
extrañar *to miss*
guardar *to keep (somewhere)*
impartir clases *to teach*
informarse *to find out*
integrarse *to integrate yourself, to fit in*
luchar por *to fight for*
mejorar *to improve*
pintar *to paint*
poner manos a la obra *to get to work*
protestar *to protest*
provocar *to cause*
recoger basura *to pick up trash*
reparar *to fix, to repair*
repartir a domicilio *to home-deliver*
respetar *to respect*
sentirse a gusto *to feel at home*
solicitar *to ask for*
sumergirse *to immerse oneself*
tener en cuenta *to take into account*
utilizar *to use*
votar *to vote*

Adjetivos
abrumado(a) *overwhelmed*
aconsejable *advisable*
considerado(a) *considerate*
cortés *polite*
de bajos ingresos *low-income*
discapacitado(a) *handicapped*
intensivo(a) *intensive*
intermedio(a) *intermediate*
personalizado(a) *personalized*
previo(a) *previous*
sin fines de lucro *non-profit*

Conjunctions, p. 456

1-63 **En el café.** You (**Estudiante B**) and your partner (**Estudiante A**) have two similar but not identical drawings. Your task is to describe them and find the differences between them without looking at each other's drawings.

- There are eight differences between the two drawings.

- The differences might include the number, kind, and location of objects, the appearance of the room, the answers to questions, or how the people feel.

- Your partner (**Estudiante A**) will begin by saying: **En mi dibujo** *(drawing)*, **los estudiantes están en un café**. To respond, you will state whether the students in your drawing are in the same place.

If you are **Estudiante A**, turn to page 45.

If you are **Estudiante B**, use this information.

Estudiante B

Las ocho diferencias:

1. _____
2. _____
3. _____
4. _____
5. _____
6. _____
7. _____
8. _____

If you are **Estudiante A**, turn to page 85.

If you are **Estudiante B**, use the information on this page.

2-59 **La invitación.** You (**Estudiante B**) and your partner (**Estudiante A**) want to go out and do something fun this week. Using the information in the entertainment guide and the appointment calendar, find an activity you both enjoy and can attend.

- **Estudiante A** will use the entertainment guide to choose an activity and invite **Estudiante B**.

- **Estudiante B** will use the appointment calendar to check his or her availability and will accept or decline the invitation.

- **Estudiante A** should start the conversation with **¿Qué tal si... ?** and propose an activity. (**¿Qué tal si vamos a un concierto?**)

- **Estudiante B** should ask about the activity (**¿Qué día es? ¿A qué hora es?**) and describe any other obligations or plans that he or she has (**El miércoles a las siete tengo que... / voy a...**).

Hora	lunes 24	martes 25	miércoles 26	jueves 27	viernes 28	sábado 29	domingo 30
9:00 AM	biología		biología		biología		
10:00 AM						correr con Ana	
11:00 AM		literatura		literatura			
12:00 PM							
1:00 PM							
2:00 PM		cálculo		cálculo: ¡examen!			
3:00 PM							
4:00 PM							
5:00 PM							trabajar restaurante Jalisco
6:00 PM					fiesta del Club Internacional		
7:00 PM							
8:00 PM							
9:00 PM	teatro		teatro				
10:00 PM							

© Cengage Learning 2016

👫 **3-57** **El árbol.** How are your powers of deduction? You (**Estudiante B**) and your partner (**Estudiante A**) have two different sets of clues. Your task is to exchange information and decipher the clues so that you completely fill out this tree for the Rodríguez family from the Dominican Republic. Write your responses in Spanish.

If you are **Estudiante A**, turn to page 125.

If you are **Estudiante B**, use this information.

Estudiante B

Las pistas (clues):

- La esposa de José tiene 68 años y los dos viven en San Cristóbal.
- Laura, una nieta de Emilia, es hija única.
- El padre de Gloria tiene 70 años y le gusta jugar al dominó.
- Julián tiene dos años más que Jesús.
- Laura tiene cuatro años más que Vanesa.
- Antonia está casada con Manuel.
- A los tíos de Jesús les gusta cantar.
- Felipe tiene un año menos que Antonia y un año más que su esposa.
- Al tío de Laura le gusta contar chistes.
- A dos de los sobrinos de Antonia les gusta leer.

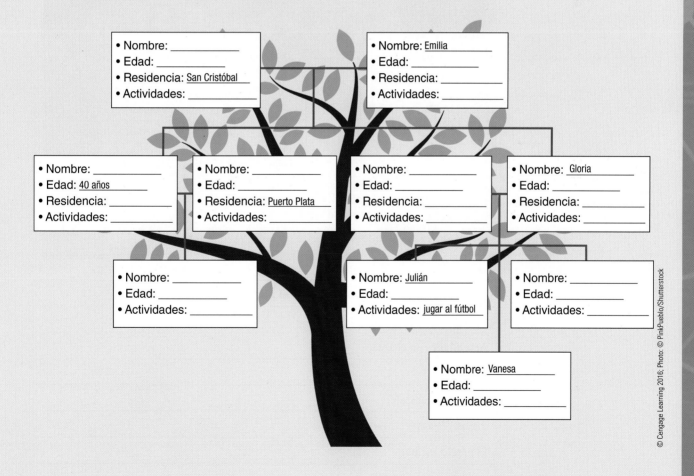

If you are **Estudiante A**, turn to page 165.

If you are **Estudiante B**, use this information.

4-57 Las vacaciones de primavera. ¿Dónde quieren Uds. pasar las vacaciones de primavera?

- Tú **(Estudiante B)** y tu compañero(a) **(Estudiante A)** tienen información sobre dos paquetes *(vacation packages)* para México.
- Primero tienen que intercambiar y apuntar *(jot down)* los detalles de los viajes.
- Después *(Then)*, necesitan comparar los dos paquetes y decidir cuál prefieren.

Estudiante B

SolMex

Paquete Especial para Estudiantes Universitarios—

La Riviera Maya

Hotel Quinto Sol

6 días 5 noches

(habitación cuádruple)

Desayuno buffet incluido
Traslados en autobús
(aeropuerto–hotel–aeropuerto)

Tour especial incluido:
Visita al parque natural Sian Ka'an
(transporte, kayaks y comida)

Solo $5500* pesos por persona

*Tarifas incluyen todos los impuestos. Precio NO incluye boleto de avión.

¡Experimenta el ambiente único de la Riviera Maya! Localizada en el extremo oriente de la Península de Yucatán, la Riviera Maya ofrece múltiples sitios para explorar: las playas solitarias con su espectacular vida marina, ríos subterráneos con fascinantes cavernas y muchas zonas arqueológicas de la antigua civilización maya.

© Cengage Learning 2016. Photo: holbox/Shutterstock

Información sobre el paquete del Estudiante A	
Destino:	
Actividades en el área:	
Hotel:	
Duración del viaje:	
Precio *(Price)*:	
El precio incluye:	
Aspectos interesantes:	

5-59 **Buenos detectives.** Ayer, a las tres de la tarde, hubo un crimen (*a crime took place*) en el barrio La Leona. El sospechoso (*the suspect*) —Jorge Ramírez— tiene una coartada (*alibi*); estuvo (*was*) con su novia Angélica Vidal. Tú y tu compañero(a) son detectives y tienen que determinar si Jorge Ramírez es inocente o culpable (*guilty*).

If you are **Estudiante A**, turn to page 205.

If you are **Estudiante B**, use this information.

■ Tu compañero(a) (**Estudiante A**) tiene fotos de las cámaras de seguridad. Tú (**Estudiante B**) tienes la declaración de Angélica Vidal.

■ Tomen turnos describiendo las actividades de Angélica y Jorge; tienen que usar el pretérito en sus oraciones. Por ejemplo: **Por la mañana, Jorge y Angélica fueron al gimnasio y corrieron.**

■ Hagan una lista de las discrepancias. ¿Es Jorge Ramírez inocente?

Estudiante B

Ayer, sábado 2 de noviembre, yo, Angélica Vidal, pasé todo el día con mi novio Jorge Ramírez.

Por la mañana me levanté temprano. A las nueve y media, encontré a Jorge en el gimnasio y corrimos juntos. Nos duchamos y nos vestimos en el gimnasio.

Luego, a las once, fuimos al mercado para comprar comida. Jorge también compró unas flores muy bonitas.

Almorzamos en mi apartamento. Nos quedamos en el apartamento toda la tarde. Hicimos los quehaceres, descansamos y miramos televisión.

A las seis de la tarde, fuimos al café de la esquina. Vimos a mi vecina, Violeta Guzmán, y hablamos por unos quince minutos.

Por la noche, Jorge y yo fuimos al club Máximo y bailamos hasta la madrugada.

If you are **Estudiante A**, turn to page 245.

If you are **Estudiante B**, use this information.

 6-58 **La cena de gala.** ¿Quiénes están en la gran cena de gala *(banquet)*? ¿Qué están comiendo? Tú y tu compañero(a) deben compartir *(share)* la información en las imágenes para contestar estas preguntas. Usa la información en estas dos imágenes; tu compañero(a) tiene que usar la información que está en la página 245.

■ Primero, tomen turnos para describir las características físicas *(physical)* de las personas y descubrir el nombre de cada uno. Por ejemplo, Estudiante A dice: **En mi página hay una señora delgada. Tiene el pelo rubio y los ojos azules. Usa gafas. Tiene más o menos 30 años. ¿Cómo se llama? Eh... ¿cómo se escribe su nombre?**

■ Luego, pregunten sobre la comida de cada persona. Por ejemplo, Estudiante B pregunta: **¿Qué está comiendo Ramón Lerma? ¿Qué está bebiendo?**

■ Anoten *(Jot down)* la información.

Estudiante B

© Cengage Learning 2016

7-64 **Diez diferencias.** Tú (**Estudiante B**) y tu compañero(a) (**Estudiante A**) tienen un dibujo de una escena en un gran almacén. A primera vista *(At first glance)* parecen idénticos, pero en realidad hay diez diferencias.

If you are **Estudiante A**, turn to page 285.

If you are **Estudiante B**, use the information on this page.

- Uds. deben compartir *(share)* la información en los dibujos para descubrir las diez diferencias, pero ¡sin mirar el dibujo de la otra persona!

- Fíjense *(Pay attention)* especialmente en las características de las personas, los estilos de ropa, los colores, el entallado *(fit)* de la ropa y la ubicación *(location)* de las cosas y las personas en el almacén. Anoten *(Jot down)* las 10 diferencias.

- Estudiante A va a empezar la conversación.

Estudiante B

If you are **Estudiante A**, turn to page 325.

If you are **Estudiante B**, use the information on this page.

8-59 **¡Vamos al festival!** Tú y tu compañero(a) están en Colombia y quieren ir a un festival. Tú (**Estudiante B**) y tu compañero(a) (**Estudiante A**) tienen información incompleta sobre el festival.

- Primero, tienen que hacerse *(ask each other)* preguntas para completar la información.
- Tu compañero(a) te va a hacer la primera pregunta: **¿Cuál es el nombre completo del festival?**
- Después, invita a tu compañero(a) a tu evento preferido.

Estudiante B

PROGRAMACIÓN
Sábado 3 de abril

Festival Iberoamericano de (1) _____ **de Bogotá**

19 de marzo al (2) _____ de abril

¡Ven a este gran festival con más de 700 funciones de 100 compañías internacionales! ¡Son (3) _____ días de espectáculos inolvidables!

Entrada General
Adultos: $8000   Niños: (4) $ _____

DANZA
Argentina
Danza Aérea
Coliseo El Campín,
(5) _____ p.m.

España
Flamenco actual
Auditorio León, 8 p.m.

TEATRO CONTEMPORÁNEO
Chile
Teatro en el Blanco presenta la obra
(6) _____
Teatro Arlequín, 6 p.m.

Estados Unidos
Corbian Visual Arts presenta *Darwin*, obra apta para todo público
Teatro (7) _____, 3 y 6 p.m.

COMEDIA
(8) _____
Luis Fernández presenta un divertido espectáculo de monólogos cómicos[1]
Teatro La Castellana, 8 p.m.

TEATRO MUSICAL
Colombia
A solas, con Margarita Rosa, combina música, video y luces
Teatro Leonardus,
(9) _____ p.m.

GRAN CONCIERTO de Concha Buika
España
Lugar: Plaza de Toros   Hora: 8 p.m.   Precio: (10) $ _____

[1]*stand-up comedy*

9-57 **En el consultorio médico.** Tú y tu compañero(a) van a dramatizar una escena en un consultorio médico. **Estudiante A** va a ser el (la) paciente y **Estudiante B** va a ser el (la) médico(a). Sigan las instrucciones.

If you are **Estudiante A**, turn to page 365.

If you are **Estudiante B**, use the information on this page.

Estudiante B: El (La) médico(a)

Tienes que:

- empezar la conversación: **Buenas tardes, señor / señorita. ¿Cómo se siente Ud.?**
- hacer preguntas sobre los síntomas, consultar la tabla y decirle un diagnóstico.
- dar consejos (con mandatos formales y el presente de subjuntivo).

Enfermedades tropicales

La fiebre morada
(*Puniceus horrrendus*)
Manifestaciones clínicas:
Síntomas:
- fiebre alta[1]
- dolor de cabeza
- tos
- dolor de garganta
- piel de color violeta

Tratamiento:
- guardar cama por diez días
- beber jugo de uva todos los días
- tomar el antibiótico Mayocina (una pastilla al día por diez días)

La dengosis
(*Tussis abominabilis*)
Manifestaciones clínicas:
Síntomas:
- fiebre moderada
- dolor de cabeza
- diarrea
- dolor de garganta
- tos continua y muy fuerte

Tratamiento:
- descansar por tres días
- beber agua y líquidos calientes
- tomar jarabe para la tos (cada cuatro horas por una semana)

La filarcosis
(*Morbus atrox*)
Manifestaciones clínicas:
Síntomas:
- fiebre moderada
- dolor de cabeza
- dolor de oídos
- dolor de garganta
- dolor de estómago

Tratamiento:
- suero intravenoso
- llevar una dieta líquida
- tomar el antibiótico Rinovinomino (dos pastillas cada ocho horas por siete días)

[1]*high*

Síntomas:

dolor de garganta	☐	tos	☐
dolor de cabeza	☐	vómitos	☐
dolor de oídos	☐	diarrea	☐
dolor de estómago	☐	fiebre	☐

Otros síntomas: _____

_____

Diagnóstico: _____

_____

If you are **Estudiante A**, turn to page 405.

If you are **Estudiante B**, use the information on this page.

10-58 **La biografía de una presidenta.** Tú y tu compañero(a) van a intercambiar información sobre una mujer muy importante: la primera en ser elegida *(elected)* a la presidencia de Argentina. Para completar la tabla, Uds. necesitan hacerse preguntas como las siguientes. Tú **(Estudiante B)** tienes que empezar el intercambio con la primera pregunta.

© AFP/Getty Images

- ¿Cuál es el nombre completo de... ? / ¿Cómo se llama... ?
- ¿Dónde / Cuándo nació... ?
- ¿En qué año se casó / se graduó / ... ?
- ¿Qué pasó / hizo en el año... ?
- ¿Qué había sido antes de ser elegida presidenta?
- (Otras preguntas originales)

Estudiante B

Nombre completo	_____ Elisabet _____ de Kirchner
Fecha y lugar de nacimiento	19 de febrero de 1953 La Plata, Argentina
Profesión	_____ y política
Datos personales	1975: Se casó con Néstor Kirchner, un compañero de la universidad. _____: Nació su hijo Máximo. 1990: Nació su hija Florencia. 2003–2007: Su esposo Néstor fue _____ de Argentina. 2010: Su esposo se murió y Cristina quedó viuda *(widow)*.
Estudios y carrera profesional	1973: Empezó sus estudios en _____ (UNLP). Fue muy activa en asociaciones estudiantiles políticas. 1979: Se graduó de la Facultad de Derecho de la UNLP. 1979–1985: Con su esposo, se dedicó a la práctica privada como _____. 1985: Empezó a ser muy activa en el Partido *(Party)* Justicialista. 1995–2007: Tuvo varios puestos nacionales, tales como _____ y _____. 2007: Fue elegida presidenta de Argentina.

11-59 ¿Qué llevamos a la isla Robinson Crusoe? Tú y tu compañero(a) van a hacer turismo en la isla Robinson Crusoe en el mes de diciembre. Tú (**Estudiante B**) y tu compañero(a) (**Estudiante A**) tienen dos páginas diferentes de una guía turística y dos listas diferentes. Hagan lo siguiente:

If you are **Estudiante A**, turn to page 445.

If you are **Estudiante B**, use the information on this page.

■ Tomando turnos, una persona pregunta si necesita llevar algo de su lista.

■ La otra persona consulta la información de su guía turística, responde a la pregunta y da una explicación.

■ Continúen intercambiando información sobre todas las cosas en las listas. Pongan una ✓ al lado de cada cosa que deben llevar.

Modelo   **Estudiante B:** ¿Tenemos que llevar pasaporte?

   Estudiante A: ¡Sí! La isla Robinson Crusoe es parte de Chile y por eso necesitamos pasaporte. ¿Tenemos que llevar... ?

Estudiante B

Mi lista:

pasaporte ❑	boleto de tren ❑	guantes y bufanda ❑
tarjeta de crédito ❑	medicamentos ❑	pantalones cortos ❑
dinero en efectivo ❑		

Isla Robinson Crusoe

LUGARES DE ATRACCIÓN TURÍSTICA

La hermosa y exuberante isla Robinson Crusoe tiene muchos lugares de interés natural e histórico. Las actividades más populares entre los turistas incluyen el buceo, el snorkel, la pesca, los paseos en kayak y nadar con los lobos marinos[1].

Parque Nacional Juan Fernández: Es Reserva Mundial de la Biosfera. Contiene especies únicas en el mundo. Actividades incluyen trekking, paseos a caballo, buceo, pesca recreativa, natación y observación de pájaros.

Puerto Inglés: Aquí pasó sus días el marinero Selkirk, el que inspiró la famosa novela *Robinson Crusoe*. Es aquí también donde se cree que hay un tesoro enterrado[2] de origen español.

San Juan Bautista: Es el único pueblo de la isla, con una población de 600 habitantes. Cuenta con hoteles pequeños y restaurantes que sirven deliciosos y frescos mariscos. Los visitantes pueden aprender sobre la pesca de langosta[3] y visitar monumentos históricos como el fuerte Santa Bárbara.

[1]*sea lions* [2]*buried treasure* [3]*lobster*

If you are **Estudiante A**, turn to page 485.

If you are **Estudiante B**, use the information on this page.

12-57 **¡A estudiar en el extranjero!** Tú y tu compañero(a) van a dramatizar una escena entre un(a) consejero(a) académico(a) y un(a) estudiante que quiere ir al extranjero el próximo verano para estudiar español.

Estudiante A: el (la) consejero(a)
Tienes que:

- hacerle preguntas sobre las prioridades y preferencias del (de la) estudiante
- usar la información sobre los dos programas para contestar las preguntas
- ayudar al (a la) estudiante a tomar una decisión (**Recomiendo que...**)

Estudiante B: el (la) estudiante
Tienes que:

- empezar la conversación: **Quisiera estudiar en el extranjero el próximo verano. ¿Qué programas me recomienda?**
- hacer preguntas y tomar apuntes
- elegir un programa

Estudiante B

	República Dominicana	Perú
Ubicación del programa		
Fechas del programa		
Precio del progama		
Cursos ofrecidos		
Tipos de alojamiento		
Visitas culturales y excursiones		
El mejor programa para mí		

Vocabulario

Nouns that end in -o are masculine and those that end in -a are feminine unless otherwise indicated.

A

a at, to; **a bordo** on board (11); **a corto plazo** short-term (10); **a cuadros** checkered, plaid (7); **a la plancha** grilled (6); **a largo plazo** long-term (10); **a menos que** unless (12); **a menudo** often (2); **¿A qué distancia está(n)... ?** How far is (are) . . . ? (11); **a rayas** striped (7); **a veces** sometimes (2); **Al final...** At the end . . . (8); **al lado de** next to, beside (1); **al máximo** the most of something (12)

abogado(a) lawyer (10)

abrigo coat (7)

abril *m.* April (4)

abrir to open (3) (4); **Abran los libros en la página (cinco).** Open your books to page (five). (P)

abrumado(a) overwhelmed (12)

abuelo(a) grandfather / grandmother (3); **abuelos** grandparents (3)

aburrido(a) boring (2)

Acabo de... I have just . . . (5)

acampar to camp (4)

accesorio accessory (7)

aceite *m.* oil (6)

aceptar to accept (8)

acogedor(a) cozy (5)

aconsejable advisable (12)

aconsejar to advise (9); **Le / Te aconsejo que...** I advise you to . . . (9); **¿Qué me aconsejas?** What do you advise me? (*informal*) (9)

acostarse (ue) to go to bed (5)

acostumbrar to be accustomed to; to customarily (do something) (8); **acostumbrarse** to get used to (12)

actor *m.* actor (8)

actriz *f.* actress (8)

acuario aquarium (11)

adelgazar to lose weight (6)

adiós good-bye (1)

adjetivo adjective (1)

administración de empresas *f.* business administration (P)

¿Adónde... ? Where . . . ? (1); To where? (2)

aduana customs (11)

aerolínea airline (11)

aeropuerto airport (4)

afeitarse to shave (5)

agente *m. f.* (airline) representative (11); **agente de bienes raíces** real estate agent (10); **agente de bolsa** stockbroker (10)

agosto August (4)

agua (mineral) (mineral) water (6)

águila *f.* eagle (8)

ahora now (6)

aire acondicionado A/C, air conditioning (4)

ala *f.* wing (8)

albóndigas meatballs (6)

alegre happy, lively (8)

alérgico(a) allergic (9)

alfombra rug (5)

álgebra *f.* algebra (P)

algo something, anything (4); **¿(Desean) Algo más?** Is there anything else (you want)? (6)

alguien somebody / someone; anybody / anyone (4)

alguna vez ever (7)

alguno(a) some, any (4)

alimento food (6)

allí there (1)

almacén, gran almacén *m.* department store (7)

almorzar (ue) to have lunch (3)

almuerzo lunch (6)

alojamiento lodging, housing (12)

alquilar to rent (11)

alquiler *m.* rental (11)

alto(a) tall (3); **alto(a) en grasa** high in fat, fatty (9)

alumno(a) student (12)

amable kind and helpful (2)

amarillo yellow (7)

ambiente *m.* atmosphere (8)

amigo(a) friend (3); **mejor amigo(a)** best friend (3)

amistad *f.* friendship (12)

análisis de sangre *m.* blood test (9)

analizar to analyze (10)

anaranjado orange (7)

anécdota personal story (8)

anfitrión *m.* host (3)

anfitriona hostess (3)

anillo ring (7)

aniversario de bodas wedding anniversary (3); **¡Feliz aniversario!** Happy anniversary! (3)

anoche last night (5)

anteayer the day before yesterday (5)

anteojos eyeglasses (3)

antes de before (5); **antes de que** before (12)

antibiótico antibiotic (9)

antiguo(a) very old (5)

antipático(a) mean, unpleasant (2)

año year (1); **Año Nuevo** New Year (8); **el año pasado** last year (5); **el año que viene** next year (4); **el próximo año** next year (4)

apagar to blow out, to turn off (3)

apartamento apartment (1)

aprender (a) to learn (how) (2)

aprendizaje *m.* learning (12)

apretado(a) (too) tight, snug (7)

apuntes *m. pl.* notes (2)

aquel (aquella) that (over there) (7)

aquellos(as) those (over there) (7)

aquí here (1)

árbol *m.* tree (8)

aretes *m. pl.* earrings (7)

arquitecto(a) architect (10)

arreglar to fix (10); **arreglarse** to get oneself ready (5)

arroba @ symbol (1); **Es... arroba... punto...** It's . . . @ . . . dot . . . (1)

arroz *m.* rice (6); **arroz con leche** rice pudding (6)

arte(s) *m. sing., f. pl.* art (P)

artesanía arts and crafts (7)

artículo article (1)

artista *m. f.* artist (10)

artístico(a) artistic (8)

asesinato murder (12)

así que so (3)

asiento de pasillo aisle seat (11); **asiento de ventanilla** window seat (11)

asignaturas academic subjects (P)

asistente *m. f.* assistant (12)

asistir a to go to, to attend (2)

aspiración *f.* aspiration, wish (10)

aspiradora vacuum (5)

asunto (legal) (legal) issue (10)

ataque terrorista *m.* terrorist attack (12)

atender (ie) to look after, to attend to (10)

aterrorizado(a) terrified (8)

atleta *m. f.* athlete (8)

atlético(a) athletic (3)

atletismo track and field (8)

atractivo attraction (11)

atraer to attract (11)

aumentar de peso to gain weight (6)

aumento (de sueldo) (salary) increase (10)

aunque although (3)

auto car (11)

autobús *m.* bus (4)

autoridad *f.* authority (12)

avanzar to move forward, to advance (12)

avenida avenue (1)

avería breakdown (11)

avión *m.* airplane (4)

avisar to let know (10)

¡Ay! Ow!, Ouch! (9)

ayer yesterday (5)

ayudar to help (5); **ayudar al prójimo** to help others (10); **¿Puedes ayudarme?** Can you help me? (*informal*) (5)

azúcar *m.* sugar (6)

azul blue (3)

B

bailar to dance (2)

baile *m.* dance (8)

bajo(a) short (3)

balanceado(a) balanced (6)

ballena whale; **observar las ballenas** to go whale-watching (11)

baloncesto basketball (2)

banana banana (6)

banco bank (4)

bandera flag (8)

bañarse to take a bath, to bathe (5)

bañera bathtub (5)

baño bathroom (4)

barato(a) cheap, inexpensive (7)

barba beard (3)

barbacoa picnic, barbecue (3)

barbaridad atrocity; **¡Qué barbaridad!** That's awful! (8)

barrer to sweep (5)

barrio neighborhood (5); **barrio histórico** historical neighborhood (11)

bastante quite, fairly, rather (6)

basura trash (5)

beber to drink (4); **¿Qué les traigo para beber / tomar?** What can I get you to drink? (6)

bebida drink, beverage (3); **bebida alcóholica** alcoholic beverage (6)

beca scholarship (10)

béisbol *m.* baseball (2)

bellas artes *f. pl.* fine arts (P)

beneficio benefit (10)

biblioteca library (1)

bien well (6); **Bien.** Fine; Good. (P); **(No) Muy bien.** (Not) Very well / Great. (1)

bienestar *m.* well-being (9)

¡Bienvenido(a)! Welcome! (5)

bigote *m.* moustache (3)

billetera wallet (7)

biología biology (P)

bistec *m.* steak (6)

blanco white (7)

blog *m.* blog (2)

blusa blouse (7)

boca mouth (9)

boda wedding (3)

boleto (de ida y vuelta) (round-trip) ticket (4)

bolígrafo pen (1)

bolso purse, handbag (7)

bonito(a) pretty, nice (3); **¡Qué día más bonito!** What a beautiful day! (4)

bosque *m.* forest (11); **bosque tropical / lluvioso** tropical forest / rainforest (11)

botas boots (7)

botella (de agua) (water) bottle (1)

brazo arm (9)

brindar to make a toast (3); **Brindo por...** Here's to . . . (3)

brócoli *m.* broccoli (6)

bromista jokester (3)

bucear to scuba dive (4)

bueno(a) good (2); **¡Buen provecho!** Bon appetit! (6); **¡Buen viaje!** Have a good trip! (4); **buena gente** a good person, "good people" (3); **¡Buena idea!** Good idea! (2); **Buenas noches.** Good evening; Good night. (1); **Buenas tardes.** Good afternoon. (1); **Buenos días.** Good morning. (1)

bufanda scarf, muffler (7)

buscar to look for (5); to seek (9); **Busco (una camiseta).** I'm looking for (a T-shirt). (7)

C

cabeza head (9)

cada (cuatro horas) every (four hours) (9)

caerse to fall (down) (9)

café *m.* coffee (4); coffee shop (1)

cafetería cafeteria (1)

cajero automático ATM , automated teller machine (4)

calcetines *m. pl.* socks (7)

cálculo calculus (P)

calendario calendar (1)

calidad *f.* quality (7); **Es de primera calidad.** It's top quality. (7)

cálido(a) hot (climate) (11)

callado(a) quiet, reserved (person) (3)

calle *f.* street (1); **Es calle..., número...** It's . . . Street . . . (1)

calor hot (4); **Hace (un poco de) calor.** It's (a bit) hot. (4); **¡Qué calor!** It's so hot! (4)

calvo(a) bald (3)

cama bed (5); **hacer la cama** to make the bed (5); **guardar cama** to stay in bed (9)

camarera waitress (6)

camarero waiter (6)

camarón, camarones *m.* shrimp (6)

cambiar to exchange, to change (4)

cambio automático / manual automatic / manual shift (11)

caminar to walk (4)

caminata hike; **hacer caminatas** to hike, to go hiking (4)

camino way (11)

camisa shirt (7)

camiseta T-shirt (7)

campanada (bell) stroke (8)

campeonato championship (8)

campo field (10); country (rural area) (11)

campus *m.* campus (1)

canción *f.* song (8)

candidato(a) candidate (12)

canoso(a) white-haired, gray-haired (3)

cansado(a) tired (1)

cantante *m. f.* singer (8)

cantar to sing (3)

cañón *m.* canyon (11)

capacidad *f.* ability (10)

cara face (5)

carácter *m.* character, personality, temperament (3)

carbohidrato carbohydrate (6)

cariño affection, love (3)

cariñoso(a) loving, affectionate (3)

carnaval *m.* carnival (8)

carne *f.* meat (6)

caro(a) expensive (7)

carrera major, degree (2)

carreta cart (7)

carretera highway (11)

carta de recomendación letter of recommendation (10)

cartas playing cards (3)

cartel *m.* poster (5)

casa house (3); **Estás en tu casa.** Make yourself at home. (5)

casado(a) married (3)

casarse to get married (10)

casi nunca hardly ever (4); **casi siempre** almost always (2) (4)

castaño(a) brown (3)

castillo castle (11)

catedral *f.* cathedral (4)

catorce fourteen (1)

celebración *f.* celebration (3)

celebrar to celebrate (8)

cena supper (3); dinner, supper (6)

cenar to have supper (5)

central central (11)

centro comercial mall, shopping center (7); **centro de orientación vocacional** career center (10); **centro estudiantil** student center (1)

cerámica ceramic (7)

cerca (de) nearby, close (to) (1); near (5)

cerdo pork (6)

cereal *m.* cereal (6)

cero zero (1)

cerrar (ie) to close (4); **Cierren los libros.** Close your books. (P)

cerro hill (11)

cerveza beer (6)

cesta basket (7)

ceviche *m.* raw fish marinated in lime juice (6)

chancletas flip flops (7)

chao bye; ciao (*informal*) (1)

chaqueta jacket (7)

charlar to chat (3)

chico(a) guy, boy / girl (3)

chimenea fireplace (5)

¡Chin chin! Cheers! (3)

chino(a) Chinese (2)

chiste *m.* joke (3)

choque *m.* crash, collision (12)

chuleta de cerdo pork chop (6)

churrasco grilled steak (6)

ciclismo cycling (8)

cielo sky (8)

cien one hundred (1)

ciencias naturales natural science (P); **ciencias políticas** political science (P); **ciencias sociales** social sciences (P)

científico(a) scientist (10)

cierto true; **(No) Es cierto que...** It's (not) true that . . . (1)

cima top, summit (8)

cinco five (1); **cinco veces** five times (5)

cincuenta fifty (1)

cine *m.* movies, movie theater (2)

cinematografía film-making (P)

cinturón *m.* belt (7)

cirujano(a) surgeon (10)

cita appointment; **pedir cita** to make an appointment (9)

ciudad *f.* city (4)

claro(a) clear (11); **¡Claro que sí!** Of course! (1)

clase *f.* class (P); **¿Qué clases tienes?** What classes do you have? (*informal*) (P)

clásico(a) classic (7)

cliente(a) customer (6)

clima climate (11)

clínica health center (1)

clóset *m.* closet (5)

club *m.* club (2)

cocina kitchen (5)

coco coconut (6)

colaborar collaborate (12)

collar *m.* necklace (7)

colonial colonial (5)

comedor *m.* dining room (5); **comedor de caridad** soup kitchen (12)

comer to eat (2)

comida food (3); meal; lunch; main meal of the day (6); **comida basura** junk food (6); **comida rápida** fast food (6)

como as, like; **como segundo idioma** as a second language (12); **como yo** like me (3)

¿Cómo? How? (2); **¿Cómo desea pagar?** How do you want to pay? (*formal*) (7); **¿Cómo está usted?** How are you? (*formal*) (P) (1); **¿Cómo estás?** How are you? (*informal*) (P) (1); **¿Cómo llego a... ?** How do I get to . . . ? (11); **Cómo no.** Of course. (10); **¿Cómo pasó?** How did it happen? (8); **¿Cómo se dice... ?** How do you say . . . ? (1); **¿Cómo se escribe tu nombre?** How do you spell your name? (*informal*) (P); **¿Cómo se llama usted?** What's your name? (*formal*) (1); **¿Cómo te llamas?** What's your name? (*informal*) (P) (1); **¿Cómo te sientes?** How do you feel? (*informal*) (9)

cómoda dresser (5)

cómodo(a) comfortable (7)

compañero(a) partner (1); **compañero(a) de clase** classmate (1); **compañero(a) de cuarto** roommate (1)

comparar to compare (12)

compartido(a) shared (12)

compartir to share (9)

competencia competition (8)

competitivo(a) competitive (10)

completamente completely (6)

comprar to buy (3)

comprender to understand (2)

comprensivo(a) understanding (3)
computadora (portátil) (laptop) computer (1)
común common, usual (6)
comunicación *f.* communication (P)
comunidad *f.* community (12)
con with (1); **¿Con qué está acompañado?** What does it come with? (6); **¿Con qué frecuencia?** How often? (2); **con regularidad** regularly (6); **con tal (de) que** provided that (12)
concierto concert (2)
concurso contest (8)
condimento condiment (6)
conducir to drive (4)
conductor(a) driver (11)
congelado(a) frozen (8)
congestionado(a) congested (9)
conjunto musical group (8)
conocer to know; to meet (4); **conocer el mundo** to travel around the world (10); **conocer nuevos lugares** to see new places (4)
conseguir (i) to get, to obtain (6); to get (10)
consejero(a) académico(a) academic advisor (12)
consejo advice, piece of advice (6) (9)
conservación *f.* conservation (12)
conservar to save (12)
considerado(a) considerate, thoughtful (12)
construir to build (5)
consulado consulate (12)
consultar to consult (6) (12)
consultorio (medical) office (9)
consumir to eat / drink; to consume (6)
contador(a) accountant (10)
contar (ue) (chistes, cuentos) to tell (jokes, stories); to count (3)
contento(a) happy, glad (1)
contestar to answer, to reply (2); **Contesten las preguntas.** Answer the questions. (P)
continuar to continue (8)
contratar to hire (10)
control de seguridad *m.* security check (11)
convencer to persuade (10)
convertir (ie) to turn, to transform (8)
coordinar to coordinate (12)
copia copy (10)
corazón *m.* heart (9)
corbata necktie (7)
cordillera (mountain) range (11)
correo electrónico email; **¿Cuál es tu correo electrónico?** What's your email (address)? (1)
correr to run (2)
corrupción *f.* corruption (12)
cortar(se) to cut, to get cut (9)
cortés polite (12)
corto(a) short (3)
costar (ue) to cost (4); **¿Cuánto cuesta (ese sombrero)?** How much does (that hat) cost? (7)
costumbre *f.* custom (8)
crear to create (12)
creativo(a) creative (10)
creer to believe (8); **Creo que...** I think that . . . (9); **No lo puedo creer.** I can't believe it. (8)
crema lotion (9)
crucero cruise; cruise ship (4)
cruzar to cross (11)
cuaderno spiral notebook (1)
cuadra block (4); **a (dos) cuadras** (two) blocks away (4)

cuadro (wall) picture (5); **a cuadros** checkered, plaid (7)
¿Cuál... ? What . . . ? (1); **¿Cuál(es)?** Which one(s)? (2)
¿Cuándo? When? (2)
¿Cuánto(a)? How much? (2); **¿Cuánto cuesta la noche?** How much does one night cost? (4); **¿Cuánto tiempo hace que... (presente)?** How long has / have . . . ? (9); **¿Cuánto tiempo hace... (pretérito)?** How long ago . . . ? (9)
¿Cuántos(as)? How many? (2); **¿Cuántos años tiene... ?** How old is . . . ? (1)
cuarenta forty (1)
cuarto(a) fourth (7)
cuarto room; **¿Cómo es tu cuarto?** What is your room like? (1)
cuatro four (1)
cubrir to cover (8)
cuchara spoon (6)
cucharita teaspoon (6)
cuchillo knife (6)
cuenta bill, check (in a restaurant) (6); **La cuenta, por favor.** The bill, please. (6)
cuento story (3)
cuero leather (7)
cuerpo body (9)
cuidarse to take care of oneself (9); **Cuídate.** Take care. (9)
cultural cultural (8)
cumpleaños *m. sing.* birthday (3); **¡Feliz cumpleaños!** Happy birthday! (3)
curioso(a) odd; **Es curioso que...** It's odd that . . . (10)
currículum *m.* curriculum vitae, CV (10)
curso course (12)

D

danza dance (12)
dar to give (4); **dar consejos** to give advice (6); **dar un paseo** to go for a walk, to stroll (4); **dar un paseo en velero** to go sailing (4)
darse un golpe to get hit (9)
datos data (10)
de from, of (1); **De acuerdo.** Okay. (2); **de bajos ingresos** low-income (12); **¿De dónde?** From where? (2); **¿De dónde es... ?** Where is . . . from? (1); **De nada.** You're welcome; No problem. (1); **De niño(a)...** As a child . . . (8); **¿De quién es... ?** Who does . . . belong to? (1); **De repente...** Suddenly . . . (8); **¿De veras?** Really? (8)
debajo de under (5)
deber must, should, ought to (4); **Debe(s) / Debería(s)...** You should . . . (9); **¿Qué debo hacer?** What should I do? (6)
débil weak (9)
décimo(a) tenth (7)
decir (i) to say, to tell (4)
decorar to decorate (3)
dedicarse to dedicate oneself to; to do (10)
dedo finger; toe (9)
dejar de to stop (doing something) (9)
delante de in front of (5)
delgado(a) thin, slender (3)
delicioso(a) delicious (6)
demasiado too much (6)
demorarse to be delayed (11)
denunciar to denounce, to condemn (12)
Depende. It depends. (8)
dependiente(a) salesclerk (7)
deportivo(a) sports-related (8)

derecha right; **a la derecha de** to the right of (5)
derecho law (P)
derechos rights (12)
desastre *m.* mess (5); **desastre natural** natural disaster (12)
desayunar to have breakfast (5)
desayuno breakfast (6)
descansar to relax (2)
desconectarse to disconnect oneself, to get away from it all (9)
descubrir to discover (12)
descuento discount (4)
deseo wish (3)
desfile *m.* parade (8)
desierto desert (11)
desorden *m.* untidiness, disorder (5)
desordenado(a) messy (5)
despacio slowly (6)
despedida farewell (1)
despedirse (i) to say good-bye (6)
despertarse (ie) to wake up (5)
despistado(a) absentminded, scatterbrained (2)
después de after (5); **después de que** after (12)
destino turístico tourist destination (11)
detrás de behind (5)
día *m.* day (2); **Día de Acción de Gracias** Thanksgiving Day (8); **Día de la Independencia** Independence Day (8); **Día de la Madre** Mother's Day (8); **Día del Amor y la Amistad** Valentine's Day (8); **Día del Padre** Father's Day (8); **Día del Trabajo** Labor Day (8); **día festivo** holiday (8)
diagnóstico diagnosis (9)
diarrea diarrhea (9)
diccionario dictionary (1)
diciembre *m.* December (4)
diecinueve nineteen (1)
dieciocho eighteen (1)
dieciséis sixteen (1)
diecisiete seventeen (1)
diente *m.* tooth (9); **dientes** teeth (5)
dieta diet (6)
dietético(a) diet (6)
diez ten (1)
diferencia diference (12)
difícil difficult (2)
dinero money (4)
dios *m.* god (8); **diosa** goddess (8)
dirección *f.* address (1); **¿Cuál es tu dirección?** What's your address? (1)
discapacitado(a) handicapped (12)
diseñar to design (10)
diseño design (7)
disfraz *m.* costume (8)
disfrazarse (de) to dress up in a costume (as) (8)
disfrutar de to enjoy (3); **disfrutar de la vida** to enjoy life (9)
disponible available (10)
dispuesto(a) willing (10)
divertido(a) fun, entertaining, enjoyable (2) (3)
divertirse (ie) to have a good time (5)
divorciado(a) divorced (3)
doblar to turn (11)
doble double (4); **doble tracción** *f.* four-wheel drive (11)
doce twelve (1)
doctor (Dr.) doctor *(male)* (P); **doctora (Dra.)** doctor *(female)* (P)
doctorado doctorate (10)

documento de identidad ID (11)
doler to hurt, to ache (9)
dolor *m.* ache, pain (9)
domingo Sunday (2); **Domingo de Pascua** Easter Sunday (8)
donativo donation (12)
donde where (11)
¿Dónde? Where? (2); **¿Dónde está... ?** Where is . . . ? (1); **¿Dónde están los probadores?** Where are the fitting rooms? (7); **¿Dónde vives?** Where do you live? *(informal)* (1)
dormir (ue) to sleep (3); **dormirse (ue)** to fall asleep (5)
dormitorio bedroom (5)
dos two (1); **dos veces** twice (5)
ducha shower (5)
ducharse to take a shower (5)
duda doubt (10); **No hay duda de que...** There's not doubt that . . . (10)
dudar to doubt (10)
dulce sweet (6); **¿Es dulce?** Is it sweet? (6)
dulces *m. pl.* candy (8)

E

económico(a) inexpensive (4)
edad *f.* age (3)
edificio building (10)
educación *f.* education (P)
ejercicio exercise (6); **hacer ejercicio** to exercise (6)
él he (1)
el the *(sing., masc.)* (1)
elecciones *f. pl.* elections (12)
electricidad *f.* electricity (12)
electrónica electronics store / department (7)
elegante elegant (7)
elegir (i) to choose (8)
ella she (1)
ellos(as) they (1)
embajada embassy (12)
emocionado(a) excited (1)
emocionante exciting (3); **¡Qué emocionante!** How exciting! (8)
empanada savory turnover (6)
empanizado(a) breaded (6)
empezar (ie) to start, to begin (3)
empleado(a) employee (10)
empleo employment (10)
emprendedor(a) enterprising (10)
empresa firm (10)
empresario(a) entrepreneur (10)
en inside, in, on (1) (5); **en caso de** in case of (11); **en caso de que** in case (12); **en cuanto** as soon as (12); **en efectivo** cash (4); **en exceso** too much (6); **en medio** in the center (5); **en moderación** in moderation (6)
encantar to love (something) (7); **Me encanta...** I love to . . . (4); **Me encantaría.** I'd love to. (3) (8)
encender (ie) to light (8)
encima de on top of (5)
encontrar (ue) to find (5)
encontrarse (ue) to be located (11); to meet (up) (8)
enero January (4)
enfermarse to get sick (9)
enfermedad *f.* illness (9)
enfermero(a) nurse (9)
enfermo(a) ill, sick (1)
enfrente de across from, facing (1)
enigmático(a) enigmatic (11)
enojado(a) angry, mad (1)

enojarse to get angry, to get mad (5)
ensalada salad (6)
enseguida right away (6)
enseñar to teach (10)
entender (ie) to understand (3); **¿Entienden?** Do you understand? *(informal)* (P)
enterarse to find out (12)
Entonces... Then . . . (8)
entrada admission, entrance (4)
entre (in) between, among (5); **entre semana** during the week, on weekdays (2)
entrenador(a) trainer (6)
entrenamiento training (12)
entretenimiento entertainment (12)
entrevista interview (10)
entrevistado(a) interviewee (10)
entrevistador(a) interviewer (10)
envolver (ue) to wrap (3)
época time of year (8)
equilibrio balance (9)
equipaje (de mano) *m.* (carry-on) luggage (11)
equipo team (8)
erupción volcánica *f.* volcanic eruption (12)
escalada climb; **hacer escalada en roca** to go rock climbing (11)
escalera staircase (5)
escaparate *m.* display window (7)
escoger to choose, to pick, to select (9)
escribir to write (2); **Escriban la respuesta.** Write the answer. (P); **¿Cómo se escribe tu nombre?** How do you spell your name? *(informal)* (P)
escritorio desk (5)
escuchar to listen; **escuchar música** to listen to music (2); **Escuchen.** Listen. (P)
escuela school (10); **escuela primaria** elementary school (12)
ese(a) that (7)
eso that *(neuter)* (7)
esos(as) those (7)
espaguetis *m. pl.* spaghetti (6)
espalda back (part of body) (9)
especialidad *f.* specialty; **¿Cuál es la especialidad de la casa?** What's the house's specialty? (6)
espectáculo show (4); **¡Qué espectáculo!** What a show! (8)
espejo mirror (5)
esperar to hope (4)
espinacas spinach (6)
esposo(a) husband / wife; spouse (3)
esquiar to ski (4)
esquina corner (of a city street) (11); **en la esquina** on the corner (4)
estación *f.* station (4), season (4); **estación de lluvia** rainy season (4); **estación seca** dry season (4)
estacionar to park (11)
estadía stay (12)
estadio stadium (1)
estampado(a) patterned, printed (7)
estante *m.* shelf (5)
estar to be (1)
estatua statue (11)
este *m.* east (11)
este(a) this (7); **Este(a) soy yo.** This is me. (3)
estilo style (5) (7); **estilo de vida** lifestyle (6)
esto this *(neuter)* (7)
estómago stomach (9)
estornudar to sneeze (9)
estos(as) these (7)
estrella star (11)
estrés *m. sing.* stress (9)
estresado(a) stressed (1)

estudiante *m. f.* student (1)
estudiar to study (2); **estudiar en el extranjero** to study abroad (10)
estudios profesionales professional studies (P)
estufa stove (5)
estupendo wonderful (10); **Es estupendo que...** It's great / wonderful that . . . (10)
evacuar to evacuate (12)
evento event (8)
evitar to avoid (6)
examen *m.* test, exam (2); **examen médico** medical examination (9)
exceso excess (6)
excursión *f.* excursion, tour (4); **¿Qué excursión nos recomienda?** What tour do you recommend (to us)? *(formal)* (4)
exigente strict, demanding (2)
éxito success (10)
experiencia experience (10)
explicar to explain (6); **¿Me puede explicar qué es (el ceviche)?** Can you explain what (ceviche) is? *(formal)* (6)
explorar to explore (4)
exposición *f.* exhibition (8)
extranjero abroad (10)
extrañar to miss (someone) (12)
extraño(a) strange, odd (8)
extrovertido(a) outgoing (3)

F

fácil easy (2)
fácilmente easily (6)
facturar to check in (11)
facultad *f.* college (1)
falda skirt (7)
Falleció hace unos años. He/She passed away a few years ago. (3)
faltar to be missing or lacking (7)
familia family (2) (3)
fantástico fantastic (10); **Es fantástico que...** It's fantastic that . . . (10)
farmacia pharmacy, drugstore (4)
fastidio bother (5); **¡Qué fastidio!** What a bother! (5)
fatal awful (9)
febrero February (4)
fecha date (4); **¿Qué fecha es hoy?** What's today's date? (4)
¡Felices fiestas! Happy holidays! (8)
¡Feliz cumpleaños! Happy birthday! (3); **¡Feliz aniversario!** Happy anniversary! (3); **¡Feliz Día de (la Madre)!** Happy (Mother's) Day! (8); **¡Feliz Navidad!** Merry Christmas! (8)
feo(a) ugly (3)
feria fair (8)
festejar to celebrate (3)
festival *m.* festival (8)
festivo(a) festive (8)
fibra fiber (6)
fideo noodle (6)
fiebre *f.* fever (9)
fiesta party (2) (3); **fiesta de cumpleaños** birthday party (3); **fiesta sorpresa** surprise party (3)
fin de semana *m.* weekend (2); **fin de semana pasado** last weekend (5)
física physics (P)
flan *m.* custard dessert (6)
flexible flexible (10)
flojo(a) (too) baggy, loose (7)
flor *f.* flower (3)

folleto brochure (12)
foto *f.* photograph (3)
fractura fracture (9)
fregadero kitchen sink (5)
fresas strawberries (6)
fresco(a) cool (4); fresh (6); **Hace fresco.** It's cool. (4); **El pescado está muy fresco.** The fish is very fresh. (6)
frijol *m.* bean (6)
frío cold (4); **Hace (un poco de) frío.** It's (a bit) cold. (4); **¡Qué frío!** It's so cold! (4)
frito(a) fried (6)
fruta fruit (6)
fuegos artificiales fireworks (8)
fuente *f.* fountain (5)
fumar to smoke (6)
furioso(a) furious (8)
fútbol *m.* soccer (2); **fútbol americano** football (2)

G

gafas eyeglasses (3)
galleta cookie (6)
ganar dinero to make / to earn money (10)
garganta throat (9)
gasolinera gas station (11)
gato(a) cat (3)
gaveta drawer (5)
generoso(a) generous (3)
gente *f.* people (4); **buena gente** a good person, "good people" (3)
geografía geography (11)
geometría geometry (P)
gerente *m. f.* manager (10)
gimnasio gym, fitness center (1)
glaciar *m.* glacier (11)
globo balloon (3)
gobierno government (10) (11)
gordo(a) fat (3)
gorra cap (hat) (7)
Gracias. Thank you; Thanks. (P); thank you (1); **Gracias por todo.** Thanks for everything. (3)
gracioso(a) funny, amusing (8)
grado degree (9)
graduación *f.* graduation (3)
graduarse to graduate (10)
grande big, large (1)
grano grain (6)
grasa fat (6)
gripe *f.* flu (9)
gris grey (7)
grupo estudiantil student organization (2)
guantes *m. pl.* gloves (7)
guapo(a) good-looking, handsome (3)
guardar to put away (5); to keep (somewhere) (12); **guardar cama** to stay in bed (9)
guardería day-care center (12)
guayaba (en almíbar) guava (in syrup) (6)
guerra war (12)
guitarra guitar (2)
gustar to like, to be pleasing to (3); **me gusta** I like (2); **¿Te gustaría ir... ?** Would you like to go to . . . ? (8)

H

Había una vez... Once upon a time . . . (8)
habilidad *f.* skill (12)
habitación *f.* room (4)
hábito habit (6)

hablar (por teléfono) to talk (on the phone) (2)
hacer to do, to make (4); **Hace muchos años...** A long time ago . . . (8); **Hace siete años que me lastimé la espalda.** I injured my back seven years ago. (9); **hace tres años** three years ago (5); **Hace una semana que me siento mal.** I've been feeling under the weather for a week. (9); **hacer rafting** to go (white-water) rafting (11); **hacer snowboard** to snowboard, to go snowboarding (11); **hacer surf** to surf (4)
Halloween *m.* Halloween (8)
hamaca hammock (7)
hamburguesa hamburger (6)
harto(a) fed up with (5); **Estoy harto(a) de...** I'm fed up with . . . (5)
hasta until (5); **Hasta luego.** See you later. (1); **Hasta mañana.** See you tomorrow. (1); **hasta que** until (12)
hay there is / there are (1); **¿Hay... por aquí?** Is there . . . around here? (4); **Hay que...** One / We / You must . . . (6)
haya there be (9)
hecho(a) a mano handmade (7)
helado ice cream (6)
herida wound, injury (9)
herido(a) wounded (person), injured (person) (12)
hermano(a) brother / sister; sibling (3)
hermoso(a) beautiful (8)
hielo ice (6); **Un (agua mineral) sin hielo.** Some (mineral water) with no ice. (6)
hijo(a) son / daughter; child (3); **hijo(a) único(a)** only child (3)
historia history (P)
hogar para ancianos *m.* nursing home (12)
hoja de papel sheet of paper (1)
hola hi, hello (P) (1)
hombre *m.* man (3); **hombre de negocios** businessman (10)
hombro shoulder (9)
hora time; hour (2); **¿A qué hora?** At what time? (2); **¿Qué hora es?** What time is it? (2); **No veo la hora de...** I can't wait to . . . (4)
horario schedule (2); **horario de oficina** office hours (2)
horno oven (5)
horror horror; **¡Qué horror!** That's awful! (8)
hostal *m.* guesthouse (12)
hotel *m.* hotel (4)
hoy today (2)
Hubo... There was . . . / There were . . . (6)
huelga strike (12)
hueso bone (9)
huésped *m. f.* guest (12)
huevo egg (6)
huir to run away, to escape (8)
humanidades *f. pl.* humanities (P)
húmedo(a) humid (11)
huracán *m.* hurricane (12)

I

idea idea (9); **Es buena idea...** It's a good idea . . . (6) (9); **Es buena idea que...** It's a good idea for (someone) to . . . (9)
ideal ideal, perfect (9)
idioma *m.* language (12)
iglesia church (8)
igualmente same here; likewise (1)
impartir clases to teach (12)

importante important (6) (9); **Es importante...** It's important . . . (6); **Es importante que...** It's important that . . . (9)
importar to care about, to matter (7); **No me importa.** I don't care. (5)
imposible impossible (10); **Es imposible que...** It's impossible that / for . . . (10)
incendio (forestal) (forest) fire (12)
incluido(a) included (11)
increíble incredible (8)
indicaciones *f. pl.* directions (11)
infección *f.* infection (9)
informal informal, casual (7)
informar to inform (10); to report (12); **informarse** to find out (12)
informática computer science (P)
informe *m.* paper, report (2)
ingeniería engineering (P)
ingeniero(a) engineer (10)
inmigrante *m. f.* immigrant (12)
inodoro toilet (5)
inolvidable memorable, unforgettable (3)
instrucción *f.* instruction (9); **instrucciones del profesor** professor's instructions (P)
integrarse to integrate yourself, to fit in (12)
intelectual intellectual (3)
inteligente smart, intelligent (3)
intensivo(a) intensive (12)
intercambiar regalos to exchange gifts (8)
interesado(a) interested (10)
interesante interesting (2)
interesar to be interested in (7)
intermedio(a) intermediate (12)
internacional international (8)
intoxicación alimenticia *f.* food poisoning (9)
inundación *f.* flooding (12)
investigación *f.* research (10); **hacer investigaciones** to research (10)
invierno winter (4)
invitación *f.* invitation (3)
invitado(a) guest (3)
invitar to extend an invitation (8)
inyección *f.* shot (9)
ir to go (1); **ir a pie** to walk, to go on foot (4); **ir de compras** to go shopping (2)
isla island (11)
izquierda left (5); **a la izquierda de** to the left of (5)

J

jamón *m.* ham (6)
Janucá Chanukah (8)
jarabe *m.* syrup (9)
jardín *m.* yard; garden (5)
jefe(a) boss (10)
joven young (3)
joyas *f. pl.* jewelry (7)
joyería jewelry (store / department) (7)
jueves *m.* Thursday (2)
jugar (ue) to play (a sport or game) (3)
jugo juice (6)
juguete *m.* toy (7)
julio July (4)
junio June (4)

K

kilómetro kilometer (11)

L

la the (*sing., fem.*) (1); **la** her (5)
laboratorio lab (1)
lago lake (11)
lámpara lamp (5)
lancha motorboat (4)
lápiz *m.* pencil (1)
largo(a) long (3)
las the (*pl., fem.*) (1)
lástima shame (10); **Es una lástima que...** It's a shame / too bad that . . . (10); **¡Qué lástima!** That's too bad! (9)
lastimarse to get hurt, to injure oneself (9)
lavamanos *m.* bathroom sink (5)
lavaplatos *m.* dishwashing machine, dishwasher (5)
lavar (la ropa) to wash (clothes) (2); **lavar los platos** to do the dishes (5)
lavarse to wash oneself (5); **lavarse los dientes** to brush one's teeth (5)
le to / for you (*sing., form.*) (6); to / for him or her (6)
leche *f.* milk (6)
lechuga lettuce (6)
leer to read (2)
lejos de far from (1); far (5)
lengua tongue (9)
lenguas languages (P)
les to / for you (*pl.*) (6); to / for them (6)
letrero sign (11)
levantarse to get up (5)
leyenda legend (8)
libertad *f.* freedom (12)
libre free, available (4)
librería bookstore (1)
libro book (1)
límite de velocidad *m.* speed limit (11)
limonada lemonade (6)
limpiar to clean (2)
limpio(a) clean (5)
lindo(a) cute, pretty (3)
líquido(a) liquid (9)
listo(a) ready (6); **¿Están listos para pedir?** Are you ready to order? (6)
literatura literature (P)
llamar to call; **¡Te llamo más tarde!** I'll call you later! (1)
llamarse to be named; **Me llamo...** My name is . . . (P) (1); **Se llama...** His/Her name is . . . (1)
llave *f.* key (5)
llavero key ring (7)
llegar to arrive (2); **¿Cómo llego a... ?** How do I get to . . . ? (11)
llenar to fill (out) (10)
llevar to wear, to carry; **llevar años aquí** to have been living here for years (3); **llevar (una vida)** to lead (a life) (6); **Me lo (la) llevo.** I'll take it. (7)
llover (ue) to rain; **Está lloviendo.** It's raining. (4); **Llueve...** It rains . . . (4)
lo him (5); **lo, la** you (*sing., form.*) (5); it (5); **Lo siento (mucho).** I'm (very) sorry. (1)
loco(a) crazy (3)
lógicamente logically (6)
los the (*pl., masc.*) (1); **los, las** you (*pl., form. in Spain*) (5); them (5)
luchar (por) to fight (for) (12)
luego then, next (5)
lugar *m.* place (4)
luna moon (8)
lunes *m.* Monday (2)
luz *f.* light (1)

M

madera wood (7)
madre *f.* mother (3)
madrugada early morning (2); **de la madrugada** a.m. (late night, early morning hours) (2)
maestría master's degree (10)
maestro(a) teacher, schoolteacher (10)
magnífico(a) magnificent (11)
maíz *m.* corn (6)
mal lousy, bad, not well (9)
malentendido misunderstanding (12)
maleta suitcase; **hacer la maleta** to pack a suitcase (4)
malo(a) bad (2)
mamá mom (3)
mandar to send (3); **mandar mensajes de texto** to text, to send text messages (2)
manejar to manage (10)
manera way, method (9)
manifestación *f.* demonstration (12)
mano *f.* hand (5) (9)
mantequilla butter (6)
manzana apple (6)
mañana tomorrow (2) (4); **de la mañana** a.m. (6 a.m. to noon) (2); **esta mañana** this morning (5); **por la mañana** in the morning (2)
mapa (del mundo) *m.* (world) map (1)
maquillarse to put on make-up (5)
mar *m.* sea, ocean (4)
mariscos seafood (6)
marrón brown (7)
martes *m.* Tuesday (2)
marzo March (4)
más more; **el (la) / los (las) más...** the most . . . (3); **más... que** more . . . than (3); **¿Quieres más... ?** Do you want more . . . ? (*informal*) (6)
máscara mask (7)
mascota pet (3)
matemáticas Math (P)
mayo May (4)
mayor (que) older (than) (3); **el (ia) mayor / los (las) mayores** the oldest (with people) (3)
me to / for me (6); me (5); **Me alegra que...** It makes me happy that . . . / I'm happy that . . . (10); **Me alegro (mucho).** That's good; I'm (really) glad. (1); **Me encanta que...** I'm delighted that . . . / It delights me that . . . (10); **Me enfada que...** It angers me that . . . / I'm angry that . . . (10); **Me gusta que...** I like the fact that . . . (10); **Me molesta que...** It bothers me that . . . (10); **¿Me permite... ?** May I . . . ? (11); **Me preocupa que...** It worries (concerns) me that . . . / I am worried (concerned) that . . . (10); **Me sorprende que...** It surprises me that . . . / I'm surprised that . . . (10)
medianoche *f.* midnight (2); **Es medianoche.** It's midnight. (2)
medicamento medicine (9)
médico(a) doctor, physician (9)
medio tiempo half-time, part-time (10)
mediodía *m.* noon (2); **Es mediodía.** It's noon. (2)
mejor better, best (3); **(mejor) amigo(a)** (best) friend (3); **mejor que** better than (3); **el (la) mejor / los (las) mejores** the best (3)
mejorar to improve (12); **mejorarse** to get better, to improve (9); **¡Que te mejores!** I hope you feel better! (*informal*) (9); **¡Que se**

mejore! I hope you feel better! (*formal*) (9)
memoria USB flash drive (1)
menor (que) younger (than) (3); **el (la) menor / los (las) menores** the youngest (with people) (3)
menorá *m.* menorah (8)
menos less (3); **el (la) / los (las) menos...** the least . . . (3); **Menos mal.** Thank goodness. (8); **menos... que** less . . . than (3)
mensaje de texto *m.* text (message) (2)
mente abierta *f.* an open mind (12)
mentor(a) mentor (12)
menú *m.* menu (6)
mercado market (4)
merienda snack (3)
mermelada marmalade, jelly (6)
mes *m.* month (4); **el mes pasado** last month (5); **el mes que viene** next month (4); **el próximo mes** next month (4)
mesa table (1); **poner la mesa** to set the table (3); **¿Una mesa para cuántos?** A table for how many? (6)
mesero(a) waiter / waitress (6)
mesita (de noche) nightstand (5)
meta goal (9)
metro subway (4); meter (11)
mezquita mosque (8)
mi(s) my (3)
microondas *m. sing.* microwave oven (5)
mientras while (5) (8); **mientras que** while (12)
miércoles *m.* Wednesday (2)
mil *m.* one thousand (4)
militar military (8)
millón *m.* million (4)
mimado(a) spoiled (3)
mío(s) / mía(s) mine (3)
mirar to look (at) (2); **mirar la tele** to watch TV (2); **Miren acá.** Look over here. (P)
mismo(a) same; **misma edad** same age (3)
mito myth (8)
mochila backpack (1)
mocoso(a) having a runny nose (9)
moda fashion (7); **a la última moda** in the latest fashion (7)
moderno(a) modern (5)
mojar to get wet (9)
mola colorful appliqué panel (7)
molestar to bother (7)
montaña mountain (4); **montaña (de ropa sucia)** pile (of dirty clothes) (5)
montar a caballo to ride a horse (4); **montar en bicicleta** to ride a bike (4)
morado purple (7)
moreno(a) dark-haired (3)
morir (ue) to die (7); **Me muero por...** I'm dying to . . . (4)
mostrador *m.* counter (11)
mostrar (ue) to show (6)
¡Muchas felicidades! Congratulations! (3)
mucho(a) a lot of, many (1); **Mucho gusto.** Nice to meet you. (1)
mudarse to move (5)
muebles *m. pl.* furniture (5)
muerto(a) dead (7) (12)
mujer *f.* woman (3); **mujer de negocios** businesswoman (10)
muñeca wrist (9)
museo museum (4)
música music (P) (2)
muy very (1)

N

nada nothing (1); nothing, not anything (4)
nadar to swim (4)
nadie nobody / no one; not anybody / not anyone (4)
naranja orange (6)
nariz *f.* nose (9)
natación *f.* swimming (8)
naturaleza nature (11)
Navidad *f.* Christmas (8); **¡Feliz Navidad!** Merry Christmas! (8)
necesario necessary (6) (9); **Es necesario...** It's necessary . . . (6); **Es necesario que...** It's necessary that . . . (9)
necesitar to need (4); **Necesito talla pequeña / mediana / grande / 38.** I need size small / medium / large / 38. (7)
negocio business (10)
negro black (3) (7)
nevar (ie) to snow; **Está nevando.** It's snowing. (4); **Nieva...** It snows . . . (4)
(ni...) ni (neither . . .) nor (4)
nieto(a) grandson / granddaughter (3); **nietos** grandchildren (3)
nieve *f.* snow (4)
ninguno(a) none, not any (4)
niño(a) little boy / girl (3)
nivel *m.* level (10)
No. No. (P); **no dejar las cosas para más tarde** not to procrastinate (9); **No entiendo.** I don't understand. (1); **No es para tanto.** It's no big deal. (9); **No está mal.** It's okay. (2); **¡No me digas!** No way! / You're kidding! (12); **No sé.** I don't know. (1)
noche *f.* night; **de la noche** p.m. (sundown to midnight) (2); **esta noche** tonight (4); **Noche de Brujas** Halloween (8); **por la noche** in the evening (2)
normalmente usually (2); normally (6)
normas de conducta norms of personal conduct (12)
norte *m.* north (11)
nos us (5); to / for us (6); **¡Nos vemos (en clase)!** See you (in class)! (1)
nosotros(as) we (1)
noticias news (12)
novela novel (2)
noveno(a) ninth (7)
noventa ninety (1)
noviembre *m.* November (4)
novio(a) boyfriend; groom / girlfriend; bride (3)
nublado(a) cloudy (4); **Está nublado.** It's cloudy. (4)
nuestro(s) / nuestra(s) our (3)
nueve nine (1)
nuevo(a) new (5)
número number (1); **Es calle..., número...** It's . . . Street . . . (1)
nunca never (2); never, not . . . ever (4)
nutrición *f.* nutrition (6)

O

o or (3); **(o...) o** (either . . .) or (4)
obligación *f.* obligation (9)
obra de teatro (theater) play (8)
observatorio observatory (11)
océano ocean (11)
ochenta eighty (1)
ocho eight (1)
octavo(a) eigth (7)

octubre *m.* October (4)
ocupado(a) busy, occupied (1)
ocurrir to happen (8)
Odio... I hate . . . (5)
oeste *m.* west (11)
oferta offer (10); **Es mi última oferta.** It's my last offer. (7)
oficina de tursimo tourist office (4)
ofrecer to offer (7); **Le puedo ofrecer (veinte dólares).** I can offer you (20 dollars). *(formal)* (7)
oído inner ear (9)
oír to hear (4)
Ojalá que... I hope that . . . , May . . . (10)
ojo eye (3) (9)
olvidarse to forget (9)
once eleven (1)
oportunidad *f.* opportunity, chance (12)
oposición *f.* opposition (12)
optimista optimistic (3)
ordenado(a) tidy, neat (5)
ordenar to tidy up (5)
oreja ear (9)
organización *f.* organization (12)
organizado(a) organized (2)
organizar to organize (12)
oro gold (7)
os you *(pl., inf. in Spain)* (5); to / for you *(pl., inf. in Spain)* (6)
otoño fall, autumn (4)

P

paciente patient (10)
padre *m.* father (3)
padres *m. pl.* parents (3)
paella (valenciana) Spanish saffron rice dish (6)
pagar (en efectivo) to pay (in cash) (4); **¿Cómo desea pagar?** How do you want to pay? *(formal)* (7); **Voy a pagar en efectivo / con tarjeta de crédito.** I'm going to pay cash / with a credit card. (7)
página page; **¿En qué página estamos?** What page are we on? (1)
país *m. sing.* country (nation) (11)
paisaje *m.* landscape, scenery (11)
paja straw (7)
pájaro bird (3)
palabras útiles useful words (P)
pan *m.* bread (6)
panorámico(a) panoramic (11)
pantalones *m. pl.* pants, trousers (7); **pantalones cortos** shorts (7)
papá *m.* dad (3)
papas fritas French fries (6)
para for; **Para mí, (la paella).** I'll have (the paella). (6); **para que** so that (12); **¿Para qué?** What for? (2)
parada (de autobús) (bus) stop (4)
paralizar to paralyze (12)
parecer to seem, to appear, to look (7); **¿Qué le parece (esta camisa)?** What do you think about (this shirt) *(formal)*? (7)
parecido(a) alike, similar (3)
pared *f.* wall (1)
pareja couple (two people) (3); **la feliz pareja** the happy couple (3)
pariente *m. f.* relative (3)
parque *m.* park (2); **parque de diversiones** amusement park (4); **parque zoológico** zoo (11)
parte *f.* part (9)

participar to participate (2)
partido game (2)
pasado(a) de moda out of style (7)
pasado mañana the day after tomorrow (4)
pasajero(a) passenger (11)
pasantía internship (10)
pasaporte *m.* passport (11)
pasar to pass; to proceed (11); **¿Cómo pasó?** How did it happen? (8); **¿Me pasas..., por favor?** Could you please pass . . . ? (6); **Pasa adelante.** Come in. (5); **pasar cerca de / por** to go near / by (11); **pasar (horas, el rato)** to spend (hours, time) (2); **pasar la aspiradora** to vacuum (5); **pasarlo bien** to have a good time; **Lo pasé / Lo pasamos muy bien.** I had / We had a great time. (3)
pasillo hallway (5)
pastel (de cumpleaños) *m.* (birthday) cake (3)
pastilla pill (9)
patio patio; courtyard (5)
patriótico(a) patriotic (8)
pavo turkey (8)
paz *f.* peace (12)
peaje *m.* toll (11)
pecho chest (9)
pedir (i) to ask for, to request (3); to order (6); **pedir ayuda** to ask for help (9); **pedir cita** to make an appointment (9); **pedir consejos** to ask for advice (6); **Te / Le pido que...** I ask you to . . . (9)
peinarse to comb one's hair (5)
pelirrojo(a) red-headed (3)
pelo hair (3)
pensar (ie) to think (3); to plan (4); **¿Qué piensas?** What do you think? *(informal)* (9)
peor (que) worse (than) (3); **el (la) peor / los (las) peores** the worst (3)
pequeño(a) small (1)
perderse (ie) to get lost (11)
perdón excuse me; sorry (1)
perezoso(a) lazy (3)
perfectamente perfectly (6)
perfecto(a) perfect (2)
perfumería perfume store / department (7)
periodista *m. f.* journalist (10)
permiso de conducir driver's license (11)
pero but (3)
perro(a) dog (3); **perro caliente** hot dog (6)
persona sin hogar homeless person (12)
personalidad *f.* personality (3)
personalizado(a) personalized (12)
pescado fish (as a food) (6)
pescar to fish (4)
pesebre *m.* manger (8)
pesimista pessimistic (3)
pez, peces *m.* fish (3)
piano piano (2)
picante spicy / hot (6); **¿Es picante?** Is it spicy / hot? (6)
picnic *m.* picnic (3)
pie *m.* foot (9); **a pie** on foot (11)
piel *f.* skin (9)
pierna leg (9)
pieza piece; item (11)
pimienta pepper (6)
pintar to paint (12)
piña pineapple (6)
piscina swimming pool (1)
piso floor; story (5); apartment *(in Spain)* (12); **de dos pisos** a two-story (5); **de un piso** a one-story (5)

pizarra (digital) (interactive) white board, chalk board (1)
placer *m.* pleasure (9)
plan *m.* plan (10)
planchar to iron (5)
planeta *m.* planet (12)
planta plant (5)
planta baja ground floor (7)
plata silver (7)
plátano plantain (6)
plato plate; dish (6); **¿Cuál es el plato del día?** What's today's special? (6)
playa beach (4)
plaza main square (of a town or city) (4)
pluma feather (8)
¡Pobrecito(a)! You poor thing! (9)
poco(a) little, not much (2); **un poco** a little (1)
pocos(as) few, not many (2)
poder (ue) to be able, can (3) (4)
política politics (12)
pollo chicken (6)
poner to put, to place (4); **poner la mesa** to set the table (3); **poner la tele / la radio** to turn on the TV / the radio (4); **ponerse (+ *adj.*)** to get (+ *adjective*), to become (5); **ponerse (+ *noun*)** to put on (clothing, perfume, etc.) (5); **ponerse en forma** to get in shape (6); **¡Pongamos manos a la obra!** Let's get to work! (12)
popular popular (8)
por for; **por dos horas** for two hours (5); **por ejemplo** for example (7); **por eso** for that reason, that's why (7); **Por eso...** That's why . . . (8); **por favor** please (1); **por fin** at last (7); **por lo general** usually (2); generally, in general (7); **por lo menos** at least (7); **por muchos años** for many years (5); **¿Por qué?** Why? How come? (2); **¿Por qué no... ?** Why don't we . . . ? (2); **por supuesto** of course, certainly (7); **por último** finally, lastly (5)
porque because (2)
posibilidad *f.* possibility (10)
posible possible (10); **(No) Es posible...** It's (not) possible that . . . (10)
postgrado graduate degree (10)
postre *m.* dessert (6)
practicar (un deporte) to play (a sport) (2)
precio price (7)
preciso necessary, essential (6); **Es preciso...** It's necessary / essential . . . (6)
preferible preferable (6) (9); **Es preferible...** It's preferable . . . (6); **Es preferible que...** It's preferable that . . . (9)
preferido(a) favorite (2)
preferir (ie) to prefer (3); **Prefiero que...** I prefer that . . . (9)
pregunta question (1)
preguntar to ask (a question) (6)
premio prize; award (8)
preocupación *f.* worry, concern (9)
preocupado(a) worried, concerned (1)
preocuparse (por) to worry (about) (5) (9); **No te preocupes.** Don't worry. (9)
preparar to prepare, to make (3)
preparativo preparation (3)
preposición *f.* preposition (1)
presentar to introduce (1); to present, to show (8); **Le presento a...** I'd like you to meet . . . (*formal*) (1); **Te presento a...** I'd like you to meet . . . (*informal*) (1)
presión *f.* pressure (9)
prestar to lend (6)

prestigioso(a) prestigious (8)
presupuesto budget (12)
prevenir (ie) to prevent (9)
prever to foresee (12)
previo(a) previous (12)
primavera spring (4)
primer, primero(a) first (7); **¿A qué hora es tu primera clase?** What time is your first class? (2)
primero first (5)
primo(a) cousin (3)
principal main (6)
principalmente mainly (6)
prioridad *f.* priority (12)
probador *m.* fitting room (7)
probable likely (10); **(No) Es probable que...** It's (not) likely that . . . (10)
probar (ue) to taste, to try (a food) (3); **probarse (ue)** to try on (7)
problema *m.* problem (10)
producto lácteo milk product (6)
profesión *f.* profession (10)
profesor(a) professor (P) (1)
prohibir to forbid, to prohibit (9); **Te / Le prohíbo que...** I forbid you to . . . (9)
pronombre *m.* pronoun (1)
pronto soon (6)
propina tip (6); **¿Está incluida la propina en la cuenta?** Is the tip included in the bill? (6)
propio(a) own (10)
¡Próspero Año Nuevo! Happy / Prosperous New Year! (8)
proteína protein (6)
protestar to protest (12)
provocar to cause (12)
próximo(a) next (3) (4)
proyecto project (10)
psicología psychology (P)
psicólogo(a) psychologist (10)
publicidad *f.* publicity, advertising (12)
público public; audience (10)
pueblo small town (11)
puente *m.* bridge (11)
puerta door (1); gate (of an airline) (11)
puerto port (11)
puesto position; job (10)
pulmón *m.* lung (9)
punto dot (1); stitch (9); **Es... arroba... punto...** It's . . . @ . . . dot . . . (1); **punto cardinal** cardinal direction (11); **punto fuerte** strength (10)
pupitre *m.* desk (1)

Q

que that; who (11)
¿Qué? What? (2); **¿Qué es esto?** What is this? (1); **¿Qué hay de nuevo?** What's new? (1); **¿Qué se puede hacer por aquí?** What is there to do around here? (4); **¿Qué significa... ?** What does . . . mean? (1); **¿Qué tal?** How's it going? (*informal*) (1); **¿Qué tal si... ?** What if we . . . ? (2); **¿Qué te pasó?** What happened to you? (*informal*) (9); **¿Qué tienes?** What's the matter? (9)
quedar to fit; to have left, to remain (7); **Me queda bien / mal.** It fits me well / poorly. (7); **quedarse** to stay (5)
quehacer *m.* chore (5)
quemarse to burn, to get burned (9)
querer (ie) to want; to love (people, pets) (3); **¿Quieres ir... conmigo?** Do you want to . . .

with me? (*informal*) (8); **¿Quieres más... ?** Do you want more . . . ? (*informal*) (6); **Quiero ir contigo.** I want to go with you. (4); **Quiero que...** I want (you) to . . . (9)
queso cheese (6)
quien(es) who (11); **¿Quién? / ¿Quiénes?** Who? (2); **¿Quién es... ?** Who is . . . ? (1)
química chemistry (P)
quince fifteen (1)
quinto(a) fifth (7)
Quisiera probar (el plato del día). I'd like to try (today's special). (6)
Quizás en otra ocasión. Maybe some other time. (8)

R

radiografía x-ray (9)
Ramadán *m.* Ramadan (8)
rápido quickly (5)
rasgos físicos physical characteristics (3)
reaccionar to react (8) (9)
realizar to carry out (8); to achieve (10)
rebajado(a) on sale, reduced (price) (7); **Está rebajado(a). / Están rebajados(as).** It's / They're on sale. (7)
recetar to prescribe (9)
recibir to receive, to get (2)
recientemente recently (6)
reclamo de equipaje baggage claim (11)
recoger to pick up (8); **recoger basura** to pick up trash (12)
recomendable advisable (6); **Es recomendable...** It's advisable . . . (6)
recomendar (ie) to recommend (4); **Te / Le recomiendo que...** I recommend that you . . . (9); **¿Qué nos recomienda?** What do you recommend? (6)
reconstrucción *f.* rebuilding (12)
recordar (ue) to remember, to recall (3)
recorrer to go all over (a place) (4)
recuerdo souvenir (4)
reducir to relieve (9)
referencia reference (10)
refresco soft drink (4)
refrigerador *m.* refrigerator (5)
refugio de animales animal shelter (12)
regalar to give (as a gift) (6)
regalo gift, present (3)
regar (ie) to water (5)
regatear to bargain (7)
regateo bargaining (7)
región *f.* region (7)
regresar to go back, to return (2)
regular so-so (1)
rehusar to decline, to turn down (8)
relaciones internacionales *f. pl.* international relations (10)
relajarse to relax (5) (9)
reloj *m.* clock (1)
reparar to fix, to repair (12)
repartir a domicilio to home-deliver (12)
repetir (i) to repeat (3); **¿Puede repetirlo?** Can you repeat that? (*formal*) (1); **¿Puedes repetirlo?** Can you repeat that? (*informal*) (1); **Repitan.** Repeat. (P)
requisito requirement (10)
resfriado cold (illness) (9)
residencia estudiantil dorm, student residence hall (1)
resolver (ue) to solve (10); to get resolved (7)
respetar to respect (12)

respirar (hondo) to breathe (deeply) (9)
responsabilidad *f.* responsibility (10)
restaurante *m.* restaurant (2)
reunión familiar *f.* family reunion; family gathering (3)
reunirse to get together (8)
rezar to pray (8)
rico(a) good; tasty; rich (6); rich, wealthy (10); **¡Qué rico(a)!** It's really good! (6)
ridículo ridiculous (10); **Es ridículo que...** It's ridiculous that . . . (10)
rincón *m.* corner (of a room) (5); **en el rincón** in the corner (5)
río river (11)
rodilla knee (9)
rojo red (7)
romper to break (7); **romperse** to break (9)
rosado pink (7)
rubio(a) blond(e) (3)
rueda wheel (6)
ruido noise (5)
ruinas ruins (11)
ruta route (11)
rutina diaria daily routine (5)

S

sábado Saturday (2)
saber to know (information / how to do something) (4)
sacar to take out (5); **sacar fotos** to take pictures (3)
sacudir to shake (8)
sal *f.* salt (6)
sala living room (5)
salario salary (10)
salida exit (11)
salir to leave, to go out (4)
salón de clase *m.* classroom (1)
saltar to skip (6)
salud *f.* health (6); **¡Salud!** Cheers! (3); **la salud de...** the health of . . . (3)
saludable healthy (6)
saludo greeting (1)
sandalias sandals (7)
sándwich *m.* sandwich (6)
sano(a) healthy (6)
satisfecho(a) full; satisfied (6); **Estoy satisfecho(a).** I've had plenty; I'm full. (6)
se debe one should (6)
Se escribe... It's spelled . . . (P)
Se lo (la) dejo en solo (treinta dólares). I'll give it to you for only (30 dollars). (*formal*) (7)
seco(a) dry (11)
secreto secret (9)
sede *f.* seat, headquarters (11)
sedentario(a) sedentary (6)
seguir (i) to follow, to continue (3); **seguir derecho** to go straight (11)
según according to (6) (8)
segundo(a) second (7)
seguro insurance (11); **No estoy seguro(a).** I'm not sure. (9); **seguro(a)** safe (5) (12); **seguro médico** health insurance (10)
seis six (1)
semáforo traffic light (11)
semana week (2); **la próxima semana** next week (4); **la semana pasada** last week (5); **la semana que viene** next week (4); **entre semana** during the week, on weekdays (2); **Semana Santa** Easter week (8)

semestre *m.* semester (2)
sencillo(a) single (4)
senderismo hiking (4); **hacer senderismo** to hike, to go hiking (4)
sentir (ie) to be sorry, to regret; to feel; **sentirse (i)** to feel (5); **sentirse (muy) a gusto** to feel at home (12)
señor (Sr.) Mr. (P)
señora (Sra.) Mrs.; Ms. (P)
señorita (Srta.) Miss; Ms. (P)
septiembre *m.* September (4)
séptimo(a) seventh (7)
ser to be (1); **ser bueno(a) en / con...** to be good at / with . . . (10); **ser un amor** to be a dear (3)
serio(a) serious (3)
servicio al cliente customer service (7); **servicio público** public service (10)
servilleta napkin (6)
servir (i) to serve (3)
sesenta sixty (1)
setenta seventy (1)
sexto(a) sixth (7)
Sí. Yes. (P) ; **Sí, enseguida.** Yes, right away. (6); **Sí, entiendo.** Yes, I understand. (9)
si if (4); **Si compra...** If you buy . . . (7)
siempre always (4)
siete seven (1)
silla chair (1)
sillón *m.* armchair (5)
simpático(a) nice (2)
sin fines de lucro non-profit (12)
sin que without (12)
sinagoga synagogue (8)
sincero(a) sincere, honest (3)
síntoma *m.* symptom (9)
sobre on top of (5)
sobrino(a) nephew / niece (3)
sofá *m.* couch, sofa (5)
sol *m.* sun (8); **Hace sol.** It's sunny. (4)
solamente only (6)
solicitar to apply for (10); to ask for (12)
solicitud *f.* application (10)
Solo estoy mirando, gracias. I'm just looking, thank you. (7)
soltero(a) single (3)
sombrero hat (7)
soñar (ue) (con) to dream (about) (10)
sopa soup (6)
soportar to stand; **No soporto (a)...** I can't stand . . . (3)
sorprender to surprise; to be surprised (10)
¡Sorpresa! Surprise! (3)
su(s) your (*formal*) (3); his/her/its (3); your (*informal / formal*) (3); their (3); **Su atención, por favor.** Your attention, please. (P)
sucio(a) dirty (5)
sudadera sweatshirt (7)
sueño dream (10)
suero intravenoso IV fluids (9)
suerte luck; **con suerte** with luck (10); **¡Qué suerte!** How lucky! (8)
suéter *m.* sweater (7)
suficiente enough; plenty (6)
sugerir to suggest (9); **Te / Le sugiero que...** I suggest that (you) . . . (9)
sumergirse to immerse oneself, to become absorbed (12)
sur *m.* south (11)
suyo(s) / suya(s) (*pl.*) yours (*inf. / form. Lat. Am. / form. Spain*); theirs (3); **suyo(s) / suya(s)** (*sing.*) yours (*formal*); his; hers; its (3)

T

tableta tablet (computer) (1)
Tal vez otro día. Perhaps another day. (2)
talla size (7)
también also, too (1) (4)
tampoco neither, not . . . either (4)
tan... como as . . . as (3); as much / many . . . as (3); **tan pronto como** as soon as (12)
tanque de gasolina *m.* gas tank (11)
tanto como as much as (3)
tardarse to take long (11)
tarde *f.* afternoon; **de la tarde** p.m. (noon to sundown) (2); **por la tarde** in the afternoon (2)
tarde late (5)
tarea homework (2); **tarea escolar** schoolwork (12)
tarifa rate (11)
tarjeta card (8); **tarjeta de crédito / débito** credit / debit card (4); **tarjeta de embarque** boarding pass (11)
taxi *m.* taxi, cab (4)
taza cup (6)
te you (*sing., inf.*) (5); to / for you (*sing., inf.*) (6)
té *m.* tea (6)
teatro theater (P) (4) (8)
techo roof (12)
técnico(a) technician (10)
tecnología technology (10)
tele *f.* television (2)
teléfono phone; **¿Cuál es tu número de teléfono?** What's your phone number? (1); **teléfono celular** cell phone (1)
televisor *m.* television, TV (1)
templado(a) mild (11)
templo temple (8)
temporada alta peak season (11)
temprano early (5)
tenedor *m.* fork (6)
tener (ie) to have (1); **tener en cuenta** to take into account (12); **tener éxito** to succeed, to be successful (10); **tener lugar** to take place (8); **tener mal genio** to be ill-tempered (3); **tener (mucha) hambre** to be (very) hungry (1); **tener (mucha) prisa** to be in a (big) hurry (1); **tener (mucha) sed** to be (very) thirsty (1); **tener (mucho) calor** to be (very) hot (1); **tener (mucho) cuidado** to be (very) careful (1); **tener (mucho) frío** to be (very) cold (1); **tener (mucho) miedo** to be (very) afraid (1); **tener (mucho) sueño** to be (very) sleepy (1); **tener que** (+ *infinitive*) to have to (do something) (1); **tener razón** to be right, to be correct (1); **Tengo...** I have . . . (P); **Tengo una pregunta.** I have a question. (1); **¿Tienes ganas de...?** Do you feel like . . . ? (2) (*informal*); **Tienes razón.** You're right. (*informal*) (9)
tercer, tercero(a) third (7)
terminar to finish, to end, to be over (2)
terremoto earthquake (12)
tiempo weather (4); **¿Qué tiempo hace?** What's the weather? (4); **Hace buen / mal tiempo.** The weather's nice / bad. (4)
tiempo completo full-time (10)
tienda store (7)
tierno(a) sweet, tender, affectionate (3)
tímido(a) shy (3)
tío(a) uncle / aunt (3)
típico(a) typical (2) (4)
título title (P)

tobillo ankle (9)

tocar to play (a musical instrument) (2); to touch (12)

tocineta bacon (6)

todavía still (5); **Todavía tengo que...** I still have to . . . (5)

todavía no not yet (7)

Todo bien. Everything's fine / okay. (1); **Todo estuvo delicioso, gracias.** Everything was delicious, thank you. (6)

todos all (of us) (3); **todos los días** every day (2) (5)

tomar to take (2); to drink (4); **tomar el sol** to sunbathe (4); **tomarse unos días libres** to take some days off (9)

tomate *m.* tomato (6)

tonto(a) dumb (3)

torcerse (ue) to sprain, to twist (9)

tos *f.* cough (9)

toser to cough (9)

tostaditas de maíz tortilla chips (6)

tostones *m. pl.* fried plantain chips (6)

trabajador(a) hardworking (3); **trabajador social** social worker (10)

trabajar to work (2); **trabajar en equipo** to work on a team (10); **trabajar para** to work for (10); **Trabajen con un(a) compañero(a) de clase.** Work with a classmate. (P)

trabajo work (9); **¿En qué consiste su trabajo?** What is his/her/your job? (10)

tradicional traditional (8)

traer to bring (4); **¿Me puede traer (otra servilleta)?** Can you bring me (another napkin)? *(formal)* (6); **¿Nos puede traer más (pan)?** Can you bring us some more (bread)? *(formal)* (6); **¿Nos trae el menú, por favor?** Can you bring us the menu, please? *(formal)* (6)

traje *m.* suit (7); **traje de baño** bathing suit (7)

tranquilamente tranquilly, peacefully (6)

tranquilo(a) quiet, peaceful (5); **Tranquilo(a).** Relax. (9)

tratamiento treatment (9)

trece thirteen (1)

treinta thirty (1)

tren *m.* train (4)

tres three (1); **tres leches** *f. pl.* cake soaked in cream (6); **tres veces** three times (5)

triste sad (1)

tú you *(sing., inf.)* (1)

tu(s) your *(informal)* (3)

tuitear to tweet (2)

turismo (de aventura) (adventure) tourism (4)

tutor(a) tutor (10)

tuyo(s) / tuya(s) yours *(informal)* (3)

U

ubicado(a) located (11)

último(a) latest, last (12); **¿A qué hora es tu última clase?** What time is your last class? (2)

un(a) a/an (1); **un poco** a little (1)

una vez once (5); **Una vez...** One time . . . (8)

unido(a) close-knit (3)

universidad *f.* university (1)

universitario(a) university (10)

uno one (1)

unos(as) some (1)

usted (Ud.) you *(sing., form.)* (1)

ustedes (Uds.) you *(pl.)* (1)

utilizar to use (12)

uvas grapes (6)

V

vacaciones *f. pl.* vacation (4); **vacaciones pagadas** paid vacations (10)

valle *m.* valley (11)

¡Vamos! Let's go! (1)

vaqueros jeans (7)

varias veces several times (5)

variedad *f.* variety (1)

vaso drinking glass (6)

vecino(a) neighbor (5)

veinte twenty (1)

vela candle (3)

velero sailboat (4)

venda bandage (9)

vendedor(a) vendor (7)

vender to sell (10)

venir (ie) to come (4)

ventana window (1)

ver to see, to watch (4)

verano summer (4)

verbo verb (1)

verdad true (10); **(No) Es verdad que...** It's (not) true that . . . (10); **La verdad es que...** Actually, . . . (5)

verde green (3) (7)

verdura vegetable (6)

vestido dress (7)

vestirse (i) to get dressed (5)

vez *f.* time, instance (5)

viajar to travel (4)

viaje *m.* trip (4)

videojuego videogame (3)

viejo(a) old (3)

viento wind; **Hace viento.** It's windy. (4)

viernes *m.* Friday (2); **el viernes pasado** last Friday (5)

villancico (Christmas) carol (8)

vino wine (6)

visa estudiantil student visa (12)

visitar to visit (2)

vista view (11)

vivienda housing (12)

vivir to live (2); **Vivo con mi familia.** I live with my family. (1); **Vivo en una residencia / un apartamento.** I live in a dorm / an apartment. (1)

vocación *f.* vocation (10)

volar (ue) to fly (8)

volcán *m.* volcano (11)

voleibol *m.* volleyball (3)

voluntariado volunteering, volunteer work (12)

voluntario(a) volunteer (10)

volver (ue) to return, to go back, to come back (3)

vómito vomit (9)

vosotros(as) you *(pl, inf. used in Spain)* (1)

votar to vote (12)

vuelo flight (11)

vuestro(s) / vuestra(s) your *(informal, used in Spain)* (3); **vuestro(s) / vuestra(s)** yours *(informal, used in Spain)* (3)

Y

y and (3); **¿Y tú?** And you? *(informal)* (P) (1); **¿Y usted?** And you? *(formal)* (P)

ya already (6) (7)

ya no no longer (6)

yeso cast (9)

yo I (1)

yoga *m.* yoga (9)

yogur *m.* yoghurt, yogurt (6)

Yom Kipur *m.* Yom Kippur (8)

yuca cassava (6)

Z

zanahoria carrot (6)

zapatería shoe store / department (7)

zapatos (de vestir, deportivos) (dress, tennis) shoes (7)

zona arqueológica archaeological site (4)

Note: The English-Spanish Glossary is found online.

Regular Verbs

Simple Tenses

Infinitive	Present Indicative	Imperfect	Preterite	Future	Conditional	Present Subjunctive	Past Subjunctive	Commands
hablar *to speak*	hablo	hablaba	hablé	hablaré	hablaría	hable	hablara	habla (no hables)
	hablas	hablabas	hablaste	hablarás	hablarías	hables	hablaras	(no) hable
	habla	hablaba	habló	hablará	hablaría	hable	hablara	hablemos
	hablamos	hablábamos	hablamos	hablaremos	hablaríamos	hablemos	habláramos	hablad (no habléis)
	habláis	hablabais	hablasteis	hablaréis	hablaríais	habléis	hablarais	(no) hablen
	hablan	hablaban	hablaron	hablarán	hablarían	hablen	hablaran	
aprender *to learn*	aprendo	aprendía	aprendí	aprenderé	aprendería	aprenda	aprendiera	aprende (no aprendas)
	aprendes	aprendías	aprendiste	aprenderás	aprenderías	aprendas	aprendieras	(no) aprenda
	aprende	aprendía	aprendió	aprenderá	aprendería	aprenda	aprendiera	aprendamos
	aprendemos	aprendíamos	aprendimos	aprenderemos	aprenderíamos	aprendamos	aprendiéramos	aprended (no aprendáis)
	aprendéis	aprendíais	aprendisteis	aprenderéis	aprenderíais	aprendáis	aprendierais	(no) aprendan
	aprenden	aprendían	aprendieron	aprenderán	aprenderían	aprendan	aprendieran	
vivir *to live*	vivo	vivía	viví	viviré	viviría	viva	viviera	vive (no vivas)
	vives	vivías	viviste	vivirás	vivirías	vivas	vivieras	(no) viva
	vive	vivía	vivió	vivirá	viviría	viva	viviera	vivamos
	vivimos	vivíamos	vivimos	viviremos	viviríamos	vivamos	viviéramos	vivid (no viváis)
	vivís	vivíais	vivisteis	viviréis	viviríais	viváis	vivierais	(no) vivan
	viven	vivían	vivieron	vivirán	vivirían	vivan	vivieran	

Compound Tenses

Present progressive	estoy estás está	estamos estáis están	hablando	aprendiendo	viviendo
Present perfect indicative	he has ha	hemos habéis han	hablado	aprendido	vivido
Present perfect subjunctive	haya hayas haya	hayamos hayáis hayan	hablado	aprendido	vivido
Past perfect indicative	había habías había	habíamos habíais habían	hablado	aprendido	vivido

Stem-changing Verbs

Infinitive / Present Participle / Past Participle	Present Indicative	Imperfect	Preterite	Future	Conditional	Present Subjunctive	Past Subjunctive	Commands
pensar *to think* **e → ie** pensando pensado	**pienso** **piensas** **piensa** pensamos pensáis **piensan**	pensaba pensabas pensaba pensábamos pensabais pensaban	pensé pensaste pensó pensamos pensasteis pensaron	pensaré pensarás pensará pensaremos pensaréis pensarán	pensaría pensarías pensaría pensaríamos pensaríais pensarían	**piense** **pienses** **piense** pensemos penséis **piensen**	pensara pensaras pensara pensáramos pensarais pensaran	**piensa (no pienses)** **(no) piense** pensemos pensad (no penséis) **(no) piensen**
acostarse *to go to bed* **o → ue** acostándose acostado	me **acuesto** te **acuestas** se **acuesta** nos acostamos os acostáis se **acuestan**	me acostaba te acostabas se acostaba nos acostábamos os acostabais se acostaban	me acosté te acostaste se acostó nos acostamos os acostasteis se acostaron	me acostaré te acostarás se acostará nos acostaremos os acostaréis se acostarán	me acostaría te acostarías se acostaría nos acostaríamos os acostaríais se acostarían	me **acueste** te **acuestes** se **acueste** nos acostemos os acostéis se **acuesten**	me acostara te acostaras se acostara nos acostáramos os acostarais se acostaran	**acuéstate (no te acuestes)** **(no) acuéstese** acostémonos acostaos (no os acostéis) **(no) acuéstense**
sentir *to be sorry, to feel* **e → ie, i** **sintiendo** sentido	**siento** **sientes** **siente** sentimos sentís **sienten**	sentía sentías sentía sentíamos sentíais sentían	sentí sentiste **sintió** sentimos sentisteis **sintieron**	sentiré sentirás sentirá sentiremos sentiréis sentirán	sentiría sentirías sentiría sentiríamos sentiríais sentirían	**sienta** **sientas** **sienta** **sintamos** **sintáis** **sientan**	**sintiera** **sintieras** **sintiera** **sintiéramos** **sintierais** **sintieran**	**siente (no sientas)** **(no) sienta** sentamos sentid **(no sintáis)** **(no) sientan**
pedir *to ask for* **e → i, i** **pidiendo** pedido	**pido** **pides** **pide** pedimos pedís **piden**	pedía pedías pedía pedíamos pedíais pedían	pedí pediste **pidió** pedimos pedisteis **pidieron**	pediré pedirás pedirá pediremos pediréis pedirán	pediría pedirías pediría pediríamos pediríais pedirían	**pida** **pidas** **pida** **pidamos** **pidáis** **pidan**	**pidiera** **pidieras** **pidiera** **pidiéramos** **pidierais** **pidieran**	**pide (no pidas)** **(no) pida** pidamos pedid **(no pidáis)** **(no) pidan**
dormir *to sleep* **o → ue, u** **durmiendo** dormido	**duermo** **duermes** **duerme** dormimos dormís **duermen**	dormía dormías dormía dormíamos dormíais dormían	dormí dormiste **durmió** dormimos dormisteis **durmieron**	dormiré dormirás dormirá dormiremos dormiréis dormirán	dormiría dormirías dormiría dormiríamos dormiríais dormirían	**duerma** **duermas** **duerma** **durmamos** **durmáis** **duerman**	**durmiera** **durmieras** **durmiera** **durmiéramos** **durmierais** **durmieran**	**duerme (no duermas)** **(no) duerma** **durmamos** dormid (no durmáis) **(no) duerman**

Verbs with Spelling Changes

Infinitive / Present Participle / Past Participle	Present Indicative	Imperfect	Preterite	Future	Conditional	Present Subjunctive	Past Subjunctive	Commands
comenzar (e → ie) *to begin* z → c before e comenzando comenzado	comienzo	comenzaba	**comencé**	comenzaré	comenzaría	**comience**	comenzara	
	comienzas	comenzabas	comenzaste	comenzarás	comenzarías	**comiences**	comenzaras	comienza (**no comiences**)
	comienza	comenzaba	comenzó	comenzará	comenzaría	**comience**	comenzara	(**no) comience**
	comenzamos	comenzábamos	comenzamos	comenzaremos	comenzaríamos	**comencemos**	comenzáramos	**comencemos**
	comenzáis	comenzabais	comenzasteis	comenzaréis	comenzaríais	**comencéis**	comenzarais	comenzad (**no comencéis**)
	comienzan	comenzaban	comenzaron	comenzarán	comenzarían	comiencen	comenzaran	(**no) comiencen**
conocer *to know* c → zc before a, o conociendo conocido	**conozco**	conocía	conocí	conoceré	conocería	**conozca**	conociera	
	conoces	conocías	conociste	conocerás	conocerías	**conozcas**	conocieras	conoce (**no conozcas**)
	conoce	conocía	conoció	conocerá	conocería	**conozca**	conociera	(**no) conozca**
	conocemos	conocíamos	conocimos	conoceremos	conoceríamos	**conozcamos**	conociéramos	**conozcamos**
	conocéis	conocíais	conocisteis	conoceréis	conoceríais	**conozcáis**	conocierais	conoced (**no conozcáis**)
	conocen	conocían	conocieron	conocerán	conocerían	**conozcan**	conocieran	(**no) conozcan**
construir *to build* i → y; y inserted before a, e, o construyendo construido	**construyo**	construía	construí	construiré	construiría	**construya**	**construyera**	
	construyes	construías	construiste	construirás	construirías	**construyas**	**construyeras**	**construye (no construyas)**
	construye	construía	**construyó**	construirá	construiría	**construya**	**construyera**	(**no) construya**
	construimos	construíamos	construimos	construiremos	construiríamos	**construyamos**	**construyéramos**	**construyamos**
	construís	construíais	construisteis	construiréis	construiríais	**construyáis**	**construyerais**	construid (**no construyáis**)
	construyen	construían	**construyeron**	construirán	construirían	**construyan**	**construyeran**	(**no) construyan**
escoger *to choose* g → j before a, o escogiendo escogido	**escojo**	escogía	escogí	escogeré	escogería	**escoja**	escogiera	
	escoges	escogías	escogiste	escogerás	escogerías	**escojas**	escogieras	escoge (**no escojas**)
	escoge	escogía	escogió	escogerá	escogería	**escoja**	escogiera	(**no) escoja**
	escogemos	escogíamos	escogimos	escogeremos	escogeríamos	**escojamos**	escogiéramos	**escojamos**
	escogéis	escogíais	escogisteis	escogeréis	escogeríais	**escojáis**	escogierais	escoged (**no escojad**)
	escogen	escogían	escogieron	escogeremos	escogerían	**escojan**	escogieran	(**no) escojan**

Verbs with Spelling Changes (Continued)

Infinitive Present Participle Past Participle	Present Indicative	Imperfect	Preterite	Future	Conditional	Present Subjunctive	Past Subjunctive	Commands
leer *to read* **i → y;** **stressed** **i → i** **leyendo** **leído**	leo lees lee leemos leéis leen	leía leías leía leíamos leíais leían	leí **leíste** **leyó** leímos **leísteis** **leyeron**	leeré leerás leerá leeremos leeréis leerán	leería leerías leería leeríamos leeríais leerían	lea leas lea leamos leáis lean	**leyera** **leyeras** **leyera** **leyéramos** **leyerais** **leyeran**	lee (no leas) (no) lea leamos leed (no leáis) (no) lean
pagar *to pay* **g → gu** **before e** pagando pagado	pago pagas paga pagamos pagáis pagan	pagaba pagabas pagaba pagábamos pagabais pagaban	**pagué** pagaste pagó pagamos pagasteis pagaron	pagaré pagarás pagará pagaremos pagaréis pagarán	pagaría pagarías pagaría pagaríamos pagaríais pagarían	**pague** **pagues** **pague** **paguemos** **paguéis** **paguen**	pagara pagaras pagara pagáramos pagarais pagaran	paga (**no pagues**) (**no) pague** **paguemos** pagad (**no paguéis**) (**no) paguen**
seguir **(e → i, i)** *to follow* **gu → g** **before a, o** siguiendo seguido	**sigo** sigues sigue seguimos seguís siguen	seguía seguías seguía seguíamos seguíais seguían	seguí seguiste siguió seguimos seguisteis siguieron	seguiré seguirás seguirá seguiremos seguiréis seguirán	seguiría seguirías seguiría seguiríamos seguiríais seguirían	**siga** **sigas** **siga** **sigamos** **sigáis** **sigan**	siguiera siguieras siguiera siguiéramos siguierais siguieran	sigue (**no sigas**) (**no) siga** **sigamos** seguid (**no sigáis**) (**no) sigan**
tocar *to play, to touch* **c → qu** **before e** tocando tocado	toco tocas toca tocamos tocáis tocan	tocaba tocabas tocaba tocábamos tocabais tocaban	**toqué** tocaste tocó tocamos tocasteis tocaron	tocaré tocarás tocará tocaremos tocaréis tocarán	tocaría tocarías tocaría tocaríamos tocaríais tocarían	**toque** **toques** **toque** **toquemos** **toquéis** **toquen**	tocara tocaras tocara tocáramos tocarais tocaran	toca (**no toques**) (**no) toque** **toquemos** tocad (**no toquéis**) (**no) toquen**

Irregular Verbs

Infinitive / Present Participle / Past Participle	Present Indicative	Imperfect	Preterite	Future	Conditional	Present Subjunctive	Past Subjunctive	Commands
andar / to walk / andando / andado	ando / andas / anda / andamos / andáis / andan	andaba / andabas / andaba / andábamos / andabais / andaban	anduve / anduviste / anduvo / anduvimos / anduvisteis / anduvieron	andaré / andarás / andará / andaremos / andaréis / andarán	andaría / andarías / andaría / andaríamos / andaríais / andarían	ande / andes / ande / andemos / andéis / anden	anduviera / anduvieras / anduviera / anduviéramos / anduvierais / anduvieran	anda (no andes) / (no) ande / andemos / andad (no andéis) / (no) anden
*caer / to fall / cayendo / caído	caigo / caes / cae / caemos / caéis / caen	caía / caías / caía / caíamos / caíais / caían	caí / caíste / cayó / caímos / caísteis / cayeron	caeré / caerás / caerá / caeremos / caeréis / caerán	caería / caerías / caería / caeríamos / caeríais / caerían	caiga / caigas / caiga / caigamos / caigáis / caigan	cayera / cayeras / cayera / cayéramos / cayerais / cayeran	cae (no caigas) / (no) caiga / caigamos / caed (no caigáis) / (no) caigan
*dar / to give / dando / dado	doy / das / da / damos / dais / dan	daba / dabas / daba / dábamos / dabais / daban	di / diste / dio / dimos / disteis / dieron	daré / darás / dará / daremos / daréis / darán	daría / darías / daría / daríamos / daríais / darían	dé / des / dé / demos / deis / den	diera / dieras / diera / diéramos / dierais / dieran	da (no des) / (no) dé / demos / dad (no deis) / (no) den
*decir / to say, to tell / diciendo / dicho	digo / dices / dice / decimos / decís / dicen	decía / decías / decía / decíamos / decíais / decían	dije / dijiste / dijo / dijimos / dijisteis / dijeron	diré / dirás / dirá / diremos / diréis / dirán	diría / dirías / diría / diríamos / diríais / dirían	diga / digas / diga / digamos / digáis / digan	dijera / dijeras / dijera / dijéramos / dijerais / dijeran	di (no digas) / (no) diga / digamos / decid (no digáis) / (no) digan
*estar / to be / estando / estado	estoy / estás / está / estamos / estáis / están	estaba / estabas / estaba / estábamos / estabais / estaban	estuve / estuviste / estuvo / estuvimos / estuvisteis / estuvieron	estaré / estarás / estará / estaremos / estaréis / estarán	estaría / estarías / estaría / estaríamos / estaríais / estarían	esté / estés / esté / estemos / estéis / estén	estuviera / estuvieras / estuviera / estuviéramos / estuvierais / estuvieran	está (no estés) / (no) esté / estemos / estad (no estéis) / (no) estén

*Verbs with irregular *yo* forms in the present indicative

Irregular Verbs (Continued)

Infinitive / Present Participle / Past Participle	Present Indicative	Imperfect	Preterite	Future	Conditional	Present Subjunctive	Past Subjunctive	Commands
haber *to have* habiendo habido	he has ha [hay] hemos habéis han	había habías había habíamos habíais habían	hube hubiste hubo hubimos hubisteis hubieron	habré habrás habrá habremos habréis habrán	habría habrías habría habríamos habríais habrían	haya hayas haya hayamos hayáis hayan	hubiera hubieras hubiera hubiéramos hubierais hubieran	
*hacer *to make, to do* haciendo hecho	hago haces hace hacemos hacéis hacen	hacía hacías hacía hacíamos hacíais hacían	hice hiciste hizo hicimos hicisteis hicieron	haré harás hará haremos haréis harán	haría harías haría haríamos haríais harían	haga hagas haga hagamos hagáis hagan	hiciera hicieras hiciera hiciéramos hicierais hicieran	haz (no hagas) (no) haga hagamos haced (no hagáis) (no) hagan
ir *to go* yendo ido	voy vas va vamos vais van	iba ibas iba íbamos ibais iban	fui fuiste fue fuimos fuisteis fueron	iré irás irá iremos iréis irán	iría irías iría iríamos iríais irían	vaya vayas vaya vayamos vayáis vayan	fuera fueras fuera fuéramos fuerais fueran	ve (no vayas) (no) vaya vayamos id (no vayáis) (no) vayan
*oír *to hear* oyendo oído	oigo oyes oye oímos oís oyen	oía oías oía oíamos oíais oían	oí oíste oyó oímos oísteis oyeron	oiré oirás oirá oiremos oiréis oirán	oiría oirías oiría oiríamos oiríais oirían	oiga oigas oiga oigamos oigáis oigan	oyera oyeras oyera oyéramos oyerais oyeran	oye (no oigas) (no) oiga oigamos oíd (no oigáis) (no) oigan
poder (o → ue) *can, to be able* pudiendo podido	puedo puedes puede podemos podéis pueden	podía podías podía podíamos podíais podían	pude pudiste pudo pudimos pudisteis pudieron	podré podrás podrá podremos podréis podrán	podría podrías podría podríamos podríais podrían	pueda puedas pueda podamos podáis puedan	pudiera pudieras pudiera pudiéramos pudierais pudieran	

*Verbs with irregular *yo* forms in the present indicative

Irregular Verbs (Continued)

Infinitive / Present Participle / Past Participle	Present Indicative	Imperfect	Preterite	Future	Conditional	Present Subjunctive	Past Subjunctive	Commands
*poner *to place, to put* poniendo **puesto**	**pongo** pones pone ponemos ponéis ponen	ponía ponías ponía poníamos poníais ponían	**puse** **pusiste** **puso** **pusimos** **pusisteis** **pusieron**	**pondré** **pondrás** **pondrá** **pondremos** **pondréis** **pondrán**	**pondría** **pondrías** **pondría** **pondríamos** **pondríais** **pondrían**	**ponga** **pongas** **ponga** **pongamos** **pongáis** **pongan**	**pusiera** **pusieras** **pusiera** **pusiéramos** **pusierais** **pusieran**	**pon (no pongas)** (no) **ponga** **pongamos** poned (no **pongáis**) (no) **pongan**
querer (e → ie) *to want, to wish* queriendo querido	**quiero** **quieres** **quiere** queremos queréis **quieren**	quería querías quería queríamos queríais querían	**quise** **quisiste** **quiso** **quisimos** **quisisteis** **quisieron**	**querré** **querrás** **querrá** **querremos** **querréis** **querrán**	**querría** **querrías** **querría** **querríamos** **querríais** **querrían**	**quiera** **quieras** **quiera** queramos queráis **quieran**	**quisiera** **quisieras** **quisiera** **quisiéramos** **quisierais** **quisieran**	**quiere (no quieras)** (no) **quiera** **queramos** quered (no queráis) (no) **quieran**
reír *to laugh* **riendo** **reído**	**río** **ríes** **ríe** reímos reís **ríen**	reía reías reía reíamos reíais reían	reí reíste **rio** reímos reísteis **rieron**	reiré reirás reirá reiremos reiréis reirán	reiría reirías reiría reiríamos reiríais reirían	**ría** **rías** **ría** **riamos** **riáis** **rían**	**riera** **rieras** **riera** **riéramos** **rierais** **rieran**	**ríe (no rías)** (no) **ría** **riamos** reíd (no **riáis**) (no) **rían**
*saber *to know* sabiendo sabido	**sé** sabes sabe sabemos sabéis saben	sabía sabías sabía sabíamos sabíais sabían	**supe** **supiste** **supo** **supimos** **supisteis** **supieron**	**sabré** **sabrás** **sabrá** **sabremos** **sabréis** **sabrán**	**sabría** **sabrías** **sabría** **sabríamos** **sabríais** **sabrían**	**sepa** **sepas** **sepa** **sepamos** **sepáis** **sepan**	**supiera** **supieras** **supiera** **supiéramos** **supierais** **supieran**	**sabe (no sepas)** (no) **sepa** **sepamos** sabed (no **sepáis**) (no) **sepan**
*salir *to go out* saliendo salido	**salgo** sales sale salimos salís salen	salía salías salía salíamos salíais salían	salí saliste salió salimos salisteis salieron	**saldré** **saldrás** **saldrá** **saldremos** **saldréis** **saldrán**	**saldría** **saldrías** **saldría** **saldríamos** **saldríais** **saldrían**	**salga** **salgas** **salga** **salgamos** **salgáis** **salgan**	saliera salieras saliera saliéramos salierais salieran	**sal (no salgas)** (no) **salga** **salgamos** salid (no **salgáis**) (no) **salgan**

*Verbs with irregular *yo* forms in the present indicative

Irregular **Verbs** (Continued)

Infinitive Present Participle Past Participle	Present Indicative	Imperfect	Preterite	Future	Conditional	Present Subjunctive	Past Subjunctive	Commands
ser *to be* siendo sido	soy eres es somos sois son	era eras era éramos erais eran	fui fuiste fue fuimos fuisteis fueron	seré serás será seremos seréis serán	sería serías sería seríamos seríais serían	sea seas sea seamos seáis sean	fuera fueras fuera fuéramos fuerais fueran	sé (no seas) (no) sea seamos sed (no seáis) (no) sean
*tener *to have* teniendo tenido	tengo tienes tiene tenemos tenéis tienen	tenía tenías tenía teníamos teníais tenían	tuve tuviste tuvo tuvimos tuvisteis tuvieron	tendré tendrás tendrá tendremos tendréis tendrán	tendría tendrías tendría tendríamos tendríais tendrían	tenga tengas tenga tengamos tengáis tengan	tuviera tuvieras tuviera tuviéramos tuvierais tuvieran	ten (no tengas) (no) tenga tengamos tened (no tengáis) (no) tengan
traer *to bring* trayendo traído	traigo traes trae traemos traéis traen	traía traías traía traíamos traíais traían	traje trajiste trajo trajimos trajisteis trajeron	traeré traerás traerá traeremos traeréis traerán	traería traerías traería traeríamos traeríais traerían	traiga traigas traiga traigamos traigáis traigan	trajera trajeras trajera trajéramos trajerais trajeran	trae (no traigas) (no) traiga traigamos traed (no traigáis) (no) traigan
*venir *to come* viniendo venido	vengo vienes viene venimos venís vienen	venía venías venía veníamos veníais venían	vine viniste vino vinimos vinisteis vinieron	vendré vendrás vendrá vendremos vendréis vendrán	vendría vendrías vendría vendríamos vendríais vendrían	venga vengas venga vengamos vengáis vengan	viniera vinieras viniera viniéramos vinierais vinieran	ven (no vengas) (no) venga vengamos venid (no vengáis) (no) vengan
ver *to see* viendo visto	veo ves ve vemos veis ven	veía veías veía veíamos veíais veían	vi viste vio vimos visteis vieron	veré verás verá veremos veréis verán	vería verías vería veríamos veríais verían	vea veas vea veamos veáis vean	viera vieras viera viéramos vierais vieran	ve (no veas) (no) vea veamos ved (no veáis) (no) vean

*Verbs with irregular *yo* forms in the present indicative

Note: The verb charts are found in Appendix p. T-1.